跨文化研究
Intercultural Research

8

U0756033

LITERATURE AND INTERCULTURALITY (1): CONCEPTS, APPLICATIONS, INTERACTIONS

文学与跨文化研究（一）：概念、应用与交流

主　编：*Michael Steppat*
　　　　Steve J. Kulich（**顾力行**）

上海外语教育出版社
外教社 SHANGHAI FOREIGN LANGUAGE EDUCATION PRESS

图书在版编目(CIP)数据

文学与跨文化研究.一,概念、应用与交流:英文 /(德)迈克尔·斯代帕,
(美)顾力行(Steve J. Kulich)主编.—上海:上海外语教育出版社,2019
ISBN 978 - 7 - 5446 - 5773 - 0

Ⅰ.①文… Ⅱ.①迈… ②顾… Ⅲ.①文学研究—世界—英文 ②文化交流—研究—
世界—英文 Ⅳ.①I106 ②G115

中国版本图书馆 CIP 数据核字(2019)第 037599 号

出版发行:上海外语教育出版社
　　　　　　(上海外国语大学内)　邮编:200083
电　　话:021-65425300 (总机)
电子邮箱:bookinfo@sflep.com.cn
网　　址:http://www.sflep.com
责任编辑:蒋浚浚

印　　刷:上海书刊印刷有限公司
开　　本:635×965　1/16　印张 32　字数 629千字
版　　次:2019 年 7月第 1版　2019 年 7月第 1次印刷
印　　数:1 100 册

书　　号:ISBN 978-7-5446-5773-0 / G
定　　价:99.00 元
　　　　本版图书如有印装质量问题,可向本社调换
　　　　质量服务热线:4008-213-263　电子邮箱:editorial@sflep.com

跨文化研究系列编委会

张雁冰（美国堪萨斯大学）

庄恩平（上海大学）

庄智象（上海外语教育出版社）

上外跨文化研究中心执行编委

张红玲（上外跨文化研究中心副主任）

王志强（上外跨文化研究中心副主任）

于朝晖（上外跨文化研究中心副主任）

周　怡（上外跨文化研究中心研究员）

翁立平（上外跨文化研究中心研究员）

迟若冰（上外跨文化研究中心研究员）

张晓佳（上外跨文化研究中心研究员）

英亚东（上外跨文化研究中心研究员）

Contents

Section One

Concepts and Orientations

Section Two
Diasporic Discourses

Section Three
Cross-Cultural Identities

Section Four
Variations of Cross-Cultural Transfer

Appendix

Intercultural Research
Series Foreword

Michael H. PROSSER
Chair of the SII International Advisory Board
(prossermichael@gmail.com)

Ancient Athens served as an intercultural and intellectual crossroads for Asia and Europe. The Greek philosopher, Socrates' famous statement "I am neither a citizen of Athens, nor of Greece, but of the world" speaks eloquently of the impact of intercultural communication, comparative analysis, and the importance of identity clarification both in his and contemporary society. Greek philosophers Socrates, Plato, and Aristotle all looked outward from their own culture, identifying or debating major world value orientations such as goodness, justice, truth, and happiness. For East Asia, multiple schools of thought developed during the Spring and Autumn Period, shaping China's cross-state communication. Confucius' *Analects* articulated the role of *ren* (benevolence and kindness), *li* (propriety and right living through ritual), *de* (moral power), *dao* (internalized moral direction), and *mianzi* or *lian* (externalized social image and harmony). These Confucian orientations were integrated into what became the fabric of not only the Chinese state, but the educational and philosophical orientation of much of East and South-Eastern Asia.

All of these early cultural conceptualizations of identities and values strongly support the potentially positive intercultural, multicultural, and global world orientations that have enhanced a dialogue of civilizations and cultures, and stress factors that are unifying rather than divisive. The challenge continues to be substantial since intercultural, multicultural, and global communication might just as easily be highly negative with increasing war, poverty, crime, and pandemics. The goal of all those interested in promoting a better local and global society vastly prefers the former.

The location from which this series originates shows some of these dynamics and contradictions. Just as each nation and people must deal with highs and lows, China is grappling both with some of the positive dialogues of modernization and internationalization, and also the challenges of divergent cultural or global discourses. From the depths of the Wenchuan earthquake in Sichuan that rallied not only the nation's, but the world's sympathy, engagement and commitment to rebuild, to the heights of the spectacularly well-orchestrated and successful 2008 Beijing Olympics; from the ongoing challenges of natural disasters like floods or human tragedies and accidents or the global financial crisis, to the futuristic development of Shanghai and its visionary and record-breaking participation and cooperation at the 2010 Shanghai Expo, we see these human and intercultural dynamics at work.

I would suggest that intercultural communication as a field has emerged to embody and embrace both these challenges of human clashes and the dialogues across cultures and civilizations. The anthropologists Edward T. Hall and Ruth Benedict serve as the symbolic grandparents of intercultural communication in North America, though neither set out to begin a new field. Others in North America in the 1960s and 1970s and coming from various viewpoints (see Vol. 2 for the complete list of influencing scholars) and I sought early to develop an intercultural communication discipline or sub-discipline, which has now spread broadly through much of the academic world.

When the field of intercultural communication began to develop rapidly in China during the 1980s and 1990s, Chinese scholars each brought and Sinocized many of these western intercultural theories and practical implications for China. Concerned international scholars have also sought to indigenize social and cultural psychology and the humanities to strengthen Chinese scholarship on intercultural communication. Currently many Chinese scholars, either in China itself, in North America, or other regions around the world, have developed robust theories and models or have postulated newer ones, as documented in the premier volume of this series, *Intercultural Perspectives on Chinese Communication* (2007).

The SISU Intercultural Institute (SII) of Shanghai International Studies University's (SISU), under Steve J. Kulich (Gu Lixing 顾力行), has accepted a mandate to undertake an *Intercultural Research* series of volumes which seeks to publish "cutting edge and seminal articles on the state of the intercultural field" in a variety of areas. As formulated in the establishment of the series, Kulich emphasized that "Each volume will focus on one primary domain and will include diverse theoretical and applied research from cultural, intercultural or cross-cultural approaches for that area, seeking to present and frame a 'state of the art' or an extended development summary on the topic."

The SII is committed to close cooperation with both Chinese and international scholars, and that was reflected since the first, where domestic scholars of the CAFIC were joined by international scholars from various disciplinary or research perspectives to contribute IC research from their respective areas of focus. SII is also committed to highlight and bring some integration to the diverse disciplines that influence, contribute to or are informed by intercultural scholarship. This is illustrated particularly by efforts in that first and subsequent volumes to invite contributions from communication studies at both the interpersonal (*jiaoji*) as well as mass communication (*chuanbo*) levels and also to include the perspectives of cultural psychology, cultural anthropology and other related fields. The interdisciplinary nature of IC motivates the SII team to identify and integrate those aspects that contribute to shared foundations for the field, especially as these reflect intercultural, multicultural human development, or in short, to "develop a discipline to develop people."

This focus on cooperation continued first with disciplinary assessment and development seminars (in 2006, 2010, 2014, 2016, a continuing hallmark of the institute), the biennial thematic IC conferences held by Shanghai Normal University, dynamic cooperation among CAFIC Shanghai Branch institutions (which also includes regular cross-city scholar forums and the annual IC outstanding MA thesis conference) and international partners like the University of Bayreuth, Bavaria, Germany (from which the collaboration for this volume has emerged). Each volume has highlighted interdisciplinary and multi-perspective scholarship on *Identity and Intercultural Communication*: focusing on *I: Theoretical and Contextual Construction* (Vol. 2), and *II: Conceptual and Contextual Applications* (Vol. 3). Other volumes in the series take up the important topic of IC values — *Value Frameworks at the Theoretical Crossroads of Culture* (Vol. 4) and *Value Dimensions and their Contextual Dynamics Across Cultures* (Vol. 5). Later volumes will focus on subsequent themes, like IC and acculturation (Vols. 6 and 7), IC and comparative literature, which now has nationally listed disciplinary status (this Vol. 8 and the next, Vols, 9 and 10), and other topics for IC disciplinary development.

Naturally, since Shanghai Foreign Language Education Press is publishing the series, Chinese academic contributions are especially encouraged, as well as those from the wider international academic community. In his foreword for the first volume, *Intercultural Perspectives on Chinese Communication* (2007), Shijie Guan noted that three features characterize the series: (1) It serves as an interdisciplinary platform for China's IC research; (2) It emphasizes the importance of scientific methodology in IC research; (3) It focuses on the localization of IC research. He concludes his remarks by saying that "The publication of this series is an occasion to celebrate for the entire Chinese community: My hope is that it develops into a series that is interdisciplinary, methodology-promoting, indigenized into the Chinese settings and blend well theories with practice (p. xvi)." As he also notes in that foreword, "In today's world, communication between various cultures have become an important task for human beings. Just as Lourdes Arizpe, chair of the Scientific Committee of the *World Culture Report*, *2000*, says, 'Cultural exchanges are in fact the axis of the new phenomena' as global cultures develop and change (p. ix)."

Since the initial books by Edward T. Hall, *The Silent Language*, *The Hidden Dimension*, *Beyond Culture*, and *The Dance of Life* began to shape the early study of intercultural communication theoretically and practically, so too, it is reasonable to assume that these volumes might provide new impetus for the academic study of various cultural contexts. The historical development, frameworks and research approaches presented both by well-established and emerging scholars in these volumes will surely move the academic understanding of key intercultural topic areas ahead. Each volume's contribution toward highlighting theoretical constructs, clarifying the "state of the art" and presenting cutting edge research and practical applications will hopefully contribute to a new apex in the field of intercultural communication. To the ongoing development of the intercultural communication discipline both in China and abroad this series is dedicated.

International Academy for Intercultural Research (IAIR)
2015 Lifetime Achievement Award Winner

Charlottesville, Virginia

Volume Preface

Meaningfully Linking Intercultural and Literary Studies: Toward the Emerging Field of Intercultural Literature

Inquiry into "Intercultural Communication" studies, which some call "IC," now has over 30 years of history in China and over 50 years internationally. Most programs of "Intercultural Communication" as a field of study usually trace their roots to the post-World-War-II U.S. diplomatic training program developed by Edward T. Hall and his associates and the publication of his book *The Silent Language* (1959). These approaches often focus on descriptive or interpretative elements of culture isolated for meaningful comparisons across cultural groups, or the social scientific examination of important cultural constructs, dimensions, or theoretical frameworks across cultures. In either case, the academic assumptions are generally rooted in functional, structuralist, positivist, social-science approaches to research. Though an "intercultural approach" to literature has at times been proposed, literary scholars often find it intellectually incongruous to attempt to link or utilize the "pragmatic" or "scientific" dimensions or theories that arise from the IC tradition in meaningful ways.

Yet, as the field of intercultural studies seeks to find its place in the Chinese disciplinary register, some proponents feel that the ongoing emphasis toward explorations of interculturality ideally fit textual studies. Based on drafts proposed in 2015, since 2016 the National Ministry of Education disciplinary register places IC within the broader framework of foreign language and literature studies. The "Direction 13" for "Comparative Literature and Intercultural Studies" identifies a field which

- is cross-language, cross-national, and interdisciplinary in orientation; it studies literary and cultural exchanges, influence, and integration in the world;
- centers on the interaction of Chinese and foreign literature, unveils the diversity and integration of literature and culture;

- includes as main research areas: the relationship between Chinese and foreign literature, transnational literature comparisons, the communication / transference of literature, the translation history of literature and culture, imagology, international Chinese culture studies (the spread of Chinese culture internationally). (Author's translation)[1]

Admittedly, these areas of emphasis are not entirely what "Intercultural Communication" studies have focused on over the years, especially in the seedbed of the field's development in North America. There and in China, where the field was formalized in 1995 with the forming of the Chinese Association for Intercultural Communication (CAFIC), the influence of communication, and cross-cultural psychology as systematic endeavors have primarily guided research initiatives toward construct definition, theory postulations, hypothesis testing, and evaluation of construct validity, reliability, and the representativeness of findings. Applications have focused primarily on intercultural teaching and training for education or international business, toward the cultivation of intercultural awareness, competence, and problem solving in individuals or cultural groups for smoother exchanges or cooperation.

Each of these emphases involve rich contents, interesting ideas, and good outcomes. But they seem somewhat remote from the approaches of textual or literary representation or analysis laid out in the disciplinary direction outlined above. How can these two expressions of "intercultural studies" be rectified, let alone integrated? That is the key question guiding the development of this volume, and each of the authors provides arguments and examples toward the potential marriage of ideas centered on interculturality as it is or can be expressed and analyzed in literary studies.

Part of the problem or gap in understanding is that past summaries about the IC field as well as the assumptions currently being advanced are limited or incomplete. The field's roots in anthropology and descriptive comparative studies and the contribution of

---

[1] The Chinese Ministry of Education document original states: "外国语言文学 13. 比价文学与跨文化研究:
比价文学与跨文化研究:比跨语言,跨国别,跨学科围导向,一世界各国文学和中外文化交流,影响与融通为对象,以中国文学和外国文学之间的互动为中心,揭示文学和文化的多元与融合。研究范围主要步及中外文学关系,跨国文学比较,文学传播郁结先后,文学语文化翻译史,形象学和国际中文化研究等。"
Available online at http://yz. chsi. com. cn/kyzx/other/201604/20160422/1530142836.html.

those who contributed to both the "interpretation of culture" and "writing culture" have too often become historical footnotes or neglected altogether.

However, there is increasing evidence that there were already earlier approaches that included the description, interaction, and creative dialogue between civilizations and cultural groups under the rubric of "intercultural" encounters or academic explorations. These include

- Terms and perspectives regarding the plurality of cultures advanced in Europe, particularly in Germany, by Johann Gottfried Herder, the von Humboldt brothers, Immanuel Kant, and others in the late 1800s (e.g., Elberfeld);
- An early series of "intercultural dialogues" among religions apparently initiated by the University of Chicago in the 1920s;
- And a social-studies "intercultural education" movement forming in the late 1920s into the 1940s (e.g., DuBois, Brown, Vickery and Cole).

Even in mainstream intercultural work, there has been a call for more nuanced re-conceptualizations of culture (see Baldwin et. al.), theorizing (Gudykunst, Dai), and critical studies (e.g., Nakayama and Halualani). Now with nearly five decades of development since the simultaneous establishment of professional divisions in associations for scholarship as well as applications in Mass Communication (ICA, 1970), Speech and Rhetoric (SCA, 1971), focused associations also in Cross-cultural Psychology (IACCP, 1972), the Society for Intercultural Education, Training, and Research (SIETAR, 1973), and the flagship *International Journal of Intercultural Relations* (*IJIR*, 1977), it is high time that the value and practice of literary studies be meaningfully rejoined with the maturing field(s) of "intercultural studies." This re-linking or revival of textual and literary analysis with intercultural studies can rekindle ferment and future developments of advantage in each of these fields, as well as enhance the emerging integrated area of study: intercultural literature. The chapters in this volume convincingly show the fertile foundations in place for the further promoting of such an endeavor.

As China begins to put "intercultural studies" on the disciplinary map, we believe that past bottlenecks and misconceptions of the limitations of IC (when it is viewed as merely a social science or functional field) can be overcome by exploring the richer historical, theoretical, conceptual, and textual contributions that exist. As these chapters show, there are a great many avenues and approaches for considering interculturality and comparative cultural interactions in literary texts.

As Homi Bhabha once posited "the location of culture" with reference to post-colonial orientations, we would argue in favor of the "re-location of culture"② with "intercultural" orientations, highlighting the broad range of foundations and foci of research that could be drawn from. By more clearly addressing the multiple levels, types, paradigms of culture and the varied processes, barriers, interventions, and outcomes of various approaches to IC, we trust that these volumes can help lay the groundwork for detangling the perceived "interdisciplinary" ambiguity or ambivalence of IC scholarship. Toward this vision, each author in these paired volumes is making an important contribution. There is great potential for a multi-faceted "intercultural literature" relevant to Chinese and international, comparative literature, as well as other forms of media/textual analysis. May these volumes contribute to moving such an academic agenda forward!

References

Baldwin, John R., Sandra L. Faulkner, Michael L. Hecht, and Sheryl L. Lindsley, eds. *Redefining Culture: Perspectives Across the Disciplines*. Mahwah, N.J., & London: Lawrence Erlbaum, 2006.

Bhabha, Homi K. *The Location of Culture*. Abingdon: Routledge, 1994.

Brown, Francis J. "Sociology and Intercultural Understanding." *Journal of Educational Sociology* 12 (Feb. 1939): 328–331.

Cole, Stewart G. "Intercultural Education." *Contemporary Jewish Record* (April-June 1941).

Dai, Xiaodong. "The Construction of Intercultural Identity in the Context of Globalization." *Identity and Intercultural Communication (I): Theoretical and Contextual Construction*. Intercultural Research Vol. 2. Eds. Xiaodong Dai and Steve J. Kulich. Shanghai: Shanghai Foreign Language Education Press, 2010. 103-121.

—. *Intercultural Communication Theories*. Shanghai: Shanghai Foreign Language Education Press, 2011.

—. "Out of a Dialogical Dilemma: The Construction of Interculturality." *Intercultural Adaptation (I): Theoretical Explorations and Empirical Studies*. Intercultural Research Vol. 6. Eds. Xiaodong Dai and Steve J.

---

② This was the title of the author's address at the 17 October 2015 International Symposium on "Literature, Comparative Studies, Interculturality: America and Beyond" at Shanghai International Studies University ("The (Re) Location of (Inter) Culture: Integrating Paradigms Toward Intercultural Literature Theorizing and Application").

Kulich. Shanghai: Shanghai Foreign Language Education Press, 2012. 97–114.

DuBois, Rachel Davis. *Get Together Americans: Friendly Approaches to Racial and Cultural Conflicts Through the Neighborhood-home Festival*. 4th ed. New York & London: Harper, 1943.

—. *Neighbors in Action: A Manual for Local Leaders in Intergroup Relations*. New York: Harper, 1950.

—. *Pioneers of the New World*. Philadelphia: Women's International League for Peace and Freedom, 1930.

Elberfeld, Rolf. "Forschungsperspektive 'Interkulturalität': Transformation der Wissensordnungen in Europa." *Zeitschrift für Kulturphilosophie* 2.1 (2008): 7–36.

Gudykunst, William B., ed. *Theorizing about Intercultural Communication*. Thousand Oaks, CA: Sage, 2005.

Nakayama, Thomas K., and Rona Tamiko Halualani, eds. *The Handbook of Critical Intercultural Communication*. Malden, Mass. & Chichester: Wiley-Blackwell, 2010.

Vickery, William E., and Stewart G. Cole. *Intercultural Education in American Schools: Proposed Objectives and Methods*. Foreword by William Heard Kilpatrick. Problems of Race and Culture in American Education. Bureau for Intercultural Education Publications. New York & London: Harper, 1943.

Steve J. KULICH, IAIR President-Elect
International Academy for Intercultural Research

Shanghai
July 2018

Crossing Bridges:
Literary and Intercultural Study

by Michael STEPPAT and Steve J. KULICH

Intercultural studies oblige researchers to be
aware of their inherited legacy, which is at times
taken for granted, as well as to constantly raise
questions about the possible cultural restraints
of their own vision and knowledge.
(Steven Shankman and Amiya Dev:
Epic and Other Higher Narratives, 2011)

Multi-perspectival Texts

An introduction to a volume on the study of literature in relation to
intercultural inquiry cannot be much more than a short one. That is
because the two fields have rarely crossed a bridge toward each
other — surprisingly enough when we recall that an intercultural
dimension has long been at home within literature itself. Even so,
literary study has hardly taken much notice of intercultural research.
Advances have been made in recent times especially regarding analytical
reflection on literature in the context of migration experience and cultural
encounter. A pioneering German volume, titled *Intercultural Literary
Studies* (2006), offers the following rationale:

> There is a special affinity of literature to the problems and potentials
> of intercultural encounters. As against the rationalistic and one-
> dimensional tendencies of social science, literature creates multi-
> perspectival texts that do justice to the complexity of a polycentric
> world. A literary text's cultural value arises from its multiple
> encoding in a plural world, as a model for dealing with complex

identities. Thus literature gains a central value for cultural self-reflection. (Our shortened translation, from Hofmann 13-14) ①

Considerations of what interculturality and foreignness mean are crucial in gaining a better understanding of cultural strangeness as a topic or condition in literature. Just as crucial is an awareness of the role played by power relations and hierarchies. Becoming acquainted with other cultures, not least among them being unfamiliar ones, and in particular with their literary production may raise readers' willingness to refrain from attempts to assimilate the Other's strangeness. Discernment of this kind forms an important feature of intercultural competence. In this context, strangeness and difference are not so much static or essentialist qualities. Rather, they emerge from a dynamic process of encounter, in the course of which participants use cultural signs for the purpose of ascribing to each other certain elements of identity and of difference. Such, at any rate, are some of the constitutive insights of intercultural literary study as they have been voiced by Hofmann and a few predecessors in a formative phase, though without directly touching on the scientific dimension of Intercultural Communication.

A similar awareness has, in fact, guided the present book series. The series has recurrently given careful attention to literature from a largely non-literary perspective rooted in the social sciences. The second of the volumes devoted to *Identity and Intercultural Communication* features a section that is designed "to broaden readers' outlooks on ethnicity" while "pushing us forward to new areas of identity research." The section includes an analysis of cultural identity construction in Bernard Malamud's *The Assistant*

---

① "Indem die Vieldeutigkeit und Ambiguität einer zeitgenössischen Subjektivität, indem deren Bestimmtheit durch verschiedenste Einflüsse und Bezugsgrößen herausgestellt wird, zeigt sich die besondere Affinität von *Literatur* zu Problemen und Möglichkeiten interkultureller Begegnung — und damit die spezifische Fragestellung der interkulturellen Literaturwissenschaft. Erstens ist gegenüber rationalistischen und eindimensionalen Tendenzen einer (gesellschafts-) wissenschaftlichen Betrachtung interkultureller Konstellationen die Möglichkeit der Literatur zu unterstreichen, multiperspektivische, ambivalente und vieldeutige Texte zu erzeugen und damit der Komplexität einer polyzentrischen Welt gerecht zu werden: 'Der kulturelle Wert des literarischen Textes [...] ergibt sich aus seiner Mehrfachcodierung innerhalb einer plural verstandenen Welt. So bietet der intertextuell geprägte Umgang mit literarischen Texten ein Modell und Trainingsfeld für den Umgang mit mehrfach codierten, komplexen Identitäten [...]' [quotation from Bronfen and Marius] [...] 'Dabei gewinnt Literatur für die kulturelle Selbstreflexion einen zentralen Stellenwert.' [quotation from Gutjahr]."

(Tian Zhang). Also, in a section that explores "the ways cultural values shape and are shaped by cultural identity struggles," a chapter shows how Lin Yutang's cultural exportism "affects cultural diversity and two-way intercultural communication" (Yige Zhu). A later volume, the first devoted to *Intercultural Adaptation*, offers a section on Intercultural Adaptation Theory which discusses what is involved in "Transforming Career via Intersectionalities and Inter/cultural Processes" (Buzzanell). Strikingly, the discussion makes use of Lionel Shriver's 2007 novel *The Post-Birthday World* to show that "inter/cultural career development processes utilize the power of narrative, bricolage (creation of something from the materials at hand), possible selves (identities), and imagination."

The Chinese Ministry of Education has approved a Direction for "Comparative Literature and Intercultural Studies" as an integrated discipline, with an interdisciplinary orientation which includes attention to literary exchanges and the communication/transference of literature. This is an especially important development as context for our focal area. As an "intellectual field," it goes beyond conventional academic disciplines (Xie 49).

We should not think that, in western literature, an intercultural theme is a new development. It has actually been written into the literature's very beginning: for our purpose we might revisit the heritage of the heroic epic, at the dawn of Greek literary history. Few works created in western literature have ever matched the poignancy of the culminating Book of *The Iliad*, ascribed to Homer.

> For ten years the Greek Argives have besieged Troy, a city of non-Greek foreignness presumably belonging to the Hittite empire and one in which recent research makes it seem likely that Luwian was spoken, until "lion-hearted" Achilles' beloved friend Patroclus is slain by the Trojan prince Hector (in league with "Far-Darter" Phoebus Apollo). This event sparks Achilles' boundless sorrow, then his implacable wrath and thirst for revenge, so much that he swallows his pride and ends a protracted and divisive quarrel with fellow leader Agamemnon in order to re-enter the war with his men, knowing well enough from a prophecy that such a decision will spell his own speedy death. Hector, "tamer of horses," is tricked by the gods into turning to face Achilles in dubious single combat, enabling the Greek hero to succeed in driving his spear through the prince's neck. In his unabating rage, Achilles refuses to accept ransom for the prince's body. Hector's aging father Priam, beside himself with grief and groveling in the mire, raves that he will somehow find a

way single-handed into the Greek camp and beg Achilles to have
compassion. His wife on behalf of the family cries out that he has
lost his mind. And indeed such a secret mission at high risk only
becomes conceivable when "all-seeing" Zeus decides to persuade
Achilles' "silver-footed" mother to intercede and try to soften her
son's heart, while Zeus' messenger Hermes at night escorts Priam
and his driver safely and undetected into the Greek camp. Reaching
Achilles' tent, Priam throws himself weeping at the fierce Greek
warrior's feet, who has just been treating Hector's body most
dishonorably by dragging it behind his chariot, and implores him to
think of his own father and finally allow the ransom. His words and
manner move the mercurial Achilles to join him in bitter weeping.

The text curiously presents Priam as behaving just like someone who
has committed a murder in his own country and has fled to seek
protection in a strange land (24.480ff): "ὡς δ' ὅτ' ἂν ἄνδρ' ἄτη πυκινὴ
λάβῃ, ὅς τ'ἐνὶ πάτρῃ/ φῶτα κατακτείνας ἄλλων ἐξίκετο δῆμον / ἀνδρὸς ἐς
ἀφνειοῦ." Thus Priam's motives in seeking out the foreign terrain
become subtly ambivalent. This final Book's conclusion devotes a
memorably empathetic focus to the Trojans' eloquent grief,
especially the lamentations of the women — Andromache, Hecuba,
Helen — while the narrative structure gradually erases the Greeks,
who after all belong to the poetic author's own language culture,
from the epic depiction. It is intriguing to speculate on the positionality
vis-à-vis the depicted cultures that the epic representation has
fashioned for the Greek listener or, later, reader.

Thus from the earliest time, the complexity of cultural Self/
Foreign encounters has received a powerful literary testimony. When
we return to our own time, we might recall that an appeal to
consider literature as being fully relevant to intercultural research
was already voiced by communication scholar John C. Condon
in 1986:

Conventional distinctions between the social sciences and the
arts — novels, plays, letters and diaries and films — cause
trouble. [...] The potential, even the likelihood, of misrepresenting
'the culture' or cultures presented is not necessarily greater for the
writer of fiction than for the social scientist. [...] A good writer in
the medium of fiction may come closer to 'reality' than a good
social scientist working within the conventions of his or her field.
[...] The student of literature must be attuned to the suggested, not
the stated, to sensing how relationships will be affected by words
and deeds, by gestures, by silence. Puffs of clouds, an unexpected

> visitor — human, animal or other: such things 'mean something' or
> the writer would not have included them. (Condon 156, 158)

It is almost as if Condon, who does not actually mention Homer, has
in mind the cloud that Homer's Apollo sends to shield Hector's slain
body from the sun's glare, or the unexpected black eagle that
appears as Priam sets off on his journey to the "land of strangers."

The "Shock" of Difference

However that may be, Condon's remarkable awareness of literature's
(and film's) value for understanding cultural relationships comes
close to meeting the by now classic concept of a paradigm
reorientation. Tracing this enables "a change in the perception and
evaluation of familiar data" (Kuhn viii-ix). As is well enough
known, Thomas Kuhn in the edition of The Structure of Scientific
Revolutions that was pertinent at this time called attention to
"achievements" in knowledge or "locus of professional commitment"
that "for a time provide model problems and solutions to a
community of practitioners" (Kuhn viii, 11); they embrace the
content of what we should observe and study, hence the objects to
consider, then the types of questions we might ask, and the nature of
how we should carry out investigations. Such achievements are not
static: a particular locus or novel way of looking at objects is
"sufficiently open-ended to leave all sorts of problems for the
redefined group of practitioners to resolve" (ibid., 10). With a new
or reoriented concept cluster, an investigator "sees differently from
the way he had seen before" (ibid., 115). Keeping this in mind, it is
important to realize that Condon's proposals — which are significant
enough to encourage an emerging research field like ours — are not
the result of coincidence.

As readers of this volume may perhaps know, a varied range of
social, political, and academic developments in the USA helped
foster some foundations upon which many of the intercultural fields
were able to prosper. A brief overview will have to suffice in this
context. It was in interdisciplinary circles at universities like
Columbia and Harvard that the study of comparative culture (as
described for instance in Leeds-Hurwitz, "Writing") developed
rapidly, building on a concept of culture as a system of learnable
patterns that can be analyzed. This form of study primarily arose out
of cultural anthropology in the 1930s and 1940s, and then the 1950s,

with additional contributions from sociology (cf. Hechter; Hitlin and Paliavin; Kulich, "Applying" and "Reconstructing"). As a primary domain of cultural analysis, such patterns can derive from anthropological, ethnographical, interpretative, or social science approaches; they can be fixed — or may alternatively be seen as dynamic and pluralized or as multicultural. Yet a visor should not focus exhaustively on the USA. Studies and applications regarding an awakening cultural sensitivity were developing with great depth elsewhere: the critical theory work of the Frankfurt school, the cultural studies approaches of the Birmingham school, or varied applications from influential French social and critical theorists or Russian philosophers and philologists. What is more, a closer look would show that the pre-history of Intercultural Communication goes back much further, into at least the mid-nineteenth century.

In the 1950s, at any rate, Edward T. Hall's works brought together a considerable variety of interdisciplinary streams — especially the cultural aspects of anthropology, linguistics, psychology, and education (see for instance Leeds-Hurwitz, "Notes") — through his training initiatives at the Foreign Service Institute (1951–55). His books and the terminologies he advanced or introduced spurred on the formation of a specific field focusing on Intercultural Communication studies and its more public application, Intercultural Communication training (cf. Leeds-Hurwitz, "Notes" and "Writing"; Pusch, "Intercultural" and *Directory*; Kulich, "Reconstructing" and "Values").[2] We will do well to heed one of Hall's characteristic insights:

> Culture is "that part of man's behavior which he takes for granted — the part he doesn't think about, since he assumes it is universal or regards it as idiosyncratic. Culture hides much more than it reveals, and strangely enough what it hides, it hides most effectively from its own participants. Years of study have convinced me that the real job is not to understand foreign culture but to understand our own. [...] The ultimate reason for such study is to learn more about how one's own system works. The best reason for exposing oneself to foreign ways is to generate [...] an interest in life which can come only when one lives through the shock of contrast and difference." (Hall, *Silent* 30)

---

[2] For a brief survey of the development of Intercultural Communication in theory and practice, see Kramsch (201–06). Kramsch notes that the Intercultural Communication field in Europe had beginnings that were different from those in the USA (202).

Literature is arguably prominent among sources of knowledge that seek to bring to light the concealed snags of what we like to take for granted, what culture "hides" from its own members. And that seek to disclose "the shock" of difference. In *The Hidden Dimension* (1966/1982), Hall goes further. He devotes a chapter to the desirability of using literary artifacts as "a key to perception." Reading "for structure rather than content" (which structuralist narratology would call discourse rather than story), one could gain data on the experience and perception of spatial distance as "a significant cultural factor," since literary works cast light on "historical trends and shifts in sense modalities" (94ff.). Hall illustrates this with examples ranging from Shakespeare's *King Lear* to Japanese fiction. The approach brings to mind the range of substantive studies that have been offered since then on spatial morphology as in American literature, and that touch on related issues (see Benesch and Schmidt, Manzanas and Benito).

Yet beyond the generally positivist, structuralist, and functionalist fields of learning of that time, important descriptive, interpretative, constructivist schools were emerging. Among these was the work of scholars who built on Dell Hymes's ethnography of communication. This has implications for the place of language in an evolutionary theory of culture and for comparative study of cross-cultural variations in verbal art. It is a framework for investigating intercultural discourse. Moreover, among the representatives of schools were those who adapted Gerry Philipsen's speech code theory in connection with Language and Social Interaction or LSI research. It enables the study of language as a medium of interaction without which social life could not develop, a carrier of culture and tool of social communication (cf. for instance Leeds-Hurwitz, *Social History*). More recently, critical approaches harking back to the Chicago, Frankfurt, and Birmingham schools of mass media and cultural studies have emerged (cf. for instance Nakayama and Halualani). Many of these employ approaches from a range of influential French, German, Italian, or Russian critical cultural theorists (prominently including Foucault's power and knowledge, Heidegger's phenomenology, Gramsci's cultural hegemony, and Bakhtin's dialogism). Conversely, advances in literary theory that consider more nuanced evaluations of identity in time and space — such as the postcolonial approaches that are evident in Said's orientalism, Fanon's existentialist humanism, Spivak's sub-alternism, Bhabha's hybridity and third space, or post-modern approaches — have fostered a sensitivity to the role of culture in literature, whether it be "inter," "trans," "cross-border," or diasporic.

An ethnography of communication invites attention to situations and uses of speaking in everyday interactions, extending to language's function as a social and cultural system in speech communities. It thus has some bearing on the study of bi- and multilingualism, which, with creative use of di-glossia with di-ethnicity, is a characteristic feature of some intercultural literary works. The creative use is, in fact, a strategically significant procedure for "minor" literature, the literature of national minorities. When di-glossia is used in the interest of a dialogic strategy to de-hierarchize an official or hegemonic culture, the growing field of Critical Intercultural Studies (as exemplified by Nakayama and Halualani, e.g., 231, 568) offers a corresponding focus. We may infer that the double focus strengthens the case for a potential merger of intercultural and migrant literary studies. What is more, Dell Hymes has studied "the shaping artistry of narrators" in oral poetic narratives mainly in North America. The aim is to understand metrical patterning, with analogues in other cultures (1994, also further essays). A recent discussion of this emphasizes that the "dialectic between narratable content and rhetorical form" which Hymes analyzed has also been "central to the development of European and modernist (ethno) poetics and literary culture": ethnopoetics as a Hymesian legacy is "at least in part an effort to destabilize or subvert certain conventional pieties of the literary establishment" (Moore 30, 32). We should add that Hymes's work has been called "instructive" and relevant to Homeric narrative art (see for instance Foley 91, 279).

Yet a meeting of the research fields is still, in most ways, a potential. It is not yet a reality. Characteristically, the interculturality of literary study is visible in another direction. After Earl Miner opened comparative study to "an eastern and a southern hemisphere" (Miner 20), Gunilla Lindberg-Wada and the editor of the *Literary History* series' first volume, Anders Pettersson, in a major undertaking offer an intercultural approach. It is defined as dealing with the "distortions that Western biases, terms and intellectual habits may introduce into Western writing of world literary history," focusing on comparisons between types of literature as they "intermingle across frontiers" (1 : x). It also focuses on intercultural interplay as the study of "encounters between literary cultures" (1 : 6). The editors go so far as to affirm that "intercultural understanding in the literary field is now more indispensable than ever before" (1 : ix). As a motto for our own enterprise, this is superb. Such an orientation in comparative study opens a rewarding enough field of inquiry. It is less concerned with a need to extend intercultural scrutiny beyond historical comparison, and toward a processual or interactive notion of culture as practice and meeting ground. Aware of this need, the present volume's participants give attention largely to literary representation of migrant situations and cultural minorities as they contribute from various angles to placing the variety of approaches in perspective. They seek to suggest ways of exploring the larger and abundantly fertile terrain where literary and intercultural study discover each other.

The Scope and Contents of This Volume

This book is divided into four sections, viz., (1) Concepts and Orientations, (2) Diasporic Discourses, (3) Cross-Cultural Identities, as well as (4) Variations of Cross-Cultural Transfer. Steve Kulich and Weng Liping have observed, in a previous volume in this series, how our cultural encounters "happen in context and with relational or interaction dynamics at play," a process which involves responses "through the experience of reading a novel" (18). Such reading of "something other than what are, all things considered, the short and simple annals of one cultural parish at one historic moment" (Miner 3) would activate a poetics that draws on intercultural evidence. With this in mind, in the following we offer a brief introduction to the chapters and the research issues that are presented in this volume.

To launch the sequence of sections, in a Prologue to "Reconsidering Intercultural Narratives" Steve Kulich inquires into an alternative to the mainstream narrative about the development of intercultural communication as a field of study.

Section One: Concepts and Orientations

The first section in this volume presents conceptual reflections that aim to provide some orientation in relating the various branches of literary study (including a comparative perspective) extending to film and of inter- as well as transcultural research to each other. The ideas presented in this section feed into the subsequent chapters, as well. The appendix of Chapter 5 introduces analytical questions for practical literary analysis.

For effective intercultural communication in our glocalized world, Mao Sihui in Chapter 1 urges moving studies of literary and cultural texts back into their social, cultural, and ideological contexts. Thus, even as we stress literature's intrinsic value, we also need to devote attention to TV, film, cartoon, and other forms of representational media. In an earlier volume in this series, in fact, there was a stress on the way "media messages play an influential role in re/constructing cultural values" and in producing meaning (Goering et al. 342). As Mao stresses, enhancing our understanding of the differences and peculiarities of literary and cultural texts from other ethnic traditions is our most challenging task.

Several chapters in the volume as a whole give some attention to matters of translation. Especially prominent is the reflection by Sandra L. Bermann in Chapter 2 on the mutual relationship between translation theory, comparative literature, and migration. Bermann briefly tracks the history of comparative literature's relationship to translation, explaining that it has only been in the context of translation's developing distinctive theoretical directions in the course of the 20th century that a recent re-union of the two fields has helped "translate" comparative literature into a more theoretically stimulating discipline. A defining issue in this context is migration: migrants have been the objects of policy making or interventions, but they have also acted as powerful cultural agents or cultural producers and brokers between cultures. In connection with migration, linguistic and cultural translation is now performing some vital sociocultural work within the frame of comparative literature.

Of key significance for the new disciplinary direction "Comparative Literature and Intercultural Studies" established by the Chinese government is a consideration of how the two components relate to each other. Zha Mingjian in Chapter 3 suggests viewing comparative literature and translation studies as sub-areas of intercultural studies, as on the one hand they belong to the scope of intercultural studies and on the other hand they can be considered as the practical rationale for intercultural theories. Comparative literature's interculturality strengthens its problem awareness and hence determines its scholarly value and significance.

Based on the idea that literature in our time is "in motion," in Chapter 4 Susan Arndt discusses the relationship of society and literature in the context of the "death of the author." She emphasizes that fiction weaves its stories and histories out of the kaleidoscope of interests of social, cultural, and political interactions. As people migrate, they take with them their (hi)stories, religions, ideas, knowledge systems, and aesthetics, and hardly anything lives out the vision of boundlessness as consistently as literature. Global interaction demands that literary studies think beyond the limitations of conventionalized areas, nations, and languages in a transcultural manner. Hence, Arndt proposes translating transtextual transculturality into an appeal for Transcultural Literary Studies.

In Chapter 5, Michael Steppat asks: Can there be a conceptual place for intercultural research when we seek a better understanding of literary culture? If images of the familiar and the foreign condition each other, analysis of literature and also film would remain barren if it did not look outside its own deceptively familiar box. Hwa Yol Jung has urged seeking a "new intercontinent of conceptualization" for adequate understanding. To facilitate that discovery, we can gain some impulses from transversal thought. It enables us to understand difficult meanings in the texts we study not as a mental act but rather as a social practice and a communicative achievement — so that textual meanings are likely to be all but meaningless outside a communicative knowledge performance. As literature itself crosses borders, three transversal operations are proposed for the progressive disclosure of a world through which words work. An Appendix translates the concept into a sequence of analytical questions for the practical task of criticism.

In Chapter 6, Zhang Longxi revisits the argumentation of his earlier essay "The *Tao* and the *Logos*," which was subsequently expanded to a book, to renew and update his critique of Derridean assumptions: is the metaphysical hierarchy of thinking, speech, and writing limited to a Western concept of language only? Ezra Pound's imagism could appear as the result of a fruitful misunderstanding of an alleged Chinese "graphic poetics," as in deconstructive anti-logocentrism. Yet there is in fact no fundamental *différance* between East and West, and beyond all distinctive features there is a clear potential for cross-cultural understanding and communication.

Section Two: Diasporic Discourses

A majority of the chapters in Sections 2, 3, and 4 explores literature that deals with migrant situations and sociocultural minorities. Partly overlapping with this, a smaller number of chapters contribute to comparative literary study and to literary adaptation as well as forms of cultural transfer. Chapters in each section exemplify the value of Intercultural Communication approaches for purposes of analysis.

The volume's second section focuses on various literary representations of the experience of diasporic spaces and conditions. Chapter 7 studies Chinese-Canadian fiction, whereas Chapters 8 through 10 devote attention to fiction and poetry relating to diasporic situations between Africa and North America (Chapters 8 and 9) and between Africa, France, and the Caribbean (Chapter 10). There are thematic connections across sections in that some chapters in the third section, too, study literary treatments of migrant and ethnic minority situations. For conditions affecting African Americans, William Starosta's comments on "Rhetoric of Racialization" and on "Eroding Centrisms" in a previous volume in this series offer useful insights.

In this section, then, Fu Lin in Chapter 7 considers individual and collective experiences of (inter)cultural encounters in Terry Woo's novel *Banana Boys* (2000), as a case study to investigate the ongoing tension between different cultural groups in Canada. The author shows how Woo introduces multiple narrative voices and perspectives to allow readers to see alternate views, a strategy that enables a focus especially on the interrelated contextual issues of racism and double consciousness.

Shola Adenekan in Chapter 8 builds on his earlier research to demonstrate how contemporary literature that is published online depicts the experience of "queerness" by trans-Atlantic characters who see Africa as their spiritual home. Whereas earlier Pan-African projects were rather reluctant in embracing "queer" desire in much of the 20th century, such desire is being robustly articulated by a new generation of African writers, many of whom are members of the professional middle classes and are themselves transnational figures, often regarded as cultural ambassadors.

In Chapter 9, Shirin Assa studies Chimamanda Ngozi Adichie's recent novel *Americanah* (2013) to show how identity tends to be in motion, under constant construction and processual negotiation. The difficulty in tracing this leads to the suggestion to replace diasporic identity, for its collective quality, with three forms of experience proposed by Rogers Brubaker and Frederick Cooper: these are commonality, connectedness, and groupness. If these are considered together with Arjun Appadurai's polyphonic portrait of space, which uses the concepts of "scapes" such as ethnoscapes or mediascapes or technoscapes instead of contraposition and determinate spaces, a fresh view of what is commonly thought of as diasporic identity becomes possible. This concept may by extension have bearing on the other topics and approaches concerning identity in the volume, as well.

Then, in Chapter 10, Patrick Oloko considers the discrepancy between Development Studies and creative writing in framing Africa's engagement with her Diaspora: whereas the former represents Africa/Diaspora relations in comparatively optimistic terms, it overlooks the complex idea of "return" and "homecoming," which is prominent in literary portraits of cultural engagements. An evolving literary genre of "homecoming" or "return" narratives, by contrast, portrays the experiences of "returning" Diaspora citizens as tending to vitiate black culture. In showing this, the author examines mainly two novels from different cultural contexts: *Juletane* (1982) by Guadeloupian/Senegalese author Myriam Warner-Vieyra and *The Hangman's Game* (2007) by Nigerian/Guyanese author Karen King-Aribisala.

Section Three: Cross-Cultural Identities

The third section studies identity problems in cross-cultural situations that extend the focus of the second section, with which it features thematic overlaps without foregrounding diasporic concepts quite as much. North America is again a prominent space: attention is given to Chinese-American writing (Chapters 11 and 13) which touches on perceptions of Chinese immigrant perceptions of values as studied by Todd Sandel and colleagues and also on Chinese-American cultural adaptation as studied by Wingkai To in previous volumes in this series. North America is likewise prominent in the depiction of Turkish and Armenian families' American experiences (Chapters 11 and 12), as well as in the anatomy of Canadian identity (Chapter 15). The postcolonial situation in Britain enlarges the geographical scope (Chapter 14).

In Chapter 11, Mine Krause compares several works by Chinese-American author Gish Jen and Turkish author Elif Shafak to explore the phenomenon of "hyphenated identities," especially for the second and third generation of immigrants in America. The phenomenon is relevant also for the African Americans (with or without an actual hyphen) who are considered in the previous section. For the perception of identity, the hyphen may either separate the two cultures in question, emphasizing an individual's cultural roots and rejecting the target culture, or it can serve as a bridge between both. The hyphen's alternative functions are investigated with regard to the function of names, the treatment of language, and eating habits: identity, as we can learn from Stuart Hall, has become a "moveable feast."

Following up on these impulses, in Chapter 12 Mine Krause examines more closely Elif Shafak's novel *The Bastard of Istanbul* (2006) with its interwoven story of two immigrant families, which depicts a clash of Eastern and Western value systems. Since research has suggested that cultural differences become especially obvious at dinner tables abroad, mainly because of the use of exotic ingredients, this chapter aims to show how culinary culture becomes interpretively significant for an identity construction process. There is thus a connection to the body discourse as analyzed in Chapter 14.

Chapter 13 offers an in-depth focus on Gish Jen's second novel *Mona in the Promised Land* (1996), which is also a topic in Chapter 10. Shen Weiwei Vivian uses this opportunity to show the potential of identity negotiation theory, as developed by Stella Ting-Toomey and also by Ronald Jackson, for critical analysis. The concept of cultural contract with its three major types as well as that of identity coordination requiring personal or internal negotiation become helpful for the purpose of literary analysis. Moreover, the novel's individual characters cannot escape the complex relations of power that inevitably shape their interactions. Jen's optimistic narration of immigrant conditions has been thought to obscure the material realities impinging on Asian Americans. Yet beneath the surface of the novel's seemingly light vein, Jen diagnoses a submerged power differential that challenges the reader's own self-image.

In Chapter 14, Yuan Mingqing investigates the transcultural communication of people of color in Zadie Smith's novel *White Teeth* (2000). It turns out that the body becomes especially significant in this process, so that the author makes analytical use of Maurice Merleau-Ponty's phenomenological understanding of the body together with Michel Foucault's analysis of the discursive production of power. The novel depicts the subtle violence which is inflicted or imposed on the fictional characters' intersubjective bodies while they desire and attempt to adapt to the metropolitan country, fusing elements of the dominant cultural discourse into their own body and its mentality — without lasting success. Yet, as the narrative shows, a bodily discourse also becomes a site where resistance and subversion can take place.

Chapter 15 turns attention to the way Canada's literary tradition of small-town fiction reflects a national psyche of "in-betweenness." Zhou Yi studies Alice Munro's "Chaddeleys and Flemings" as a case example, for the difference between a connection to "England and history" and a physiocracy tradition of Scotland, Ireland, and France. Canada's identity and security appear as a rivalry between Europe's elitist tradition and U.S.-style consumer culture. From its position in a non-central "in-betweenness," Canada resists the possibility of cultural assimilation by fostering distinctive regional literatures.

Section Four: Variations of Cross-Cultural Transfer

The fourth section devotes attention to the transfer of cultural artifacts and practices across borders, including instances of literary and theater adaptation, comparative study, and translation. When objects are transferred or transformed, ideas and values are usually transported with them. Chapters in this section show how the concerns of intercultural study are relevant to the literary production of "a reasonably full historical range" (Miner 3), with asymmetrical parameters, to provide a context for the literature of our own time. The historical dimension is especially important if we do not want to suggest that intercultural experiences and their representation are merely phenomena of the present. Cultural transfer in this sense is always a transfer across borders, as the heading makes explicit, and these may be temporal as well as topographical. Yet it is important to be aware that a form of transfer which may appear as cultural empathy can function as a trans- or imposition of one's own cultural horizon on the alien. Such empathic transposition is especially difficult to avoid.

It is not surprising that drama and theater have a share in the domain of intercultural adaptation theory: as we can learn from Donal Carbaugh's work on "cultures in conversation," when dialogue is carried on or discussed, those taking part hear messages conveyed about institutions such as "theater, opera" (128). In Chapter 16, Michael Steppat illustrates the conceptual arguments presented in Chapter 5 with a fresh assessment of the non-commercial, Shakespearian civic masque *Caliban By the Yellow Sands*. Chiefly devised by New York dramatist Percy MacKaye, it was produced in New York in May 1916 while world war was threatening to engulf the U.S., and subsequently in Boston. The masque project, which employed well over a thousand players, was intended to empower immigrant communities to operate through "constructive imagination" for the purpose of "creating the international mind" — and for "the horizon of cosmopolitan promise." It has been argued that the masque subjects immigrants to neo-colonial obligations of an Anglo-Saxon culture in America. Reassessing such a perception becomes possible by means of careful attention to the resources of intercultural research.

In Chapter 17, Sun Yan contributes significantly to the volume's concern with comparative literary study when she reads the Chinese Yuan-based drama *He Tong Wen Zi* or *The Contract* together with William Shakespeare's comedy *The Merchant of Venice*. Like the previous chapter, this focus also speaks to the analysis of drama. Each of the plays develops its action and thematic significance around a "contract," and each resolves the major dramatic conflict in a courtroom. Closer examination reveals both convergences and divergences regarding legal culture between the two plays. The divergence is subtly strengthened in a leading modern Chinese translator's rendering of the court scene in *The Merchant of Venice*, which overwrites English legal thought with Chinese legal philosophy.

Inge van de Ven and Tom van Nuenen in Chapter 18 consider transfer in an alternative way, calling attention to the recipient's inclination to transpose her or his cultural and ethical horizon into the unfamiliar text, the other's mind. This is an inadvertent effect of the ethical orientation in literary studies: critics such as Martha Nussbaum and Wayne Booth argue that literary narratives can make us more empathic, by offering the experience of living vicariously through the textualized Other — which is clearly relevant for intercultural contact zones. Yet the authors show how, unlike these, Hans-Georg Gadamer's ontological hermeneutics avoids the effect of transposition. They endeavor to rethink the notion of intercultural and interpersonal empathy with the textualized Otherness of characters, by means of a new reading of McEwan's award-winning novel *Saturday* (2005).

Words of Appreciation

As we conclude these introductory statements, we would like to express our thanks and appreciation to all those who have supported the endeavor and helped us to bring about this volume. We are beholden to Prof. Feng Qinghua, Vice President of Shanghai International Studies University (SISU), for opening and addressing the international symposium " Literature, Comparative Studies,

Interculturality" in 2015, which gave us important stimuli for our cooperative research. We wish to give our strong appreciation to Prof. Zha Mingjian, Dean of the Graduate School and Dean of the School of English Studies at SISU, for his personal initiative in furtherance of our work and in organizing that symposium, with untiring and valuable support from Prof. Wang Xin, School of English Studies at SISU. Prof. Mao Sihui, Executive Director of the International Association for Intercultural Communication Studies (IAICS), has not only strengthened the said symposium with his own prominent participation, but has given us essential impulses for our work. Prof. Zhang Hongling and the staff of the Office for International Cooperation and Exchange at SISU deserve thanks for decisive support in enabling the various stages of our cooperation. The Intercultural Institute staff at SISU has contributed very helpful service to our endeavor all along. What is more, the program organizers of the 22nd IAICS Conference in 2016 have enabled an especially fruitful environment for stimulating exchanges of ideas benefiting our work. In Germany, the Bavarian Academic Center for China has granted a generous fund to enable the formative stage of our cooperative research cluster, with the additional backing of the Vice-President and the International Office of the University of Bayreuth as SISU's partner institution. Doctoral student groups especially in Shanghai and in Bayreuth have contributed useful debates and ideas to our inquiry. A productive research environment has been provided by the Bayreuth Institute for American Studies for our cooperative work from the beginning. We owe great thanks, moreover, to Shanghai Foreign Language Education Press for its professional excellence in the printing of the volume.

We wish to take this opportunity to express our profound gratitude to each of the contributors to this volume, for having prepared excellent scholarly essays and engaging with us in fruitful discussion. Building on this experience, we feel strongly encouraged in looking forward to further explorations together.

References

Benesch, Klaus, and Kerstin Schmidt, eds. *Space in America: Theory, History, Culture*. Architecture Technology Culture 1. Amsterdam & New York: Rodopi, 2005.
Bronfen, Elisabeth, and Benjamin Marius. "Hybride Kulturen: Einleitung zur

anglo-amerikanischen Multikulturalismusdebatte." *Hybride Kulturen*. Eds. Elisabeth Bronfen and Marius Benjamin. Tübingen: Stauffenburg, 1997. 1-29.

Buzzanell, Patrice M. "Transforming Career via Intersectionalities and Inter/cultural Processes." *Intercultural Adaptation (I): Theoretical Explorations and Empirical Studies*. Intercultural Research Vol. 6. Eds. Xiaodong Dai and Steve J. Kulich. Shanghai: Shanghai Foreign Language Education Press, 2012. 75-96.

Carbaugh, Donal. "Cultures in Conversation: Cultural Discourses of 'Dialogue' in Global, Cross-Cultural Perspective." *Intercultural Adaptation (I): Theoretical Explorations and Empirical Studies*. Intercultural Research Vol. 6. Eds. Xiaodong Dai and Steve J. Kulich. Shanghai: Shanghai Foreign Language Education Press, 2012. 115-133.

Condon, John. "Exploring intercultural communication through literature and film." *World Englishes* 5.2-3 (1986): 153-161.

Foley, John Miles. *Homer's Traditional Art*. University Park: Pennsylvania State UP, 1999.

Goering, Elizabeth, Andrea J. Krause, and Liu Yifei. "The 'Collective Programming of the Mind': A Thematic Analysis of Values Re/Constructed in Reality Courtroom Television Programs in the United States, Germany, and China." *Value Dimensions and Their Contextual Dynamics Across Cultures*. Intercultural Research Vol. 5. Eds. Steve J. Kulich, Weng Liping and Michael H. Prosser. Shanghai: Shanghai Foreign Language Education Press, 2014. 337-364.

Gutjahr, Ortrud. "Alterität und Interkulturalität: Neuere deutsche Literatur." *Germanistik als Kulturwissenschaft: Eine Einführung in neue Theoriekonzepte*. Eds. Claudia Benthie and Hans Rudolf. Velten, Reinbek: Rowohlt, 2002. 345-369.

Hall, Edward T. *The Hidden Dimension*. 1966; New York: Anchor Books, 1982.

—. *The Silent Language*. 1959; New York: Anchor Books, 1981.

Hechter, Michael. "Values Research in the Social and Behavioral Sciences." *The Origin of Values*. Eds. Michael Hechter, Lynn Nadel and Richard T. Michod. New York: Aldine/Walter de Gruyter, 1993. 1-30.

Hitlin, Steven, and Jane Allyn Piliavin. "Values: Reviving a Dormant Concept." *Annual Review of Sociology* 30 (2004): 359-393.

Hofmann, Michael. *Interkulturelle Literaturwissenschaft*. Paderborn: Wilhelm Fink, 2006.

Homer. *The Iliad*. Web. 17 July 2016. http://www.perseus.tufts.edu/hopper/text? doc = Perseus:text:1999.01.0134:book = 1:card = 1

Hymes, Dell. "Ethnopoetics, Oral-Formulaic Theory, and Editing Texts." *Oral Tradition* 9.2 (1994): 330-370.

Kramsch, Claire. "Intercultural Communication." *The Cambridge Guide to Teaching English to Speakers of Other Languages*. Ed. Ronald Carter. Cambridge UP, 2001. 201-206.

Kuhn, Thomas S. *The Structure of Scientific Revolutions*. 2nd ed. Chicago: U of Chicago P, 1970.

Kulich, Steve J. *Applying Cross-cultural Values Research to "the Chinese": A Critical Integration of Etic and Emic Approaches*. 2011. Web. 17 July 2016. http://d-nb.info/1018232532/about/html

—. [Special Issue Introduction] "Reconstructing the histories and influences of 1970s intercultural leaders: Prelude to biographies." *International Journal of Intercultural Relations* 36.6 (2012): 744-759. Web. 17 July 2016. http://dx.doi.org/10.1016/j.ijintrel.2012.08.004

—. "Values Studies: The Origins and Development of Core Cross-Cultural Comparisons." *Value Frameworks at the Theoretical Crossroads of Culture*. Intercultural Research Vol. 4. Eds. Steve J. Kulich, Michael H. Prosser and Liping Weng. Shanghai: Shanghai Foreign Language Education Press, 2012. 33-70.

Kulich, Steve J., and Weng Liping. "Introduction: Value Dimensions, Dynamic Contexts, and Beyond." *Value Dimensions and Their Contextual Dynamics Across Cultures*. Intercultural Research Vol. 5. Eds. Steve J. Kulich, Weng Liping and Michael H. Prosser. Shanghai: Shanghai Foreign Language Education Press, 2014. 1-24.

Leeds-Hurwitz, Wendy. "Notes in the history of intercultural communication: The Foreign Service Institute and the mandate for intercultural training." *Quarterly Journal of Speech* 76 (1990): 262-281.

—, ed. *The Social History of Language and Social Interaction Research: People, Places, Ideas*. Cresskill, NJ: Hampton P, 2010.

—. "Writing the Intellectual History of Intercultural Communication." *The Handbook of Critical Intercultural Communication*. Eds. Thomas K. Nakayama and Rona Tamiko Halualani. Malden, Mass. & Chichester: Wiley-Blackwell, 2010. 21-33.

Lindberg-Wada, Gunilla, ed. *Literary History: Towards a Global Perspective*. 4 vols. Berlin & New York: de Gruyter, 2006.

Manzanas, Ana María, and Jesús Benito. *Cities, Borders, and Spaces in Intercultural American Literature and Film*. New York: Routledge, 2011.

Martin, Judith N., and Thomas K. Nakayama. *Intercultural Communication in Contexts*. 6th ed. New York: McGraw-Hill, 2013.

Miner, Earl. *Comparative Poetics: An Intercultural Essay on Theories of Literature*. Princeton: Princeton UP, 1990.

Moore, Robert. "Reinventing Ethnopoetics." *The Legacy of Dell Hymes: Ethnopoetics, Narrative Inequality, and Voice*. Eds. Paul V. Kroskrity and Anthony K. Webster. Bloomington: Indiana UP, 2015. 11-36.

Nakayama, Thomas K., and Rona Tamiko Halualani, eds. *The Handbook of Critical Intercultural Communication*. Malden, Mass. & Chichester: Wiley/Blackwell, 2010.

Pusch, Margaret D. "Intercultural Training in Historical Perspective." *Handbook of Intercultural Training*. Eds. Dan Landis, Janet M. Bennett and Milton J. Bennett. 3rd ed. Vol. 2. Thousand Oaks, CA: Sage, 2004. 13-36.

Pusch, Margaret D., and SIIC. *Directory of Selected Resources*. Portland, OR: Summer Institute of Intercultural Communication (SIIC), Intercultural Communication Institute (ICI). July 2012. Web. 17 July 2016. http://www.intercultural.org/documents/SIICResources.pdf

Sandel, Todd L., Anna Wong Lowe and Wen-Yu Chao. "What Does It Mean to Be 'Chinese'? Studying Values as Perceived by Chinese Immigrants to the United States and by Their Children." *Value Frameworks At the Theoretical Crossroads of Culture*. Intercultural Research Vol. 4. Eds. Steve J. Kulich, Michael H. Prosser and Liping Weng. Shanghai: Shanghai

Foreign Language Education Press, 2012. 529–558.

Starosta, William J. "Expanding the Circumference of Centrisms: On the Reframing of Identity." *Identity and Intercultural Communication（I）: Conceptual and Contextual Applications*. Intercultural Research Vol. 2. Eds. Xiaodong Dai and Steve J. Kulich. Shanghai: Shanghai Foreign Language Education Press, 2010. 53–68.

Tian Zhang. "Bewilderment and Rebirth in Jewish Identity: Cultural Identity Construction in The Assistant by American Jewish Writer Bernard Malamud." *Identity and Intercultural Communication（II）: Conceptual and Contextual Applications*. Intercultural Research Vol. 3. Eds. Steve J. Kulich and Xiaodong Dai. Shanghai: Shanghai Foreign Language Education Press, 2012. 353–362.

Wingkai To. "Chinese American Culture and Identity: Adaptation, Conflict, and Change." *Intercultural Adaptation（I）: Theoretical Explorations and Empirical Studies*. Intercultural Research Vol. 6. Eds. Xiaodong Dai and Steve J. Kulich. Shanghai: Shanghai Foreign Language Education Press, 2012. 283–295.

Xie, Ming. *Conditions of Comparison: Reflections on Comparative Intercultural Inquiry*. New York & London: Continuum, 2011.

Yige Zhu. "Lin Yutang's Cultural Exportism and Cultural Diversity." *Identity and Intercultural Communication（II）: Conceptual and Contextual Applications*. Intercultural Research Vol. 3. Eds. Steve J. Kulich and Xiaodong Dai. Shanghai: Shanghai Foreign Language Education Press, 2012. 155–165.

Reconsidering Intercultural Narratives: Prologue to Research on Rachel Davis DuBois and Early Textual Approaches to Interculturality

Steve J. KULICH

Shanghai International Studies University

Summary: Intercultural communication and literary studies share more commonality, assumptions, and supportive content than may commonly be acknowledged. The academic field of intercultural communication has generally adopted a particular mainstream narrative about its development, linked to post-World-War- Ⅱ conditions and perspectives. Yet there is another important earlier narrative that has been largely, if not almost entirely, overlooked by this field, which this chapter seeks to explicate and introduce. The kinds of narratives that we adopt and pass on will have bearing on the research field's future development. This currently evolving project seeks to map the contours of an alternative history which finds its roots in the work of Rachel Davis DuBois and her colleagues in the Intercultural Education Movement (1929–1950) and other approaches to cultural texts and drama.

Introduction

In this pioneering volume, we seek to re-integrate two important fields of study, that of the well-established field of literary studies with the more recent efforts at examining intercultural relations and intercultural communication between or among groups. It may seem to some to be an uneasy alliance between the descriptive, imaginative, and creative art of literature with the applied, practical, everyday challenges of people of different cultures seeking to understand or communicate with each other. But in putting together this volume, we argue that both fields of study share more commonality, assumptions, and supportive content than may commonly be acknowledged, and that, both historically and for future developments, literary and intercultural studies have important points of contact and mutuality.

At whatever points in the "ABC" model of attitudes (see Rosenberg) that is often attributed to Clyde Kluckhohn (though Rachel Davis DuBois was already implementing it several decades earlier), most scholars in each field would agree that the study of Behavioral or Cognitive processing needs an understanding of the Affective at the outset. In her review of the early intercultural education initiatives of Rachel Davis DuBois, Cherry McGee Banks notes:

> She designed a curriculum that included three approaches for changing intergroup attitudes: the emotional approach, the situational approach, and the intellectual approach (DuBois, 1942). DuBois believed that reducing prejudice and developing an appreciation for ethnic differences required that students connect emotionally with people from different ethnic groups. (81)

The personal and cultural sentiments that guide both our intergroup interactions and our art are rooted in how we feel about our own, family, group, or cultural narratives. And the literary or filmed encapsulation, representation, or examination of narratives, whether it be a poem, short story, novel, or one's reflective cultural story, is often where the affective can be best illustrated, expressed, or intuited, without ignoring the cognitive.

Narrative is a powerful cultural transmission process and product. The narratives we construct, notice, frame, retell, and propagate inadvertently or intentionally contribute to the cultural story that we eventually adhere to — they become part of our cultural group's identity and ethos. Each narrative emphasizes events or elements that we deem to be important to our interpretation of the world we experience, and conversely provides a reading that leaves out or de-emphasizes other aspects not considered as meaningful or important.

Those of us who have grown up in the academic field of intercultural communication have generally adopted a mainstream narrative: that this field was given impetus from the pioneering intercultural training work of Edward T. Hall. Roots of our academic and applied craft are traced to Hall's team's work at the Foreign Staff Institute (FSI), which was an American government initiative to deal with post-World-War-Ⅱ issues of seeking to understand the context of diverse countries and how those moving internationally could make sense of variations across national cultures. Hall's work at the FSI and his book *The Silent Language* (1959) have become both the dominant narrative of the field and the straw man that those who take issue with certain themes, generalities, or oversights in the field seek to counter or complement. Yet, it needs to be noted, this is but one narrative. We can learn important lessons from Chimamanda Ngozi Adichie about what it means to have stories and to realize their origins: "How they are told, who tells them, when they're told, how many stories are told, are really dependent on power" (TED Talk July 2009). We should beware, indeed, of "the danger of a single story."

If intercultural and intergroup research is to expand, it needs to uncover another important narrative that has been largely, if not almost entirely, overlooked by the field of intercultural communication. The founders of this forerunner considered their work to be very "intercultural," making strong use of pertinent terminology, and developed an influential movement called "intercultural education" in the 1930s that persisted through the 1950s. A project now evolving and related to this volume seeks to map the focus and development of that initiative and to show that intercultural literature was already a key part of the corpus, one that needs to be and in fact is being rediscovered and reconceptualized.

Rachel Davis DuBois and Intercultural Education

A key player in the alternative story is Rachel Davis DuBois (1892－1993). The *New York Times* obituary describes her as "Educator Who Promoted Value of Diversity." The article explains:

> Counter to the philosophy of the time that promoted ethnic assimilation, Dr. DuBois was among the few educators preaching that differences should be celebrated. Her work drew on her own Quaker background and her discovery of children in southern New Jersey who felt inferior and ashamed of their Italian heritage. [...] She developed a widely copied technique called group conversation that uses a common experience, like spring festivals, for people to learn about each other's customs. [...] At New York City schools,

she organized festivals on the music, dance and food of different cultures and presented plays portraying friction and harmony. (Lambert, 2 April 1993)

DuBois received a doctoral degree from Columbia, and in the book that arose from her dissertation (*Get Together Americans*, 1943) she speaks of literary sources that inspired or were used in her group dialogue "Neighborhood-Home Festival" method (for her neighborhood concept, see Looker 38). This happens mainly in Chapter 3 ("Appreciating Our Cultural Ingredients"), and includes Antoine de Saint-Exupéry's *Flight to Arras* (1942), Jerre Mangione's *Mount Allegro* (1943), Thomas Mann's *Joseph and His Brothers* (1933ff.) and his son Klaus Mann's autobiography *The Turning Point* (1942), Langston Hughes's "I Too" in his *First Collection* (1926), W. E. B. DuBois's essays and sketches in *The Souls of Black Folk* (1903) and his *Dusk of Dawn: An Essay Toward an Autobiography of a Race Concept* (1940), MacKinley Helm's biography *Angel Mo' and Her Son, Roland Hayes* (1942), Rabindranath Tagore's poetry collection *Gitanjali* (1910). She cites *Playwrights Present: Problems of Everyday Life* (1942), excerpts of classic and modern drama edited by Harry H. Giles (who became a later leader of the Bureau of Intercultural Education) and Robert J. Cadigan, a volume which reflects a key emphasis of the application of the method in schools and communities to dramatize culture so that it could be observed and experienced.

To enhance intercultural understanding further, DuBois cites Maxwell Anderson's "The Arts as Motive Power; Certain Reflections on the State of the World and Upon the Position of the Artist in It: VARIED REFLECTIONS UPON THE ARTS AS MOTIVE POWER" (*New York Times* 17 Oct. 1937), Marjorie Patten's *The Arts Workshop of Rural America: A Study of the Rural Arts Program of the Agricultural Extension Service* (1937), John Dewey's *Art as Experience* (1934), and Daniel Prescott's *Emotion and the Educative Process* (1938) (*Get* 105). For a project on "Passage Here — What We Brought," DuBois announces: "Vicarious living through drama and art will be used in the project as much as possible" (ibid., 35). She records a strong classroom demand for information about different cultural groups, so that the teachers of various subjects (including literature, social science, and home economics) "found themselves teaching co-operatively" (ibid., 37). This led to a continuous process of curriculum revision in the schools which DuBois describes. By 1941, she and her colleagues of the Service

Bureau of Intercultural Communication (SBIC) had put together and made available a list of more than 50 titles that served as resources for enhancing an understanding of various cultural groups (see the Service Bureau's *Publications*).

In *Neighbors in Action* (1950), DuBois expands the record of "word pictures of American family life," a "list of books so that the reader may start his own intercultural quest" (Chapter 6). The list includes novels about conditions in Ireland (143), fiction and poetry about African American life (151) and in another section James Weldon Johnson's collection of African American poetry as well as folk tales from different cultures, including China (280).

Varied Sources of Culture

DuBois's interest in literature can be seen prominently in *National Unity Through Intercultural Education*. This is an Education and National Defense pamphlet (1942) prepared in cooperation with the U.S. Department of Education by DuBois as director of the Intercultural Education Workshop, New York. It offers an opportunity for her to detail her ideas for education at several age levels. These are by no means all about literature, but since that is a prominent element I will focus in the following especially on her suggestions for literature.

Under the heading "The School Should Pave the Way," DuBois declares that the school "should recognize the value of all the varied sources of American culture" including, among others, the "Oriental descent on the Pacific coast" (6). Without appreciating his cultural background, James Weldon Johnson "could not have put into permanent poetic form, through his classic *God's Trombones* [1927], the primitive Negro sermons" (ibid.). Louis Adamic, originally from Slovenia, who wrote travelogues and fiction, is a further instance. In a curricular section "In the Language Arts," fifth-grade students are depicted "writing a play on the basis of Marco Polo's story": "The returning Polos were talking to the incredulous woman who opened the door of their old home in Venice." DuBois extends this to affirming that "[m]any short stories and poems can be used to suggest intercultural themes"; this can extend to ballads and folk literature (ibid., 9). "Many of the familiar masterpieces of literature included in the English curriculum" enable "intercultural appreciation," such as Dorothy Canfield Fisher's novel *The Bent*

Twig (1915), and also Sir Walter Scott's *Ivanhoe* (ibid., 10); DuBois commends Adamic's literary quarterly *Common Ground*, which, appearing since 1940, was devoted to intercultural relations and includes short stories and poetry.

In foreign language teaching, DuBois for instance suggests a focus on "French influence in American life and culture," including attention to literature and music, as a curricular element that is equally important in all language subjects (ibid., 11). "Writing original stories and verses" is highlighted as a school exercise, beginning at a rudimentary level: "Short stories and verses about friends of other lands and races," to be used as supplementary reading material (ibid., 16). At higher level, DuBois records that "[t]he use of creative or documentary playwriting has proved effective for intercultural education," as done by classes in English and/or social studies: "some aspect of the cultural heritage of the American community," if possible pertinent to their own local community, should be chosen (ibid., 25).

In her autobiographical work *All This and Something More* (1984), DuBois recalls: "As far as I know we were the first to use the term intercultural education" (76). Circa 1935.

DuBois's emphasis on "all the varied sources of American culture" rests on her resistance against the "melting pot" image of American society. In a better-known passage of *Get Together Americans*, she memorably writes:

> The melting pot idea, or "come-let-us-do-something-for-you" attitude on the part of the old-stock American was wrong. For half the melting pot to rejoice in being made better while the other half rejoiced in being better allowed for neither element to be its true self. [...] The welfare of the group [...] means [articulating] a creative use of differences. Democracy is the only atmosphere in which this can happen, whether between individuals, within families, among groups in a country, or among countries. This kind of sharing we have called cultural democracy. Political democracy — the right of all to vote — we have inherited. [...] Economic democracy — the right of all to be free from want — we are beginning to envisage. [...] But cultural democracy — a sharing of values among numbers of our various cultural groups — we have scarcely dreamed of. Much less have we devised social techniques for creating it. (5–6)

With this emphasis on a "creative use of differences," DuBois had become a pioneer of the Cultural Gifts Movement in education (see James Banks 518ff.). She was convinced that each ethnoracial group made significant contributions to the fabric of culture in America, so that a program of assimilation would be an error (see also Selig 70).

Her approach becomes apparent in the initiative to create a national radio program, which had support from the federal government but owed most to DuBois's energies. She was looking for a way to counter the impact of Father Charles Coughlin's radio broadcasts propagating America as a country for white Christians (see the account in Savage 24, also Schneider 189). The federal commissioner of education, John Studebaker, who was interested in institutionalizing intercultural education, was the right person to approach. CBS offered its New York production studios and assigned the scriptwriting to the influential cultural critic Gilbert Seldes, based on research and dramatic material which DuBois and her team would contribute.

It turned out, however, that Seldes insisted on highlighting the unifying aspects of American cultural groups and communities (already in his 1936 book *Mainland*), whereas DuBois believed in "dramatizing the contributions" of America's cultures, focusing on one such group at a time to reveal the "most common misconceptions held toward each specific group" (qtd. in Savage 25). For DuBois, "[t] he governing metaphor of the series was the gift. These immigrants come bearing gifts for the nation. And the gifts they bring are their own special talents" (Goodman 37). The result of Seldes and DuBois pulling in different directions was a series of compromises rather than a unified concept. With the title "Winning freedom/Americans all, immigrants all," and directed by Earle McGill, the product was at any rate launched in December 1938 and ran for 26 weeks with a range of actors, billed as

> " Radio broadcasts of dramatic skits highlighting immigrant contributions to building America; in part with music. Prepared and produced by the United States Department of the Interior, Office of Education, with the cooperation of the Columbia Broadcasting System and the Service Bureau for Intercultural Education and with the assistance of the Works Progress Administration." (www.worldcat. org/title/americans-all-immigrants-all-program-no-5-winning-freedom)

Once it got underway the broadcast project was " highly self-critical," especially regarding Seldes's scriptwriting skills (ibid., 38). For all the limitations, with her substantial work on this broadcast series DuBois did all she could to advance her idea of making "creative use of differences." University of Melbourne historian

David Goodman has recently affirmed that "[t]his program really seemed to exemplify what the Federal Radio Education Committee was all about" (Goodman 36). It promoted greater cultural understanding in a time of increasing suspicion and insecurity.

Exploring Cultures Through Fiction and Documentary Plays

Soon after DuBois gave an overview of literary sources to support her neighborhood festival concept in *Get Together Americans*, Joseph S. Roucek, chairman of the Department of Political Science and Sociology at Hofstra College, cooperating with Alice Hero and Jean Downey, published his extensive listing of *The Immigrant in Fiction and Biography* (1945). The publisher was the Bureau for Intercultural Education in New York, which DuBois had initially launched as the "Service Bureau" nearly a decade earlier. By 1945, as a woman and a Quaker pacifist, she had been pushed out to make way for leaders who supported melding cultures and uniting America under the war effort. Nevertheless, this work provided an annotated bibliography, organized by immigrants' source cultures, which reads like an expanded and systematized version of DuBois's overview.

The extensive "Fiction" part begins with works relevant to "Immigrants from Many Lands" and proceeds alphabetically from Armenians to Yugoslavs, including the Chinese. The very first section includes Willa Cather's *O Pioneers!* (1913); the section on Chinese features Richard T. LaPiere's *When the Living Strive* (1941) and Charles R. Shepherd's *Lim Yik Choy: The Story of a Chinese Orphan* (1932). It is clear that these sections cannot be thought of as complete, but they provided a literary starting point for cultivating intercultural understanding of varied cultural groups. The bibliography could function at least partly as a resource guide to assist teachers in making appropriate selections for classes; titles marked with * by Dr. Lou LaBrant, Professor of English Education at New York University, are considered suitable for junior high school students. The compilation, on the whole, represents a significant initiative of the Bureau for Intercultural Education that furthered DuBois's vision.

In 1943 William Vickery and Stewart Cole sought to systematize what DuBois had started, and proposed objectives and methods for intercultural education. In several contexts, they also include literary materials in their recommendations for selecting and organizing classroom materials at the senior high school level. For instance, studying Chinese culture in American cities, especially regarding the second and third generation of immigrants, aims to create "a true picture of Chinese culture" with a comparative focus on fictional stories and motion pictures (102–103). For a better understanding of African Americans in American life, a curricular unit for "Studies of the Negro's place in American literature" is suggested: "Negro poets and writers should be studied in their historical context and their work compared with their contemporaries' achievements" (ibid., 105). In a chapter on "Methods and Techniques in Intercultural Education," the authors point out that "[t]he literature dealing with race and culture group relations is as varied in type as it is voluminous," so that educators are better able than ten or fifteen years earlier to "select reading material which presents accurate accounts of cultural differences" (ibid., 110). Accordingly, they recommend,

> Novels, short stories, biographies, and poems which express democratic ideals in relation to minority groups, or present an accurate and sympathetic picture of life in other lands and among culture groups in America, are as important in intercultural education as factual surveys and reports. This type of material does much to build desirable attitudes, particularly if the students read it voluntarily and because their interest has been aroused rather than because it appears on the "required list" of collateral reading. (Ibid., 111)

In 1945 the Bureau published Spencer Brown's *They See For Themselves*. It describes an extensive project that makes use of "the documentary or factfinding method" (2), exemplified in eleven high schools in and around New York. Students chose their subject matter, "wrote their material as scenes of a play, then put the play together, cast, and produced it themselves" (ibid., 3). The method is that of functional theater, inspired by the Federal Theatre Project (ibid., 8) and often using personal interviews as source material (Chapter 3). An important educative aim is to discern "levels of meaning," explained partly with the help of I. A. Richards's *Practical Criticism: A Study of Literary Judgment* and illustrations from literary classics. The resulting documentary play becomes a "Living Newspaper," a form cultivated in the Federal Theatre, and is described as drawing on the heritage of dramatic satire as far back as Aristophanes (Brown 57) and as having forebears in the Epic Theater as developed by Bertolt Brecht (ibid., 61). An Appendix prints three such documentary plays as composed by high school students, as models for intercultural teaching and learning.

Appreciating Cultures through Theater: Initiatives of Percy MacKaye

There are other narratives to explore, especially concerning a further theatrical genre that one could consider in this context, though it is not within the Bureau's scope. New York dramatist and poet Percy MacKaye (1875–1956), member of the National Institute of Arts and Letters, so far as we know had no direct contact with DuBois, but in some ways they were pursuing similar agendas. In his early work *The Playhouse and the Play and Other Addresses Concerning the Theatre and Democracy in America* (1909), MacKaye diagnoses

> a world of democracy, which concerns itself little, or not at all, with the interests of aesthetics, artistry, craftsmanship. The world of art complains that democracy ignores the concerns of beauty. Democracy complains that the world of art ignores the concerns of citizenship. [...] true democracy is vitally concerned with beauty, and true art is vitally concerned with citizenship. (190–191)

DuBois's concept of "cultural democracy" is not far from this. As for MacKaye, in a reconceived ceremony for new citizens he speaks of "those enlightened ideals of *the new citizenship* which stand not for the levelling away of all world-cultures to leave bare an American mediocrity, but for the welcoming of all world-cultures to create an American excellence" (*New* 14). Like DuBois, he claims to value the different immigrant cultures: the dramatic art of American diversity "shall be the richer and mightier for every positive contribution of distinctive experience and tradition which each member shall conserve from his own inheritance and bring to it — the Asiatic, the European, the American, each contributive of his peculiar zone and meridian of wisdom [...]" (*Playhouse* 93). Accordingly, he declares in 1912 that he wishes to widen his art "by the inexhaustible store of material awaiting the dramatist's muse in the folk-lore which is poured from overseas into America through our immigrant population, now ignored or stamped out by ignorant derision" (*Civic* 75). DuBois's engagement in education and broadcasting thus correlates with an earlier movement in American theater, both based in New York.

That movement expresses a concern with public education as well as neighborly activity: MacKaye explains that his ideas are designed "for a new method of community building, for a dynamic, cooperative means of education in community aims, for a loyalty to those aims at once spontaneous and disciplined, for a purposeful efficiency of neighborliness" (*Community*, Preface). And neighborhood engagement goes beyond one's own national culture: "Neighborliness in a little town may beget the neighborliness of nations. The International Mind is the neighborly mind, though the neighborhood be but a village" (ibid., 18). The theater has "the mightiest potentiality for civic enlightenment and education in America," as "drama is a contemporaneous civic force" (*Playhouse* 127).

Conclusion

This chapter has illustrated the importance of narratives related to intercultural inquiry and textual explorations which have been largely ignored in the ever-expanding field of intercultural communication studies. As "intercultural studies" are now incorporated into the disciplinary register in China and linked to "comparative literature" (see the author's Preface in this volume), there is thus considerable potential for inquiry into this alternative story, not only related to the development of intercultural communication, but also its varied foci and the frameworks from which some unsung pioneers operated. The project that has begun will be presented more fully within our series, and will be further explored for a better perception of how these developments affect and modify an updated profile of this important research field and how both comparative literature and intercultural communication can be integrated meaningfully and academically.

References

Adichie, Chimamanda Ngozi. The Danger of a Single Story. TED July 2009. Web. https://www.ted.com/talks/chimamanda_adichie_the_danger_of_a_single_story? language = en

Banks, Cherry A. McGee. " A Historical Perspective on Intercultural/ Multicultural Education in the United States." *Mapping the Broad Field of Multicultural and Intercultural Education Worldwide: Towards the Development of a New Citizen*. Eds. Nektaria Palaiologou and Gunther Dietz. Newcastle upon Tyne: Cambridge Scholars Publishing, 2012. 78–92.

Banks, James A., ed. Encyclopedia of Diversity in Education. Vol. 1.

Thousand Oaks, CA: SAGE, 2012.

Brown, Spencer. *They See for Themselves: A Documentary Approach to Intercultural Education in the High School*. Problems of Race and Culture in American Education. Bureau for Intercultural Education Publication Series. New York & London: Harper, 1945.

DuBois, Rachel Davis. *All This and Something More: Pioneering in Intercultural Education*. Bryn Mawr, Penn.: Dorrance, 1984.

—. "Conserving Cultural Resources." *Americans All: Studies in Intercultural Education*. The Department of Supervisors and Directors of Instructors of the National Education Association, The National Council of Teachers of English, and The Society for Curriculum Study. Washington, DC: The Department of Supervisors and Directors of Instruction, National Education Association, 1942. 148–159.

—. *Get Together Americans: Friendly Approaches to Racial and Cultural Conflicts Through the Neighborhood-home Festival*. 4th ed. New York & London: Harper, 1943.

—. *National Unity Through Intercultural Education*. Education and National Defense Series Pamphlet No. 10. Washington, DC: U. S. Government Printing Office, 1942.

—. *Neighbors in Action: A Manual for Local Leaders in Intergroup Relations*. New York: Harper, 1950.

Goodman, David. "Hearing 'Immigrants All.'" Saving America's Radio Heritage: Radio Preservation, Access, and Education. Library of Congress Panel, Feb. 2016. 23–42. Web. June 2017.

Kluckhohn, Clyde et al. "Values and Value-Orientations in the Theory of Action: An Exploration in Definition and Classification." *Toward a General Theory of Action: Theoretical Foundations for the Social Sciences*. Eds. Talcott Parsons and Edward A. Shils. Cambridge, MA: Harvard UP, 1951. 388–433.

Lambert, Bruce. "Rachel D. DuBois, 101, Educator Who Promoted Value of Diversity." *The New York Times* 2 April 1993. Web. June 2017.

Looker, Benjamin. *A Nation of Neighborhoods: Imagining Cities, Communities, and Democracy in Postwar America*. Chicago & London: U of Chicago P, 2015.

MacKaye, Percy. *The Civic Theatre in Relation to the Redemption of Leisure: A Book of Suggestions*. New York: Mitchell Kennerley, 1912.

—. *Community Drama: Its Motive and Method of Neighborliness. An Interpretation*. Boston & New York: Riverside P, 1917.

—. *The New Citizenship: A Civic Ritual*. New York: Macmillan, 1915.

—. *The Playhouse and the Play and Other Addresses Concerning the Theatre and Democracy in America*. New York: Macmillan, 1909.

Rosenberg, Milton. *Attitude Organization and Change: An Analysis of Consistency Among Attitude Components*. New Haven: Yale UP, 1960.

Roucek, Joseph S. *The Immigrant in Fiction and Biography*. In Cooperation with Alice Hero and Jean Downey. New York: Bureau for Intercultural Education, 1945.

Savage, Barbara Dianne. *Broadcasting Freedom: Radio, War, and the Politics of Race, 1938–1948*. Chapel Hill & London: U of North Carolina P, 1999.

Schneider, Dorothee. *Crossing Borders: Migration and Citizenship in the*

Twentieth-Century United States. Cambridge, Mass.: Harvard UP, 2011.

Selig, Diana. *Americans All: The Cultural Gifts Movement*. Cambridge, Mass.: Harvard UP, 2008.

Service Bureau for Intercultural Education (Rachel Davis DuBois and Stewart G. Cole), eds. *Publications: Books, Reports of Projects, Classroom Units, Teacher's Plans, Bibliographies, Plays*. New York: Service Bureau for Intercultural Education, 1941.

Vickery, William E., and Stewart G. Cole. *Intercultural Education in American Schools: Proposed Objectives and Methods*. Foreword by William Heard Kilpatrick. Problems of Race and Culture in American Education. Bureau for Intercultural Education Publications. New York & London: Harper, 1943.

Section One

Concepts and Orientations

1

Interfacing Literature, Culture, and (Intercultural) Communication Studies in the Digital Era

Mao Sihui
Shantou University

Summary: According to Roland Barthes, all literary and cultural texts (written, audio-visual texts, and social contexts) are "semiological systems." For effective intercultural communication in our glocalized world, we have to move studies of literary/cultural texts back into their social, cultural, and ideological contexts from intra- and inter-cultural perspectives. While we continue to stress literature's intrinsic value, we should devote attention also to TV, film, cartoon, and other forms of representational media. An essential task of scholars in intercultural communication and in literary and cultural studies is to create a critical space where we recognize the tremendous impact of the digital revolution on all aspects of our culture, to ensure that certain humanistic values prevail in this digital age. Enhancing our understanding of the differences and peculiarities of literary and cultural texts from another country/culture/tradition is one of the most challenging tasks. The example of Stephen Frears's *My Beautiful Launderette* (1985) shows how conventional boundaries between classes, races, sexes, and cultures can be effectively deconstructed.

1. Representational Text and Critical Space

The long-standing separation of literature, culture, and (intercultural) communication studies has been one of the *mythologies* that still haunt the teaching profession and academia but need to be carefully re-thought and re-examined. Perhaps it is necessary to re-state that literature is an inseparable part of a culture and all literary and cultural texts (written, audio-visual texts, and social contexts) are, according to Roland Barthes, "semiological systems" (41). The values, norms, and taboos of a society, and the ideas, feelings, and identities (personal, national, political, sexual, or cultural) of a particular group of people are constructed and communicated through the use of literary/non-literary, verbal/non-verbal languages. In other words, studies of literary/cultural texts within and also across languages in this increasingly *glocalized* world (going through the dual processes of *globalization* and *localization*) have to be put back into their social, cultural, and ideological contexts from intra- and inter-cultural perspectives so as to maximize the cultivation of one's cross-cultural pragmatic competence and critical faculty for effective intercultural communication.

But, first of all, let's unpack a couple of issues related to literature, culture, media, and communication. The very term *Literature* conjures up a host of contradictions and conflicts. In the last three decades, there has been a general deep concern over the declining and increasingly marginalized status of *Literature* (with a capital L), be it Chinese, English, French, or German, in the university curriculum. At the Graz Conference on English Literature and the University Curriculum (Austria) in 1989, Wolfgang Zach (11) asked a provocative yet truly important question: "Are literary scholars today in the situation of dinosaurs on the verge of extinction?"

Indeed, teachers of English Literature have strongly felt that there exists a disconcerting insecurity about the function or "use or usefulness" of literature in our fast-moving postmodern world. Almost every department of English/foreign languages in Chinese universities today, for example, has experienced tremendous pressures for curriculum change under the powerful impact of commercialization of universities and the devastating forces of what has been called "Socialist Market Economy with Chinese Characteristics." Take for instance a top university for foreign language studies in Southern China. To meet the needs of the mushrooming foreign business enterprises, multinational corporations, new media companies/ firms, hotel and tourism industries in Southern China, especially the coastal areas, the former Department of English at the university has split into four schools/colleges over the last two decades: the Faculty of English Language and Culture (with B.A., M.A., and Ph.D. programs in linguistics, literary/cultural and translation studies), the School of English for International Business (with degree programs in international business management, economics, trade, law, and English), the School of Interpreting and Translation Studies (with B.A., M.A., M.T.I., and Ph.D. in interpreting and translation studies), and the School of English Education (with B.A. and M.A. programs in English Education). These schools (which used to be the Department of English Language and Literature) have been offering "fashionable" programs and courses such as Marketing, Economics, Tourism Management, Information Technology, Strategies in Business Negotiations, Stock Exchange ABC, International Law, Accounting, and many many others. The well-established one-year (40 weeks) English Literature Course (a history of English literature and selected readings) for the 4th-year undergraduate students has been reduced to a one-semester course. And because of "gloomy" employment prospects, the number of students who are "willing" to take the literature course has been shrinking, thus being regarded as an "endangered species," much less protected than our endangered giant pandas.

What's more, teachers of literature seem to be suffering from an "identity crisis" brought on by an array of factors: the newly-granted high prestige of natural sciences and other "practical" subjects in our society, central and local governments' "unequal" (meaning "unfair") allocation of funds for the arts and humanities (particularly for literary studies), the utilitarian way of thinking and practice of our society with its quasi-American dollar-chasing aesthetics and emphasis on employment prospects among students, parents, and school administrators, and the socially dominant position of audiovisual mass media. To a certain extent, the developments of cultural studies, regional studies, digital media studies have also contributed to the devaluation of the long-standing special status accorded to "the Great Literary Tradition" or the Canon.

In *The Western Canon* (1994) Harold Bloom, in an openly contemptuous tone, criticizes most of the modern theoretical schools — Feminism, New Historicism, Deconstruction, Lacanism and Semioticism — and lumps them together as *the School of Resentment* whose influence, according to Bloom, has made the study of literature an ideological act at its most fruitful or simply a kind of left-wing censorship at its worst. These theorists, if they consider creating a new canon at all, in Bloom's view will merely choose books by authors who "offer little but the resentment they have developed as part of their sense of identity" (7). Bloom's book opens with "An Elegy for the Canon" and ends with an "Elegiac Conclusion." How about the future? Bloom writes:

> What are now called "Departments of English" will be renamed departments of "Cultural Studies" where *Batman* comics, Mormon theme parks, television, movies, and rock will replace Chaucer, Shakespeare, Milton, Wordsworth, and Wallace Stevens. Major, once-elitist universities and colleges will still offer a few courses in Shakespeare, Milton, and their peers, but these will be taught by departments of three or four scholars, equivalent to teachers of ancient Greek and Latin. (519)

In short, scholars like Bloom believe that, as far as *Literature* is concerned, the glory is gone, the present wretched, the future bleak. And this is almost true of the situation now in most English departments in China. However depressing "the Literature scene" may be, it would not make us feel any better if we go on sentimentalizing over these powerful shifts and changes in the arts and humanities. We may try to defend the noble humanistic objectives as well as the established paradigm in the literary. But the reality is: we have been, more or less, *conditioned* by the moving image over the last few decades, although we may declare that we have never given up our resistance. It is a fact that the younger generations of scholars and students have been brought up on television, computer, Hollywood, animated films, 3D blockbusters, Facebook, Twitter, Weibo, WeChat, and a million and one mobile apps. We are forced, therefore, to ask some crucial questions such as those asked by Wolfgang Zach (11):

> (1) How should we react to the ever-increasing impact of the "new" media in the modern world?
>
> (2) Should we simply ignore them in the teaching of literature, or should the study of literature be turned into media studies to keep pace with the development in the social environment?
>
> (3) Is it justifiable to use them in an ancillary function to literary studies?

Probably, few people would disagree that our world would be extremely impoverished if it were deprived of great masters like

Homer, Sophocles, Dante, Shakespeare, Milton, Whitman, and T. S. Eliot, who are part of the accumulated wisdom of humanity stored in the printed word over the centuries. But I personally believe that, while we continue to stress the intrinsic value of *Literature*, its important role in attaining our students' linguistic, cultural competence and problem-solving capability, and its "latent emancipatory, liberating force [...] as a residue of complete freedom, of self-realization and human solidarity" (Zach 12), TV, film, cartoon, and other forms of representational (now mostly digital) media just cannot be ignored — precisely because they are central to people's lives today as the most essential source of information and entertainment. For our educational and critical objectives, they provide us with an enormous range of texts[①] for comparative studies which can, when *creatively employed*, lead to interesting findings about the different signs and codes, and also to a deeper, more balanced understanding of the texts, literary or non-literary, *referential* (texts that inform) or *representational* (texts that involve) (see McRae 1–7). What I am suggesting here is that we should get out of the constraints of traditional definitions of *Literature* with a capital "L", and expand it to include other representational texts that open up, call upon, stimulate, and use areas of the mind from imagination to emotion, from pleasure to pain. This has been popularly termed as *literature* with a small "l". In other words, "literature" denotes a rather comprehensive and subdivided field that neither just means nor excludes the Canon. This is the very space where literature, culture, media, and communication studies interface with one another.

The ever more rapid flows of capital, information, ideas, images, and people, with an increasingly popular adoption and acceptance of new/digital media technologies across the globe, as Anna Everett and John T. Caldwell point out, are "revolutionizing our sensory perceptions and cognitive experiences of being in the world. In the process, new visual, aural, linguistic, and literary

---

① There are, according to Bassnett and Mountford (14), three major text types: A) Visual Texts (film, TV, cartoon, photographs, drawings, advertisements, etc.); B) Verbal (spoken & written) Texts (interviews, spoken drama, film/ TV commentaries, radio programs, poetry, novels, play scripts, journalism, newspapers, academic writings, brochures, pamphlets, etc.); C) Musical Texts (vocal/instrumental records, CDs, LDs, etc.). For a fuller discussion of texts in relation to text-types, text-tokens, formal and material properties of texts, effects of texts on the reader, and texts, contexts and circumstances, see especially Chapter 3 of Durant and Fabb (49–65).

codes and signifiers are emerging that require new hermeneutic responses" (vi).

Indeed: the internet, e-commerce, migration, multinational corporations, and mega trans-continental projects represent challenges as well as assaults on all kinds of geopolitical, socio-cultural and psychological boundaries, beliefs, and systems. As educators and scholars in intercultural communication and literary and cultural studies, one of our essential tasks is to create a critical space where we learn to recognize the tremendous impact of the digital revolution on all aspects of our education, culture, and society, to maintain a proper balance between issues of practices, ethics, discourses of the new media and the *digitextual* monopolies of the English-speaking world — and to ensure that certain humanistic values prevail in this digital age, whether these values are encoded in the Canon or the alternative literature, traditional or digital forms of media, an Arab fairy tale or a Disney animated movie, an ancient Chinese stone tablet or a controversial note by Donald Trump on Facebook. Undoubtedly this has tremendous implications for today's intercultural communication and also literary and cultural studies.

One of the many possible ways to ensure a fair degree of success in the decoding of a literary/cultural text (such as a movie) is the comparative approach: asking ourselves *linguistic*, *literary*, *cultural*, *and ideological questions* from an intercultural perspective. One of the very fruitful areas in this regard has been the interdisciplinary study of (the intertextuality in) literature and films (see Cancalon and Spacagna, Stam and Raengo). But it should be noted that there hardly exists a clear dividing line between what is purely linguistic, literary, or cultural, since one is quite often intrinsically related to, or embedded in, the other.

2. An Illustration

Let's take films as an example. We all have films that we love for what they present to us: laughs, thrills, stunning audio-visual effects, haunting images of horror, or touching moments of romance — for visual power and visual pleasure (see Mirzoeff 9 – 13). Films frequently elicit physical, emotional, psychological, and intellectual reactions to themes, characters, images, symbols, sound, music, lighting, costume, and other formal cinematic strategies. Since it uses different ranges of linguistic, emotional, and cultural references and social attitudes, a film can be read as a powerful representational text. Compared with many other kinds of texts, films offer more direct and imaginative stimuli for the viewers to think about the world that they live in and the world each film presents: the history (e.g., the turbulent 1960s in Alan Parker's *Mississippi Burning*, 1988), the culture (e.g., the state of art and identities in Chen Kaige's *Farewell My Concubine*, 1993), the society (e.g., the bitter cry against poverty and the Establishment in Vittorio de Sica's *Bicycle Thieves*, 1948), and the human complexity (e.g., the multi-layered making of Schindler in Steven Spielberg's *Schindler's List*, 1993). Reading them as texts, we can, for example, see Charles Chaplin's *Modern Times* (1936) as a light-hearted yet powerful satire on industrial technology and its dehumanizing effects, Spielberg's *E.T.* (1982) as a touching celebration of love (allegory) full of religious subtexts with a divinely childlike faith, Stephen Frears's *My Beautiful Laundrette* (1985) as an extremely entertaining, insightful, and ruthless examination of both race relations and the economic state in Thatcher's Britain in the 1980s as well as national, ethnic, and sexual identities, and Ang Lee's *Life of Pi* (2012) as a fantastic visual attempt to reflect on important issues such as Faith, Courage, and Truth. Sitting in the dark for two hours gazing at images of light and shadows, who can remain undisturbed, for instance, by the sheer masculine energy and unfussy presentation of Rambo as a pain-proof fighting machine, or untouched by the sense of alienation and loneliness in Shirley Valentine's good-humored monologues and the great joy of rebirth she finally finds in herself?

Apart from these "big" thematic responses to films with "a touch of imagination" (McRae 31), we can also take a film, "chop it up" and select some (both verbal and non-verbal) discourses for detailed study, for linguistic, semantic, pragmatic, and cinematic analysis. To illustrate this point, let us examine briefly a scene from *My Beautiful Laundrette* just before the opening of the newly-furnished laundrette. In front of us, we see a laundrette which glitters like a Hollywood picture palace (perhaps a postmodernist parody of the commercial dream and sexual fantasy Hollywood represents). The camera, with a classical piece of music as background, cuts between and also connects three very telling images: the love-making of Omar (son of a faded Pakistani socialist living in South London) and Johnny (a white ex-National Front hoodlum) in the back room, the dancing of Nasser (Omar's uncle, the smoothest of the smooth commercial operators in the Thatcherite era) and his mistress Rachel (white, middle-class, and middle-aged) in the spacious and elegant laundrette, and the eager customers (mainly local folks) waiting outside the door. In the inner room, hidden from the public, Omar calmly makes his bitter complaints about the vicious prejudice the Asian immigrants suffered at the hands of the establishment and the racist National Front, and Johnny begins to touch, kiss, and undress Omar. Then the camera cuts to the outside: Nasser and Rachel entering the big laundrette hand in hand and cheerfully starting to dance (actually their last waltz). The next few cuts shift mainly between the two couples and the sequence basically consists of close-ups and medium shots:

— Johnny and Omar kissing more passionately.
— Nasser and Rachel waltzing faster.
— Johnny and Omar drinking and sharing wine from mouth to mouth.
— Nasser and Rachel kissing each other like a gentleman and a lady.
— Understanding smiles and laughter from the customers.
— Johnny spots Nasser through the window. Nasser leaves Rachel and comes to the back room.
— Nasser: (*Seeing the two boys dressing in panic*) What the hell are you doing? Sun-bathing?
— Omar: Er ..., sleep, Uncle. We were shut out. Where's Papa?
— Nasser is speechless for a moment and then leaves the boys.

An objective camera shifts to the outside in a deep focus: Johnny, Nasser, and Rachel sharing champagne and starting the ribbon-cutting ceremony; near the camera, Omar playing a music tape; in the distance, customers filing into the laundrette. In these shots, apart from interesting exchanges of discourses (e.g., Omar's use of "Where's Papa" to change the topic and fend off further questions), images of the public and the private, the affirmative, and the subversive are ingeniously brought together. The conventional (typically British) boundaries between classes (working-class and middle-class), races (white and coloured), sexes (heterosexual and homosexual), and cultures (classical music/waltz and washing, making telephone calls, and socializing) are effectively deconstructed, and analyzing the cinematic language and verbal/non-verbal discourses in the film does make us *think* about important issues of class and socio-cultural and sexual identities — what it means to be Asian and British in Thatcher's Britain in the late 1980s and early 1990s.

In our *glocalized* world where intercultural communication is a daily practice as in "global production" of films which generates "global discourses" (Harbord 93–116), learning to understand another culture is an important, dynamic, and complex process. Misunderstandings and conflicts in cross-cultural situations are very often caused by the lack of socio-pragmatic cultural competence in the interlocutors. The enhancement of our awareness of the differences and peculiarities of the literary and cultural texts from another country/culture/tradition presents itself as one of the most essential as well as challenging tasks for scholars in intercultural communication and literary/cultural studies in the digital era. This task calls for a new approach to understanding and critiquing intercultural communication and literary/cultural texts, and redefining shifting traditional boundaries between/among diverse academic disciplines, thus helping us enter a new collection of different spaces for intercultural dialogue, (self-)identity negotiation, and socio-cultural navigation.

References

Barthes, Roland. "Theory of the Text." *Untying the Text: A Post-Structuralist Reader*. Ed. Robert Young, trans. Ian McLeod. New York: Routledge and Kegan Paul, 1981. 31–47.

Bassnett, Susan, and Alan Mountford. *British Studies: Designing and Developing Programmes Outside Britain*. London: British Council, 1993.

Bloom, Harold. *The Western Canon: The Books and School of the Ages*. London: Macmillan, 1994.

Cancalon, Elaine D., and Antoine Spacagna, eds. *Intertextuality in Literature and Film: Selected Papers from the Thirteenth Annual Florida State University Conference on Literature and Film*. Gainesville: UP of Florida, 1994.

Durant, Alan, and Nigel Fabb. *Literary Studies in Action*. London: Routledge, 1990.

Everett, Anna, and John T. Caldwell. *New Media: Theories and Practices of Digitextuality*. London: Routledge, 2003.

Harbord, Janet. *Film Cultures*. Thousand Oaks, CA: Sage, 2002.

McRae, John. *Literature with a Small 'l'*. London: Macmillan, 1991.

Mirzoeff, Nicholas. *An Introduction to Visual Culture*. London & New York: Routledge, 1999.

Stam, Robert, and Alessandra Raengo, eds. *A Companion to Literature and Film*. Malden, MA: Blackwell, 2008.

Zach, Wolfgang, ed. *English Literature and the University Curriculum*. Frankfurt am Main: Peter Lang, 1992.

2

Comparative Literature Meets Translation Theory[①]

Sandra L. BERMANN
Princeton University

Summary: Comparative literature has long been a field that is not univocal but that offers different emphases and healthy debates. Within this relational network, translation is among the particularly active nodes. Initially, during the 19th century, comparative literature flourished in collaboration with translation. But by the early 20th century, translation came to be marginalized in a discipline that, focusing on Europe, prized readings " in the original." Somewhat later, however, translation studies developed in distinctive theoretical directions, enabling a recent re-union of comparative literature with translation which has helped "translate" comparative literature into a field more interesting and important for our times. The chapter briefly traces the history of this disciplinary relationship. Building thereon, the author argues that each translated text has a story, indeed a travelogue, and literary migrations through translation into different languages and cultures can be revolutionary. Translation and transtextuality affect every culture, even the most seemingly pure; they make us not only who we are, but somewhat other than who we think we are. A defining issue in

---

① This chapter was originally presented as a talk in Shanghai at the International Association for Intercultural Communication Studies (IAICS) and at the Summer School for Criticism and Theory at Cornell University. Some portions of this chapter appeared in an earlier version in Bermann, "World."

this context is migration: migrants have historically been powerful cultural agents as well as the objects of policy making or interventions. They may be victims, but also cultural producers and brokers between cultures. In connection with migration, linguistic and cultural translation is now performing some vital sociocultural work within the framework of comparative literature, engaging in questions that affect the public sphere.

I. Comparative Literature — Present and Past

Comparative literature as practiced in the US and abroad has had an active — and changeful — past. Perhaps because of the different emphases now current and because of the healthy debates they foster, the field today does not generally claim to be univocal, with a single, universally accepted object or method of study. Rather, its breadth and variety are salient. As one major US university explains on its web site, "Comparative literature is the study of literature and other cultural expressions across linguistic and cultural boundaries [...] Department offerings and research make frequent use of linguistics, film, painting, music, philosophy, history, sociology, political science and even medicine. Courses span the cultures of the world and historical periods from antiquity to current time."②

The many voices of this expansive field have created what might best be described today as a mobile network of approaches, where both relationality and differentiation play a role (see Felski and Friedman). Inquiring into texts and media, as well as their transmission and translation over time, language and place, comparatists frequently approach broad human issues such as race, gender, imperialism and human rights as well as more traditional literary topics. In the course of wide-ranging inquiries, they also reflect theoretically, bringing new focus not only to *what* we interpret but *how*.

In this sense, comparative literature often acts as "the laboratory or workshop of literary studies, and through them, of the humanities" (Greene 143 – 144). Breadth coupled with innovation have made comparative literature both energetic and protean. Well established in a good number of individual undergraduate and graduate programs

---

② www. brown. edu/academics/comparative-literature/aboutus/. Accessed 31 Oct. 2016.

and departments in Europe, the US and, increasingly, around the world, its methodologies undergird scholarship and teaching in departments of English, the modern languages, cultural studies, and more.

If the metaphor of the laboratory or workshop aptly describes the field, its arena has by now been extended to the website. Here, hypotheses and results are shared and tested. This is certainly one of the reasons why the American Comparative Literature Association's current "Report on the Profession," displayed on its web site, is particularly effective. It captures not only the range of research but also the discursive, dialogical, and overtly experimental mode of this mobile network, allowing each reader to view and critically interact with the different voices that comprise the multiplicity (the Babel?) of the field.

A. Current Nodes of Interest

Within this relational, virtually conversational, network, there seem to be several particularly active nodes: colonialism and postcolonialism; gender, sexuality, race and the politics of identity; interdisciplinarity (including law and human rights); intermediality and the digital humanities; world literature; and translation. All are important, indeed essential, to the discipline as we know it today.

But I choose to focus here on translation (and particularly translation theory) because of all of these various and important nodes of interest, translation has a particularly close, if not vexed, historical kinship to the discipline of comparative literature — and, I believe, an especially important role in its current unfolding.

Let me turn briefly to one well-known narrative of the history of comparative literature (there are others, depending on geographical site, moment, and political perspective). This one emphasizes the field's early expressions in 19th-century Europe, where it initially served as an antidote to a growing nationalism. At that point, it flourished in collaboration with translation. But by the early 20th century, translation was deliberately marginalized in what had become a highly Eurocentric discipline that prized readings "in the original," and largely of "major" European languages. Only in the late 20th century did comparative literature once again meet — and warmly embrace — the field of translation. This happened well after translation theory had itself developed in distinctive theoretical directions. I would argue that this relatively recent meeting — or re-union — of comparative literature with translation not only resulted in a fruitful expansion of literary studies to include new, previously less read, texts. Rather, translation theory's own growing insights into ethics, history, and an active involvement in the world has helped "translate" comparative literature into something worldlier and more potentially transformative — as well as more theoretically interesting — than before.

Let's take a closer look at this disciplinary history before returning to some of these present, disciplinary "translations" (and I am using the term here in both its restricted, inter-linguistic sense and its more metaphorical one):

B. Disciplinary Beginnings

Though "comparative literature" was a term used in a few teaching manuals in France as early as 1816 (see Bassnett 12), the idea of comparative literature as a literary study crossing national boundaries was by this time clearly "in the air." It found much of its initial theoretical inspiration in 19th-century Germany. Goethe, for instance, advocated looking beyond national contexts to see literature as the "universal possession of mankind." His words, recorded by Eckermann in 1827, are "National literature is now a rather unmeaning term; the epoch of world literature is at hand and everyone must strive to hasten its approach."③ His view was largely proleptic, a discussion of a broader view of literature that he hoped would come after the clearly nationalizing tendencies of his day. It would occur through the transmission and translation of texts across different national contexts — and discussion among authors in an internationalizing age.

In fact, the European interest in translations and adaptations in the late 18th and 19th centuries was already producing some of the cosmopolitanism Goethe hoped to see. He himself translated, read widely in translation, theorized about it, and particularly enjoyed reading his own works in other languages. Translations of Chinese novels as well as the ghazals of Hafiz inspired Goethe's own writing and served to acquaint European readers with other literary cultures, bringing these texts literally within the broader "possession of mankind" (or of those with the freedom, leisure, and education to read them).

---

③   The connections of the term "world literature" to translation (as well as to Comparative literature) are also important and bear further scrutiny than there is space for here.

In the context of 19th-century Europe's wars, its emerging nation-states, and its rapid colonial expansion, such ideals of trans-national literary study, augmented by an intensified effort to translate — and re-translate (the re-translation of Greek texts was especially prized) — contributed to what soon became a growing field of interest, if not yet of regular university study. They played a role in the *bildung*, or self-cultivation, of the cosmopolitan individual. Together, they marked out a way to consider literary and cultural issues at this moment of political transformation, a way that would consider national literatures as they migrated across national borders and linguistic differences, challenging but also enriching one another.

At times, such early transnational literary study ended by advancing nationalizing interests (consider the Grimm brothers in Germany). But at others, comparative writings were unusually broad and transnational. Such was the case, for instance, with the first comparative literature journal, *Acta Comparationis Litterarum Universarum* edited by the Transylvanian scholar Hugo Meltzl de Lomnitz (1877). Publishing articles in a variety of languages (ten official ones) and engaging with topics such as literary histories, the role of translation, and the importance of multilingualism, the journal clearly foreshadowed 21st-century concerns. The book *Comparative Literature* (1886), by the Irishman Hutcheson Macauley Posnett (living in New Zealand), likewise marked out a wide-ranging comparativism, though with an evolutionary, more hierarchical approach (see Damrosch et al. 41–60).

C. Comparative Literature in the European Academy

If translation played an essential role in early 19th-century renditions of comparative literature, this partnership, and the rangy cultural vision that sustained it, soon began to dissolve as comparative literature became an academic discipline. By the early 20th century in France, when comparative literature first secured a place in the academy, the field was already turning in more positivist directions where only "rapports de fait" between two texts, in two different (European) national languages, could bear the name "comparative literature." Studies including more tended to be categorized as "general" or "world" literature (both something lesser) (Bassnett 28–30). Moreover, when studying such "rapports de fait" (specific influences, contacts), research was to be done in the original languages — most definitely not in translation. This "French school" and its constraints — both on the global reach of literary study and on the uses of translation — long dominated.

The early 20th-century German tradition of comparative study developed differently, often concerned with folk and oral cultures. Though it might have provided a strong transnational force in Germany after World War I (at least in the hands of scholars such as Ernst Robert Curtius), colleagues such as Leo Spitzer and Eric Auerbach were forced to flee during the Nazi rise to power. Migrating first to Turkey and then the United States, they used their scholarly work to retrieve the European culture left behind. They also became instrumental in founding a US version of comparative literature.

D. Comparative Literature in the U.S. Academy

What was this New World version? Developing at a safe distance from the warring European nation-states, comparative literature in the US from the late 19th and early/mid 20th century generally offered a less politicized, more idealistic view of the field (see Bassnett 32–37). It clearly tended toward more open, interdisciplinary practices. (As Henry Remak states in 1961: "Comparative Literature is the comparison of one literature with another and comparison of literature with other spheres of human expression.") (Stallknecht and Frenz 3).

Yet in practice, the field of comparative literature in the US as well as Europe nonetheless concentrated for decades primarily on the "major" European literatures — to be read in the "major" European languages. These tendencies were reinforced by funding from the US National Defense Education Act that supported strong European language departments in most US universities and also by the postwar rise of the New Criticism, with its insistence on a close reading of original texts. In this context, translation was not generally acceptable for teaching and learning in the field, and theorizing about it remained uninteresting. If we have any doubts about this, we need only turn to the various reports issued by the American Comparative Literature Association (ACLA).

In its 1969 Report (edited by Harry Levin), the ACLA suggests: "We need not be too much concerned with the problem of foreign literature in translation, if we distinguish clearly between such courses and courses in Comparative Literature [...]" (Bernheimer 23). A somewhat later Report by Tom Greene (1975) worries even more, and more explicitly, about the prospect of literature in translation: "At the undergraduate level, the most disturbing recent trend is the association of Comparative literature with literature in translations. Many courses taught today under the rubric Comparative literature are in fact not properly labeled" (Bernheimer 35).

This rejection of translation was tied in part to positivist philological expectations inherited from the French School, in part to strong European language departments in the US, but also to ideological (often colonialist) assumptions about non-European literatures — and to theoretical and methodological constraints. As long as texts were European, they could, it was believed, be effectively studied with the theoretical tools at hand, themselves drawn from the heritage of European philosophy, theory, and literary criticism. Other texts received only intermittent attention within the field and so were far less well-known (though a few departments, or individuals within them, did attempt to bring East Asian literatures together with the European).④ Concern about the potential theoretical as well as linguistic difficulties of a more global study often limited desires for broader exploration. Greene put it plainly in that same 1975 Report: "we are still lacking the concepts and tools that permit us truly to study literature at the global level. These concepts and tools will gradually materialize" (Bernheimer 36).

They did, and in part, I would suggest, through translation theory itself.

E. The Transitional Years

Between the mid-1970's and the 1990's, comparative literature grew and changed dramatically. Theory, largely but not only European, became a major interest, and soon a defining feature. First structuralism and then poststructuralism — particularly deconstruction — revolutionized it, transforming the ways individual texts were read and how they might be read comparatively. It often did so through probing insights into the question of language itself. Cultural studies emerged as another strong, if sometimes conflicting current, carrying with it a keener sense of historical and political contexts. As the century progressed, not only did postcolonial studies grow in importance, but also gender and sexuality studies, new historicism, race and ethnicity studies, trauma studies, and translation studies; all

---

④ Earl Miner, teaching at Princeton in the Department of Comparative Literature as well as in English and East Asian Studies, was a particularly well-known example.

expanded the global range of texts read as well as the theoretical assumptions brought to them. Certain figures, including René Etiemble (France) and Earl Miner (US), worked specifically to include a broader group of literatures and comparative theories to study them.

A more planetary comparative literature also found expression through new comparative literature associations throughout the world. In addition to those in Canada, Western Europe, and the US, active societies in Africa, China, Eastern Europe, India, Japan, Latin America, and elsewhere brought distinct, often quite different perspectives to the field. The International Comparative Literature Association, established in 1955, encouraged this process while joining scholars for broad international projects. Focusing in part on their own complex literary cultures, these organizations used their perspectives to see — and at times substantially revise — assessments of dominant European and North American literatures (see Bassnett 37–38). In the same years, important new work produced by scholars from many parts of the world, including that of Edward Said, Swapan Majumdar, and Mikhail Bakhtin entered into circulation, disrupting past assessments, opening new insights into empire and postcolonialism, and increasing an awareness of the planet's many diverse literary traditions as well as their European and US representations.

Though these several developments joined to radically transform the identity of comparative literature, making it far more supple and inclusive, only in the 1990's did the field (or the dominant Euro-American branch I've been describing) "officially" embrace a more extensive linguistic and cultural reach. At the same time, it opened the door to translation. At this juncture, Charles Bernheimer's 1993 ACLA Report made a disciplinary recommendation that reflected the dimensions of the change. It advocated reading more literatures from more parts of the world. In order to do so, it insisted on more language learning — not only of a select group of European languages, but of other languages as well. The report also registered a dramatic new openness to reading in translation: "While the necessity and unique benefits of a deep knowledge of foreign languages must continue to be stressed, the old hostilities toward translation should be mitigated." And in contrast to the past, it further suggested that translation might even be one of comparative literature's long-awaited theoretical "tools" for studying the newly "global" sphere. Indeed, it could, so it seemed, help define the field: "Translation can well be seen as a paradigm for larger problems of understanding and interpretation across different discursive traditions. Comparative literature, it could be said, aims to explain what is lost and what is gained in translations between the distinct value systems of different cultures, media, disciplines and institutions" (Bernheimer 44).

In short and to conclude this historical narrative, by the close of the 20th century comparative literature had met translation once again, and had begun mending the rifts created over the years. Changes in the "real world" clearly played a significant role in this, as the increasingly global reach of financial and military systems as well as information technologies prompted a sometimes urgent rethinking of cultural, linguistic, and translation issues — on a world scale. 9/11 came as a powerful wake-up call to many scholars, and a new linguistic and literary cosmopolitanism began to be debated in the 21st-century context of war, religious and political confrontation (see Apter). Due in large part to this, as well as to changing developments in the field itself, some of which I've tried to outline here, comparative literature reached the turn of the 21st century with far greater engagement with more of the world's texts — and with translation as a partner once again. Haun Saussy's 2004 ACLA report was clear. Comparative literature would now be described through its tendency toward encounter and relation — with other texts, cultures, disciplines. Its reach would be increasingly global, and translation, in its growing theoretical complexity, would figure prominently (see Saussy 3–42).

It's important to note that by this time, "translation studies" had developed into a discipline in its own right, and one that had already moved from a predominantly linguistic to a "cultural" phase (see Bermann and Porter 1–11). Interested at this point not only in the linguistic descriptions of translation but also in the cultural role of translators and translation, and therefore in the issues of power, hegemony, identity (of various kinds), empire and postcolonialism, translation studies and comparative literature could very easily join forces. They did. Comparative literature soon became engaged, even deeply engaged, in "thinking translation."

II. Comparative Literature Meets Translation Studies

Among the many testimonies to comparative literature's renewed

interest in translation at the turn of the century, one might mention
Susan Bassnett's 1993 *Comparative Literature: A Critical Introduction*;
Gayatri Spivak's much discussed essay "The Politics of Translation,"
also in 1993; Larry Venuti's 1995 *The Translator's Invisibility* and
his first publication of *The Translation Studies Reader* in 2000;
J. Hillis Miller's article in *Diacritics* in 2001 identifying "the question
of translation as the central problematic in comparative literature";
and Emily Apter's 2006 book *The Translation Zone: A New
Comparative Literature*.

In works such as these, translation studies brought to comparative
literature a deepening sense of linguistic and cultural critique, and a
specific theorizing of translation in its relation to literary and
cultural study. True, as Antoine Berman insisted in his own
groundbreaking look at translation theory's history in 1984,
theorizing about translation had in fact begun more than a century
before, precisely in 19th-century Germany, where a version of
comparative literature (as *Weltliteratur*) was also first being
described. But what was fragmentary in translation theory then
developed much more fully in the late 20th century. It was a
theorizing that not only manifested the importance of translation as
a practice and a theoretical domain — an achievement important in
itself. It also brought with it some specific emphases: a strong ethical
dimension, underscoring translation's relation to other peoples,
texts, and cultures; also, a renewed sense of literary history.
Another emphasis, and one that has increasingly emerged, is an
experiential engagement with language issues, and a reassertion of
their importance within broader literary, political, and
humanitarian concerns.

Let me pause briefly on each of these sites of contemporary
partnership between comparative literature and translation:

A. Ethical Imperative

As Schleiermacher clearly described in the 19th century, a
translation stands in a pivotal but ambiguous relationship to the
target language and its source. It can be appropriative and
ethnocentric in its strategies, bringing the foreign text seamlessly but
reductively to the reader. Here, homogenization and hierarchy
predominate. This is, however, only one way to proceed.
Translation also has the potential to open a relation with the Other,
to transform our selfhood as well as our intellectual hypotheses
through the experiential mediation of what is Foreign (Berman esp.

43–69). By producing an opening, a dialogue, with another text and culture, translation is capable of achieving its highest ethical potential. It is perhaps above all, this bit of hope for — and action toward — a more "relationary" and indeed even "disturbatory" space that translation proposes. Though the roots of this commitment reach as far back as 19th-century Germany, its 20th and 21st-century effects when joined with comparative literature, particularly in its postcolonial work, have been groundbreaking (see Spivak, Bhabha, and Venuti for examples).

In the process of reinforcing some of comparative literature's own recent ethical concerns about language, power and the translator's work, "thinking translation" can also extend the well-honed practice of close reading, so intrinsic to the profession, to the translation as well as source, allowing the reader to note what has been "gained," as well as "lost," in translation. Reading closely, we can note, for instance, what Goethe called the "regeneration" of the original that arises through translation (Berman 66–67). Benjamin later speaks famously of the text's "survival" or "afterlife" in translation (Benjamin 77), an idea effectively elaborated by Derrida: "translation augments and modifies the original which, insofar as it is living on, never ceases to be transformed and to grow. It modifies the original even as it also modifies the translating language" (Derrida, *Ear* 122). For as has often been noted, a translation can show us an "other side" of the original text,[5] aspects of it that had previously remained hidden or unnoticed. In this sense, translation revivifies the target language but also the language and the literary tradition of the source.

It is also in the context of an ethics of the Other that the theoretical issue of "untranslatability" arises. Untranslatability has long been a theme surrounding specific sacred texts that it intends to protect and to mark as sacred. It also marks spaces of literary sacredness and of individual untranslatability — literary or personal texts considered too precious or too painful (as in cases of traumatic memory) — for dissemination.

But there is, of course, another sort of underlying untranslatability, one very often discussed in the translation of literary, and especially poetic, texts: the untranslatability that inheres in language itself — evident in the lack of exact semantic and cultural equivalence

---

[5] As Tymoczko notes in passing (22), the Chinese word *fan yi*, related to the English word *translation*, itself suggests this.

between languages — and the different ways in which sound and sense, letter and meaning join in each. This is the source of a quite inevitable untranslatability which knowledgeable translators — and readers — recognize all too clearly. On a practical level, translators can, of course, deal with it in different ways. They can ignore it, reducing the text's complexity. Or they can expand the potential of the target language as well as the source by transposing the "original" though calques and new syntactic turns that capture, albeit only partially, the sense of the untranslatable within the source. In this practical effort, a task more of creative transposition than an establishing of equivalence, we may begin to discover what Benjamin called the kinship of languages — or simply extend the potential meanings that languages allow, always knowing that the process is in fact endless (see Berman 190).

Such rendering of the "untranslatable" is, of course, not a simple or intuitive process on the part of the translator. It requires an extensive knowledge of the entire historical range of the languages involved and a keen awareness of their dialogical potential. It heightens our awareness not only of different languages but also of language itself — its quality *as* language — and its multiple roles in our daily lives, in our larger human history, and the politics of our day.

B. History and the Constitutive Powers of Translation

Thinking about language and the role of translation can transform an awareness of literary and cultural history. This is at least in part due to the constitutive power of translation. In a very practical sense, translation underlies history and at times dramatically constitutes it. As Bella Brodzki puts it, "Translation today is seen to underwrite all cultural transactions from the most benign to the most venal" (Brodzki 2). In certain fields, such as religion and philosophy, translation's historical power is particularly salient. Consider, for instance, translations of religious texts that have themselves created powerful new interpretations and even religious institutions. Martin Luther's German translation of the Latin Vulgate offers one dramatic example. The Chinese translations and commentaries on Buddhist texts provide another (as Martha Cheung has eloquently shown).

Or consider the history of philosophy as it evolves, for instance, through Heidegger's re-readings of the Greek philosophers and his re-translations of their primary terms. Or Derrida's more recent translations and re-interpretations of philosophical issues and terms (such as "relève" for "Aufhebung") (see Derrida, "What"). *The Dictionary of Untranslatables* by Barbara Cassin, now translated into English by Emily Apter, Jacques Lezra, and Michael Wood, tracks some of these particularly intriguing translation histories (with their many ambiguous turns) that have in fact constructed what we think of as contemporary philosophy.

The importance of the history of translation to a global literary history is only beginning to be explored. Yet it has much to recommend it. Let me simply mention that each translated text has a story — indeed a travelogue and one from which we can learn. In fact, in their quiet ways, such literary migrations through translation into different languages and cultures can be quite revolutionary. They can reveal the longstanding transnationalism and transtextuality of acclaimed national classics, and the surprising polyculturalism of inherited national cultures.

An example such as the *Arabian Nights* is a case in point with its several translations across languages and cultures, translations that often include textual additions and transformations (see Horta). A work of many hands and several cultures — Persian, French, Arabic — its changes over time and place reveal the complexity of its history. But foundational texts of European cultures are also surprisingly transnational. Cervantes' *Don Quixote* is a well-known example. So is Dante's *Inferno*.

Indeed, the *Inferno* reveals a particularly interesting — and linguistically constitutive — translational travelogue (for a fuller discussion, see Bermann, "In"). We could begin by following the winding trade routes of Dante's own translations, beginning with what he read from Latin and French and heard in various Italian dialects, as he constructed the plurilinguistic vernacular that we today call Italian. But we could also travel in another direction, looking to all the translations and adaptations of Dante's text that have journeyed over time, place and by now, some seventy languages. A third step might be to examine how translations and adaptations have become interwoven with recipient cultures, increasing the transtextual quality of their poetry: in the Anglophone context we might look, for instance, to the work of T. S. Eliot or of Derek Walcott, where Dante appears prominently through translation and intertextual allusion. Such translation histories can also be traced in the migration of poetic forms and genres: the sonnet, the ghazal form, the haiku all offer intriguing examples.

The real gain would be to rethink the literary history of several global literary traditions, noting not their static qualities, but their adventurous encounters and interweavings that make us aware that translation, transmission, and transtextuality affect every culture — even the most seemingly pure, and even 'our own,' directly and often irremediably. They make us who we are and also somewhat other than who we think we are. They make us — have long made us — "post-national" — if not exactly in the way Goethe envisioned. And they have done so since the very beginnings of our literary histories. As Edouard Glissant has suggested, "foundational" texts frequently reveal a nomadism, complete with stories of exile and errantry, rather than a simple rootedness (see Glissant 14 – 16). Looking to translation histories forcefully reminds us of their further linguistic and geographical wanderings. Such a study remains to be written, but some of the literary migrations have often been pointed out and the ways in which they constitute our transnational histories noted. In such historical contexts, translation in the restricted sense becomes transtexuality and, at times, the basis for a heightened awareness of our interwovenness.

C. Engagement

Let me turn in conclusion to the aspect of translation that might be called its potential for engagement with a broader public sphere. There are many examples of this today — from fan-subbing to translating political protests (see Baker). But I will focus here on a single current example: translation and migration — a topic that challenges us to think through comparative literature and translation issues from ethical, historical, and experiential standpoints.

Migration — and I speak now not only of migrating texts and cultures but of peoples — is clearly a defining issue of our time (as well as of our historical past), and it is likely to remain one well into the future. It is, in a sense, the human face of globalization, expressing not only our much publicized mobility, but also the encounters and interdependence that increasingly shape our lives. Often, they call for conscious engagement.

As we know, large-scale human migration dominates many regions of the world today, and the media flood us with images and stories of peoples on the move, often with tragic beginnings — and equally tragic ends. Humanitarian issues arise on a daily basis — in Greece, Turkey, Africa, the Middle East, and the Americas — raising concerns about shelter, food, medical attention, and simple protection from harm. In 2015 the United Nations counted 244 million international migrants worldwide. Many more remain uncounted. And the number is rising.

For a comparatist interested in language and translation, the movements of people, their languages, and their cultures across borders immediately raise a number of threshold questions — intellectual and humanitarian. Some are quite speculative and statistical: important questions about language use, the dominance of English, the potential loss of smaller languages. Others are far more practical and individual, and equally essential to consider.

At the most basic level, we might ask for instance how not knowing a particular language alters the lives of international and national migrants, sometimes affecting their very survival. What are the most critical instances of this? How, and in what specific contexts, do linguistic translations occur and what are their effects? Who produces them? How do differing political and cultural power structures figure within them — and how do these affect the subjectivities of migrating peoples?

Some linguistic issues have a particularly strong political and legal valence. Who is defined as a "migrant," a "refugee," an "asylum seeker" or "a guest"? And what entity provides the definitions? How do *changing* boundaries (such as those within the Soviet Union and its dissolution or those resulting from European colonialism) as well as simply *crossing* boundaries bring new meanings to these terms? How does the clandestine trafficking of human bodies enter into this set of terms and calculations? How do recipient communities react to the influx of people, whether their coming is publicized in newscasts, print media, and on the web — or carefully hidden? How can human rights issues relating to migration be addressed, given the juxtaposition of starkly differing views of social organization in different nation states and, to return to our initial issue, the different languages in which these are often expressed? Here, translation can be raised as a humanitarian need and an ethical question: is the translation linguistically and culturally competent, and is it being performed in dialogue with, rather than in hierarchical relation to the speaker or writer? How are national identities, bureaucracies, and legal vocabularies negotiated? How does the migrant's status as alien relate to her/his eventual categorization within a legal and political system? How can the migrant's own voice be heard within the translations required for legal and national recognition? (see Giordano).

Migration also places before us issues of resettlement, education, and integration. Many of these again concern translation, both linguistic and cultural. How can migrants become effective agents in a culture and educational system in ways that allow them to live, work, and reach their human potential? How will educational systems in host cultures be transformed by new groups, their new languages and cultures? How do translations of literary texts, memories, music, and art arise and move within and through cultures, and how do these translations reveal and affect broader "cultural translations" and cultural histories? Which texts are not, or cannot be translated — and what are the reasons for this?

In these and other ways, language and translation reveal much about the nature of migrant and home communities, but also about the multiple roles migrants play — as family members, legal or illegal citizens, job seekers, students, workers, targets of police activity, objects of resettlement and re-education, artists, and translators, often self-translators (see Polezzi). As some of these roles and observations already suggest, the linguistic effects *of* the migrant are also important — both as an individual and as representation. Migrants, that is, have historically been powerful cultural agents as well as the objects of policy making or interventions. They are cultural producers and brokers between cultures, not only victims — and this often emerges through writing and the arts. Think of the way migration has changed the human sciences in the past. Could we imagine a history of modern democracy without Hannah Arendt? Or conservative argument without Leo Strauss? Or comparative literature without Erich Auerbach? What about the prominence of the literary memoir in the globalizing world, where memory so regularly draws with it stories of migration and displacement, as in Michael Ondaatje's *Running in the Family*? Or the powerful transformative role of language itself, placed center stage in the work of Ngugi wa Thiong'o? In all of these, migration can serve not only a connecting, but also a disrupting function. It can disrupt older coordinates and dichotomies (about nation and citizenship; identity and otherness; borders and policing; gender, sexuality, race, ethnicity; human rights) and it invites new kinds of discussion, provokes ethical debates, and creates new histories.

Migration can also produce transformative effects on language itself. It can highlight sites of apparent untranslatability, and also at times serve as a springboard to linguistic creativity. Think of Dante in exile, moving from city to city, dialect to dialect, transforming and creating his own "volgare illustre." Consider the creoles, pidgins, multilingualisms, Spanglishes, Chinglishes, as well as the everyday anti-grammaticalities and countercultural argots that arise as people move and languages intersect — intentionally in the rap of Pitbull or unintentionally in multiple "language acts" on the street.

Such common linguistic results of migration can disrupt what we have learned to think of as given national languages as they underscore the very strangeness of language itself and its relationship to the political order. Through migration and translation, language can produce, that is, surprising plurilinguistic and polycultural zones, spaces in which old connections are challenged, where multiplicity is the rule, and where something new may be born — experimental works of art, and new theoretical reflections on language, literature, nation, and self (see Bhabha). Such linguistic effects of migration produce — and change — cultural history as they redraw the boundaries not only of languages and cultures in particular national and international environments, but also the borders between the disciplines in which we work, creating more transversal conversations. They make space in which new interdisciplinary research and teaching can fruitfully take place.⑥

In ways such as these, translation (viewed in its relation to migration) is already performing some very worldly work within the capacious literary framework of comparative literature. It fits well with the discipline's broad border-crossing remit, its interests in ethics and history, and its increasing engagement with questions affecting the public sphere. The interdisciplinary projects it inspires might help us to theorize more adequately and respond more humanely to the complex topic of migration — while providing a closer look at the role of comparative literature now paired with translation studies and active in a broader global context.

References

Apter, Emily. *The Translation Zone: A New Comparative Literature*. Princeton & Oxford: Princeton UP, 2006.
Baker, Mona. "The Changing Landscape of Translation and Interpreting

---

⑥ Princeton's new interdisciplinary research community, "Migration: People and Cultures across Borders," is just one such example of scholarly and pedagogical collaboration.

Studies." *A Companion to Translation Studies*. Eds. Sandra Bermann and Catherine Porter. Chichester, West Sussex: Wiley Blackwell, 2014. 15–27.

—, ed. *Translating Dissent*. London: Routledge, 2016.

Bakhtin, M. M. "Forms of Time and of the Chronotope in the Novel: Notes toward a Historical Poetics." *The Dialogic Imagination: Four Essays*. Ed. Michael Holquist. Trans. Caryl Emerson and Michael Holquist. Austin: U of Texas P, 1981. 84–258.

Bassnett, Susan. *Comparative Literature: A Critical Introduction*. Oxford: Blackwell, 1993.

Benjamin, Walter. "The Translator's Task." *The Translation Studies Reader*. Ed. Lawrence Venuti. 3rd ed. London: Routledge, 2012. 75–83.

Berman, Antoine. *The Experience of the Foreign: Culture and Translation in Romantic Germany*. Trans. S. Heyvaert. Albany: State U of New York P, 1992.

Bermann, Sandra. "In the Light of Translation: On Dante and World Literature." *Foundational Texts of World Literature*. Ed. Dominique Jullien. New York: Peter Lang, 2011. 85–100.

—. "World Literature and Comparative Literature." *The Routledge Companion to World Literature*. Eds. Theo D'Haen, David Damrosch, and Djelal Kadir. London & New York: Routledge, 2012. 169–179.

Bermann, Sandra, and Catherine Porter, eds. *A Companion to Translation Studies*. Chichester, West Sussex: Wiley Blackwell, 2014.

Bernheimer, Charles. *Comparative Literature in the Age of Multiculturalism*. Baltimore: Johns Hopkins UP, 1995.

Bhabha, Homi K.*The Location of Culture*. London & New York: Routledge, 1994.

—."The Third Space: Interview with Homi Bhabha." *Identity: Community, Culture, Difference*. Ed. Jonathan Rutherford. London: Lawrence & Wishart, 1990. 207–221.

Brodzki, Bella. *Can These Bones Live? Translation, Survival, and Cultural Memory*. Stanford: Stanford UP, 2007.

Cassin, Barbara. *A Dictionary of Untranslatables: A Philosophical Lexicon*. Trans. Emily Apter, Jacques Lezra, and Michael Wood. Princeton: Princeton UP, 2014.

Cheung, Martha, ed. *An Anthology of Chinese Discourse on Translation*. Vol. 1: *From Earliest Times to the Buddhist Project*. Manchester: St. Jerome, 2006.

Damrosch, David, Natalie Melas, and Mbongiseni Buthelezi, eds. *The Princeton Sourcebook in Comparative Literature: From the European Enlightenment to the Global Present*. Princeton: Princeton UP, 2009.

Derrida, Jacques. *The Ear of the Other: Otobiography, Transference, Translation*. *Texts and Discussions*. Ed Christie McDonald. Trans. Peggy Kamuf. Lincoln: U of Nebraska P, 1985.

—. "What is a 'Relevant' Translation?" *The Translation Studies Reader*. Ed. Lawrence Venuti. 3rd ed. London: Routledge, 2012. 365–388.

Felski, Rita, and Susan Stanford Friedman. "Introduction." *Comparison: Theories, Approaches, Uses*. Eds. Rita Felski and Susan Stanford Friedman. Baltimore: Johns Hopkins UP, 2013. 1–12.

Giordano, Cristiana. "Practices of Translation and the Making of Migrant Subjectivities in Contemporary Italy." *American Ethnologist* 35.4 (2008):

588–606.

Glissant, Edouard. *Poetics of Relation*. Trans. Betsy Wing. Ann Arbor: U of Michigan P, 1997.

Goethe, Johann Wolfgang von. *Conversations with Eckermann* (*1823 – 32*). Trans. John Oxenford. San Francisco: North Point, 1984.

Greene, Roland. "Their Generation." *Comparative Literature in the Age of Multiculturalism*. Ed. Charles Bernheimer. Baltimore: Johns Hopkins UP, 1995. 143–154.

Horta, Paulo Lemos. *Marvellous Thieves: Secret Authors of the Arabian Nights*. Harvard UP, 2017.

Majumdar, Swapan. *Comparative Literature: Indian Dimensions*. Calcutta: Papyrus, 1987.

Miller, J. Hillis. "Literary Study Among the Ruins." *diacritics* 31.3 (Fall 2001): 57–66.

Ondaatje, Michael. *Running in the Family*. Toronto: McLelland & Stewart, 1982.

Polezzi, Loredana. "Translation and Migration." *Translation Studies* 5.3 (2012): 345–356.

Said, Edward. *Orientalism*. London: Routledge, 1978.

Saussy, Haun, ed. *Comparative Literature in an Age of Globalization*. Baltimore: Johns Hopkins UP, 2006.

Schleiermacher, Friedrich. "On the Different Methods of Translating." *The Translation Studies Reader*. Ed. Lawrence Venuti. 3rd ed. London: Routledge, 2012. 43–63.

Spivak, Gayatri Chakravorty. "The Politics of Translation." *Outside in the Teaching Machine*. London & New York: Routledge, 1993. 179–200.

Stallknecht, Newton P., and Horst Frenz, eds. *Comparative Literature: Method and Perspective*. Carbondale: Southern Illinois UP, 1961.

Tymoczko, Maria. "Reconceptualizing Translation Theory: Integrating Non-Western Thought about Translation." *Translating Others*. Ed. Theo Hermans. Vol. 1. Manchester: St. Jerome, 2006. 13–32.

Venuti, Lawrence, ed. *The Translation Studies Reader*. London: Routledge, 2000.

—. *The Translator's Invisibility: A History of Translation* . London: Routledge, 1995.

3

Comparative Literature, Translation, and Intercultural Studies: Interaction and Mutual Enhancement

ZHA Mingjian
Shanghai International Studies University

Summary: Comparative literature, translation studies, and intercultural studies, being three independent disciplines, possess distinctively individual research targets, contents, and methodologies. Nevertheless on a macro level, comparative literature and translation studies can be viewed as sub-areas of intercultural studies, as on the one hand they belong to the scope of intercultural studies and on the other hand they can be considered as the practical rationale for intercultural theories. This is essential for the new disciplinary direction "Comparative Literature and Intercultural Studies" established by the Chinese government. The interculturality of comparative literature strengthens its problem awareness and hence determines its scholarly value and significance. Language is the carrier of culture. The cross-linguistic nature of translation enables it to be cross-cultural at the same time. Translated work is the product of the encounter, negotiation, and communication of different cultures, embodying the nature of inter-culture. In the intercultural domain, literary texts not only produce new texts but also represent the reproduction of the relationship between literary meaning, literary intertextuality, and cultural intertextuality. From the perspective of the relationship between the three aspects mentioned above, cross-cultural vision and intercultural problem awareness are the prerequisites for research in comparative literature and translation studies. One of its main research objectives is to investigate the cross-cultural nature of literary intertextuality. Meanwhile, the findings from comparative literature and translation studies can enrich the theories and methodologies for interdisciplinary intercultural research. These three disciplines are closely related and also interact in such a way as to expand each other's research scope.

Comparative literature, translation studies, and intercultural studies, being three independent disciplines, possess distinctively individual research targets, contents, and methodologies. Nevertheless, on a macro level, comparative literature and translation studies can be viewed as sub-areas of intercultural studies, as on the one hand they belong to the scope of intercultural studies and on the other hand they can be considered as the practical rationale for intercultural theories. Interculturality is one of the properties of comparative literature. Intercultural studies is not only the disciplinary provision and basic requirement of comparative literature, but also the route and method to deepen the research in comparative literature. Meanwhile, the findings from comparative literature research can enrich and expand intercultural studies. From such a perspective, this chapter explores the relationship between these two disciplines.

I. Intercultural Studies: Basic Requirement of Comparative Literature

What is comparative literature? The well-known British comparative literature scholar Susan Bassnett says at the beginning of her book *Comparative Literature: A Critical Introduction*:

> Sooner or later, anyone who could claim to be working in comparative literature has to try and answer the inevitable question: What is it? The simplest answer is that comparative literature involves the study of texts across cultures, that it is interdisciplinary and that it is concerned with patterns of connection in literatures across both time and space. (1)

In other words, comparative literature is the study of texts across cultures.

In the textbooks of comparative literature in China, comparative literature is defined as literary studies across languages, nations, and cultures. Language is the carrier of culture. To some extent, nations have their own distinct culture, while cultures also extend beyond single nations and manifest themselves at ethnic and regional levels (see also Sandra Bermann's chapter in this volume). Therefore, the cross-linguistic and cross-nation requirement for comparative literature can be summarized as "cross-culture." Cross-culture is the fundamental nature of comparative literature as well as the basic prerequisite for conducting research in this area. Comparative literature is the intercultural and literary study of various literary relationships and similar literary phenomena with a comparative awareness in the domain of world literature. The research objective of comparative literature is firstly to reveal the distinctive features of national literature and secondly to look for the common patterns of world literature, also known as common poetics.

Literature is the concentrated representation of culture. Regarding the exploration of literary phenomena, one has to go beyond the surface and enter into discovering and probing on the cultural level so as to reveal the characteristics of national literature and the reasons for it to come into being and develop. The results of comparative literature research have to be further analyzed on the cultural level in order to find and summarize the common problems and common lines of development in literature.

Research in comparative literature is conducted with an intercultural scope. Interculturality is the basic condition and requirement for research in comparative literature. The homogeneity and heterogeneity of human culture are the prerequisites that determine the feasibility of comparative literature.

1. *The homogeneity of cultures:* the homogeneity of human culture provides comparative literature with the precondition for comparing. If we look at human societies from different theoretical perspectives, we will find that they all possess something in common. For instance, from the perspective of Marxist historical materialism, human society is destined to evolve from primitive society to slave society, from feudal society to capitalist society and eventually to communist society. According to the value of human behaviors and motivations in cultural anthropology, different national groupings have experienced the process of moving beyond a tradition-led society.

   Therefore, on the macro level, the development of nations to a large extent bears some similarities. This suggests the homogeneity of culture, hence the foundation for comparative literature. As Russian comparatist Viktor Zhirmunsky once pointed out, the development of a certain commonality and regularity in human society provides the prerequisite for comparative studies in literature.

2. *The heterogeneity of cultures:* On the micro level, in the process of human civilization development, different nations produce cultures with distinctive features, which cause cultural differences. During the time around 800 BC to 200 BC, which is regarded as the Axial Age by philosophers such as Karl Jaspers, various civilizations experienced a great cognitive leap. It is during this period of time that China, India, Babylon, and ancient Greece, the four ancient civilized regions, all developed new perceptions and understanding of the universe and the situation of human beings. The differences of perception and understanding enabled the four representative human civilizations to develop into the beginning of world culture. This is a cultural heterogeneity predicated on cultural homogeneity. Greek culture produced clearly defined philosophies in terms of nature, order, and their significance: this included a concept of Logos, the method of bisection, and also a notion of Absolute Spirit (substance) as later conceptualized by Hegel. Socrates, Plato, and Aristotle were representatives of such rational cognition, on the basis of which Greek culture began to prosper and later became an important element of western culture. The Bible emphasizes the concept that God created the world and rules everything. All these concepts are visible in the development of Christianity, together with certain elements in Greek culture, forming the major cultural foundation of the western world. The core concepts of Indian culture are Karma and Reincarnation. It perceives the experiential world and practical life as illusion, like the moon reflected in water. Thus it advocates transcending the current life, along with hope for the future. Chinese culture emphasizes the fact that man is an integral part of nature, stressing the harmony between man and nature as well as the belief in universal order. It considers that the four cardinal virtues (empathy, shame, modesty, and conscience) exist in people's hearts and are connected with nature, preserving mental constitution, nourishing nature, and understanding destiny.

These core concepts in different cultures are reflected in their literary masterpieces: Homer, the Old Testament, The Four Vedas (The Rig Veda, The Sama Veda, The Yajur Veda, and The Atharva Veda), and *The Book of Poetry*.

Once again, then: literature is the concentrated representation of culture. The homogeneity of cultures makes it possible for different nations and regions to compare. Because of the heterogeneity of culture, comparison becomes necessary. The homogeneity and heterogeneity of cultures thus determine the inevitability of the existence of comparative literature and the possibilities for its development.

Although different nations and regions have different cultures and life styles, as human beings we encounter similar problems, as commonness is shared in our human nature: literature is based on that commonness. The felt experience of life, such as love, destiny, sense and sensibility, the pain of growth, the temporariness of life, the contradictions between expectation and reality, misery and traumatic memory, grievance, loneliness, nostalgia, etc. are all included in literature, becoming the target of literary expressions, forming the basic themes of world literature, and reflecting the universality of human nature.

II. Intercultural Research and the Significance of Comparative Literature

From the perspective of comparative literature as a discipline, interculturality is not only the prerequisite for comparative literature but also where its disciplinary significance resides. Interculturality demands that research in comparative literature should be deepened.

The method of parallel study in comparative literature particularly emphasizes the question of "comparability." Ming Xie (Chapter 2) has illuminated the conceptual difference between comparison and comparativity. Parallel studies target literary works with no obvious influence or connections existing between each other, investigating their similarities in literary concepts, themes, genres, portrait of characters, and means of artistic expressions etc. They explore the differences in such similarities, and they analyze the reasons behind those similarities and differences in terms of history, society, culture, and aesthetics. Parallel studies have raised the bar very high for researchers. Qian Zhongshu has explained that to a certain extent, everything can be compared, whereas on another level, nothing can be compared. This emphasizes the importance of problem awareness in parallel studies. Not everything can be compared. On which grounds does one compare two given literary works or authors? What points does one intend to make? This is what should be considered before conducting parallel studies. Only problems with a particular kind of value should be approached, which brings about the issue of "comparability." "Comparability" concerns the scholarly value and significance of parallel studies: parallel studies are expected to analyze issues which are normally invisible in other forms of literature research, and the conclusions of parallel studies should deepen the understanding of different features between, for instance, Chinese and western literatures. If there is only a listing of similar literary phenomena, there will be "comparing for the sake of comparison," which is the "X + Y" mode that has been frequently criticized. Its shallowness and its tendency to draw a forced analogy cause the loss of its scholarly value.

For example, one could think of making a comparison between Anna in Leo Tolstoy's *Anna Karenina* and Fan Yi in Cao Yu's play *Thunderstorm*, considering that these two women have similarities: they both have a wealthy family with high social status; they both lack love in their marriage; and they both desire to break their marriage and pursue true love. Also, one could try to draw a comparison between Zhu Bajie in *A Journey to the West* and Falstaff in Shakespeare's *Henry IV* plays, with the belief that both of them are fat, funny, and essentially comic characters. It can be perceived that such a comparative process is simply one of listing some shallow features of similarity without possessing any scholarly value. It is just literature comparison, instead of comparative literature.

The French comparatist Jean-Marie Carré has famously pointed out that "Comparative literature is not literary comparison" (Préface): while literary comparison finds similarities and differences between texts on the surface, comparative literature surpasses the apparent listing to explore the more fundamental essence and question the causes contributing to such similarities and differences. In order to pursue that purpose, it is necessary for a comparatist to conduct in-depth research on the respective cultures in which different literatures are produced.

A more profound explanation of the differences and similarities found in literary comparison can be reached only through developing in-depth research on the cultural dimension. To place the analysis of the literatures produced in different cultures in a cultural dimension, one must deploy the cultural comparison from the perspective of cross-cultural studies. Therefore, to develop from literary comparison to comparative culture becomes an inevitable process for the further development of comparative literature; to be armed with cross-cultural awareness is a basic requirement for a comparatist.

The interculturality of comparative literature strengthens the problem awareness in comparative literature and thus determines its scholarly value and significance. The intercultural research vision requires conducting comprehensive literary *and* cultural research, based on a combination of the internal poetic issues in literary texts with external cultural issues. It is on the basis of analyzing literary similarities and differences that we can find their cultural origins and explain those similarities and differences profoundly and appropriately. It is only through the intercultural interpretation that we can discover the cultural commensurability and the common foundation towards the construction of common poetics.

The purpose of comparative literature is to find out the universal principles of literature, what Qian Zhongshu calls the common "poetic heart" and "literary mind" (see Yue 66). To realize this purpose, it needs to find out the commonality of literature in different cultural systems and the common discourse in literary dialogue.

It is the literary commonality and common discourse that constitute the interculturality of literature. Conversely, we can also find the common contents and correspondence among different literatures in light of interculturality. The concept of interculturality itself — taking the interconnection between literary phenomena as the core characteristics — is the foundation of the theoretical construction of comparative literature research as well as the basic feature of comparative literature's thinking mode. As René Wellek once said, from the viewpoint of comparative literature, the coherent Western literary tradition has been interwoven in innumerable cobwebs of interrelationships.

The theory of intertextuality argues that the signs in any piece of work are related to other signs which do not appear in it, so that every text is interwoven with other texts; there are no independent texts; texts are all "inter-text." Besides obvious allusion and borrowing, all language signs constituting the text will form differences with other signs outside the text, and therefore demonstrate their own special characteristics. Intertextuality can be understood in both narrow and broad senses, which are discussed also by Susan Arndt in this volume. The narrow definition is represented by Genette, who believes that intertextuality refers to the relationship between one text and other texts existing in this text (whose existence should be proved). The broad definition is represented by Barthes and

Kristeva, who believe that intertextuality refers to the relationship between any text and the knowledge, codes, and signifying practices that in total form the text's meaning, so that the knowledge, codes, and signifying practices form a network with limitless potential. The theory of intertextuality not only focuses on the inter-functions and influences between texts, but also attaches importance to the forming process of a text's content and the codes whose sources cannot be traced — the influence of cultural tradition everywhere (see Culler 102).

The theory of intertextuality can be used as the starting point for theoretical and case studies of the intercultural explanation in comparative literature, particularly translation studies in the context of comparative literature.

III. Translation Studies, Intercultural Context, and Interculturality

Traditional translation is an applied form of study aiming for faithfulness to the original. It aims to guide translation practice, provide criteria for the practice, and criticize the quality of the translated version. Its core issue is: how to translate, and how to be seamless with the original text. In the late 1970s, a "culture turn" appeared in translation studies, shifting the focus from the original texts to the translated versions. The school of culture within translation studies believes that translation does not happen in a vacuum. It is not a simple transformation of words, nor a linguistic conversion behavior independent of the register of the target language culture. Rather it is an intercultural process. The whole process of translation, from selection to actual translation, to translation strategies, and finally to the circulation and evaluation of the translated versions (mainly not the evaluation of the quality of the translated works), is limited and influenced by various elements from the target language. Therefore, translation is a manipulation of the target language culture and a rewriting of the original text. The "cultural turn" of translation studies is to focus on how literary works are constrained and influenced by the target culture when they make their entry into a new context. This is in accordance with the translation studies of comparative literature.

Translation studies in the field of comparative literature focus on the occurrence, production, communication, and acceptance of translated literature in a specific target cultural context, as well as on the literary and cultural relationship enacted in this process. They require exploring the determining cultural factors behind phenomena occurring during the contrastive analyses of translated texts, including deletion, addition, over-interpretation, and misinterpretation etc., instead of being satisfied with a superficial analysis of the translated works. They aim to reveal the manipulation and impact of politics, ideology, literary values, economic aspects etc., in a target language culture on literary translation, and then move on to the analysis of the relationship between literature and culture in a particular period of time, probing into the literary and cultural functions of literary translation and its significance.

David Damrosch's rediscovery of world literature begins from the perspective of the intercultural communication of literary texts. He redefines world literature in *What Is World Literature?*. His fundamental view is "world literature is not an infinite, ungraspable canon of works but rather a mode of circulation and reading" (5). He argues that "world literature is writing that gains in translation" (ibid., 281). Without translation, literature couldn't have been circulated and world literature couldn't have existed. World literature is the product that "gains in translation"; this seems to be self-evident common sense. It was not Damrosch's intention to argue for the common sense; his intention was to explore how works, via translation, make their entry into the space interwoven by two cultures. The conflicts, exchanges, compromises, and dialogues between the two cultures develop along with translating and reading the works.

Damrosch sees world literature in terms of dynamic literary relations. These relations form a novel dimension, as the site where world literature comes into existence. He uses the analogy of "elliptical refraction" to describe the world literature dimension, "[...] the source and host cultures providing the two foci that generate the elliptical space within which a work lives as world literature, connected to both cultures, circumscribed by neither alone" ("World" 514). The literary dimension is filled with magnetic forces of different cultures. A literary dimension is therefore a cultural magnetic field. The literary works in the field are constrained by different cultures. Their mode of existence and their forms are the products of the co-effects of various cultures. Therefore, the literary works in the field have already changed in terms of content and form. They are no longer what they originally were. Instead, they retain the features of the source language literature while they reflect the features of the target language culture: "All works cease to be the exclusive products of their original culture once they are translated; all become works that only 'began' in their original language" (*What* 22). This is not only true for the nature of translated works, but also for the reading of translated works: "We encounter the work not at the heart of its source culture but in the elliptical field of force generated among works that may come from very different culture and eras" ("World" 530). And: "Works of literature take on a new life as they move into the world at large, and to understand this new life we need to look closely at the ways the work becomes reframed in its translations and in its new cultural context" (*What* 24).

Literary translation is not simply a switch between languages, but (once again) a rewriting of literary texts in the intercultural context. Translation is the encounter, negotiation, and conversation between different cultures; the translated texts thus become new texts not only with the elements from the original culture but also with the reflections of the target culture, embodying the nature of inter-culture. Analyzing how the new text is created, and investigating its form, can be seen as a starting point of intercultural studies.

In the cross-cultural field, literary translation not only produces the new texts and their meanings but also reproduces literary and cultural intertextuality. If the choice of translation and the process of translating can be understood as a production of meanings of cross-cultural discourse, then when the translated works enter into their circulation, they will expand the scope of cross-cultural dialogue and enrich the connotation of new cultural dialogues. That is what we call the reproduction of meaning in cross-cultural dialogue.

IV. Conclusion

Based on the relationship between comparative literature, translation studies, and intercultural studies, we can consider intercultural vision and intercultural problem awareness as the prerequisite for comparative literature and translation studies. One of the main research objectives is then to explore the intercultural connotation of literary intertextuality. The research findings of comparative literature and translation studies can further enrich the theories and methodologies of intercultural research. These three disciplines are closely related, and also interact in such a way as to expand each other's research scope.

References

Bassnett, Susan. *Comparative Literature: A Critical Introduction*. Oxford:
Blackwell, 1993.
Carré, Jean-Marie. "Préface." *La littérature comparée*, by Marius-François
Guyard. Paris: Presses Univ. de France, 1951.
Culler, Jonathan. *The Pursuit of Signs: Semiotics, Literature, Deconstruction*.
London: Routledge & Kegan Paul, 1981.
Damrosch, David. *What Is World Literature?* Princeton & Oxford: Princeton
UP, 2003.
—. "World Literature, National Contexts." *Modern Philology* (Toward World
Literature: A Special Centennial Issue) 100.4 (May 2003): 512–531.
Wellek, René. "The Crisis of Comparative Literature." *René Wellek:
Concepts of Criticism*. Ed. Stephen G. Nichols, Jr.. New Haven & London:
Yale UP, 1963. 282–295.
Xie, Ming. *Conditions of Comparison: Reflections on Comparative Intercultural
Inquiry*. New York & London: Continuum, 2011.
Yue, Daiyun. *China and the West at the Crossroads: Essays on Comparative
Literature and Culture*. Trans. Geng Song and Darrell Dorrington.
Singapore: Springer, 2016.

4

Literary Studies and Transtextual Transculturality[①]

Susan ARNDT
University of Bayreuth

Summary: The chapter explores the idea that literature is "in motion," in connection with the concepts of "homo migrans" (Bade) and "literary studies as a life science" (Ette). The author discusses the relationship of literature and society in the context of the "death of the author," then the significance of literary transculturality in the context of migration and globalization, followed by the concept of transtextuality. The polysemy of the prefix "trans" makes it possible to think across borders of individual literary texts, conceptualizing literature in the context of other fictional imaginations, non-fictional texts, and social contexts. Culture always emerges as a Babel of collective and individual identities which create rhizomic cultural spaces, in complex "glocal" negotiations. *Transculturalism* comes closest to this dynamic, as a sign of culture's cross-border mobility which entangles local and translocal dynamics beyond spatial and temporal borders. Ottmar Ette's "literature in motion" is intertwined with Gayatri Spivak's "planetarity" and Edouard Glissant's "poétique de la relation." With this in mind, the author proposes translating transtextual transculturality into a plea for Transcultural Literary Studies.

Literature is in motion, writes Ottmar Ette (*ÜberLebenswissen* 238).

---

① This chapter is adapted from Arndt (2016).

That is because it keeps itself and the social processes linked to it in action. Literature is (in) motion — because it stays true to itself by transforming itself and these processes. However, literature is also (in) motion because of complex processes of migration. The *homo migrans* (Bade) travels through *space-time*, accompanied by ideas, texts, and discourses. What does this mean for "literary studies as a life science" (Nünning and Basseler) that has "literature in motion" as its very subject?

To answer the question, I will first discuss the relationship of literature and society in the context of the "death of the author." I will then delve into transculturality (and literature) within the context of migration and globalization, to prepare for introducing the concept of transtextuality. Finally, I will propose translating transtextual transculturality into a plea for Trans * cultural Literary Studies in general and Trans * cultural Anglophone Studies, in particular.

1. Literature in Times of the "Dead Author"

British literary critic Terry Eagleton has popularized Roman Jakobson's definition of literature as "organized violence" in everyday speech (2). This formalistic approach places language, aesthetics, and *belles lettres* at the center of conceptualizing literature. Indeed, literature pleases, entertains, and enriches — in socially encoded and yet individual ways. Yet it startles, too. Theodor Adorno has posed the question whether it would not be barbaric to write poetry after/on Auschwitz (cf. Kiedaisch). But ultimately, there is nothing that cannot be embraced by the fictional imagination — be it familiar or unfamiliar, loved or detested, visionary or barbaric to the imaginative mind. Literature can comprehend or not; cause sympathy or deny it. Jonathan Littell's 2006 novel *The Kindly Ones* shows that literature does not have to be just *belle* and agreeable; it can and must also be irritating, disturbing, shocking, and jolting. In fact, literature can even speak and "muse through" (Barham) where other forms of language are trapped in silence. Essentially, it is concerned with knowledge: literature knows and aims to (make) know(n).

The practically endless freedom of aesthetically formed thoughts only seemingly absolves literary worlds of responsibility for social realities. Conversely, it is diverse realities that are responsible for the textual worlds that are poetically created. It is out of the kaleidoscope of interests of social, cultural, and political interactions that fiction weaves its stories and histories. Literature talks about people and their societies, about the story of their having-become and the future of their contemporary actions, as well as about power and its social implications. Fictional characters, their (speech) acts, conflicts, and visions do not spring from a vacuum, they emerge instead from a coordinate system of symbolic categorizations of age, nation, religion, gender, race and ethnicity. It meets with that of readers in polylogue.

La mort de l'auteur is relevant — on the one hand, because readers' interpretations lend imaginations their own and yet fragile meanings (cf. Barthes, Foucault). No one reading is like the other, it is always the reader's (current) position in symbolic systems and discourses that has more than (just) a little to say about what the text says and does not say, and what it provokes. Interpretation is free. And powerful.

La mort de l'auteur — on the other hand, because literature lives in, and as, discourse so that there is no literature beyond discourse. However, no author was ever simply a powerless and mindless marionette of her * his time. We do not have magical feathers (as in J. K. Rowling's popular *Harry Potter* series) or text-generating algorithms to thank for literature but *agency*, the power to act *imaginatively*. It is watchful eyes and conscience-controlled actions that, in and through fiction, view and inspect symbolic orders and the discourses that frame them, interweave or undo them, defend or judge them. Every fictional work introduces its own accents, probes nuances and underlying differences. Yet the priority of the focus only gains shape out of what remains unsaid and is concealed.

Thus, literature does not mirror social processes; it lives and influences them, right in their very heart. Social dynamics are not simply represented, they are also shaped. In this way, literature remains of "vital significance" for the future of coexistence "in peace and difference " in times of migration, globalization, and transculturalism (Ette, *TransArea* 5).

2. Interculturalism. Multiculturalism. Transculturalism.

Migration affects people and their societies as much as their life knowledge, experiences, and languages. "The 'Homo migrans' has existed since there was a 'Homo sapiens'," writes Klaus Bade, "because migrations are as vital to the human condition as birth, reproduction, sickness, and death." The claim of the existence of a "golden age" of a homogeneous society is about as true as a claim that globalization is a most recent phenomenon. According to Ette (*TransArea* 7), this is a continuous process that has gone through four acceleration phases since the early modern era (1. Colonial expansion at the start of the early modern era; 2. Mid-18th century — early 19th century; 3. Last third, 19th century — 1910; 4. 1980 — 2020). I would hypothesize that the digital revolution and the refugee movements as caused by global responsibilities seem to set a fifth acceleration phase in motion, which proceeds out of the fourth and accelerates beyond it. We live in a networked world, and these global networks are to be found in every curve of the globe in an even more intense way. They affect concepts of self-image based on nation, society, and culture even as they affect risks, crises, and conflicts. There have never been monocultures. Cultures are *glocal*: with local traces in global contexts, as well as global designs shared and reified in local spaces. Yet how does one aptly describe social effects around migration, globalization, and glocalization? Intercultural, multicultural, and transcultural have developed as terminologies to describe these processes — similar and yet different in their priorities.

Intercultural places the emphasis on the interaction between two cultures. In doing so, the term "intercultural" stays caught in the intellectual pitfall of assuming that it is actually possible to hermetically seal off cultures from each other — Chinese culture over here, German culture over there; culture A meets culture B. Thus framed, the focus is directed at methods of communication, mutual understanding, and tolerance *between* cultures. As virulent as cultural differences may be in certain terms, both in individual and intersectional terms, one cannot clearly place any pure German culture onto a narrow *that-is-(only)-typically-German* shelf (cf. Ibáñez, Nussbaum). Therefore, the term "intercultural" fails to meet the complex entanglements within and beyond cultures.

The concept "*multicultural*" is somewhat more consistent in conceiving cultures as reciprocal parts of a commonly shared and geopolitically mapped spacetime, a nation for that matter (cf. Nagle, Parekh, Reitz et. al, Trotman). Yet ultimately, the multicultural paradigm rather conceptualizes cultures additively as coexisting in terms of "parallel societies," such as *white* * German, Turkish * German, and Afro * German "cultures." Thus, the notion that cultures can be defined and distinguished clearly and stored by clear-cut categories like containers on a cargo ship remains undisturbed. Hence, multiculturalism may be a helpful vocabulary in certain political contexts, yet conceptually, its scope is far too narrow.

Properly understood, culture is always a Babel of collective and individual identities which create *rhizomic* cultural spaces (see Deleuze and Guattari, Glissant) in complex glocal negotiations. *Transculturalism* comes closest to this dynamic (cf. Datta, Epstein, Schulze-Engler, Welsch). Here, culture is conceived in the plural form and as *per se* polyphonic. The semantic potential of the prefix "trans" firstly opens the possibility to think beyond cultural boundaries and to describe the formation of something new, which is fundamentally different from the mere summing up of cultural elements. Secondly, the "transcultural" concept provides the opportunity to think beyond the limitations of culture. This includes reading the word's root via its prefix subversively, with a double thought movement that leads away from reading culture in essentialist terms and toward understanding culture as a critical category of knowledge. Third and lastly, the "transcultural" acts as a hypernym of culture. Here, transculturalism is a sign of culture's cross-border mobility, which entangles local and translocal dynamics beyond spatial and temporal borders and thus gives credit to interactions of culture and society (cf. Hühn et al.).

Admittedly, transculturalism offers room for approaches involving a *myth of sameness* (see hooks 167–168). They focus on global migrations and networks of people, cultures, and imaginations in a way that is somewhat inattentive to power relations that matter here (cf. for instance Welsch). Analogously, the concept of cosmopolitanism has come under criticism because it attaches too little importance to global and political power constellations and their histories, presents, and futures (cf. for instance Appiah). As a critical intervention into this desideratum, my conceptualization of trans * culturalism marks cultures (also via its asterisk) as polydirectionally entangled. In doing so, it is in keeping with Dipesh Chakrabarty's *Provincializing Europe*, Shalini Randeria's work on entangled histories, and concepts of hybridity from Homi Bhabha to Kien Nghi Ha, so as to identify global (literary) encounters and their power contexts, deconstruct, and re-situate them.

3. Transculturalism and Literature

People migrate — and with them their (hi)stories, religions, ideas, knowledge systems, and aesthetics. Hardly anything lives out the spaciousness of the vision of "boundlessness" as consistently and enigmatically as the concept of "world literature." Poetics and literary ideas flow globally and connect with artists who are located in the world's libraries, and in video and media centers, reinforced by the digital revolution of communication, knowledge transfer, and the fictional imagination. Beyond any fantasy of hermetically sealed cultures, words weave fictional nets that can only be understood as the literary products of interlinked histories, nations, and languages. Here, genres and media, discourses and knowledges, imaginations and aesthetics interlock and continuously reinvent themselves as well as nations and languages in the process. The world's cultures meet to interlink and change in irreversible and unpredictable ways.

When it does speak, literature knows no boundaries; it is translocal and universal, transtemporal and timeless. As a local of *space-time*, it resides in conventionalized interstices of time and space without neglecting to reliably unhinge them. Its ideas, poetics, and characters are not only at home in their respective original texts, but wander and migrate to live in various textual residences. Borne by the freedom of fictional imagination, they emancipate themselves of things that contribute to the world's stuffiness such as geopolitically powerful border fences, which decide about belonging or exclusion. Here, one can neglect the circumstance that readers may not understand (the native language of) literary ideas, poetics, and characters: literature's fragmented Babel is self-translating. The *Nibelungenlied* does not have to limit itself to Germany or to Richard Wagner's castle, as the German epic equally boldly embraces for instance its Malian sibling-epic *Sundjata*. Familiar cartographies are not simply transcended but are turned on their heads. This does not mean, however, that there are no borders, nor that literature does not create any itself, and certainly not that borders are unimportant. Necessary as they are for making meaning, boundaries always need interrogation, being "interested instances of power, specific constructions, with real material consequences" (Barad 182). They are indeed leading factors when literary texts surmount their own limits to weave themselves into any other existing or future text.

At this point, conceptually, we are right in the middle of intertextuality. Significantly influenced by the Bulgarian-French post-structuralist Julia Kristeva (and following Bakhtin's concept of "dialogicity"), a first, broad interpretation of intertextuality says: everything is language, all that is language is text, and all that is text is intertextual. Be it phonetic, graphic, or visual fabric, owing to its global network every notion of the singular is misplaced. Texts that have never "met" or will never do so, know each other, interconnect. Discourses live through centuries and leave traces in texts, which in turn leave traces and remember history into the future. Thus each text knows another text, and is indeed related to it. Fabrics, or texts, that unexpectedly grow in *rhizomic*, multi-dimensional ways develop in such a manner, and in doing so celebrate the order in chaos. The sheer endlessness of textual worlds is like that of the oceans. Like waves, texts rise out of these worlds to merge with them again and later, elsewhere, take shape as newly formed waves.

Removed from the expanses of the oceans, movements and encounters between individual waves can be mapped — and this is the second and more specific understanding of intertexuality. Distancing itself from Kristeva, it is more specific and endeavors to set limits. This interpretation reads texts as closed word-spaces that open up to and confide in each other. Yet beyond the vast reach of texts and intertexts, the concreteness of bi- and multilateralism and of artistically created dia- and polylogicity is at work. Texts speak to each other because generations that follow seek dialogue with senior ones in order to preserve the old, or design the future anew. Copies develop in this way, which occasionally dismantle the original. Furthermore, intertextuality creates analogies in this sense, which sustain a particular logic or even go against its grain. Ultimately, such an interpretation of intertextuality is concerned with references that allude to their godparents so as to credit them, denounce them, or both. The aim is, therefore, to seek out intended meanings and references. Complex relationship levels are peeled back, layer by layer. Palimpsests divulge well-hidden stories in exchange for new futures.

Both understandings of intertextuality agree in one main aspect: literature sets off polylogues that are constantly changing and, in the process, represent and shape aesthetics' dynamic Histories of Knowledge. Yet this begs the question, is it not more meaningful to conceive of such polylogues in motion as being "transtextual"?

The polysemy of the prefix "trans" makes it possible, firstly, to think across borders of individual literary texts, beyond the mere adding up of literary elements — literature as a transtextual amalgam. Secondly, a concept of "transliterarity" offers the opportunity to think beyond literature. This includes reading the word's root subversively and conceptualizing literature in the context of other fictional imaginations, non-fictional texts, and social contexts. Transtextuality as polylogue in motion combines diverse media forms and genres as well as *space-times*. Like a hypernym of literature, the concept of transliterarity highlights literature's cross-border mobility, which entangles local and translocal dynamics in society and fiction beyond the borders of genres and media forms.

4. Literary Studies and Transtextual Transculturalism

Literary studies as a "life science" adapts itself to literature (as a strand of human knowledge-making) and not vice versa. How then should literary studies react to literature's transtextual transculturalism?

The field of literary studies explores cultural processes. It does so by co-conceptualizing them with social and political processes, thereby contributing to a complex understanding of these dynamics. The "death of the author" centralizes discourse as a flow of knowledge through *space-time*, and with it the power of interpretation (cf. Jäger). "All things are subject to interpretation; whichever interpretation prevails at a given time is a function of power and not truth." Black British author Bernardine Evaristo prefaces her novel *Blonde Roots*, which reinterprets Maafa, with these words adapted from Friedrich Nietzsche.

It is precisely through the power of interpretation that literary studies become a life science, which de/constructs knowledge from (fictional) texts, as well as their past and future. Literature exists in the "political unconscious," as Frederic Jameson calls it, until core discourses are made visible. Naturally, this can be accomplished by reading in private. However, it is the duty of literary studies to systematize and professionalize the process by building on linguistic, theoretical, and methodological skills.

Global interaction and literature's transtextuality demand that literary studies think beyond the limitations of conventionalized *areas*, nations, and languages in a transcultural manner. To this end, they require a seminal terminology. The idea of "world literature" does not seem to be sound enough in this case as, with

Johann Wolfgang von Goethe (cf. Koch), Erich Auerbach, Pascal Casanova, und David Damrosch, a canonization of *white* north American and European mainstream literatures is conceptually inherent within it. Here, Ottmar Ette's "literature in motion" introduces new accents, in conceptual entanglement with Gayatri Spivak's *planetarity* and Edouard Glissant's "poétique de la relation":

> Et il me semble que c'est seulement une poétique de la Relation, c'ést-à-dire un imaginaire, qui nous permettra de "comprendre" ces phases et ces implications des situations des peuples dans le monde d'aujourd'hui. [...] (Glissant 24)

This is to consider literature's global presence and its unforeseeable diversity and polyphonic dialogicity in equal measure to the power relations that frame it. Édouard Glissant emphasizes:

> [L]es cultures du monde mises en contact de manière foudroyante et absolument consciente aujourd'hui les unes avec les autres se changent en s'échangeant à travers des heurts irrémissibles [...] Dans la rencontre de cultures du monde, il nous faut avoir la force imaginaire de concevoir toutes les cultures comme exerçant à la fois une action d'unité et de diversité libératrices. (Glissant 14, 71)

The Martiniquan writer and literary theorist finds the metaphor of the rhizome fitting to describe the idea of a "unité-diversité" (ibid., 12). A rhizome networks as a root system and spreads out over a surface, instead of digging itself into the depths like a root with a single origin. Literature is conveyed in the rhizome's network-like structure, to connect and entangle with other texts (see ibid., 59, 63, 69). Glissant continues: "[J]e rêve une nouvelle approche, une nouvelle appréciation de la littérature, de la littérature comme la découverte du monde, comme découverte de Tout-monde" (91).

This philological transformation consists of more than an opening of individual literatures. Avoiding exclusions is only one aspect. Considering historically grown, discursive, and structurally anchored entanglements — together with their hierarchies — is also part of it. The history and future, hybridity and polyphony, diversity and difference of "literature in motion" correlate well with what Ottmar Ette calls literary studies "with no fixed abode" (*ÜberLebenswissen* 238). This has been methodically washed with the waters of transculturalism and transtextuality. In academic polylogy, the concept links linguistically or regionally framed areas of literary studies, while at the same time considering and transcending the borders, histories, and geopolitics of nations and of languages. It employs familiar approaches and theories, structures and categories, concepts and terminologies with the aim of turning them around. Instead of narrow and outdated philological categorizations, literary thought is guided by epistemological requirements that are limited only by the demands of various established levels of expertise and linguistic skills. While translations are their own works of art, they can in this case expand the empirical framework (ibid., 88–92).

Some may argue: that is what General and Comparative Literary Studies are all about. Indeed, this field would seem to be perfect for the task; yet it is often more theoretical than practical. Yet this approach is part and parcel of keeping the one-nation-one-language literary studies paradigm working. What is more, at General and Comparative Literary Studies' very core, one finds (as in the concept of "world literature") a *white* and Western canon, which considers the Rest of Color as better placed in Area Studies, and often views literature's rhizomic globality in a one-dimensional manner. In *Death of a Discipline*, the Indian-American literary theorist Gayatri Spivak has criticized this narrow nature of her home discipline, as well as that of Area Studies and any One-Nation-One-Language-Only-Discipline: "It is time, in globality, [...] to put the history of Francophony, Teutophony, Lusophony, Anglophony, Hispanophony *also* — not *only* (please mark the difference) — in a comparative focus" (12). According to Spivak, comparative work should not be left to General and Comparative Literary Studies alone. The discussion is not about the task of regional literary studies, but about intensifying and extending their dialogicity, the result of which is that comparative transculturalism becomes a universal method with a power-sensitive global orientation. Whether comparative literature or Romance language studies, English literature or African studies: they must all undergo a paradigm shift, which redefines, restructures, and reclassifies literary subjects. The global perspective on literary history and genres as offered by Lindberg-Wada has been going in a similar direction.

In this context, Mary Louise Pratt makes use of a visionary allegory borrowed from George Orwell's *Animal Farm*. She views literary theorists as animals in the chicken coops and enclosures of a farmer who has retired — not before leaving all the doors and gates open:

> What do we want to do? The foxes now have access to the henhouse; the hens, however, are free to go somewhere else. Animals will move from pasture to pasture and pen to pen; strange

matings will occur and new creatures [be] born. The manure pile will be invaded and its winter warmth enjoyed by all. It will be a while till new order and new leadership emerge. But the farmer won't be back. (Pratt 58)

It is true that we cannot understand literatures by squeezing them into suffocating corsets, which are determined by factors such as languages, nations, or continental borders. New creatures and new farmers of literary studies are needed. In this respect, Ette's visionary *TransAreas* (2012) are cutting-edge. However, as heirs of Babylon, we have also learned to remain modest cobblers sticking to their last — and so have our language skills, which (to a limited extent) can be complemented by translations. Ultimately, we cannot do more than split complex global entanglements into small, manageable pieces so as to see and understand them within the necessary complexity of the larger mosaic. Yet to be oriented by the respective objective while mapping the empirical material, i.e., the corpus, is far more convincing than to rely on patterns and algorithms rooted in nations here and areas there.

5. Holistic Readings

One of these new TransAreas that can rise like a phoenix from the ashes is Transcultural English Studies or (in German) "Transkulturelle Anglistik." Frank Schulze-Engler, one of its most important representatives, writes:

Exploring the prospects and contours of "Transcultural English Studies" [...] does not entail giving free rein to metadisciplinary ambitions but, rather, reflects a set of common challenges and predicaments that in recent years have increasingly moved centre-stage not only in New Literatures in English but also in British and American Studies. (x)

While the idea of Transcultural English Studies overcomes the praxis of classifying literatures in terms of nation, the focus on one-language-only gets stuck. Therefore, it is more consistent to speak of Transcultural Literary Studies. As "transareal" *and* "translingual" literary studies in motion, alongside Ette's TransArea, Spivak's *planetarity*, and Glissant's "poétique de la relation," it nudges peripheral literatures into various centers — and vice versa. This interlocking of center and periphery negates categories of binary logic such as "the West" and "the Rest of Color." Thus, Transcultural Literary (or English) Studies is a field that has the tools at hand to enable an understanding of African literatures as borne by complex migratory movements and located in dynamic African diasporas, which are (for instance) a part of Britain and of Germany, and which can be multilingual or reflexive (cf. Zabus).

I would like to add two other aspects to my conceptualization of Transcultural Literary (or English) Studies. On the one hand, English is used as a global coordinate, but it is also transcended. English is included as the core language in a complex coordinate system of other languages and the global polylogy of literature. "[I]l faudrait," writes Glissant, "que toutes ces langues s'entendent à travers l'espace, aux trois sens du terme entendre: qu'elles s'écoutent, qu'elles se comprennent et qu'elles s'accordent" (91). This offers a framework to consider multilingual "TransAreas" such as Africa as a continent, or for example Cameroon or India as countries, in a more holistic manner, or even to understand English texts by German, Chinese, or Palestinian authors within the contexts of their countries of origin.

On the other hand, Transcultural Literary (or English) Studies offer a methodology to "provincialize" British and other Western literatures in Dipesh Chakrabaty's sense, meaning that the *white* canon is complemented by other literatures. In the process, impacts of global literatures on *white* (British) writing and vice versa are identified and analyzed. This implies that — in an integrative and complementary approach to literatures of Color — Transcultural Literary (or English) Studies will read canonical texts anew. These range from Aristotle and Wolfram von Eschenbach to William Shakespeare and Jane Austen, then right up to Joanne K. Rowling and Jonathan Littell, analogously to critical categories such as intersectional postcolonialism.

But does the epistemological net profit of Transcultural Literary (or English) Studies go beyond the fact that empirical areas are only becoming more planetary? What value can a transcultural view of literatures add? Literary studies that speak about the global networking of world literatures speak of the global representation of knowledge within the context of mediation and negotiation. The prefix "trans" not only insists on poly-directional and rhizomic literary relationships. In addition, it focuses on the fact that social discourses and their histories are globally entangled — not least, borne and influenced by literary fictions. The profile of Transcultural

Literary (or English) Studies allows for a holistic reading of literature as the flow of represented "survival knowledge" (Ette) through diverse *space-times* (by way of the ideas of *totalité-monde*, Glissant's one-world, and Spivak's planetarity).

Detached from mono-lingual or mono-national language grids, accompanied by its complementary closeness to linguistics, and empowered by relationships with concepts such as transnationality, translocality, and transmigration, Transcultural Literary Studies can direct our gaze to overall cultural, social, and political contexts. It is in dialogue with Ottmar Ette's vision of "transareal" literary studies. Polylogues have begun, and these beginnings will look for new polylogues, multi-vocally.

References

Appiah, Kwame. *Cosmopolitanism: Ethics in a World of Strangers*. New York: Norton, 2006.

Arndt, Susan. "Literaturwissenschaft und Transtextuelle Transkulturalität. Überlegungen zu Ottmar Ettes Visionen einer zukunftstragenden LebensWissenschaft." *Literatur Leben*. Eds. Albrecht Buschmann, Julian Drews, et al. Berlin: Walter Frey, 2016.

Auerbach, Erich. "Philologie der Weltliteratur." *Gesammelte Aufsätze zur Romanischen Philologie*. Eds. Fritz Schalk und Gustav Konrad Bern. München: Francke, 1967. 301–310.

Bade, Klaus J. *Europa in Bewegung*. *Migration vom späten 18. Jahrhundert bis zur Gegenwart*. München: Beck, 2000.

Bakhtin, M[ikhail] M. *The Dialogic Imagination: Four Essays*. Ed. Michael Holquist, trans. Caryl Emerson and Michael Holquist. Austin: U of Texas P, 1981.

Barad, Karen. "Meeting the Universe Halfway: Realism and Social Constructivism Without Contradiction." *Feminism, Science, and the Philosophy of Science*. Eds. Lynn Hankinson Nelson and Jack Nelson. Dordrecht: Kluwer, 1996. 161–194.

Barham, Nabil. *Poets of the Unseen; Musing Through Loss and Displacement in Identity Formation in and around the Palestine/Israel Conflict*. PhD Thesis, Univ. of Bayreuth, 2016.

Barthes, Roland. "La mort de l'auteur." *Le Bruissement de la langue*. *Essais Critiques 4*. Paris: Éditions du Seuil, 1984. 61–67.

Bhabha, Homi K. *The Location of Culture*. Abingdon: Routledge, 1994.

Casanova, Pascal. *La république mondiale des lettres*. Paris: Éditions du Seuil, 1999.

Chakrabarty, Dipesh. *Provincializing Europe: Postcolonial Thought and Historical Difference*. Princeton & Oxford: Princeton UP, 2007.

Damrosch, David. *What is World Literature?* Princeton & Oxford: Princeton UP, 2000.

Datta, Asit, ed. *Transkulturalität und Identität: Bildungsprozesse zwischen*

Exklusion und Inklusion. Frankfurt am Main: IKO — Verlag für Interkulturelle Kommunikation, 2005.

Deleuze, Gilles, and Felix Guattari. *A Thousand Plateaus: Capitalism and Schizophrenia*. Trans. Brian Massumi. Minneapolis & London: U of Minnesota P, 1987.

Eagleton, Terry. *Literary Theory: An Introduction*. 2nd ed. London: Blackwell, 1996.

Epstein, Mikhail. "Transculture: A Broad Way between Globalism and Multiculturalism." *The American Journal of Economics and Sociology* 68.1 (2009): 327–351.

Ette, Ottmar. *Literature on the Move*. Trans. Katharina Vester. Amsterdam & New York: Rodopi, 2003.

—. *TransArea*. Berlin: de Gruyter, 2012.

—. *ÜberLebenswissen: Die Aufgabe der Philologie*. Berlin: Kadmos Kulturverlag, 2004.

—. *Writing-between-Worlds: Transarea Studies and the Literatures-without-a-fixed-Abode*. Trans. Vera M. Kutzinski. Berlin: De Gruyter, 2016.

Evaristo, Bernardine. *Blonde Roots*. London: Penguin, 2008.

Foucault, Michel. "Qu'est-ce qu'un auteur?" *Bulletin de la société française de philosophie* 62 (1969): 73–104.

Glissant, Édouard. *Introduction à une poétique du divers*, Paris: Éditions Gallimard, 1996.

Ha, Kien Nghi. *Ethnizität und Migration reloaded*. Berlin: wvb, 2004.

—. *Hype um Hybridität*. Bielefeld: transcript, 2005.

Hooks, bell. *Black Looks: Race and Representation*. Boston: South End P, 1992.

Hühn, Melanie, Dörte Lerp, Knut Petzold and Miriam Stock, eds. *Transkulturalität, Transnationalität, Transstaatlichkeit, Translokalität: Theoretische und empirische Begriffsbestimmungen*. Berlin: Literatur Verlag, 2000.

Ibáñez, Beatriz Penas, and Carmen López Sáenz, eds. *Interculturalism: Between Identity and Diversity*. Bern: Peter Lang, 2006.

Jäger, Siegfried. *Diskursanalyse: Eine Einführung*. Münster: Unrast, 2015. (First pub. 1993.)

Jameson, Frederic. *The Political Unconscious*. Ithaca, NY: Cornell UP, 1981.

Kiedaisch, Petra, ed. *Lyrik nach Auschwitz? Adorno und die Dichter*. Stuttgart: Reclam, 1995.

Koch, Manfred. *Weimaraner Weltbewohner: Zur Genese von Goethes Begriff "Weltliteratur"*. Tübingen: Niemeyer, 2002.

Kristeva, Julia. "Bachtin, le mot, le dialogue et le roman." *Critique* 23 (1972): 438–465.

Lindberg-Wada, Gunilla, ed. *Literary History: Towards a Global Perspective*. 4 vols. Berlin & New York: de Gruyter, 2006.

Littell, Jonathan. *Les Bienveillantes*. Paris: Gallimard, 2006.

Nagle, John. *Multiculturalism's Double-Bind: Creating Inclusivity, Cosmopolitanism and Difference*. 2009. London & New York: Routledge, 2016.

Nietzsche, Friedrich. *Nachgelassene Fragmente 1885 – 1887*. Vol. 12. Eds. Giorgio Colli and Mazzino Montinari. München: Deutscher Taschenbuch Verlag de Gruyter, 1988.

Nünning, Ansgar, and Michael Basseler. "Literary Studies as a Form of 'Life Science': The Knowledge of Literature." *New Theories, Models and Methods in Literary and Cultural Studies*. Eds. Greta Olson and Ansgar Nünning. Trier: WVT, 2013. 189–212.

Nussbaum, Martha C. *Cultivating Humanity. A Classical Defense of Reform in Liberal Education*. Cambridge, Mass.: Harvard UP, 1997.

Orwell, George. *Animal Farm*. London: Secker and Warburg, 1945.

Parekh, Bhikhu. *Rethinking Multiculturalism: Cultural Diversity and Political Theory*. Cambridge, Mass.: Harvard UP, 2000.

Pratt, Mary Louise. "Comparative Literature and Global Citizenship." *Comparative Literature in the Age of Multiculturalism*. Ed. Charles Bernheimer. Baltimore: John Hopkins UP, 1995. 58–65.

Randeria, Shalini. "Geteilte Geschichte und verwobene Moderne." *Zukunftsentwürfe: Ideen für eine Kultur der Veränderung*. Eds. Jörn Rüsen, Hanna Leitgeb, and Norbert Jegelka. Frankfurt am Main: Campus, 1999. 87–96.

Reitz, Jeffrey G., Raymond Breton, et al. *Multiculturalism and Social Cohesion: Potentials and Challenges of Diversity*. Springer Science + Business Media, 2009.

Schulze-Engler, Frank. Introduction. *Transcultural English Studies*. Eds. Frank Schulze-Engler and Sissie Helff. Amsterdam & New York: Rodopi, 2009. ix–xvi.

Spivak, Gayatri Chakravorty. *Death of a Discipline*. New York: Columbia UP, 2003.

Trotman, C. James, ed. *Multiculturalism: Roots and Realities*. Bloomington: Indiana UP, 2002.

Welsch, Wolfgang. "Transculturality: The Puzzling Form of Cultures Today." *Spaces of Culture: City, Nation, World*. Eds. Mike Featherstone and Scott Lash. London: Sage, 1999. 194–213.

—. *Transkulturalität: Zwischen Globalisierung und Partikularisierung. Mainzer Universitätsgespräche Interkulturalität. Grundprobleme der Kulturbegegnung*. Mainzer Universitätsgespräche, 1998.

Zabus, Chantal. *The African Palimpsest: Indigenization of Language in the West African Europhone Novel*. Amsterdam & Atlanta: Rodopi, 1991.

5

Performances of Meaning: A Transversal Inquiry

Michael STEPPAT
University of Bayreuth

Summary: Can literature become useful for any of the branches of Intercultural Communication? Conversely, can there be a conceptual place for intercultural research when we seek a better understanding of literary culture? We encounter these two connected questions when we seek ways to understand the dynamic circulation of interculturally shaped ideas and value notions, as driven by literary culture. The second question, which has hardly been tackled, is this chapter's main focus. Most of us are likely to be aware that, as forms of mental modeling with respect to culture, images of the familiar and the foreign mutually condition each other. In a similar way, we can assume that analysis of literature and also film would remain barren if it did not look outside its own deceptively familiar box. If literary culture can be said to offer multiperspectival works that allow insight, better than any other kind of articulation, into a polycentric world's complexity, we will need a "new intercontinent of conceptualization" (Hwa Yol Jung) for adequate understanding. There is a pathway intersecting this inquiry: comparative study. In historical research, it has been using "intercultural" as a suggestive attribute. Nonetheless, we plainly need a processual and interactive approach to culture in order to explore Intercultural Communication's significance for the study of literature. Living in an age when any clear boundary between one's own culture and foreign cultures is lost owing to mutual permeation, we have surely all become growingly aware that literature crosses borders — not unlike the way concepts of boundary and of transculturation as cultural interfusion have become central in constructing Intercultural Communication theories.

In light of this double awareness, we should look for coefficient operations from transversal rationality that we can adapt for reconsidering literature. That is because *textual meanings are likely to be all but meaningless outside a communicative knowledge performance*. That kind of performance targets exactly the praxial involvement that intercultural research embodies.

Building on the conceptual arguments, without being directly dependent on them, an Appendix offers a sequence of analytical questions for a focused research agenda. The questions are designed for the practical work of literary investigation. They can be used without consideration of the conceptual arguments.

1. Connecting Dots

The study of literature has hardly taken notice of Intercultural Communication research. Yet the latter has shown itself aware in striking ways of literature's significance. Among such cases is an earlier volume in this series, *Identity and Intercultural Communication II* (2012). The exploratory volume speaks of Ethnicity and Cultural Identity, Value Orientations and Cultural Identity, and also Language Teaching. But hardly anybody would expect one of the chapters to be devoted to American literature, another to a discussion how English and German romantic poetry and philology advanced cultural identity in 18th- and 19th-century Europe. With this topic network, the volume shows how sensitive issues of cultural identity construction are addressed not only in Intercultural Communication but equally in the study of literature. Isn't it strange, then, that there has been little substantial interchange? The volume could be said to speak to the awareness of a conference organized by the American studies institute at the University of Bayreuth (Germany), as partner institution of Shanghai International Studies University (SISU). The conference issued a call to "Connect the Dots: Structures — Networks — Systems": the idea is to communicate, connect ideas, exchange thoughts on areas that include narrative structures. When we respond to such impulses, our research task will be a cognate one — to try to understand the dynamic circulation of interculturally shaped ideas and value notions.

Literature has emerged as an important means of worldmaking, of constructing the norms and values by which we live (see Baumbach et al.). At the same time, value frameworks and dimensions have been extensively studied in Volumes 4 and 5 of the present book series. Indeed, "values research is a very active, current, and contributing part of the intercultural and related disciplines" (Kulich, "Preface" 29) — inviting partnership, surely, with the literary discipline. We might recall that there is a "specific feat of literature": "[...] it can divide its narrative into enunciation and *énoncé* (that is, into story and discourse) and thereby reveal its own means of constructing values. [...] [L]iterature opens up a space where new possibilities of meaning- and value-making can be explored" (Neumann 136–137). Comparative cultural values study, for its part, reveals how values can be investigated as "abstract or latent structures that are modifiable by experience and that exert their effects via associative networks" of attitudes and beliefs (Feather 114). It's hard to believe that such studies have nothing to offer to literary scholars.

In approaching our research task, we light on two interlocking questions:

— Can literature become useful for any of the branches of Intercultural Communication?
— Or, conversely: Can there be a conceptual place for intercultural research when we seek a better understanding of literary culture?

These are two complementary ways of looking at the same phenomenon. But since the second, unlike the first, has hardly been tackled it will for now become the chief focus. I will argue that there is indeed such a conceptual place, and that, as several suggestive contributions in the present volume illustrate, the study of literature (which extends to film) has much to gain from intercultural research. My own additional piece, "All the races," aims to offer just one such practically oriented illustration.

An Appendix to this chapter offers a series of analytical questions for the practical work of literary investigation. Any reader who is less interested in the conceptual groundwork could skip the following pages (Sections 2–7) and go straight to the brief section 8 and to the chapter's Appendix. The questions offered there are not directly dependent on a grasp of the conceptual argumentation.

2. Outside the Box

When we consider cultural connections and encounters, we cannot escape a focus on time, on historical inquiry, at least for a moment. It is likewise represented in the SISU volume spoken of above. We cannot but be aware that when people from different cultural backgrounds meet, backgrounds that inevitably have a temporal compass, the differences can hamper communication in ways that are usually hegemonic but may not be easy to trace. Perhaps "intercultural (mis)communication" is a more suitable term for the research object (Mao, "Translating Popular" 159). Culture, of course, is more than ethnicity. It is certainly more than nationality. In each case, cultural interactions move in a kind of fractal network, relating larger to smaller social circles, which is formed of ways in which the present responds to the past. Doesn't history keep intervening in the present we would like to shape (see also Bharucha 252)? From cultural-group history to social history, also in diasporic and in minority situations, the pastness of the past is elusive. Zygmunt Bauman stresses that the lack of "shared recollections" means that "the meeting of strangers is *an event without a past*," a shared past, almost "a *mis*-meeting" (95). And surely mis-meetings of all kinds, with their impact, are common objects of literary representation. It's not far from there to a complementary proposition: like the future, the past for Gilles Deleuze doesn't "have much meaning, what counts is the present-becoming," which is set in a spatialized "middle and not the beginning or the end" (Deleuze and Parnet 23). Or: "All is always now" (T. S. Eliot, "Burnt Norton"). A present-becoming constitutes what is past.

The Becoming process merges with that of identity building: in particular, it is likely to bring home a crucial inquiry. In what ways and with what effects do we construct the spatiotemporal *familiar* as knowable in relation to the *foreign*? That question escapes simple answers. It is especially elusive when we consider what Sigmund Freud disclosed as the "immanence of the strange within the familiar" (Kristeva 182–183). Hence we need the whole story, which goes further — we need to question the familiar's static character. The interrogation is in tune with Maurice Merleau-Ponty's lateral approach of "learning to see what is ours as alien and what was alien as our own," setting ourselves at a distance from our own society (*Signs* 120). And it is in tune with Ming Xie's proposition that being on both sides of a mirror enables us to see *how* we see (3, 20). The images of both the familiar and the foreign that suggest themselves are forms of mental modeling, ones which become capable of mutually conditioning each other. They appear as reciprocal images, not as functions of demarcation against each other. It is when appropriating the foreign becomes a mode of self-critical shaping of the familiar that the latter as such comes into being. The familiar in turn needs a conscious re-appropriation, in mutual exchange with the foreign Other. The process is that of an "incessant testing of the self through the other person and the other person through the self" (Merleau-Ponty, ibid.). In Edouard Glissant's poetics of relation, each identity is "extended through a relationship with the Other" (11); the extension yields rhizome-identities. It ought to be rewarding to study interdependencies between the cultural self and the foreign, with borderlines that create bridges between identities. A mere dualism of the familiar and foreign would remain sterile, static.

Incessant testing requires us to think of culture not as an essentialist entity that exists on its own terms, originating at some period in the past and thence transferred to members of a collective. It is rather a category of critical thought if not knowledge, a dynamic process (see Blioumi 6, 90), this being "the diverse, complex, contextual living situation that needs to be constantly mediated" as well as "negotiated and interpreted" (Kulich, "Constructing" 118). Accordingly, "it takes exposure to 'otherness' to unravel or cause us to reflect on 'own-ness'" (Kulich, "Values" 36). Only then can we know what our own culture is (ibid.). Hegel's *Science of Logic* (1812 version; e.g., 21.106, 21.113) is heavy reading. But it does appear to cast light on our query, when it enables us to claim that no existence "is not itself an other." This means that otherness is "contained" in as well as separated from any something, as "the other of itself and so the other of the other." Thus, something and other are "inherently joined together," something indeed "has passed over into otherness," so that "something is just as much an other as the other is." Or indeed, in the words of Zhuangzi: "'That' comes out of 'this' and 'this' depends on 'that' — which is to say that 'this' and 'that' give birth to each other" (10). With such concepts in mind, can we bring to light how preconceptions and stereotypes are formed about phenomena from other cultures?

The Multiperspectival Text

That issue is thematized and problematized nowhere as much as in fiction. It is a vital programmatics in literary comparison and likewise in film. Surely, "[...] discussions around stereotypes are the very issues which novels like those of [Chimamanda Ngozi] Adichie are all about; and such novels succeed splendidly in entering fully into the complexities which are important in the quest for intercultural awareness" (Holliday, *Understanding* 35). Fictional literature as such is particularly significant in "working beyond the established imaginations about cultural description," for "[b]uilding a picture of complex personal cultural trajectories in dialogue with national structures" (Holliday, *Intercultural* xi, 30). Conversely, then, once again: can there be a conceptual place for intercultural research, especially with a communicative thrust, to help us discern meanings? So far none has been discovered to any extent — while all around us, disturbing questions keep arising about the consequences of cultural encounters for forming cultural, social, and personal identities through difference. The Intercultural Research volume spoken of above outlines a range of applications for identity concepts. There are "efforts to preserve traditions, learn new cultures, [...] choose language or cultural convergence, as well as by attempts at self-adjustment, saving face or constructing a public image, developing an awareness of oneself and others, and establishing relationships" (Kulich and Dai, "Introduction" 29–30). They are hardly specific to intercultural research, and indeed we don't have to look far to find each powerfully represented in literary culture.

So we might ask whether analysis of literature will not be barren if it does not look outside its own deceptively familiar box. In our case it would look to social science and what one might perhaps call non-text-based cultural study as seemingly extraneous patterns of discourse. Such connecting of dots has happened recurrently, with the sociology of literature or with the theories of psychoanalysis or of gender. As a scientific imaginary, for that matter, string theory is gaining cultural currency (as in Sean Miller). But as we look toward conditions of interculturality, we have a novel situation of cultural sensitivity, and it's one that challenges our responsibility. We are likely to realize that literature has a unique potential: it offers multiperspectival texts, ones that arguably enable insight, perhaps better than any other kind of articulation, into a polycentric world's complexity. Such a postulate makes it inevitable to ask whether we might not need what has quite recently been called a "new intercontinent of conceptualization" (Jung, "Transversality" 153). The neologism is suggestive, calling attention to the challenge we are facing vis-à-vis the domains of the tried and tested.

3. "To See Differently"

The task involves more than just looking over a neighbor's fence. Contrasting with fictional narrative, Intercultural Communication's focus is on interpersonal relations, on interactivity. It is similar with Transcultural Communication's field of competence, which is designed to "help people" communicate in "a wide range of intercultural situations" (Ting-Toomey, *Communicating* 261). Yet transcultural communication can go beyond face-to-face interactions when it studies media, specifically "communicative figurations in globalized, mediatized worlds" (Hepp 11). What might literary students gain from such communicative sciences that they would not readily gain elsewhere? There are difficulties. For one thing, it's not easy to demarcate the disciplinary field precisely. Intercultural Communication itself, far from being unitary *tout court*, is an edifice with many apartments not all of which might lend themselves to a conjunctive strategy. Just one instance: in Europe alone, one overview of interculturality research ignores literature, while another gives it due attention (see Elberfeld, Lüsebrink). What's more, no-one would deny that any paradigms or categories teased out by Intercultural (or Transcultural) Communication, as a research field that is at least partly at home in the social sciences, may need to become tailored and adjusted before one can weigh their relevance for literary analysis. The relationship between the inter-, cross- and transcultural is usefully discussed by Ming Xie (3–5; see also Jiang and Huang).

So are there any good reasons to consider the usefulness of Intercultural Communication research for literature? It is hardly the field of received literary theory that suggests doing so. We hear from American poet-critic Eugene Jolas in 1929 that "[t] he writer expresses. He does not communicate" (*Critical* 112). That is not exactly encouraging. Nor has literary scholarship created suitable precedents, though encounters between literary cultures are certainly studied. Comparative literature study cuts across our inquiry. As a pioneer of intercultural and comparative poetics, Earl Miner opened comparative study to an eastern and a southern hemisphere (see

Comparative 20) — only to warn, a few years later, that "[i]ntercultural literary study has numerous hazards and may be fundamentally impossible. Nobody, not even that French wizard [and Sinologist], René Etiemble, really knows enough literatures, has enough ideas of literature" ("An Allegory" 81).

The knowledge in question is that which enables comparisons. Beyond individual wizardry, collaboration and teamwork can open a new pathway. It's that of (for instance) Japanese studies scholar Lindberg-Wada, who offers an intercultural approach to the topic of literary genres in the context of a global literary history: "intercultural understanding in the literary field is now more indispensable than ever before" (1 : ix). That is a compelling insight, which we can adopt for the present volume. In the same historical project, Anders Pettersson speaks of transcultural literary studies that "transcend the borders of a single culture in their choice of topic" (1 : 1). Could this open a dialogue with the concept of transculturation, understood as cultural interfusion and hybridization (see Guo-Ming Chen, "Theorizing" 62–63)? Zhang Longxi calls attention to the value of studying thematic affinity across cultures (see "Two Questions" 58). In a comparative discussion of genres, Mineke Schipper declares that intercultural literary theory deals with oral and written literatures "from different cultures," while she cautions that it may be working with "concepts or methods from one culture that are used in the study of another culture" (67). What is more, Shankman and Dev offer comparative studies of epic and other higher narratives.

Overlapped Lenses

But research agendas like those mentioned do not necessarily, or consistently, depend on what one might call a processual and interactive approach to culture (for culture as process, see Faulkner et al. 40–43, also Kulich and Weng 17). Let us look more closely. We can view phenomena as intercultural, very generally, when strains of different cultures become "intertwined" (as explained for instance in Eoyang 5). Going Across and Happening Between are key processes (see Kulich and English 23 – 24, who pay attention to fictional figures). For theater theorist Patrice Pavis, this takes shape in the metaphorical hourglass of intercultural "transposition" (*Theatre* 16), when one compares theatrical forms and practices that are capable of being "engaged and *intertwined* with each other (instead of merging together)" (ibid., 18; cf. Bharucha's reminder (245) that there may be members of a source culture in a target audience).

Thus, a valuable *Asian Shakespeare Intercultural Archive* has been created and continues to expand < http://a-s-i-a-web.org >. Yet "intercultural" can become politicized, turning into an undesirable quality. That happens when it is suspected of being in league with a subtle cultural imperialism that doesn't satisfy the ideal of "equal cultural exchange" in some Shakespearean productions. While content by Shakespeare is supposed to combine with form by non-Western theatrical traditions, in practice often "even the form is dominated by Western realist theatre" (Im 237, 239). Countering this, the alternative of transculturated Shakespeare should acknowledge that it "easily falls into a director's theatre" (ibid., 242). In turn, a simplistic imperial/colonial allegation has been rebutted in favor of a dramatic adaptation's "perpetual dialogue" with the original's continuing presence, as a Derridean supplement (Thurman 16). For theater, this in itself is a fertile research terrain.

In another vein, an interactive approach has been offered for instance by Heidi Rösch in 1992: the study of interethnic communication especially involving marginalized cultures (see 66ff.). In American studies, too, interculturality research "is primarily interested in the consequences of migration and the ensuing transformation of existing societies," so that "intercultural and transcultural forms of co-existence look for the possibilities of communication between ethnic groups" (Hornung xii). In the same context, intercultural terms "suggest reciprocity and mutuality," with "sharing or experiencing by each of the persons or parties concerned"; the idea of postethnic living "should be discarded in favor of *intercultural* because people living together just can't get beyond their ethnicity" (Lubbers 258, 282). Indeed, anyone who wishes to solidify the communicative moment toward Intercultural Communication, with an eye to social science, might test this.

Could such a venture gain impulses from Johann Georg Hamann's drawn-out wrestling with the idea that "Reason is language — Logos" (1784; Dickson 333)? It suggests that the rationality of social knowledge has a kinship with the verbal practice which is a formative part of reality ... and which writers then put to incisive use. But that wouldn't carry far enough. We could note that narratives have, in passing, been called literary forms of Intercultural Communication when they render as warning symbols the effects of a hatred of foreignness (see Vancea 188). We could read this as gesturing toward phenomenology — if literature and culture are defined as "the progressive awareness of our multiple relationships with other people and the world" (Merleau-Ponty, *Sense* 152), with the other people of the world. The root of this understanding, we may assume, is Friedrich Nietzsche's insight in 1876 – 1877 that a competent person gains maturity several times by experiencing a variety of cultures ("verschiedene Culturen durchlebt"), each of which needs to be comprehended (*Nachlass* 23 [145]: 455).

But we need to strengthen this further. We can find sturdy material in advanced foreign language education: research in this field shows the importance of literature for cross-cultural comparison (see Mao, "Interfacing" 175–176). The research offers a concept of "third places" in a learning process, so that "the intersection of multiple native and target cultures" becomes the site of interpretation (Kramsch 233, 257). Also, seeing other cultures through "overlapped lenses" enables an intercultural stance, one which helps learners to "develop a decentred perspective" for "discovering the logic of their interlocutors' utterances" (Ware and Kramsch 203). The concept is to some degree adaptable for literature. If we take readers *per se* as learners and introduce them to "the cultural codes" active in different cultural communities, can we employ Intercultural Communication research for decoding? (Delanoy 279) If we think of readers as lifelong learners, Merleau-Ponty's lateral "learning to see" and even Ming Xie's seeing "*how* one sees" (quoted farther above) move on a converging pathway. So the focus of language education is helpful, while it remains complementary. It's much less tangential, at any rate, than the idea that literature emphasizes social awareness, as occasionally summarized in the term socioliterature and applied for instance to the documentary novel, or the observation that it fosters "intercultural exploration" (Walsh 11).

Reversals of the Familiar

As yet, then, we haven't come across material sound enough for bridging the disciplinary gap. It's no coincidence that such bridging has rarely been tried. In consequence, we should remove to a subtending, infradisciplinary level of reasoning. If we step back from any immediate consideration of Intercultural Communication, we can revisit Friedrich Nietzsche. We'll do well to be mindful of his appeal in *Genealogy of Morality* (1887):

> [L]et us, particularly as knowers, not be ungrateful toward such resolute reversals of the familiar perspectives and valuations with which the spirit has raged against itself all too long now, apparently

wantonly and futilely; to see differently in this way for once, to want to see differently, is no small discipline and preparation of the intellect for its future "objectivity" [...] so that one knows how to make precisely the difference in perspectives and affective interpretations useful for knowledge. [...] There is only a perspectival seeing, only a perspectival "knowing"; and the more affects we allow to speak about a matter, the more eyes, different eyes, we know how to bring to bear on one and the same matter, that much more complete will our "concept" of this matter, our "objectivity" be. (85)

Any rigid division of the arts would be foreign to Nietzsche's thought, while his evocation of "wanting to see differently" from a plurality of perspectives as enabling usable knowledge is germane. Not only that, it is timely. Not too long ago, Douglas Kellner has proposed a related strategy for the range of cultural studies, including literary study, which should become multiperspectival: "[T]he more interpretive perspectives one can bring to a cultural artifact, the more comprehensive and stronger one's reading may be" (98). The connecting of dots is as valid for literature as it is for feature films.

Though no-one would claim that just adding up several approaches will automatically yield improved insight, "a variety of critical perspectives utilized in a proficient and revelatory fashion provides the potential for stronger (i. e. more many-sided, illuminating, and critical) readings"; one should allow the various perspectives to "inform and modify each other" (ibid., 99). As Chimamanda Adichie would remind us, we ought to avoid *the danger of a single story*. Since literary students are obviously concerned with stories, with cultural artifacts and critical reading, the proposition is an appeal to them — to us. Does it tie in with any other, related ones that are now current? Since we are asking about bringing together, lying across: perhaps with the concept of transversal rationality?

4. "Literature Speaks Science"

What is perhaps the key question for a literary study agenda is in fact addressed in the transversal thought of Calvin Schrag: how can we deal with such resistant blocks as "an irruptive portion of discourse, an unanticipated meaning in a text"? (Schrag, "Transversal" 74) Clearly, that is the kind of blockage we stumble upon in a literary artifact. It speaks to phenomenology's fundamental tenet: "Because we are in the world, we are condemned to meaning" (Merleau-Ponty, *Phenomenology* xxii). Can we think of the resistant block as *rupture de sens*, as in a foreign tongue (see Zarate 230), in a translation venture? Transversal thought meets that of interculturally oriented literary scholars when they call for closer attention to a mode of radical aesthetic alienness within literary texts, which is apparent in language's poetic function (see Leskovec 86). We are dealing with the basic question of how to read, an adequate manner of reading. If we assume that literature represents processes of ascribing meaning, does that make sense especially when communicative acts occur between persons who identify themselves by means of cultural signs as different from each other? (see Gutjahr 353)

In any such case, from transversal thought we might acquire a way to understand the lack of anticipation in the meaning: it's an effect of the "isolated mental act of cognition" when it meets the "otherness" of "a play of forces that act upon us, that obtrude, thrust themselves forward without warrant or request" (Schrag, "Transversal" 74). Cultural forces, as is easy to realize, thrust themselves on the reader of the *Jinshan geji* poems in San Francisco as much as on the reader of, say, Chinua Achebe's *No Longer at Ease*.

Is the isolated mental act in danger of being auto-recursive, as it were, having to feed on itself from within a discipline? From the sciences' vantage point, we might note that Bruno Latour endorses logologist Ludwik Fleck's early perception that the idea of there being "a mind facing an object above the abyss of words and world" is ready for demolition (Latour 93). It's the isolated discursive subjectivity which is at stake, since that subjectivity is at a loss for the requisite tools to cope with the textual obtrusion of the foreign and alien. Looking afresh at the obtrusion arguably has fundamental value for our line of questioning, since comparative and literary study keeps challenging cognitive energy ... without taking note of what Intercultural Communication research has to offer as it seeks to cast light on the cultural forces' interplay.

Myth-making and Storyworld

Conversely, the picture is different. For the methodological foundations of multiculturally oriented communication theory, there are calls for giving attention and credibility to allegories, novels, and poems (see Miike 52); also calls for "richly textured qualitative inquiry," for "bodily-based communicative experiences" such as storytelling, drama, and song (Gordon 92, 96). At times, researchers use reconstructed narratives which are stories, or allegories (see Holliday, *Intercultural* xi). Edward Hall already found the study of literary artifacts desirable as "a key to perception," to gain data on the experience and perception of spatial distance as "a significant cultural factor" (Hall 94). John Condon somewhat later proposed that "[a] very good way to explore issues of intercultural communication and cultural patterns of communication would seem to be through literature and film" (153).

That can become quite specific. The fictional achievement of Chimamanda Adichie for intercultural awareness was already mentioned. We have to look no farther than the present book series to find a comparative study of rhetoric speaking of Du Fu and other Chinese poets (see Gu 170, 172–173); studying cultural identity and value orientations enables a focus on the work of Lin Yutang (see Zhu). On intercultural adaptation, a study of career design processes calls attention to narrative fiction, viz. Lionel Shriver's novel *The Post-Birthday World* (see Buzzanell 85, 91–92). A study of motivationally distinct values operates with a little fictional narrative of its own making (see Schwartz 320). Elsewhere, the communication theory of culture makes effective use of a science-fiction-oriented text version of Shakespeare's *Hamlet* Act 3 Scene 1, to show how cultures develop in response to shared events and language (see Carbaugh 79). Social constructionism speaks of narrative and of film (see Leeds-Hurwitz 893 – 894). Numerous studies work with little fictional scenarios, a form of narrative, as an accepted method (just one example: Straub and Loch 20). Social and literary researcher Li Mengyu finds that "[l]iterary works can serve as good materials for the research of intercultural communication; however, the perspective has often been ignored" (Li 113–114). In a major way, psychology scholar Paul Rosenblatt in 2014 is among those who make use of "literature as social science," as he analyzes a range of fictional works accordingly: novels "potentially can help to fill the gap in the social science literature" for studying the impact of racism; they may turn out to be "especially valuable resources"; "both fiction and apparently objective social research rest on subjectivities" about choosing aspects of the subject matter, about witnesses' accounts, about finding the right language for description, and about interpreting; we should think of "novelists as like social scientists in being astute observers of the social world" (2, 3, 7).

Literary analysis of the fiction can gain new insights from the social scientist's "thematic conceptual categories" gleaned from textual data (ibid., 17).

It's worth staying aware of Jolas's declaration in 1929, which has bearing on the use of scenarios, that all narrative is "the projection of a metamorphosis of reality" (*Critical* 111). From another angle, sociologist Bauman curiously reflects that sociologists "ought to come as close as the true poets do to the yet hidden human possibilities": joining forces with poets, social scientists should "pierce the walls of the obvious and self-evident," since "the walling up of possibilities belies human potential while obstructing the disclosure of its bluff" (203). Much earlier, in a seminal move Henri Bergson proposed that a closed society can only open itself to "humanity in general," that is to "all other men," by means of myth-making, of the achievements of art especially in terms of fiction, drama, and poetry (20–22, 88–89).

From these various voices, we can gather that "[l]iterature speaks science, which reencounters narrative, which, suddenly, anticipates science. [...] knowledge is never cut up into crystalline continents, strongly defined solids. [...] no instruction is possible, no transformation without this fluid whirlpool" (Serres, *Troubadour* 56). And we can reactivate the call for a "new intercontinent of conceptualization." A freshly ontological orientation in narrativity was contributed by Kurt Ranke in the 1960s, who introduced the influential concept of *homo narrans*. As David Carr explains, narrative has its first role in "the pre-literary structuring and shaping of real life," before any literary embodiments which have a cognitive/aesthetic purpose (72). The *before* is more logical than temporal in character. In consequence, narrativity has become part and parcel not only of branches of social science, but of transversal thought. Speaking to the same extension of received notions of narrative, cognitive narratology's concept of storyworld reaches beyond a narrowly conceived literary domain (see, for instance, Herman).

Decentering the Subject

If "literature speaks science," we run across a far-reaching suggestion. The attainment of "unanticipated meaning" is not a mental act but much rather "a social practice and a communicative achievement" (Schrag, "Transversal" 71). Communication discourse itself, with its intercultural purview, has embarked on an overdue move toward stressing the embedded character of agency. It recognizes an inherently relational nature of human individuality, urging participants to practice changing "dominant monologic" communication patterns toward "dialogic ones" (Stewart and Zediker 227; cf. Gehrke). The attainment of meaning, we can gather, eludes any search that is not communicatively situated and oriented, between our institutional and discursive practices, our disciplinary boundaries. The meaning may turn out to be meaningless without that communicative orientation. With due adjustments, studying some contemporary literature — with origins in Chinese or American or African cultures — might gain a few insights for instance from semantic differentials developed in the cross-cultural study of affective meaning, or in the study of shared conceptions and sentiments between cultures (see Osgood, Heise).

As Ludwik Fleck realized very early, without "social conditioning" no cognition is possible, so that "a thought collective" becomes indispensable (43). Or: if Cartesian *cogito* is open to question, "why don't you try *cogitamus*?" (Latour 97) Exploring cultural translation, Mao Sihui urges scholars to engage with colleagues in other countries in discussions and reflections (see "Translating the Other" 281); from an intercultural approach to studying literary genres, Mineke Schipper not too differently urges cooperation with experts who are working "in and on the respective cultures" (67). We shouldn't imagine this to run like clockwork. Seeing that different communities may focus attention on different matters, professional communication across group lines "is likely to be arduous, often gives rise to misunderstanding [...]" (Kuhn 296). Many may have experienced this. Hence, beyond the sciences, we should hasten to note that there is still room for inscribing an agentive subject or solitary ego on the performance of meaning (see Schrag, *Resources* 88) — reassuring for most literary students.

But that subject is not where we might expect. It becomes "decentered and resituated" in communicative praxis, and is now shown to be "an emergent from the patterns of meaning and lines of force" (ibid., 66; cf. Guo-Ming Chen's Taoist explanation regarding free movement between subject and object: "Identity" 40). In its emergence, the subject turns into a feature of what we can still think of as a present-becoming. By analogy, for Michel Serres a center is "absent and unlocatable"; "[w]e neither know how to nor can we inhabit this fault line, this axis or this vortex: who would build his house in the middle of a current?" If the flowing lines of force deny any centered fixity, no knowledge is founded on what actually turns out to be a "mobile place — which is the ultimate foundation and founds nothing" (Serres, *Troubadour* 27).

It's not all that far, as we can easily find, from the lines of force to the chief emphasis of social constructionism. Allied to interpretive Intercultural Communication, this concept describes a process by which people "jointly construct" their understanding of social life, thus developing meanings "in coordination with others" (Leeds-Hurwitz 2: 891). Social interaction and co-construction are the key terms in this branch of communication theory both within and across cultures. It is true that an emphasis on existential and interminate communication, with an intersubjective shift, was advanced earlier by Karl Jaspers, at least in the west. Thus it is not necessarily an original achievement either of transversality or of social constructionism.

Yet the point here is a precise one. We can understand a communicative project as one that takes its resources from "dialogic transactions and institutional forms," the practices of "various communities of investigators and interpreters" who attempt to understand configurations of meaning (Schrag, *Resources* 57; cf. Dai's concept in defining dialogue: 98–101). As Zhang Longxi and Sir Geoffrey Lloyd have observed, there is (after all) a "multidimensionality" of data, phenomena, and styles of inquiry, and investigators are likely to have a common language to gauge transitions of meaning (see Zhang "Complexity"). A community of interpreters may be located at what Kramsch has described as the intersection of multiple native and target cultures (see above). Academically and institutionally various, such communities may well be culturally various to boot. The agenda is then to acknowledge "the weight of alterity, the incursivity of disclosure": we will see what this means. The agenda involves responding to "that which is at once other and alien" (Schrag, *Resources* 170). It calls for reconceiving *unity-within-diversity*.

5. The Other of Thought

Can the "weight of alterity" become fruitful for our question? As a quality of unanticipated meaning, alterity is indeed the object, within as much as between literary works. But here, a decisive effect is pointed out not by transversalism but by Glissant: we should conceive of the principle of alterity as *the Other of Thought*. This is more than meets the eye. It requires that a subject who or which indulges generously enough in some *Thought of the Other* (thinking of the other) not rest content with doing so. Instead, since that subject is not where we might expect, it needs to alter course, with otherness of thought prizing the subject open, thus "changing me within myself"; "[t]hen I have to act" — "an aesthetics of turbulence" (Glissant 154–55). The act is "a relocation" in and across individual mapping because our place becomes "disquieting" (Gonçalves Matos 63). That happens within, and it happens in encountering, a literary text which is characterized in its singularity by "otherness to the cultural conditions" of any specific moment and place (Attridge 34). Every culture, we could also say, "has its own unthought implicit to its episteme" (Xie 44).

When we encounter a text characterized by otherness, we may feel urged to create what emerge as new scholarly narratives. When we do so, Mineke Schipper declares, we need to "revise, or reject" ideas we have received from our predecessors, both "within and across cultures" (81). It's thus that the movement of responding to what is other and alien affords an opening, almost an episiotomy, for the emergence of comparative study as pursued by Schipper and colleagues. Such responding has a purpose. When literature offers the aesthetic encoding of a pluralized and transformed reality, it is for the sake of aiding participation in sociocultural discourses. Running parallel to a poeticizing universalism (as in offering a dialectic comparison between Labîd ben Rabi'a and Mallarmé), participation is likely to be an enactment of minority experience. As such, it becomes an option affecting a majority, as described by Emily Apter in terms of global *translatio* (44–46).

Some Objects

That explains how the analytical process finds its agenda. In practical terms: objects of comparative inquiry will then be scenarios such as fictional biographies shaped by diverse cultural experiences, depicted cultural co- or interexistences of ethnic groups, regions that are characterized by pluricultural involvement. The representation of migrant and sojourner situations, response to borders or boundaries (as characterized by Spivak), difficulties of cultural mixing, multiple identities and their linguistic shaping are among such objects, *not* only in the literary production of our own present time. Earlier literature can sharpen our awareness of a wider range of interactive possibilities in such circumstances. Moreover, it is a common experience that textual structures tend to be heterogeneous in themselves, rather than self-contained. They speak and respond to others, so that within them socially or subculturally hybrid semiosis may create a space of transfer. The perceiving and communicating subject is one of the dots to be interactively transferred, connected. And that happens in the fractal network, as it were, to achieve a polysemic alignment which operates "*between* forms of knowledge" and is thus "transversal to the differentiated culture-spheres [i.e., such as art and science], lying across their disciplinary constitutions" (Schrag, *Resources* 147−148) — but without reaching coincidence (ibid., 149; see also Xie 49−51). The culture spheres meet, but do not coincide. Such an alignment forms an open texture, an "intertexture" that regulates its inner shape (ibid., 81, 94). In an important way, it is poetic. By Jolas's definition in 1929, the poet "brings together realities far removed from each other, that seem without any organic relationships, that are even tending to mutual destruction" (*Critical* 181). One activates the *otherness of thought* as "one moves across the borders and boundaries of the several disciplinary matrices" (Schrag, "Transversal" 65): in our case, across from literature to interrogate interculturality's communicative thrust. Borders, after all, need interrogation as "interested instances of power" (Barad, "Meeting" 182).

Contact Zone and Chronotope

But what does interculturality actually mean for our concern? Speaking of Intercultural Communication activities, Mao Sihui offers an understanding of contact space as "the zone where textual and visual representations of ideology and culture come into discursive contact with each other and establish dynamic relations" ("Translating the Other" 281). Similarly, Dai Xiaodong: interculturality forms "an intersecting space where individuals from different cultures encounter and interact with each other" (106); it "highlights the significance of inbetween space, which embraces terms such as contact zone, interface, intersection, or interactive area in intercultural dialogue" (109). An almost identical approach is presented by Pearson-Evans and Leahy (xv−xvi). It is an adversarial space, which may be characterized by confrontation (see also Xie 16, 163); it separates at the same time as it connects (see Waldenfels 71). And it is where (for instance) the concepts of Coordinated Management of Meaning or Communication Accommodation belong.

There is another way of putting this spatial concept. To liberate the imagination, in the tendency of cultures to meet "there opens up a multiply dispersed zone in which we are gripped by vertigo [...] the shiver of a beginning, confronted with extreme possibility" (Glissant 109). This amplifies the curious sound of Jolas's macaronic: "We were in the wild melting pot of the fekterjas/Nous étions dans un vertige à perte de vue" (*Words*). It follows from the contact zone idea that the concept of boundary becomes "the center" for Intercultural Communication theory (Chen, "Theorizing" 58) — while transversality avers, with good reason and with less centralizing force, that social practices are informed by boundaries along with durations, moments, or places (see Schrag, *Resources* 157). We can only note in passing that Wolfgang Welsch has critiqued concepts of interculturality for positing cultures as separate islands or spheres in a Herderian traditionalism (196). That spatial isolation is less traceable in the recent approaches that are relevant to our focus on literature.

Intriguingly, the intersecting space is not only the home of interculturality. When it is concretized in language and in history, a space thusly described becomes the site of interpretive rationality in transversal thought. This means: it comes with a focus on interpretation that forms a bridge toward hermeneutics. In this concretization, it's not difficult to see that literature has a dwelling. But here we need a word of caution. The concretization is not exhausted in the spatial dimension which is tropically dominant. For Schrag, rather, who speaks of durations and moments as informing social practice, interpretive rationality is *chronotopal* — even as reason's claims retain a measure of spatial relevance as they "move across the sites, localities, and regions of our varied communicative practices" (*Resources* 83). As a Bakhtinian marker of connectedness, which transversal thought employs, the chronotope has an advantage. It is not bound to the possibly reductive implication of a Deleuzian present-becoming as spoken of earlier, and the reason for this may be that it is at home in literary study.

That is a noteworthy origin: a powerful literary concept nourishes transversality. We can gather that the intersecting spacetime, which takes a distinct shape in different disciplines, is the location of some crucial unanticipated textual meanings. It should enable the speedy travel that we need, whenever a *rupture de sens* threatens, from the deceptive familiarity of chronotopal reading to intercultural research. Or enable us to toggle between them. We should not forget that, like culture, literature has a strongly historical and thus temporal dimension — intriguing representations of cultural encounter don't occur only in the literature of our time. It is vital to retain this perspective if we are not to narrow the literary corpus to a synchronous spatiality. We can think of the past as "another culture" (Tatlow 5).

6. Operations

Affinity between literary study and intercultural-communicative research, accordingly, does not have to imply fusion. Here, we need to avoid a misunderstanding. Moving across does not mean simply linking up the originary practices, protocols, or thinking patterns that are proper to each research field, as if we were moving to cross out or erase the distinctions. We do not, that is, have to buy into ditching the aesthetically informed study of literature in favor of cultural discourses, textualities, or information carriers. But do we have to surrender the study of artifacts to social science? To answer that, we need ...

the first of three coefficient operations:

Moving across rather means making full allowance for enabling modification or transformation of any specific intercultural research concept, even acknowledging the possibility of contrasts and collisions all the way to what may turn out to be "a veritable rupture and incommensurability" in a few cases (as we can gather from Schrag, *Resources* 70). A subtly political dimension is enfolded here, though transversalism never speaks of it. Inquiring and deciding in each analytical case which of the options is the right one, whether linkage or tweaking is called for after purely literary methods of analysis have failed to unearth meaning, is the operation of "praxial critique": an exercise of "discernment in our discursive and institutional engagements" (ibid., 57).

In this concept, praxis stands not just for practice as an application of some theory, but rather treats "social practices as performances of meaning" (ibid., 58). We need such discerning critique in any multiperspectival effort as commended by Douglas Kellner. For instance, does the theory of Intercultural Identity Negotiation or that of Coordinated Management of Meaning really harbor a line of continuity with (say) a Sino-American novel? Or with a work of fiction informed by African cultural experience? In terms of a comparative approach: with a dual-optic focus on both? Or, alternatively, does such a negotiation theory need some degree of transformation?

Fitting Together

In any such case, it is vital that the discernment, with its decisions, is not carried out by isolated subjective cognition. It's a performance, one that appears in the shape of ...

the second of the three operations:

that of "articulating configurations of meaning" (Schrag, ibid., 81). It holds an inseparable emphasis on articulating as enunciating but also as fitting together (*con*). It thus extends the scope of Paul Ricoeur's "mise en intrigue," drawing a configuration out of a narrative succession, beyond narrative constitution (*Temps et récit*). Configuration is an act that stretches across the research fields such as literary study and Intercultural Communication, across their institutional imprints, if need be at a topographical and *a fortiori* cultural distance. Its purpose is to disclose meaning by discerning the terms of their mutual engagement. It works as a communicative endeavor within social practice, one that brings the participants together — across cultural or national borders if that's the nature of the case. The methodology presented by Tötösy de Zepetnek (1998) goes in this direction, but the scope is larger than an empirical approach.

　　We can find a bridge toward a critical Foucaultian perspective: "Semantic contentfulness is not achieved through the thoughts or performances of individual agents but rather through particular discursive practices" — which "define what counts as meaningful statements" (Barad, "Posthumanist" 819). After all, the literary study of intercultural relations is focused on a "struggle for cultural dominance" and "hierarchical stratification based on cultural oppositions" (Ben-Porat 179–180). What is more, transculturality for its part may be ambivalently characterized by violence accompanying the experience or assertion of subjectivity, uprooting some earlier culture (see Marotta 94–95). For our purposes, we are looking at an encounter between specific variants of culture, viz., cultures of knowledge. We could think of it as a transculturation process. If we do, the term can be meaningful if the process places cognitive advance within a broad social relevance, and thus aims for a potentially counter-hegemonic legitimacy of knowledge production. In this sense, encountering and moving across suggest each other. Articulation of meaning "always travels with a saying something *to* and *with* the other" (Schrag, *Resources* 88).

This has immediate bearing on the knowledge acquisition pathway. It is crucial to grapple with a counter-intuitive and perhaps somewhat heterodox proposition: that in the sciences there is never a "gap between representations and reality" (Latour 94; see also the discussion in Xie 113−117). To understand this, it's vital to grasp a phenomenon which turns out to have key significance for cognitive energy. It's the experience that, in the shortest formulation, both the objects of knowledge and the knowledge of them are in flux, together subject to specific historicities. Mathematician Alfred North Whitehead has argued in his weighty *Process and Reality* (65): "Real potentiality is relative to some actual entity, taken as a standpoint whereby the actual world is defined. It must be remembered that the phrase 'actual world' is like 'yesterday' and 'tomorrow,' in that it alters its meaning according to standpoint." And as a consequence (79), "[t]he simple notion of an enduring substance sustaining persistent qualities, either essentially or accidentally, expresses a useful abstract for many purposes. But whenever we try to use it as a fundamental statement of the nature of things, it proves itself mistaken." (Perhaps we should note that *real potentiality* is a Hegelian category that depends on time and place data, but happily we don't need the processual specifics when we try to grasp the concept's relevance.) Knowledge is "always a view from somewhere" (Barad, "Meeting" 180). With due regard for cultural distance, the *standpoint* recalls Zhuangzi's playful assertion that he knows what fish enjoy — "by standing here beside the Hao [river]" (Zhuangzi 138).

Railroads and Stormy Waters

What's the point of this? In the various sciences, just as in literary study in a large cultural sense, it tells us that "flux" (Latour) submits both the objects and the knowledge of them to the same conditioning. The Schragian travel metaphor resembles this, introducing a temporal dimension on a transitional scale. The objects themselves (in our case the unanticipated meanings) change in accordance with the manner of the cognitive operations (cf. Gaskin 154ff.), being agents in the production of knowledge. We have a new way to understand the correspondence theory which speaks of a representation's correlation with the represented object, the initial form of which was advanced by as early a thinker as Carneades. Kant assumed that we can have cognition of no object as a thing in itself (Preface to *Critique of Pure Reason*, 2nd ed.). In this context we can consider the concepts advocated by Karen Barad, as in the inseparability of observed object and agencies of observation ("Posthumanist"): *"observations do not refer to objects of an independent reality"* ("Meeting" 170).

The pathway trope gives this a temporal aspect. The knowledge generation process forms a successive path between several or serial versions of a knowledge claim — at initial time t a claim can't yet be decided, but more likely at time $t + 1$ or $t + 2$ along the path (see Latour 88). That is the path of configuration: our second operation.

Perhaps this is easier to understand if we analogize it with a railroad system, since a correspondence theory as just sketched needs a complex network of well-run stations which allows for many correspondences to be set up (ibid., 96), forming a rhizomic figure. Hence, though Latour doesn't say so, the successive path turns out to be a chronotopal figure, a Bakhtinian track across the discursive engagements.

Accordingly, there is no longer "a determinable *what*" of content that is decisive for meaning. There is rather an articulation of "*how* our conglomerate beliefs and practices hang together, bind and separate" (Schrag, "Transversal" 71). Discernment of meaning, that is, becomes inseparable from the *how* of configurative display. We have a conjunctive mode that travels along the real potentiality. It's the "question of the validity of knowledge," of "How *can* I know" anything about cross-cultural understanding (Zhang, "Translating" 29, 32).

Hwa Yol Jung has recently characterized the performance as having to "navigate the stormy waters" of intercultural and interdisciplinary border crossings (*Transversal* xii, 22). Is this where we get Glissant's aesthetics of turbulence (Glissant 155)? Jung's nautical image is justified in that the border-crossing of *disciplinary* matrices, traversing literature in moving toward intercultural inquiry, becomes a border-crossing of the heavy seas of *cultural* matrices: "The end product of transversality in the fusion of cultural (and disciplinary) horizons is hybridity or creolization" (Jung, *Transversal* xiii, 29). Or, as Patrice Pavis has described intercultural theater and performance: "It is at the crossing of ways, of traditions, of artistic practices that we can hope to grasp the distinct hybridization of cultures [...]" (*Theatre* 6) ... enabling, among other forms, Creolized theater ("Intercultural" 8).

Competence in communicating across cultural barriers has been controversially urged by Jürgen Habermas, and is supported by empirical evidence showing how it is "sometimes" possible — "despite very real difficulties" (Fokkema and Ibsch 178). The transversal product, we should hasten to add, does *not* level out, nor does it deny tweaking or even rupture. Fusion doesn't paste over diversity, which, as Nietzsche already suggested, has its own value. But in denaturalizing a monolingualizing process, in showing such a process to be "an artificial arrest" of language transit and exchange, Creole can become a suggestive emblem of mutual engagement, even of a comparative approach to literature (as in Apter 245 or with less emphasis Mecklenburg 435–436).

Journey of Reading

We were talking about a successive *path*, the spatiality of *moving across*. That evokes geometry. The move targets intersections where two or perhaps more lines of thought and action meet, where it becomes "a journey of difference without arrival" (Jung, *Transversal* 32). On the journey, that is, difference is such that it preserves the integrity of the foreign and alien. Would it be more accurate to speak of *trans*difference? This concept gives more precision to allowing for the absence of any purpose which would involve getting captured within binary polarities (cf. Zhang, *Tao* xvii). It also does justice to the notion that signifying systems are palimpsests wherein what is erased or repressed remains present, so that excluded alternatives do not just evaporate (see Breinig). One should, accordingly, be alert to finding "similarities in differences as well as differences within similarities" (Chang 144) — a recommendation also strengthened by Zhang Longxi in the present volume. Arguably, the palimpsestic analogy enables another way to understand the present-becoming, spoken of earlier.

We can pursue the travel trope a little further. Serres declares that 'to read and to journey are one and the same' (*Jouvences* 12 translated); Schrag (quoted above) that articulation of meaning always travels with the Other. Intercultural adaptation, for that matter, has spatial features of "landscapes and learner movement, which suggest stages of travel" in intercultural theory (Cortazzi and Jin 403). And thinking travel, "going away from *chez soi*," means "building a home on cultural crossroads" (Bauman 206).

We are close to the earlier idea of moving across, and close to considering translation. Reading/journeying brings us to the site of an ethics of difference in modern translation theory. It seeks to retain a sense of a source text's strangeness in translation, "receiving the Foreign as Foreign" without domestication (Berman 241). It's especially relevant when one considers that rewritings, to which translations belong, for good or bad inevitably reflect "a certain ideology and a poetics," and as such "manipulate literature to function" in a given way in any society: "Rewriting is manipulation, undertaken in the service of power [...]" (Bassnett and Lefevere xi; similarly Hickey 1). This, of course, is exactly the kind of matter studied in Intercultural Communication's critical branch. A source text, then, is not to be surrendered wholly to the *dispositif* of reception. "Opacities must be preserved; an appetite for opportune obscurity in translation must be created. [...] The framework is not made of transparency" (Glissant 120). An illustrative instance is offered by Zhang Longxi (see also *Tao* 27).

We can tease out two polarities: either stepping into another's language culture without feeling an urge to displace it by *taking it back home*, or giving in to a humanist will to translate and share any common roots and codes. In between, there is a negotiable space in which the challenge of identifying translatable meaning, interrogating what is familiar from the mirror of the foreign, is likely to push isolated mental acts of cognition into the background.

7. The Border Zone

As the journey of difference suggests, all understanding is comparative, looking toward "what is not (yet) given, or pre-given" (Xie 2). Comparison is "the source and resource of discovering the limits of the self's discourse in light of the foreign other who is always more or less exotic" (Jung, *Transversal* 17). From the foreign and different other, it is only a short distance to Nietzsche's urging of reversals of familiar perspectives (as quoted above). From thence, in turn, we have the transversal movement across our culture-spheres — it enables adjustment or even abandonment of deceptively familiar practices, for the sake of "the forging of new and untried perspectives" (Schrag, *Resources* 178). If the perspectives are untried, they are clearly empowered by what then appears as rationality's protentional and hence anticipative vector. It is one that doesn't just recollect and look to what's already accomplished (ibid., 83; Schrag, "Transversal" 71); it works through a configurative operation as outlined above. To be sure, the expectation of a scientific theory's predictive and also causal-explanatory quality will still be unlike the mostly "interpretative, hermeneutic, narrative, metaphorical, semantically overdetermined " range of literary theories (see also Norris 406). Yet the protentional vector should help to bridge the gap.

But where does all this leave our query about the relevance of Intercultural Communication? Have we lost it along the way? On the contrary. This is a good place to recall that "[n]ew ideas are often generated at the cultural interface, and new meanings are produced on the border zone between different and opposed positions" (Dai 111). We need these considerations to understand ...

the decisive matrical operation, the third,

which is the one we need most. Its place is that of service to the others, in mutual conditioning. The two performances of (1) critique and (2) configurative display as discussed serve to clarify, even to follow from, a referential " *responsiveness* [...] to that which is 'other,'" which means to the irruption or incursion of phenomena as they happen to be encountered (Schrag, *Resources* 111). By responding to the interstices of social interaction, we move beyond notions of pantextualism. But there's a simpler version of this. We need to acknowledge that "words neither create the world nor reflect it, but work *in* and *through* it" (Schalkwyk 17). Or: where "matter and meaning" meet, we have a "fully contextual be-in" (Barad, "Meeting" 179). If we hold on to our awareness that the subject is heterocentric, as discussed above, displaced from its erstwhile vantage point, we will find that it's the world's incursive foreignness, rather than any isolated cognitive act, that triggers the operation (see also Jung, *Transversal* 43, 77).

Our purpose is still that of refiguring irruptive and unanticipated meaning in literary artifacts. And that purpose gives us a matrical agenda: to reveal or, better, disclose the fissures of social interaction, the "displayed world of praxial involvements" (Schrag, "Transversal" 73). That world is transtextually represented, not exhausted in textual circularity. It is arguably unlocked by the social sciences, and thus by Intercultural Communication, in a performance of referentiality. After all, we should remember, we can think of literary culture as a progressive awareness of "our multiple relationships with other people and the world" (Merleau-Ponty, as quoted above) — a progressive disclosure of a world through which words work. As suggested at the beginning of this chapter, both literature and Intercultural Communication are strongly concerned with processes of constructing the norms and values by which we live. An "ethics of knowing," then, calls for responsibility (Barad, "Meeting" 183), just as literary study can be called a "life science" (Nünning and Basseler).

But we should pedal back for a moment. Will everything encountered actually be capable of display and disclosure? Some of what is disclosed as encountered strangeness will become perceivable enough. Yet a *facies absconditus* will escape such presence (as Schrag for his part is careful to note in *Resources* 111). Here, can we assume that the well-known iceberg metaphor of which Edward T. Hall speaks, with its deeper layers of cultural beliefs and values that are concealed beneath verbal and nonverbal symbols, offers tools, though not self-sufficient ones, from Intercultural Communication to aid a disclosive rationality (see Ting-Toomey, *Communicating* 10–11)?

At this point, it may become especially easy for the literary student to discover a textual opening with interculturality shining through. As a regular experience, we recall, the sociocultural interactions that are symbolically figured in literature cast strange meanings in our way. These compel us to seek a route, to navigate stormy waters, working around the unanticipated in a search for disclosure — which arguably turns out to be exactly the praxial involvement that intercultural science embodies. And this can serve well enough as a chief proposition.

Forking in Time

From that juncture, our geometric diagonal cuts right across to the demand for critique and for rendering a configurative account (that is, to the operations). The cut may appear to be spatial. But that should not mask its assimilation with time: a historical discursivity dwells within both the literary canon and interpretive performance. It doesn't necessarily dwell within the methodology of social science as such, but as we have seen there's no need to transfer that 1 : 1 to the study of literary representation. Schrag's transversal reasoning itself has a limitation. It doesn't go much further than to endorse Paul Ricoeur's proposal of a *temps raconté* or "third" time in narrative. That concept interweaves historical experience and invention, with a corresponding initial focus on historical narration (*Resources*, as on 156–157). Yet it should be clear that the idea of *homo narrans* or that of historical fiction by no means exhausts literature, just as cultural encounters are not the domain only of the literature and the experience of our time.

When we embark on the three operations, that is, we need to reclaim the multiple valences of temporal disposition, and to do so across the range of literary genres and their intertextual as well as intergeneric folds. Then, we need to adjust our articulative praxis accordingly. There is a good reason for this: "[T]he challenge of reading, into the present of a specific cultural performance, the traces of all those diverse disciplinary discourses and institutions of knowledge that constitute the condition and contexts of culture" requires a "disjunctive" cultural temporality that is "at once ours and other" (Bhabha 233–234).

Time-as-trace, that is, forces adjustment: it harbors the strangeness of a temporality that we cannot claim as an element of our reading. At least we cannot before we communicate across the terrain of discursive diversity. Arguably, the straight transversal diagonal then reveals another face when it turns out to be more like the "forking paths" in the garden of Jorge Luis Borges' famous tale. These, however, are actually a "forking in time." Can we reclaim the diagonal's mobile energy? And follow it to where we may gain encouragement, if not a challenge, to engage in communicative performance from literature and also film toward intercultural praxeology? If so, our journey will empower a dialogic exchange across our cultural and disciplinary borders.

8. Some Possibilities

The exchange would enable us to gain enhanced awareness of possibilities such as the following:

(a) Since literature gives shape to the reality that exists within a literary work, to factual as well as possible experience, we can study the manner of mimetic engendering of literary images of other cultures, images embodying a cultural grouping or its members, as a methodology of comparative inquiry. Such semiotic images, which may be in the form of allegory, parable, myth or other figurations, typify ideas about one's familiar surroundings *in relation* to foreignness.

(b) For a trajectory that cuts across comparative and intercultural study, we will also want to inquire about some key developments: literary exchange and transfer, intercultural reception, and multilingual author positions (see also Schiewer 362, 380). They may involve "creative misunderstanding" (Williams 156, also Zhang Longxi). In certain periods, significantly including ours, a clear boundary between one's own and foreign cultures is lost owing to mutual permeation, external networks, and hybridizations. In such a period, one will become growingly aware that literature crosses borders, that, as Susan Arndt's chapter in this volume illuminates, it is *on the move* (Ottmar Ette). One will become aware that its marginality affects and modifies the culture of the supposed centers — dissolving spatial fixity in favor of mobile configurations of cultural knowledge.

A practical dimension directly follows from these proposals for conceptual siting. What specific questions can Intercultural Communication research help us to ask meaningfully about literary forms that, in a variety of ways, figure or represent cultural encounter? A methodology that builds on such questions may be comparative. Or it may seek to understand cultural interplay involving dialogic border-crossing *within* literary works, to train awareness of such artifacts' cognitive potential for coping with problems of cultural identity. The procedure is extendable, with minor adjustments, to film.

Our team has thus far developed an initial sequence of question cycles on interconnected (t)issues: see the Appendix to this chapter.

References

Apter, Emily. *The Translation Zone: A New Comparative Literature*. Princeton & Oxford: Princeton UP, 2006.

Attridge, Derek. "Ethics, Otherness, and Literary Form." *The European English Messenger* 12.1 (2003): 33–38.

Barad, Karen. "Meeting the Universe Halfway: Realism and Social Constructivism Without Contradiction." *Feminism, Science, and the Philosophy of Science*. Eds. Lynn Hankinson Nelson and Jack Nelson. Dordrecht: Kluwer, 1996. 161–194.

—. "Posthumanist Performativity: Toward an Understanding of How Matter Comes to Matter." *Signs: Journal of Women in Culture and Society* 28 (2003): 801–831.

Bassnett, Susan, and André Lefevere. "General editors' preface." *Translation, History, Culture: A Sourcebook*. Ed. André Lefevere. London: Routledge, 1992.

Bauman, Zygmunt. *Liquid Modernity*. Cambridge: Polity, 2000.

Baumbach, Sibylle, Herbert Grabes and Ansgar Nünning, eds. *Literature and Values: Literature as a Medium for Representing, Disseminating and Constructing Norms and Values*. Giessen Contributions to the Study of Culture 2. Trier: WVT, 2009.

Beller, Manfred, and Joep Leerssen, eds. *Imagology: The Cultural Construction and Literary Representation of National Characters. A Critical Survey*. Amsterdam: Rodopi, 2007.

Ben-Porat, Ziva. "Cultural Relativism and Models for Literary Studies." *The Search For a New Alphabet: Literary Studies in a Changing World*. Eds. Harald Hendrix, Joost Kloek et al. Amsterdam & Philadelphia: John Benjamins, 1996. 177–181.

Bergson, Henri. *The Two Sources of Morality and Religion*. Trans. R. Ashley Audra and Cloudesley Brereton. London: Macmillan, 1935.

Berman, Antoine. "Translation and the Trials of the Foreign." 1985. *The Translation Studies Reader*. Ed. Lawrence Venuti. 3rd ed. Abingdon: Routledge, 2012. 240–253.

Berry, John W., Uichol Kim and Pawel Boski. "Psychological Acculturation of Immigrants." *Cross-cultural Adaptation: Current Approaches*. (International and Intercultural Communication Annual 11.) Eds. Young Yun Kim and William B. Gudykunst. Newbury Park: Sage, 1987. 62–89.

Bhabha, Homi K., and Jonathan Rutherford. "The Third Space: Interview with Homi Bhabha." *Identity: Community, Culture, Difference*. Ed. Jonathan Rutherford. London: Lawrence & Wishart, 1990. 207–221.

Bhabha, Homi K. *The Location of Culture*. Abingdon: Routledge, 1994.

Bharucha, Rustom. *Theatre and the World: Performance and the Politics of Culture*. London & New York: Routledge, 1993.

Blioumi, Aglaia. *Interkulturalität als Dynamik: Ein Beitrag zur deutsch-griechischen Migrationsliteratur seit den siebziger Jahren*. Tübingen: Stauffenburg, 2001.

Borges, Jorge Luis. *Ficciones*. 1944. Madrid: Alianza, 2006.

Breinig, Helmbrecht. Introduction. *Multiculturalism in Contemporary Societies: Perspectives on Difference and Transdifference*. Ed. Helmbrecht Breinig. Erlangen: Universitätsbund, 2002. 11–36.

Burgoon, Judee K., and Ebesu Hubbard. "Cross-Cultural and Intercultural Applications of Expectancy Violations Theory and Interaction Adaptation Theory." *Theorizing About Intercultural Communication*. Ed. William B. Gudykunst. Thousand Oaks, CA: Sage, 2005. 149–171.

Buzzanell, Patrice M. "Transforming Career via Intersectionalities and Inter/cultural Processes." *Intercultural Adaptation (I): Theoretical Explorations and Empirical Studies*. Intercultural Research Vol. 6. Eds. Xiaodong Dai and Steve J. Kulich. Shanghai: Shanghai Foreign Language Education Press, 2012. 75–96.

Carbaugh, Donal. "A Communication Theory of Culture." *Inter/Cultural Communication: Representation and Construction of Culture*. Ed. Anastacia Kurylo. Thousand Oaks, CA: Sage, 2013. 69–87.

Carr, David. *Time, Narrative, and History*. Bloomington: Indiana UP, 1986.

Chang, Hui-ching. "Touring the Field of Intercultural Communication: Finding Differences and Commonalities." *Identity and Intercultural*

Communication (*I*) : *Theoretical and Contextual Construction*. Intercultural Research Vol. 2. Eds. Xiaodong Dai and Steve J. Kulich. Shanghai: Shanghai Foreign Language Education Press, 2010. 125–149.

Chen, Guo-Ming. "On Identity: An Alternative View." *Identity and Intercultural Communication* (*I*) : *Theoretical and Contextual Construction*. Intercultural Research Vol. 2. Eds. Xiaodong Dai and Steve J. Kulich. Shanghai: Shanghai Foreign Language Education Press, 2010. 23–51.

—. "Theorizing Intercultural Adaptation." *Intercultural Adaptation* (*I*): *Theoretical Explorations and Empirical Studies*. Intercultural Research Vol. 6. Eds. Xiaodong Dai and Steve J. Kulich. Shanghai: Shanghai Foreign Language Education Press, 2012. 51–73.

Condon, John. "Exploring intercultural communication through literature and film." *World Englishes* 5.2–3 (1986): 153–161.

Cortazzi, Martin, and Lixian Jin. "Journeys of Learning: Insights into Intercultural Adaptation." *Intercultural Adaptation* (*I*): *Theoretical Explorations and Empirical Studies*. Intercultural Research Vol. 6. Eds. Xiaodong Dai and Steve J. Kulich. Shanghai: Shanghai Foreign Language Education Press, 2012. 399–420.

Dai, Xiaodong. "Out of a Dialogical Dilemma: The Construction of Interculturality." *Intercultural Adaptation* (*I*): *Theoretical Explorations and Empirical Studies*. Intercultural Research Vol. 6. Eds. Xiaodong Dai and Steve J. Kulich. Shanghai: Shanghai Foreign Language Education Press, 2012. 97–114.

Delanoy, Werner. "'Come to Mecca' — Assessing a literary text's potential for intercultural learning." *Experiencing a Foreign Culture*. Eds. Werner Delanoy et al. Tübingen: Gunter Narr, 1993. 275–302.

Deleuze, Gilles, and Claire Parnet. *Dialogues II*. Revised ed. New York: Columbia UP, 2007.

Dickson, Gwen Griffith. *Johann Georg Hamann's Relational Metacriticism*. Berlin & New York: De Gruyter, 1995. (Quotes Hamann's *Briefwechsel*, eds. Ziesemer/Henkel, here 5 No. 753.)

Elberfeld, Rolf. "Forschungsperspektive 'Interkulturalität': Transformation der Wissensordnungen in Europa." *Zeitschrift für Kulturphilosophie* 2.1 (2008): 7–36.

Eoyang, Eugene, ed. *Intercultural Explorations*. Vol. 8 of the Proceedings of the XVth Congress of the International Comparative Literature Association "Literature as Cultural Memory" Leiden 16–22 Aug. 1997. Amsterdam & New York: Rodopi, 2005.

Ette, Ottmar. *Literature on the Move*. Trans. Katharina Vester. Amsterdam & New York: Rodopi, 2003.

Faulkner, Sandra L., John R. Baldwin, Sheryl L. Lindsley, and Michael L. Hecht. "Layers of Meaning: An Analysis of Definitions of Culture." *Redefining Culture: Perspectives Across the Disciplines*. Eds. John R. Baldwin, Sandra L. Faulkner, Michael L. Hecht, and Sheryl L. Lindsley. Mahwah, N.J., & London: Lawrence Erlbaum, 2006. 27–52.

Feather, Norman T. "Values, Valences, Actions, Justice, and Emotions: The Flinders Program of Research on Values Forty Years On." *Value Frameworks at the Theoretical Crossroads of Culture*. Intercultural Research Vol. 4. Eds. Steve J. Kulich, Michael H. Prosser and Weng Liping. Shanghai: Shanghai Foreign Language Education Press, 2012. 103–136.

Fleck, Ludwik. *Genesis and Development of a Scientific Fact*. 1935. Eds. Thaddeus J. Trenn and Robert K. Merton. Trans. Fred Bradley and Thaddeus J. Trenn. Chicago: U of Chicago P, 1979.

Fokkema, Douwe, and Elrud Ibsch. *Knowledge and Commitment: A Problem-Oriented Approach to Literary Studies*. Amsterdam & Philadelphia: John Benjamins, 2000.

Gaskin, Richard. *Language, Truth, and Literature: A Defence of Literary Humanism*. Oxford UP, 2013.

Gehrke, Pat J. "Before the One and the Other: Ethico-Political Communication and Community." *Philosophy of Communication Ethics: Alterity and the Other*. Eds. Ronald C. Arnett and Pat Arneson. Lanham, Md.: Fairleigh Dickinson UP, 2014. 55–73.

Giles, Howard, and Tania Ogay. "Communication Accommodation Theory." *Explaining Communication: Contemporary Theories and Exemplars*. Eds. Bryan B. Whaley and Wendy Samter. Mahwah, NJ: Lawrence Erlbaum, 2006. 293–310.

Glissant, Edouard. *Poetics of Relation*. Trans. Betsy Wing. Ann Arbor: U of Michigan P, 1997.

Gonçalves Matos, Ana. "Literary Texts: A Passage to Intercultural Reading in Foreign Language Education." *Language and Intercultural Communication* 5.1 (2005): 57–71.

Gordon, Ronald D. "Beyond the Failures of Western Communication Theory." *Journal of Multicultural Discourses* 2.2 (2007): 89–107.

Gu, Jiazu. "Rhetorical Clash between Chinese and Westerners." *Identity and Intercultural Communication (I): Theoretical and Contextual Construction*. Intercultural Research Vol. 2. Eds. Xiaodong Dai and Steve J. Kulich. Shanghai: Shanghai Foreign Language Education Press, 2010. 161–176.

Gutjahr, Ortrud. "Alterität und Interkulturalität: Neuere deutsche Literatur." *Germanistik als Kulturwissenschaft: Eine Einführung in neue Theoriekonzepte*. Eds. Claudia Benthien and Hans Rudolf Velten. Reinbek: Rowohlt, 2002. 345–369.

Hall, Edward T. *The Hidden Dimension*. 1966; New York: Anchor Books, 1982.

Hegel, Georg Wilhelm Friedrich. *The Science of Logic*. First pub. 1812. Trans. and ed. George di Giovanni. Cambridge UP, 2010.

Heise, David R. *Surveying Cultures: Discovering Shared Conceptions and Sentiments*. Hoboken, NJ: John Wiley, 2010.

Hepp, Andreas. *Transcultural Communication*. New York: Wiley-Blackwell, 2015.

Herman, David. *Story Logic: Problems and Possibilities of Narrative*. Lincoln: U of Nebraska P, 2002.

Hickey, Leo. Introduction. *The Pragmatics of Translation*. Ed. Leo Hickey. Clevedon: Multilingual Matters, 1998. 1–9.

Holliday, Adrian. *Intercultural Communication and Ideology*. Thousand Oaks, CA: Sage, 2011.

—. *Understanding Intercultural Communication: Negotiating a Grammar of Culture*. Abingdon, Oxon.: Routledge, 2013.

Hornung, Alfred. "Intercultural America: Introduction." *Intercultural America*. Ed. Alfred Hornung. Heidelberg: Universitätsverlag Winter, 2007. ix-xix.

Im, Yeeyon. "The Lure of Intercultural Shakespeare." *Medieval and Early Modern English Studies* 15.1 (2007): 233–53.

Imahori, Tadasu T., and William R. Cupach. "Identity Management Theory: Facework in Intercultural Relationships." *Theorizing about Intercultural Communication*. Ed. William B. Gudykunst. Thousand Oaks, CA: Sage, 2005. 195–210.

Jameson, Daphne. "Reconceptualizing Cultural Identity and Its Role in Intercultural Business Communication." *The Journal of Business Communication* 44 (July 2007): 199–235.

Jiang, Fei, and Kuo Huang. "An Attempt to Clarify the Differences between the 'Two Categories and Four Means' of Theoretical Study on Intercultural Communication." *China Intercultural Communication Annual* 2 (2017): 143–165.

Jolas, Eugene. *Critical Writings, 1924 – 1951*. Eds. Klaus H. Kiefer and Rainer Rumold. Northwestern UP, 2009.

—. *Words from the Deluge*. New York: Gotham Book Mart, 1941.

Jung, Hwa Yol. *Transversal Rationality & Intercultural Texts*. Athens, OH: Ohio UP, 2011.

—. "Transversality and Public Philosophy in the Age of Globalization." *Journal of Political Criticism* 12 (2013): 139–188.

Kellner, Douglas. *Media Culture: Cultural Studies, Identity and Politics Between the Modern and the Postmodern*. London & New York: Routledge, 1995.

Kim, Young Yun. "Cross-Cultural Adaptation Theory." *Encyclopedia of Communication Theory*. Eds. Stephen W. Littlejohn and Karen A. Foss. Thousand Oaks, CA: Sage, 2009. 244–248.

Kramsch, Claire. *Context and Culture in Language Teaching*. Oxford: Oxford UP, 1993.

Kristeva, Julia. *Strangers to Ourselves*. Trans. Leon S. Rudiez. New York: Columbia UP, 1991.

Kuhn, Thomas S. *The Essential Tension: Selected Studies in Scientific Tradition and Change*. Chicago: U of Chicago P, 1977.

Kulich, Steve J. "Constructing Dynamic Theoretical Frames for Contextual Intercultural Identity Analysis." *Identity and Intercultural Communication (II): Conceptual and Contextual Applications*. Intercultural Research Vol. 3. Eds. Steve J. Kulich and Xiaodong Dai. Shanghai: Shanghai Foreign Language Education Press, 2012. 105–154.

—. "Preface to the Two Values Volumes." *Value Frameworks at the Theoretical Crossroads of Culture*. Intercultural Research Vol. 4. Eds. Steve J. Kulich, Michael H. Prosser and Weng Liping. Shanghai: Shanghai Foreign Language Education Press, 2012. 18–30.

—. "Values Studies: The Origins and Development of Core Cross-Cultural Comparisons." *Value Frameworks at the Theoretical Crossroads of Culture*. Intercultural Research Vol. 4. Eds. Steve J. Kulich, Michael H. Prosser and Weng Liping. Shanghai: Shanghai Foreign Language Education Press, 2012. 33–70.

Kulich, Steve J., and Alexander S. English. "Introduction to the Second *CIC Annual* Volume: IC Roots, Research, Relevance." *China Intercultural Communication Annual* 2 (2017): 17–32.

Kulich, Steve J., and Weng Liping. "Introduction: Value Dimensions,

Dynamic Contexts, and Beyond." *Value Dimensions and Their Contextual Dynamics Across Cultures*. Intercultural Research Vol. 5. Eds. Steve J. Kulich, Weng Liping and Michael H. Prosser. Shanghai: Shanghai Foreign Language Education Press, 2014. 1–24.

Kulich, Steve J., and Xiaodong Dai, eds. *Identity and Intercultural Communication (II): Conceptual and Contextual Applications*. Intercultural Research Vol. 3. Shanghai: Shanghai Foreign Language Education Press, 2012.

—. Introduction. *Identity and Intercultural Communication (II): Conceptual and Contextual Applications*. Intercultural Research Vol. 3. Eds. Steve J. Kulich and Xiaodong Dai. Shanghai: Shanghai Foreign Language Education Press, 2012. 29–38.

Latour, Bruno. "A Textbook Case Revisited — Knowledge as a Mode of Existence." *The Handbook of Science and Technology Studies*. Eds. Edward J. Hackett, Olga Amsterdamska et al. 3rd ed. Cambridge, Mass.: MIT Press, 2008. 83–112.

Leeds-Hurwitz, Wendy. "Social Construction of Reality." *Encyclopedia of Communication Theory*. Eds. Stephen W. Littlejohn and Karen A. Voss. Vol. 2. Los Angeles: Sage, 2009. 892–895.

Leskovec, Andrea. *Fremdheit und Literatur: Alternativer hermeneutischer Ansatz für eine interkulturell ausgerichtete Literaturwissenschaft*. Berlin: Lit, 2009.

Li, Mengyu. *Intercultural Communication*. [Title also in Chinese.] Qingdao: China Ocean UP, 2011.

Lindberg-Wada, Gunilla, ed. *Literary History: Towards a Global Perspective*. 4 vols. Berlin & New York: de Gruyter, 2006.

Lubbers, Klaus. "*The Virgin's Seed*: A Note on Intercultural Perspectives in American Art." *Intercultural America*. Ed. Alfred Hornung. Heidelberg: Universitätsverlag Winter, 2007. 257–83.

Lüsebrink, Hans-Jürgen. *Interkulturelle Kommunikation: Interaktion, Fremdwahrnehmung, Kulturtransfer*. 4te Auflage. Stuttgart: Metzler, 2016.

Mao, Sihui. "'Interfacing language and literature': with special reference to the teaching of British cultural studies." *Language, Literature and the Learner: Creative Classroom Practice*. Eds. Ronald Carter and John McRae. London: Routledge, 1996. 166–184.

—. "Translating Popular Culture: Feng Xiaogang's Film *Big Shot's Funeral* as a Polynuclear Text." *Translation, Globalisation and Localisation: A Chinese Perspective*. Eds. Wang Ning and Sun Yifeng. Topics in Translation 35. Clevedon: Multilingual Matters, 2008. 155–173.

—. "Translating the Other: Discursive Contradictions and New Orientalism in Contemporary Advertising in China." *The Translator: Studies in Intercultural Communication* (Manchester) 15.2 (2009): 261–282.

Marotta, Vince. "The multicultural, intercultural and the transcultural subject." *Global Perspectives on the Politics of Multiculturalism in the 21st Century: A case study analysis*. Eds. Fethi Mansouri and Boulou Ebanda de B'béri. Abingdon, Oxon.: Routledge, 2014. 90–102.

Mecklenburg, Norbert. "Interkulturelle Literaturwissenschaft." *Handbuch Interkulturelle Germanistik*. Ed. Alois Wierlacher. Stuttgart: Metzler, 2003. 433–439.

Merleau-Ponty, Maurice. *Phenomenology of Perception*. Trans. Colin Smith.

London & New York: Routledge, 1958.

—. *Sense and Non-Sense*. Trans. Hubert L. Dreyfus and Patricia Allen Dreyfus. Evanston: Northwestern UP, 1964.

—. *Signs*. Trans. Richard C. McCleary. Evanston: Northwestern UP, 1964.

Miike, Yoshitaka. "Toward an Alternative Metatheory of Human Communication: An Asiacentric Vision." *Intercultural Communication Studies* 12.4 (2003): 39–63.

Miner, Earl. "An Allegory on the Banks of the Nile and Other Hazards of Intercultural Literary Comparison." *College Literature* 23.1 (1996): 81–92.

—. *Comparative Poetics: An Intercultural Essay on Theories of Literature*. Princeton: Princeton UP, 1990.

Neumann, Birgit. "What Makes Literature Valuable: Fictions of Meta-Memory and the Ethics of Remembering." *Ethics in Culture: The Dissemination of Values through Literature and Other Media*. Eds. Astrid Erll, Herbert Grabes and Ansgar Nünning. Berlin: de Gruyter, 2008. 131–152.

Nietzsche, Friedrich. *Nachlass 1875 – 1879*. Kritische Studienausgabe. Eds. Giorgio Colli and Mazzino Montinari. Vol. 10. Berlin: de Gruyter, 1988.

—. *On the Genealogy of Morality*. 1887. Trans. Maudemarie Clark and Alan J. Swensen. Indianapolis & Cambridge: Hackett, 1998.

Norris, Christopher. "Literary theory, science and philosophy of science." *The Cambridge History of Literary Criticism*. Eds. Christa Knellwolf and Christopher Norris. Vol. 9: Twentieth-Century Historical, Philosophical and Psychological Perspectives. Cambridge: Cambridge UP, 2001. 401–417.

Nünning, Ansgar, and Michael Basseler. "Literary Studies as a Form of 'Life Science': The Knowledge of Literature." *New Theories, Models and Methods in Literary and Cultural Studies*. Eds. Greta Olson and Ansgar Nünning. Trier: WVT, 2013. 189–212.

Osgood, Charles E., William H. May and Murray S. Miron, eds. *Cross-Cultural Universals of Affective Meaning*. Urbana, IL: U of Illinois P, 1975.

Pavis, Patrice. "Intercultural Theatre today (2010)." *Forum Modernes Theater* 25.1 (2010): 5–15.

—. *Theatre at the Crossroads of Culture*. Trans. Loren Kruger. London & New York: Routledge, 1992.

Pearce, Barnet. "The Coordinated Management of Meaning (CMM)." *Theorizing About Intercultural Communication*. Ed. William B. Gudykunst. Thousand Oaks, CA: Sage, 2005. 35–54.

Pearson-Evans, Aileen, and Angela Leahy, eds. *Intercultural Spaces: Language, Culture, Identity*. New York: Peter Lang, 2007.

Pettersson, Anders. "Introduction: Concepts of Literature and Transcultural Literary History." *Literary History: Towards a Global Perspective*. Ed. Gunilla Lindberg-Wada. Vol. 1. Berlin & New York: de Gruyter, 2006. 1–35.

Ranke, Kurt. *Die Welt der einfachen Formen: Studien zur Motiv-, Wort- und Quellenkunde*. Berlin: de Gruyter, 1978.

Rösch, Heidi. *Migrationsliteratur im interkulturellen Kontext*. Frankfurt/ Main: Verlag für interkulturelle Kommunikation, 1992.

Rosenblatt, Paul C. *The Impact of Racism on African American Families: Literature as Social Science*. 2014. London & New York: Routledge, 2016.

Schalkwyk, David. *Literature and the Touch of the Real*. Cranbury, NJ: Rosemont & Associated UP, 2003.

Schiewer, Gesine Lenore. "Interkulturelle Philologie am Beispiel der

Interpretation von Chamisso-Literatur: Ansätze der Linguistik unter Berücksichtigung der Mehrsprachigkeitsforschung." *Literatur interpretieren: Interdisziplinäre Beiträge zur Theorie und Praxis*. Ed. Jan Borkowski et al. Münster: mentis, 2015. 361–388.

Schipper, Mineke. "Genres: An Intercultural Approach." *Epic and Other Higher Narratives: Essays in Intercultural Studies*. Eds. Steven Shankman and Amiya Dev. New Delhi: Longman, 2011. 64–82.

Schrag, Calvin O. *The Resources of Rationality: A Response to the Postmodern Challenge*. Studies in Continental Thought. Bloomington: Indiana UP, 1992.

—. "Transversal Rationality." *The Question of Hermeneutics*. Ed. Timothy J. Stapleton. Dordrecht: Kluwer/Springer, 1994. 61–78.

Schwartz, Shalom H. "Robustness and Fruitfulness of a Theory of Universals in Individual Values (The PVQ)." *Values Frameworks at the Theoretical Crossroads of Culture*. Intercultural Research Vol. 4. Eds. Steve J. Kulich, Michael H. Prosser and Weng Liping. Shanghai: Shanghai Foreign Language Education Press, 2012. 295–338.

Seih, Yi-Tai, Michael D. Buhrmester, Yi-Cheng Lin, Chin-Lan Huang and William B. Swann, Jr. "Do people want to be flattered or understood? The cross-cultural universality of self-verification." *Journal of Experimental Social Psychology* 49 (2013): 169–172.

Serres, Michel. *Jouvences sur Jules Verne*. Paris: Minuit, 1974.

—. *The Troubadour of Knowledge*. Trans. Sheila Faria Glaser and William Paulson. Ann Arbor: U of Michigan P, 1997.

Shankman, Steven, and Amiya Dev, eds. *Epic and Other Higher Narratives: Essays in Intercultural Studies*. New Delhi: Longman, 2011.

Spivak, Gayatri Chakravorty. *Death of a Discipline*. The Wellek Library Lectures Series. New York: Columbia UP, 2003.

Stewart, John, and Karen Zediker. "Dialogue as Tensional, Ethical Practice." *Southern Communication Journal* 65 (2000): 224–242.

Straub, Detmar, Karen Loch et al. "Toward a Theory-Based Measurement of Culture." *Journal of Global Information Management* 10.1 (2002): 13–23.

Swann, William B. "The self and identity negotiation." *Interaction Studies* 6.1 (2005): 69–83.

Tatlow, Antony. *Shakespeare, Brecht, and the Intercultural Sign*. Durham, NC: Duke UP, 2001.

Thurman, Chris. "Generation S: 'Southern' Shakespeares across Time and Space." *South African Essays on ' Universal ' Shakespeare*. Ed. Chris Thurman. Farnham, Surrey & Burlington, VT: Ashgate, 2014. 1–16.

Ting-Toomey, Stella. *Communicating Across Cultures*. New York: Guilford Press, 1999. 2nd ed., 2019.

—. "Communicative resourcefulness: An identity negotiation theory." *Intercultural Communication Competence*. Eds. Richard L. Wiseman and Jolene Koester. Newbury Park, CA: Sage, 1993. 72–111.

Tötösy de Zepetnek, Steven. *Comparative Literature: Theory, Method, Application*. Amsterdam & Atlanta: Rodopi, 1998.

Vancea, Georgeta. *Toleranz und Konflikt: Interkulturelle Dimensionen der deutschsprachigen Gegenwartsliteratur*. Heidelberg: Universitätsverlag Winter, 2008.

Waldenfels, Bernhard. *Phenomenology of the Alien: Basic Concepts*. Trans. Alexander Kozin and Tanja Stähler. Evanston, Ill.: Northwestern UP, 2011.

Walsh, John. "Socioliterature: contemporary teacher in culture learning." *Culture and Language Learning Newsletter* (East-West Center) 1 Dec. (1973): 10−11.

Ward, Colleen A. Acculturation Theory, Research and Application: Working with and for Communities. *International Journal of Intercultural Relations* 34 (Special Issue). Amsterdam: Elsevier, 2010.

Ward, Colleen A., Stephen Bochner and Adrian Furnham. *The Psychology of Culture Shock*. 2nd ed. London: Routledge, 2001.

Ware, Paige D., and Claire Kramsch. "Toward an Intercultural Stance: Teaching German and English Through Telecommunication." *The Modern Language Journal* 89.2 (2005): 190−205.

Welsch, Wolfgang. "Transculturality: The Puzzling Form of Cultures Today." *Spaces of Culture: City, Nation, World*. Eds. Mike Featherstone and Scott Lash. London: Sage, 1999. 194−213.

Whitehead, Alfred North. *Process and Reality*. 1929. Corrected ed., eds. David Ray Griffin and Donald W. Sherburne. New York: Free Press, 1985.

Williams, R. John. "Modernist Scandals: Ezra Pound's Translations of 'the' Chinese Poem." *Orient and Orientalisms in US-American Poetry and Poetics*. Eds. Sabine Sielke and Christian Kloeckner. Frankfurt/Main: Peter Lang, 2009. 145−165.

Xie, Ming. *Conditions of Comparison: Reflections on Comparative Intercultural Inquiry*. New York & London: Continuum, 2011.

Zarate, Geneviève, et al. *Médiation culturelle et didactique des langues*. Centre européen des langues vivantes, Editions du Conseil de l'Europe. Strasbourg, 2003.

Zhang, Longxi. "The Complexity of Difference: Individual, Cultural, and Cross-Cultural." *Interdisciplinary Science Reviews* 35.3−4 (2010): 341−352.

—. *The Tao and the Logos: Literary Hermeneutics, East and West*. Durham, N.C. & London: Duke UP, 1992.

—. "Translating Cultures: China and the West." *Chinese Thought in a Global Context: A Dialogue Between Chinese and Western Philosophical Approaches*. Ed. Karl-Heinz Pohl. Leiden: Brill, 1999. 29−46.

—. "Two Questions for Global Literary History." *Studying Transcultural Literary History*. Ed. Gunilla Lindberg-Wada. Komparatistische Studien/ Comparative Studies 10. Berlin: de Gruyter, 2006. 52−59.

Zhu, Yige. "Lin Yutang's Cultural Exportism and Cultural Diversity." *Identity and Intercultural Communication (II): Conceptual and Contextual Applications*. Intercultural Research Vol. 3. Eds. Steve J. Kulich and Xiaodong Dai. Shanghai: Shanghai Foreign Language Education Press, 2012. 155−165.

Zhuangzi. *The Complete Works*. Trans. Burton Watson. New York: Columbia UP, 2013.

Appendix   Questions of Intercultural Communication for Literary Studies

Whenever the following paragraphs include references to personae in literary works or films, it should be understood that (as distinct from social science) these are products and effects of textual or fictional construction, and hence of such elements as (inter)action, setting, narrative level, style, intertext, montage, genre, and related ones. Accordingly, they are just one component among several that are mutually dependent in the construction of a fictional work, and other components may likewise merit analysis according to the categories specified below. While *The Living Handbook of Narratology* focuses on "speakers" and "characters" in explaining identity construction (http://www.lhn.uni-hamburg.de), these are not the only relevant components. It is assumed that fictionally constructed personae, like actions and situations, have a potentially referential quality that is subject to interpretation.

The intercultural research titles are listed among References. For an explanation of the relevant research, please see the Appendix to this volume.

(0–1)   ECOCULTURAL BACKGROUND

Is there any representation of the cultural background patterns (culture(s) of origin) of personae as constructed by text or film, or narrators, i.e. any representation of the cultures that influenced them and their place therein, for instance by means of description of settings? Is there any representation of other cultures' (nations, regions, ethnic groups) attitudes toward the cultural background patterns, as hetero-images? What predispositions and stereotypes are shown regarding ingroup and outgroup identification factors? If no background patterns and/or predispositions are depicted at all, what reason could there be? By what literary means or tropes and stylistic features are the auto-images of 0–1 represented, if at all? Are allegorical representations amenable to the same analytical procedure, throughout, as socially realistic genres?

(0–2)   CULTURAL CONSTRUCTION: OWN CULTURE AWARENESS

How aware, if at all, are textually or filmically constructed personae (or narrators) of any of 0–1? Is there a seamless transition between individual embodiment of a culture and the meaning-generating activities of an individual's social identity group? What is the relationship between them? What triggers or initiates any "cocktail of awareness" (Aldous Huxley) regarding the origin and function of predispositions and stereotypes, to perform distanciation? How and with what methods or narrative levels is this shown? Assuming that meanings are developed in coordination with others, hence in co-construction: Are any events and situations that result in "expectancy violation of interaction positions" (Judee K. Burgoon) involved in triggering or accelerating awareness? Is the interaction research on tendencies to form structures of opportunity for self-confirmation (William B. Swann) relevant?

(0-3)   PERSONAL MEDIATING FACTORS
Are there differences between 0–1 and culture(s) of socialization? If so, what are they? In case there are differences, do personae develop orientations in the shape of personal mediation between these two cultures, and if so how? Furthermore, does the culture (s) of socialization differ from culture(s) of formation? If so, how? Do personae ever "cleanse the doors of perception" (William Blake) and transform any features of 0–1? Does such a transformation pertain to any outgroup/Other perception? How are these aspects shown, by indirect or direct characterization methods and by specific methods of literary or filmic representation?

(0-4)   SELF-OTHER PERCEPTION/AWARENESS
Following from the previous: Do individuals perceive and respond to differences in others, and if so how? Does the perception include any form of subjective experience involving the human body? How do they consider Others/Strangers in relation to themselves? Do they perceive similarities as well as differences, and what is the relationship between similarities and differences? Is the perception a positive or a negative experience, or some of both? Do "untold" or "unheard" narratives (Barnett Pearce) occur in any depicted situation, and do they affect the perception process? Is there any readiness, and at what stage in a process, to consider outgroups and Others as co-cultures? Is there any form of interpenetration or interfusion between the self and the alien (e.g., as in the concept proposed by Guo-Ming Chen)?

(0-5)   VALUE CLUSTERS
Does research in cross-cultural psychology on value dimensions that consistently cluster together (Shalom H. Schwartz), rather than appearing as single elements, have relevance for analyzing the literary work(s) in question? If so, how?

(0-6)   IDENTIFICATION COMPONENTS
What relative weight do personae and actants attach to any of the major components of cultural identification, for their culture of origin or a culture of contact: social class, geography, vocation, "philosophy" (= religion or politics), language, biological traits with cultural aspects (ethnicity, gender ...) (as proposed by Daphne Jameson)? Is that weight consistent, or does it vary? How do personae valorize any of the components?

(0-7)   IDENTIFICATION SCALES
In the fictional construction, which scales are relevant in forming (inter)cultural identification concepts:
(A) social association: individual, small social circles, larger social circles ...?
(B) volition: full personal intention or choice, ascribed or accepted roles, externally imposed roles?
(C) activity: accepting sociocultural conditions, assenting to efforts to modify them, proactive in seeking to modify them?

What combinations of these, if any, are relevant to the literary work(s)? Are the scales stable and consistent, or do they vary? Is there any correlation with 0–6?

(1–1) ACCULTURATION/ADAPTATION
Do personae find ways to cope with or adapt to a new cultural context (to culture(s) of contact) that confronts them, within a situation familiar or unfamiliar to them? If so, what ways do they find? Does Colleen Ward's distinction between a psychological (i.e., level of comfort in a new environment over time) and a sociocultural adaptation model (i.e., a sojourner's increasing ability to effectively interact with members of the host society) have relevance for any depicted situation? Does a convergence versus divergence strategy of communicative interaction (Howard Giles) have relevance for any depicted situation? Is there any depiction of a search for interpersonal and relational identity (Tadasu Imahori and others) for fictional communication partners, to renegotiate apparently fixed or distinct cultural identities? Are alternative ways suggested to cope with new cultural context, from which a selection becomes possible in any situation? Does the interpretation that socioculturally subordinate personae or actants give to their conduct differ from the interpretation of that conduct by any dominant ones? Is a choice of the acculturation strategies as conceptualized by John W. Berry (assimilation/separation/integration/marginalization) depicted, and are the strategies consistent in personal and less personal life domains? Is any integrative theory of cross-cultural adaptation toward an intercultural identity (as developed by Young Yun Kim) relevant?

(1–2) SITUATIONAL MIXING
Do the persone or actants at any point find themselves on an unfixed and heterogeneous "medio" level of situational mixing across hybridized (or: non-hybridized) groups? If not, what alternative is depicted?

(1–3) APPROPRIATENESS/FUNCTIONALITY
How might personae adequately function in each situation of cultural encounter, whether they do or not? By what literary means of representation is this suggested, if at all?

(1–4) CONFLICT/RESPONSE TO SITUATIONS
In what ways do personae respond to confusing ambiguity, cognitive or situational dissonance, personal challenges, interpersonal conflict with cultural contexts? Is there any suggestion how they might respond constructively, and if so, by what means is this suggested? Does face negotiation theory (with differential conflict communication styles) as developed especially by Stella Ting-Toomey become relevant?

(1–5) COPING WITH BARRIERS
Is there any representation of perceived or real barriers that prevent cultural understanding, and if so, how do personae cope with them? Do they affect or impact on such barriers in any way? Are there

cultural elements that apparently cannot be easily changed, and if so, how are they dealt with?

(1–6) POWER INEQUITIES

Following from 1–5: Are any perpetuated and institutional or discursive factors shown that might impede agentic change? By what representational means? If there are socio-cultural center/periphery distinctions with a hegemonic dimension, are these static or is there any scope for dynamic transformation? Does such transformation have an equivalent in the literary means of representation? Do power inequities affect any other of these question cycles, and if so, how?

(2–1) MODERATING ETHNOCENTRISM

Do personae or actants impose any assumed cultural superiority on their efforts to deal with aspects of 0–2 through 1–6? Or do they refrain from such imposition, and if so, do they refrain consciously? Does there appear a possibility to engage with others to reflect on one's cultural constructions, including dissonant elements between constructions? (compare 0–2)

(2–2) PERSONAL/INTERCULTURAL DEVELOPMENT

Do any personae seek to get comfortable in a newly negotiated sociocultural niche with a newly acquired set of operational procedures? Do such procedures remain static? Or do any personae seek to keep growing in their personal and psychic development, in dealing with differences and building on similarities? By what means is this shown?

(3–1) LITERARY RECEPTION

Are any literary methods used to guide readers' responses to any of the above, and if so, which methods? Are any methods used to guide readers toward an awareness of their own intercultural positionality or subjectivity? In other words, what reader positions are constructed in the work(s)? Are all readers taken to respond in a similar way, or are there any assumed differences between groups or types of readers? In other words, what recipient types or groups does the work (or do the works) target?

(3–2) INTERTEXT/INTERLITERARINESS

Are any of the above question cycles represented so as to include intertextual marking? And so as to suggest transtextual relationships? Are any of the cycles treated in comparable ways in different literary artefacts, including ones from each of the cultures depicted? If so, what additional signifying value does the comparison contribute to the cycles? Do any features of "interliterariness" appear to apply to the work(s) in question?

(3–3) LITERARY GENRES

The question cycles apply to all relevant literary genres, from prose narrative fiction (including historiographic fiction or historiographic metafiction), poetry, drama, to motion picture genres. Assuming it is clear to what genre the work(s) to be analyzed belong: how do generic conventions and characteristics affect analysis of the representation's tropes? Are there intergeneric and intermedia effects?

(4-1) LITERARY CONTEXTUALIZATION
What is the contextual relationship between the ontological perspective of the fictional or possible world shown in the literary work(s), in cycles 1-2, and the reference world of sociocultural propositions (the extraliterary environment) in which the work(s) seek(s) to intervene? How is this relationship represented or adumbrated within the work(s), as mediated aesthetic contextuality? How strong is the semantic potential of the fictional or possible world that is placed at the center of the literary work's modal system?

(4-2) NARRATIVITY AND TEXTUAL MARKERS
The analytical methods needed for intra- and extraliterary communication processes are obviously not identical. We can understand narratives evoked in everyday conversation as storyworlds (David Herman) no less than fictional narratives in literature and film, as mental models of what is being represented. Even so, the analytical processes require differentiation. Concerning narrative forms, there are several layers in the simplified structuralist communication sequence: Sender 1-Recipient 1 ("rhesis", perhaps closest to extraliterary communication), S2-R2 ("diegesis"), S3-R3, and S4-R4. Also, there may be an extra- and an intradiegetic narrative level, which "communicate" with each other as well as with the recipient. There is a partly analogous differentiation in drama. Variant focalizations (zero, external, internal, variable) and narratorial person positions (auto-, homo-, heterodiegetic) communicate differently with recipients. We might ask, what textual markers set in motion what inferences about intercultural storyworlds, and possibly reference worlds, and how do they do so?

(4-3) NEGATIVITY
If any of the above cycles, especially in 1 and 2, are not traceable in the literary work(s) that figure or represent cultural encounter, what might be possible reasons?

The questions will be revised and developed in light of continuing intercultural research.

6

The Tao and the Logos Revisited

ZHANG Longxi
City University of Hong Kong

Summary: By a most intriguing coincidence, the Greek word *logos* and the Chinese word *tao*, though different in many aspects, share the same duality of meaning, that is, both signaling thinking and speaking. In both Greek and Chinese philosophical thinking, there is a metaphysical hierarchy of inner thinking over outer expression, and thus the debasement of language, particularly writing. While Jacques Derrida criticized this as logocentrism and phonocentrism, he insisted that logocentrism is purely Western and, following Ernest Fenollosa and Ezra Pound, that the largely non-phonetic Chinese writing offers an alternative to Western thinking and language. This creates an opposition that fits in the usual East-West divide, and thus a serious impediment to cross-cultural understanding and communication as a desire to find or create a cultural Other suppresses the reality of that Other. I offered a critique of Derrida's dichotomous view almost 30 years ago. Looking back at that debate, I see an even greater importance today to argue not only for the necessity, but for the validity of cross-cultural communication across the linguistic and cultural gaps that suggest differences between China and the West. A larger context of comparison between cultures should enable a recognition and identification of difference.

More than thirty years ago, in March 1985, my essay, "The *Tao* and the *Logos*: Notes on Derrida's Critique of Logocentrism," was published in the University of Chicago journal *Critical Inquiry*, based on the Eberhard L. Faber Class of 1915 Memorial Lecture I had delivered at Princeton University one year earlier. That essay contained the initial idea that later developed into my first book in English, *The Tao and the Logos: Literary Hermeneutics, East and West*, published by Duke University Press in 1992. The mid-1980s was a time when Jacques Derrida's name was ringing loud in every comparative literature department in America, and deconstruction and *différance* were major catchwords of the day in literary studies. The emphasis — or rather, as I saw it, an overemphasis — on difference of all kinds predominated all disciplines in the humanities and social sciences: gender difference, racial or ethnic difference, difference in sexual orientation, class difference, cultural difference, and of course difference between the East and the West. The last was nothing new, for the poet of the British Empire, Rudyard Kipling, had long been famous for his often-quoted line: "Oh, East is East, and West is West, and never the twain shall meet." Surely nineteenth-century imperialism and colonialism, the whole ideological apparatus of racism, national hygiene and eugenics, were all propped up on the theoretical foundation of racial and cultural differences. Not even the linguistic difference was new in any fundamental sense, for Hegel had already argued in his preface to the second edition of *Science of Logic* that in Western languages "prepositions and articles denote relationships based on thought," but the Chinese language is underdeveloped, for it is "supposed not to have developed to this stage or only to an inadequate extent," whereas German in particular has "many advantages over other modern languages; some of its words even possess the further peculiarity of having not only different but opposite meanings" (*Science* 32). *Aufhebung* was Hegel's favorite example. For Hegel, German and Western phonetic languages in general are superior means of expression when the self-consciousness of the knowing self tries to find articulation.

According to Hegel, the ideal possession of knowledge is attained when truth or *logos* is consciously grasped as articulated logical knowledge, as self-presence of self-consciousness. "The force of mind is only as great as its expression," says Hegel; "its depth only as deep as its power to expand and lose itself when spending and giving out its substance" (*Phenomenology* 74). When the mind tries to express itself, however, it necessarily suffers from the process of alienation, for there is a gap between inner thinking as self-consciousness and language as outer expression. Inner thinking always suffers a loss when it gets into the form of an outer expression. Hegel argues:

> Language and labour are outer expressions in which the individual
> no longer retains possession of himself *per se*, but lets the inner get
> right outside him, and surrenders it to something else. For that
> reason we might just as truly say that these outer expressions
> express the inner too much as that they do so too little. (Ibid. 340)

Following Plato and the entire tradition of philosophical idealism,
Hegel does not so much denigrate language *per se* as he does its outer
form, what he calls the "physiognomy and phrenology" of
expression, that is, writing. In contrast, living speech is the form in
which the inner self directly speaks and is immediately present.
Speech, says Hegel, is

> the form in which *qua* language it exists to be its content, and
> possesses authority, *qua* spoken word. ... Ego *qua* this particular
> pure ego is non-existent otherwise; in every other mode of
> expression it is absorbed in some concrete actuality, and appears in
> a shape from which it can withdraw; it turns reflectively back into
> itself, away from its act, as well as from its physiognomic
> expression, and leaves such an incomplete existence (in which
> there is always at once too much as well as too little), lying
> soulless behind. Speech, however, contains this ego in its purity; it
> alone expresses I, I itself. (Ibid. 530)

Using the analogy of the written language as physiognomic or
outer expression and speech as the body or the inner character,
Hegel argues that speech expresses the self "in its purity," whereas
the written form of language is always inadequate, always expresses
"at once too much as well as too little," an outer form that does not
contain the self and its living voice. In Hegel's view, Chinese as a
largely non-phonetic language exemplifies this concrete actuality
with little or no potential for metaphysical thinking, whereas
German and Western alphabetic writing in general are far superior in
registering the sound of the living voice. Chinese writing is not fully
developed, says Hegel, because it "does not express, as ours does,
individual sounds — does not present the spoken words to the eye, but
represents (*Vorstellen*) the ideas themselves by signs" (*Philosophy*
135).

What Hegel articulates here is of course the metaphysical
hierarchy in the Western tradition, the alienation of inner thinking
in speech and writing, which Derrida strongly criticizes as
"*logocentrism*: the metaphysics of phonetic writing" (Derrida 3).

Thus deconstruction is first and foremost a radical critique of this logocentrism, the metaphysical hierarchy of thinking, speech, and writing, and in carrying out this critique, Derrida follows Nietzsche and Heidegger as predecessors in such radical philosophizing. The emphasis on fundamental differences, however, is where Derrida and Hegel unexpectedly converged, because when it comes to the difference between Chinese and Western writing, Derrida is in total agreement with Hegel in his understanding of the nature of Chinese as a language fundamentally different from that of the West. If Hegel denigrates Chinese as trapped in the outer form of writing without containing sound or the living voice, Derrida praises Chinese precisely for getting rid of the living voice, for having no *logos* as the phonocentric presence of the thinking self, the Cartesian *cogito*. Derrida's praise of Chinese as a language is diametrically opposed to Hegel's dismissal of Chinese, but both agree that Chinese exemplifies a graphic linguistic system fundamentally different from that of the West, thus both solidifying the East-West dichotomy, which has of course a long tradition in the Western conceptualization of China as its Other (see my "Myth," later revised to become Chapter 1 of *Mighty*).

Relying on Ernest Fenollosa and Ezra Pound and their peculiar understanding of the Chinese written characters as presenting concrete *things* directly rather than representing abstract ideas and sounds, Derrida finds in the non-phonetic Chinese writing "the testimony of a powerful movement of civilization developing outside of all logocentrism" (Derrida 90). In other words, he considers logocentrism to be uniquely Western. Within the Western tradition itself, he admires Pound's imagism and Mallarmé's symbolist poetics as something similar to the deconstructive effort to get outside the logocentric and phonocentric biases. Fenollosa took Chinese written characters to be "shorthand pictures of actions and processes," which are thought to be valuable for their pictorial values (Fenollosa 8). "The Chinese written language, it appeared, was undeviatingly concrete. Every word was an image; the line was a succession of images," says David Perkins in describing the effect of Fenollosa's view on Pound. "Pound must have wondered how he might achieve an equivalent in English." Pound's imagism, therefore, conceived of poetry as "a succession of images without the less active, more abstract parts of language that ordinarily connect and interpret them and it afforded speed, suggestiveness, and economy" (Perkins 463). That was, of course, how Fenollosa and Pound understood Chinese poetry and thought Chinese written characters to be a most appropriate medium for poetry; and in Pound's imagistic, "graphic poetics," Derrida found an anti-phonocentric and anti-logocentric breakthrough. So Derrida declares:

> This is the meaning of the work of Fenellosa [*sic*] whose influence upon Ezra Pound and his poetics is well-known: this irreducibly graphic poetics was, with that of Mallarmé, the first break in the most entrenched Western tradition. The fascination that the Chinese ideogram exercised on Pound's writing may thus be given all its historical significance. (92)

The connection here of Fenollosa and Pound with Chinese written characters as the basis of an "irreducibly graphic poetics" is indeed a well-known story in the study of modern Western poetry, but it is well-known among Sinologists as a serious misunderstanding and among students of modern poetry as a "creative misunderstanding." The Sinologist George Kennedy dismissed Pound's translation of the Confucian *Analects* as "bad translation," even though he acknowledged it as "fine poetry," while the literary scholar Laszlo Géfin praised Pound's use of Chinese in his ideogramic poetics as "the most fruitful misunderstanding in English literature" (Kennedy 462, Géfin 31). Both agreed, however, that Pound's idea of Chinese as concrete images was a "misunderstanding." Pound is undoubtedly an influential figure in modern poetry, but insofar as the Chinese language is concerned, he should be the last person to rely on for understanding how that language actually works. The fact is that the majority of Chinese written characters contain a phonetic part to indicate its pronunciation. Relying on Pound and seeing Chinese writing as fundamentally different from the Western phonetic writing, Derrida is thus not so different from Hegel and the traditional view of the East-West divide.

The more fundamental question is, however, whether logocentrism or the metaphysical hierarchy of thinking, speech, and writing is limited to a Western concept of language only? Or is logocentrism — the privileging of the *logos* and the debasement of writing — symptomatic only of Western metaphysics? I chose to speak of the *tao* and the *logos* because in these two important terms we find some astounding similarities and unexpected affinities quite revealing of the ways in which thinking and language are conceptualized in the philosophies of the East and the West. *Logos*, as is well-known, is a Greek word that means both thinking (*Denken*) and speaking

(*Sprechen*) (Ritter s.v. "Logos"). Interestingly, the Chinese word *tao* (or *dao* in the now widely adopted pinyin system for transcribing Chinese), which is so crucial in traditional Chinese historical and philosophical thinking, also means thinking and speaking, thus signaling the duality of idea and articulation. The duality of thinking and speaking contained in one and the same word in Greek (*logos*) and in Chinese (*tao*) is quite remarkable, and we may wonder whether the similarities between the *tao* and the *logos* are really a matter of pure coincidence or serendipity.

Taoism was an important philosophical school in Chinese antiquity more than two thousand years ago. When its originator, the great philosopher Laozi, was asked to write a book to expound his ideas, the first thing he did was to point out the futility of writing a book to expound his ideas. This is put in the significant, paradoxical first line in the *Laozi* or *Tao Te Ching*: "The *tao* that can be spoken of is not the constant *tao*; the name that can be named is not the constant name" (Wang Bi Ch. 1 p. 1). It is important to realize that the verb translated here as "be spoken of" is also *tao* in the original text, and that the subtle play on the meanings of this word is totally lost in most English translations, which usually render this line as "the way that can be spoken of is not the constant way." Here the word "way" as a noun and "speak" as a verb are all *tao* in the Chinese original. The same syntactic structure becomes clear when one reads the parallel line: "The name that can be named is not the constant name." In order to highlight Laozi's punning on the word *tao*, I deliberately kept *tao* as a verb in my otherwise strange translation by transliterating the word, rather than rendering it either as "way" as a noun or as "speak" as a verb. My translation thus reads:

> The *tao* that can be *tao*-ed ["spoken of"]
> Is not the constant *tao*;
> The name that can be named
> Is not the constant name. (Zhang, "The *Tao*" 391).

It would be helpful to know the circumstances under which the book of the *Laozi* or *Tao Te Ching* was written, for the great historian Sima Qian (145?−90? b. c. e.) tells us in his biography of Laozi that the philosopher was requested to write a book about his philosophy, and he was rather reluctant to write:

> Lao Tzu cultivated the *tao* and virtue, and his teachings aimed at
> self-effacement. He lived in Chou for a long time, but seeing its

decline he departed; when he reached the Pass, the Keeper there was pleased and said to him, "As you are about to leave the world behind, could you write a book for my sake?" As a result, Lao Tzu wrote a work in two books, setting out the meaning of the *tao* and virtue in some five thousand characters, and then departed. None knew where he went to in the end. (Sima Qian, qtd. in *Tao Te Ching* 9)

From this we realize that Laozi wrote the *Tao Te Ching* for the sake of laymen who were little equipped to have intuitive understanding, and the first thing he reminded his reader is that language is inadequate to express what the concept of *tao* really means. As an important commentator, Wei Yuan (1794–1856), explains,

> The *tao* cannot be manifested through language, nor be found by following its trace in name. At the coercive request of the Pass Keeper, he was obliged to write the book, so he earnestly emphasized, at the very moment he began to speak, the extreme difficulty of speaking of the *tao*. For if it could be defined and given a name, it would then have a specific meaning, but not the omnipresent true constancy. (Wei Yuan 1)

The most illuminating commentary to date comes from the great modern scholar Qian Zhongshu (1910–1998), who not only points out the significant punning on the word *tao* (or *dao* in the pinyin transliteration) that highlights the difficulty of speaking of that which cannot be spoken, but also relates this to the Greek word *logos* with a similar duality of meaning:

> "The *dao* that can be spoken of (*dao*) is not the constant *dao* "; here the first and the third character *dao* is the *dao* as in *dao-li* [reason], and the second *dao* is the *dao* as in *dao-bai* [speech], or as in the line "*buke dao ye* [cannot be told]" in the poem "There is Thistle on the Wall" in the *Book of Poetry*, that is, words and speech. We may compare this with the ancient Greek word *logos*, which means both "reason" (*ratio*) and "speech" (*oratio*); in more recent times, some have argued that the proverbial statement that "man is the animal of reason" originally meant that "man is the animal that speaks." (Qian Zhongshu 2: 408)①

It is interesting that, as most important philosophical terms in

---

① Qian gives references in this passage to Ullmann 173. Cf. Hobbes, Chapter 4 "The use of speech" and "Universal," and Heidegger "Der Mensch zeigt sich als Seiendes, das redet" (165).

classical Chinese and in ancient Greek, the *tao* and the *logos* contain the duality of thinking and speech, the idea and its articulation, in one and the same word; and that in both traditions, thinking or the idea is thought to be beyond speech or language. Laozi tells us that *tao* is ineffable; that even the word *tao* is not its real name: "I do not know its name, so I arbitrarily call it *tao*"; thus "*tao* always remains nameless" (Wang Bi, Chapters 25 and 32, pp. 14, 18).②
Moreover, in both traditions, we find a similar tendency to denigrate language as outer expression, particularly writing. Language is considered inadequate in expressing the inner concept, and *tao* as speech is inadequate to speak of *tao* as the ineffable idea. That is the point Laozi made at the beginning of his book, namely that it is impossible and futile to present the philosophical idea of *tao* in a book, even though he was, paradoxically, about to write that book. In other words, the debasement of writing is an idea very much imbedded in the non-phonetic Chinese tradition as well.

This is also the point made by another great Taoist philosopher Zhuangzi in a famous story about the wheelwright Pian, who tells Duke Huan, when he finds the Duke reading in a hall, that the book he is reading contains "nothing but the dregs of the ancients!" (Guo Qingfan 217). The Duke is not pleased and demands an explanation. The wheelwright then remarks that he found it impossible to teach even the art of wheel-making, presumably a much simpler matter than extracting wisdom from ancient books. "I can't even teach it to my son, and my son can't learn it from me," says the wheelwright. "The ancients and what they could not pass on to posterity are all gone, so what you are reading, my lord, is nothing but the dregs of the ancients" (ibid. 218). Here the wheelwright's remark presumes a hierarchy of speaking over writing, because teaching to his own son how to make a wheel is of course conducted orally, and if that fails to do it, how could the Duke, the wheelwright asks, learn anything from the dead written language in a book? For Zhuangzi, written words are harmful to intuitive understanding and memory. He says in another famous passage often alluded to in classical Chinese poetry and philosophy:

> It is for the fish that the trap exists; once you've got the fish, you forget the trap. It is for the hare that the snare exists; once you've got the hare, you forget the snare. It is for the meaning that the

---

② Unless otherwise noted, all translations of Chinese are mine. Wang Bi lived from 226 to 249.

word exists; once you've got the meaning, you forget the word.
Where can I find the man who will forget words so that I can have a
word with him? (Ibid. 407)

The point of Zhuangzi's question is of course that most people
tend to *remember the word* but forget the meaning. So he is searching
for a man who will *forget his words* so as to remember his meaning.
Isn't that also the point Plato makes in *Phaedrus* when Socrates tells
the story about the invention of writing? The Egyptian god Theuth
presented his invention of writing to king Thamus, and the king
commented on the invention, saying: "If men learn this, it will
implant forgetfulness in their souls; they will cease to exercise
memory because they rely on that which is written, calling things to
remembrance no longer from within themselves, but by means of
external marks. What you have discovered is a recipe not for
memory, but for reminder" (Plato, *Phaedrus* 275a, p. 520).

In the seventh philosophical letter, Plato puts it very clearly
that "no intelligent man will ever be so bold as to put into language
those things which his reason has contemplated, especially not into a
form that is unalterable — which must be the case with what is
expressed in written symbols" (*Letter vii* 343a, p. 1590). The idea
expressed here is indeed very close to what Taoist thinkers thought of
language, particularly writing. "This passage," as Qian Zhongshu
says after quoting it, "may almost be translated to annotate the
Laozi" (2: 410).

From the numerous quotations of philosophers of the East and
the West we may conclude that the debasement of writing, the
metaphysical hierarchy of thinking, speech, and written symbols,
the critique of the inadequacy of language, particularly of writing,
are indeed common in both the East and the West. Derrida is
therefore *not* correct in regarding logocentrism as a uniquely
Western phenomenon and in seeing Chinese as the opposite of
Western alphabetic writing and exemplifying a sort of fundamental
différance from the West.

Derrida, of course, did not think so. In fact, I had a chance to
meet Derrida and talk about my article before its publication in
Critical Inquiry. He was lecturing in Yale at the time, and I gave
him the manuscript of my essay. We met in his office at Yale and
had a long talk in one afternoon. Derrida admitted that he did not
know Chinese, but when he was writing *Of Grammatology*, he said,
he happened to be interested in the work of Fenollosa and Pound. I
explained to him that Pound was definitely an important poet, but

his understanding of Chinese was unreliable. On that point, because he did not know Chinese himself, Derrida could not have much of an argument with me, but eventually he asked me a loaded question: "Are you saying that Taoism and logocentrism are the same?" "No," I replied, and I tried to contextualize the question. "You are the *maître de différance*," I said. "When we say A *and* B, the two of course cannot be the same, but because you are saying that logocentrism is exclusively Western, I have to point out that the metaphysical hierarchy of thinking, speech, and writing exists in China as well. Suppose you or somebody with your influence were saying that logocentrism is exactly the same as Taoism, I would probably take a different stance and say, hey, wait a minute, there are significant differences between the two."

So it all depends on the context or situation of our argument, and the situation I saw in the American academic world at the time was an overemphasis on difference, particularly between China and the West. That explains why I wanted to point out some of the similarities between Taoist and Western ideas about language, speech, and writing. In China, as I also argued in my article, the importance of writing and of calligraphy as a form of art had in some sense already deconstructed the metaphysical hierarchy long before deconstruction became hot and popular in American universities.

For Derrida, how the Chinese language actually operates was not the concern, for he was more interested in seeing Chinese writing as an alternative to the Western tradition of logocentrism. The desire to find a cultural Other was so strong that the reality of the Other hardly mattered, and when the reality contradicted the imaginary Other, the real Other was to be ignored. A Chinese tradition without the irksome logocentric-phonocentric baggage was just such a desideratum, in Derrida's view, to be cherished and admired, even though that was precisely the reason why Hegel thought Chinese was inadequate, underdeveloped, and unfit for philosophizing. The very different views and attitudes towards philosophy or what counted as philosophy created a problem, and that problem came to the surface in an interesting episode when Derrida visited China in September 2001. Nicolas Chapius, writer, translator, and diplomat, then the French Consul-General in Shanghai, arranged a lunch meeting for Derrida to meet Professor Wang Yuanhua, a well-respected senior Chinese scholar. As we read in an interview with Professor Wang, the meeting was not so successful, because "in their conversation that lasted more than two hours, the focus was around a remark Professor Derrida made at the lunch table that 'there is thought in China, but no philosophy'" (Wang Yuanhua, *Qingyuan* 26). That remark was meant to be a compliment, of course, but Wang Yuanhua was not particularly pleased. He understood Derrida's point, but he disagreed nonetheless, for he later wrote:

> Derrida's remark that China had no philosophy, only thought, has caused some to have misunderstood him as denigrating Chinese culture. In fact, what he called philosophy was that which resembles Western philosophy in nature. He regarded Western philosophy as originating in Greece and centered on logos, which was precisely what he tried to deconstruct. Having said this, however, I believe that he made such a remark probably because few in the West had studied the metaphysical school of the Wei-Jin period, and therefore had overlooked it. (Wang Yuanhua, *Si* 244)

If philosophy is exclusively conceptualized as "that which resembles Western philosophy," which was "originating in Greece and centered on logos," then there would be no philosophy anywhere in the world except in the West, and there would be no possibility of comparative philosophy or any cross-cultural comparative work. Such exclusive conceptualization of any concept rules out any attempt at cross-cultural understanding and reduces all comparisons to differences that are often claimed to be untranslatable and incommensurate. But if that is not a grossly Eurocentric prejudice, what is? Why should all philosophies be defined along the lines of a narrowly understood Greek model? In China, there is of course no Greek philosophy, just as in China people speak Chinese, not Greek or French. But can such banality constitute any discovery in knowledge and count as serious scholarship? And yet, in talking about fundamental differences between the East and the West, scholarly argument often boils down to precisely that.

As an expert on the famous work in Chinese literary criticism, Liu Xie's (465?–522) *Literary Mind or the Carving of Dragons*, Professor Wang Yuanhua has paid special attention to the ideas of the Wei-Jin period in Chinese history, roughly of the third to the fifth centuries, because that was a period of relatively free thinking when the Confucian orthodoxy set up in the Han dynasty collapsed after four hundred years as a predominant ideology, and Taoist metaphysics rather than Confucian ethics and politics became intellectually influential and stimulating, reviving to some extent the lively philosophical debates from the pre-Qin antiquity. "The debates about the essence and the minutiae, about being and nothingness, and about language and meaning all concern ontological issues," says Professor Wang when commenting on the lively debates and intellectual activities of that period (Wang Yuanhua, *Si* 243). One of the most important philosophical debates of that time made inquiries into the nature of language and its adequacy, which becomes an important issue much discussed in contemporary philosophy in our time. So for Professor Wang Yuanhua as for many other Chinese scholars, to say that there is no philosophy in China is simply wrong, no matter whether this is meant to be a dismissal as by Hegel or a compliment as by Derrida.

We have now entered the second decade of the 21st century with important changes taking place globally, which put many of the old concepts and ideas in question. We are now also facing many new problems out of age-old discord and conflicts, which makes clear that the overemphasis on racial and cultural differences is likely to lead to horror and disasters. The East-West divide, the fundamental cultural differences between China and Europe, should certainly be reexamined and rethought. The *tao* and the *logos* are of course different and have played important roles in the formation of very different cultures and traditions, but as I have argued, differences are a matter of degree, not of kind; though we can find all sorts of differences in focus and emphasis, beyond all the differences there is always the possibility of cross-cultural understanding, the possibility of translation and communication, and there is always a larger context of comparison within which differences can be recognized and identified as such.

"Differences make all of us distinct as individuals, as groups, communities, and nations, but despite and beyond all the differences, we share the same globe as human beings and as neighbours," as I wrote in another place. "The universalist's denial of individual and cultural differences obviously gives us a false picture of the world, and the relativist's insistence on all difference without similarity equally distorts the true condition of our world, the possibility of cross-cultural understanding and cooperation. The reality is always more complex than such either/or dichotomy would lead us to believe, and we may do well to choose to know the complexity of reality than to believe in the false picture of either all unity or total difference" (Zhang Longxi, "Complexity" 350). I believe the point made here is valid and relevant because the overemphasis on difference, particularly between China and the West, is still visible in much discussion in the humanities and social sciences and prevents us from getting out of the dichotomy of a simplistic East-West divide.

To come back to the *tao* and the *logos*, I would acknowledge that the differences between the two are obvious and not to be overlooked. The *tao* has important implications not just for Taoism, but for other Chinese philosophical schools as well, and *logos* energized the entire Western tradition not only as the philosophical notion in ancient Greece, but as the Word of God in its New Testament embodiment in Christian theological tradition. In other words, they have played a significant role in fashioning the different traditions in China and the West. In considering the duality of thinking and speech as contained in one word, however, the shared or common philosophical issues, even though dealt with differently in different traditions, are what makes the hidden affinities between the *tao* and the *logos* discernible and significant. In our effort to reach out for others for understanding and peaceful coexistence, the comparability of the *tao* and the *logos*, I hope, may guide us to a better future for the whole of humanity.

References

Derrida, Jacques. *Of Grammatology*. Trans. Gayatri Chakravorty Spivak. Baltimore: Johns Hopkins UP, 1976.

Fenollosa, Ernest. *The Chinese Written Character as a Medium for Poetry*. Ed. Ezra Pound. Square Dollar Series. San Francisco: City Lights Books, 1969.

Géfin, Lazlo. *Ideogram: History of a Poetic Method*. Austin: U of Texas P, 1982.

Guo Qingfan. *Zhuangzi jishi* [*Variorum Edition of the Zhuangzi*]. *Zhuzi jicheng* [*Collection of Masters' Writings*], 8 vols. Vol. 3. Beijing: Zhonghua shuju, 1954.

Hegel, Georg Wilhelm Friedrich. *The Phenomenology of Mind*. Trans. J. B. Baillie. 2nd rev. ed. New York: Harper & Row, 1967.

—. *The Philosophy of History*. Trans. J. Sibree. New York: Willey, 1900.

—. *Science of Logic*. Trans. A. V. Miller. New York: Humanities P, 1976.

Heidegger, Martin. *Sein und Zeit*. 11te Auflage. Tübingen: Niemeyer, 1967.

Hobbes, Thomas. *Leviathan Parts I and II*. Ed. A. P. Martinich. Ontario: Broadview Editions, 2005.

Kennedy, George A. "Fenollosa, Pound, and the Chinese Character." *Selected Works of George A. Kennedy*. Ed. Tien-yi Li. New Haven, Conn.: Yale UP, 1964. 443–462.

Perkins, David. *A History of Modern Poetry: From the 1890s to the High Modernist Mode*. Cambridge, Mass.: Harvard UP, 1976.

Plato. *The Collected Dialogues, including the Letters*. Eds. Edith Hamilton and Huntington Cairns. Princeton: Princeton UP, 1961.

Qian Zhongshu. *Guan zhui bian* [*Pipe-Awl Chapters*]. 5 vols. Beijing: Zhonghua shuju, 1979.

Ritter, Joachim, and Karlfried Gründer, eds. *Historisches Wörterbuch der Philosophie*. Vol. 5. Basel: Schwabe, 1980.

Tao Te Ching. Trans. D. C. Lau. Harmondsworth: Penguin, 1963.

Ullmann, Stephen. *Semantics*. Oxford: Blackwell, 1964.

Wang Bi. *Laozi zhu* [*Laozi with Annotations*]. *Zhuzi jicheng* [*Collection of Masters' Writings*], 8 vols. Vol. 3. Beijing: Zhonghua shuju, 1954.

Wang Yuanhua. *Qingyuan jinzuo ji* [*Collection of Recent Works*]. Shanghai: Wenhui, 2004.

—. *Si bian lu* [*Dialectical Reflections*]. Shanghai: Shanghai guji, 2004.

Wei Yuan. *Laozi ben yi* [*The original meaning of the Laozi*]. Shanghai: Shanghai guji, 1955.

Zhang, Longxi. "The Complexity of Difference: Individual, Cultural, and Cross-Cultural." *Interdisciplinary Science Reviews* 35.3–4 (2010): 341–352.

—. *Mighty Opposites: From Dichotomies to Differences in the Comparative Study of China*. Stanford: Stanford UP, 1998.

—. "Myth of the Other: China in the Eyes of the West." *Critical Inquiry* 15.1 (Autumn 1988): 108–131.

—. "The *Tao* and the *Logos*: Notes on Derrida's Critique of Logocentrism." *Critical Inquiry* 11.3 (March 1985): 385–398.

Section Two

Diasporic Discourses

7

Cultural Encounters in the Diaspora: Intercultural Communication and Identity in Terry Woo's *Banana Boys*

Fu Lin
University of Bayreuth/Shanghai

Summary: The chapter investigates individual and collective experiences of (inter) cultural encounters as represented in Terry Woo's novel *Banana Boys* (2000). Taking into account the importance of literary representations as vehicles of intercultural communication, this chapter focuses on two interrelated contextual issues that problematize intercultural contact: racism and double consciousness. It argues that ongoing intercultural communication forcefully engages diasporic subjects in the negotiation of their cultural identities and cultural belongings in the context of multiculturalism. Adopting a pluralistic approach that brings in critical vocabularies of culture, intercultural communication, cultural identity, racism, and double consciousness, the chapter seeks to explore the impact that intercultural communication has on cultural identities of diasporic subjects and their well-being. As such, the research contributes to the growing body of intercultural communication studies by providing insights into the potential that fiction has for increasing our understanding of both dynamic tensions and advantages that intercultural encounters present.

Introduction

The ever-increasing mobility of people and the multifaceted nature of intercultural contact have prompted growing interest in the study of intercultural communication across a broad spectrum of disciplines such as sociology, psychology, anthropology, linguistics, media studies and business studies, among others. In this chapter, I propose the idea of employing literature as a medium to study intercultural communication and cultural identity. In dealing with these two concepts, one can hardly overlook the widely theorized yet still challenging concept of culture. For instance, Hofstede (13) sees culture as the "collective programming of the mind." Gudykunst and Kim (13) consider culture as "'systems of knowledge' shared by a relatively large group of people." Schwartz (138) perceives culture as "the rich complex of meanings, beliefs, practices, symbols, norms, and values prevalent among people in a society." He claims that the prevailing "cultural ideals" (values that are considered appropriate and desirable) that are emphasized in a society are the most central traits of culture. The notion of culture, thus, indicates a set of static essences that are acquired, shared and historically transmitted from one generation to the other, namely core values, beliefs, behavioral characteristics and customs. Seeing culture in a more dynamic manner, Clifford and Marcus view culture as a constructed, flexible, changing and plural concept. Rather than focusing on the commonalities, anthropologist Anthony Wallace (28) has offered an alternative view of culture as an "organization of diversity." For him, what members of the same culture have in common is their ability to infer behaviors, recognize patterns of thought, and make predictions despite the fact that they may have divergent standpoints. In the interdisciplinary field of linguistic anthropology, Duranti (33) proposes seeing culture as a "system of signs" that represents the world where cultural products must be communicated "in order to be lived." Seen in this light, culture is a product of human interaction that is open to interpretation and negotiation. Cultural products, thus, are acts of communication. The communicative aspect of culture enriches our lives and facilitates the connection of people across different geographical locations.

Globalization deterritorializes the conventional concept of nation-state, blurs the borders of nations, and challenges the strict distinctions of cultures. The increasing intercultural contact associated with relocation, displacement, and massive migration has generated ongoing uncertainties and debates around the conceptualization of culture and cultural identity. Similarly to the concept of culture, cultural identity has been widely studied by scholars from diverse disciplines of the humanities. A review of academic research on the concept reflects a range of perspectives. Hall (435), for instance, points out that there are at least two different views of cultural identity. The first viewpoint highlights a "collective self." It emphasizes the unity of people with shared history and cultural codes. Such group distinctiveness allows particular communities to differentiate themselves from others. Moreover, in the context of diaspora, when collective meanings are strategically assigned to a diasporic community, cultural identity then emerges as a political concern, highlighting power imbalance in the new land as well as the shared historical experiences and membership of the community. A second standpoint, however, recognizes that even when people with similar cultural background share certain similarities, there are still crucial and significant differences among them that endow individuals with distinctive characters. Collier and Thomas see cultural identity as a dynamic composition of multiple identities including nationality, ethnicity, gender, and race, so that whichever identity dominates over the others depends primarily on the given context or situation. Although varied in contexts and theoretical backgrounds, what these theorists share in common is the understanding that the formation of cultural identity is an ongoing, dynamic process that engages individuals and cultural groups in constant negotiation of their sense of self when especially the way they perceive themselves is not necessarily the same as what others ascribe to them. Constructed and rendered in cultural encounters, cultural identity undergoes continuous transformation.

The fluid process of identity negotiation occurs in the process of communication. Communication situations are perceived as being intercultural when communicators carry different cultural attributes. Communication can take place between individuals; it also exists between two cultural systems. Whether consciously or unconsciously, as cultural carriers, people integrate their cultural attributes into their communication patterns. The German-born American anthropologist-linguist Edward Sapir (515) points out that every individual is, to some extent, "a representative of at least one sub-culture which may be abstracted from the generalized culture of the group of which he is a member." Thus, all communication is, to some extent, intercultural. Like other forms, intercultural communication significantly involves communicators exchanging and interpreting narratives. With this in mind, in the present study, intercultural communication is perceived primarily as in-person or virtual communication between or among individuals or groups with different cultural backgrounds.

Considered as a form of communication, literature with its aesthetic structures can engage formally, stylistically, and metaphorically with intercultural themes and promote intercultural awareness. Literature that tackles intercultural issues often (re-)creates real-life situations, calling attention to the dynamics of and the problems associated with intercultural encounters. I will use Terry Woo's novel *Banana Boys* (2000) as a case study to investigate the ongoing tension between different cultural groups in Canada. It addresses two interrelated issues that problematize the intercultural contact: racism and double consciousness.

As a national policy in Canada, multiculturalism allows people from diverse cultural backgrounds to preserve their cultures within well-regulated limits. As a notion, it denotes an "acknowledgement of the co-existence of multiple cultures and peoples within one space, generally the space of the nation-state" (Ang 14). However, in real life, the idea of multiculturalism is often in collision with social dynamics, as Ien Ang argues: the policy does not take account of "the dynamism that occurs when different groups come to live and interact together." The social challenges that arise from the interactions among different groups cannot be overcome by a multiculturalism policy. Hence, as a policy, it cannot solve problems such as racism.

1. *Banana Boys*: General Observations on Plot and Narrative Perspective

Written by Chinese-Canadian author Terry Woo, this novel is set in Toronto, Canada in the 1990s. Narrated by five "Banana Boys" (i.e., yellow on the outside, white on the inside) and one Banana Boy's sister, the novel provides an account of the lives of five Chinese Canadian protagonists — the Banana Boys: Luke, Dave, Sheldon, Rick, and Mike. As each individual account unfolds, readers learn that Luke quits his studies at university and becomes a DJ at a radio station; Dave is a software tester and a frequent victim of racism; Sheldon works as a gas line inspector, who has grown up without the torment of racism; as a consultant at a management consulting firm, Rick deliberately abuses anti-depressants and alcohol to maximize his performance in his personal and professional life; Mike is a graduate student in Biology, who wishes to become a writer. Formulated as a Word document, the novel consists of six segments — "thanatopsis," "hi there!", "neurosis," "hysteresis," "catharsis," and "kenosis." Narrated by Rick's sister, Shirley, the prologue "thanatopsis" begins with the death of one Banana Boy, Rick; the end is an epilogue "kenosis," which signifies a new beginning. The four main sections of the novel are further subdivided into five personal accounts of each Banana Boy's life. Rather than adopting an omniscient narrative strategy, the multiple narrative voices and perspectives allow readers to see alternate views and to construct a comparative mental picture of the "Banana Boys." In doing so, the multiple narrative voices alleviate the limitation of a single point of view by unfolding supplementary events. After the reunion at Rick's funeral, each of the Banana Boys initiates his story. The constant shift in time and perspective disturbs narrative cohesion and a chronological order of a linear narrative. The disrupted narrative exemplifies the disassociated memory of perplexity and struggle that each Banana Boy has undergone over the years.

2. Racial Grief

The concept of "race" is a socially constructed fallacy that has been affecting human lives pervasively at individual and social, discursive and structural levels. The concept was invented by Europeans in the late 1600s and 1700s to rationalize European Imperialism, colonial expansion, and to define *white* people's alleged superiority (Feagin 68). Although a number of scholars have attempted to define *racism* and to identify its multifaceted forms, the common insights lie in the understanding that the term refers to the beliefs in "races"[1] and *white* supremacy. Albert Memmi (78) suggests that racism emerges from diverse situations, rather than simply as an ideology: "Racism does not limit itself to biology or economics or psychology or metaphysics;

---

[1] 'Race,' 'white,' and 'black' are used in single quotation marks here to refer to biologistic constructs "whenever these terms are categories of 'race theories'"; when written in italics, they refer to "social positions and/or as analytical categories." See Arndt 167–189.

it attacks along many fronts and in many forms, deploying whatever is at hand, and even what is not, inventing when the need arises." The naturalization of racism is often manipulatively reinforced through varied social and cultural forms to justify and rationalize *white* supremacy as well as discriminatory and unfair treatment toward People of Color. The rationalization of *white* supremacy is for the benefit of *white* people. For Memmi (112), *racism* is prevalent; it is a "cultural discourse" that has been surrounding people since their early childhood — it exists in diverse cultural productions to which people are exposed. The cultural discourse plays a key role in influencing people's beliefs. Racism permeates everyday life, as Philomena Essed (2) explains: "As a process it is routinely created and reinforced through everyday practices." Given its pervasive nature, it is not surprising to see its reflections in social practices. Since many *white* people are unaware of their privilege of being *white*, their actions, without vicious intentions, may unsettle the well-being of People of Color (see also Pulido 467).

Racism-related incidents can happen unexpectedly to people, although they may possess the knowledge of the existence of racism. Cumulatively and repetitively, a series of such incidents may have the potential to damage the victim's emotional and psychological well-being (see Bryant-Davis and Ocampo, "Racist" 484; Harrell; Sanchez-Hucles). For instance, in *Banana Boys*, Dave is the only Chinese Canadian boy without a Chinese name. Growing up in Canada enables Dave to feel that he has "become more Canadian than the average Canadian" (Woo 45). His father attempts to make him a real Canadian by naming him after the "Leafs captain of the late sixties and early seventies, Dave Keon" (Woo 38). In addition, by drinking massive amounts of Canadian alcohol and becoming a hockey fan, Dave's father seeks to embrace his Canadianness; however, despite all his efforts to integrate himself and his son into mainstream Canadian society, Dave is often the target and victim of racism:

> When I was younger, I guess I wanted to be just like everyone else [...]. But, obviously, I wasn't ... couldn't be, could never be. You're looking at a victim of the R-word, beat up on a regular basis, subjected to racial taunts, general abuse, evidently because the sons of the local Hatfields thought I had slanty eyes (*I did?*) and yellow skin (*it was?*). Case in point: do you remember that classic rhyme? *Me Chinese/ Me play joke/ Me go pee pee in your Coke ...?* Well, imagine hearing it upwards of three times a day,

often culminating in fat lips, black eyes, wounded pride. (Woo 38)

The confessional, homodiegetic tone accompanied with a self-questioning mode suggests that Dave's experience is found to be sudden, uncontrollable, and unexpected without his understanding the motives behind the racial attack. He sets out to live an ordinary life in a country which takes pride in its official multiculturalism policy and in celebrating its cultural diversity, yet his incessant victimization experiences of racial assault in both derogatory verbal and abusive physical forms resulting from his skin color and facial feature signify that citizenship and voluntary assimilation do not warrant membership in the mainstream *white-dominated* community. Under the guise of the joking song lies his damaged psyche, with a sense of isolation, helplessness, and reflexive vexation. The repetitive singing of the song indicates that the racial assault is not a single incident, but multiple and prolonged incidents that haunt, stress, and torment him insidiously, unsettling his fundamental sense of self, integrity, self-esteem, self-worth, and security. By supplementing a self-questioning rhetorical interrogation, a sense of humor is integrated into a presumably serious and afflictive situation. In Dave's narration, he employs humor as a device to come to terms with the situation, and to emphasize his mental shock owing to the occurrence of racist incidents targeting his physical being.

Dave's experience does not stand alone; with the internet permeating everyday life, digital form of racist messages are communicated in an anonymous yet equally abusive way that constantly erodes the Chinese minority's psychic well-being. As Mike reads from an online Asian-Canadian forum:

* bullshit * when you know * full and well * that this country is falling to pieces because of all the fucking immigration. [...] If having reasonable neo-conservative views makes me a racist, then I say just send all the chinks back to the eastern cesspools and opium dens from whence they came. (Woo 188)

In the digital era, the perceived racism has been transformed to a defamatory discourse on the internet. Under the guise of pseudonyms, racist messages are publicized to further encourage *white* supremacy and to despise equality among citizens. The impact of such digital assault and menace is in no way less pernicious to one's psychological tranquility than the assault in real life, as Mike painfully writes:

You're born here. You're raised here. You raise a family, earn the respect of your friends and colleagues. You work hard, play fair, shoot straight, pay your taxes — you're a normal, productive member of Canadian society. And yet with a lone word from a single prejudiced freak, you are immediately degraded [...].

It hurts.

I hate *it*.

You think, *It's so unfair*. You think, What's the point of it all? You think, *screw you guys*, *I'm going home*. Except that you are home. All that blood, sweat, tears, anthems, and you're *still* treated like garbage by garbage. In your own home. (Woo 188–189)

These lines are powerfully written in the second-person perspective to address readers directly. The unconventional second-person narrative mode allows readers to be interactively engaged in Mike's ongoing struggle, bearing witness to his life in Canada, feeling his pain of being stigmatized as unwanted and non-legitimate citizen, and identifying with his predicament of being at home yet not being perceived as being at home. The pronoun "you" provides an intimate and personal sense of urgency, indicating that the racism-based grief is not experienced by Mike alone, but possibly shared collectively by those who are reading his story, and those who are seeking the precise language to convey this affliction. By addressing readers directly, the narrator creates a "community kinship" with readers whose integrity and vitality have constantly been trampled on and deprived by the ongoing humiliation of a hostile environment. Mike's convincing tone also illustrates that despite official multiculturalism policy, racist actions persist; the internet serves as a communicative platform for people to incite, spread, promote, and rationalize racial hatred and culturally-intolerant resentment. Moreover, the enduring affliction resulting from exposure to sustained racial hatred and denial of their equality is ingrained in the collective consciousness of People of Color, and each new racist incident, no matter in what form it occurs, reignites these victims' past pain, ravaging their fundamental sense of self and generating more scars in the psyche.

Although speaking Chinese with a "Russian or Scottish" accent, and self-identified as "more Canadian than the average Canadian," who deliberately resists the "Chinesey" thing, Dave is actively engaged in defending social justice and justifying racial equality. For instance, Dave witnesses one incident when an elderly Chinese woman who barely speaks English is found to be verbally insulted by a local grocery store worker. Irritated by the racial assault, Dave threatens, "Listen, you stupid cracker, if I ever catch you mocking

Chinese people like that again, I'm gonna rip your fucking arms off and stuff them down your throat. You understand — 'buddy'?" (Woo 137). Although Dave's aggressive response carries a life-threatening message, his reaction reflects the sudden outburst of the accumulated and destructive rage that has been suppressed internally over the years, as Dave bitterly recounts: "I've heard enough cries of 'chink!' and 'slope!' to last me several lifetimes. It still burns me up how this sort of shit can happen when all you're doing is picking up hot dogs, Kraft Dinner and a lousy head of bok choy" (Woo 138). These racist remarks are frequently uttered in public places where Dave least expects them. Instead of being shocked to turning mute and frozen or singing a joking song as how he coped with similar situations when he was a teenager, the adult Dave adopts a furious reaction, which represents one type of self-defensive mechanism to which members of a diasporic group may resort in coping with mounting stress and cumulative minor insults from hostile situations. Dave's aggression can also be seen as a form of resistance against racial assault. Such resistance is a natural response of victims of racism; it helps them to gain redress for the humiliation they have suffered. Dave's explosion of rage suggests that a manifestation of racism-related stress is beyond the capacity limit of what his psyche can accommodate and tolerate, so that one minor racist incident can ignite his rage.

3. Double Consciousness

Not only do these Banana Boys have to cope with racism-related stress, they also have to wrestle with double consciousness. In fact, racism and double consciousness are interlinked; racism causes double consciousness since racism legitimizes the status of People of Color as racialized *other*. The awareness of being *othered*, on the other hand, affects the way People of Color position themselves.

In *The Souls of Black Folk* (originally published in 1903), Du Bois (11) discusses the concept of "double consciousness": "this sense of always looking at one's self through the eyes of others, of measuring one's soul by the tape of a world that looks on in amused contempt and pity"; the sense of "twoness," of being "an American, a Negro; two souls, two thoughts, two unreconciled strivings; two warring ideals in one dark body." Within the twoness, one element is a self-identified soul, thought and striving, whereas the other is ascribed and imposed in Du Bois's context from the "Other," namely, *white* Americans. Although today Du Bois's concept of "double consciousness" has attained general currency in academia when engaging in the discussion of what it means to be Black in America, the term itself did not originate with him. For instance, Dickson D. Bruce Jr. assumes that Du Bois's use of the notion indicates his familiarity with both American Transcendentalism and psychology, although there is no irrefutable evidence that shows which source inspired him the most. From a transcendental perspective, the term is associated with Emerson, who employs the notion in a figurative approach to delineate the dilemma one encounters when he views the lives of "the understanding" and "the soul" through the lens of Transcendentalism (see Bruce 237). Seen in this light, the two lives share little commonality with each other, and double consciousness from this perspective elicits "a set of oppositions" (ibid. 238, also for the following).

For Du Bois, "double consciousness" refers to an internal struggle of preserving the African soul while living in a "materialistic, commercial world of white America." It is this precise conflict that resonates with Emerson's "double consciousness." Although the spiritual aspect of African identity is in opposition to American materialism, the mergence of the two is mutually complementary, as Du Bois (11) writes: "He would not Africanize America, for America has too much to teach the world and Africa. He would not bleach his Negro soul in a flood of white Americanism, for he knows that Negro blood has a message for the world." The gifted African soul that is associated with African civilization can be seen as a spiritual alternative to *white* Americanism, although meanwhile it serves as a source to the double consciousness. From Du Bois's standpoint, the "veil" and the gifted "second-sight" are central to the construction of African American double consciousness. The veil, seen as both corporal difference and racializing lens, has impacted African Americans' lives fundamentally. The veil's racializing lens hinders *white* Americans from viewing African Americans as "authentic" Americans; it also obstructs African Americans from viewing their true selves, since the *white* gaze is overwhelmingly unbearable. The gifted "second-sight" allows them to wander in two cultures, obtaining insights from two perspectives: the Africans and the *white* Americans, although the process of reciprocating views is often accompanied by befuddlement, frustration, and vexation. Such a conception of "double consciousness" implies a positive connotation. However, in my analysis of Chinese Canadian characters' double consciousness, I focus more on the notion's negative aspect, stressing the ruptured self which battles two imposed identities.

As a medical term in psychology, "double consciousness" refers to a "Duality of Person in the same Individual" (Bruce 241). The dual personalities are not only distinct from each other, but evidently opposed to each other (see Bruce 242). Bruce Jr. infers that during the time Du Bois was constructing the concept of coexisting African and American identities, there was a compelling indication that he was inspired by this medical term, since his notion suggests a distinctive state of mind that is characterized by a predicament of the coexistence of one ascribed identity and one's own sense of self trapped in one integrated body. Although the predicament distresses African Americans' lives, this unique state of mind should not be perceived as inferior or abnormal; rather, it entails a sense of uniqueness which allows African Americans to be granted a knowledge of both cultures, denying the precedency of one culture over the other and also the renouncement of either. The inosculation of two coexisting selves carries the potency to construct a better self.

Although Du Bois's double consciousness was set in the American context over one century ago, referring specifically to African Americans being compelled to view themselves through the contemptuous gaze of *white* Americans while struggling to maintain their own self-identities, the same condition can find its correlation with writings on colonialism and People of Color in other contexts. For instance, Frantz Fanon illustrates colonized people's experiences:

> "Speaking as an Algerian and a Frenchman." Stumbling over the need to assume two nationalities, two determinations, the intellectual who is Arab and French, [...] if he wants to be sincere with himself, chooses the negation of one of these two determinations. Usually, unwilling or unable to choose, these intellectuals collect all the historical determinations which have conditioned them and place themselves in a thoroughly "universal perspective." (Fanon 155)

The psychic dilemma of being unable and unwilling to choose between the two interwoven identities appears to run parallel with Du Bois's unsettling double consciousness. The dilemma is the consequence of colonialism and suppression by the colonizer. The common state of double consciousness among downtrodden people in and outside the U.S. demonstrates the ongoing condition of living with privileged people's misjudgments and misrepresentations. When this troubled state of mind is only experienced unilaterally by oppressed people, it can be traumatic, since under the condition of two conflicting identities coexisting in one self, a substantial amount of time and vigor are inevitably invested in negotiating the true self and mediating the internal conflicts inflicted by external force. Hecht and Jackson similarly speak of the ways in which biculturalism may lead to fragmentation and dysfunction owing to pressures of shifting identity; Deaux and Ethier have explored the problem of threats to identity "as a consequence of stigmatization."

The agitating condition of double consciousness has found its vestige and validity in *Banana Boys*. The collective awareness of double consciousness can be seen as a shared cultural condition among People of Color who strive to assimilate in a *white*-dominated society. Like African Americans, the Chinese Canadian characters struggle to define themselves throughout the novel. The consciousness of being "Bananas" is largely formed through their experiences as Chinese Canadians growing up in Canada, and through retrospective interaction with *white* Canadians and the Chinese who grew up in China. By viewing themselves through the eyes of the other, these five protagonists encounter the opposing identities imposed on them: seen from the perspective of *white* Canadians, they are "Chinese," who have no difference from recent Chinese immigrants; however, for the Chinese who have grown up in China, they are "hollow bamboos," who "have no consistent culture, no substance, no essence" (Woo 11). The ongoing denial of their cultural authenticity by both *white* Canadian and Chinese communities has left indelible marks on their psyche, disrupting their sense of self and sense of belonging, as Shirley illustrates: "They stand between two groups, not quite Canadian, and certainly not Chinese, marginal and maybe kind of messed up, belonging to and accepted by neither" (Woo 104).

The constant reminder of how their own self-definition collides with the identities imposed on them can be seen as a stressor that causes tensions in their psyche, as they often feel marginalized by both *white* Canadians and Chinese communities. The misrepresentation of their images by mainstream Canadian culture based on their physical difference has become a psychological burden that impedes them from fully identifying themselves as Canadians. In this light, double consciousness can be viewed as having potentially detrimental impacts on the psyche of these characters, confounding their self-definitions. Although the notion is not explicitly employed by Mike, the condition of double consciousness is reflected in his retrospection of the "Essence of the Banana": "Something was ... *there*. Something that bugged us, nagged at us, kept us all slightly off-kilter. It was like an undefined burden of some sort, kind of hard to describe" (Woo 104). Under the guise of their seemingly prosperous lives lies their inner pain, which "always came back to us in one way or another like that darned cat. Every time someone slipped up, we all paid for it. Somehow. Somewhere" (Woo 104). The predestinate tone as well as the compulsively repetitive pattern of this double consciousness has become a psychic burden that keeps haunting the way these Banana Boys define themselves as Chinese Canadians and as regular human beings. Despite their desire to announce their own place in the world, they are constantly compelled to negotiate the identities inscribed to them and to define themselves unwillingly. Driven by the double sense of alienation and the crisis of their identities, they strive to reconcile two cultures and to negotiate their true selves, only to find that their true selves are not confined to either ascribed identity.

Moreover, the very sense of double consciousness enables them to be both an insider and an outsider of two cultures, as Shirley writes:

> They pronounce the "j" in words like jook. They eat burgers and steaks one day and funky foods, like chicken feet and pigs intestines, the next. They listen to Country-Western and Heavy Metal, and despise karaoke. [...] They cook bacon with chopsticks, and read Hong Kong magazines only for the pictures flipping pages left to right. (Woo 11)

Their common distinctiveness in pronunciation, eating habits, cooking style, music taste, and reading behavior all suggests their shared cultural traits that bear traces of two different cultures, although they are not fully conformed to either. Through these unique cultural practices, whether consciously or unconsciously, their common cultural traits have become distinctive symbols that differentiate them from other groups. The natural adoption of both cultural traits is the outcome of being raised in Canada by Chinese-born parents.

Although they are equipped with knowledge and insights from both Canadian and Chinese cultures, the term "Banana Boys" carries a derogative connotation of being "inauthentic" and having no "essence" of two ascribed identities, namely, Chinese and Canadian. In Rick's word: "Bananas are the intersection — messed up, hyposensitized, marginalized, somewhere in between — and we all know that most car crashes occur at intersections" (Woo 185). The intersection disrupts the exclusive assimilation to one cultural system, and the fact that these Banana Boys have often been stigmatized as "hollow" and culturally inferior has challenged their own self-identifications. Dual alienation resulting from their "yellow on the outside" image and their "white on the inside" social upbringing sets the stage for their traumatic sense of double consciousness, which is often closely affiliated with their fractured and fragile psyche — "miserable, frustrated, alone" (Woo 381).

Conclusion

The intersection of racism and double consciousness as represented in the novel illustrates the ongoing challenges faced by diasporic subjects in their intercultural encounters. In the novel, all Banana Boys realize the undefinable nature of their identities by rejecting the restraining labels externally imposed on them. They struggle between two cultural identities, only to realize that neither can sufficiently define them. Their double consciousness on the one hand causes their collective melancholy; on the other hand, it equips them with the necessary cultural sensitivity that enables them to decode cultural specificities while switching between cultures. If there are no "independently existing objects with inherent characteristics," the meaning of such a cultural position is achieved "through particular discursive practices," in "an ongoing performance" (Barad 816, 818, 821). Through the case study of *Banana Boys*, I hope to expand scholarly dialogues on intercultural communication that often adopt a social-psychological approach. Although that approach has been proven to generate critical ideas on intercultural communication, given the multi-faceted nature of intercultural interaction, a single approach may not be sufficient to acknowledge its complexity and raise awareness of intercultural understanding. With its aesthetic reach, diverse points of view, and emotional engagement, literature can powerfully diagnose real and deeply-felt experience that lies just beneath the surface of extrafictional reality. As an important site of cultural transmission, literature provides an alternative framework for us to understand the fluid nature of culture and the dynamics of cultural identities in relation to intercultural contact and communication.

The chapter is a revised version of a chapter in the author's dissertation "Trauma in Chinese North American Fiction", accepted at the University of Bayreuth in 2015.

References

Ang, Ien. *On Not Speaking Chinese: Living Between Asia and the West*. London & New York: Routledge, 2001.

Arndt, Susan. "Whiteness as a Category of Literary Analysis: Racializing Markers and Race-Evasiveness in J.M. Coetzee's *Disgrace*." *Word & Image in Colonial and Postcolonial Literatures and Cultures*. Ed. Michael Meyer. Amsterdam: Rodopi, 2009. 167–189.

Barad, Karen. "Posthumanist Performativity: Toward an Understanding of How Matter Comes to Matter." *Signs: Journal of Women in Culture and Society* 28 (2003): 801–831.

Bruce Jr., Dickson D. "W. E. B. Du Bois and the Idea of Double Consciousness." *The Souls of Black Folk: Authoritative Text, Contexts, Criticism*. Eds. Henry Louis Gates Jr. and Terri Hume Oliver. New York: W. W. Norton, 1999. 236–244.

Bryant-Davis, Thema, and Carlota Ocampo. "Racist incident-based trauma." *The Counseling Psychologist* 33 (2005): 479–500.

—. "The Trauma of Racism: Implications for Counseling, Research, and Education." *The Counseling Psychologist* 33 (2005): 574–578.

Cheng, Anna Anlin. *The Melancholy of Race: Psychoanalysis, Assimilation, and Hidden Grief*. New York: Oxford UP, 2001.

Clifford, James, and George E. Marcus, eds. *Writing Culture: The Poetics and Politics of Ethnography*. Berkeley: U of California P, 1986.

Collier, Mary Jane, and M. Thomas. "Cultural identity: An interpretive perspective." *Theories in Intercultural Communication*. Eds. Young Yun Kim and William B. Gudykunst. International and Intercultural Annual 12. Newbury Park, CA: Sage, 1988. 99–120.

Deaux, Kay, and Kathleen A. Ethier. "Negotiating Social Identity." *Prejudice: The Target's Perspective*. Eds. Janet K. Swim and Charles Stangor. New York: Academic P, 1998. 301–324.

Du Bois, W. E. B. *The Souls of Black Folk: Authoritative Text, Contexts, Criticism*. Eds. Henry Louis Gates, Jr., and Terri Hume Oliver. New York: W. W. Norton, 1999.

Duranti, Alessandro. *Linguistic Anthropology*. Cambridge: Cambridge UP, 1997.

Essed, Philomena. *Understanding Everyday Racism: An Interdisciplinary Theory*. Newbury Park, CA: Sage, 1991.

Fanon, Frantz. *The Wretched of the Earth*. New York: Grove P, 1968.

Feagin, Joe R. *Racist America: Roots, Current Realities, and Future Reparations*. New York: Routledge, 2010.

Gudykunst, William B., and Young Yun Kim. *Communicating with Strangers: An*

Approach to Intercultural Communication. 2nd ed. New York: McGraw-Hill, 1992.

Hall, Stuart. "Cultural Identity and Diaspora." *The Post-Colonial Studies Reader*. Eds. Bill Ashcroft, Gareth Griffiths and Helen Tiffin. 2nd ed. London & New York: Routledge, 2006. 435–438.

Harrell, Shelly. "A multidimensional conceptualization of racism-related stress: Implications for the well-being of people of color." *American Journal of Orthopsychiatry* 70.1 (2000): 42–57.

Hecht, Michael L., and Ronald L. Jackson II. *African American Communication: Exploring Identity and Culture*. 2nd ed. Mahwah, N.J. & London: Lawrence Erlbaum Associates, 2003.

Hofstede, Geert H. *Culture's Consequences: International Differences in Work-related Values*. Thousand Oaks, CA: Sage, 1980.

Memmi, Albert. *Racism*. Trans. & ed. Steve Martinot. Minneapolis: U of Minnesota P, 2000.

Pulido, Laura. "Rethinking Environmental Racism: White Privilege and Urban Development in Southern California." *American Studies: An Anthology*. Eds. Janice A. Radway et al. Malden, MA: Wiley/Blackwell, 2009. 465–475.

Sanchez-Hucles, Janis. "Racism: Emotional abusiveness and psychological trauma for ethnic minorities." *Journal of Emotional Abuse* 1 (1998): 69–87.

Sapir, Edward. "Cultural Anthropology and Psychiatry." *Selected Writings of Edward Sapir in Language , Culture and Personality*. Ed. D. G. Mandelbaum. Berkeley & Los Angeles: U of California P, 1949. 509–521.

Schwartz, Shalom H. "A Theory of Cultural Value Orientations: Explication and Applications." *Comparative Sociology* 5. 2–3 (2006): 137–182.

Wallace, Anthony F. C. *Culture and Personality*. New York: Random House, 1961.

Woo, Terry. *Banana Boys*. Toronto: Riverbank P, 2000.

8

Middle-Class, Mobile, Queer and African: Transnationalism in Online Writing from Nigeria and South Africa

Shola ADENEKAN
University of Bremen

Summary: In *African Literature in the Digital Age*, the author has carried out a survey mapping the agenda of same-sex desire in African literature, arguing that some members of the older generation of African writers used fictional homosexual characters as part of a larger project of decolonizing the African body as well as that of the diasporic black body. Despite this agenda, their writing gave us a good insight into the figure of the African homosexual and how this figure relates to other black queer figures outside the continent. For some of Africa's emerging literary voices, as this chapter aims to show, queerness, class, and transnational spaces intersect, while their work suggests that the earlier Pan-African projects contributed to a silencing of queer desire which we witness in much of the last century. While literature in the print age has helped articulate the idea of nationhood and Pan-Africanism, online literature, the rise of the African middle classes, as well as the increase in transnational movements are now arguably the catalyst for the development of African queer identities. This chapter studies how the literature that is being published online depicts the experience of queerness by characters who see Africa as their spiritual home. Queer desire is being articulated by a new generation of African writers, many of whom are members of the professional middle classes and are themselves transnational figures, often seen by many as cultural ambassadors. Their writing indicates that the figure of the queer African is central to our understanding of the implicit problems of transnationalism and Pan-Africanism.

The Queer Twin

When Wole Soyinka was creating the character of Joe Golder in *The Interpreters* (1965), he probably did not know that Golder would become the precursor to many transnational black queer characters some four decades later — in the age of the internet. As a matter of fact, one can argue that Soyinka gave some of the currently emerging African voices literary narratives to build on, because over forty years ago he helped usher in a new model of a queer African genre in which alienation is collective rather than idiosyncratically personal. Most importantly, from Soyinka's generation to this new (third) generation, the trope of non-straight African is regularly navigated through transnational characters that possess the right kind of education, European language skills, and the financial clout to move easily between the countries of Africa and the West. This seems to suggest that homosexuality and queerness exist only in unfixed spaces, of which transnational spaces are an ideal metaphor. Like intercultural spaces, they are interstitial, located "between fixed identifications" (Bhabha 4), with flexible borders (see also Cohen); "overlapping geographies" result in "oscillating identities" (Massaquoi 51). Non-straight desire seems to be what middle-class Africans who have had western-style education tend to harbor. Sexual deviation appears to go hand-in-hand with the notion of transnationalism, as does sexual freedom. In this way, foreignness is ascribed to queerness. For example, Golder in *The Interpreters* is an African American lecturer working at a Nigerian university, but his masculinity is often called into question by his intellectual friends because of his supposed queerness. He becomes an object of constant ridicule because of his sexuality, so much so that this African American in Africa often expresses his frustration by singing the African-American spiritual "Sometimes I feel like a motherless child."

Golder's lamentation is similar to the evocation of home and diaspora that emanates in the poems and fictional narratives that form the case studies for this chapter; works that were published in a digital PDF format by *Outliers* (2008). *Outliers* is a ground-breaking trans-Atlantic project that articulates and theorizes homo-erotic choices from a Pan-African perspective by bringing together writers and thinkers who are based in Africa and North America. The audacious project came about as part of the intellectual discourses that continue to respond to the notion of the un-Africanness of homosexuality by certain sections of the black diaspora. As recent scholarly studies such as those by Okpewho and Nzegwu (2009) suggest, more Africans are emigrating to North America than ever before since the end of the trans-Atlantic slave trade. The link I want to make here speaks to the intertextual dialogue that Paul Gilroy (1993) famously refers to as the Black Atlantic — the centuries-old continuous movement of texts and people between Africa and its diaspora in the New World. Susan Arndt (2013) aptly points out that, whether consciously or unconsciously, texts across different media, genres, and generations talk to one another due to the fact that they "seek to enter into dialogues with their predecessors to conceptualise and shape new futures" (4). Therefore, one can argue that the groundwork for the current digital age's quest for gay rights and the currently emerging articulation of what it means to be a queer African was laid down by works published decades earlier. I have previously theorized on the remarkable uptake of digital technologies on the African continent — with more mobile phone users than in the whole of Europe and North America — and how this trend is impacting on the way literature is produced and consumed. I also analyzed the way in which class, sexuality, politics, and literature intersect in the digital age (see Adenekan, *African*). This chapter, therefore, aims to contribute to understanding the intricate link between the forces of globalization, class, gender, and sexuality.

The notion of queer transnational intertextuality I am arguing for can be seen in Terna Tilley-Gyado's short story *Spinning With Longing* and in Rudolph Ogoo Okonkwo's *Prisoners of the Sky* (both 2008). These two cybertexts revisit the trans-Atlantic queer discourse which Soyinka initiated in *The Interpreters* (1965). In these two online stories, we get the classic trope of alienation that a queer black body may experience within this trans-Atlantic space. For example, the protagonist in *Spinning With Longing* remarks that as a Nigerian American living in the U.S., she "was never the desired, only ever a witness to other women desiring each other. I didn't understand why I couldn't seem to get a foothold into this world I so much wanted to be part of. I didn't know there was really any other world for girls like me" (Tilley-Gyado 8). For the protagonist in America, her black queer body has a double connotation: her queerness challenges the homophobia she meets in America, while her blackness does the same for the racism she meets with. Additionally, her black body conforms neither to mainstream America's ideal of female beauty nor to its white hegemony. A highly-educated young middle class woman, the protagonist should have been able to fit right in with the Beltway crowd. Instead, due to America's racism and homophobia, like Golder in *The Interpreters*, she aches for "*home, home, home, home*" (ibid., 9).

Like Golder, the protagonist in *Spinning With Longing* has experienced racism and alienation in America. Consequently, she goes to Africa in search of home in Nigeria, with the warning from her Nigerian-born mother ringing in her ears — that Africans do not "believe in homosexuality, bisexuality, whatever. White people brought that thing with them. It is not natural for Africans" (ibid.). In Nigeria, the homophobia that she encounters is fiercer than in America, so that she has to confront the reality that the idealized image of home she has conjured up while being raised in America is not ready for a Black queer. Instead, Nigerian politicians are bent on building on the anti-sodomy law inherited from the colonial government half a century earlier. She laments "the certainty of moral high ground magnified on the faces of those who believe such laws safeguard the souls of the nation" (ibid., 10). Men "toast" her (the Nigerian youth slang for flirting), but she can't bring herself to tell them she is a lesbian. Instead, she partakes in compulsory heterosexuality by not publicly querying the societal pretentiousness that there are no gays and lesbians in Nigeria, and that all grown-up daughters eventually seek men to marry. Her timidity in not outing herself as a queer person in Nigeria means that she perpetuates a culture of silence. As in Soyinka's *The Interpreters*, this particular story problematizes the idyllic imagination of homeland in popular diasporic productions (such as reggae songs and sometimes black cinema) because the physical space of Africa does not necessarily resemble the image that has been conjured up within the Atlantic world to seek a way leading back to Africa.

The protagonist's desire for home and her disappointment in what she witnesses in Nigeria give us a good view of the impact of colonial legacy on contemporary African thinking. Oyeronke Oyewumi

(1997) argues that colonial modernity adversely impacted on African concepts of sexuality and gender by introducing not only new types of gender but a stratified straight versus non-straight sexual binary, without anything in between and outside of this gender and sexual convention. Through this imposition, Oyewumi argues that colonial discourses reduced the complex ways in which social ideologies and cultural practices once operated in many African societies. Using Oyewumi's hypothesis, one can argue that non-straight black (African) bodies disrupt ideas of hetero-normativity that emerged from the project of colonial modernity. In this (post)colonial dispensation, those who deviate from the norm are seen as just that — deviants.

As Sagoe, Joe Golder's journalist friend in *The Interpreters*, views Golder's behavior with suspicion because he is gay, the lesbian protagonist's mother in *Spinning With Longing* warns her daughter: "What kind of clothes are you taking? You can't just dress any way you want. It's not America. People will notice. Where are you going with these trousers? [...] You better not chase people's daughters over there oh" (Tilley-Gyado 8). Forty-two years before this story, Sagoe, the fictional Nigerian journalist in *The Interpreters*, expresses a similar disapproval of Golder when he sees a copy of James Baldwin's novel, *Another Country*, lying on the back seat of Golder's car, by remarking "Why is this lying on the car seat? So when you give lifts to students you can find an easy opening for exploring?" (Soyinka 200). While Baldwin as a gay writer represents America's perversion to Sagoe, it is organic cotton trousers that become a symbol of queer perversion for the protagonist's mother in *Spinning With Longing*.

What literary representations — from print to online — have shown over the course of more than half a century is that some members of the middle classes, who despite the fact that they have studied and lived in America, still see America as a pervasive site of sexual perversion, while Nigeria is seen as the antithesis of supposedly American decadence. The protagonist evokes W. E. B. Du Bois's (1903) double consciousness, when she speaks of not belonging in either of these two trans-Atlantic spaces as "the queer twin" (Tilley-Gyado 10) talking across two spaces — the Old World (Africa) and the New World (America). The online, including *Outliers*, is also a space that enables an examination of the idea of transculturality. For writers, it allows not just the fusing of different aesthetic traditions (Nigerian and American as well as African and Western), it also enables a robust display of how young Africans are negotiating national, class, racial, and global identities. A topographic twinning illustrates how "the anxiety of our era has to do fundamentally with space" (Foucault 23). African and queer, being visible and being invisible, one twin able to speak only in America whereas the other "aches deeply for home" to be found, or rather not to be found, in Africa: these twinned conditions of (inter)cultural space become impossible to reconcile. Forty years after Joe Golder in *The Interpreters* could not find a lover on either side of the Atlantic, the lesbian protagonist in *Spinning With Longing* hints at the end of the story that she finally has a girlfriend in America (ibid.) — after she experienced "a terrible affair in the end" (ibid., 8). The fictional events signify the experience that black kinship, shared history, and geographical location do not necessarily result in either stable relationships or stable identities, even or especially in the age of Facebook and Twitter (see Macharia, "Slicing"). For the protagonist in *Spinning With Longing*, the "real" Africa becomes an impossibility; similarly to the case of Joe Golder in *The Interpreters*, notions of "home," "freedom," sexual desire, and "mother" all become elusive. Sigmund Freud has warned us in *The Uncanny* (1919), as is well enough known, about the *un-heimlich* dimension concealed within the idea of home.

If one of the things *Spinning With Longing* is trying to show us is that racial identity *can* be a practice of queer intimacy, Rudolf Ogoo Okonkwo's online fictional piece for *Outliers*, *Prisoners of the Sky*, actually makes this happen. It's a story of another young Nigerian-American woman, Nkechi, who is found frolicking by her parents in the back of a limousine with another girl on her high school's senior prom night. To her parents, her homosexuality is a sign of western corruption, a belief Nkechi thinks is incredible, given that her parents are university professors. Her father informs her and us that she has "staged the last stunt of your teen years here in America" (Okonkwo 17), and dispatches her straight to the University of Nigeria, Nsukka. It does not take Nkechi long to realize that, contrary to her parents believing that Nigeria will cure her lesbianism, queers actually exist in Africa. Her freshman year's roommate soon becomes her lover.

Like *Spinning With Longing*, this cyberstory moves the discourse of queerness beyond sexuality by focusing on the construction of home and diaspora, both in the sense of domestic intimacy (in Nigeria: in the dormitory of the University in Nsukka) and in the sense of trans-Atlantic belonging. When Nkechi was sent to Nigeria, little did her parents know that she would find the love of her life in Nkem, whom we are told comes from a humble background: "Her mother was a petty trader and her father was a carpenter in their village of Ideani. She went to Queen's College, Enugu, on a scholarship" (ibid., 18). Homosexuality thus cuts across class, and Nkem harbors a middle-class queer ambition: she wants to move to America, and waxes lyrical about the prospect of the state of Massachusetts legalizing gay marriage. She gladly asks Nkechi, "Does the gay marriage law passed in Massachusetts mean that you as an American can marry me and then take me to America?" (Ibid.).

Of course, that is not to be. Nigeria's compulsory heterosexuality means that the only way in which Nkem can realize her American dream is by falsely agreeing to marry Nkechi's U.S.-based cousin. In a dramatic ending, the two women came out by kissing in full glare of the public and before their relatives (who have come to welcome the bride to be) at an American airport. While same-sex desire cannot be achieved in Nigeria, America simultaneously becomes a site of tolerance and of perversion. These movements between Africa and North America speak to African and diasporic queers' search for meaning. They force us to think through domestic spaces as sites of colonial and postcolonial queer intimacies.

London with a Hint of Gugulethu

The speaker in Cary Alan Johnson's (2008) online poem entitled "Outlier" expresses the anguish of the black gay man in America, his stance against the essentializing of the queer black body, and the longing of that queer figure for home in Africa, away from the objectification of his body in America:

> I rail against any attempt to see my sexuality, my sex, my sexing as
> mainstream.
> Normally, I'm abnormal [...]
> I am a brother of Samuel Delaney's Time Square Red,
> Time Square Blue. Tell the truth.
> There were dicks. They were sucked. It was lovely.
> I'm a freak of brother from the People's Republic of Brooklyn who
> has chosen to live my life in Africa (dark, Dark Continent)
> loving brothers loving brothers
> knowing sisters (really knowing/ trying).
> Black men loving black men remains a revolutionary act. (Johnson 28)

Like the two short stories, this poem illustrates how the black queer body becomes a tool of resistance across the diaspora. The sexuality that is foregrounded becomes multiply dispersed as sexuality/sex/ sexing, the latter together with the variability of Red/Blue indicating a moveable enunciative process, one that is intertextually produced in and from the memoir-like essays of Samuel Delany [sic] to shape its own "square," its own critical topography as sexing becomes a spatial thirding. The transnational space spoken of at the beginning turns out to be "a space of resistance and permanent struggle," so that it becomes "a meeting point, a hybrid place, where one can move beyond the existing borders. It is also a place of the marginal women and men, where old connections can be disturbed and new ones emerge. A Thirdspace consciousness is the precondition to building a community of resistance to all forms of hegemonic power" (Soja 56). The African diaspora in America gave birth to the "Black is Beautiful" slogan of the 1960s and 1970s, but the black queer body within that diasporic space is not (yet) accepted as beautiful. These creative works make us look at bodies that still remain hidden within trans-Atlantic histories and narratives — bodies which a contemporary gendered code refuses to integrate on both sides of the Atlantic. Macharia ("More Notes") tells us that these bodies will remain a part of the postcolonial nationalistic projects and diasporic discourses for generations to come. These fictional authors can contribute to our understanding of how various forms of border crossing shape representations of sexuality in African literature.

It is obvious that, for a growing number of young Africans straight or gay, as well as for many across the continent of Africa, the internet is ensuring that knowledge once privileged and situated within the confines of higher education has never been more free, more plentiful, or more available; information technologies afford connection, mitigate isolation, and even make way for social movements. Eve Sedgwick (1997) enables a realization that capitalism relies on stimulating or creating consumer interest and participation, and through some of these emerging narratives in the online writing space, we are seeing how the internet, as a product of capitalism, has become a tool for generating contemporary queer identity in Nigeria and Kenya. More precisely, it is the middle class gays' preoccupation with living and negotiating what Rosemary Coombe (1993) refers to as "the everyday life of consumer capitalism and the way in which affluent gays and lesbians employ mass culture in quotidian practices" (16) that the fictional protagonist's lifestyle evokes. Given the representations in many of these online queer writings, we may indeed assume that material culture has become implicated in the construction of queer identity. Queer performances in some of the online fiction often leave little space for the expression of lower and underclass queer experience, since these groups have already been excluded by the barrier of language (the inability to read and write in European languages on which the internet is mostly based), and many may not be able to afford regular internet access due to subscription cost and bandwidth limitation. The protagonist in *Shades of the New South Africa* (2007), an online short story by the Oxford-University-educated South African writer Eusebius McKaiser, recognizes the omission of destitute gay Africans from the continent's mainstream gay culture, as he depicts a would-be lover's unconcern about the plight of young, poor, gay, black men in Cape Town:

> Sifiso seems totally oblivious. These street kids are just part of the familiar landscape of Seapoint; to be negotiated but never to be acknowledged ... such honesty may ruin your appetite while sitting at Newscafe enjoying the morning's paper and overlooking the gorgeously blue ocean but for the aesthetic blotch of stray dogs and streetkids ...

The "negotiation" speaks of a joint, inseparable experience between a utopia and the distancing gaze at the "aesthetic blotch": a mirror in which "I discover my absence from the place where I am," making me visible in seeing myself "where I am absent" (Foucault 24). The conceptualization of a queer project is, after all, "a utopian story" of courage, power, and resistance (Massaquoi 52), but it hardly accounts for the mirror function. State control of the media across the African continent has been widely discussed and studied by scholars (examples include Ebenezer Obadare, 2006; Nadine Dolby, 2006; George Ogola, 2011). Online African literature is showing us is that we also need to focus our attention on the potential level of control that access to the new media space gives to the educated class, and how those who are in the new information network may unconsciously use the medium to their sole advantage — so much so that the unconnected may not be heard at all. Cultural and economic power thus matters in our articulation of the way in which same-sex and queer desire are being represented. Our attention should not just be on the state and on business corporations; we should also focus on powerful stakeholders beyond these two entities. Furthermore, some of the emerging African queer texts are showing us how the lower classes can easily be excluded and displaced from global cultural consciousness, and how this invisibility has been carried over into the online writing space: much of the new queer fiction in this medium speaks to the middle-class African queer experience, while fictional characters of lower economic status are seldom portrayed. The lifestyle of transnational young African writers who are easily at home in Lagos, London, and Los Angeles is now being transplanted into fictional gay characters.

The gay protagonist in *Shades of the New South Africa* attests to this phenomenon:

> So there I am in Joburg in Cape Town. Celebrating thirty years of survival. The crazy world refuses to stop and acknowledge my tenacity. I am invisible in a space littered with twig-figured girls and boys with bulging muscle, as sexy as Popeye after a can of spinach, about to rescue his beloved twig-figurine, Olive. They are all draped in Diesel, Levi's, CK and other funk-indicating labels I cannot pronounce, let alone spell. They dance and giggle and strut around the dance floor, moving skilfully to local house beats, the imported cosmopolitan sounds of London mixed with a hint of Gugulethu, to mask the victory of cultural imperialism. This is the new resistance politics. I inhale the sweet, horny smells of booze and cigarettes and sweat and hormones and youth and promise and life ... the intoxicating aroma of the new south africa [sic]. I sit in a corner, making love to a bottle of Castle while scanning the room. For sex. For escapism. I choose my strategy. I try hard to look "upwardly mobile" ... yet chilled. The popular look seems to say "I'm-an-assistant-MD-but-have-loxion-kulca-flowing-through-my-soul". I realise I am screwed. (Or rather I won't be.) I'm not darkie enough to ooze even an ounce of loxion kulca through my coloured veins. I'm not rich enough to ooze assistant-MD. I'm not scrawny enough to masquerade the lie of "youthful innocence". How did I sneak past the doorman? It must have been my coconut twang, I guess -- but that brand seems so last year, as stale as the "I-spent-a-gap-year-in-London" gag.

The protagonist depicts the pretension of affluence with "funk-indicating labels," gay men and women who affect foreign "twang" and like to display their collection of foreign clothes and other luxuries so as to be accepted into the gay scene. The speaker's "invisible" quality reveals a positional identity as it (once again) "enables me to see myself there where I am absent" (Foucault 24). The London-Gugulethu mix is less an intercultural space than one of class division, a world that is far removed from the South African townships and a million miles away from most villages in Nigeria and Kenya. But this world is real to many middle-class writers. In this new century, as in the last, class remains a very important factor in literature's representation of queer African life, because what literature is imitating is the fact that class embodies the experience of most African writers, with a middle-class queer experience that is manifesting itself overwhelmingly in the new media space to create its form of "cultural imperialism" — which is paradoxically indistinguishable from "resistance politics." Stevi Jackson (2011) points out: "Morality and taste are implicated in the maintenance of class boundaries" (17). As capital has bestowed on middle-class writers the opportunity of modern education and the affordability of the internet, the social relationships that fictional queer characters form online mirrors the communities that writers themselves form in cyberspace. A global middle-class identity is thus projected as the norm for non-straight Africans, in a continent in which many are indigent. Digital capital is therefore becoming the cultural capital. It contributes to creating "counter-sites, a kind of effectively enacted utopia in which the real sites, all the other real sites that can be found within the culture, are simultaneously represented, contested, and inverted" (Foucault 24). Rarely do we see fictional narratives or poems that capture the experience of African homosexuals who live in rural areas, or who are struggling to make ends meet in urban areas. Instead, fictional gay characters like real-life writers are often affluent, educated, and socially mobile. The protagonist in *Shades of the New South Africa* expresses frustration at the limited pool of lovers, and tells us that he is used to "being spoiled by choice gay hangouts on Christopher Street in New York and Old Compton Street in London." We hear his complaint because he has the financial capability to enter the gay metropolis, as both the character and the writer who created him come from the same world — that of the professional African middle class. Furthermore, these short stories in the new media space confirm Robert Cover's assertion that capital labor is linked to both same-sex desire and homophobia. Through these fictions, we are seeing the way that capital labor leads to social exclusion for many Africans, in this case, lower-class queers — people who cannot afford to pay for internet dating, who are excluded from many queer activities for instance in Nigeria and

Kenya. The media space functions as a Foucaultian mirror between a utopia and the heterotopia that thrives on its distance from and its marginalizing energy against queer existence among the lower classes.

Cyberspace is a construct of both reality and fiction. As Michelle Kendrick (1996) argues, it "foregrounds the ways in which technology intervenes in our subjectivity" (143). The urban gay lifestyle is no different from the lifestyle that middle-class straight characters lead in the fictional narratives being produced by some of Africa's notable transnational literary figures such as Chimamanda Adichie and Teju Cole — they are immersed in Blackberry phones, bling, popular music, and digital connectivity. Just as these writers spend much of their time in the metropolitan spaces of Lagos and New York, so do the fictional characters they give us. Nkem, the closeted lesbian lover in Okonkwo's *Prisoners of the Sky*, arrives in America from Nigeria, sporting "sparkling gold bracelets dangled around her neck and wrists" (20). As he enters a gay club in downtown Cape Town, the protagonist in *Shades of the New South Africa* takes in the bar staff and surmises straight away: "I can just imagine the job ads: 'Fat and ugly men need not apply'. The gay market is tough. Certainly no place for oldies or fatties."

The world of most fictional African queer characters appears to be that of CNN, the music of the American R&B singer R. Kelly, physically-fit gay lovers, and luxurious hotel rooms in Abuja and Cape Town — two of the most expensive cities in the world. And since affordability equals accessibility, a subscription to Gaydar.com and a bottle of wine in a trendy Cape Town gay bar may well be beyond the reach of many less affluent gays and lesbians. The affluent lifestyle in addition to the internet and the expensive mobile phones that these fictional characters often carry as emblems in these online short stories represents the way in which many middle-class Africans are part of the global capitalist system, as people who possess cultural and economic capital. These elements symbolize the transnational and globalized identity of many members of this social group.

Two-Step Skip by Crispin Oduobuk-Mfon Abasi, in *Outliers*, is a narrative that shows the way in which this growing quest for a connection with the outside world by Africans with disposable incomes may lead to exploitation. Organizations like Gaydar.com (www.gaydar.com) appear to be a place where middle-class gay Africans congregate, and since the narrator is emotionally and geographically separated from his family and community, he is prone to capitalist exploitation since he has no choice but to buy companionship on the internet and can be induced to lead an ostentatious gay lifestyle. Music by US artists Fat Joe and then Angie Stone is shown to be subtly relevant to a desperate, possibly homicidal effort to "two-step skip" and thus escape a sexual predator — only to grow aware that there are more waiting (Abasi 16). Cover suggests when global online companies sell to the middle class from the non-West, they hope to get some level of brand loyalty in return. This is how some of the world's most dynamic, far-sighted cultural organizations are enhancing their income and securing their future by linking with young African professionals — that most affluent, influential, sought-after demographic. In cyberspace, the queer African body thus simultaneously reveals and signifies the obscenity of materialism and exploitation.

Conclusion

The inter-connectedness between different literary spaces, especially between the metropolitan centers of Africa and North America, has helped advance the cause of gay rights movements in postcolonial Africa. Yet literature depicting transnational figures also shows the challenges faced by people whom many would deem privileged due to the economic and cultural power they possess. Given the fact that many African national leaders and their followers wrongly perceive homosexuality as being un-African, literature helps to undermine this notion by bringing to the fore nuanced representations of queerness and same-sex desire in an African context. Transnational characters who criss-cross these fictional spaces, moreover, reveal the experience that homophobia is not just an African dilemma but is very active in North America, especially for black queers. For these characters, the experience of being different or queer is not fully mitigated by their being members of the global middle classes, as they are not fully accepted in Africa and in North America.

Even so, fictional narratives seem to completely ignore the phenomenon that there are very likely working-class Africans who are gays, lesbians, transgender, and queers; much of the depiction online and in print seems to center on middle-class characters many of whom have the ability to travel between countries in Africa and the West, and many of whom speak European languages as well as possessing the capital to indulge in expensive taste.

References

Abasi, Crispin Oduobuk-Mfon. "Two-Step Skip." *Outliers: Theorizing (Homo) Eroticism in Africa: A Collection of Essays and Creative Work on Sexuality in Africa* 1 (2008): 11–16. Web. 20 May 2016.

Adenekan, Shola. *African Literature in the Digital Age: Class and Sexual Politics in New Writing From Nigeria and Kenya*. Diss. Univ. of Birmingham, 2012.

—. "New Voices, New Media: Class, Sex and Politics in Online Nigerian and Kenyan Poetry." *Postcolonial Text* 11.1 (2016). Web. 20 May 2016.

Alexander, Bryant Keith. "Reflections, Riffs and Remembrances: The Black Queer Studies in the Millennium Conference." *Callaloo* 23.4 (2000): 1285–1305.

Arndt, Susan. Introduction. *Intertextuality: Dialogues in Motion*. Bayreuth: BIGSAS Festival of African Diasporic Literatures (2013): 1–8.

Bhabha, Homi K. *The Location of Culture*. Abingdon: Routledge, 1994.

Cohen, Anthony P. *The Symbolic Construction of Community*. 1985. London: Routledge, 1993.

Coombe, Rosemary. "Publicity Rights and Political Aspiration: Mass Culture, Gender Identity, and Democracy." *New England Law Review* 26 (1992): 1221–1280.

Cover, Robert. "Queer with Class: Absence of the Third World Sweatshop in Lesbian/Gay Discourse and a Rearticulation of Materialist Queer Theory." *Ariel: A Review of International English Literature* 30.2 (1999 & 2003): 29–48.

Dolby, Nadine. "Popular Culture and Public Space in Africa: The Possibilities of Cultural Citizenship." *African Studies Review* 49.3 (2006): 31–47. Web. 20 May 2016.

Du Bois, W. E. B. *The Souls of Black Folks*. 1903. Web. 20 May 2016. http://www. wwnorton. com/college/history/give-me-liberty4/docs/WEBDuBois-Souls_of_Black_Folk-1903.pdf

Foucault, Michel. "Of Other Spaces." *Diacritics* 16.1 (1986): 22–27.

Gilroy, Paul. *The Black Atlantic: Modernity and Double Consciousness*. London: Verso, 1993.

Jackson, Stevi. "Heterosexual Hierarchies: A Commentary on Class and Sexuality." *Sexualities* 14.1 (2011): 12–20.

Johnson, Cary Alan. "Outlier." *Outliers: Theorizing (Homo) Eroticism in Africa: A Collection of Essays and Creative Work on Sexuality in Africa* 1 (2008): 40–41. Web. 20 May 2016.

Kendrick, Michelle. "Cyberspace and the Technological Real." *Virtual Realities and Their Discontents*. Ed. Robert Markley. Baltimore & London: John Hopkins UP, 996. 143–160.

Macharia, Keguro. "'How does a girl grow into a woman?': Girlhood in Ngugi wa Thiong'o's *The River Between*." *Research in African Literatures* 43.2 (Summer 2012): 1–17. Web. 20 May 2016.

—. "More Notes on Queer Africa: Toward an Intellectual Project." *Gukira*.

10 Jan. 2010. Web. 20 May 2016. <http://gukira.wordpress.com/2010/01/10/more-notes-on-queer-africa-toward-an-intellectual-project/ >

—. "'Slicing the Hunger': Queering Diaspora in Melvin Dixon's *Change of Territory*." *Callaloo* 32.4 (Fall 2009): 1262–1273. Web. 20 May 2016.

Massaquoi, Notisha. "The Continent as a Closet: The Making of an African Queer Theory." *Outliers: Theorizing (Homo) Eroticism in Africa: A Collection of Essays and Creative Work on Sexuality in Africa* 1 (2008): 50–60. Web. 20 May 2016.

McKaiser, Eusebius. "Shades of the New South Africa." *African-writing.com*. 2007. Web. 20 May 2016.

Obadare, Ebenezer. "Playing Politics with the Mobile Phone in Nigeria: Civil Society, Big Business and the State." *Review of African Political Economy* 33/107 (March 2006): 93–111. Web. 20 May 2016.

Ogola, George. "The Political Economy of the Media in Kenya: From Kenyatta's Nation-building Press to kibaki's Local-Language FM Radio." *Africa Today* 57.3 (2011): 77–95. Web. 20 May 2016.

Okonkwo, Rudolph Ogoo. "Prisoners of the Sky." *Outliers: Theorizing (Homo) Eroticism in Africa: A Collection of Essays and Creative Work on Sexuality in Africa* 1 (2008): 26–34. Web. 20 May 2016.

Okpewho, Isidore, and Nkiru Nzekwu, eds. *The New African Diaspora*. Bloomington & Indianapolis: Indiana UP, 2009.

Oyewumi, Oyeronke. *The Invention of Women: Making an African Sense of Western Gender Discourses*. Minneapolis: U of Minnesota P, 1997.

Sedgwick, Eve. *Novel Gazing: Queer Readings in Fiction*. Durham, NC: Duke UP, 1997.

Soja, Edward W. "Thirdspace: Toward a New Consciousness of Space and Spatiality." *Communicating in the Third Space*. Eds. Karin Ikas and Gerhard Wagner. New York: Routledge, 2009. 49–61.

Soyinka, Wole. *The Interpreters*. London & Ibadan & Nairobi: Heinemann Educational, 1965.

Tilley-Gyado, Terna. "Spinning With Longing." *Outliers: Theorizing (Homo) Eroticism in Africa: A Collection of Essays and Creative Work on Sexuality in Africa* 1 (2008): 15–26. Web. 20 May 2016.

9

The Death of Identity: The Representation of Black Diasporic "Identity" in *Americanah*

Shirin Assa
University of Bayreuth

Summary: Any operation of transcultural criticism that uses a concept of identity meets with the difficulty that identity tends to be in motion, under constant construction and processual negotiation. One highly debated and recent strand is diasporic "identity." It appears strongly relevant to the latest novel by Chimamanda Ngozi Adichie, *Americanah* (2013), which narrates the story of a young Nigerian woman by the name of Ifemelu who flees from her politically restless and post-independent country to pursue her studies in the United States. Metonymically, the narrative of her relocation is part of the founding of Nigerian diasporas. A generation of meaning in association with the writing process receives central attention in the novel. The chapter, accordingly, aims to analyze (dis)continuities in the diasporic identity of Ifemelu's character and the narrative situations which help to shape it. In order to do so adequately, the chapter suggests moving away from any concept of identity and exploring whether, from the perspective of transcultural literary studies, instead three forms of experience proposed by Rogers Brubaker and Frederick Cooper can be adapted: these are commonality, connectedness, and groupness. These may enable a better understanding of how *Americanah* offers a polyphonic representation of black diasporic lives.

Introduction

In critical writing involving matters of identity, the concept at times appears to be carelessly applied and ambiguously treated. A process of analysis aiming for maximum proximity to clarifying the concept has to cope with an accumulation of implications. Hence tackling identity concepts is a complex task, as its lexicon is convoluted and the meaning, more often than not, lost in what might seem merely word play. Usefully, Brubaker and Cooper (6-8) enumerate the key definitions of identity as (1) a contrast to "interest" and a basis of social and political action; (2) a collective phenomenon; (3) a foundational and abiding peculiarity; (4) a processual and interactive development that make collective action possible; and lastly (5) a term to frame the fragmented nature of the contemporary "self." The definitions, as they note, noticeably overlap and hold tensions as against each other. For example, on the one hand, the second and third are in line with an essentialist and fixed notion of identity, whereas the fourth and fifth define identity as fluid and in process. On the other hand, the couplet of the second and third is contradictory to the fourth and the fifth definition. We may accordingly gather that the vicissitudes of identity are entangled with the politics and poetics of such questions as who identifies an animate or inanimate entity as what/who, in which spacetime, why, and with what effects. These inquiries are related to the structures and discourses of positioning and identifying collectivities in relation to their respective individuals. Individual and collective identity appears as resting on a consensus between identification and positioning.

Identity, we might assume, is a matter of what we could call meaning in motion, as indicating that it is under constant construction and processual negotiation, of notions of Self and its constitutive Other(s). Clearly, then, different strands of identity coexist and become entangled. They are complementary and/or contrasting, individual and collective, cultural and political. One of these highly debated and recent strands of identity is diasporic "identity" (see especially Hall "Cultural"; also Jackson 1: 221-226). It appears strongly relevant to the latest novel by Chimamanda Ngozi Adichie, *Americanah* (2013), which narrates the story of a Nigerian by the name of Ifemelu who flees from politically restless and post-independent Nigeria to pursue her studies in peace in the United States. Metonymically, her relocation is part of a larger displacement of her generation across cultures, mainly to the United States and Britain, and the founding of Nigerian diasporas. Thus framed, identity in motion, generating meaning in association with the writing process, can be said to receive central attention in the novel, and in this chapter accordingly I aim to analyze (dis)continuities in the diasporic identity of Ifemelu's character.

Substituting Identity

Similarly to Rogers Brubaker and Frederick Cooper, I would put the concept of identity under erasure. With respect to their proposed methodological rigor, I propose burying identity (as it were) and instead making use of the experiences of commonality, connectedness, and groupness. They designate "the emotionally laden sense of belonging to a distinctive, bounded group, involving both a felt solidarity or oneness with fellow group members and a felt difference from or even antipathy to specified outsiders" ("Beyond" 19). By focusing especially on selected representations of recent and older black diasporic identity in *Americanah*, I will scrutinize the way commonality, connectedness, and groupness become useful in breaking up and superseding identity. Can we, from the perspective of transcultural literary studies, adopt or adapt in literary analysis the three related categories as a substitute for and improvement on identity? In which ways and to what extent do they address the vicissitudes of identity practices?

What is Diaspora?

To move ahead from these questions, we need to clarify the diaspora concept. Brubaker (5–7) takes account of three common components of diaspora: (1) dispersion, (2) homeward orientation, and (3) boundary-maintenance. He adds that "diasporas have been seen to result from the migration of borders over people, and not simply from that of people over borders" (ibid., 3). Diaspora, for the present context, is a collective displacement and border crossing of individuals who are, on the one hand, (un)consciously tied to narratives and politics of their former spacetime — in the name of "home," "origin," "nation," and similar categories — and on the other hand consciously involved in narratives and politics of (un) belonging in their receiving spacetime. Therein lies a potentiality: an active negotiation of meaning which takes place beyond borders and between such a community with its positionality and lateral connections to other diaspora (s). Such a consciousness is most certainly not bounded and bordered: it flows in different spacetimes. Consistently with this, Appadurai (296) challenges inside-outside divisions such as center/periphery. Instead, he presents a polyphonic portrait of space. Appadurai rejects "objectively given relations" and the apriori existing spaces which are static, strictly bordered, and "look the same from every angle of vision." It is worth noting that hybrid models are, as well, based on the premise of two (or more) separate spaces. However, Appadurai depicts spaces as "deeply perspectival constructs, inflected very much by the historical, linguistic and political" positionalities (ibid.). Thus, Appadurai proposes prefixes of scapes, in particular (1) ethnoscapes, (2) mediascapes, (3) technoscapes, (4) finanscapes, and (5) ideoscapes in order to break with the former assumption of sealed levelers/communities/spaces (as found in the work of Saffran, Cohen, Sheffer and like-minded scholars) and thus, he acknowledges the encountering spacetimes.

Diasporic "Identity"

Diasporic "identity" is a collective identity for those displaced, despite the exiled condition, and has a collective modality by definition. The concept offered by Stuart Hall is widely known:

> The diaspora experience as I intend it here is defined, not by essence or purity, but by the recognition of a necessary heterogeneity and diversity; by a conception of "identity" which lives with and through, not despite, difference; by *hybridity*. Diaspora identities are those which are constantly producing and reproducing themselves anew, through transformation and difference. (Hall, "Cultural" 235)

It is promoted as a site of resistance, represented as a creative and liberating force of modern life, but also regarded as traumatic experience. Diasporic identity oscillates between politics of "boundary-maintenance" and "boundary-erosion" (Brubaker 6-7) and, thus, defined, can be synonymized with or mistaken for "hybridity." Moreover, diasporic identity is not automatically a feature granted to all displaced groups; that is, not every group — beyond individuals —

possesses or seeks identity. In other words, an intergenerational, active negotiation and consciousness must be incorporated by diasporic groups in order to realize diasporic identity. Diaspora and its identity, as John Armstrong indicates, is a practice of "longue durée" (206–213) which reaches out for a coalition of successive generational communities. In the literature of diaspora, diasporic identity is celebrated as "harbinger of globalized futures" (Zeleza 35). Furthermore, diasporic identity is translated into positionalities of communities and their respective social actors along spectrums of history, culture, politics, development and economics, globalism, postcolonialism, and further areas. This is the diasporic codification of identity.

A Conundrum of Coherence

There exists a tension in defining identity that would demand further contemplation. Identity can be solid and sacred as heritage, vast as history, vague as nation, inclusive as culture, personal as sex, performative as gender, political as "race," economical as class ... How can it remain intact or coherent in the face of the contested implications, varying associations, and multiplied intersections? Identity has, in fact, cast off many essentializing and general implications. As a consequence, individuality, fluidity, and performativity have been vociferously celebrated. While identity and its politics are undoubtedly salient, Brubaker and Cooper perceive it as a menace for analysis. They aptly discern between a category of practice and a category of analysis, and demonstrate the probability of (ab)using these domains interchangeably (5). In order to avoid this possible threat, Brubaker and Cooper respond to these developments by proposing three sets of analytical alternatives in an attempt to "parcel out the work to a number of less congested terms" (14): (1) Identification and categorization; (2) Self-understanding and social location; and as already noted (3) Commonality, connectedness, groupness.

Toward Analysis

Commonality, connectedness, and groupness chiefly highlight the collective modality of identity, which is consistent with racial, national, ethnical, religious, and related "identities." Analogously, and building on this premise, diasporic identity is likewise collective. In the following I will ask, how do individual and group identities interact? How much agency and awareness are involved in the process? Is identity essential for groupness? Is collective identity concomitant with an unlimited membership in a group, and does it therefore impose a lasting homogeneity? These questions will hopefully unravel some difficulties just beneath the surface of the rubric of collective identity. To enable this, I will discuss "a sense of belonging" in relation to Weber's *Zusammengehörigkeitsgefühl* below. It may also be useful to remain aware that relational connectedness is not essential for forging a group (see Brubaker and Cooper 20).

Emotional entanglements concurrently generate opposing tendencies, especially inward convergence and outward divergence. This can be called a bilateral politics of (un)belonging, which bears witness to a construction of self-understanding vis-à-vis the Other. The Self-Other relation in connection with a poetics of identity is discussed, as is well known, by Stuart Hall (*Questions*). In the same vein, paradoxically, diasporic belonging can turn out to be unbelonging — or, in the sense that Derrida appropriates it, it is an "aporia," a way of saying that there is only impossible belonging: "When we speak of 'belonging,' we speak also of a certain kind of denial: of a shortfall or lack, of exclusion [...]" (Fernandez 34). We thus have a duet between rejection and being rejected, in which both cases are *per se* the negation of belonging. What is perceived to be closeness between members of a group is, of course, relative in comparison to the constitutive Other. Hence, the internal affinities within a group by no means blur the lines of authority and differences within the group, or disconnect them from parallel memberships and solidarities. This underscores how intertwined, multiplied, and paradoxical the poetics of identity can become. In contrast to Stuart Hall, who refers to identity as "the meeting point" (*Questions* 19), Brubaker and Cooper break it down into the range of experiences and terms as specified above (20). In their concept, commonality alludes to shared particularit(y/ies), while connectedness stands for relational ties, intersubjectivity within groups. In the former, the discussion is centered on categories as sites of identification: the Middle class, Iranians, blacks, transgender people, queers, Muslims, above/under 40 year-olds are a few examples of the implication of categories with which people identify or are identified. Whether a person or agent identifies her/himself with a category or is being identified by others can become a crucial question, but is not the issue in our immediate context (Brubaker and Cooper devote sustained attention to it). To indicate a category of consciousness, I will make use of the term self-understanding.

The term becomes significant when we consider how *Americanah* benefits from meta-narration. By that I mean to call attention to the omniscient narrator, who narrates the story of Ifemelu as protagonist at one level, and Ifemelu who articulates herself at another level. Owing to her blog "Raceteenth or Various Observations About American Blacks (Those Formerly Known as Ne [ ]) by a Non-American Black" (Adichie 4), Ifemelu verbally utters her self-understanding in relation to number of contested categories such as race, gender, nationality, class, and a few more. Though in the narrative, Ifemelu declares that use of Ne[] or Ni[] "depends on the intent and also on who is using it" (ibid., 138), in order not to reproduce the hate speech with which this term is heavily loaded, I will employ the abbreviation. Being a victim of hate speech after her first speech, Ifemelu discerns between her audiences and her readers analogously to her self-representation and her self-understanding.

> And so, in the following weeks, as she gave more talks at companies and schools, she began to say what they wanted to hear, none of which she would ever write on her blog, because she knew that the people who read her blog were not the same people who attended her diversity workshops. During her talks, she said: "America has made great progress for which we should be very proud." In her blog she wrote: *Racism should never have happened and so you don't get a cookie for reducing it*. (Ibid., 305)

The artistic juxtaposition of the subject who speaks and the subject who is spoken of grants the reader an ultimate proximity in order to examine Ifemelu's "emotional [...] sense of belonging to a distinctive, bounded group" of diaspora, which is a major constituent of collectivity (Brubaker and Cooper 19). This felt solidarity is somewhat tantamount to Weber's notion of *Zusammengehörigkeitsgefühl*, to which I will return. Prior to that, however, I discuss notions of and relations between commonality, connectedness, and groupness, starting with the relations between commonality (shared peculiarities) and groupness (feeling of belonging together) and then, connectedness and groupness. These are not identical. Then, I will scrutinize the couplet of commonality and connectedness in respect to groupness. Ultimately, I will discuss the implications of Max Weber's term between group members.

Commonality and Groupness

A considerable portion of the novel is interdigitated (one could say) with the rhetoric of race in American society. There are various discussions — mostly but not exclusively — around racial categories. In one of the blog's entries, Ifemelu narrates

> [...] there is an oppression Olympic going on. American racial minorities — blacks, Hispanics, Asians, and Jews — all get shit from white folks, different kinds of shit, but shit still. Each secretly believes that it gets the worst shit. So, no, there is no United League of the Oppressed. However, all the others think they're better than blacks because, well, they're not black. (Adichie 205)

She goes on to note how racial minorities aspire to whiteness, with the unanswered query "then what do WASPs [White Anglo-Saxon Protestants] aspire to?" (ibid). She pins down both ends of the racial spectrum, and designates their white-ward orientation. Meanwhile, Ifemelu makes use of non-blacks' and non-whites' in-between racial categories to equally drain respective poles of "whiteness" and "blackness." This, in itself, is nothing new. However, playing with the slipperiness of such an active social leveler in the United States, Ifemelu overinflates both poles of the racial spectrum in order to contest them:

> There's a ladder of racial hierarchy in America. White is always on top, [...] and American Black is always on the bottom, and what's in the middle depends on time and place. [...] So in undergrad, we had a visiting speaker and a classmate whispers to another, "Oh my God, he looks so Jewish," with a shudder, an actual shudder. Like Jewish was a bad thing. I didn't get it. As far as I could see, the man was white, not much different from the classmate herself. [...] You see, in America's ladder of races, Jewish is white but also some rungs below white. A bit confusing but I knew this straw-haired, freckled girl who said she was Jewish. How can Americans tell who is Jewish? How did the classmate know the guy was Jewish? (Ibid., 184–185)

What lies beyond this criticism is neither to abandon race as a category nor to identify with it, rather to contest and transform it from the quintessence of collective identity or a component thereof into a mere attribute. Whether a group or a person identifies with an attribute or is being ascribed to it by an Other, is then not enough solely to form groupness, not to mention a collective identity.

Connectedness and Groupness

Connectedness (the relational ties) refers to the social network within which a person is caught up, viz. a web of friends and family, a network of people who are socially related: whether it be as a teacher with students and other teachers, as a patient with doctors and nurses, as an immigrant with other citizens, and further categories. Instances of such networks abound in *Americanah*. Yet I would like to underline a particular network in the sense of technoscapes (Appadurai 297) and then build an interpretive argument thereon. I would argue that Ifemelu's "Raceteenth or Various Observations" is an embodiment of technoscapes. Inspired by her friend Wambui, and in order to get some distraction from a recent breakup with her white boyfriend Curt, Ifemelu starts her weblog with a different name and targets "other people [who] had become black in America," whom she intends to "unzip" (Adichie 296, 307). As the writing progresses, new spaces and links are inserted, molding the presupposed conditions of the weblog along with its writer:

> The blog had unveiled itself [...]. Its readers increased by the thousands, from all over the world, [...] and yet she had not imagined any of this [...]. E-mails came from readers who wanted to support the blog. Support. That word made the blog even more apart from her, a separate thing that could thrive or not, sometimes without her and sometimes with her. So she put up a link to her PayPal account. Credits appeared, [...] as regular as a pay cheque [...]. (Ibid., 303)

Her weblog becomes advertised. She receives invitations to give lectures and organize events on the subject of diversity. Ifemelu gets to be interviewed, photographed, and titled as "The Blogger." These representations are new to her, and she has not yet formed a self-understanding based on them: "[...] a part of her always stiffened with apprehension, expecting the person on the other end to realize that she was play-acting this professional, this negotiator of terms, to see that she was, in fact, an unemployed person [...]" (ibid., 304).

Ifemelu finds a voice. Owing to blogging, she is heard. She

makes a living, gains social status, and becomes spatially mobile. Ifemelu fluidly moves into scapes of self-understanding. She compares and contrasts them. This transition from merely "being" to becoming is made possible by a proliferation of the "to do" options for her, turning her into an active agent. This used to be one of the major differences she had felt with her white privileged boyfriend, Curt: "He was always thinking of what to *do* and she told her that it was rare for her, because she had grown up not doing, but being" (ibid., 207). Rather than uniting people over their commonalities, she discerns them despite their commonalities, and demands recognition. More than assimilatory narratives of the residing country and canon models of diasporas, namely African Americans, Ifemelu deplores assimilation. There are moments in which Ifemelu is confronted with assimilatory practices that are offered to her and her relatives by narratives of their country of residence, be it America or other canonized diasporas. The first time Ifemelu witnesses Auntie Uju's adaptive practices, it strikes her. Bearing in mind that names are sites of identity in language (De 187), "Aunty Uju's cell phone rang. "Yes, this is Uju." She pronounced it *you-joo instead of oo-joo*. "Is that how you pronounce your name now?" Ifemelu asked afterwards. "It's what they call me." Ifemelu swallowed the words "Well, that isn't your name" (Adichie 104). On one occasion, when she adopts an American accent, Ifemelu becomes conscious of it and stops her phony self-representation (ibid., 173–176). However diffused, another example is centered in the interactions between Ifemelu and her African American lover Blaine, through which she distinguishes between American Africans who have newly migrated to the United States and African Americans who are African descendants although they are born, raised, and based in America (ibid., 310–312). Given more space, one could explore at greater length the matter of "relaxing hair" in the novel, a dense motif which is fairly prominent.

Ifemelu, at any rate, explores moments of resistance and articulates them, negotiates with words and meanings, and attains more options of being different. In registering the platform which Ifemelu has created, we should note that it becomes advocated merely as a network that we should not mistake for a community. On the one hand, connectedness *per se* does not generate a sense of belonging together; on the other hand, groupness is substantially reliant on just this feeling. We may assume that Ifemelu and her readers very likely share some resemblances, not least with regard to their constitutive Other. It is legitimate for Ifemelu to address such commonalities. However, there is a difference between empathy and belonging, and she does not stretch tokens so as to form a group. Hence we should emphasize that networks are not accountable for groupness.

Groupness

Having looked at differences between commonality and connectedness, we should examine the relationship between them. For Brubaker and Cooper, the couplet of commonality (shared particularities) and connectedness (relational ties) does not constitute groupness (the feeling of belonging together). However, the latter can be a component thereof. We should consider two contrasting results of the couplet. The first is the example of HAPPILYKINKYNAPPY.COM. This is a technoscape that, despite Ifemelu's blog, which remains under the rubric of connectedness, evolves as a group notably for its dynamics and concentrated interactions. Ifemelu observes this group:

> They were done pretending that their hair was what it was not [...]. They complimented each other's photos and ended comments with "hugs". They complained about black magazines never having natural-haired women in their pages, about drugstore products [...]. They traded recipes. They sculpted for themselves a virtual world where their coily, kinky, nappy, woolly hair was normal. And Ifemelu fell into this world with a tumbling gratitude. Women with hair as short as hers had a name for it: TWA, Teeny Weeny Afro. [...] She ordered products from women who made them in their kitchens and shipped them with clear instructions [...]. (Ibid., 212)

The common ground between "them," which soon becomes "us," is black beauty in general and black hair in particular. It's the token which Ifemelu as someone occupying the black body possesses. Like others, she is an active, conscious, and voluntary participant, and belongs to this world both consciously and unconsciously. This community is represented as an autonomous space which transcends notions of beauty, norm, and their by-products in society, and last but not least in language. I want to emphasize that this space is not merely a site of information; it is interwoven with mobility, production, creativity, resistance, solidarity, and belonging.

As the narration proceeds, a delicate point is laid out that is worth dwelling upon. When a black man compares Ifemelu's hair to a "jungle" (ibid., 213), she considers relaxing her hair again. Being empowered by the virtue of belonging to HAPPILYKINKYNAPPY, she endures the force of norm. Getting the products needed to relax her hair,

> [t]hen she [i.e., Ifemelu] remembered a post by Jamilah1977 — *I love the sista who love their straight weaves*, but *I'm never putting horse hair on my head again* — and she left the store eager to get back and log on and post on the boards about it. She wrote: *Jamilah's words made me remember that there is nothing more beautiful than what God gave me*.

A few days after that, "[...] she looked in the mirror, sank her fingers into her hair, dense and spongy and glorious, and could not imagine it any other way. That simply, she fell in love with her hair" (ibid., 313). On this site, pain is transformed to pleasure, and a former disadvantage becomes celebrated as a new source of re(de)fining beauty.

The second result of the commonality-connectedness couplet can be seen in the African-American community to which Ifemelu is linked via Blaine, her lover. They are black and Ifemelu is their "chocolate sister" (ibid., 311), yet that does not compensate for her non-Americanness: "She [Ifemelu] had been with Blaine for more than a year, but she did not quite belong to his friends" (ibid., 322). This sense of un-belonging is not restricted to her self-identification. It is reinforced by others. Shan, Blaine's sister who holds famous *salons* that primarily connect the African-American community and reinvigorate their African-American consciousness, identifies Ifemelu as an outsider by saying, "[...]she's African. She is writing from the outside. She doesn't really feel all the stuff she's writing about. [...] If she were African American, she'd just be labelled angry and shunned" (ibid., 336). Later, in the course of an argument with Blaine which was primarily ignited by Ifemelu's not participating in the protest that he had organized so as to support a fellow African American, she articulates the diagnosis: "She recognized, in his tone, a subtle accusation, not merely about her laziness, her lack of zeal and conviction, but also about her Africanness; she was not sufficiently furious because she was African not African American" (ibid., 345). It is beyond question that she is identified as a black person like African Americans are. It is equally undeniable that she is closely connected to this community. However, Ifemelu simply is not "black enough": being "black enough" supersedes "black." This is not a matter of commonality *per se*, rather of its degree and form which diminish a sense of belonging together mutually for Ifemelu and other group members.

On the matter of groupness, there is a final important point. Brubaker and Cooper underscore that

> [...] categorical commonality and relational connectedness need to be supplemented with a third element, what Max Weber calls a *Zusammengehörigkeitsgefühl*, a feeling of belonging together. Such a feeling may indeed depend in part on the degrees and forms of commonality and connectedness, but it will also depend on other factors such as particular events, their encoding in compelling public narratives, prevailing discursive frames, and so on. (20)

Already touched upon above, this sense of belonging incorporates powerfully felt allegiances that may be imagined or intrinsic, recently emerged or historical, transitory or permanent. This sense of belonging together compensates the varying degrees of commonality and different forms of connectedness. With this in mind, Ifemelu's manner of belonging to an African-American community finds a new twist by a "particular event": the 2008 presidential election in the United States, which was a historical step for black Americans and non-black Americans due to the candidacy of Barack Obama. "Their [i.e., Ifemelu and Blaine's] union was leached of passion, but there was a new passion, outside of themselves, that united them in an intimacy they had never had before, an unfixed, unspoken, intuitive intimacy: Barack Obama" (Adichie 352). This new referential source of belonging holds Blaine, his friends, and Ifemelu together as they almost all — "[e]xcept for Michael, who always wore a Hillary Clinton pin on his breast" (ibid., 355) — support Obama. In this regard, "Ifemelu no longer felt excluded" (ibid., 352). The community that is brought together by Barack Obama's nomination advances single bodies as well as concentrated, unidirectional groups like Blaine's and Shan's. The event's encoding in public United States narratives overrides commonalities and connectedness. During the speech Obama holds for having won his party's nomination, among Obama's supporters, Ifemelu notices that they all belong together for sharing a belief. Ifemelu studies the black man next to her and the "thick crowd" around them:

> [...] all glowing with a strange phosphorescence, all treading a single line of unbroken emotion. They believed. They truly believed. It often came to her as a sweet shock, the knowledge that there

> were so many people in the world who felt exactly as she and Blaine
> did about Barack Obama. (Ibid., 356–357)

Such a sense of belonging extends to and engages successive
generations. After Obama's victory in the election, Dike, Ifemelu's
cousin, and a representative of the second generation of African
immigrants in the United States, texts her saying: "*I can't believe it.
My president is black like me*" (ibid., 360). Groupness generates and
associates meaning for its social actors, and includes them in the
public and cultural idiom of America and beyond.

Conclusion

Identity is an elusive concept indeed. Its connotation is dense,
paradoxical, and unclear. Literary criticism has been so busy answering
"what is 'identity'?" that it sometimes seems to have forgotten that
identity is dead — being overburdened by meaning. There exists no
'entity' in 'identity'; if anything, there are Appadurai's scapes.
When identity has to endure such transformation, why do we still
address it? Brubaker and Cooper point up the conundrum, asking:

> If it is fluid, how can we understand the ways in which self-
> understandings may harden, congeal and crystallized? If it is
> constructed, how can we understand the sometimes coercive force
> of external identification? If I is multiple, how do we understand the
> terrible singularity that is often striven for — and sometimes
> realized — by politicians seeking to transform mere categories into
> unitary and exclusive groups? How can we understand the power
> and pathos of identity politics? (1)

Grappling with these questions, I would say that what is regarded as
black diasporic identity is an amalgam of culture, history, race and
resistance, economics of (un)belonging, politics of discrimination,
and the like issues. Yet still, black diasporic identity is a "we don't
know!" that always comes down to race. We should remain aware
that race is a positioning, not an identity; there is no cut delineating
it as object from agencies and positions of observation (cf. Barad
170). The real menace is less the (ab)use of race as a category, and
more the stretching of that category as an identity.

  Americanah, then, offers a polyphonic representation of black
diasporic lives in America and beyond. It frames the degrees of
commonalities and forms of connectedness. It illustrates that neither

commonality nor connectedness alone are accountable for forming groupness. It shows how a commonality *per se* is contested by people who share it. *Americanah* depicts the diffused as well as the concentrated networks none of which guarantees groupness. It also shows ways in which groupness is reliant on a sense of belonging together. What is occluded under the rubric of black diasporic identity is a flow of consciousness that can be concentrated into different practices, like sharing a commonality and/or a connectedness which sometimes *may* lead to groupness. The flow is neither an identity nor a quality, it is merely a practice. And that is as close as we can get to the meaning of collectivity and community in discussing diaspora, by "valuing, measuring, the spaces between our fingers while still feeling connected to the hand/body" (Fernandez 36).

References

Adichie, Chimamanda Ngozi. *Americanah*. London: Fourth Estate, 2013.

Appadurai, Arjun. "Disjuncture and Difference in the Global Cultural Economy." *Theory Culture Society* 7 (1990): 295–310.

Armstrong, John Alexander. *Nations Before Nationalism*. Chapel Hill: U of North Carolina P, 1982.

Arndt, Susan, and Marek Spitczok von Brisinski, eds. *Africa, Europe and (Post)colonialism: Racism, Migration and Diaspora in African Literatures*. Bayreuth: Breitinger, 2006.

Barad, Karen. "Meeting the Universe Halfway: Realism and Social Constructivism Without Contradiction." *Feminism, Science, and the Philosophy of Science*. Eds. Lynn Hankinson Nelson and Jack Nelson. Dordrecht: Kluwer, 1996. 161–194.

Brubaker, Rogers, and Frederick Cooper. "Beyond 'identity.'" *Theory and society* 29 (2000): 1–47.

Brubaker, Rogers. "The 'diaspora' diaspora." *Ethnic and Racial Studies* 28.1 (2005): 1–19.

Cohen, Robin. *Global Diasporas: An Introduction*, Seattle, WA: U of Washington P, 1997.

De, Aparajita. "What's In a Name? Tropes of Belonging and Identity in *The Namesake*." *South Asian Review* 28.2 (2007): 182–200.

Fernandez, Jane. "Framing the Diaspora: The Politics of Identity and Belonging." *Diasporas: Critical and InterDisciplinary Perspectives*. Ed. Jane Fernandez. Oxford: Inter-Disciplinary, 2009. 29–39.

Hall, Stuart. "Cultural Identity and Diaspora." *Identity: Community, Culture, Difference*. By Jonathan Rutherford. London: Lawrence & Wishart, 1998. 222–237.

Hall, Stuart. *Questions of Cultural Identity*. Eds. Stuart Hall and Paul Du Gay. London: Sage, 1996. 1–17.

Jackson, Ronald L., II, ed. *Encyclopedia of Identity.* 2 vols. Thousand Oaks: SAGE, 2010.

Safran, William. "Diasporas in modern societies: Myths of homeland and return." *Diaspora* 1.1 (1991): 83–99.

Weber, Max. *Economy and Society.* Ed. Guenther Roth and Claus Wittich. New York: Bedminster P, 1968.

Zeleza, Paul Tiyambe. "Rewriting the African Diaspora: Beyond the Black Atlantic." *African Affairs* 104.414 (2005): 35–68. Web.

10

"You May Enter But You Will Never Be Inside": Diasporic Constructions of Stasis and Progress in the African Homeland

Patrick OLOKO
University of Lagos

Summary: Development Studies and creative writing are increasingly framing Africa's engagement with her Diaspora in competing tones. Development Studies represents the Africa/Diaspora relations in comparatively optimistic and hopeful terms of a flow of resources and transnational linkages, which ensure an equitable redistribution of global wealth. In such perceptions, the idea of "return" and "homecoming," which is complex in literary portraits of cultural engagements, is simply overlooked. Yet an evolving literary genre, tagged "homecoming" or "return" narratives, portrays the experiences of "returning" Diaspora citizens as tending to vitiate a real or imagined transnational black culture, with a "vicious circle" of *angst* that often characterizes cultural relations between Africans and their Diaspora cousins. This chapter examines mainly two novels from different cultural contexts: *Juletane* (1982) by Guadeloupian/ Senegalese author Myriam Warner-Vieyra and *The Hangman's Game* (2007) by Nigerian/Guyanese author Karen King-Aribisala. These encode marriages across cultures as metaphoric alliances between Africa and her Diaspora. As the narratives show, the way the individual mind's barriers ease to allow cultural adjustment contrasts sharply with the reluctance of social systems to ease their culture's bounds.

Introduction

Interest in the subject of Africa's engagement with her Diaspora is enjoying a renewed cycle of interest and expositions in creative writing and in Development Studies. This is happening as concerns grow about how to solve the increasing problems of poverty, diseases, and political instability in Africa. The two domains of representation are increasingly framing the subject in competing and discordant tones. Creative writers imaginatively cast contact experiences between people in the two geographies in pessimistic and culturally gloomy portraits. An evolving genre of literature, tagged "homecoming" or "return" narratives (see Secovnie), portrays the experiences of "returning" Diaspora citizens as tending to vitiate a real or imagined transnational black culture. The idea of an overarching "black culture," the assumptions of similarity and solidarity woven around Blackness in holisms such as Négritude and Pan-Africanism are, in the narratives, negated in the "vicious circle" of angst that often characterizes cultural relations between Africans and their Diaspora cousins (see Borman, Blake).

Development Studies represents the Africa/Diaspora relations in more optimistic and hopeful terms. Regarded as having transcended or coped well with their subaltern positions in the western hemisphere, Diaspora Africans have become "increasingly confident" in the way they "yearn for Africa [and] want to speak and work for Africa in its moment of crisis" (Mohan and Zack-Williams 205). Such views and conclusions, sourced largely from the quantum of remittances by African migrant workers in the industrialized world, present the African Diaspora, the other half/side of the Black Atlantic (see Gilroy), as part of a new and interestingly "virtuous circle" (see Bakewell, Patterson) in the flow of resources and transnational linkages, which ensure an equitable redistribution of global wealth. This optimistic narrative draws attention to the role that the African Diaspora can play in changing the fortunes of a continent consistently represented as always in dire need of "change" and development in order to level up with other parts of the world (see for instance Adebayo et al., Akyeampong, Patterson, Styan). The extant, historically entrenched image of a space of marginalization and oppression is varied and even reversed in this discourse in the way its agency is highlighted. There is an implicit irony, not always bookmarked well enough, of a restructured world order in which the oppressed are being empowered in the very locations/spaces of their oppression. To the extent that black people are involved, it is being suggested that there is a shift in the global economic and social order with new ideas about social justice and reparations for past and present social wrong. Where the old discourse formulates a "return" to Africa, with spatial relocation as an imperative for the survival of the African Diaspora citizen, there is a new fixation with rootedness in the Western hemisphere as crucial to Africa's existence. Black slaves, once seen as involuntary migrants who were "uprooted" from the motherland in Africa, are now implicitly construed as heroes and harbingers of a struggle to foster inclusion and entrench racial diversity in the world outside Africa. As Patterson and Kelley have observed, "[r]acial capitalism, imperialism, and colonialism — the processes that created the current African diaspora — shaped African culture(s) while transforming Western culture itself" (13). As a result, the Black Atlantic is important as "an integral part of the formation of the modern world as we know it" (ibid.).

1. Narratives of Intercultural Marriage and Their Contexts

Metaphoric Alliances

Even though this conception of "kinship" signals a new turn in Africa/Diaspora engagements, some problems are notable in the analysis. Firstly, the broadened reconceptualization of the Diaspora to include African migrant workers in the western hemisphere threatens traditional and mainstream diasporic identities. It submerges and obliterates what has been described as "overlapping diasporas" (Patterson and Kelley). The problem with this sweeping inclusion is that it ignores other particularities of the engagements: the idea of "return" and "homecoming," which is complex in literary portraits of cultural engagements, is simply overlooked. Importantly as well, the discourse centralizes Africa's contemporary economic and political problems in a way that tends to expose the continent as the site of continuous, economically and politically corrective mediations. In this way, it feeds into or even links up with older ideas of racism in the way it re-historicizes location as the cause as well as the solution to the problem of Blackness. In other words, issues of cultural stasis and progress as well as continuities and their obverse reappear in current as in earlier discourses of Africa in connection with her Diaspora engagement. Finally, Development discourse positions Diaspora Africans as possible agents of change and transformation in Africa, in a business relationship that bears all the traditional marks of the continent's engagement with the west. As history tells us, that relationship cast the western investor as a tourist and outsider who was welcomed only within a formally secure economic space (see for instance Bochner, Janssens). A point like that of contributions which "a black globality" (Patterson and Kelley 24) can make to the pool of investible global capital and other resources appears to be clear in such an image of the relationship. However, it threatens to reproduce colonization in another character in a land whose inhabitants have become adept in resisting colonization. So, while the capital and goodwill of Diaspora Africans are needed to develop and transform Africa, what are the cultural terms of an Africa/Diaspora engagement and linkage under conditions of the obvious cultural hybridity or "difference" of the Diaspora African?

This chapter examines how narratives of marriage can offer us snapshots of intercultural relations between Africa and her Diaspora from a variety of perspectives, to understand what has been characterized as "the uniqueness and the commonality of the African experiences on both sides of the Atlantic" (Zack-Williams 349). I will analyze mainly two novels from different cultural contexts: *Juletane* (1982), written by Guadeloupian/Senegalese author Myriam Warner-Vieyra, and *The Hangman's Game* (2007) by Nigerian/Guyanese author Karen King-Aribisala. These frame the Africa/Diaspora engagements from the perspective of "overlapping Diasporas." My immediate objective is to delineate the outlines and dimensions of transcultural black cooperation as framed in metaphoric alliances between Africa and her Diaspora, in the marriages encoded in the narratives. My overall conclusion aims to show how discourse of "progress" in the African Diaspora assumes a dysfunctional Africa in order to make sense and to make its point, in the same way that the idea of Africa as "home" rested on the notion of a dysfunctional African Diaspora seeking security and rehabilitation in the "motherland." The fate of these regions, like that of conjoined twins, appears to be tied together in a collective and reflexive production of survivalist significations.

Rhetoric and Reality

The narratives of cooperation and of conflict articulated in the imaginaries and enquiries described above derive from assumptions about a common progenitorial identity that was developed to deal with the historical experience of Africa and her descendants. Blackness, "the privileging of African origins as the basis of black culture" (Wade), is the first important basis of a proven connection between Africa and her Diaspora. It is the worldview and marker of a stable identity of Africans and their descendants as a people in a continuously changing, browning, and diverse contemporary world (see Pabst "An Unexpected"). It is also an embodiment of ideologies, histories, and experiences that have defied the boundaries of nation-states and continents in many self-evident ways, to categorize Africa and her descendants or to isolate them for categorization (again see Pabst "An Unexpected"). Historically, Blackness positioned the black race to speak out to the white race from the margins of power or from a region of political and cultural insignificance. The origination of the idea in resistance against domination and in a struggle for inclusion in the racial mainstream inevitably meant that Blackness was always defined against or in relation to Whiteness (see Fanon [1967], cited in Moten 178, also Pabst "Blackness"). Pan-Africanism, Négritude, the Black Panther movement and other ideological groups that thrived in the nineteenth and twentieth centuries were curated as intellectual props or gravitational points for mobilizing energies around race and color, to enable a united political and cultural action against racism and colonialism. That is, the corollary of an assumed, culturally uniform *white* racial force that can inflict racism and colonialism is a counterforce that becomes naturally constituted in the contrary color of Blackness. A collegial and expansive view by Léopold Sédar Senghor constructs Blackness as an insertion to promote diversity in the pool of "a Civilization of the Universal, a Civilization of Unity by Symbiosis" that would bring together a "divided but interdependent world" (see description by Banoum).

Naomi Pabst has illustrated how much this idea persists in public consciousness and drives the discourse of intergroup relations:

When the *New York Times* ran an article that referred to Nelson Mandela as an African American, it became clearer than ever how much we still needed the broader term *black*. And it became clearer than ever that the designations *black* and *African American* should not be conflated. Visual appearance aside, how, based on his heroic life legacy and given his Herculean struggle against white supremacy, could we argue in seriousness that Mandela is not black? ("An Unexpected" 117)

In other words: Blackness as an ideology has come to inspire a simple assumption that cultural homogeneity is bound up with race. The idea of an African "homeland" in Diaspora thinking is undoubtedly linked to this assumption, and has been the basis of a firmer psychic connection between the African Diaspora and Africa. The contradiction then becomes clear. While Blackness functioned as a difference-instantiating construct in the struggle to frame "the modern world as we know it" (Patterson and Kelley 187), its unintended, but significant *realpolitik* aftermath is clearly as a difference-neutralizing philosophical formulation. But, as Pabst has noted, "if there is one thing about blackness that quickly gets exposed upon juxtaposition of geographical contexts, it is intraracial difference" ("An Unexpected" 117). That is, beyond the unifying politics signified in exterior "Blackness," there is a deeper set of entrenched disparities, differences, and discontinuities that are dredged to the surface during moments of intra-black contacts, especially at personalized relationship levels such as marriage. A succinct problematization of the issue, following Pabst, which is at the heart of the analysis of texts in this chapter is seen in the question posed by Fred Moten: if "the black cannot be an other for another black, if the black can only be an other for a white, then is there ever anything called black social life?" (178).

In the social exchanges within and around the Black Atlantic, would Blackness neutralize the obvious difference between culturally-hybrid Diaspora Africans and their culturally "pure" Africans cousins domiciled in the "homeland" — should an occasion arise for the former to "return"? The very question raises another contradiction relating to the place of Africa in a "neo-liberal" world order. To what extent has Africa modernized her institutions or developed the necessary outlooks that are required of participants in a real or imagined and culturally tolerant world, one that has been hewn into shape with the active participation of Diaspora citizens?

Homeland and Cosmopolis

In seeking answers, we should consider literary inscriptions of the interface between Africa and her Diaspora. They are converse to the optimism of Development discourse. Where Development-studies analysts define the motivation for African Diaspora charity in terms of kinship ties, literary narratives frame social incidents and experiences within the cultural relations between people of the two regions, enabling a testing and verification of ties. As Karen Barad reminds us, science is "movement between meanings and matter, word and world, interrogating and redefining boundaries [...] in 'the between', where knowledge and being meet" (185); reality itself is "constituted by the 'between'" (181). In this constitution of the forms of knowledge, literature demonstrates how culture is pivotal to development, by contextualizing migrations and presenting diverse perspectives of the Black Atlantic in interfaces of relationships. If race and color or ideas associated with them are harnessed as a needful model of identity at specific times in a people's history, creative writers may key into the conversation. But they will furnish readers with representations of social experience to show that cultural and other differences do not easily or necessarily get submerged just because there is an urgent political objective at hand.

A growing literary awareness of the political and cultural phenomenon discussed above has been trending in a number of works since 1965, when Ama Ata Aidoo published her play titled *The Dilemma of a Ghost*. We should briefly consider these before turning to the novels. Such works offer social snapshots of West Africa, the usual migration destination of the Diaspora character, and its response to globalization, multiculturalism, and other neo-liberal ideas upon which the increasing perceptions of the world as interconnected and interdependent are based. They convey a sense of being organized on the assumption that, while slavery imposed a condition of forceful migration from the homeland, globalization and its modernities have made a free world possible to ensure a reverse, voluntary migration or return. Thus a general pattern in the plot is that heterosexual characters fall in love, get married, and move to live in West Africa, where they learn unexpected lessons in cultural adjustment in ways that enable the reader or audience member to reach conclusions about mind-sets as against mind-shifts regarding cultural relations between Africa and the African Diaspora. The characters' cultural adjustment situations vary, depending on whether the writer is African or Diaspora African. A brief synopsis of major works describing such situations will hopefully illuminate how West African writers portray the subject of intercultural relations relative to their Afro-Caribbean or Diaspora counterparts.

In Aidoo's *Dilemma of a Ghost* (1965) Eulalie, an African American, marries the Ghanaian Ato Quayson in the United States where he had gone for further studies. They later relocate to Ghana, where Eulalie faces a variety of adjustment challenges caused largely by misunderstanding based on prejudice and cultural perceptions about slavery. Soon, Ato's mother identifies him as the source of conflict. The play ends when Ato's mother, in a show of understanding and tolerance, leads Eulalie offstage. Tess Onwueme in her play *The Missing Face* (1992) then varies Aidoo's plot by portraying the experience of African American Ida Bee, who travels to Nigeria in search of her husband Momah. Upon their reconnection, a struggle for understanding and acceptance begins, with Momah's parents and relatives showing more feeling and understanding than the "culturally translated" husband. Mariama Bâ's fiction *Scarlet Song* (1986) extends the pattern's racial scope in her portrait of Mireille, a French girl whose Senegalese husband Ousmane marries a second wife because a "toubab" or white/foreigner will not understand the Senegalese notion of obligations that a wife owes her mother-in-law. The story ends tragically rather like the way *Juletane* ends — as we shall see. Works showing intercultural relations set in Francophone and Islamic societies tend to end in a specific way which is different from works set in Anglophone and Christian cultural regions. Isidore Okpewho's narrative *Call Me By My Rightful Name* (2004) appropriates the quest motif of Alex Haley's *Roots* (1976) to tell the story of Otis Hampton, an African American who goes to Nigeria to rediscover his African roots, in order to be fully reconciled to his African American social experience.

As far as cultural relations are concerned, these works' predominant tone suggests that West African writers tend to imagine and characterize Diaspora Africans as expecting a culturally relativized Africa. They are portrayed, that is, as seeking a "homeland" in the mold of multicultural cities in the western hemisphere such as Paris, London, and New York. This clearly amounts to ignoring the important contradiction, in cultural and geographic terms, between ideas associated with "homelands" and cosmopolises. And because there is not always an easy reconciliation between the Diasporic Africans' notions of a pristine African "homeland" and their expectation of a reception therein in cosmopolitan terms, their immersion and cultural (re)membership processes become rhizomatic, spawning a series of unpleasant experiences that give rise to an awareness of the differences among black people. Social relationships and experiences enacted by West African writers therefore tend to imply that hybridity (in the sense of being black but behaving differently from other black people in a specified "homeland" social space) can problematize the adjustment processes for the "returning" Diaspora citizen. Thus, when Senegalese in Dakar choose to assimilate rather than integrate Mireille and Juletane respectively in Bâ's and Warner-Vieyra's narratives, they are (un) consciously resisting attempts to transform their "homeland" into a cosmopolis. The Senegalese action is consistent with the idea of identity preservation — the very reason for the promotion of "Blackness" and its precipitate of a "return" to Africa. We should not overlook, however, that in their portraits of intra-black cultural relations West African writers imply that racial similarity and cultural homogeneity can reinforce each other with minimum effort. These are subject to the normal infractions and integration difficulties that often characterize migrations and resettlement.

2. (Re)settlement Spaces

Liminal Presences

Afro-Caribbean writers such as Maryse Conde, Miriam Warner-Vieyra, and Karen King-Aribisala in their carefully curated rendering of experiences suggest that the extant cultural atmosphere in the "homeland," or the integration conditions, require the Diaspora returnees to literally remake themselves in the image and likeness of Africans before they can transact any profitable existence. They portray social experiences from the point of view of victims. They thus imply in their enactments that the portrait offered by West African writers is the usual view of a sympathetic but unaffected chronicler who is free from the depersonalizing terms of adjustment and integration into African "homeland" cultures.

In Warner-Vieyra's *Juletane* (1982), the eponymous character is a Guadeloupian Christian. She meets and marries a Senegalese Muslim, Mamadou, in Paris. Cosmopolitan Paris mutes their palpable religious and cultural differences. When they relocate to Dakar in Senegal, their overlooked orientations return to haunt them and to generate a series of tensions, conflicts, and crises that eventually lead to Juletane's tragic situation of becoming literally a refugee in the African homeland.

In King-Aribisala's *The Hangman's Game* (2007), the nameless female protagonist travels to Nigeria with clearly drawn notions of Africa's relations with her Diaspora: "I want to see for myself why slavery, the slave trade, occurred in the first place [...] I want to know why blacks sold their fellow blacks into slavery and I want to know why God allowed it" (10). This is the novel's stated objective, into which the writer in a balanced plot weaves and embeds the political and the personal. Upon arrival in Lagos, she meets her nameless guide at the airport; they fall in love and promptly proceed to marry. The marriage thrusts the protagonist, in a Dickensian manner, into the open and politically volatile society to observe and report the pre-modern governance practices of a postcolonial African state. The device of namelessness is a distancing strategy to resist cultural inclusion or submersion. However, the writer's real aim and unstated objective is to depict what has been described in another context as "the divide that often erupts between Africans and their diaspora" (Secovnie 128). For reasons relating to craft, as I shall show below, it is possible to discern an intertextual connection between *Juletane* and *The Hangman's Game* wherein the two novels act as prequel as well as sequel to one another.

These novels insert the Afro-Caribbean dimension into the narrative discourse of migration in two significant ways. The first is a re-routing of the transcontinental path of the historical journey into slavery to signify a tri-Atlantic return to Africa. Juletane, the eponymous character of Warner-Vieyra's novel, departs from Guadeloupe and arrives in Dakar via Paris, while the nameless protagonist of King-Aribisala's novel arrives in Lagos from Guyana via London, urged on by her idealistic quest for the "truth" of slavery. These characters' presence within and between historical as well as contemporary realities is liminal. It thus (dis)places them to negotiate and manage their existence in ways that reveal the "homeland," their destination, as a complex reality of progress versus stasis. The second shows how the liminality of the characters' position in the "homeland" cultural space interrogates, and therefore complicates, our notion of their cultural transactions. Given the pervasive commonalities between these Diaspora returnees and their homeland cousins, are we to interpret the formers' experiences as "intra," "inter," or "trans"cultural? And: given that they frame black cultural experiences to reveal what Gayle has observed in another context to be "the internal complexities contained within the signifier 'Black'," what promise and possibility does the spectrum of West African and Afro-Caribbean narratives as synopsized above offer in terms of a (re)turn of the gaze from intergroup to intragroup relations — or vice versa — in the expected multicultural and tolerant new world order?

Marital Space

Intercultural narratives have been observed as, among other things, specifically foregrounding the challenges of integration, which are inherent in the migration experience of an interface between the foreign and the familiar (see for instance Zimmermann). Each category's perspective in this pair as it defines *the other* in the encounter can prompt self-reflection. That could lead to significant shifts of mind as well as of border in defense of if not countering tolerance, as attitudes change or adjustments together with coexistence become imperative. The two novels enact perspectives of social relationships affirming this view *as* intercultural relations. In the narratives we find characters adjusting to new social and physical spaces and conditions, incidences of their (in)tolerance of strangers or *the other* and vice versa, as well as many other acts of cultural negotiation and transaction. All these bear clear marks of human relation practices across cultures. They occur in a (re)settlement space in which exchange processes are constituted into a dialogic discourse of cultural identities necessitated by migration. In *Juletane* Ndèye, Mamadou's third wife, declares boldly, "I can't bear strange people" (42). Even though this statement is commensurate with her portraiture as an assuming woman, the word "strange" as she uses it also by transfer describes the refugee-like condition of an Afro-Caribbean protagonist who has decided to shut herself into a literal as well as metaphoric inwardness when adjustment to the culture of polygamy and integration into Dakar's Islamic society seem to make no sense to her.

A barometer for probing the depth of cultural (dis)affiliation at the micro and macro levels — and indeed the preferred literary technique for encoding intercultural liaisons — is heterosexual marriage. Silva, Campbell, and Wright have pointed to the increasing phenomenon of intercultural marriage. Yet they observe that the success rate of intercultural marriages depends on two factors. On the one hand, similarity of cultural orientation between couples, or the degree of their shared values, can significantly influence the way they manage the relation: "[...] the decision to enter an intercultural marriage may be more easily made when the partners' cultures are similar or when the couples can find complementary values amidst their different backgrounds" (859). On the other hand, the abode or geographical space where the couples meet or where they choose to live is crucial to the success of the marriage: "[...] the more open and neutral a community is to intergroup contact, the more likely individuals are to meet and form long-term relationships with people from diverse backgrounds" (ibid.).

Following Silva, Campbell, and Wright, we may assume that progenitorial and historical circumstances play a crucial role in bringing together and shaping the (mis)fortune of the protagonists and other major characters in *Juletane* and *The Hangman's Game*. They receive formal cultural orientations in relatively homogeneous societies such as Guadeloupe, Guyana, and Senegal. Then they later move on to modern cosmopolitan settings where skin color, shared political circumstances, history, and other assumptions of kinship help them to forge and to shape their intercultural connections and emotional relationships. For example, in the case of Juletane and Mamadou Paris, where they meet and marry, is constructed as a flexible space where various ethnic, religious, and other social interests and circles intersect in ways that orientate the individual away from absolute commitment to a group. Thus, even though the cosmopolitan dazzle of Paris can dissolve and neutralize differences, it highlights the couple's "Blackness" against the city's predominantly racial hue of whiteness, enabling the characters' common racial ties to bind them together in this liberal city, while also blinding them to their cultural differences.

Earlier, and in the same way, Paris had brought together the three "fathers" of Négritude (according to Banoum), viz., Léopold Sédar Senghor (Senegal), Léon-Gontran Damas (French Guiana), and Aimé Césaire (Martinique). Despite their national and cultural differences, these men united along the black color line to pursue a political and intellectual battle for independence and for reclaiming the values of "Blackness." *Juletane*, set in postcolonial Dakar, can be read as an experiment aimed at testing the extent to which cultural cooperation between Africa and her Diaspora is coterminous with the political cooperation between Senghor and his Afro-Caribbean counterparts in their charting of a new course for their postcolonial, "black" Francophone nations.

In principle, a marriage promotes or is expected to promote co-existence, inclusion, and mainstreaming. In practice, however, as West African writers and their African Diaspora counterparts often portray the experience, it is different: the way the mind's borders and barriers ease up to allow the promise or profits of cultural adjustment and co-existence when individuals of different cultures fall in love and marry often contrasts sharply with communities' and social systems' willingness to ease their culture's borders and barriers to accommodate them. The location of the marital space within a family unit's close circuit at the micro level of culture makes it easier to detect the threats posed by some intercultural marriages to community and cultural values. It is in marriages that anxieties, estrangement, and alienation build up to generate conflict that either threatens or is perceived to threaten the wider society. Thus, even though a marriage is intercultural, it is often subordinated to cultural interests, and relativized to accord with the dominant spouse's personal and political interests. Personal interests and social considerations need to be balanced in the all-important choice of a marital partner. As is often the case in imagined intercultural marriages, the complexity of intercultural relations and encounters is deepened in narratives of cross-cultural marriages.

3. *Juletane:* Re-centering the "Homeland"

When Juletane and Mamadou are sent to Dakar to test and practice their Parisian training in liberalism together with tolerance, the city resurrects and re-centers the cultural prejudice of "homeland" in Mamadou. In contrast to Paris, Dakar is a culturally fixed and stable scenario, where the terms of accommodation and integration are, in Warner-Vieyra's depiction, extremely assimilating and depersonalizing. As the experience of Hélène, a young Antillean social worker in Senegal, illustrates in the novel (which I will refer to as *J*), Dakar is more tolerant of tourists and other cultural outsiders who make less visible demands on its scarce resources and who experience the society from a distance. For outsiders like Juletane who seek inclusion and cultural participation, the society frames a set of conditions for reception. Two of these stand out in terms of how they delineate the adjustment circumstances of Juletane and of the nameless protagonist of *The Hangman's Game*, accounting for their exclusion/inclusion from the cultural mainstream. The first is Juletane's realization that being married to a Muslim correlates with accepting polygamy as a normal part of life. On the journey from Paris to Dakar, Juletane comes to understand that her husband has another wife with whom she is expected to share him. Later, he marries a third, and the expectation again is that they would all coexist happily in a homestead. Thus the first and important condition for integration and membership in the society is tolerance of rivalry in marriage. In Juletane's Catholic and western-oriented culture, marriage is regarded as a hallowed personal and emotional space, to be shared by a heterosexual couple in a monogamous union. Because she does not understand this strange and irrational world in which co-wives share a husband and live happily, she descends into loneliness — and loses her mind.

A definitive turn in the plot of the narrative comes when Juletane is informed that she would never be able to have children again, after she had a miscarriage occasioned by her being hit by a vehicle. At this point, the awareness strikes her that she has "failed" the second and crucial test of integration, and must now expect the consequences:

> I used tears, tantrums, special dishes, coquetry, indifference, to try to dissuade Mamadou from bringing Awa to Town. His mind was made up. Whenever we discussed it, he tried to persuade me to accept this very natural solution [...] we would be a big happy family, Awa's children would be my children. (*J* 36)

Prior to this development, Mamadou had rationalized polygamy to Juletane as being culturally foisted on him. He had been largely successful in managing the situation to Juletane's advantage by keeping Awa away from their home in the city. But even though Mamadou fulfills his duties to Awa within the minimum limits required by custom, it becomes clear at this point that Awa has more wifely capacities than Juletane, especially in the crucial areas of childbearing and tolerance of polygamy. This informs Mamadou's decision to bring her to the city to share the marital space with Juletane. Juletane describes the situation:

> Awa was the real mistress of the house. I could find no fault with her. When she came home from the hospital after the birth of her baby son, Alioune, she came to see me and told me: "take him, he is yours." (Ibid., 38)

> Mamadou's happiness made me sad. If I had had the child he wanted so much, our life would have been quite different. (Ibid., 39)

What Mamadou regards as a "natural" solution is in fact a cultural provision to ameliorate conditions that cannot be helped, such as the biological condition that confronts Juletane. Such strategies have been carefully built into the cultural system, and "insiders" such as Awa and Ndèye have been socialized to understand, tolerate, and cope with them. This is why Ndèye can become Mamadou's third wife, even though the protagonist-narrator portrays her in a bad light throughout the novel. This is also why Awa can hand over her child to Juletane for adoption, even though she has good reasons not to trust her capacity for motherly devotion.

But the novel's crisis, which leads to its tragic outcome, lies in the delicate question of how far the needs of a cultural "outsider" must be taken into consideration. It is easy for Juletane to expect her husband to accept her childlessness and cling to him for understanding and support, which is how such situations are managed in her western, Christian-oriented culture. But the issue is whether Mamadou, now located in Dakar, a West African Islamic hub known for observing Islam's least restrictive demands (see *J* 68), will or can consent to providing that support and understanding, which would mean forgoing the tempting cultural alternatives that would be of benefit to him, to Juletane, and to his society. When Juletane, in her deranged state of mind, proceeds to obliterate Mamadou's family without even knowing that she has done so, the reader is confronted with the crucial question of tolerance and sacrifice: who in this narrative is intolerant? Is it Juletane herself, who expects Mamadou to sacrifice his being in a society where such a sacrifice is clearly untenable? Or is it Mamadou, who chooses to close his eyes to the special needs of the cultural "outsider," the stranger in his care?

4. *The Hangman's Game*

"It All Connects"

The needs of the cultural "outsider" are familiar to the author of *The Hangman's Game*, who is Guyanese by birth and Nigerian by marriage and naturalization. Having lived in Lagos all her adult life, Karen King-Aribisala understands quite well that her individuality or "otherness" is an inevitable portent of social isolation or exclusion. She observes:

> Anywhere there is a group there will always be an "other." For instance, I have always lived as an "other" it seems to me. *I've always been apart from the group*, including when I was the only Black in an English boarding school. (Eghagha, emphasis added)

She has reinforced this view in a recent article titled "What Is Africa to Me Now? The Sweet, the Bitter ..." (2015). Therein, she uses her own experiences of living in Europe as well as in West Africa to voice a fear of imagined and actual conditions of intercultural marriage. When, for instance, her husband's parents asked that she submit herself to purification by washing her legs in a bowl of water as part of the rites in her marriage to a Nigerian of the Yoruba ethnic group, her own parents' fears were heightened:

> If the Nigerians could be so culturally chauvinistic right here in Rome, how would their daughter fare when she was actually in Nigeria? She would no longer be protected by foreigners of expatriate land. She would as an adult be subjected to cultural horrors, alienation; and my Nigerian husband, whatever his principles and his love for their daughter, would not be able to withstand the cultural pressures that would definitely increase once we lived in Africa. (18)

Fortunately, as King-Aribisala makes clear in the article, her own marriage has not fitted neatly into the pattern of Juletane's to justify these fears. As she puts it, "I have been blessed, been fortunate that when the group pressure tries to assert itself against our union, Femi [her spouse] has responded as an individual who is part of a group but is nonetheless sensitive to my individuality" (ibid.). Nevertheless, as she articulates elsewhere, such fears inevitably tinge the consciousness of African Diaspora writing, particularly her own:

> [...] you are writing and it's like you are drawing things out of a bank, things that you've heard, things that you've read, conversations that you have had [...] and experiences that you've had, *and it all connects*. (Eghagha, emphasis added)

Her technique in *The Hangman's Game* is to circumvent the reality of Juletane's experience by re-centering Juletane's pre-Dakar imagination of intercultural social relations in order to recover and restore a measure of optimism and hope in the human condition.

Women in Control

The idea of connections between one's writing and what one has heard, seen, or read is particularly useful in linking King-Aribisala's novel with Warner-Vieyra's in order to ascertain the role that art can play in mediating the sociocultural experience. A careful scrutiny of *The Hangman's Game* would reveal implicit intertextual connections with *Juletane* in characterization. The diary-like narrative structure of *Juletane* allows the eponymous character to be written out of the novel, so that another character going into another intercultural marriage could evolve to revise or update Juletane's experience.

Hélène is prepared for that role in the way she gains valuable insights about how to manage her upcoming marriage to Ousmane. For his part, Ousmane is prepared for a role different from Mamadou's in being characterized as pliable and emotionally committed to a marriage based on justice and respect for the female spouse's rights. Considering Hélène's experience from previous relationships and her resolve to marry for the simple reason of having a child, it is arguably logical to presume that she morphs into the nameless character of *The Hangman's Game* (which I will refer to as *HG*), while Ousmane is a morph of her liberal spouse here depicted in terms of the Book of Genesis:

> In his talking and in his words, spirit-filled, I know I have met the bone of my bone and the flesh of my flesh. In one month I know this. I love my man ... and he loves me ... *I can tell him the worst about me and be mind-naked with all my faults upfront* ... We are married before we are married. (*HG* 12, emphasis added)

The Hangman's Game tells two stories which are differentiated by typeface and temporal setting, but unified by the presence and what Eghagha has called the "control" of a female narrator and protagonist. Its main concern, which keys into the prevailing trend of social and political criticism in Nigerian writing, is to show how "control" figures literally and symbolically as both idea and tool in the governance practices of postcolonial Nigeria under military rule and in colonial/slavery-era Guyana. This striking regional similarity horrifies the narrator, who declares: "[...] I feel hemmed in by present and past; by country and country. I look at my dress and I'm still thinking of hemming" (ibid., 81). The second, less obvious subject is intercultural spousal relations, which the author started in her first work of fiction, *Our Wife & Other Stories* (1990). There is a new sense of confidence and expertise in the handling of cultural integration issues in this novel to justify a return to the subject. The caution, fears, and overwhelming resignation to the forces of assimilation which characterize the intercultural encounters in the short stories are significantly reviewed and pepped up in the novel.

The narrator and protagonist achieves a measure of liberation through a manner of absorption with the self, in order to gain the required presence of mind to cope with her condition of "otherness." She deals with the haunting presence of employees and family members by anonymizing and submerging them in generic identities

such as "Driver," "Nurse," "Gardener," "Husband," and "Daughter."
Through this method of detached presence, she maintains a "control"
that is crucial to her mental survival — unlike Juletane, who submits
to a destructive self-absorption. A critic has pointed in this regard to
the way in which King-Aribisala's "works deal primarily with women
who are either in control or aspire to be in control of their lives. In
King-Aribisala's fiction, a new voice emerges. This is the voice of
the African in the Diaspora attempting to find a place in a home that
is not truly home" (Eghagha). The reference to the author as
"African in the Diaspora" is not clear. However, King-Aribisala's
portrayal of characters who seek control of their lives in the African
"homeland" space shows the careful calibration of her imagination to
justify a reference to her as "a new voice." The distinctiveness of this
voice is seen in the re-characterization of the African male spouse
from a muscular and haunting cultural presence that overrides his
spouse's claim to an identity and personhood, to a caring and
sensitive male who provides the necessary cultural translation that
may enable his spouse to cope with her difference.

Imagination Against Barriers

The grim outcome in *Juletane* points to how the predominantly
Islamic culture of Senegal mediates intercultural spousal relations so
as to foreground what its author depicts as characters' simple assumptions
about cultural modernization in Africa. In *The Hangman's Game*,
the narrative gaze shifts to another dominant religion, Christianity,
in a cosmopolitan urban setting. King-Aribisala shows how an
ingenious management scheme by the cultural outsider produces a
less fatal result in intercultural relations. The nameless spouse of the
equally nameless protagonist in the novel is represented as "trading"
in *the word*: he combines his job as a Professor of Linguistics with
lay preaching in a Christian ministry. In actual life, King-Aribisala's
husband is a Christian and a scholar, and they have been living in
Lagos where she holds a teaching position in a local university (see
King-Aribisala "What," Eghagha), while he runs a Pentecostal
church as well as writing regular columns on political and Christian
subjects in local newspapers. King-Aribisala makes much of her
Christian conviction by ensuring that it is writ large in her fiction
(see also Gibbs). In *The Hangman's Game*, she calibrates the
religion to serve the female spouse's interest in the way Islam is made
to advance the male's interest in *Juletane*. To a significant extent,
the narrative is heavily autobiographical without being less creative,

as the following suggests:

> Nurse is a Christian. So am I. So is my husband. We are all, all Christians. Not the Sunday-only-Church-going-type of Christian you understand. We try to live the teachings of Christ daily. It's not easy. As a matter of fact, you could say Nurse came into my household in response to our faith, complete with a tiny cross hanging around her neck. She had been introduced to us by her mother, a deaconess in the church [...] The deal was that in exchange for helping me with the housework, we'd pay for her university education. I planned to give her an education she would never forget. (*HG* 35)

Unlike *Juletane*, *The Hangman's Game* does not depict a tortured and self-absorbed character who fails to attain the ideal in an African interreligious marriage. Yet this is not an attempt to glamorize Christianity as promoting harmony in intercultural marriages. On the contrary, the protagonist appropriates Christianity to serve her personal interest of maintaining "control" of her environment, in a way that compares with how political leaders in slavery-era Guyana and postcolonial Nigeria use the institution to achieve personal and political goals. Similarly, the novel's depiction of how its protagonist is insulated from the traumas and other adjustment shocks of a typical intercultural marriage does not necessarily mean that Lagos, unlike Dakar, has attained the level of cosmopolitanism and cultural modernization required for easing the pain of alienation faced by cultural outsiders. King-Aribisala's entire oeuvre is so overtly devoted to exploring the perceived cultural and political spectacle that is Lagos and Nigeria that only an insignificant lineament of her narratives would sync with such a view. Christianity is made to function in the novel as part of the infrastructure for gaining the crucial control required for survival.

Indeed, the novel hangs on "control," or the need for it, as a predominant motif uniting the actions taken by the narrator and the political leaders she criticizes. Colonial rulers and postcolonial military dictators in the West Indies and West Africa are represented as using their political power to manipulate citizens in order to maintain their power, positions, and privileges. King-Aribisala, for her part, uses an author's vast discretionary powers to steer the narrative toward ameliorating the tragic experiences of the African Diaspora female spouse/victim. All fictional events and characters are drawn so as to enable the narrator to be in control. Thus unlike Juletane, who goes to Dakar after her marriage to Mamadou, this novel's narrator arrives in Lagos ostensibly with a return ticket, and getting married is only incidental to the clearly defined goal she had set out to achieve:

> I wanted, desperately, to understand the reasons behind our ancestral enslavement. What better way than to get a visa to Nigeria, a country that had trafficked in slaves, and live among its people and discover first hand why hands exchanged silver for the likes of me. (HG 9)

When she marries, she chooses a man characterized as significantly free from the overbearing influence of family. This is unlike Mamadou, who is informed by his uncle upon arrival that culture requires him to deal fairly with his local and foreign wives. Here, the protagonist enjoys an affectionate relationship with her husband, and ensures she has her way in crucial issues relating to the achievement of her objectives. When she decides, for instance, that they should go to a part of the city considered unsafe, her husband frets for their safety. But she gets her way when "my face bullies him into moving the car onto the Third Mainland Bridge" (ibid., 80). And even though her retinue of hired servants is represented as made of powerful and important actors in Nigeria's political drama and debacle, they are subjected to the protagonist's cultural adjustment program.

The author has spoken volubly of how "imagination" has been a crucial tool in resolving the pain of cultural alienation, which is defined as happening when "female protagonists [who] often [...] hail from Europe and the West Indies [...] become embroiled in Nigerian societal values and situations" (Preface to Our):

> I think imagination is a very powerful tool for changing all that is warped with the world. [...] Why are there these divisions between clans, between ethnic groups, between kindred? [...] Why are there so many barriers in the world? Can we get rid of them? And you have to imaginatively, both in style and in content, lend yourself to break down barriers if we are going to be healed of the things which are walls between us all over the world. (Eghagha)

Accordingly, when King-Aribisala describes herself as having "a great imagination" because "[t]o create a poem, a story, a novel you have to use reality in an imaginative way" ("What" 24), the contexts of her "use" of reality become clearer, especially her attempt to mediate the harsh reality of West African intercultural marital relations toward healing denouements.

Conclusion

The narratives of "return" as evident in the foregoing consist of two parts. The first, as discussed in the above synopses, is written by West Africans and focuses clearly and squarely on the difference or "otherness" of Diaspora Africans from their home-based kin. Even so, what emerges in the portraits are sympathetic delineations that suggest negotiated acceptance and tolerance of the returning Diaspora citizens. The second, to which much attention is paid, is written by black people of African descent and portrays the "return" experience of Diaspora citizens by focusing on the adjustment challenges they often face in social relationships on account of their "otherness." Taken together, the narratives reveal how writers across the Black Atlantic have been part of the intellectual efforts to shape a collective identity for Africa and its descendants in the way that they attempt to unionize them, as it were, as "black" people in formal social and cultural relationships. As the Introduction shows, this approach differs from the Development Studies model of intra-black cooperation through business relationships. That the unionization experiment represented in creative writing tends to reveal an unevenness of "black" culture which often produces catastrophic results demonstrates the need for cultural and soft-power diplomacy, such as that attempted in King-Aribisala's novel, as a *sine qua non* for any lasting economic cooperation.

The increasing ease of travel and migration in our time has no doubt buoyed the phenomenon of "return" narratives. Through these, "black" people see themselves in relation to one another and also see how they figure within the larger global order of an evolving and contested multiculturalism. The narratives subsist largely within postcolonial literary frameworks, firstly in that the returning African Diaspora citizens' social experiences are re-imagined and defined along the lines of political and moral tensions of Africa/Europe contact experiences, and secondly in the way their re-insertion of the Us/Them model of identity fits the colonial relation paradigm. Finally, the narrative remodeling of the conflicts of classic postcolonial texts invites readers to reflect on the deeply complex and political nature of the simple "assumption of natural kinship" (Secovnie 128) of "black" people.

References

Adebayo, Samson B., Ezra Gayawan et al. "Modelling Geographical Variations and Determinants of Use of Modern Family Planning Methods Among Women of Reproductive Age in Nigeria." *Journal of Biosocial Science* 00 (2012): 1–21.

Akyeampong, E. "Africans in the Diaspora: the Diaspora and Africa." *African Affairs* 99.395 (2000): 183–215.

Bakewell, Oliver. "Keeping Them in Their Place: the ambivalent relationship between development and migration in Africa." International Migration Institute (Univ. of Oxford) Working Paper 8 (2007).

Banoum, Bertrade Ngo-Ngijol. "*Négritude.*" *Africana Age: African & African Diasporan Transformations in the 20th Century.* 2011. Web. 20 June 2016.

Barad, Karen. "Meeting the Universe Halfway: Realism and Social Constructivism Without Contradiction." *Feminism, Science, and the Philosophy of Science.* Eds. Lynn Hankinson Nelson and Jack Nelson. Dordrecht: Kluwer, 1996. 161–194.

Blake, Cecil. "An African Nationalist Ideology Framed in *Diaspora* and the Development Quagmire: Any Hope for a Renaissance?" *Journal of Black Studies* 35.5 (2005): 573–596.

Bochner, Stephen. "The Social Psychology of Cross-cultural Relations." *Cultures in Contact: Studies in Cross-cultural Interaction.* Ed. Stephen Bochner. Oxford: Pergamon, 1982. 5–44.

Borman, David Michael. *Literature of Return: Back to Africa, Belonging, and Modernity.* Open Access Dissertations (Univ. of Miami), Paper 1226. 2014.

Eghagha, Hope. "Bridges Across Cultures: The Writing of Karen King-Aribisala." 10 May 2005. Web. 8 July 2016. <http://www.lhcolloquy.com/HE%20article.htm>.

Gayle, Addison, ed. *The Black Aesthetic.* New York: Anchor-Doubleday, 1971.

Gibbs, James. Review of *Kicking Tongues* (1998). *World Literature Today* 73.4 (1999): 801.

Gilroy, Paul. *The Black Atlantic: Modernity and Double Consciousness.* London: Verso, 1993.

Janssens, Maddy. "Evaluating international managers' performance: parent company standards as control mechanism." *The International Journal of Human Resource Management* 5.4 (1994): 853–873.

King-Aribisala, Karen. *The Hangman's Game.* Leeds: Peepal Tree, 2007.

—. *Our Wife & Other Stories.* Lagos: Malthouse, 1990.

—. "What Is Africa to Me Now? The Sweet, the Bitter ..." *Research In African Literatures* 46.4 (2015): 15–25.

Mohan, Giles and Alfred B. Zack-Williams. "Editorial: Africa, the African Diaspora and Development." *Review of African Political Economy* 29 (2002): 205–210.

Moten, Fred. "The Case of Blackness." *Criticism* 50.2 (2008): 177–218.

Pabst, Naomi. "Blackness/Mixedness: Contestations over Crossing Signs." *Cultural Critique* 54 (Spring 2003): 178–212.

Pabst, Naomi. "An Unexpected Blackness." *Transition* 100 (2008): 112–132.

Patterson, Tiffany Ruby and Robin D. G. Kelley. "Unfinished Migrations: Reflections on the African Diaspora and the Making of the Modern World." *African Studies Review* 43.1, Special Issue on the Diaspora (2000): 11–45.

Patterson, Trista et al. "Tourism and Climate Change: Two-Way Street, or Vicious/Virtuous Circle?" *Journal of Sustainable Tourism* 14.4 (2006): 339–348.

Secovnie, Kelly O. *Translating the Transatlantic: West African Literary Approaches to African American Identity*. Ph.D. diss., State U of New York at Albany. PQDT Open. 2009.

Silva, Luciana C., Kelly Campbell and David W. Wright. "Intercultural relationships: Entry, adjustment, and cultural negotiation." *Journal of Comparative Family Studies* 43.6 (2012): 857–870.

Styan, David. "The security of Africans beyond borders: migration, remittances and London's transnational entrepreneurs." *International Affairs* 83.6 (2007): 1171–1191.

Wade, Peter. "Defining Blackness in Colombia." *Journal de la société des Américanistes* 95.1 (2009): 165–184. Web. 20 June 2016.

Warner-Vieyra, Myriam. *Juletane*. Paris: Présence africaine, 1982.

Zack-Williams, Alfred. "Development and diaspora: separate concerns?" *Review of African Political Economy* 22 (1995): 349–358.

Zimmerman, Christian von. "Kulturthema Migration und Interkulturelles Schreiben." *recherches germaniques*. Ed. Christine Maillard. Revue Annuelle Serie 3, 2006. 7–25.

Section Three

Cross-Cultural Identities

11

From Separating to Uniting Hyphen: "Hyphenated Identities" in Gish Jen's and Elif Shafak's Novels

Mine KRAUSE (Paris)

Summary: Chinese-American author Gish Jen and Turkish author Elif Shafak are both female immigrants who write novels in English and live in English-speaking countries, i.e., the United States and England respectively. This chapter aims to explore the phenomenon of "hyphenated identities" as depicted in Gish Jen's *Typical American* and *Mona in the Promised Land* as well as in Elif Shafak's *The Saint of Incipient Insanities* and *The Bastard of Istanbul*. All four novels describe various kinds of inner conflicts that immigrants experience as soon as they decide to live in the U.S. The sensation of a life between two cultures and feeling torn apart appears as an important issue especially for the second and third generation of immigrants. For the perception of identity, the hyphen has different functions: it can either separate the two cultures in question, emphasizing one's cultural roots and rejecting the target culture. Or it can serve as a bridge between both cultures, pointing to their similar aspects and seeing "the Other" as an enriching element. It is in the characters' perception of names, language, and eating habits that the positive or negative impact of the hyphen becomes particularly visible. When names are mispronounced abroad, when one's linguistic limits in a foreign language become visible, and when another country's culinary culture appears exotic, one's former sense of belonging is lost and a phase of suffering from alienation begins.

These periods of acculturative stress either lead to a biased approach toward the target culture, or to the development of an open mind that does not judge other cultural elements as threatening but regards them as enriching. During and after a confrontation with this kind of stress, it becomes clear whether the hyphen is a separating or a uniting signifier.

Introduction

Chinese-American, Jewish-American, Armenian-American, Mexican-American ... Immigrant groups in the United States are often characterized by a "hyphenated identity" (Çağlar) of which the feeling of being American seems to be the uniting basis. The expression "American" behind the hyphen stands for this common national aspect, while the adjective before the hyphen still leaves enough room for the cultural particularities foreigners want to keep from their homeland.① From a visual point of view, this hyphen has opposite functions with regard to identity perception. It might either separate the two cultures in question or serve as a bridge between them.

Depending on the respective interpretation, the understanding of one's own identity changes considerably. Those who subconsciously focus more on the separating function of the hyphen, and by doing so cling to their origins, can be described as separators. Their reactions to the target culture, i.e., the culture of a new country, are mostly negative since they are frequently going through phases of acculturative stress (also called culture shock). Those who, however, concentrate on the uniting force of the hyphen are global souls characterized by a state of intercultural personhood. They are

---

① Arjun Appadurai is of the opinion that the concept of hybridity should replace the idea of hyphenation, claiming that "the formula of hyphenation (as in Italian-Americans, Asian-Americans, and African-Americans) is reaching the point of saturation, and the right-hand side of the hyphen can barely contain the unruliness of the left-hand side" (Appadurai 424). However, when it comes to the sensation of being in-between cultures, the different functions of the hyphen gain importance in the identity reconstructing process. My article aims at illustrating that living in a country like America which consists of immigrants also means constantly dealing with "hyphenation." "Unhyphenated Americans" (Byers 107) do not exist, or as Hackney puts it: "The 'hyphenated American' — African-American, for example, or Italian-American — is part of American tradition" (Hackney 218f.).

not assimilators, since they do not completely reject their own cultural heritage, but are still open-minded enough to continuously reconstruct their identity by taking in elements of different cultures.

When abroad, the experience of being a foreigner has a considerable impact on one's sense of belonging. Chinese novelist Gish Jen and Turkish novelist Elif Shafak, both writing in English, describe different aspects of this homelessness and "in-between-ness" in their works. The impression of being nowhere at home is of particular relevance when it comes to the characters' names, their approach to language, and also their perception of culinary habits, all of which are essential elements of their identity.

In the following, I will apply certain identity-related theories, among them Deleuze's and Guattari's, Hall's as well as Braidotti's ideas of fluidity, Kim's concept of intercultural personhood, Berry's notion of acculturative stress, and Pearce's Coordinated Management of Meaning Theory (CMM), to Gish Jen's novels *Typical American* and its sequel *Mona in the Promised Land* as well as to Elif Shafak's *The Saint of Incipient Insanities* and *The Bastard of Istanbul*.[2] The narrative style of both writers is humorous, and their way of describing the phenomenon of in-between-identity is rather similar. What Gish Jen and Elif Shafak also have in common is their perception of Eastern versus Western, traditional versus modern, and individual versus collective identity concepts of immigrant families. Their vision of identity as a fluid construct that can potentially evolve toward intercultural personhood is also more or less the same. However, with regard to their approach to hyphenated identity, Gish Jen more often underlines the separating function of the hyphen, whereas Elif Shafak emphasizes its uniting power. This tendency also becomes clear in the answers with which both writers kindly provided me regarding their perception of intercultural identity. I have taken these into account for my analysis.

Nomadic Existence: Open, Fluid Identities

The nomad is not at all the same as the migrant; for the migrant goes principally from one point to another, even if the second point

---

2. In referring to Gish Jen's and Elif Shafak's novels, I will use the following abbreviations: *TA* for *Typical American*, *ML* for *Mona in the Promised Land*, *SI* for *The Saint of Incipient Insanities* and *BI* for *The Bastard of Istanbul*.

is uncertain, unforeseen, or not well localized. But the nomad goes from point to point only as a consequence and as a factual necessity; in principle, points for him are relays along a trajectory. (Deleuze and Guattari 44)

Considering Deleuze's and Guattari's definition in *Nomadology*, some of Gish Jen's and Elif Shafak's characters can doubtlessly be regarded as nomads who constantly wander around in-between cultures, thus confirming the observation that "[...] the life of a nomad is the intermezzo" (ibid.). In *Nomadic Subjects*, Rosi Braidotti describes the nomad's identity in a similar way, highlighting the aspect of discontinuity: "Nomadic consciousness [...] consists in not taking any kind of identity as permanent: the nomad is only passing through; [...] he never takes on fully the limits of one national, fixed identity" (Braidotti 64). With the expression "volatility of identities," Bauman hints at the same phenomenon (178). In many respects, Braidotti's concept of the nomad whose identity is "made of transitions, successive shifts, and coordinated changes without an essential unity" (Braidotti 57) corresponds to Elif Shafak's notion of global souls who do not feel homeless but instead are under the impression of belonging everywhere despite their fragmented selves.

In both *Nomadology* and *Nomadic Subjects*, the authors state that nomads tend to cross cultural boundaries and are not concerned about the destination of their identity journey. Having no passport or too many of them, nomads are "cutting across different kinds and levels of identity" (Braidotti 64), which can sometimes result in a fragmentation of self. Stuart Hall calls this loss of a fixed identity "dislocation or de-centering of the subject," which means "de-centering individuals both from their place in the social and cultural world, and from themselves" (Hall 597). Keupp defines this pluralization of self that consists of multiple identities as "patchwork identity," an expression that Wolfgang Welsch also uses in his description of "transcultural identity."③ A crisis of identity can be the consequence in certain cases. It is the internal hybridity of cultures that has a considerable impact on the individual identity evolution. Welsch regards this phenomenon as "inner plurality,"

---

③ Wolfgang Welsch uses the expressions "cultural hybrids" and "patchwork identity" while explaining his own concept of "transcultural identity": "Die Menschen sind in ihrer kulturellen Formation zunehmend durch *mehrere* kulturelle Herkünfte und Verbindungen bestimmt, sind kulturelle Mischlinge. Heutige kulturelle Identität ist patchwork-Identität" ("Kultur" 151).

describing the idea of being transcultural within one's own self.④ In her book *Der Multikulti-Irrtum*, Seyran Ateş uses this concept to point at the link between globalization and the development of transcultural identities. Especially in the course of intercultural communication, different cultural elements mix and new, more complex identities develop, which can be regarded as "transcultural." Armanoush in Elif Shafak's *The Bastard of Istanbul* puts the same sensation into the following words: "Plurality means the state of being more than one" (*BI* 117).

During periods of identity crises, these patchwork elements might threaten the individual's sense of belonging and existential coherence. However, in the case of nomads, the initial feeling of homelessness later generally leads to a wish to overcome integration problems by accepting one's identity as something fluid, flexible, and always open for change. As Schultermandl and Toplu state, "protagonists [...] learn, often at crucial moments in their character development, that only by embracing a fluid sense of self can they reach a sense of belonging amidst this hyper-mobility" (Schultermandl and Toplu 13). In *The Saint of Incipient Insanities*, Elif Shafak depicts nomads as "noble and restless": "On the saddle of a nomad's horse there was no room for memento mori, family albums, childhood photos, love letters, or adolescence diaries [...]. Only freedom that merits the name, so pure and plain, could ride a nomad's horse" (*SI* 19).

In terms of identity, nomadic existence means freedom of choice, fluidity, flexibility, constant movement, and renewal. This perception of identity can remind us on the one hand of Robert J. Lifton's idea of a "protean self" which is defined as "fluid and many-sided" (Lifton 1), and on the other hand of Bertalanffy's "General System Theory" (1968), on which Kim's concept of "intercultural personhood" is based. Chen's and Collier's approach also highlights the constantly changing elements of identity despite a generally solid social embedding: "Cultural identities are understood as socially constructed, structurally enabled or constrained, discursively constituted locations of being, speaking, and acting that are enduring as well as constantly changing, multiple yet nonsummative, and political as well as paradoxical" (Chen and Collier 45).

Ludwig von Bertalanffy argues that all human beings can be

---

④ "Heutige Menschen sind zunehmend in sich transkulturell" (Welsch, "Kultur" 152).

regarded as "open systems" that are able to interact freely with their environment and never stop evolving. As this openness, according to Welsch, makes identity more "permeable"⑤ and suitable for "interlocking" ("Durchdringungen und Verflechtungen"), identity transformations continuously take place. Being an "open system" allows us to pick and reunite different cultural elements which sometimes seem to be incompatible. Mona's following observations about America and being American illustrate this patchwork concept in Gish Jen's *bildungsroman Mona in the Promised Land*: "American means being whatever you want, and I happened to pick being Jewish" (*ML* 49); "This is America. I can remember what I want, I can be what I want, I can —" (*ML* 248). As Parikh correctly observes, "to be American, from Mona's perspective, refers to the *process* rather than the *content* of identity" (Parikh 40). The idea of constant movement and change is inherent to this perception.

Armanoush in Elif Shafak's *The Bastard of Istanbul* is also aware of the flexible nature of identity, which she clearly articulates by using the expression "fluctuating": "I do know how it feels to be torn between opposite sides, unable to fully belong anywhere, constantly fluctuating between two states of existence" (*BI* 116). Here, seeing identity as an open system means unlimited freedom of choice, but also insecurity because of an instability that is caused by the sensation of being "in-between." Not without reason, Lai states that "nomadic desire is essentially about connection and renewal" (Lai 12) by highlighting at the same time the element of "discontinuity."

Part of the acculturation process are so-called "behavioral shifts (e.g., in ways of speaking, dressing, eating, and in one's cultural identity)" (Berry 702). Depending on the individual case, the impression of "living in between" and always being on the move can either have more positive or more negative connotations, including uncertainty, anxiety, and even depression. The identity of those who are characterized by a non-judgmental open-mindedness toward other cultures is generally fluid. These "nomads" easily engage in intercultural dialogue, communicate across cultures, and even succeed in transcending cultural boundaries, which increases the probability of achieving a state of "intercultural personhood"

⑤ In her article, Çağlar also uses the expressions "permeable" and "fluid" to describe the new openness of identity: "A growing number of people define themselves in terms of multiple national attachments and feel at ease with subjectivities that encompass plural and fluid cultural identities" (Çağlar 169).

described by Young Yun Kim as "a way of relating to others that conjoins and integrates, rather than separates and divides" (Kim, "Intercultural" 405). Most "moved-to-here" and "born-here" immigrants have in common that they sooner or later undergo a "nomadic journey of identity" (Lai 1). During the nomad's identity journey, parts of the old self are lost or transformed, so that a new identity can arise: "It's not so easy to get rid of your old self. On the other hand, nothing stands still. All growth involves change, all change involves loss" (*ML* 268). It is the immigrant's individual perception of identity that decides whether the impression of growth or that of loss dominates the integration process.

The Notion of "Home" and the Sensation of Loss

Together with being a nomad there comes, at first, inevitably a sensation of loss. As Friedman correctly points out, "home comes into being most powerfully when it is gone, lost, left behind, desired and imagined" (Friedman 202). In order to understand what might have been lost, it is necessary to define "home" as such. Welsch states that one needs to confirm home by choosing it as one's home once again, despite other geographic possibilities. To be able to do so, home must be left behind and seen from another perspective while being abroad. If, after this experience of being away, home is still regarded as home, it becomes a "cultural and human category."⑥

When Gish Jen's and Elif Shafak's characters talk about their ideas of "home," we can clearly observe, now and then, the notion of "loss" or of "missing" something familiar. Ralph in Jen's *Typical American*, for instance, seems to be under the impression of belonging nowhere: "He missed his home, missed having a place that was home. Home! And yet his life there, no: it didn't begin to fill the measure of his hopes for a life" (*TA* 33). Visibly, home has turned into a source of nostalgia for him, but at the same time it cannot be considered his real home as it no longer fulfills his expectations. According to Barnett W. Pearce, one of the founders of the Coordinated Management of Meaning Theory (CMM), the source of this nostalgia lies in pluralism that "is often experienced at

---

⑥ Home only turns into one's real home "wenn man sich (angesichts auch anderer Möglichkeiten) bewusst zu ihr entschieden, sie nachträglich eigens gewählt und bejaht hat. Nur dann ist ‚Heimat' keine naturwüchsige, sondern eine kulturelle und humane Kategorie" (Welsch, "Transkulturalität" 62).

first as a great liberation; after a while it may come to be felt as a great burden. There appears then a nostalgia, a yearning for the comforting certainties of the past. Pluralism, the erstwhile liberator, now becomes an enemy, the 'great satan' who must be fought in the name of timeless truths" (Pearce 36).

The fact that home is neither here nor there on the one hand results in disorientation and a sensation of loss, but on the other in a certain freedom of adding different cultural elements to one's identity and thus completing it. Whereas Ralph does not make much use of this opportunity, Ömer in Elif Shafak's *The Saint of Incipient Insanities* does. At the beginning, he feels as confused as Ralph: "'Lost' was precisely what [Ömer] was, and what he had been more than anything for the last five, ten, fifteen years of his life ..." (*SI* 14). But during his stay in America he gradually learns to appreciate his new nomadic identity, which allows him to be whoever he wants to be (an idea also elaborated in Gish Jen's *Mona in the Promised Land*): "He was a nobody to each and all of them, so pure and immaculate — absolutely nameless, pastless, and, thereby faultless. And because he was a nobody, he could be anybody" (*SI* 81f).

The sensation of loss is especially striking when it comes to names, language, and culinary culture. Identity is threatened when names are mispronounced or misspelled, when we can no longer use our mother tongue in order to express our thoughts or feelings, and when we are unfamiliar with the food we come across in another country. Experiencing one of these losses can already trigger a serious identity crisis, but when two or even all three elements come together, frequently the result is a so-called culture shock. Kim uses this expression in the context of her "stress-adaptation-growth dynamic," whereas Berry prefers the term "acculturative stress." In his article "Acculturation: Living successfully in two cultures," Berry points out that the idea of "shock" has quite negative connotations, while the word "culture" suggests that this shock is a reaction to one culture only (cf. Berry 708). In contrast, the expression "acculturation" implies the interaction of at least two cultures, during which phases of acculturation (learning) and deculturation (unlearning), integration and disintegration, as well as progression and regression alternate. "Acculturation" includes both positive and negative aspects, thus matching Kim's "stress-adaptation-growth dynamic" with its alternating draw-backs and leap-forwards.

Unlike Berry, Kim describes acculturation as "a process over which each individual has a degree of freedom or control, based on his or her predispositions, pre-existing needs and interests" (Kim, "Globalization" 87). However, it is rather questionable whether, in situations where important reference points are lost and acculturative stress occurs, individuals confronted with another culture are really able to control their identity development.

Regarding the concept of hyphenated identity, the experience of acculturative stress can underline the hyphen's separating function if the impression of having lost an essential part of oneself remains predominant. If, despite this loss, the individual's focus still lies on the enriching aspects of living abroad, the hyphen can be regarded as a bridge between two (or more) cultures. Gish Jen's and Elif Shafak's characters deal with the sensation of loss in different ways, depending on whether they are separators, assimilators, or global souls. In the following, I will examine the topics "names," "language," and "culinary culture" with regard to the association of loss.

Loss of Name — Change of Identity

"Names are the welcoming bridges to the significant other's castle of existence [...]. That is how it is with names, the easiest thing to learn about human beings, yet the most difficult to possess" (*SI* 23f.). Indeed, maybe one of the most traumatizing changes Gish Jen's and Elif Shafak's characters experience when they come to America is the transformation of their names, often causing a "draw back" in their identity development. In terms of spelling and pronunciation, an adaptation of their original name to "Western standards" is expected from Chinese immigrants, for example. In her novel *Typical American*, Gish Jen describes how in an instant Yifeng turns into Ralph for purely administrative reasons. Having no English name to write down on his forms, he asks the university secretary Cammy to choose one for him. Cammy runs through the names of her ex-boyfriends and finally picks "Ralph" for him. This arbitrary way of naming him shortly afterwards results in Ralph's first existential crisis, which is the reason why "his stomach puckered with anxiety" (*TA* 11). The fact that he feels "anxiety" and in *Mona in the Promised Land* still suffers from a "trouble with his stomach" (*ML* 243) already highlights his fear of losing an essential part of himself. He cannot identify with a name that does not at all resemble his former one (and thus his former self).

While on the one hand, Ralph leaves his Chinese name behind because he wants to fit in by "trying to be like other people" (*TA* 11), his language skills and cultural background at the beginning make it impossible for him to feel American: "He refused to be made an American citizen. He thumbed his nose at the relief act meant to help him, as though to claim his home was China was to make China indeed his home" (*TA* 23). It is therefore not surprising that his change of name causes inner conflicts. For Ralph's wife Helen, the gap between her Chinese and American name is smaller, as her real name "Hailan" (*TA* 52) phonetically resembles her new one. Such similarities can also be observed between "Kailan" and its American variation "Callie", as well as between "Mengna" and its American version "Mona". Even though in all cases the poetic meanings of these names ("Sea Blue", "Open Orchid" and "Dream Graceful") get lost, the alienation effect seems to be less striking than between the names "Yifeng" and "Ralph" which have strictly nothing in common.

In her novel *The Saint of Incipient Insanities*, Elif Shafak describes a similar link between names and identity. The individual change Turkish student Ömer experiences is certainly less radical than Ralph's, but he nevertheless seems to be traumatized by the transformation of his name — a topic that accompanies him throughout the novel: "[...] Ömer knew exactly what he had left behind: his dots! Back in Turkey, he used to be ÖMER ÖZSİPAHİLİOĞLU. Here in America, he had become OMAR OZSIPAHILIOGLU" (*SI*, 5). Ömer and Ralph share the impression of having lost a part of their identity together with the adaptation of their names to the new country. This idea of loss, which also has an impact on one's sense of belonging and understanding of home, is summarized in the following statement:

> As names adjust to a foreign country, something is always lost — be it a dot, a letter, or an accent. What happens to your name in another territory is similar to what happens to a voluminous pack of spinach when cooked — some new taste can be added to the main ingredient, but its size shrinks visibly. It is this cutback a foreigner learns first. The primary requirement of accommodation in a strange land is the estrangement of the hitherto most familiar: your name. (*SI*, 6)

The feelings caused by this change are predominantly negative, described by words like "lost," "shrinks," "cutback," and "estrangement." According to a theory by Berry, the identity development that is related to the transformation of a name could be regarded as the result of the melting pot phenomenon⑦ which is defined as "assimilation [...] sought by the dominant acculturating group" (Berry 706). In the cases of Ralph, Ömer, and also of his roommate Abed who is called "Abdoul" (*SI* 177, 201) or "Halid" (*SI* 115, 125) by Ömer's American girlfriends, a part of the "fitting in process" is (involuntarily) forced on the individual by the outside world during which their names are mispronounced and thus transformed. What sounds unfamiliar is either adapted to more American phonetic "standards" or — in an attempt to protect its exoticness — made even more exotic.

The links between names and identity which Elif Shafak describes in *The Saint of Incipient Insanities* are numerous. It is especially Ömer who seems to define himself through his name and often "lament[s] his lost dots" (*SI* 216), but at the same time he understands that this loss can also be his gain when it comes to his integration process: "His dots were excluded for him to be better included. After all, Americans, just like everyone else, relished familiarity — in names they could pronounce, sounds they could resonate, even if they didn't make much sense one way or the other" (*SI* 5). Throughout the novel, it becomes quite clear that this transformation on the one hand has been a trauma for Ömer, but on the other hand serves as a superficial means of adaptation which he sometimes even tries to accelerate: "Foreigners are people with either one or more parts of their names in the dark. [...] Ömer had replaced his name with the less arduous and more presentable Omar or Omer, depending on the speaker's choice" (*SI* 6). Similarly to Ralph, he abandons a part of himself with his original name in order not to be immediately categorized as a stranger. Now and then, the sensation of loss leads to an identity crisis, as is demonstrated by Ömer's following questions: "Who am I, what do I want, do I really have to want ... someone, something ... do I really have to be ... someone, something?" (*SI* 262). How to be true to one's former self but still adapt to a new culture is one of the fundamental issues Elif Shafak deals with here.

In contrast to the imposed transformation of names spoken of

---

⑦ Kim describes the link between melting pot and identity as follows: "Replacing the traditional 'melting pot' metaphor with newer ones such as 'mosaic,' 'quilt,' and 'salad bowl,' the pluralistic construction of personhood has elevated collective interests as a concern to the individual above their implications for personal self-interest" (Kim, "Globalization" 85).

above, Ralph's daughter Callie, who is a second-generation Chinese-American, decides to change her name in order to become more Chinese. Even though she does not speak a word of Chinese and has never been to China, Callie feels a certain nostalgia for the homeland of her parents (maybe also because some of her physical features make it difficult for her to feel a 100 percent American). In her endeavor to belong somewhere, she even becomes more Chinese than the Chinese,[8] starts to wear cloth shoes that are no longer used in China and calls herself "Kailan":

> And why does she call herself Kailan? So much trouble to find her a nice English name, why does she have to call herself something no one can spell? She says she's proud to be Asian American, that's why she's using her Chinese name. (Her original name, she calls it.) But what in the world is an Asian American? That's what Ralph and Helen want to know. (*ML* 301)

In Callie's case, there is an obvious overemphasis of the Asian and a clear rejection of the American which makes the connecting hyphen between Asian and American disappear. In contrast to this separator-like behavior, the identity development of Callie's sister Mona goes in the exactly opposite direction. Having accepted the feeling of belonging nowhere, being "a stranger in a strange land" (*ML* 33), Mona gradually becomes so flexible in her perception of identity that she starts to belong anywhere. While Callie clings to her new/original name Kailan, Mona is always on the move and constantly changes names during her nomadic existence. For her, America is the country of endless possibilities, which is why she can turn from Mona into Callie or from Chang into Changowitz. She can even lead the life of "a more or less genuine Catholic Chinese Jew" (*ML* 44) called "Ruth." Unlike her sister, Mona seems to feel at home in America because this is the country where she can be whoever she wants to be.

A similar flexibility in terms of names and identity can be observed in Elif Shafak's character Armanoush. On the one hand, her American mother Rose decides to change "Armanoush" into "Amy" to wipe out all thought of her Armenian ex-husband's family. This Americanization of her name forces Armanoush to act like an American in every imaginable way, which includes the obligation to

---

[8]   A similar phenomenon can be observed in Zadie Smith's *White Teeth*, where second-generation immigrant Magid becomes "more English than the English" (Smith 406).

eat exclusively American food in her mother's house. On the other hand, her real name "Armanoush" automatically makes her a part of the Armenian community even though she does not speak the Armenian language. Armanoush herself chooses the name Madame My-Exiled-Soul (a tribute to Armenian novelist Zabel Yessaian who spent most of her life in exile) as her chatroom identity, which clearly reflects her sensation of homelessness. Like Mona, Armanoush adapts to her respective names, acting as American "Amy" with her mother, as Armenian "Armanoush" in her grandmother's house and as an Armenian-American on the search for her identity when she is Madame My-Exiled-Soul, i.e., a hyphenated existence. While having a conversation in the chatroom, she describes this back and forth between her identities as follows: "You guys were all born into the Armenian community and never had to prove you were one of them. Whereas I have been [...] constantly fluctuating between a proud but traumatized Armenian family and a hysterically anti-Armenian mom" (*BI* 119).

The impression of "fluctuating in between" names and different cultural worlds corresponds to the concept of "open systems" and "nomadic identities" discussed above. Depending on the context, Armanoush's identity focus and thus her sense of belonging and home changes, which becomes particularly obvious when she arrives in Turkey. While looking for her family's past, she suddenly feels more Armenian than American: "I am Armenian ... well, Armenian American" (*BI* 157). There are times like these when there seems to be no uniting hyphen between her two identities, but toward the end of the novel, the Armenian and American cultural elements gradually become more connected and turn Armanoush into a global soul. In her, Mona's, and Ömer's cases, the hyphen eventually starts to serve as a bridge between cultures.

Lack of Words, Loss of Identity

Besides the transformation of names, the change of language also plays an important part with regard to a foreigner's identity development abroad. In *Nomadic Subjects*, Rosi Braidotti dedicates the chapter "By Way of Nomadism" partly to the language development of a polyglot whom she describes as a "linguistic nomad" (Braidotti 29) always being "in between languages" (Braidotti 41). Just as those who have a nomadic identity need to adapt to the constant, rather arbitrary transformation of their names, they also need to live with the fact that the nature of language is "treacherous" and that "words have a way of not standing still, of following their own ways" (Braidotti 29). When abroad, a direct confrontation with the arbitrariness of language takes place which we hardly ever notice while speaking our mother tongue but of which we become very much aware when learning or practicing another language.

Being an immigrant means — at least initially — losing one's linguistic roots and points of reference. According to Braidotti, this experience can lead to "resignation or despair" (Braidotti 29). Additionally, the sensation that home can no longer be found in one's native language is increased by another fact: immigrants belonging to the category of "hyphenated subjects" often use words and formulations that are neither part of their mother tongue nor of standard English, but can be considered "a concoction of their own making" (Braidotti 59 f.). In Elif Shafak's *The Saint of Incipient Insanities*, the difficulties foreigners are facing when trying to communicate in a language that is not their own are described in a humorous way. The lack of words in another language results in a certain linguistic creativity which, despite the circumstances, enables a more or less efficient dialogue: "That was the second best thing about a foreigner conversing with another foreigner in a language that was foreign to both. When one of them couldn't find a particular word and neither could the other, still they would be able to understand each other entirely" (*SI* 10).

As time goes by, nomads who constantly wander around between different cultures and identities develop a more flexible perception of language in general. In *By Way of Nomadism*, Braidotti correctly observes that the nomad is "in transit" between languages (Braidotti 39) and does not focus on the importance of a steady mother tongue for the identity building process. Real nomads sooner or later seem to lose the sensation of having a mother tongue, as they continuously navigate between languages and sometimes are not even able to recall in which language they sing, dream or love (cp. Braidotti 40). For them, language turns into a mere tool of communication and exchange, having no longer the function of creating a sensation of home. Resulting from the gradual disappearance of their mother tongue, nomads often develop their own kind of language, i.e., their individual way of speaking. Between foreigners, in particular, the lack of nuances and other linguistic difficulties lead to new forms of communication, in which paradoxically mutual understanding is achieved in spite of all missing words.

Articulating a Fragmented Self

In Gish Jen's and Elif Shafak's novels, some characters (like Ralph and Helen in *Typical American* or Abed in *The Saint of Incipient Insanities*) speak broken English with a strong accent while others are able to express themselves more or less fluently. However, in the United States, English is the mother tongue of second- and especially third-generation immigrants who no longer understand the language of their ancestors. In many cases, language turns into a limiting factor when trying to put one's whole self (and particularly one's emotional states) into precise words and define one's identity. Only bilinguals might have experienced the sensation of feeling equally at home in two languages, but neither Gish Jen nor Elif Shafak present the reader with such a character. As Elif Shafak describes in *The Saint of Incipient Insanities*, living abroad leads to a gradual loss of nuances in one's mother tongue, which has a considerable impact on one's identity development. This sensation of loss is expressed in the following extract:

> Just like patients still feeling their amputated limbs long after the surgery, people who have been entirely and brusquely cut from their native tongue, and have henceforth learned to survive in a foreign language, somehow continue sensing the disjointed words of their distant past, and try to construct sentences with words they no longer possess. (*SI* 11)

While some words are lost in the native tongue, new ones are found in the target language. During this learning process, the experience of culture shock seems to be stronger for those who do not speak English well enough to express themselves without much difficulty, such as for instance Ralph in Gish Jen's novel *Typical American* whose lack of understanding and whose faulty pronunciation immediately make him feel uncomfortable and embarrassed: "'Name?' he repeated, or rather 'nem,' which he knew to be wrong. He turned red, thinking of his trouble with long a's, th's, l's, consonants at the end of words" (*TA* 9). This feeling of shame as a consequence of insufficient linguistic competence can often be observed during the first confrontations with another culture abroad. Resulting from his problems with the English language, Ralph starts to "hate the alphabet" (*TA*, 9), which doubtlessly reflects a phase of acculturative stress.

In *The Bastard of Istanbul*, a confrontation with Turkish,

Armenian, and English as a foreign language takes place quite frequently during intercultural encounters. As a result of limited or entirely lacking linguistic skills, "the Other" is sometimes regarded as a threat. In certain cases, the characters also seem to lose a part of their identity and with it their sense of belonging, since they are not able to express and define themselves. Language barriers often lead to emotional ones which can only be overcome after a period of stress that is part of the "stress-adaptation-growth dynamic" described by Kim. Mustafa's sister Banu, for example, faces such a stressful situation the moment she hears the sound of English with which she is not familiar: "'What are you whistling?' Auntie Banu asked suspiciously. She didn't know any English and was deeply distrustful of any language that made her miss something obvious" (*BI* 69). The expressions "suspiciously" and "deeply distrustful" indicate that Banu is afraid of "the Other" hidden behind words she does not understand.

The Armenian-American Armanoush experiences a similar sensation during her stay in Turkey. It is the contrast between having just heard her native language English on the phone while speaking with her mother, and the "exotic" reality around her that triggers a feeling of alienation: "When she hung up Armanoush looked around her and felt a deep estrangement. The Turkish rugs, the old-fashioned bedside lamps, the unfamiliar furniture, books and newspapers that spoke another language ... Suddenly she felt a panic that she hadn't felt since she was a small child" (*BI* , 167). Negative emotions like "estrangement" and "panic" underline the unpredictable impact of the unfamiliar. Ralph, Banu, and Armanoush thus all three have the sensation in common that their respective mother tongue is threatened during a confrontation with "the Other."

Accents as Indicators of Foreignness

In another language, the "proof of foreignness" (*SI* 213) can be found in the difficulty of handling nuances. We define through precise words who we are, but the moment these words lose their meaning in a different country and are replaced by others that we are not able to use and pronounce like a native speaker, a feeling of disorientation and alienation is the natural consequence. In the course of time, the fact of constantly living abroad and between countries leads to the impression that nomads are no longer in possession of "that vast and yet familiar land called Mother-tongue" (*SI* 13) which once had a reassuring effect since it created a sense of belonging. They even start to have an accent in every language they speak, which at times contributes to their sensation of having lost their home and can trigger different forms of identity crises. Rosi Braidotti describes this phenomenon as follows: "A sort of polymorphous perversity accompanies a polyglot's accent, which reveals the capacity to slip in between the languages, stealing acoustic traces here, diphthong sounds there, in a constant and childlike game of *persiflage*" (Braidotti 40).

With regard to their mother tongue Turkish, Elif Shafak's characters Ömer and Mustafa experience such a linguistic in-between state, after having spent several years in the United States. The day they decide to visit their home country, their way of speaking Turkish has changed so much that natives do not even consider them Turks. Such a vehement change naturally also has a direct impact on their identity perception, which becomes clear in the following description: "Although Ömer had talked with him in Turkish several times, the boy still seemed to refuse to take him for a Turk" (*SI* 324). It even happens to Ömer that he no longer knows when to speak Turkish and when to speak English: "Ömer had spoken Turkish with Gail and English with Defne" (*SI* 284). In the streets of Istanbul, he is often taken for a tourist and immediately categorized as American: "Somehow Gail's presence was sufficient to render them both Americans" (*SI* 330).

Mustafa's fate is similar to Ömer's, the only difference being that from the very beginning his aim is to concentrate on losing his accent in English and to forget all his Turkish. Howard Giles's Communication Accommodation Theory (CAT), which is an extension of his Speech Accommodation Theory, explains that people have a tendency to "adapt to each other's communicative behaviors in terms of a wide range of linguistic-prosodic-nonverbal features including speech rate, pausal phenomena and utterance length, phonological variants, smiling, gaze, and so on" (Giles 7). This so-called "convergence," which can also be applied to intercultural face-to-face interactions, seems to occur especially during intercultural interactions in which the foreigner tries to imitate the native speaker's accent. This turns out to be true in Mustafa's case and can also be applied to Gish Jen's Sherman in *Mona in the Promised Land*.⑨

⑨ The case of Gish Jen's Sherman in *Mona in the Promised Land* also proves Giles's theory, as the following extract demonstrates: "It is like old times, except that Sherman's English is [sic!] so greatly improved that his voice itself seems somehow to have improved along with it. Apparently that's what immersion in another culture will do" (*ML* 227).

Motivated by the desire to leave his past behind, Mustafa succeeds in completely assimilating to American culture: "Armanoush's stepfather was thought to be American, presumably from the Midwest" (*BI* 93). But just like Ömer, Mustafa also has moments of confusion when, after having spent many years in America, he is suddenly confronted with the Turkish language: "For a split second Mustafa hesitated, not because he didn't know what he would like to drink but because he didn't know which language to reply in" (*BI* 289). For assimilators like him who are "caught in an in-between state," the past appears a burden bearing "a fossilized definition of language" (Braidotti 59). The shifts between different accents "oscillating madly between nonpresence and omnipresence" (*SI* 4) can certainly have destabilizing psychological effects.

However, with Gish Jen's characters, the situation is slightly different: Ralph especially does not make a real effort to work on his English accent (even though he tries to improve his grammar), insisting on saying "Tank you" (*TA* 12) and systematically speaking Chinese with his wife at home. According to Giles's Communication Accommodation Theory, the linguistic behavior of Ralph and also of Abed in Elif Shafak's *The Saint of Incipient Insanities* can be called "divergence," i.e., the (mostly subconscious) tendency to underline their difference and their "us-versus-them"-attitude by using a strong accent. The impression of feeling at home neither in one's mother tongue nor in a foreign language naturally also has a considerable impact on the perception of one's own identity.

Once the first experiences of acculturative stress are overcome, the positive aspects of such a "linguistic loss" can be noticed. In America, Mustafa, Ömer, Ralph, Helen, and other characters learn that new words contribute to the evolution of more flexible identities in another country. Abed, Piyu, and Ömer all show the same reaction, for instance, when the American Gail speaks English with them. They "absorbed her jargon like a dry sponge absorbs water. The argot they snatched from her, expressions they heard for the first time, they thrust into their pockets, and once outside the house, they instantly tried to use these words, like a child eager to skate with his new skates" (*SI* 289).

The behavior of all three foreign students shows that once the phase of linguistic stress is overcome, the stage between adaptation and growth begins. New English words are "absorbed," "snatched," and used actively at the first possible occasion. This is one step forward toward a successful intercultural interaction. However, draw-backs can occur at any time, as Ömer's following spontaneous exclamation in Turkish shows: "'Arroz, çekil üstümeden.' Bizarre but true. With animals, plants, and babies, foreigners speak in their native tongue when there is no one around" (*SI* 241).

Searching for Linguistic Roots

Especially for the children of immigrants who do not speak the language of their ancestors, this linguistic lack can turn into a major identity problem. English is the mother tongue of the second and third generation immigrants to the United States. However, there is always a part of their identity for which they are consciously or unconsciously searching in their parents' and/or grandparents' home country. In Gish Jen's *Mona in the Promised Land*, Callie and Mona look Chinese, which is why people take it for granted that they also speak the language of a country they have never seen: "'Of course, she speaks it,' says Eliot when Sumner asks. 'Open your eyes'" (*ML* 182). The fact that neither of them understands enough Chinese to be able to rearrange their aunt's books is reason enough to trigger Callie's identity crisis: "What did they mean? Callie, leafing through one particularly marked-up volume, began to cry. The clothes had been easy, familiar; this belonged to a stranger" (*TA* 290).

It is not surprising that traumatizing experiences like these make Callie want to learn the language of her parents. But while the Chinese they speak changed during their stay in America, the "Harvard Chinese" Callie is picking up seems to be an entirely different language: "They sense that the language she's learning to speak is not their language at all" (*ML* 128). Having started to take Chinese lessons, everything about Callie becomes more and more Chinese, until almost nothing of her former "American-ness" is left. This development is a strong indicator of an ongoing identity crisis during which Callie tries to find her roots and understand her "second self."

Like Callie, Armanoush in Elif Shafak's *The Bastard of Istanbul* is looking for her personal history by searching for traces of her Armenian family in Istanbul. She does not understand or speak enough Armenian to build herself a home in the Armenian-American community. As she points out to Armenian-Americans in the chatroom, she feels "on this threshold since the day I was born" (*BI* 119), and needs to take a trip toward her past in order to learn more about her "Armenian-ness." When she comes across Aram, the Armenian boyfriend of Mustafa's sister in Istanbul, she understands for the first time that it is possible to live with a fluid, constantly changing identity without suffering from it: "[...] Aram could *not* be Armenian or Turk or any other nationality. Aram could only be Aram, entirely sui generis" (*BI*, 247).

While Callie tries to learn the language of her ancestors in order to become more Chinese, Armanoush does not undertake any such linguistic endeavors. Thanks to her intercultural exchange with Aram, she understands that "global souls" speak a universal language comprehensible to other global souls. Learning a foreign language, even though it can help in the process of discovering another culture, is not indispensable when it comes to acquiring intercultural personhood.

Individualistic versus Collectivistic Culinary Cultures

The impression of feeling at home abroad is not only increased by hearing one's own name correctly pronounced or by communicating in one's mother tongue, but also by eating familiar food. It is no coincidence that in their novels, both Gish Jen and Elif Shafak refer to the kitchen as a place that creates a sense of belonging. Berry, among others, states that the process of acculturation entails "sharing each other's food preferences" (Berry 700). While in America eating is rather an individualistic action, China, Turkey, and Armenia are characterized by collectivistic culinary cultures. It is exactly this cultural clash between individualistic and collectivistic eating habits that can lead to phases of culture shock, especially at the beginning of one's stay abroad. The contrast between individualistic and collectivistic culinary cultures is pointed out in *Mona in the Promised Land* in the following way: "Or is it just that other people grew up eating their individual portions from their individual plates; whereas the Changs help themselves from bowls in the middle of the table, and no one can leave until everyone else is done" (*ML* 67).

Similar observations concerning collectivistic culinary habits can be made in *The Bastard of Istanbul* where Mustafa's sister tells her daughter: "But do not forget, my dear, [...]that you are a Kazancı, not a vegetarian! [...] And we Kazancıs love red meat! The redder, the greasier, the better!" (*BI* 74). The culinary rituals of "we Kazancıs" doubtlessly has a considerable impact on the development of an equally collectivistic identity. The same is true in the case of Mona's family where no one "is allowed to prefer not to eat something" (*ML* 29). When members of such collectivistic cultures are confronted with the individualistic American way of life or when Americans suddenly have to deal with collectivistic eating habits, they lose their culinary references. Whereas assimilators try to eat only typically local dishes and do not want to be reminded of the food that is characteristic of their home country, separators — after a period of acculturative stress — start to cling even more to their own culinary culture. Such "draw-back" reactions can appear at any time, but can also be overcome by positive experiences with certain "exotic" dishes, as is illustrated in Gish Jen's and particularly in Elif Shafak's works.

Kitchen Rituals and Sense of Belonging

As Kittler et al. point out in *Food and Culture*, "[f]oods that demonstrate affiliation with a culture are usually introduced during childhood and are associated with security or good memories" (Kittler et al. 5). Fischler argues in a similar way, saying that "food and cuisine are a quite central component of the sense of collective belonging" (Fischler 280). In Gish Jen's and Elif Shafak's works, dishes typical of the respective home countries are associated with identity elements of a former life. They often create a feeling of home and can thus serve as a source of comfort.

For example, Ömer in *The Saint of Incipient Insanities* tries to promote his roommates' sense of belonging of by bringing home specialties of their respective countries, "couscous with lamb and sweetened figs as a favor to Abed" and "soft beef tacos with salsa" (*SI* 107) for Piyu. In addition, being in a kitchen that smells like one's childhood to a certain extent seems to put the feeling of alienation caused by being abroad into perspective. In the case of Piyu's girlfriend Alegre, this connection between "kitchen" and "belonging" is summarized in the following way: "Alegre does not know if being in the kitchen makes her happy or not. But perhaps that's not the point anyway. Homelands are not, she senses, about happiness after all. In any case, the only thing she can be sure of is that here, in the kitchen, she belongs" (*SI* 338). When Amed's mother Zahra comes over to America for a visit, she immediately takes over that place of the house and turns it into "*her* kitchen" (*SI* 184) in order to create a home for herself abroad. Having her own territory where nobody can "interfere" (*SI* 184) makes her feel more secure.

In their chapter "Acculturation of Food Habits," Kittler et al.

state that in contrast to learning another language or adapting to certain dress codes, "culturally based food habits are often among the last practices people change through acculturation" (Kittler et al. 6). This observation turns out to be true in Gish Jen's *Typical American*, for instance, where Ralph's rather open-minded sister Theresa is surprised to see Helen focus exclusively on Chinese food: "When she could not have Chinese food, she did not eat" (*TA* 62). The fact that Helen always cooks and eats "Chinese style" (*TA* 228) and no longer tolerates any other kinds of flavors shows that she does not feel at home in America: "'In Shanghai you ate foreign food,' Theresa said [...]. 'Why shouldn't you eat it here?' Still, for a long time, Helen would not, which they both thought would make her sick. She was not at home enough, though, even to fall ill" (*TA* 62 f.). This clinging to one's original culinary culture is easier than clinging to one's name or native language since "eating is usually done in the privacy of the home, hidden from observation by majority culture members" (Kittler et al. 6).

In collectivistic cultures, a sense of community is created in the kitchen, whereas in America this place of the house has rather a pragmatic purpose. While abroad, the loss of a particular kitchen atmosphere and the familiar culinary routines that accompany it can have a destabilizing effect as far as identity is concerned. Ralph's "digestive problems" (*TA* 9) and homesickness (*TA* 57) as well as Ömer's diarrhea (*SI* 257) could, by the way, be regarded as a general psychological consequence of deculturation. When it comes to certain kitchen rituals, however, even assimilators sometimes experience moments of draw-backs, which can be seen in Mustafa's case. Mustafa feels the need to bring some collectivistic atmosphere into the individualistic kitchen of his American wife Rose to make the place cozier and more comfortable: "He didn't like the stools and instead kept two solid-wood honey pine dining chairs in the kitchen, one for him and the other for him too" (*BI* 265). He finds it "soothing" (*BI* 292) when Rose prepares pancakes or other dishes in this kitchen, and thus creates a sensation of home that resembles the one he was used to as a child.

Mona, who at times is torn between her American and Chinese identities, also experiences the kitchen as calming: "How different the kitchen air feels from the air outside! It smells different too, of course — like sesame oil today. But mostly she notices how enveloping it is, how moist, and warm. She feels as though she breathes differently in this house, her home. ... All this is familiar"

(*ML* 293). It is the "food security"[10](Koç and Welsh 9) subconsciously associated with the kitchen atmosphere that plays a considerable role in the perception of one's identity abroad. The moment collectivistic and individualistic rituals as well as flavors of different culinary cultures start to mix in a kitchen, the acculturation process can be regarded as successful.

Eating Together as a Social Event

"Food plays a key role in human socialization" (Koç and Welsh 1), and especially so in collectivistic cultures. This also explains why intercultural communication mostly takes place at the dinner table. Sharing a meal is a "social event" (cp. Krusche 194) during which all kinds of topics (ranging from superficial gossip to serious issues) are discussed with both family members and guests. In her novels, Elif Shafak illustrates how the dinner table is indeed the ideal place for intercultural exchange, where different concepts ranging from the Muslim sabr to the verb aguantar in Spanish can be discussed (cp. *SI* 144). When it comes to food, it is not necessary to speak the same language in order to understand each other.

Koç and Welsh state that "otherness" is identified through food, whereas "others sharing 'our' taste, offer us [a] symbolic welcome" (Koç and Welsh 9). This means that the action of enjoying a meal together abroad eliminates certain cultural barriers and makes "the Other" appear less frightening. "Do you like the food?" (*SI* 331) might therefore be one of the first questions foreigners have to answer in collectivistic cultures. If they appreciate the dishes that are presented to them, they have already made the first step in the process of turning from "the Other" into "one of us."

Such a scene in which food turns into a common ground for intercultural exchange can be found in Elif Shafak's *The Bastard of Istanbul*, where Armanoush, even though she does not speak a word of Turkish, engages in a conversation about some dishes she recognizes on the table of her Turkish hosts: "'What a gorgeous table.' She beamed. 'These are all my favorite foods. I see you have made hummus, baba ghanoush, *yalanci sarma* ... and look at this, you have baked *churek*!'" (*BI* 156). The fact that Armanoush knows some food-related words in Turkish because of her Armenian

---

[10] Dietrich Krusche also includes the yearning for continuity and sameness in his perception of food security: "Sicherheit/Kontinuität/Gleichheit" (Krusche 202).

heritage shows how universal the culinary language is: "I do not speak the Turkish language, unfortunately, but I guess I speak the Turkish cuisine" (*BI* 156). In *The Saint of Incipient Insanities*, we come across a similar scenario where Ömer's American girlfriend Gail manages to discuss the use of saffron in Ottoman-Turkish dishes with the taxi driver despite their respective language problems: "'And no Turkish saffron?' the driver asked in broken English [...]. But Gail seemed ready for the question. In a second, she was naming Ottoman-Turkish dishes made with saffron, widening the smile on the driver's face with each name she pronounced in her broken Turkish" (*SI* 346). Both examples illustrate that the language of food is accessible to everyone. Exchanging ideas about culinary diversity generally creates a peaceful atmosphere that also awakes interest in and promotes discussions of other cultural particularities.

Dong-Lin Zheng correctly observes that Mona in Gish Jen's *Mona in the Promised Land* speaks the language of Chinese food like an expert even though she does not understand a word of Chinese (cp. Zheng 79): "Mona tells her she knows Chinese." "*Byeh fa-foon*," she says. "*Shee-veh. Ji-nu.*" This is Shanghai dialect, meaning, "Stop acting crazy. Rice gruel. Soy sauce" (*ML* 5f). Such a natural identification with the culinary culture of their ancestors is also described in *Typical American* where both Mona and Callie naturally say the Chinese names of certain dishes during their visit to Chinatown:

> English-speaking or not, Mona and Callie knew this much Chinese:
> *da bao* were big buns with chicken and egg and juicy chunks of
> Chinese sausage [...]; *cha shao* was roast pork. *Zongzi* were lotus
> leaf-wrapped bundles of sticky rice [...]. *Jiaozi* were the pork
> dumplings they went down the block to eat with *jiang you* and
> vinegar [...]. (*TA* 132)

In this extract, it becomes obvious that the dishes which are associated with one's childhood remain part of one's cultural heritage. After all, certain kinds of food we know from our childhood define an essential part of our identity, as shown in the cases of Armanoush, Mona, and Callie. For those having "hyphenated identities," food can sometimes even be the only cultural connection to the country of their ancestors. This observation is not surprising, since eating habits mostly develop during childhood and are strongly influenced by one's parents, especially in collectivistic cultures. This is the reason why Armanoush fluently speaks the "language of Armenian cuisine" while Mona and Callie know how to pronounce the names of Chinese dishes.

Culinary Culture and Identity

In *Food and Culture*, Kittler et al. highlight the link between culinary culture and identity as follows: "Beyond self-identification, incorporation can signify collective association. What one eats defines who one is, culturally speaking, and, conversely, who one is not" (Kittler et al. 5). Koç and Welsh underline the same aspects by claiming that "as we learn what to eat, how to eat, when to eat, we learn 'our' culture, 'our' norms and 'our' values and through this process we learn who 'we' are" (Koç and Welsh 1). In Gish Jen's *Mona in the Promised Land*, this connection between eating habits and identity is clearly stated: "'Think about what she grew up eating,' they say. 'That's who she is, you can't deny it'" (*ML* 56). Jennifer Ann Ho also stresses this connection when analyzing Mona's "food stories" or "food tropes": "Like Mona's ethnic identity, food is both a fixed, yet fluid variable, one used to ostensibly fix her place in American society, as food is often believed to signal essentialism. However, it reveals its instability through its mutability, since food, like people, can assume a variety of ethnic guises" (Ho 126). When arriving in another country, the loss of one's culinary references that formerly created a sense of belonging can lead to a feeling of disorientation and anxiety. The culinary habits experienced abroad often have a considerable impact on the perception of one's identity, as Fischler points out in "Food, Self, and Identity": "If one does not know what one is eating, one is liable to lose the awareness or certainty of what one is oneself" (Fischler 290). Sharing a meal can serve to bridge cultural gaps, claims Jennifer Ann Ho with regard to Gish Jen's novel *Mona in the Promised Land* — an observation that is also valid for Elif Shafak's novels.

For those leading a nomadic existence between different cultures, this link between losing one's culinary references and having to redefine a part of one's identity can become a source of inner conflicts. Depending on the respective phase of the "stress-adaptation-growth dynamic," i.e., "draw-back" or "leap-forward," the confrontation with exotic dishes can trigger various reactions ranging from aversion to curiosity.[①]

[①] Krusche describes this wide range of reactions toward exotic food, including the perception of unfamiliar dishes as source of confusion, doubt, pride, anger, gratitude, and even self-loss (cf. Krusche 198): "Erfahrungen höchsten Genusses wie tiefsten Ekels — Glück und Bei-mir-Sein ebenso erleben wie Verlorenheit, Leere, Verzweiflung — bis hin zu dem, was man Selbstverlust nennt" (Krusche 202).

In both Gish Jen's and Elif Shafak's novels, certain culinary experiences and identity changes go hand in hand. The day Callie decides to become Chinese, she bans all American ingredients from her everyday diet: "Instead of Wheaties or an English muffin, Callie is eating *shee-veh*, with assorted pickled and deep-fried condiments, something like what their parents used to eat in China" (*ML* 168). This tendency of overemphasizing one culture while completely rejecting the other is typical of those who feel torn between identities. A similar behavioral pattern can be observed in *The Bastard of Istanbul*, where the American woman Rose after her traumatizing marriage with an Armenian throws out all exotic ingredients as a kind of symbolic action after her divorce. She keeps the "Armenian cuisine as far from the borders of her kitchen as possible," and cannot hinder herself from "vilifying it to her neighbors and friends" (*BI* 100). Kittler et al. point out that distinguishing certain types of food as foreign or exotic can serve to "maintain group separation" (Kittler et al. 5). Focusing on one cuisine only means making a clear identity statement, i.e., in Callie's case becoming more Chinese, in Rose's case going back to being "purely American."

Together with the change of eating habits, often triggered by a negative intercultural experience, comes a general aversion against "the Other." However, the contrary can also occur: where intercultural culinary exchange is successful, the perception of a foreign culture can even turn separators into global souls. In this case, the concept of identity is revisited and reconstructed, while a new, larger sense of belonging gradually develops: "The multicultural cuisine may offer us a glimpse of widening notions of identity, self, and belonging" (Koc and Welsh 10). Abed in *The Saint of Incipient Insanities*, for instance, does not like to mix culinary cultures and wants to put national labels on every kind of food. For him, something like "*ChineseVietnameseBurmeseJapanese cuisine*" (*SI* 140) is not an option, whereas his mother Zahra observes American eating rituals with curiosity and is of the opinion that "The guest eats what the host offers" (*SI* 182). As these examples show, food preferences and resistance to certain kinds of food can reflect tendencies of acculturation, assimilation, adaptation, or integration (cp. Koç and Welsh 1).

In *An Ethics of Betrayal*, Parikh claims that "to be American is to let [the past] go, to forget, or better yet, not to ever have known" (41). Being an assimilator, Mustafa not only "unlearns" the

Turkish language, but also the Turkish cuisine, thinking that he can free himself from his cultural heritage and become entirely American. When, after 20 years of staying abroad, he comes back to Istanbul for a family visit with his American wife Rose, he dies from food poisoning while eating his favorite childhood dessert *ashure*. Without doubt, this cause of death has a deeper symbolic meaning. Despite all attempts of assimilation, it is impossible to completely escape one's cultural roots which shaped an essential part of one's identity. Rejecting one's cultural heritage sooner or later kills an important part of oneself.

Instead of wiping out one culture in order to overemphasize another (as shown in the cases of Elif Shafak's Mustafa and Gish Jen's Callie), there is a healthier option which consists of simply enlarging one's "culinary vocabulary." Before taking the plane to Istanbul, Rose fills her bags with American snacks at the airport in order to create some food security and thus be "on the safe side" (*BI* 287). However, Mustafa's family welcomes her so warmly by offering her a wide variety of Turkish dishes that Rose opens up and starts to engage in an intercultural dialogue about cultural particularities in general. Gail in *The Saint of Incipient Insanities* has a similar experience when arriving in Turkey: "Everywhere they went Gail was offered something to eat or to drink, but usually both. Foreigners had to be fed!" (*SI* 331). In both cases, "the very best of Ottoman-Turkish cuisine" (*SI* 332) as a warm culinary welcome seems to facilitate the process of gradually becoming a global soul, which also proves Koç and Welsh's statement that "changes in food preferences may also reflect changes in broader cultural perceptions and practices" (Koc and Welsh 9).

Gish Jen's and Elif Shafak's Perceptions of "Hyphenated Identity"

The hyphen's function in "hyphenated identity" is interpreted in different ways by Gish Jen and Elif Shafak. Taking Karen Barad's understanding of meaning into account, these differences are not so surprising: "Meaning is not a property of individual words or groups of words. Meaning is neither intralinguistically conferred nor extralinguistically referenced. Semantic contentfulness is not achieved through the thoughts or performances of individual agents but rather through particular discursive practices" (Barad 818). Barad goes further in her explanation by highlighting that meaning is "an ongoing performance of the world in its differential intelligibility" (Barad 821). Depending on the questions we ask and on the respective approach we use, each literary work and the situations to which it calls attention appear in a different light. In other words, if we apply an intercultural communication theory, the conclusions we draw will differ from those we would have drawn if we had used a different theory from the social sciences. This is one of the reasons why Barad underlines "the inseparability of 'observed object' and 'agencies of observation'" (Barad 814).

Gish Jen's and Elif Shafak's approaches clearly differ from one another. The reactions which the characters show toward "the Other" in Gish Jen's *Typical American* and *Mona in the Promised Land* as well as in Elif Shafak's *The Saint of Incipient Insanities* and *The Bastard of Istanbul* already give us an idea about the writers' own perceptions of hyphenated identity. During a short email exchange, Gish Jen was so kind as to provide me with some answers on her view of the hyphen's function. When I asked her whether the hyphen in, for example, "Chinese-American" was there to unite or to separate the home and target culture, she stated that she did not believe in using a hyphen between Chinese and American. From this observation, it could be concluded that the two cultures stand separately, without a bridge in-between.

Taking a closer look at Gish Jen's novels, this separating function of the hyphen becomes quite clear. Neither the first generation of immigrants (Ralph, Helen, and Ralph's sister Theresa) nor the second generation (Callie) try to combine cultural elements of both countries in a harmonious way. Ralph's, Helen's, and Theresa's way of commenting on everything negative as "typical American" highlights their acting like separators who do not accept the new culture with which they are confronted. Only during a transitional phase do they seem to be partly drawn toward their heritage culture while at the same time making an effort to find a modus vivendi in America. Callie, however, evolves from being American toward being more Chinese than her own parents. During this process, she separates both cultures and stresses the "Chinese" in Chinese-American while getting rid of the "American." Only Mona can be regarded as a global soul who likes to combine different cultures and religions to get an entirely new vision of the world. She is open for everything that "the Other" can teach her, to a point where she easily switches from being Catholic to being Jewish. The fact that she likes to constantly change her identity makes her a nomad who sees flexibility as enriching when approaching other cultures.

Elif Shafak's attitude toward the hyphen's function differs from Gish Jen's. In her novels, building bridges between cultures is one of the most important aspects. In an interview entitled "Creating the Story Together," she clearly points out that one of her priorities as a writer is creating connections and synthesis: "My work is about combinations and connections. I like to connect things, stories, cultures ... I believe in the power and beauty of syntheses" (Shafak, "Interview" 12). Despite various difficulties, Shafak's characters who are torn between two or more cultures sooner or later come to the point where they succeed in harmonizing different, sometimes even opposing cultural elements and thus reconstructing their own identity. In-between identities like Armanoush and Aram in *The Bastard of Istanbul* or Ömer and Abed in *The Saint of Incipient Insanities* can serve as examples of this identity development which follows the steps of the "stress-adaptation-growth dynamic" as described by Kim. As soon as the periods of draw-backs are overcome, mutual understanding can be achieved: "If we can build genuine bridges through culture and art, bridges that extend across cultures, we can all learn from each other" (Shafak, "Interview" 13).

Being a world citizen while protecting one's cultural roots may be one of the most striking characteristics of Shafak's nomads. Her way of describing them reflects her own nomadic identity, which she summarizes as follows: "I commute between languages the way I commute between cultures. I am a commuter, a nomad. For me writing fiction is about 'journeys' anyhow" (Shafak, "Interview" 13). We can thus conclude that the hyphen in "hyphenated identities" unites local and universal aspects of different cultures in Elif Shafak's works.

When one feels torn between two cultures, the experience of having a "hyphenated identity" can cause culture shock. With regard to this sensation, Gish Jen states in her message to me: "I don't think in terms of culture shock." However, she also adds that "I do think the tension between more individualistic and more collectivistic cultures far more vexing than many people realize." In both *Typical American* and *Mona in the Promised Land*, a clash between individualistic and collectivistic cultures can certainly be observed. Some of Gish Jen's characters show reactions of resentment, discomfort, or shame, when confronted with cultural habits with which they are not familiar. The fact that Ralph has to replace his Chinese name by an American one triggers "anxiety" (*TA* 11), which proves that he undergoes a phase of acculturative stress. Classifying everything negative as "typical American" might be another indicator of culture shock that is typical of separators, who glorify their home while regarding the customs of the target country as disturbing at best: "'Typical American no-good,' Ralph would say; Theresa, 'typical American don't-know-how-to-get-along'; and Helen, wistfully, 'typical American just-want-to-be-the-center-of-things'" (*TA* 67). Seeing America as a country of "no morals" (*TA* 67), Ralph, Helen, and Theresa often use attributes like "just-dumb" (*TA* 67), "no-manners" (*TA* 76), "unreliable" (*TA* 78), "wasteful" (*TA* 103) or "good-for-nothing" (*TA* 126) to characterize Americans in general. It is the unlimited freedom one can experience in America that seems to be the primary cause of culture shock in the case of these first-generation immigrants.

While Gish Jen personally does not seem to acknowledge the concept of culture shock, Elif Shafak hints at this sensation by using the expression "estrangement" which nomads can feel when going back and forth between various cultures: "A nomad or a commuter is always wandering. Wherever he goes he carries within a sense of estrangement. Paradoxically, he is equally 'at home' in different places" (Shafak, "Interview" 16). Among others, Armanoush, Ömer, and Amed go through phases of culture shock which also lead to temporary alienation. However, Elif Shafak's focus lies not so much on the negative aspects of intercultural encounters but rather on the learning process that is triggered by cross-cultural exchange. Therefore, in her novels the "leaping-forward" of the "stress-adaptation-growth dynamic" is generally made more visible than the "draw-back."

Taking the statements of both writers and the identity concepts in their works into account, we could conclude that Gish Jen does not necessarily believe in the uniting function of the hyphen in the case of in-between identities, whereas for Elif Shafak this hyphen almost always serves as a bridge between different cultures, regardless of whether they are individualistic or collectivistic. After all, building various kinds of intercultural connections seems to be the key strategy for Shafak in order to achieve mutual understanding, as becomes clear in her following statement: "Xenophobia is 'fear of the Other' and fear usually stems from not really knowing the Other. We need to listen to each other more and build more connections of trust, peace and coexistence" (Shafak, "Interview" 15).

The Hyphen's Fluidity: Toward a Positive "In-Between" State

In terms of terminology, Çağlar correctly observes that there exist some identity concepts including "hybrid," "creolized," "hyphenated," and "diasporic" which more or less describe the same identity type: "These concepts aim to capture the complexity of the practices, cultural configurations and identity formations of translocal and culturally nomadic groups" (Çağlar 170). The important nuance which needs to be taken into consideration is whether these concepts focus on similarities or rather on differences between cultures. The notion of "hyphenated identity" might be the only one that makes both approaches possible, depending on the way the hyphen is interpreted, either as separating or uniting element.

Underlining these different functions of the hyphen, contemporary Turkish writer Ece Temelkuran, whose works have been translated into various languages, has stated in an email to me: "The hyphen for sure is there to connect and to unite, but it also makes the distinction between two belongings visible. The hyphen is there to pile up different belongings while making sure that they don't get intersect." Elif Shafak shares this observation, explaining her vision on identity politics in an interview with the BBC:

> Instead of using identity, I prefer to use "belongings", plural. I think it's possible to feel attached to more than one place, one city, one culture, one language. There is a metaphor the poet Rumi uses: he talks about living like a drawing compass. One leg of the compass is quite static, it is based somewhere, but the other leg meanwhile draws a huge, wide circle around it. And just like that, I think it's possible to be from somewhere but also to be from everywhere, to be a world citizen, a global soul. I have a deep attachment to Istanbul, but also to London. I think it's possible to have multiple homes and multiple homelands. [...] We are a mixture of multiple selves, multiple voices.

Having a "hyphenated identity" can turn into a burden if it creates the impression of being trapped between two or more cultures. In this case, the fact of leading a nomadic existence goes hand in hand with various sensations of loss, including loss of name, native language, and culinary references,[12] as described in Gish Jen's and Elif Shafak's novels. Especially in the state of acculturative stress, the notion of "in-between-ness" is experienced as a source of conflict, but as Elizabeth Grosz points out in her chapter "In-Between," "the in-between is the only space of movement, of development or becoming: the in-between defines the space of a certain virtuality, a potential that always threatens to disrupt the operations of the identities that constitute it" (Grosz 92–93).

As Elif Shafak correctly observes in her article "Dreaming in more than one language," "[c]ultural connections are ripples that travel far and wide, reaching unmapped shores" (22). Here, she also points out that "[w]e can only have a better, safer, and more peaceful world if we build strong cultural connections that transcend religious, national or ethnic boundaries" (ibid.). The concept of "hyphenated identity" can stand for the positive aspects of such a cultural mix, if the focus lies on its capacity of building bridges between cultures and promoting intercultural exchange. Both Gish Jen and Elif Shafak use food as a metaphor for this kind of interculturality, Gish Jen "Peking duck, Westchester style" (ML 186), Elif Shafak the dessert ashure. In the first case, the typically American drink Pepsi-Cola serves to add an exquisite taste to a traditional Chinese dish. Thus, American and Chinese culinary habits begin to mix. The idea to "stuff the turkey with stir-fried rice stuffing" and to carve the turkey "with a knife and chopsticks" (ML 41) equally shows that the two cultures are starting to become more connected through the hyphen, and not only on a culinary level. As Jennifer Ann Ho correctly observes, food thus also "becomes a useful metaphor [...] to discuss the limits and freedoms of identification because it also embodies the duality of being associated by natality with certain regions, yet it adapts to various cooking techniques and additions" (Ho 126).

The dessert ashure, which Elif Shafak uses in The Bastard of Istanbul, equally stands as a metaphor for this intercultural blend. Being made of many different ingredients that need to be cooked separately, this sweet dish gets a unique taste the moment all ingredients are mixed together. The same is true for intercultural encounters: when people from various cultural backgrounds start to

---

[12] The sensation of loss as a consequence of nomadic existence is not only an essential topic in Gish Jen's and Elif Shafak's but also in Zadie Smith's novels. This would merit further study.

interact and exchange their experience, they together create a particular atmosphere which can make the fear of "the Other" disappear.

In his article about transculturality, Welsch highlights the advantages which people characterized by a hyphenated identity have to offer. According to him, nomads whose identities consist of many different cultural elements are more open-minded and thus more likely to understand "the Other." Consequently, they are often successful in intercultural encounters, since a state of inner transculturality facilitates dealing with everything that seems unfamiliar.[13] While separators underline the uncertainty and disorientation that comes with this in-between-state, global souls rather concentrate on the positive potential of identity development with which intercultural encounters provide them. Çağlar herself states that "new, more flexible definitions of culture are needed, concentrating more on the aspect of fluidity" (Çağlar 169). This more flexible definition of culture naturally also includes a more flexible definition of identity, making it possible to belong everywhere instead of in-between.

As globalization continues, the concept of identity becomes more and more fluid. The challenge lies in seeing the positive aspects of the losses that come along with the experience of staying abroad. The loss of one's name, native language, and culinary culture, as pointed out in this chapter, does not necessarily mean the loss of one's entire self but rather leads to reconstructing identity as a whole. Having a hyphenated identity can either mean feeling at home nowhere or belonging everywhere, depending on the interpretation of the hyphen's function. Both cultures, that which comes before and that which comes after the hyphen, can be combined in order to reach a synthesis. The only problem that might occur when identity becomes too fluid is alienation, which in Mona's case is described as follows: "[...] so easily open is she that she almost does not know who is this Mona Chang" (*ML* 234). However, it is this open concept of identity that makes it possible to

---

[13] Welsch describes the advantages of transculturality as follows: "Denn aus je mehr Elementen die kulturelle Identität eines Individuums zusammengesetzt ist, umso größer ist die Chance, dass zumindest eine gewisse Schnittmenge mit der Identität anderer Individuen besteht. Von da aus können diese Individuen statt einer Haltung der Abwehr Praktiken der Kommunikation entwickeln. Darin liegt einer der großen Vorteile des Übergangs zu Transkulturalität" (Welsch, "Kultur" 152).

enjoy the challenges of a "hyphenated world" where identities are constantly in the process of being "performatively renegotiated" (Byers 114) and where an unlimited number of cultures can be added — by simply using a hyphen.

We live in an age in which the question "where are you from" gradually shifts toward "where you are at" (Gilroy 3), describing one's present "cultural location" instead of one's national origin. Stuart Hall correctly observes that the identity of the "post-modern subject" can be "formed and transformed continuously in relation to the ways we are represented or addressed in the cultural systems which surround us" (Hall 598). As such, identity has become a "moveable feast," which means that there is "no fixed, essential, or permanent identity" (Hall 598): "As the systems of meaning and cultural representation multiply, we are confronted by a bewildering, fleeting multiplicity of possible identities" (Hall 598). It is exactly this multiplicity of possible identities that promotes intercultural dialogue. The hyphen facilitates a certain fluidity between identities without losing the culture of origin on the way. As a consequence, the tension between the global and the local gradually disappears and it becomes easier to see the hyphen's uniting aspects, thus creating an identity that resembles "a house with no walls between the rooms" (*ML* 208).

References

Appadurai, Arjun. "Patriotism and Its Futures." *Public Culture* 5.3 (1993): 411–429.

Ateş, Seyran. *Der Multikulti-Irrtum: Wie wir in Deutschland besser zusammenleben können*. Berlin: Ullstein, 2010.

Barad, Karen. "Posthumanist Performativity: Toward an Understanding of How Matter Comes to Matter." *Signs: Journal of Women in Culture and Society*, 28 (2003): 801–831.

Bauman, Zygmunt. *Liquid Modernity*. Cambridge: Polity, 2000.

Berry, John W. "Acculturation: Living successfully in two cultures." *International Journal of Intercultural Relations* 29 (2005): 697–712.

Berry, John W., Uichol Kim and Pawel Boski. "Psychological Acculturation of Immigrants." *Cross-cultural Adaptation: Current Approaches*. Eds. Young Yun Kim and William B Gudykunst. (International and Intercultural Communication Annual 11.) Newbury Park: Sage, 1987. 62–89.

Braidotti, Rosi. *Nomadic Subjects: Embodiment and Sexual Difference in Contemporary Feminist Theory*. New York: Columbia UP.

Byers, Michele. "Material Bodies and Performative Identities: Mona, Neil, and the Promised Land." *Philip Roth Studies* 2.2 (2006): 102–120.

Çağlar, Ayşe. "Hyphenated Identities and the Limits of 'Culture'." *The Politics of Multiculturalism in the New Europe*. Eds. T. Modood and P. Werbner. London: Zed Books, 1997. 169–185.

Chen, Yea-Wen, and Mary Jane Collier. "Intercultural Identity Positioning: Interview Discourses from Two Identity-Based Nonprofit Organizations." *Journal of International and Intercultural Communication* 5.11 (2012): 43–63.

Deleuze, Gilles, and Félix Guattari. *Nomadology: The War Machine*. Trans. Brian Massumi. 1986. Seattle: Wormwood Distribution, 2010.

Fischler, Claude. "Food, Self and Identity." *Social Science Information* 27 (1988): 275–292.

Friedman, Susan Stanford. "Bodies on the Move: A Poetics of Home and Diaspora." *Tulsa Studies in Women's Literature* 23.2 (2004): 189–212.

Giles, Howard, Nikolas Coupland and Justine Coupland. "Accommodation Theory: Communication, Context, and Consequence." *Contexts of Accommodation*. Eds. Howard Giles, Justine Coupland and Nikolas Coupland. Cambridge: Cambridge UP, 1991. 1–69.

Gilroy, Paul. "'It Ain't Where You're From, It's Where You're At': The Dialectics of Diaspora." *Third Text* 13 (1990/91): 3–16.

Grosz, Elizabeth. *Architecture from the Outside: Essays on Virtual and Real Space*. Cambridge, Mass.: Massachusetts Institute of Technology P, 2001.

Hackney, Sheldon. *One America Indivisible: A National Conversation on American Pluralism and Identity*. Washington, DC: National Endowment for the Humanities, 1999.

Hall, Stuart, David Held, Don Hubert and Kenneth Thompson, eds. *Modernity: An Introduction to Modern Societies*. Cambridge: Polity, 1996.

Ho, Jennifer Ann. *Consumption and Identity in Asian American Coming-of-Age Novels*. New York: Routledge, 2005.

Jen, Gish. *Mona in the Promised Land*. New York: Alfred A. Knopf, 1996.

—. *Typical American*. London: Plume, 1992.

Kim, Young Yun. "Beyond Cultural Identity." *Intercultural Communication Studies* 4.1 (1994): 1–23.

—. "Cross-Cultural Adaptation Theory." *Encyclopedia of Communication Theory*. Eds. Stephen W. Littlejohn and Karen A. Foss. Thousand Oaks: Sage, 2009. 244–248.

—. "From Culture to Interculture: Communication, Adaptation, and Identity Transformation in the Globalizing World." *Intercultural Communication: A Reader*. 14th ed. Eds. Larry A. Samovar, Richard E. Porter, Edwin R. McDaniel and Carolyn Sexton Roy. Boston: Cengage Learning, 2015. 430–437.

—. "Globalization and Intercultural Personhood." *Intercultural Communication: A Reader*. 13th ed. Eds. Larry A. Samovar, Richard E. Porter and Edwin R. McDaniel. Boston: Cengage Learning, 2012. 83–94.

—. "Ideology, Identity, and Intercultural Communication: An Analysis of Differing Academic Conceptions of Cultural Identity." *Journal of Intercultural Communication Research* 36.3 (2007): 237–253.

—. "Intercultural Personhood: An Integration of Eastern and Western Perspectives." *Intercultural Communication: A Reader*. 14th ed. Eds. Larry A. Samovar, Richard E. Porter, Edwin R. McDaniel and Carolyn Sexton Roy. Boston: Cengage Learning, 2015. 405–417.

Kittler, Pamela Goyan, Kathryn P. Sucher and Marcia Nahikian Nelms. *Food and Culture*. Belmont: Wadsworth, 2012.

Koç, Mustafa, and Jennifer Welsh. "Food, identity and the immigrant experience." *Canadian Diversity* 1.1 (2002): 46–48.

Krusche, Dietrich. "Die fremde Mahlzeit. Zum Spannungsfeld zwischen Gastlichkeit und Fremde". *Gastlichkeit: Rahmenthema der Kulinaristik*. Ed. Alois Wierlacher. Berlin: LIT, 2011. 194–205.

Lai, Chung-Hsiung. "Nomadic Desire: The Schizo-Identity in *Mona in the Promised Land*." *Intergrams* 10.2–11.1 (2010): 1–19.

Parikh, Crystal. *An Ethics of Betrayal: The Politics of Otherness in Emergent U.S. Literatures and Culture*. New York: Fordham UP, 2009.

Pearce, Barnett W. "The coordinated management of meaning." *Theorizing about Intercultural Communication*. Ed. William B. Gudykunst. Thousand Oaks, CA: Sage, 2005. 35–54.

Schultermandl, Silvia, and Sebnem Toplu. *A Fluid Sense of Self: The Politics of Transnational Identity*. Wien & Berlin: LIT, 2010.

Shafak, Elif. *Baba ve Piç*. Istanbul: Doğan Kitap, 2012.

—. *The Bastard of Istanbul*. London: Penguin, 2007.

—. "'Creating the Story Together': An Exclusive Interview with Elif Şafak." *Journal of Turkish Literature* 6 (2009): 9–20.

—. "Dreaming in more than one language." *The Morning After: The future of the UK's cultural relationship with other European nations*. The British Council. 2016. Web. 20 July 2016.

—. *The Saint of Incipient Insanities*. New York: Farrar, Straus and Giroux, 2004. Smith, Zadie. *White Teeth*. London: Penguin, 2000.

Welsch, Wolfgang. "Kultur aus transkultureller Perspektive." *Lehr- und Lernmaterialien zur Vermittlung kultureller Kompetenzen*. Eds. Dietmar Treichel and Claude-Hélène Mayer. Münster: Waxmann, 2011. 149–158.

—. "Was ist eigentlich Transkulturalität?" *Hochschule als transkultureller Raum? Kultur, Bildung und Differenz in der Universität*. Eds. Lucyna Darowska, Thomas Lüttenberg and Claudia Machold. Bielefeld: transcript, 2010. 39–66.

Zheng, Dong-Lin. "Perplexity and growth: An analysis on the initiation theme of *Mona in the Promised Land*." *Sino-US English Teaching* 7.12 (2010): 78–81.

Video

Elif Shafak on identity: "multiple cultures, multiple homelands" (18 April 2016). http://www.bbc.co.uk/programmes/p03rg78s

12

Tasting Interculturality: Culinary Visions of America in Elif Shafak's *The Bastard of Istanbul*

Mine KRAUSE (Paris)

Summary: In Turkish writer Elif Shafak's concept of "insular" and "global souls," cultural misunderstandings are understood as an essential element of our age of migrations. Clashes between the two souls can easily occur. In Shafak's novel *The Bastard of Istanbul* (2006, first in English), cross-cultural interactions between insular and global souls are frequent. The interwoven story of two families depicts a clash of Eastern and Western value systems, impacting on the characters' general perception of identity. In this context, different approaches to culinary culture play a crucial part. Culinary practice carries a wide range of cultural topics of debate, in this case including a foreigner's particular vision of America that is closely linked to corresponding identity concepts. Partly making use of the "difference-as-problem approach" (Xu) and of research on "acculturative stress" (Berry) as well as "food security" (Koç & Welsh), this chapter aims to show how culinary culture is interpretively significant for the identity construction process.

Elif Shafak's Identity Concept: "Insular" and "Global Souls"

During the Campagna-Kerven Lecture Series at Boston University,

Turkish writer Elif Shafak① introduced the idea of "insular" and "global souls" representing two opposite tendencies in today's world. According to her perception, our age is characterized by movements, migrations, renewals and nomadic existences. As we travel more frequently and become familiar with other cultures, we keep reconstructing ourselves and gradually turn into "global souls."② It is true that intercultural encounters can now be considered an indispensable part of many people's lives. However, there are still many "insular souls" who prefer to stay in their cultural and mental ghettos rather than being confronted with mentalities about which they do not know anything. As a result, this age of migrations can also be regarded as an age of cultural misunderstandings. Elif Shafak states that a writer's role consists in bringing different, sometimes even seemingly incompatible cultural elements together in order to achieve a kind of cosmopolitan energy.

Intercultural interaction between insular and global souls can be observed in *The Bastard of Istanbul*.③ The expression "bastard" in the title at first sight has a negative connotation and could be associated with symbolic meanings like "hybrid" or "dubious origin," thus highlighting the dominant topic of in-between identities. It reflects the feeling of being trapped between different cultures, to a point where one's own sense of belonging gradually disappears together with one's cultural roots. Shafak's novel is set in San Francisco, Tucson, and Istanbul, and tells the story of two families, the Turkish Kazancıs and the Armenian-American Tchakhmakhchians. Cross-cultural interactions between insular and global souls often take place here. As the fates of both families become more and more interwoven, a clash of Eastern and Western value systems can be noticed, which also has an impact on the characters' general perception of identity. In an interview with Serdar Korucu, Elif Shafak states that food and culinary culture play an essential part in this book, also with regard to the definition of identity.④ Coming from very different cultural and religious backgrounds, the novel's characters sit down at the same table and share a meal whilst

---

① The original Turkish spelling is Şafak.
② The video of this lecture called "East, West and Global Souls" can be found under the following link: < http://www.youtube.com/watch? v = qMkdRqYeXk8 >. The global soul concept Elif Shafak proposes here is not the same as Pico Iyer's focus on worldwide displacement in *The Global Soul*.
③ The Turkish title is *Baba ve Piç*.
④ < http://www.elifsafak.us/roportajlar.asp? islem = roportaj&id = 133 >.

exchanging their ideas about controversial topics like abortion, the Armenian genocide, patriarchy, or a woman's role in society. During their conversations, some of the family members get to know those better by whom they initially felt threatened, and start to overcome certain prejudices. Once they manage to immerse themselves into another culture, rethink their view of the world and develop empathy for the Other, these intercultural dialogues at the dining table enable them to add "global soul elements" to their identity.

My chapter will focus on various culinary visions of America as described in *The Bastard of Istanbul*, putting Elif Shafak's global soul concept in relation with some theories on intercultural identity and culinary cultures. I will examine American food, eating habits, the role of women, and different perceptions of kitchens and dining rooms with regard to their impact on shaping individual and collective identities. I will equally take into account the universal language of food as a means of establishing a cross-cultural dialogue and "global connections" (Shafak, "Interview" 13) between America and Turkey. Shafak's own feelings about America are part of this analysis, considering her answer to one of my questions regarding this topic during a broadcast of the BBC World Book Club. In the course of the novel, the reader not only finds out more about how Americans and immigrants see the United States from a culinary point of view, but also gains an insight into intuitive approaches to other countries. Ideally, the (mostly culinary) intercultural encounters described here result in a fruitful exchange illustrating Elif Shafak's conviction that "[i]t is possible to be local and universal all at once" (Shafak, "Interview" 13).

Rose: American Eating Culture as Indicator of Identity

In their article "Emotion and intercultural communication," David Matsumoto, Jeffrey Leroux and Seung Hee Yoo point out that conflicts often become inevitable as soon as people from different cultural backgrounds start to engage in a dialogue. Individual reactions to misunderstandings that result from intercultural encounters can be more or less vehement, depending on the degree of negative experience involved. In the case of the American woman Rose, who is introduced in the second chapter of *The Bastard of Istanbul*, this degree of negative experience is quite high. Having been brought up in a small Kentucky town with "no multicultural background" (58), she soon learned to focus on local traditions. During her marriage with Barsam, Rose gets traumatized by the omnipresence of her husband's Armenian family and feels more and more threatened by cultural differences. Clearly, she still considers her former in-laws' judgment of her housewife and mother qualities as transgressions against her own value system, which is upsetting to her self-perception. Americans normally do not measure a wife's value by her performance in the kitchen.

Being constantly under the impression of failing in her household duties, Rose develops an aversion to exotic food which metaphorically stands for the time-consuming activity of cooking in an Armenian woman's life. As a consequence of these two opposing perceptions, a cultural clash between Rose and her female in-laws cannot be avoided. Taking her past into account, her following thoughts in the international food section of an American supermarket are not surprising: "No more *patlijan*! No more *sarmas*! No more weird ethnic food! Even the sight of that hideous *khavourma* twisted her stomach into knots" (39). As Alois Wierlacher points out in *Architektur interkultureller Germanistik*, cultural differences become especially obvious at dinner tables abroad, mainly because of the use of exotic ingredients which trigger all sorts of reactions.⑤ It is therefore not surprising that Rose continues to associate unfamiliar dishes with the traumatic experiences she had at her in-laws' house, where she always felt like an outsider.

The Experience of Culinary Clashes: Difference as Problem

The expressions "resentment" (38), "weird," "hideous" (39), "anger and melancholy," "horrendous" (40), as well as "confusion" (42) describe Rose's derogatory attitude not only toward exotic food, but also toward cultural diversity in general. Her negative reactions neatly fit into Matsumoto, Leroux and Yoo's observation that dealing with difference can often lead to "anger, frustration, or resentment" (Matsumoto et al. 16). Shafak's own definition would make Rose fall into the category of "insular souls" since her unpleasant memories hinder her from seeing the "Other" as enriching for or complementary to her own identity. According to Berry, Kim and Boski's theory of intercultural adaptation and adjustment, both Rose and her former in-laws could be classified as

---

⑤ "Kulturelle Andersheit und Fremdheit wird besonders gut an fremdkulturellen Tischen und ihren Ingredienzien erfahren" (Wierlacher 380).

"separators," as proved by their categorical refusal of certain dishes associated with the other's culture. Contrary to "assimilators," who completely abandon their own cultural identity in order to resemble members of the target culture, the so-called "separators" feel an urgent need to protect their traditions and are against taking in elements from other cultures because they feel threatened by them.

If we apply Berry, Kim and Boski's classification, Rose's identity development would consist of four phases: as a child, Rose was not taught to be open-minded toward cultural alternatives. For this first phase, Xu Kaibin's "difference-as-problem approach" (Xu 380) is also valid, making her see her own culture as the norm and the other's culture as an exception to the rule. As a consequence of her biased attitude, which makes her a "separator" and an "insular soul," Rose experiences moments of acculturative stress (sometimes called culture shock) when she marries into an Armenian Catholic family. During her marriage — the second phase — she starts to cook Armenian dishes, trying to adapt to this culture and thus briefly becoming more "global." However, as her ex-husband's family (the Tchakhmakhchians) keeps calling her "*non-Armenian*" by using a derogatory Armenian expression, she does not feel accepted: "Rose had always felt like an outsider there, always aware of being an *odar* — this gluey word that had stuck on her from the very first day" (38). As a result of her negative experiences with Armenian culture, her third phase is characterized by an "us against them" (Kim, "Ideology" 240) attitude, starting right after she leaves her marital life behind. Her aversion against the Other (in this case the Armenians) leads to an over-emphasis on everything that her own culture has to offer — an act of defiance that can also be observed in the Tchakhmakhchian family.

The Impact of Culinary Culture on Identity Development

A radical change is equally reflected in Rose's culinary habits after her divorce. Once she leads the life of a single mother, she immediately goes back to exclusively cooking "real Kentucky dishes" (39) in order to get back the part of her American identity she partially had to suppress during her marriage. By banning "exotic" ingredients from her home, she keeps the "Armenian cuisine as far from the borders of her kitchen as possible," and even years after her divorce still enjoys "vilifying it to her neighbors and friends" (100). For Rose, being an American woman obviously implies having the right to put fast food or simple dishes on the table instead of cooking a complicated meal. She is used to eating whatever she wants whenever and wherever she wants, either in company or not, at her own choice. The Tchakhmakhchians accuse her of "being a slip-shod wife and a terrible mother" (36) or an "irresponsible mom" (39) because she does not fulfill a woman's traditional role in the household. This results in constant intercultural misunderstandings related to different attitudes toward food in general and the functions of family members in particular. While the Oriental family concept corresponds to the so-called "family of security" which with its traditional role distribution is clearly patriarchal, the American "family of freedom" (Kallenberg-Schröder 4 f.) is characterized by the independence of each family member. Especially when it comes to a woman's role in the household, the rather dominant Tchakhmakhchians incorporate the values of a "family of security" which are incompatible with Rose's mentality. These opposing approaches show that the activity of eating goes hand in hand with either collective or individual perceptions of identity.

During this phase, the sharp contrast between American fast food and traditional Armenian dishes to a certain extent symbolizes Rose's inner conflicts and identity struggles that came along with her marriage. As a kind of backlash against the Tchakhmakhchians' traditional views, Rose over-emphasizes her "insular" American character traits in order to restore her original identity that she until then partly had to deny. The fact that she starts working at the Cactus Grill after her divorce can, for instance, be seen as a kind of protest reaction against her former in-laws. For the same reasons, she only buys typically American products in the supermarket which would never enter the Tchakhmakhchians' kitchen because of their artificial flavor, including those that have no equivalent in Oriental cultures such as "Carb Watchers Gourmet Sugar-Free Vanilla Crème Flavor Dark Chocolate" (36) and coconut marshmallows. In the "junk food" (36) supermarket aisles where other American women also do their grocery shopping, Rose neither feels judged nor inadequate and can thus restore some of her self-confidence. Similarly, cooking and eating "real Kentucky dishes" (39) in her typically American kitchen provides her with a sense of belonging and security. The fundamental change of her eating habits seems to underline the end of her former life and helps her "become a new woman" (37) which is actually her former self.

Another obvious change in Rose's eating habits occurs when she decides to travel to Istanbul with her second husband Mustafa to take her daughter Armanoush back home from her Turkish in-laws. In this fourth phase that starts at the Tucson airport, she is suddenly in desperate need of American food that — in a figurative sense — serves as an indicator of identity and creates a feeling of home. By buying a lot of provisions before leaving the U.S., she shows a "separator"'s typical focus on local dishes, trying to take her traditional eating habits abroad with her because she is afraid of cultural disorientation. The thought of unfamiliar eating rituals in a foreign country immediately creates a sensation of anxiety in her: "This being her very first trip to a country where English wasn't the primary language and people did not eat maple syrup-soaked pancakes in the morning, Rose found herself simultaneously excited and distressed" (282). During her Turkish Airlines flight from San Francisco to Istanbul, she has an intercultural experience that once again involves food. The words "THERE ARE NO PORK PRODUCTS IN OUR FOODS" (288) have a destabilizing effect on her, making her feel guilty since she has bacon combos in her bag. This indirect sign of respect for other customs and traditions proves that she is not always as "insular" as it might have appeared at first glance.

The Impact of Food on Insular Souls

During her flight to Istanbul, Rose finds out that she likes Turkish food and, as a consequence, also becomes more open to intercultural encounters. This interesting link between culinary culture and cultural perceptions has been observed and summarized by Koç and Welsh in their article "Food, identity and immigrant experience," where they state: "Changes in food preferences may also reflect changes in broader cultural perceptions and practices" (Koç and Welsh 46). Making her develop some global soul characteristics, Rose's positive culinary experience on the plane has a considerable impact on her general behavior toward Mustafa's family. Her attitude toward her new in-laws, the Kazancıs, is different from what it was toward the Tchakhmakhchians, because Rose starts to understand that her identity is not threatened by them. When she meets the Kazancıs, her first approach to Turkish culture and family life is again a culinary one: "Rose and Mustafa spent their first two days in Istanbul eating" (330).

In contrast to the "American way of life" which also includes the option of eating alone once in a while, having a meal together in the Turkish and Armenian tradition is an event no family member is allowed to miss. Sitting around the dinner table, sharing the day's news and making small talk is a social and "entirely synchronized event" (186). Even though the Kazancıs bombard Rose with questions about America while she is trying exotic dishes, she does not feel uncomfortable and even seems to enjoy her first intercultural dialogue in another country. Her reactions show that her love for her daughter — as was once the case with her devotion to her first husband Barsam — can sometimes make her forget her narrow-minded Southern mentality and help her develop more global soul characteristics. With this character, Elif Shafak illustrates that intercultural encounters can help insular souls to become more curious about other cultures and also more flexible in their formerly rather static perception of identity.

Mustafa: An Immigrant's View of American Women and Kitchens

If we apply Berry, Kim and Boski's theory, Mustafa's case would be an example of "acculturation," where physical and biological changes (including a new nutritional status) are involved (Berry et al. 64). At the same time, this Turkish character can be regarded as an "assimilator" since he wants to leave his cultural identity behind and become as American as possible. For this purpose, Mustafa is determined to learn how to speak English without an accent, so that nobody will be able to identify him as an immigrant: "One day [...] I will speak in such a way that no one will ask this rude question because they will not believe, even for a minute, that they are talking to a foreigner" (46). As it is for Rose, American food becomes an indicator of identity for Mustafa, even though for entirely different reasons. Frozen spinach, pizza, and soup cans contrast with his former life in which he never had to prepare a meal on his own⑥ and in which eating fast food was not accepted. At the beginning of his time in the United States, he feels "like a dethroned king living in exile" (44) because the women of the house are no longer at his service. For his mother Gülsüm as for the women of the Tchakhmakhchian household, America's fast food culture obviously is a threat, as to a certain extent it seems to be a metaphor for the decline of the traditional family. For Gülsüm (as for Rose's former mother-in-law Shushan), cooking local dishes means resisting

---

⑥ Similar observations about the division of roles between men and women can be found in Elif Shafak's novel *Honour*.

American influences in general which are associated with artificiality and decadence. Strikingly, Mustafa quickly forgets about his mother tongue and can also perfectly live without Turkish dishes, but even after two decades in America he subconsciously still clings to the conservative idea of a woman's place behind the stove. Having married Rose, he gradually has to accept that being a wife in the Western world does not necessarily include doing chores.

A Woman's Role in Eastern and Western Kitchens

Already in his early childhood, Mustafa learned that a woman's responsibilities should be limited to the kitchen. The considerable gender gap which can be observed regarding the education of Turkish boys and girls is summarized in the following extract:

> Until [Mustafa] came to the United States, he had never had to cook in his life. Every time he labored in the small kitchen in his two-bedroom student apartment, he felt like a dethroned king living in exile. Long gone were the days when he was served and fed by a devoted grandmother, mother and four sisters. Now, dishwashing, room-cleaning, ironing, and especially shopping were a huge burden for him. It wouldn't be as difficult if he could only rid himself of the feeling that someone else should be doing these things for him. (44)

In traditional Oriental families, boys are spoilt like little princes by their mothers and sisters. Mustafa associates the activity of cooking automatically with one or several women, and — as the only man of the family who got all the attention — cannot easily cope with his new role in an American household, both alone as a student and later also during his marriage with Rose. While none of the Kazancı women — regardless of their educational backgrounds and beliefs — rebels against society's implicit expectations of them, Mustafa's American wife is no longer ready to make the sacrifices she once made during her first marriage. In her house, neither the kitchen nor the dinner table are places of social interaction as they are in Turkey, but rather have an aesthetic and functional value.

For Rose, it is above all the modern design that counts, and not so much the familiar atmosphere.⑦ She likes to spend time with

---

⑦　In Elif Shafak's novel *Honour*, it is also obvious that the kitchen does not play an essential role in a Western household: "Tariq had a theory about British kitchens: that they were deliberately made tiny and gloomy so that everyone would have to make do with takeaways" (46).

decorating and remodeling her kitchen by "adding pull-out shelves" (265) because she wants it to have "class written all over it" (167). Mustafa, however, obviously prefers its cozy and comfortable aspects: "He didn't like the stools and instead kept two solid-wood honey pine dining chairs in the kitchen, one for him and the other for him too" (265). Interestingly, this man who assimilates to U.S. culture from the very beginning of his stay abroad, can never entirely get used to the independence a woman has in an American household. After many years in this country he still subconsciously associates the kitchen with a place where women have long conversations in private while preparing a meal. Seeing his wife make pancakes or any other dish has a "soothing" (292) effect on him, as this sight reminds him of his mother and creates a feeling of home.

Denial of Cultural Roots: Assimilation as Escape

Turkish culinary culture and Turkish language — both being part of his identity — are the two major elements Mustafa tries to forget as quickly as possible in order to get rid of his past. In the end, Mustafa denies his origins and creates a new identity for himself. His stepdaughter Armanoush's friends believe him to be American, "presumably from the Midwest" (93), which proves that over the years he managed to lose one of the indicators of his original identity, i.e., his accent. Even his name, which has always been a part of himself, undergoes a slight transformation toward "Mostapha" (49). America in general and American cuisine in particular can here be regarded as a form of escape and a kind of prison at the same time. While on the one hand Mustafa is the ideal immigrant, who systematically assimilates without questioning anything, on the other hand he lets go of all traditions of his own culture that could have provided him with some emotional stability (as is, for instance, the case with Rose when she finally gets back to cooking Kentucky dishes). The day he returns to his home country after having spent twenty years abroad, he is confronted with the Turkish cuisine and, ironically, not long afterwards dies from a poisoned Turkish dessert. Since eating in Turkey is a collective experience (rather than an individual one as in America), Mustafa's action of eating his last dish alone obtains a particular meaning. A culture he tried to forget about for such a long time eventually takes revenge in the form of his favorite childhood dessert that kills him in the end, thus reminding him of his real identity for the very last time.

The identity theories that match Mustafa's character best are those described by Berry, Kim and Boski in their article "Psychological Acculturation of Immigrants." In the course of this "psychological acculturation" (Berry et al. 63), Mustafa adapts his cultural and social characteristics (including his eating habits) to "American standards" in order to fit perfectly into his new environment. He thus undergoes a "sociocultural process," altering his behavior in order to fit in with a changed environment (cf. Matsumoto et al. 17). According to Berry, Kim and Boski, immigrants can choose between "assimilation, integration, separation, and marginalization" (Berry et al. 65). Their definition of assimilation corresponds to the behavioral patterns Mustafa develops in America, given that he indeed relinquishes his own cultural identity and quickly becomes alienated from his home culture. His assimilation with regard to American fast food also stands for this general tendency, corresponding to Kim's assimilationism-pluralism-integrationism-separatism theory (Kim, "Ideology" 239). Even though assimilation can be imposed by the dominant groups of a society,[8] this does not apply in Mustafa's case as he deliberately chooses assimilation, i.e. adjustment without questioning, over the less radical form of adaptation. However, considering his attitude toward a woman's role in the kitchen, there are now and then phases of "separation" in his behavior. It could be useful to review empirical research that underpins assimilation theories in order to find out whether it is really possible to assimilate to 100% to the target culture. In my opinion, phases of "separation" may always occur in moments of unexpected confrontations with one's original culture.

Armanoush-Amy: A Global Soul Between Hamburgers and Pastirma

The Armenian-American girl Armanoush can be regarded as one of the global souls in Elif Shafak's *The Bastard of Istanbul*. While her mother Rose — still traumatized by the Armenian culture — wants her daughter above all to be American and for this purpose even changes her name to Amy, Armanoush herself (although she does not speak Armenian) feels torn between both cultures. When it comes to determining identity, food again plays a significant role.

---

[8] "Assimilation, when sought by the dominant acculturating group, is termed the 'melting pot'" (Berry 706).

Lady Peacock/Siramark's test is supposed to measure degrees of "Armenianness," listing 15 questions about Armenian traditions and attitudes. Depending on the answers given, the results range from being an "outsider" or an "inside-outsider" to being an Armenian or a "proud Armenian." The test mentions some culinary elements that are part of Armanoush's life and make her "a proud Armenian" (115). However, when she takes a trip to Mustafa's family in Istanbul to find out more about her past, she soon learns that identity cannot be put into such clearly defined categories. Sitting down at the Kazancıs' dinner table for the first time, Armanoush starts to understand that, according to the food-related criteria which seemed to rate her "Armenianness," she might just as well have been Turkish. Not only Armenians but also Turks know the taste of *mantı*, "the curse of *bastırma*" and "the smell of *sudžuk*" (114) of which the Turkish equivalents are *mantı*, *pastırma* and *sucuk*. Very similar eating rituals can be found in both countries, where it is also common practice for "relatives to keep shoveling food into your mouth" (115).

The Armenian and the American cuisine are both equally present in Armanoush's life. The fact that for Rose a "perfect meal" (39) needs to consist of hamburgers, fried eggs, maple-syrup-soaked pancakes, hot dogs with onions, or a mutton barbecue indirectly has a considerable impact on her daughter's definition of identity. Quickly Armanoush learns the cultural differences between hamburgers and *pastırma*, local and exotic dishes, "us" versus "them" and eventually also between Amy and Armanoush. In contrast to her mother, Armanoush seems to be rather a global soul by nature, as she easily goes back and forth between American and Armenian mentalities. Dividing her time between Rose's and her grandmother's house, she is used to always adapting to the respective circumstances. Both fast food and exotic dishes have become an essential part of herself, making it difficult for her clearly to determine her identity.

Food as Universal Language

As Armanoush does not speak a word of Turkish, food becomes her universal guide. This can be proved by her following statement: "I do not speak the Turkish language, unfortunately, but I guess I speak the Turkish cuisine" (156). For global souls like her, successful intercultural interaction does not necessarily require linguistic competence. Cultural diversity for them means first to focus on similarities rather than on differences, and to see other cultures as an enrichment rather than as a threat. With this attitude, acculturative stress that triggers negative emotions can be largely avoided. As described in Bean and Stevens's *America's Newcomers and the Dynamics of Diversity*, global souls are able to adapt without assimilating by protecting their own origin and adding elements from other cultures to it. This approach may be the best starting point for experiencing a fruitful intercultural dialogue. In America, Armanoush does not feel the need for any kind of categorization, such as labeling people as Armenian, Turkish, American etc. Her mentality is also reflected in her way of seeing dishes not as national possessions, i.e., as typically Armenian or typically Turkish. Whereas some of the novel's characters are divided into Turkish, Armenian, and American food lovers or haters, global souls like she is do not put a national label on what they are eating. In her case, different kinds of dishes seem to correspond to different identities: the Armenian to Armanoush, the American to Amy, and everything in between to her My-Exiled-Soul-personality which stands for the culinary and general curiosity of a world citizen.

In *The Location of Culture*, Homi Bhabha argues that attributes like "ambivalent," "nomadic" and "in-between" are characteristic of cultural identities (cf. Xu 382) — an observation that fits Elif Shafak's global soul concept and matches Armanoush in particular, who states that "[p]lurality means the state of being more than one" (117). She understands that accepting the Other is helpful in constructing or rather completing her own identity. For her, using intercultural dialogue at the same time is a means to learn more about herself. At the beginning, her "multiple and competing identities" (Xu 385) are at times a source of instability, and result in a fragmented self. Observations like "[b]ecause of her fragmented childhood, she had still not been able to find a sense of continuity and identity" and her own statement "I know how it feels to be torn between opposite sides, unable to fully belong anywhere, constantly fluctuating between two states of existence" (116) prove that Armanoush has not yet found the right way to live in peace with her global soul characteristics. However, in the course of time she learns to deal with the many, sometimes contradictory elements of her personality. Just as she enjoys eating Armenian and American food as well as an "Asian fusion with a touch of Caribbean influence" (107) in an exotic restaurant, she soon manages to unite different cultures in herself.[9] Since Armanoush looks for different pieces of her identity in various places and sees the enriching sides of cultural particularities, Matsumoto, Leroux and Yoo's theory about "multicultural identities and multiple perspectives" (Matsumoto et al. 17) probably matches her character best.

Toward Intercultural Personhood

Another theory that is appropriate in Armanoush's case is Young Yun Kim's concept of intercultural personhood. She goes through a "stress-adaptation-growth dynamic," which consists of alternating phases of acculturation (i. e. learning) and deculturation (i. e. unlearning), integration and disintegration, as well as progression and regression. Old and new cultural patterns blend and lead to a continuously reinventing process of identity. As a result of her numerous intercultural experiences, Armanoush develops an "intercultural identity" and could be described as a "world citizen" who "acknowledge[s] the interconnectedness among all peoples" (Pitts 397). All of these ideas are also part of Elif Shafak's own global soul concept. While working, living and/or traveling abroad, intensive intercultural encounters can take place that are often stressful and strenuous. In the course of time, the confrontation with difference might be regarded as valuable, making communication, mutual understanding, and adaptation possible. With Armanoush, this is exactly what happens: at first, she feels under pressure, torn between her father's family and her mother, since they all want to impose their own culture on her.

During this period, emotional stress often dominates over the positive impressions that could be evoked by intercultural exchanges.

---

[9] An interesting parallel between food and identity as experienced by Armanoush can also be found in a statement by Kerra in Elif Shafak's novel *The Forty Rules of Love*: "If we can eat the same food, [...] why shouldn't we be able to live together? [...] Ours is an ever-liquid world where everything flows and mixes" (178). This idea of constant "flowing" that has a considerable impact on our identity development can also be found in Zygmunt Bauman's *Liquid Modernity*: "[I]dentities cannot but look fragile, temporary and 'until further notice', and devoid of all defences except the skills and determination of the agents to hold them tight and protect them from erosion" (Bauman 178). A similar-sounding idea is expressed by Robert Jay Lifton in *The Protean Self*, who like Elif Shafak — and in contrast to Bauman — highlights the positive aspects of flexible identities: "We are becoming fluid and many-sided. [...] This mode of being [...] enables us to engage in continuous exploration and personal experiment" (Lifton 1).

As she is not sure who she really is, Lady Peacock/Siramark's identity test plays an important role for her, providing her with some orientation. However, as soon as she decides to go to Istanbul and learns more about her family's past, her "cultural empathy and openness toward embracing cultural and group diversity" (Pitts 398) increases and she focuses more on the positive aspects of multi- and interculturality. In the end, Armanoush's interest in any kind of cuisine as well as her way of seeing the similarities between Armenian and Turkish dishes instead of constantly highlighting differences to a certain extent also stand for her general, rather unbiased approach to other cultures. This way of refocusing on similarities is "a forgotten path" of Intercultural Communication research, whereas they "should become an integral part of the identities of intercultural researchers and the field," since "it is this underlying foundation that gives rise to cultural idiosyncrasies" (Chang 137, 139).

Food for Armanoush is closely related to intercultural experiences which make her lose "her sense of place. She felt like she could be in Europe or in the Middle East or in Russia" (253). Whereas the American cuisine for Rose creates a sense of belonging and makes her "feel at home" (292), her daughter is able to enjoy exotic smells and flavours without becoming anxious or destabilized. Armanoush does not choose between one or the other, but accepts what she is being offered, as is the case in one of Istanbul's taverns: "*This must be the style here*, Armanoush figured out, *instead of choosing from a menu, the whole menu comes to you*" (253). Food-related actions like her eating the eighth *simit* ⑩(302) given to her as a welcome gift at the Kazancıs' breakfast table are symbolically relevant as they create a bond between cultures. As a consequence of her positive intercultural experiences, Istanbul starts to turn into "something edible" (246) — an "edible city" (Poole 224) full of smells that bring Armanoush closer to her real identity, which is a mixture of many different ingredients.

The Dessert *Ashure*: A Metaphor of Coexistence

The moment Armanoush sits down at the Kazancıs' dinner table in Istanbul, an interesting intercultural dialogue starts to take place

---

⑩   A sesame ring.

which partly gives insights into Turkish-Armenian history, but also into the Turks' vision of America and the Americans. While Armanoush wants to "become an Armenian-American" (119) like the ones she knows from the chatroom Café Constantinopolis, the Kazancıs seem to have no doubt about her identity: for them she is simply an "American girl" (156) called Amy. The focus of the conversation lies first on life in America in general before shifting toward Armanoush's national identity and the controversial topic of the Turkish-Armenian past. Armanoush's observation that "there are different Americas" (157) perfectly corresponds to her global ideas of plurality and coexistence. Just as she finds nuances important and therefore sees America and its people from different perspectives, she also tries to highlight the multicultural aspects of Armenian and Turkish culture. In this context, it is essential to notice that Armanoush once again tends to underline the similarities between Armenians and Turks rather than the differences. "So that's one more thing in common" (159), she gladly exclaims when she comes across words in Armenian and Turkish that have the same roots. While Rose, the Tchakhmakhchians and also some members of the chatroom Café Constantinopolis are characterized by their "us against them" mentality (Kim, "Ideology" 240) which can cause polarization, Armanoush obviously prefers the idea of coexistence, of which the dessert *ashure* ⑪ becomes a symbol toward the end of the novel.

"Both-and" vs. "Either-or": A Culinary Mix

The notions of successful intercultural interaction are recurrent in Elif Shafak's novels. In *The Bastard of Istanbul*, America is a place where a kind of peaceful coexistence seems to be possible. In this "melting pot" as described by Kim in the article "Ideology, Identity, and Intercultural Communication," minorities like "Greek Americans, Sephardim Americans, and Armenian Americans" (111) live together side by side just as was once the case in Istanbul. The cook of a fish restaurant describes the formerly so colorful Turkish society as follows: "This city was so cosmopolitan once. [...] We had Jewish neighbors, lots of them. We also had Greek neighbors, and Armenian neighbors. [...] You know, we were all intermingled" (170). The concepts of cosmopolitanism, multiculturalism ("çokkültürlülük")

---

⑪ The English spelling is *ashure*, the Turkish *aşure*.

and multiple voices ("çokseslilik"[12]) are illustrated by an Armenian sweet dish called *anuschabur* (Անուշապուր) or its Turkish equivalent *aşure*.

Every chapter of the novel is named after one of its ingredients, which play an essential role in the lives of one or several characters. The particularity of the recipe is that all ingredients need to be cooked separately. Even though they taste delicious on their own, the unique flavor of *ashure* can only be achieved by mixing them all. In a figurative sense, a similar observation can be made for the novel's characters: they all have their own, often very original personalities, but despite their differences they manage to coexist, sometimes even under the same roof. However, the more they try to interact and "mix," which mostly takes place around the dinner table (also across national borders), the richer and more fascinating their lives become. Out of successful interactions and intercultural dialogues, real global souls can be born who do not feel the need to choose between an "either-or" but will always opt for a "both-and."

Cuisine "Without Borders"

An "us against them" versus a "both-and" mentality is also reflected in the characters' eating habits. As pointed out earlier, after her traumatic marriage Rose focuses on the American cuisine and only opens herself to other culinary experiences toward the end of the novel. The behavior of the Tchakhmakhchian family is very similar: apart from the Armenian they never accept another kind of cuisine. Even though they have been living in the United States for a very long time, they consider American food in general as artificial and not worth a try. The same rule seems to apply to their social contacts, since they live in a ghetto to which only family members have access. An American like Armanoush's date Matt Hassinger is treated like an exotic guest. Seeing their "inquiring gazes" makes him feel uncomfortable: "He lost his confidence and broke into a sweat" (106). In contrast, different kinds of people can easily coexist in Armanoush's life, just like different kinds of cuisine (including American, Armenian, Asian-Caribbean, and later also Turkish dishes).

An important intercultural exchange about identity and coexistence takes place between Armanoush and the companion of Mustafa's

---

[12] Elif Shafak explains her *ashure* metaphor in the interview with Serdar Korucu (in Turkish): <http://www.elifsafak.us/roportajlar.asp?islem = roportaj&id = 133>.

sister Zeliha, Aram, around a dinner table in an Istanbul tavern. Like the cook of the fish restaurant, Aram describes an Istanbul where plurality was not just accepted but cherished: "Armenian Istanbulites belong to Istanbul, just like the Turkish, Kurdish, Greek, and Jewish Istanbulites do. We have first managed and then badly failed to live together. We cannot fail again" (254). Even though Armanoush can in general be regarded as a global soul, in her conversation with Aram she unexpectedly shows some "insular" character traits. In terms of national identity, this man cannot be categorized as either Armenian or Turkish, since he has a very multicultural background and does not want to be reduced to one nationality. Speaking English with a British accent, he belongs to the rare people who can adapt to different cultures and still remain true to themselves. Thinking that the Turks might be "oppressing" (254) him, Armanoush proposes that Aram should leave Istanbul and start a new life in the United States, where he could be integrated into an Armenian community (an idea a "separator" would have had). Although she has a "culinary vocabulary" (252) that knows no national borders and reflects her open mind, she subconsciously associates only America with a notion of absolute freedom. Aram makes her understand that it is possible to be yourself even if you cannot exactly determine where you belong to: "[...] Aram could *not* be Armenian or Turk or any other nationality. Aram could only be Aram, entirely sui generis" (247). Various identities — just like the various ingredients of the sweet dish *ashure* — can coexist in one single person. The result is the sensation of being "displaced but not placeless" (255).

Elif Shafak's Vision of Coexistence in America

By showing that it is not only possible to add exotic ingredients to dishes but also cultural diversity to people's lives, Elif Shafak makes her point as a supporter of cosmopolitanism. The dessert *ashure* serves both as an "epitome of survival, solidarity, and cornucopia" (288) as well as a metaphor for "plurality" (117) and coexistence, of which the ideas of tolerance and empathy are an essential part. The predominant idea is one of sharing and creating harmony which is also underlined by Banu's *ashure*-story.⑬ One could even go a step

---

⑬ Aksoy points out that *ashure* (also called "Noah's pudding"), in achieving a "fusion of incompatible parts" (56), can also be regarded as a metaphor for "a coming together of clashing and colliding flavors that manage to create harmony" (45).

further and claim that for Elif Shafak this sweet dish to a certain extent stands for America. At the BBC World Book Club program that was broadcast on 2nd March 2015, she answered my question about what America emotionally means to her as follows:

> In a way, what I see in America is this collective identity that is supernational, bringing together different national, ethnic and religious backgrounds. There is this commonness, this common identity that binds people together. There aren't many places in the world that achieve that the way America did, so as a Turk to me it is intriguing what they have achieved in America, or — let me put it this way — what the English language has achieved. [...] Just like in cultures, I believe in languages as well. I support cosmopolitanism.⑭

Like the dessert *ashure*, which is made of many different ingredients, the rich, delicious and unique taste of America consists in its cosmopolitan people who speak various languages, have their own culture, and contribute to intercultural dialogues with their individual ideas. Without doubt, in this kind of exchange as presented in *The Bastard of Istanbul* the most universal language is the culinary one. As is shown in the case of Rose, who at the end of the novel starts to enjoy eating dishes with which she is unfamiliar, positive culinary experiences can open one's mind and increase one's curiosity for other cultures. During the rather intuitive act of eating, questions can be asked that eventually make prejudices disappear, such as the Kazancıs' stereotypical vision of America: "Was it true that Americans survived on mammoth portions of fast food, only to go on a diet in TV contests?" (330). Showing interest in the other's culture is the first step toward leaving behind an "us versus them" mentality and gradually becoming a global soul.

However, as Elif Shafak points out in a recent essay,

> [u]nfortunately, not everyone can be a globetrotter or a nomad. Alarming numbers of people never set foot in "other lands" or come face to face with someone of another cultural, religious or ethnic background. Isolation breeds xenophobia. Where there is a cognitive gap between "us" and "them", it is much easier to make generalisations that feed fears, clichés and stereotypes. There is nothing more dangerous for a human being than failing to notice they

---

⑭ The interview is available under the following link: <http://www.bbc.co.uk/programmes/p01sqlxs>.

have been engulfed by a single narrative. The first thing undemocratic societies deny their citizens is multiplicity. ("Dreaming" 22)

It is this gap between "us" and "them" that literature aims to overcome. The act of sharing a meal with "the Other" is one of various ways to approach different cultures without fear. While politics increases the gap between "us" and "them," literature counteracts this development: "Politics burns bridges. Literature builds them. Politics divides people into categories. Literature challenges and dissolves them. Politics thrives on the assumption that 'We are better than them'. Literature whispers: 'The other is me'" (ibid.).

Culinary Culture As a Mirror of Identity

The American Rose, the Turkish immigrant Mustafa, and the Armenian-American Armanoush have all very different visions of America which directly or indirectly shape their identity. As illustrated in this chapter, identity and culinary cultures are closely related: the characters' perceptions of life are often reflected in their eating habits and sometimes also in their way of preparing certain dishes. In some cases, eating and cooking can even have a therapeutic function, such as filling a void or dealing with internal conflicts. While Rose eats marshmallows to compensate for her emotional distress, Mustafa's sister Banu works in the kitchen to distract herself from an existential crisis by "reorganiz[ing] the cereal jars lined on the shelves, mopp[ing] the floors, bak[ing] raisin-walnut cookies, wash[ing] the plastic fruits on the counter, and painstakingly spong[ing] an ossified mustard stain at the corner of the stove" (195). Taking these observations into account, the characters' culinary habits in this novel can often be interpreted as a mirror of their souls.

Rose represents American (or Western) women who often experience strict household obligations as a burden and sometimes even as a threat to their individuality. From an Oriental point of view, however, the act of cooking and eating traditional dishes together strengthens family bonds and creates a sense of belonging. The former is an individualistic, the latter a collectivist approach — both of which are explained in Ting-Toomey's face negotiation theory. One of the scenes highlighting the consequences of such a collectivist attitude for the individual might be the following, where Zeliha tells her daughter: "But do not forget, my dear, [...] that you are a Kazanci, not a vegetarian! [...] And we Kazancis love red meat! The redder, the greasier, the better!" (74). Just as culinary preferences are often dominated by family members in Oriental cultures, each individual's identity is also defined by and to a large extent dependent on them. By refusing to eat some dishes that are imposed on them at the dinner table, Asya and Armanoush show that they have their own personality and a freedom of choice, not only as far as food is concerned.

Food Security and Multicultural Cuisine

For most of the characters, Koç and Welsh's analysis of the relation between food and identity is appropriate. In their article, they state that "food security is part of 'feeling at home'" and also observe that "the multicultural cuisine may offer a glimpse of widening notions of identity, self and belonging" (Koç and Welsh 47). Various identity theories can be linked to particular culinary cultures and also to some of the characters described in *The Bastard of Istanbul*. As pointed out earlier, Berry, Kim and Boski's concept of intercultural adaptation and adjustment matches Rose, the Tchakhmakhchians and Mustafa. Rose and her former in-laws belong to the category of "separators." They generally refuse to become familiar with the Other, sometimes as a consequence of negative experiences with different cultures. Mustafa, on the contrary, can be regarded as an "assimilator" who denies his own cultural identity in order to fit in totally abroad. Both extremes are destabilizing in terms of identity, as there is no healthy balance between traditional and new cultural elements. Elif Shafak's global soul concept eventually applies to those who — while coping with intercultural confrontations and the resulting acculturative stress — can adapt to one or several cultures without assimilating. Armanoush and especially Aram belong to this third group. Young Yun Kim's concept of intercultural personhood is the most adequate one as far as their identity development is concerned. In a broader sense, global souls can also be seen as people who question the existing order and break certain rules to take in new cultural influences, but at the same time remain true to themselves.

The path from peaceful coexistence to efficient interaction via intercultural dialogue is long and difficult. Not only in *The Bastard of Istanbul*, but also in *Honour*, *The Forty Rules of Love* and *The Saint of Incipient Insanities*, Elif Shafak shows that love, compassion and empathy can serve as means to overcome the fear of the Other which is often caused by cultural misunderstandings and a general sense of insecurity. America as depicted in *The Bastard of Istanbul* is a society of multiple and sometimes clashing cultural identities. By building bridges between food and culture, community and the individual, traditions and modernity, East and West, and also between past and present, Elif Shafak proves that it is possible to leave our mental ghettos and become global souls in an age of mobility. If what we want to achieve is a form of mutual understanding across national borders, it is necessary to learn how to "celebrate difference, otherness, and plurality" (Xu 379). Xu Kaibin's observation perfectly corresponds to Elif Shafak's ideas of diversity, intercultural dialogue, and cosmopolitanism. Only by striving for cultural diversity is it possible to spice up and add a fresh taste to our lives. Once the Other is seen as a source of inspiration (and not of anxiety), we can start to work toward the unique taste of interculturality together.

References

Aksoy, Can. "Urban Claustrophobia: A Reading of Familial Interaction in *The Bastard of Istanbul.*" *Journal of Turkish Literature* 6 (2009): 45–58.

Bauman, Zygmunt. *Liquid Modernity.* Cambridge: Polity, 2000.

BBC World Book Club. "Elif Shafak — The Forty Rules of Love." Online video clip. 2 Mar. 2014. Web. 12 Dec. 2015. http://www.bbc.co.uk/programmes/p01sqlxs

Bean, Frank D., and Gillian Stevens. *America's Newcomers and the Dynamics of Diversity.* New York: Russel Sage, 2003.

Berry, John W. "Acculturation: Living successfully in two cultures." *International Journal of Intercultural Relations* 29 (2005): 697–712.

Berry, John W., Uichol Kim and Pawel Boski. "Psychological Acculturation of Immigrants." *Cross-cultural Adaptation: Current Approaches.* (International and Intercultural Communication Annual 11.) Eds. Young Yun Kim and William B. Gudykunst. Newbury Park: Sage, 1987. 62–89.

Bhabha, Homi K. *The Location of Culture.* London: Routledge, 1994.

Boston University. "East, West, and Global Souls." Online video clip. https://www.youtube.com/watch?v = qMkdRqYeXk8. 3 May 2011. Web. 12 Dec. 2015.

Chang, Hui-Ching. "Touring the Field of Intercultural Communication: Finding Differences and Commonalities." *Identity and Intercultural Communication (I): Theoretical and Contextual Construction.* Intercultural Research Vol. 2. Eds. Xiaodong Dai and Steve J. Kulich. Shanghai: Shanghai Foreign Language Education Press, 2010. 125–149.

Gibson, Margaret A. *Adaptation Without Assimilation: Sikh Immigrants in an American High School.* New York: Cornell UP, 1988.

Gudykunst, William B. "Cultural variability in communication." *Communication*

Research 24 (1997): 327–346.

Iyer, Pico. *The Global Soul: Jet Lag, Shopping Malls, and the Search for Home*. New York: Alfred Knopf, 2001.

Kallenberg-Schröder, Andrea. *Die Darstellung der Familie im modernen amerikanischen Drama*. Frankfurt am Main: Peter Lang, 1990.

Kim, Young Yun. "Beyond Cultural Identity." *Intercultural Communication Studies* 4.1 (1994): 1–23.

—. "Cross-Cultural Adaptation Theory." *Encyclopedia of Communication Theory*. Eds. Stephen W. Littlejohn and Karen A. Foss. Thousand Oaks: Sage, 2009. 244–248.

—. "From Culture to Interculture: Communication, Adaptation, and Identity Transformation in the Globalizing World." *Intercultural Communication: A Reader*. 14th ed. Eds. Larry A. Samovar, Richard E. Porter, Edwin R. McDaniel and Carolyn Sexton Roy. Boston: Cengage Learning, 2015. 430–437.

—. "Globalization and Intercultural Personhood." *Intercultural Communication: A Reader*. 13th ed. Eds. Larry A. Samovar, Richard E. Porter and Edwin R. McDaniel. Boston: Cengage Learning, 2012. 83–94.

—. "Ideology, Identity, and Intercultural Communication: An Analysis of Differing Academic Conceptions of Cultural Identity." *Journal of Intercultural Communication Research* 36.3 (2007): 237–253.

—. "Intercultural Personhood: An Integration of Eastern and Western Perspectives." *Intercultural Communication: A Reader*. 14th ed. Eds. Larry A. Samovar, Richard E. Porter, Edwin R. McDaniel and Carolyn Sexton Roy. Boston: Cengage Learning, 2015. 405–417.

Koç, Mustafa, and Jennifer Welsh. "Food, identity and the immigrant experience." *Canadian Diversity* 1.1 (2002): 46–48.

Korucu, Serdar. "Elif Şafak ile röportaj.". 22 May 2006. Web. 12 Dec. 2015. http://www.elifsafak.us/roportajlar.asp? islem = roportaj&id = 133

Krause, Mine. "The Culinary Language of Insular and Global Souls in Elif Safak's *The Bastard of Istanbul*." *Journal of Turkish Literature* 10 (2013): 88–107.

Lifton, Robert J. *The Protean Self: Human Resilience in an Age of Fragmentation*. Chicago: U of Chicago P, 1993.

Matsumoto, David, Jeffrey Leroux and Seung Hee Yoo. "Emotion and Intercultural Communication." October 2005. Web. 12 Dec. 2015. http://www.kwansei.ac.jp/s_sociology/attached/5288_44277_ref.pdf

Pitts, Margaret Jane. "Intercultural Personhood." *Encyclopedia of Identity*. Eds. Ronald L. Jackson II and Michael A. Hogg. Thousand Oaks, CA: Sage, 2010. 398–402.

Poole, Ralph J. "Bastardized History: Elif Shafak's Transcultural Poetics." *Real Yearbook of Research in English and American Literature* 26 (2010): 213–230.

Shafak, Elif. *Baba ve Piç*. Istanbul: Doğan Kitap, 2012.

—. *The Bastard of Istanbul*. London: Penguin, 2007.

—. "'Creating the Story Together': An Exclusive Interview with Elif Şafak." *Journal of Turkish Literature* 6 (2009): 9–20.

—. "Dreaming in more than one language." *The Morning After: The future of the UK's cultural relationship with other European nations*. The British Council. 2016. Web. 20 July 2016. https://www.britishcouncil.org/sites/

default/files/the_morning_after_eng.pdf

—. *The Forty Rules of Love*. London: Penguin, 2010.

—. *Honour*. London: Penguin, 2012.

Ting-Toomey, Stella, and John Oetzel. "Face Concerns in Interpersonal Conflict: A Cross-Cultural Empirical Test of the Face Negotiation Theory." *Communication Research* 30.6 (2003): 599–624.

Wierlacher, Alois. *Architektur interkultureller Germanistik*. Munich: Iudicium, 2001.

Wierlacher, Alois, and Regina Bendix. *Kulinaristik: Forschung — Lehre — Praxis*. Berlin: LIT, 2008.

Xu, Kaibin. "Theorizing Difference in Intercultural Communication: A Critical Dialogic Perspective." *Communication Monographs* 80.3 (2013): 379–397.

13

Identity Negotiation in Gish Jen's
Mona in the Promised Land

SHEN Weiwei Vivian
Hangzhou Medical College and Shanghai
International Studies University

Summary: We can use Gish Jen's second novel *Mona in the Promised Land* (1996) to show the potential of identity negotiation theory for critical analysis. The work has been ranked as one of the best novels by *The New York Times* and among the Top 10 by the *Los Angeles Times* in the year of its appearance. Jen's optimistic narration of immigrant conditions and her apparently easy resolution of ensuing cultural conflicts has been thought to elide a consideration of material realities impinging on Asian Americans. Yet it appears illuminating, for a better understanding, to consider the concepts of identity negotiation as developed by Stella Ting-Toomey and also by Ronald Jackson. The novel shows how, owing to prevailing and asymmetrical relations of force, efforts to function as a multicultural person may be stressful and isolating. The concepts of cultural contract with its three major types as well as of identity coordination requiring personal or internal negotiation become helpful for the purpose of literary analysis. Beneath the surface of the novel's seemingly light and witty vein, Jen diagnoses a submerged power differential that challenges the reader's own self-image.

Introduction: Postmodernist Reading?

We can use Gish Jen's second novel *Mona in the Promised Land* (1996) to show the potential of identity negotiation theory for critical analysis, as against other approaches. As a Chinese-American woman writer, Jen is very popular in Asian American literature. This work has been ranked as one of the best novels by *The New York Times* and among the Top 10 by *Los Angeles Times* in the year of its appearance. Set in upstate New York in the late 1960s, *Mona in the Promised Land* (to which I will refer as *M*) continues Jen's first novel *Typical American* (1991), which introduces Chinese immigrants who come together to form the Chang family, and it chronicles the *bildungsroman* of teenager Mona Chang. She is the pancake restaurant owners' second daughter, and her family moves into a prosperous Jewish neighborhood in its quest for upward social mobility. However, Mona's behavior for the pursuit of an American dream turns out to develop beyond their wish.

An important debate among critics involves, on the one hand, the postmodernist reading of the novel: the story is read as focusing to a significant extent on identity fluidity in connection with American multiculturalism. The novel's first chapter speaks of "the blushing dawn of ethnic awareness" (*M* 3): while African Americans are turning Chinese, Jews are turning black, and some Chinese girls are turning more Chinese, Mona is turning Jewish — much to her parents' worry. Therefore, the story is interpreted, though with different degrees of emphasis, as exploring or highlighting identity transformation (see Gilbert, Eder, Gilman, Ho, Zheng, Feng, Liu), as the American multicultural discourse favors a newly fashioned, ever-transforming, fluid subjectivity. For instance, Zheng Dong-lin declares that in this novel "Jen explores the identity problem of Chinese immigrants and insists that identity is changeable, fluid and chosen rather than born" (78). Pin-chia Feng reads the novel as testing the idea of "the fluid nature of ethnic identity and the possibility of an interethnic coalition based on true understanding and actual practice" (83); Jen "uses Mona's exploration of fluid identity to criticize the demand of ethnic authenticity by mainstream society" (86).

On the other hand, several scholars (Wong "But," Chen, Partridge, Li) do not share this emphasis or even disagree, developing different categories though partly overlapping with the scholars mentioned above. With reference to "subjectivity-shuttling," Wong in an earlier context declares "I can't see how an interstitial, shuttling exercise of power is done": if one were to adopt a concept of Asian American fluidity and interstitiality, instead of strengthening an Asian American voice in American culture extending to politics, "certain segments of the Asian American population may be left without a viable discursive space" ("Denationalization"19). For the novel, Wong ("But") accordingly argues for the importance of considering socioeconomic class in reading representations of ethnicity. She pinpoints class as the center of family conflicts surrounding Mona's conversion to Judaism, which is motivated by an idealistic desire for social change together with filial desire to improve her family's social standing. Similarly, Li maintains that anxiety in Jen's characters is engendered by their uncertain identities, since Chinese immigrants have achieved little in trying to integrate into mainstream culture in America no matter how hard they have tried. For Asian Americans, anxious identities appear to be their destiny. A significant perspective that has been used for interpretation is the postcolonial concept of hybridity. Partridge makes use of this, while he also recognizes the naivety in Mona's concept "American means being whatever you want" (*M* 49): individual identity formation is not self-determined or works independently from the rest of society (see Partridge 185). He argues that social class is the great marker of difference in Jen's two novels, *Typical American* and *Mona in the Promised Land*. Social class also receives due attention in the reading offered by Chen: though acknowledging the politics of multiple and shifting identifications with free choice to identify with a proliferation of differences, he examines the identity construction through which each major character's subjectivity is performatively enacted. He argues that, although performers try to disavow class antagonism in their performance of identity of differences, class secretly overdetermines other differences in political identity, and that class antagonism still predominates in the struggle for hegemony (Chen 56). The failure of Camp Gugelstein (an experiment in interethnic Chinese/Jewish/white/black communalism in which all are equal) is the best evidence to show readers how utopian it is to build a house without walls between the rooms: class in connection with ethnic antagonism breaks out as a flask is missing and the Negro is suspected to have stolen it.

Communication as "Rubbing off"

Such difficulties can be understood from an anti-essentialistic view of identity. Stuart Hall argues that identities are never unified, especially in modern times, in which identities are increasingly fragmented and fractured; identities are never singular but are multiply constructed across different, often intersecting and antagonistic, discourse, practices and positions. They are constantly in a process of change and transformation (see Hall 4). Does this, as in the case of postmodernist reading, open any chances for ethnic minority people to choose their cultural identity according to their own wish? Homi Bhabha asserts that "hybridity" opens possibilities for apparently homogeneous national cultures, the consensual or contiguous transmission of historical traditions, or "organic" ethnic communities to transform (Bhabha, *Location* 5-8). In this view, hybridity is marked by the "in-betweenness" and "interstitiality" caused by continuous negotiation between the foreign and the familiar. Thus, the process of identity formation is ongoing. In this way, culture and identity are redefined as a fluid, dynamic process of change and creolization, rather than a homogenizing whole. Several critics (Gonzalez, Ho, Partridge) have noticed the dynamic, hybrid transformation of cultural identity in the novel and accepted Bhabha's hybridity theory as making sense for interpreting the novel. However, as we shall see, what they have neglected is Bhabha's discussion of hybridity in relation to critical forms of the communication process, of resistance and struggles in terms of the exercise of coercive power imposed on the underprivileged.

Postmodern sociologist Zygmunt Bauman could be understood as an advocator of liquid life and fluid identity. However, he is fully aware that in the globalizing world, "[u]npredictability breeds anxiety and fear" (*Individualized* 122). Since the globalizing world is full of dangerous forces of coercion, "accidents and surprises," one must never let vigilance lapse. Therefore, in the course of an individual life, forces that keep people constantly struggling, that cause "anxiety and fear," always make themselves felt. The key lies in how people handle these difficulties: with "ambition and resolve"? What strategy could intercultural communicators, privileged or underprivileged, dominant or marginalized, upper class or lower class, adopt in the pluralist and globalizing world? Relevant to understanding fluid identity is Confucius's recommendation (*Analects*

13: 23) that "The *junzi* acts in harmony with others but does not seek to be like them" (Robert Eno) or, in an older rendering, "the superior man is affable, but not adulatory" (James Legge). This provides an adequate place for individuals' desire to be unique persons. It provides us with a view of the dynamics of convergence and divergence in intercultural communication: individuals converge to develop commonalities in order to reach mutual understanding and meaningful dialogue with others. They diverge to maintain self-identification. The two complimentary but different processes are at work in the identity negotiation process.

When she was asked about what she wants her readers to learn from *Mona in the Promised Land*, Jen explained,

> [...] ethnicity is a very complicated thing, not a stable, unified thing. Right now many people hold the view that if you're a Chinese American, that is far and away the most important fact about you. That is what you were born and will be forever. To try to make yourself something else is being false to your true self. I think that's entirely wrong. I think that all the groups in America have rubbed off on each other, and that no group is pure. [...] To imagine that being just one thing is the be-all-and-end-all truth about yourself is pretty naive. (Partridge 173–174)

Jen in another interview highlights "the whole American experience" as "all the many groups kind of jostling and intermingling and banging against each other and coming together both. *Bill Moyers:* Like bumper cars? *Gish Jen:* It is like bumper cars" (Jen, "Becoming"). While she does justice to postmodern ideas about ethnicity and also about stereotyping that affect some prevailing literary discourses, she is aware that individuals from different groups "rub off" to (re)construct their identities. There is a dialogic process in which ethnic groups need to jostle against each other for conflictual resolution. During this dynamic process, each group is ever-changing and, as it were, impure. We need to pay attention to the communicative process of "rubbing off" in society, as well as the ethnic groups' bumping and banging together.

In speaking of identity formation in connection with migration, the "promised land" theme functions at various levels in the novel. It refers to the land which, according to Genesis 15: 18 – 21, was promised by the Hebrew God to Abraham and then his descendants, and came to be associated with a hope for salvation and liberation. The theme of pursuing such a land later became an important source of hope for the various immigrant groups who came to the United States to search for a new and better life. However, this search for a promise is full of dangers, conflicts, and contradictions for the marginalized minority. For instance, Mary Antin's autobiography *The Promised Land* (1912) describes the difficulties and low social status of Jewish American women. Pin-chia Feng believes that Jen's novel, to a certain extent, rewrites Antin's classic work when it shows Mona's conversion to Judaism.

A "General Politics" of Truth

No strategy available to intercultural communicators may be able to move ahead without antagonisms. For Michel Foucault, "[p]ower is everywhere; not because it embraces everything, but because it comes from everywhere." It is "the multiplicity of force relations immanent in the sphere in which they operate" (*History* 93). Thus, individuals cannot escape the complex and self-reproducing relations of power that are embedded in social life and that inevitably shape interactions. In cross-cultural encounters, as in any others, the truth of "true self" dwells within this network:

> Truth is a thing of this world: it is produced only by virtue of multiple forms of constraint. And it induces regular effects of power. Each society has its regime of truth, its "general politics" of truth: that is, the types of discourse which it accepts and makes function as true; the mechanisms and instances which enable one to distinguish true and false statements, the means by which each is sanctioned; the techniques and procedures accorded value in the acquisition of truth; the status of those who are charged with saying what counts as true. (Foucault, "Truth" 131).

There are two interrelated levels of power operating simultaneously in any given situation (see also Kurylo 166). The first level is macroscopic, which is the way power is set up in a given culture or society at a particular time in history. At this level, power circulates so as to embrace government and politics, social policy and the law, religious institutions, educational systems, health care institutions, family and kinship systems, mass media, and other social institutions. This level of power is generally created by an influential group of people, and affects the lives of almost everyone in the society. The second level is microscopic, which occurs in individual and social transactions on a smaller scale — in conversations with others, interpersonal relationships, or inter/cultural encounters. Together, the two levels of power operate simultaneously in people's lives, in their relationships with particular others, and with the larger social group.

The "force relations" become equally significant in the concept of Antonio Gramsci. He has developed a three-dimensional concept for such relations in society:

1. A relation of social forces independent of human will, i.e., social classes which have specific functions in the production process.
2. A relation of political forces. This refers to the degree of homogeneity, self-consciousness, and politicization of the social classes. There are various degrees of self-consciousness, from a simple awareness of subjective and immediate interests to the point where one becomes conscious of one's objective class interests.
3. A relation of military forces. Gramsci also terms it "politico-military" forces as in the case of the state's military forces. This refers to the state's oppressive apparatus. (Gramsci, *Selections* 180–183)

Not all of these may be equally relevant to an analysis of the novel. For Gramsci, at any rate, voluntarism is meaningless. In a Marxist sense, "will" means making a distinction, hence it serves the identification of a class. It means a class's political life independent from other classes: a compact organization that is disciplined toward its own specific goals (see Gramsci, *History* 11). Therefore, to Gramsci, voluntary action and the human will are only meaningful when they are the collective will of many, a class's compact will. He sees power as directly linked to the ideological hegemony of a society's dominant classes. For an individual, to be conscious of the complex social network — its hegemonic forces — within which an individual realizes him/herself already generates power (see Daldal 149).

How does such an emphasis relate to Bhabha's postcolonial approach? While Bhabha's concepts of hybridity and Third Space tend to be better known, he describes the "emergence of a dialogical site — a moment of enunciation, identification, negotiation — that was suddenly divested of its mastery or sovereignty in the midst of a markedly asymmetrical and unequal engagement of forces" (Bhabha, "In the Cave" x). The dialogic approach is a negotiation in which communicators in a "moment of enunciation" strive for equal rights against the experience of a deprivation of power:

[F]or me the importance of hybridity is not to be able to trace two original moments from which the third emerges, rather hybridity to me is the "third space" which enables other positions to emerge. This third space displaces the histories that constitute it, and sets up new structures of authority, new political initiatives, which are inadequately understood through received wisdom. (Rutherford 211)

In the discourse of intercontinental migrants entering a new and dominant culture, as in Jen's novel, the "asymmetrical and unequal engagement of forces" between the marginal individual and the native creates a meeting point in which the borderline is transgressed, old cultural representation is disrupted, and both sides' identity becomes a "site of negotiation." What positions, then, become able to emerge? In the novel, Mona reinvents her ethnicity by converting to Judaism, the religion of her peers. Superficially, multicultural reinvention may well be attractive to us, suggesting free choice of belief and value regardless of biological differences, no-one being excluded, everyone being equal. However, behind this alleged utopian fluidity is the hardship and discrimination from which Asian Americans actually suffer, in which power, race, and identity politics are embedded.

A further problem arises: if identity so fluidly changes over time, how can we consider this chameleon-like identity as being authentic (see Cohen)? In Mona's case, "[...] so easily open is she that she almost does not know who is this Mona Chang" (M 234). She is so capable of transforming that she herself is almost unable to recognize an underlying individual. A closer examination of Mona's life, moreover, reveals many traces of power, discriminations, and stereotypes. Where Mona and Callie used to live, rocks were thrown at them as a peculiar kind of welcome. The narrator satirically remarks that "[t]heir group hasn't always been the oppressed. They used to be the oppressor; and that makes them, as a minority, rank amateurs" (ibid., 36). "Their group" refers to the Chinese minority, who can in more or less subtle ways turn against some group members. As members' identities need to become shaped and reshaped by interactions with members of different groups, in this "hyphenating world" such identities are doomed to enter a constant process of (re)negotiation; what appears to be fluidity may be caused by a lack of choice for dealing with imposed, asymmetrical force.

Does Jen's optimistic narration of immigrant conditions and her easy resolution of ensuing cultural conflicts elide a consideration of material realities impinging on Asian Americans, viz., the role of race, class, and gender in the working of identity politics in America? She has been criticized for such elision (see Wong "But," Chen, Wang). While postmodernist readings of the novel provide a basis for a critique of what they perceive to be politically correct, a close reading of the narrative and a careful study of Jen's own statements will reveal that neither has she been wholly uncritical of dominant ideologies and of multiculturalism, nor has she rejected identity dynamics or the difficulties of class mobility:

> I want to question why it's funnier for an Asian-American woman to consider switching identities like that than it would be for, example, an Irish-American. There's some racist component to that formulation. [...] Asian-Americans are held up to a different standard in that regard than Caucasian Americans, and there's an assumed power differential there that I want to question. [...] People have found the book hilarious, from what they've been saying to me during the tour, but there are also serious issues there that I hope they'll consider as well. (Jen, "So")

The novel's comic and "funny" mode, which makes reading attractive, is thus to be understood as harboring a question for the reader — that of "why" the Asian-American switching is thought so funny. Appealing to the reader in this question extends the experience of loss of "familiar signs" of which Stella Ting-Toomey speaks in her concept of identity negotiation.① Concepts of belonging to a social "set" without objection, of "reticence" in connection with "class" determinants, and of "selfhatred" all have their place in the narrative, but do they suggest an eliding of material realities? What I read therein is the hard work that Asian Americans invest in their desire to blend into American society, to be accepted into the dominant circle of cultural identity and class with similar privileges, without being put aside as either a "model minority" or a yellow peril.

The "new structures of authority" that are claimed for hybridity and the political life of social classes with a focus on collective or compact will go further beneath the textual surface than the postmodernist emphasis, but do not have much more explanatory

---

① For the potential difficulties of relating literary and Intercultural Communication studies to each other, see also the Excursus section in the Appendix on "Intercultural Concepts of Identity" in this volume.

potential for our purpose. Bhabha speaks of "[h]ybrid hyphenations" of cultural identification with an emphasis on "the performative nature of differential identities," a "negotiation of those spaces" that open out, "remaking the boundaries" as in marriages between a Chica-riricua and a Hassidic Jew (*Location* 217 – 218). Is such a negotiation process similar to what is depicted in the novel I am analyzing? It appears illuminating, for an understanding of the connection, to consider the concept of identity negotiation as developed by Stella Ting-Toomey and also by Ronald Jackson.

Gain, Loss, Exchange

Ting-Toomey calls attention to the way each "intercultural contact can bring about identity dissonance or stress" owing to "interaction unpredictability" (7); the result can be "identity shock" (ibid., 27), as people's attempt to become members of another culture can lead to an experience of "identity vulnerability" with a "degree of stress or perceived threat individuals experience in an unfamiliar situation" (ibid., 181). Losing "familiar signs and symbols of social discourse" can result in anxiety (quoted ibid., 246). The "concept of 'power' underscores many of the interplays between 'dominant' and 'non-dominant' group relations" in society (ibid., 172). In Jen's novel, Mona's parents, originally from wealthy families in pre-1949 Shanghai, put pressure on their children to be high-achieving "model minorities," or "New Jews," in order to recover their lost class privileges. Accordingly, they reject people-of-color rhetoric which would align them with non-dominant groups such as lower-class blacks and Latinos. The family members' efforts to weather and overcome adaptive stress and perceived identity threats can be understood as entering into a bargaining mode, "a transactional interaction process [...] whereby individuals in an intercultural situation attempt to assert, define, modify, challenge, and/or support their own and others' desired self-images" (ibid., 40; reformulated a little in the 2nd ed.). Since the communicators in the process may attempt to "challenge" the others' identity, the issue of dominance is built into the negotiation. Ting-Toomey has turned against the implication contained in intercultural competence concepts that a stranger should always adapt to a host, regardless of variable contextual conditions. Many Intercultural Communication scholars (e.g., Hecht, Jackson, and Ribeau) agree in assuming that identities are dynamic, not static, and are influenced by interaction with others. At the same time, critical Intercultural Communication scholars (ibid., 242; Moon) contend also that identities are not simply conceded while communicating; there is an attempt to hold onto and then negotiate aspects that define who one is.

Based on Ting-Toomey's concept, Ronald Jackson defines the negotiation process as

> a bargaining process in which two or more individuals consider the exchange of ideas, values, and beliefs [...] a process in which one considers the gain, loss, or exchange of their ability to interpret their own reality or worldview. If it is discovered that one has negotiated part or all of her cultural identity, then that can be translated to mean that she has conceded a dimension of her cultural locus of control. As a natural consequence of this negotiation, it can be argued that she has also, in the process, forfeited certain cultural values, traditions and/or norms (which serve to define who she is) within that communication episode. (*Negotiation* 10)

Hecht, Jackson, and Ribeau speak of negotiation as "an important metaphor to describe the process of identity recognition, relational coordination, and value exchange via interaction" (222). They agree with Ting-Toomey that the attempt to function as a multicultural person may not always be profitable; "it is often stressful, shocking, and isolating" (ibid., 230). Accordingly, "intercultural relationships may or may not be coordinated, depending upon the dynamics involved (such as power, boundaries, cultural loyalty, group identification, maturity, etc.)" (Jackson, "Cultural" 361).

Contracts and the Prior Self

Based on Starosta's and Olorunnisola's meta-model for "negotiation of a third culture" (Chen and Starosta, 1998), Jackson contends that a process by which two interactants become creators of a hybrid "third culture" and abandon their primary cultures is possible (*Negotiation* 5). He proposes several tenets for investigation, among which cultural identities as well as multiple identities within daily interactions can shift (for the following, see ibid., 5–6). Negotiation occurs during interaction, and it may be the result of one's feelings of submissiveness to another who possesses more power; or it may be simply a reaction to societal norms and expectations. Identity negotiation precedes identity shifts, while both strongly impact one's decision to consider sacrifice of one worldview (or reality interpretation) in exchange for another. Even when one becomes the other, or separates from a primary culture, there are still remnants of one's prior self, so that although one has changed, one still remains the same. This is one way in which cultural representatives rationalize their decisions to negotiate and shift their cultural identities. One's prior self is not lost, and in a suitable context one's earlier self may reappear.

Jackson distinguishes three cultural contract types, for "personally and socially" explored identity (see Hecht, Jackson, and Ribeau 226–227): Ready-to-Sign (assimilation), Quasi-Completed (adaptation), and Co-Created (mutual valuation). Ready-to-sign cultural contracts are prenegotiated, so that unlike the other types no further negotiation is allowed. Such contracts are designed to promote assimilation or maintain one's own worldview. This kind of contract is what dominant groups often make the marginalized group "sign." Quasi-completed contracts are partly prenegotiated and partly agreements to relationally coordinate one's identities with those of another. This appears to be the most common type of cultural contract, although they are short-term or temporary episodes of identity shifting. "Signers" of a quasi-completed contract are usually not ready to fully co-create, and do not rule out maintaining their own worldview. They "straddle the fence" in terms of a commitment for harmonious relationship and coordination. Some quasi-completed contracts are signed as self-protection in order to avoid stress. The final type, co-created contracts, are fully negotiable, the parameters being personal preferences or requirements. Co-created contracts are the ideal kinds of social agreement with cultural others, because they provide the optimal means of relational coordination across cultures and signal that the relationship is fully negotiable and open to differences. If a cultural contract is co-created, there is full acknowledgment and valuation of cultural differences.

Negotiating With the Self

Since identity needs to be both "personally and socially" explored, the dynamic variables do not operate without the individual's internal process, which may occur subconsciously and rapidly or may be protracted: "This coordination is initiated after an initial negotiation with the self [...] identities, whether social, cultural or otherwise, have meaning for the individual when they are first negotiated personally" (Jackson, "Cultural" 361). Racial identity may be ascribed as defining an individual, yet such an "identification referent takes on significance when its meaning is negotiated within the self." Only when an ontological reorientation is completed, after "intrapersonal adjustments," will it be carried over into external relations with others, in which cultural difference makes itself felt. Such difference "does not have to be conflictual, but often times, just as in a new marriage, interactants must come to terms with value distinctions if the relationship is to be successful" (ibid.). Bhabha's example of an intercultural marriage thus occurs again here, with attention to internal negotiation. We should, however, not lose sight of the terms of gain and loss, because we may assume that "mutually enhancing interaction between unequals is not probable"; conflict may turn out to be inevitable (Miller 79).

The landscape of cultural identity is obviously a complex and multi-disciplinary field. Intercultural communication scholar Steve Kulich's Identity Matrix Theory may shed some further light on it. In the context of cross-cultural negotiation and conflict resolution, Kulich proposes a dynamic model to include fruits from different disciplines and perspectives:

> Individuals in any social interaction (or anti-social reaction) are actually operating with (hiding or to some degree enacting) multiple identity sets (some congruous or related, but others contradictory) on a multi-level, multi-dimensional playing field (complex scaled options), playing a gambit between individual- and social-level influences and goals, a range of personal choices and societal ascriptions (power domains), and cognitive tensions (assessment of the situation) between affective meanings (hoping for security and satisfaction) and behavior outcomes (functional acts, some of which may be deemed appropriate, but others that risk being uncomfortably inappropriate). (73)

This concept brings a measure of integration to intercultural identity theories. It offers a dynamic framework in which all levels, sub-levels, propositions, or overlapping categories can co-exist and become defined within the constructs of each (cross-) cultural interaction. It pays especial attention to the power domain, which has long been neglected in such contexts and is crucial in the identity formation process. It thus enables a dynamic integration of identity choices which are made affectively, behaviorally, and cognitively. The individual and the social negotiation levels become closely intertwined, with power domains making themselves felt on both.

Helen's Vulnerable Identity

In the novel, identity vulnerability and anxiety are written into the depiction of Mona's and her sister Callie's mother. In Chinese American literature, mother-daughter relationships are often narrated as a cultural conflict between Chinese values and traditions versus newly assimilated American ones. Jen's narrative avoids such a paradigm, because the mother character is quite assimilated, whereas her two daughters are fighting for their own answers to the question of belonging. Ethnicity is contested and constantly changing. In *Mona*, the parent characters Helen and Ralph belong to the first-generation Chinese immigrants who struggle for what they hope will be a decent life in their host land. As immigrants, the Changs have had their difficult diasporic experience in adapting to the U.S., as is narrated in *Typical American*. Their seemingly "melting into" the host society, adapting to the privileged White Anglo-Saxon Protestant (WASP) model, has indeed enabled an acceptable life with economic success. Helen's wish is to help her two daughters achieve a higher social status and economic sufficiency, as her well-to-do familial position in pre-revolutionary China would lead her to expect.

Actually her assimilation has a deep root in class anxiety. Born of an upper-middle-class family in Shanghai, as we learn from both novels, Helen was clearly privileged and hence perhaps belonged to a minority, but not one that was placed on the social margin. In pre-revolutionary China, she owned a car, had servants, and enjoyed a position in society by virtue of her family history. Since such a status was swept away by the success of the Chinese revolution, Helen's whole outlook in the present including her attitude to her daughters is ultimately shaped by the Gramscian relations of political and military forces spoken of above. Accustomed to affluence as they grew up in Shanghai, both Helen and Ralph were influenced by music, dress, lifestyle, and ideas of life and education that can be deemed Western. Helen grew up with Christmas trees, which formed a tradition. She ate bagels for breakfast in the morning, and studied at a convent school run by French missionaries. As her daughter Mona explains,

> "[...] She said it's all a matter of manners. You have to know how to stand, how to sit. She said people in Shanghai knew who you

were right away, you didn't have to open your mouth."
"And is that true?"
"I think you also had to wear a lot of jewelry." (*M* 53)

Thus it is hard for Helen to find out there is a great divide between life in her former country and life in the new, as a Chinese immigrant. Helen expects her daughters to act like the privileged mainstream, especially "in a place where people might look down on you" (ibid., 280). A constant fear of being the object of "looking down" exemplifies the vulnerability of their identity. Nonetheless, owing to her assimilationist propensities, Helen learns to adapt to the dominant cultural practice and apply her diasporic understanding to Chinese American life: she "never intended that they [the Changs] should be a minority" (ibid., 52).

Repeated statements such as "We own this restaurant," "We live in Scarshill," the neighborhood of a Jewish middle and upper class community, and "You should see our tax bracket" all bespeak a thinly veiled identity anxiety. To Helen, Chinese immigrants who are economically established through hard work are distinguished from other minorities: they are "a model minority and Great American Success. They know they belong in the promised land" (ibid., 3). She boasts about her high-standard earlier life to show her higher social identity (ibid., 41–42); she insists her daughters work hard and choose a profession that enables them to make money (ibid., 129), and wants Callie to become a doctor (ibid., 235). Her daughters should adopt the dominant WASP-related values — to adjust to the ideological hegemony of the society's dominant classes, as spoken of above, to "act in harmony with others." This extends to a race-biased mindset when she worries about Callie's college rooming arrangement with a girl named Naomi, whom she takes as likely to be black and thus of lower-class status, while the girl reassuringly turns out to be a "brownish black" (ibid., 37). Helen sees herself as a parent who is Westernized enough not to order her daughters to speak Chinese (ibid., 48). At the beginning she is confident that her daughters will obey her wishes, due to her installation — paradoxically countering the assimilationist bent — of the traditional Chinese value of filial piety. The hope is presumably that a collective will might enable an exercise of power, absorbing the individual. Yet such imposition does not carry very far. When she is forced to realize Mona's determination to convert to Judaism, Helen is afraid that her daughter has lost her Chinese identity and their social/ethnic status could drive them out of their Great Success in the promised land. Helen's seemingly flexible and performative identity program, resulting from class-based identity anxiety, only locks her up in what her daughter at one point calls "Fort Chang" (ibid., 269). Will the girl gain a new freedom after leaving the fort?

Escaping From the Fort

> In short, if I am inescapably Chinese by descent, I am only sometimes Chinese by consent. When and how is a matter of politics.
>
> (Ien Ang 36)

What Mona's case illustrates is a decisive "initial negotiation with the self," which cultural contracts theory urges tracing. From the first few pages, the narrator gradually moves closer inside her mind, so that before long we hear "Mona begins to realize [...]" Much of the narrative then tracks the erratic process of initial negotiation, as she comes to consider her family context as "Fort Chang." Mona confesses to her boyfriend that she is never at home because she is not WASP, not black, not as Jewish as Jewish can be, and not from Chinatown either (*M* 231). At the beginning she tries to be more Chinese, then American, then Jewish, without much success as she experiences the hybridity of different ethnic influences in her identity formation process. For a time, she seems to have a somewhat blithe understanding of identity switch: "Like I could become Jewish, if I wanted to. I'd just have to switch, that's all" (ibid., 14). A conversion process appears like a fairly simple technical procedure not requiring much adjustment. And indeed, a crucial turn comes about when she eventually claims a paradoxical Chinese-Jewish-American identity. Against the discrimination experience that is familiar to her family, this Chinese girl knows that her neighbors are "rich and Jewish": a "Great American Success" that clearly belongs in the promised land. In the United States, and in the fictional neighborhood, the most common Jewish population is that of Ashkenazim coming originally from Eastern Europe or Germany. According to Marc Lee Raphael, Jews generally are among the highest socioeconomic groupings in the US (1) the country has long been seen as "'Protestant, Catholic, and Jewish,' as if Jews constituted something like a third of the religious population and Muslims did not exist" (ibid., 4). Scarshill, where the Changs now live, belongs to "the upstanding-citizen type" associated with well-to-do Jews, much better than where the Changs (who would like to be "New Jews") used to live, though "a bit down the hill from the private-plane set" (*M* 4). Mona's best Jewish friend Barbara Gugelstein "is her own separate accounting unit"; while she gets paid to do housework at home, Mona and Callie "are slave labor" (ibid., 26).

Mona finds the life of her Jewish boyfriend Seth Mandel's step-mother Bea ideal: she has a big house and a stock portfolio (ibid., 117), with a social conscience that enables her to fight for black civil rights. Bea not only defends her own rights, she tries to improve society and actually shares with the poor a portion of her properties. Bea's fluid balance between the rich and the poor, the black and the white, the privileged and the underprivileged, is thoroughly desirable for Mona, an identity formation that her own mother does not have. As she describes it, "my parents would never even go marching for themselves, much less for a bunch of blacks" (ibid., 117); "[i]n China, there is a compound wall; in America, there is lawn" (ibid., 236–237). Mona believes this makes Americans more "approachable," while she does not realize that the lawn is a sign of upscale status that may in turn need defending. She explains her mother's position: "[...] in China, people mostly try to stay out of trouble. Keep their heads down. The tallest tree catches all the wind, they say. Sweep the snow from your own doorstep" (ibid., 236).

While Mona has no wish to be locked inside Fort Chang, she knows that leaving it would be a form of betrayal in her parents' eyes. With growing intensity, Helen and her daughter challenge each other's self-image. Mona is near enough to "the pain of immigration" as Scarshill shows "both the Chinese and the Jews as Scarred peoples" (Rody 90). In this dilemma, an attempt to emulate Bea appears a possible solution — one that necessitates her conversion to Judaism. The idea of religious freedom is bound up in what Foucault has called a "'general politics' of truth." While Mona's conversion may subjectively and from one perspective appear to be a form of free and individual choice, we should not overlook that it actually operates as what Jackson calls a "ready-to-sign cultural contract," one in which the dominant group makes next to no concession to adapt or adjust to the newcomer. For critical analysis, this may well be a case of "situated knowledge," in that "knowledge is always a view from somewhere" (Barad 180). Consequently, for the conversion a notion of "remaking the boundaries" as spoken of earlier turns out to have rather narrow limits. The remaking concept itself, like that of fluid and choosable identity, is a form of knowledge that functions as "a condensed node in an agonistic power field" (Haraway 577).

The conversion effort inevitably meets with her parents' strong disapproval, coupled with a renouncing of their assimilation history. On the High Holy Days, which are alliteratively associated with Helen's lofty claims, Helen accuses her daughter of being a troublemaker:

> "That's enough Jewish," she says. "Forget about services. Not funny anymore. You know where all the trouble started? All the trouble started from you become Jewish."
>
> "Mom," Mona says. "It's a free country. I can go to temple if I want. In fact, if I wanted to, I could go to a mosque ..."
>
> "Forget about free country," she says.
>
> "What do you mean? This is America. I can remember what I want, I can be what I want, I can ... It's a free country, I can talk however I want. It's my right."
>
> "Free country! Right! In this house, no such things!"
>
> "That's exactly the problem! Everywhere else is America, but in this house it's China!"
>
> "That's right! No America here! In this house, children listen to parents!" (Ibid., 248–250)

At the heart of the situation is a clash of values: a Chinese value of family and filial piety conflicts with a foregrounded American value of individual freedom of choice. Helen can accept her daughter's adapting to an American, dominant value for social advancement, but not in becoming a Jew. Driven away from home, just as she always keeps searching for a home that becomes elusive (see also Lai), Mona becomes homeless. Wandering around Grand Central Station, she finds a lady sitting next to her on a bench: "This lady has laid herself down, stretched herself out — and now, sure enough, is making herself comfortable" (ibid., 255). When she stirs, with a dangling leg losing its mooring, we have a symbolic indication that Mona herself might be dragged into an *unheimliche* condition. She is made to feel "as though she stands at the pointy start of time. Behind her, no history. Before her — everything. How arrogant! As if you have no mother! As if you come out of thin air!" (ibid.) The air is the emptiness of social vacancy, without family roots. There is a threat of degradation that she has not considered: "Is this life outside of high school?" (Ibid.) The homeless lady with dirty clothes is a mirror for Mona. Actually she serves as a stand-in for Helen: when Mona offers her a better place to rest, she is also reaching out to her mother, who meets her upon her return in clothing that recalls the homeless woman (see Black 131). In any case, Mona persists in her determination, and luckily encounters Bea — who gives her money for a sustainable escape. That escape is not simply a movement toward any other cultural community. On the last day of his stay in America, Mona's Japanese boyfriend Sherman asks her to marry him. But she responds, "How can I be Japanese?" (*M* 18) His answer seems logical in his terms: "Like you become American. Switch" (ibid., 19). Yet such an oriental, almost arbitrary switch would not serve her social class mobility.

Thus Mona's socioculturally assimilative negotiation continues, until at the novel's end she marries Seth — adopting neither his family name nor hers, but creating the integrative and witty name Changowitz. Nothing could more clearly speak of a fusion of cultures, in tune with the novel's "*jouissance* of boundary-crossing in itself" (Rody 90). The unique name perhaps does justice to the recommendation that, while acting in harmony, "the *junzi* does not seek to be like others" (as quoted above). There are both inherited and performative aspects of identity, existing "simultaneously in a crowded self"; accordingly, as Shameem Black argues, "Mona is not Chinese until she becomes Jewish" (124). While Bhabha had highlighted "remaking the boundaries" as in marriages between a Chica-riricua and a Hassidic Jew (*Location* 217–218), analyzing the novel requires careful attention to the stages of the narrative unfolding of an "initial negotiation with the self."

The inherited and performative aspects are passed on to Mona's little daughter Io, the figure from Greek myth who is constantly on the move without rest. The narrator asks, "For what else would be the favorite cuisine of a child part Jewish, part Chinese, barely off breast milk?" The answer: "But of course, Italian" (*M* 303) — prompting Mona to muse that (supported by an amusing "Nes and Yo") she could easily change her name, like her own, if she wished to do so. Affiliation, abandonment, and adoption become related options in a fluid cultural negotiation (see Anshaw 9).

Making One's Own Choices?

Callie's case is carefully depicted to contrast with Mona's. Callie cannot be understood without attention to her African-American roommate Naomi. Naomi is "a Renaissance woman" who grew up in a working-class Chicago neighborhood, spent her teen years in a fancy New England prep school, and understands Chinese culture even better than Callie and Helen. An ideally hybrid persona in U.S. multicultural society, she studies Mandarin, practices yoga and Taiji (while she also likes black cultural icons and cooking). Being good friends, Callie and Naomi work together on a book. But the book is only credited to Naomi, as the editor of the book ignores Callie by taking it as "one person's" book — Naomi's. Callie seems to negotiate the incident quite well by explaining to her sister, "We're not book material. Naomi's experience has an import, ours just doesn't. After all, blacks are the majority minority. Also they've been slaves and everything" (*M* 270). However, Callie is encouraged by the editor to write books about Chinese culture, though she has "never been to China" (ibid.). Though Naomi understands China and Chinese culture better than Callie, the editor is not interested in acquired knowledge but in genetic heritage. Naomi becomes entangled in contradiction: on the one hand, she cherishes a freedom to choose whoever she is, constructing hybrid roots for identification. She suggests that Callie could just forget her parents and connect instead with ancestors, who may or may not be genetically related to her (ibid., 129). Yet on the other hand, Naomi tells Mona "You are yellow. A yellow person, a yellow girl" (ibid., 170). That opens a semiotic gap of its own, since Mona's "summertime color is most definitely brown, and the rest of the year she is not exactly a textbook primary" (ibid.). Naomi's assignment of ethnic identity in literal terms of color subverts her insistence on choice (see also Yuan's study of the body in this volume). Possibly this shows a reappearance of an earlier self in a suitable context, as Jackson has diagnosed the separation from a primary culture.

As for Callie, we should remain aware that the concept of model minority, the stereotype that the U.S. mainstream imposes on Asian Americans, becomes one that Callie consciously or not adopts. Callie chooses to perform in this way in exchange for being accepted into society, a choice which involves refraining from any disruption of power relations: one can concede, accommodate in identification, or negotiate a social relationship anew. In her case, too, the narrative structure traces her internal negotiation process, in various stages, though not to the same degree as with her sister (for the context of traumatizing experiences in the process, see Krause's chapter in this volume). Callie accepts her name not appearing in the book she has co-authored with Naomi, since the editor encourages her to write a book on Chinese culture — her negotiation strategy is a smart win-

win strategy for better chances of social adaptation. When she declares "I'm my own person" and "I made my own choices" (ibid., 302), and succeeds in becoming a pediatrician and raising a family, she also changes, becomes "more Chinese," and renames herself Kailan. Chen critiques her "pseudo-individuality" since she is being "merely submissive to traditional authority"; her performance poses no subversive threat to the society's power structure (18). But that does not do full justice to her negotiation process, which Callie appears to have understood as a carefully calibrated trade-off, weighing loss against gain, in the sociocultural marketplace.

Suggestions of subversiveness seem rather to be written into the depiction of Naomi, who appears capable of adjusting that quality to suit her needs. She preaches to Mona about resistance to colonial or race-related oppression, while she boasts her freedom to choose whoever she may be and what she can become. Naomi practices daily meditation and yoga, drinks Chinese tea, cooks "an authentic tea-smoked duck" (*M* 186), and even speaks a clear Mandarin much better than either of the sisters. It hardly matters that meditation does not belong only to Chinese culture, or that yoga was not invented by the Chinese, but by Indians: Naomi believes it will make her "closer to Buddhist" (ibid., 169). Naomi fuses cultures, each of which has "rubbed off" on the other: she likes jazz, potato pie, Chinese dumplings, diet soda, Scrabble, film noir, star gazing, soccer, and other preoccupations. Mona so admires Naomi that she "does everything Naomi says. She strives to think the way Naomi thinks" (ibid., 170).

Yet there are problems. Naomi's notion of identity choice is punctured in her emphatic imposing of a "yellow girl" label on Mona, as quoted above. Her self-concept is hardly subversive. While working in Scottish dress as waitresses in Rhode Island, Naomi and Callie usually respond to people's inquiry "What part of Scotland are you from?" in wittily subversive tones, claiming that one is from "deepest, darkest Wales" and the other from "the Far Eastern part" (ibid.). They take it as a way to challenge an ethnic stereotype. But when Naomi serves Mona and her friends, the Ingle family, she responds to the same question "So what part of Scotland are you from?" merely with "I'm not from Scotland" (ibid., 178). When Mona is disappointed, Naomi ignores her "as though she has never seen Mona before in her life" (ibid.), for the sake of "purposefully letting the Ingles enjoy a particularly leisurely dinner" (ibid., 180). This is a submissive strategy: the rich Ingles enjoy a high social status. We hear that "if Eloise [Ingle] disappears, every policeman on the East Coast is going to be out searching for her" (ibid., 185). If submissiveness is a performance, just like the witty elusiveness, it nonetheless denies any consistent effort to shake up clichés of ethnicity. Jen records and reveals the priority of social distinctions, allowing the reader to witness the difficulty of remaking boundaries.

Playing the WASP Game

In the novel, several characters are capable of negotiating multiple identities, an activity which is contingent on context. Mona's best friend Barbara first tries to perform the role of a typical American teenager. She wants to appear cool by performing less politely than Mona; she wants to be popular among her peers by having "big boobs" and using a Lord & Taylor charge card. Yet she suddenly declares herself to be a Jew (ibid., 30) attending Jewish ritual and traditions. Her abrupt behavior results from her thinking that "being Jewish is great" and "there's something special about being Jewish she wouldn't want to give up" (ibid., 135). However, when her father is in danger of being fired, her selfhood's inner vulnerability (as in Ting-Toomey's analysis) becomes exposed when she turns to correcting her "Jewish" nose and changes back to a mainstream American identity again, that of a "WASP": "A little Jewish is fine, but my mom says too much is too much — look at what happened in Munich" (ibid., 222). She is afraid of being attacked by extremists or territorists (ibid.). Eloise Ingle's father, a successful and wealthy businessman, tells the great lesson of life: "You've got to know how the game is played" (ibid., 177), to take advantage of different cultures and identities in any contingent context.

The most skilled performer and identity-switcher, Mona's boyfriend and finally husband, submits no less to social reality. Mona accuses Seth of being a man with no manners (ibid., 121); adopting anti-bourgeois values, Seth lives in a teepee, uses chopsticks, does yoga, sleeps on a tatami mat, wears dashiki, displays an exquisite Zen-like melancholy, believes in a possible previous life in which he was Japanese, and endeavors to behave as "an authentic inauthentic Jew." Self-centered, he seems to have no consideration for others. Seth believes that "between the inside person and the outside person there should be no difference" (ibid.). He explains that he is "in the process of becoming an inauthentic inauthentic Jew," still searching for his identity and to be "not confused with an authentic Jew" (ibid., 112). Yet when Mona argues that "without the world of outer politeness, you cannot have a world of inner richness" (ibid., 237), Seth finally acts and "moves differently" and negotiates a different self (ibid., 275–276), playing "the game." He goes to university, against his previous inclinations when he wanted to pursue a true self (ibid., 112). He ultimately becomes a professor and "generally noble type" with tenure prospects (ibid., 298), hence very promising in terms of Helen's social expectations. He has negotiated his own way as member of a model minority, with a clearly "WASP"-ish perspective (see also Chen).

No Walls Between the Rooms?

But are not the lower classes unlikely or ineligible to "switch" their cultural and social identities? Mona and her middle-class friends Seth and Barbara refuse to accept this. They attempt to prove their hypothesis by building an open space for a multicultural project of "a house with no walls between the rooms" — in Barbara's parents' spacious house in which they have discovered tunnels, a site which they name Camp Gugelstein. In the camp, the lower classes are represented by a black and a Chinese illegal immigrant, whom Mona and her friends observe and on whom they conduct experiments (see *M* 194). Among their findings is that when white men fight back against oppression, they're heroes, but when black men do, they're savages (ibid., 195). And they wonder "which is worse — not speaking English and having no visa and leaving your family behind to be forced to drink their own piss or having a black face and living in a project and having a great-grandmother who was a slave?" (ibid., 139). The girls try to persuade black Alfred to convert to Judaism: the "whole key" to this religion is "to ask, ask, instead of just obey, obey," so that Alfred will learn how to have "a big house and a four-bay garage and a gardener" (ibid., 137). Mona's own hope to find a "switch" to upward mobility would be replicated in this "key," when a black man performs a parallel move. Yet Alfred knows better: "We're asking and asking, but there ain't nobody answering. And nobody is calling us Wasp, man, and nobody is forgetting we're a minority, and if we don't mind our manners, we're like as not to end up doing time in a concrete hotel. We're black, see. We're Negroes" (ibid.). And indeed, the camp itself proves as much; the socially conscious group collapses as soon as a silver brandy flask is missing, forcing the lower-class men to leave.

This socio-ethnic experiment is a significant event in Mona's process of "initial negotiation with the self" as described by Jackson, where it becomes a feature in the reader's corresponding negotiation with the identity formations which the novel offers for attention. Mona realizes, "If people lived in houses with no walls between the rooms, there would have to be a lot of rules" (ibid., 208) — ones that would presumably derive from and implement a Gramscian "relation of social forces," hence a fresh structure composed of high walls. A black lower-class man is no Eloise Ingle: "[...] she is not your friend Alfred. Nobody cares what happens to Alfred. If Eloise disappears, every policeman on the East Coast is going to be out searching for her" (ibid., 185). The fictional structure itself demonstrates that "nobody cares" about the likes of Alfred: the epilogue accounts for the recent developments of major characters, all of whom have promising futures. Yet Alfred's socio-ethnic group all but disappears into silence.

Conclusion

If there "ain't nobody answering," the prospect for social as well as (inter)cultural communication appears dim. Will a character like Alfred end up in a "concrete hotel" rather than a room without walls? Is a black cook's diagnosis valid: "Some things just be's that way"? (ibid., 301) In a satirical vein, Jen mocks all characters in individual ways, doing so from the perspective of the model minority to which she herself belongs — which means accepting American dominant core values of the individual's resourcefulness in tearing down the walls between rooms. In an interview, Jen affirms:

> In the beginning, you want acceptance. And then later on you want self realization. Maybe that is a way of being like everybody else here in America.
>   ***Bill Moyers:*** Well, that's very American, isn't it?
>   ***Gish Jen:*** It is.
>   ***Bill Moyers:*** The business of inventing ourselves?
>   ***Gish Jen:*** Yeah, it is. But one hopes that one will somehow bring some inner essence out and make it manifest. (Jen, "Becoming")

Social identity formation, as Jackson has observed, requires "initial negotiation with the self"; an "inner essence" would thus become "manifest" in the person's social identity.

The manifestation fuses cultural and social positions. We can consider the case of young Barbara's decision to alter her Jewish nose by an operation. She desires to become an invisible minority (which Mona cannot), to appear indistinguishable from a WASP in order to avoid ethnic discrimination. Since her family's social status is much more solid than Mona's, in her form of border-crossing (inscribed on the body) an ethnic issue is inextricably bound up with class considerations. When an Intercultural Communication textbook observes that "the individuals in a given culture are not identical, which suggests that any culture is replete with cultural struggles" (Martin and Nakayama 91), the struggles are more than cultural: "[C]ulture, social class, and communication work together to reproduce the contemporary social structure" (ibid., 70). As several scholars have pointed out (see Dirik, McAlister, Wong *Reading*), cultural conflicts cannot be solely interpreted from a cultural perspective.

Nor can they be understood without attention to gender, when we consider objectivity as bound to "limited location" and knowledge as invariably "situated" (Haraway 583): Barbara's identity is less dynamic than that of Seth, so that the difference between individuals in their ethnic group would need examining in light of gendered positions. So would the case of African-American Naomi, just beyond the novel's end, if we consider that minority girls and women, perhaps even more than men, have opportunities of upward class mobility through interracial marriage (see Qian, Blair and Ruf 557, Shinagawa and Pang 127). But Jen creates a notable counter-instance in the case of the marriage between Alfred and Barbara's cousin Evie, which enables him to move upward a notch or two on the social ladder, with the Jewish community "rubbing off" on him. In this novel's seemingly light and witty vein, Jen diagnoses the challenges to one's self-image that dwell in the prospect for ethnic minorities' social rising, without concealing the notion that it is a person's grasp of occasion or opportunity that makes a difference and without pretending that it would be readily available to all members of a community. As Rabbi Horowitz recommends, "people are supposed to be their own rabbi and do their business directly with G-d" (*M* 34). Yet the notion of a person's grasp is not necessarily a showcasing of individualism: it harbors, as Jen ("So") has clearly articulated, a submerged "power differential" that challenges the reader's own self-image, to provoke considering *why* it seems to be so funny for an Asian-American woman to think of switching identities. As "object of knowledge," the novel thus turns out to be "an actor and agent," engaging in "a power-charged social relation of 'conversation'" with its reader (Haraway 592 – 593). The conversation is a communication process, with readers who are likely to be inevitably Others to at least one of the novel's multiple cultural communities — be it Chinese, Catholic, Jewish, or African American. It could become a "co-created" contract of "mutual valuation," as described by Ronald Jackson, pointing up the restrictive type of "ready-to-sign" contract which is all that is available to Mona.

The writing of this chapter was supported by in part by Zhejiang Federation of Humanities and Social Sciences [Grant number 2016N61M].

References

Ang, Ien. *On Not Speaking Chinese: Living Between Asia and the West*. London: Routledge, 2001.

Anshaw, Carol. "The 21st-Century Family." *Women's Review of Books* 22.2 (2004): 8–9.

Barad, Karen. "Meeting the Universe Halfway: Realism and Social Constructivism Without Contradiction." *Feminism, Science, and the Philosophy of Science*. Eds. Lynn Hankinson Nelson and Jack Nelson. Dordrecht: Kluwer, 1996. 161–194.

Bauman, Zygmunt. *Culture in a Liquid Modern World*. Cambridge: Polity, 2011.

—. *The Individualized Society*. Cambridge: Polity, 2001.

—. *Liquid Life*. Cambridge: Polity, 2005.

—. *Thinking Sociologically*. 2nd ed. Oxford: Blackwell, 2001.

Bhabha, Homi K. "In the Cave of Making: Thoughts on Third Space." *Communicating in the Third Space*. Eds. Karin Ikas and Gerhard Wagner. New York & Abingdon, Oxon.: Routledge, 2009. ix-xiv.

—. *The Location of Culture*. London: Routledge, 2004.

Black, Shameem. *Fiction Across Borders: Imagining the Lives of Others in Late Twentieth-Century Novels*. New York: Columbia UP, 2010.

Chang, Yi-Fan. "*Identity Switch: a Study on Gish Jen's Mona in the Promised Land*." MA thesis. National Sun Yat-sen University. 2010.

Chen, Fu-Jen. "Performing Identity in Gish Jen's *Mona in the Promised Land*." *The International Fiction Review* 34.1–2 (2007): 56–70.

Chen, Guo-Ming, and William J. Starosta. *Foundations of Intercultural Communication*. Boston: Allyn and Bacon, 1998.

Cohen, Anthony P. *Signifying Identities: Anthropological Perspectives on Boundaries and Contested Values*. New York: Routledge, 2000.

Confucius. *The Analects*. Trans. Robert Eno. 2015. Web. 17 July 2016. http://

www.indiana.edu/~p374/Analects_of_Confucius_(Eno-2015).pdf

—. *The Analects*. Chinese Text Project. Trans. James Legge. Web. 17 July 2016. http://ctext.org/analects

Daldal, Asli. "Power and Ideology in Michel Foucault and Antonio Gramsci: A Comparative Analysis." *Review of History and Political Science* 2.2 (2014): 149–167.

Dirik, Arif. "Culturalism as Hegemonic Ideology and Liberating Practice." *The Nature and Context of Minority Discourse*. Eds. Abdul R. JanMohamed and David Lloyd. New York: Oxford UP, 1990. 394–431.

Dong, Lan. "From Changowitz to Bailey Wong: Mixed Heritage and Transnational Families in Gish Jen's Fiction." *Growing up Transnational: Identity and Kinship in a Global Era*. Eds. May Friedman and Silvia Schultermandl. Toronto: U of Toronto P, 2011. 210–221.

Eder, Richard. "Review of *Mona in the Promised Land* by Gish Jen." *Los Angeles Times* 26 May 1996: Book Review 2.

Feng, Pin-chia. *Diasporic Representations: Reading Chinese American Women's Fiction*. Berlin: LIT, 2010.

Foucault, Michel. *The History of Sexuality: An Introduction*. Trans. Robert Hurley. London: Penguin, 1978.

—. "Truth and Power." *Power/Knowledge. Selected Interviews and Other Writings by Michel Foucault, 1972 – 1977*. Ed. C. Gordon. Brighton: Harvester, 1980. 109–133.

Gilbert, Matthew. "Gish Jen, All-American: The Cambridge Novelist Doesn't Like to Be Labeled — Except As a Big-Mouth." *The Boston Globe* 4 June 1996: 53.

Gilman, Sander. "'We're Not Jews': Imagining Jewish Bodies and Jewish History in Contemporary Multicultural Literature." *Modern Judaism* 23.2 (2003): 126 – 155. *Jewish Frontiers: Essays on Bodies, Histories, and Identities*. New York: Palgrave Macmillan, 2003. 169–206.

Gonzalez, Begona Simal. "The (Re)Birth of Mona Changowitz: Rituals and Ceremonies of Cultural Conversion and Self-Making in *Mona in the Promised Land*." *MELUS* 26.2 (2001): 225–242.

Gramsci, Antonio. *History, Philosophy and Culture in the Young Gramsci*. Eds. Pedro Cavalanti and Paul Piccone. Saint Louis: Telos P, 1975.

—. *Selections from the Prison Notebooks*. 6th ed. London: Wishart, 1980.

Hall, Stuart, and Paul du Gay, eds. *Questions of Cultural Identity*. London: Sage, 1996.

Haraway, Donna. "Situated Knowledges: The Science Question in Feminism and the Privilege of Partial Perspective." *Feminist Studies* 14.3 (1988): 577–599.

Hecht, Michael L., Ronald L. Jackson II, and Sidney A. Ribeau. *African American Communication: Exploring Identity and Culture*. 2nd ed. Mahwah, NJ: Lawrence Erlbaum Associates, 2003.

Ho, Jennifer Ann. *Consumption and Identity in Asian American Coming-of-Age Novels*. New York: Routledge, 2005.

Jackson, Ronald L. II. "Cultural Contracts Theory: Toward an Understanding of Identity Negotiation." *Communication Quarterly* 50.3–4 (2002): 359–367.

—. *The Negotiation of Cultural Identity: Perceptions of European Americans and African Americans*. Westport, CT: Praeger, 1999.

Jen, Gish. "Becoming American: Personal Journeys. Interview with Gish

Jen." 2003. Web. 12 July 2016. http://www.pbs.org/becomingamerican/ap
_pjourneys_transcript1.html

—. *Mona in the Promised Land*. New York: Alfred A. Knopf, 1996.

—. "So, aren't you going to ask if I'm Jewish?" Interview with Ron Hogan.
The Beatrice Interviews. 1996. Web. 12 July 2016. http://www.beatrice.
com/interviews/jen/

—. *Typical American*. Boston: Houghton Mifflin/Seymore Lawrence, 1991.

Kulich, Steve J. "Toward an Integrated Identity Matrix Theory (IIMT):
Proposals for a Dynamic Cultural Identity Framework." *Identity and
Intercultural Communication (I): Theoretical and Contextual Construction*.
Eds. Xiaodong Dai and Steve J. Kulich. Shanghai: Shanghai Foreign
Language Education P, 2010. 69–102.

Kurylo, Anastacia. *Intercultural Communication: Representation and
Construction of Culture*. Los Angeles: Sage, 2013.

Lai, Chung-Hsiung. "Nomadic Desire: The Schizo-Identity in *Mona in the
Promised Land*." *Intergrams* 10.2–11.1 (2010): 1–19.

Li, Hongyan. "Anxious Identities in Gish Jen's Novels." Ph.D. Dissertation,
Suzhou Univ. 2011. In Chinese.

Liu, Zhe. "The Pursuit and Construction of Ethnic Identity." *Journal of
Tianjin Foreign Studies Univ*. 19.4 (2012): 72–75.

Martin, Judith N., and Thomas K. Nakayama. *Intercultural Communication
in Contexts*. 5th ed. New York: McGraw-Hill, 2010.

McAlister, Melani. "(Mis) reading *The Joy Luck Club*." *Asian America:
Journal of Culture and the Arts* 1 (1992): 102–118.

Miller, Jean Baker. "Domination and Subordination." *The Social Construction
of Difference: Race, Class, Gender, and Sexuality*. Ed. Paula S. Rothenberg.
New York: St. Martin's P, 1992. 73–80.

Moon, Dreama G. "Critical Reflections on Culture and Critical Intercultural
Communication." *The Handbook of Critical Intercultural Communication*.
Eds. Thomas K. Nakayama and Rona Tamiko Halualani. Malden, Mass. &
Chichester: Wiley-Blackwell, 2010. 34–52.

Partridge, Jeffrey F. L. "Beyond Multicultural: Cultural Hybridity in the
Novels of Gish Jen." *Bloom's Modern Critical Views: Asian American
Writers*. Ed. Harold Bloom. New York: Infobase, 2009. 169–192.

Qian, Zhenchao, Sampson Lee Blair and Stacey D. Ruf. "Asian American
Interracial and Interethnic Marriage: Differences by Education and
Nativity." *The International Migration Review* 35.2 (2001): 557–586.

Raphael, Marc Lee. *Judaism in America*. New York: Columbia UP, 2003.

Rody, Caroline. *The Interethnic Imagination: Roots and Passages in
Contemporary Asian American Fiction*. Oxford UP, 2009.

Rutherford, Jonathan. "The Third Space: Interview with Homi Bhabha."
Identity: Community, Culture, Difference. Ed. Jonathan Rutherford.
London: Lawrence and Wishart, 1990. 207–221.

Shinagawa, Larry Hajime, and Gin Yong Pang. "Asian American
Panethnicity and Intermarriage." *Amerasia Journal* 22.2 (1996): 127–152.

Sorrells, Kathryn. *Intercultural Communication: Globalization and Social
Justice*. Los Angeles: Sage, 2013.

Ting-Toomey, Stella. *Communicating Across Cultures*. New York & London:
Guilford P, 1999. 2nd ed. 2019.

Wang, Chih-ming. "'An Identity Switch': A Critique of Multiculturalism in

Gish Jen's *Mona in the Promised Land.*" *Crossing Oceans: Reconfiguring American Literary Studies in the Pacific Rim*. Eds. Noelle Brada-Williams and Karen Chow. Hong Kong: Hong Kong UP, 2004. 139–154.

Wang, Han-sheng. "Ethnic Identity in Gish Jen's *Mona in the Promised Land.*" *Applied Linguistic Journal of Kaoshiung First University of Science and Technology* (2007): 113–130.

Wong, Sau-ling Cynthia. "But What in the World Is an Asian American? Culture, Class and Invented Traditions in *Gish Jen's Mona in the Promised Land.*" *European and American Studies* 32.4 (2002): 641–674.

—. "Denationalization Reconsidered: Asian American Cultural Criticism at a Theoretical Crossroads." *Amerasia Journal* 21.1–2 (1995): 1–27.

—. *Reading Asian American Literature: From Necessity to Extravagance*. Princeton, NJ: Princeton UP, 1993.

Zheng, Dong-lin. "Perplexity and Growth: An Analysis on the Initiation Theme of *Mona in the Promised Land.*" *Sino-US English Teaching* 7.12 (2010): 78–81.

14

Power Relations and the Body in Transcultural Communication: Reading Zadie Smith's *White Teeth*

Yuan Mingqing
University of Bayreuth

Summary: This chapter aims to integrate Maurice Merleau-Ponty's phenomenological understanding of the body and Michel Foucault's analysis of the discursive production of power in order to analyze the transcultural communication of people of color in Zadie Smith's novel *White Teeth* (2000). It is through the body that migrants perceive the world, experience it, construct and interpret themselves and their relations with the world to which they respond and with which they interact. The subtle violence imposed on the fictional characters' intersubjective bodies for instance through eyeing and through naming meets with a desire to adapt to the metropolitan land, which drives them unconsciously and without lasting success to fuse elements of the dominant discourse into their own body and its mentality. Yet when bodily discourse inflicts forms of violence, it turns out that the process is not simply where characters' self-abjection comes from, but also where their resistance and subversion can take place.

Introduction

With the fast development of technology in conjunction with massive global migration, transcultural communication or transculturality has become a buzzword in many disciplines. The concept of transcultural communication evolves from those of international communication, cross-cultural communication, and intercultural communication, but it differs from them by more strongly acknowledging and calling attention to the problematic concept of the nation state, the ambiguity of (cultural) boundaries, the ongoing dynamics of encounters, and the multilayered intersectionality of identity and cultural space. As Marwan Kraidy explains, transcultural communication is based on a belief that "all cultures are inherently mixed," while cross- or intercultural communication "tends to study contacts between individuals from different cultures that are assumed to be discrete entities," and international communication is mainly built upon national territorial divisions (194). This implies that transcultural communication, on the one hand, is not limited to interpersonal communication, but operates more on social and cultural levels; on the other hand, it does not focus on differences of nation states or regions, but delves into various layers of hybridity (ibid., 1).

Yet transcultural communication, which is crucial in the formation of hybridity, in fact "strengthens the agency of those with the means to translate and name the world, while weakening the agency of other participants" (ibid., 152). Accordingly, as a result and also a reflection of globalization, transcultural communication may have the effect of enhancing a dominant discourse and silencing the suppressed and their attempted subversion. And transculturation, as a result of transcultural communication, always involves a process not only of acquiring another culture, but also the deculturation of losing or being uprooted from a previous culture; it consequently leads to "new cultural phenomena" (Fernando Ortiz in 1970, qtd. in Hepp 15). We may gather from these explanations that the concept of hybridity does not necessarily entail only a positive interpretation. Instead, a matrix of power relations is embedded in the formation of hybridity (see for instance Kraidy 9, 14ff., Hepp 20ff.), and transcultural communication serves as an ongoing, changing, and interactive terrain of power struggles.

This leads to a general questioning of the concept and evaluation of hybridity. According to Homi Bhabha, hybridity emerges from "a doubling, dissembling image of being in at least two places at once which makes it impossible for the devalued, insatiable évolué […] to accept the coloniser's invitation to identity" (117). However, as Ania Loomba observes, "the split, ambivalent, hybrid colonial subject" in Bhabha's conceptualization is "curiously universal and homogeneous" (150). To be sure, hybridity speaks of a conflicted, ongoing, and changing identity, but hybrid features within hybridity and differences beneath its surface are hardly discussed. The concept of hybridity thus appears to have covered all internal differences and taken postcolonial syncretism as a benchmark with which all other identities or subjectivities should compare. Only a hybrid or integrated identity in this sense, in a multicultural era, appears as successful transculturation/acculturation. To some extent, then, the celebration of hybridity could be said to impose a form of domination on the mitigating conciliation of painful identities, all but ignoring deeper reasons that may lead to a "non-hybrid" identity. This raises the questions: what is the standard to judge the success or failure of transculturation? And what is the relation between a hybrid identity and transculturation?

Embodying Communication

All these questions may be explored, experienced, and even answered by a focus on the human body, if the body is

> no longer conceived as an object of the world, but as our means of communication with it, [...] the world no longer conceived as a collection of determinate objects, but as the horizon latent in all our experience and itself ever-present and anterior to every determining thought. (Merleau-Ponty, *Phenomenology* 106)

As against Descartes' dualism, Merleau-Ponty highlights the unity of the body and consciousness. This enables what Hwa Yol Jung has called the interpretive art of "*carnal hermeneutics*": Ways of embodiment are "the silent spring of everything we do and think," as the body "*is* communication itself" (148). At the same time, ever since Friedrich Nietzsche spoke of the body as a "social structure composed of many souls" and even a "political structure" (ibid., 233), the body can be read as "*social inscription* in the world" (ibid., 148). Thus, as the body becomes "an effective agent and, thereby, [...] the very basis of human subjectivity," embodied subjectivity is intersubjective, placed in specific forms of institutional and historical order (Crossley, "Merleau-Ponty" 45). As Philip Hancock declares, the body is "a contested terrain on which struggles over control and resistance are fought out" (1). This perception correlates with Michel Foucault's accounts of how the body is forged through discourse and imprinted by history.

In this sense, people of color who migrate to dominantly *white* societies (italicized to show an analytical category) sometimes find it very difficult to integrate into the country of residence. They obviously carry with them their own histories, their own perspectives, their own perceptions. They may be constantly struggling between inner self and outside world, between the past and present, between how they see themselves and how they are perceived in a dominantly *white* society. It is through the body that they perceive the world, experience it, construct and interpret themselves and their relations with the world to which they respond and with which they interact. Their transculturation and identification in the new land are exactly where the body and discursive power meet in the process of transcultural communication.

Zadie Smith's novel *White Teeth* (2000), which is set in London, develops around three families from three different cultural backgrounds over three generations, and is filled with metaphors of bodies, appears as eminently suited to illustrate the relationship between the body as "political structure" and transcultural communication. Thus, with a transcultural reading of *White Teeth*, I aim to examine how the bodies of people of color from a previous colonial space are pained, violated, and maimed by a dominantly *white* discourse, how this influences their identification and transculturation/transcultural communication process, and how they try to negotiate and change boundaries — to resist, subvert, and rebel against the dominant power discourse through their body.

Intersubjective Gazing

For an understanding of institutional and historical order, Michel Foucault's discussion of the production and institutionalization of power is relevant. In *Discipline and Punish*, he uses Jeremy Bentham's panoptic prison to explain how power works through seeing and being seen: "he who is subjected to the field of visibility, and who knows it, assumes responsibility for the constraints of power; [...] he inscribes in himself the power relation in which he simultaneously plays both roles; he becomes the principle of his own subjection" (202 – 203). In this sense, the subject experiences the power relation (being seen), installs the power scheme through himself (knowing being seen), and is defined and remains in the surveillance of power (staying being seen). However, Foucault has been criticized for presupposing that the subject is "sentient, and capable of visual meaning," together with "intersubjectivity and the subject of intersubjectivity" (Crossley, "The Politics" 405), without being able to provide a non-contradictory explanation for the assumptions. More precisely, Foucault points to the power mechanism of gazing, but he fails to explain on which basis it works. He only claims "an inspecting gaze which each individual under its weight will end interiorizing to the point that he is his own overseer, each individual thus exercising this surveillance over, and against himself" (Foucault, "Body/Power" 155). If gazing is a way of executing power, being gazed upon is to expose oneself under the surveillance of power, so that it can be internalized as a restraint upon oneself. This is to some extent intersubjective, since the body senses and also is sensed within a self/other relation, but it is not the focus of any explanation by Foucault.

This is where Merleau-Ponty's understanding of perception and the body becomes useful. Since Foucault focuses on articulating how the power mechanism works throughout history instead of explaining agency and perceptual capability, the concept of perception, which is made of things we have perceived (Merleau-Ponty, *Phenomenology* 5), consolidates the presupposition of sentient ability and intersubjectivity (things-and-we). The body is the way in which we get to know the world, and an inner consciousness is actually "a meaningful configuration of sensations" (Crossley, "Merleau-Ponty" 46). Among all the sentient capabilities, gazing is the one which can produce a feeling of anxiety and alienation, but the look, which objectifies the person, "takes the place of a possible communication" (Merleau-Ponty, *Phenomenology* 361) — even as "the refusal to communicate is still a form of communication" (ibid). As in transcultural communication, body language sends a large amount of information; the look is "effected in the action of a surveyor and communicated (by virtue of its visible/cultural form) to a surveyed" (Crossley, "The Politics" 415), being both intersubjective and intercorporeal.

In *White Teeth*, such a concept has analytical value. Since the beginning of the novel, Samad, a Bangladeshi soldier in the British army, is at the center of the others' "eyeballing." Though he wears the same uniform as others, his comrade "couldn't help but stare" at him for almost one week (Smith 83). Samad's different appearance attracts not only their gaze, but also Captain Dickinson-Smith's "passion over [his] arse" as well as over "two slender muscular arms that could only make sense wrapped around a lover; also those luscious light green/brown eyes" (ibid., 84). From the day when he begins serving in a tank, Samad is the object of being gazed upon, as object of desire. His different physicality distinguishes him, sets him off as the Other. Samad experiences his difference through being gazed upon. His identity as a soldier and capable fighter is ignored, while being a person of color causes attention and stands out. His body becomes feminized in the colonial context, as it were, and is projected as an object of homosexual desire. A virtually patriarchal power relation is mirrored in the body of colonial subjects.

Since the look is not simply objectifying, but also intersubjective, Samad's being marked out and looked at causes him anxiety and alienation; it disempowers him, distances him, and generates in him a feeling of a coercive self/other relation. The gaze is an execution of power, a ventilation of desire, and being looked at is the moment of Samad's realization of his difference, the construction of his body through a "political structure," the institution of power. He becomes more aware of prejudice and discrimination against him, of hostility in the dominantly *white* discourse. This awareness correlates with Merleau-Ponty's view of intersubjectivity, and shows how a hybrid identity is never only a personal matter, but always a "social inscription" with a specific cultural attribute.

From the body experience, Samad is pinned to an inferior position in the dominantly *white* discourse, and he has internalized the inferiority. His sense of lack resembles his crippled right hand, "a broken thing" (Smith 10): the absence of a capable body, a mark inscribed on the body by a historical discourse that began its existence long before he was born. What is crippled is not only his hand, but also his sense of himself, his psyche, and his "faith," which constitute a postcolonial power relation while they are constituted by colonial discourse. Born in a colonial time and space, he is destined not to have a whole self; he is constantly maimed, crippled by the power structure. His crippled hand is a permanent scar, a trauma, a perception created, imposed, and strengthened by the dominant discourse and then represented, displayed, and memorized by the body.

The eyeballing also effects itself through Irie's excessive concern over her own body. She constantly worries about her skin color, her body shape, and her hair. She feels undesired, unwelcomed, and lacks self-esteem out of her dissatisfaction with her body. She always has the impression that she is too big, "loaded with pineapples, mangos and guavas; [...] big tits, big butt, big hips, big thighs, big teeth" (Smith 265). This idea is strengthened by an advertisement on a lamp-post announcing "lose weight to earn money" (ibid.), which creates a link between body shape and social class. Her body seems to fall into a mutually dependent category of ugliness and lower class, which shows how the prevailing power grid employs conjunctive categories to function and how a body aesthetics is imprinted and shaped by sociohistorical context to ensure a western dominance. If the eyeballing of Samad can be seen as a reflection of racism and colonialism during World War II, in Irie's case the matter of "race" appears to fade gradually into the cover and disguise of multiculturalism, which lauds the diversity of cultures, replacing ethnicity with distinctions of social class and seemingly innocent aesthetic standards.

Since the body and its perceptions are always intersubjective or intercorporeal, Irie, who was born and grows up in the dominantly *white* discourse, unconsciously or willingly imposes that discourse on herself, "interiorizing" the "inspecting gaze" (Foucault, as quoted above) — or, in Frantz Fanon's words, "[a]fter having been the slave of the white man, he enslaves himself" (Fanon 136). Irie seems to be a willing victim of the *white* discourse. She wears all kinds of tight clothes to reduce her belly, her breast, and her hips, so as to lose weight and to look slimmer, even though she still cannot change the fact that her body is "genetically designed with another country in mind, another climate" (Smith 266). She has nightmares of being so "big" and dreams that one day her Jamaican-style body will transform into an "English Rose."

Her dissatisfaction with her body not only generates self-abjection, an ineffably low self-esteem that always makes her very submissive, lacking confidence and forever following others around, but also produces a sense of estrangement and alienation. She always feels "[t]here was England, a gigantic mirror, and there was Irie, without reflection. A stranger in a stranger land" (ibid.). Her dissatisfaction does not come from her body as such, but from the dominantly *white* discourse, hence from the social gaze, the body norms, and the aesthetic standards that limit her realization of her own value and beauty. Instead of accepting her natural body as a different kind of beauty, Irie always feels ashamed and depressed by her own body. It seems to be a matter of body shape, but in fact, it is more a matter of the discursive practice of power constituting and constituted through the body.

Transcultural communication is not only an interaction or communication among different cultural groups but also a process of transculturation, hybrid identification, and competition as well as compromise of cultures. The body, which experiences and animates perceptions of the world, is both production and agency in the discursive context. That is why the body's intersubjectivity and intercorporeality influence identification, by which they are in turn influenced. Perhaps this might help to explain migrants' eagerness to transculturate in their residential environment, but also the resulting difficulties they encounter. In each case, the social reality needs to be seen in bodily terms: "To be social is first and foremost to be intercorporeal" (Jung 233).

Naming and Norming

If the body is "anterior to every determining thought" (Merleau-Ponty, as quoted above), language as a means to exchange messages not only reflects histories, cultures, or values, but also determines thinking patterns and social interactions. For Merleau-Ponty, language is not "an external force or subject which determines thought from without. Language is the very means, the very mode of structured praxis, through which thought is achieved" (Crossley, "The Politics" 412), from within the body. In a dialogue, for instance, "the objection which my interlocutor raises to what I say draws from me thoughts which I had no idea I possessed, so that at the same time that I lend him thoughts, he reciprocates by making me think too" (Merleau-Ponty, *Phenomenology* 413). This not only shows intersubjectivity happening in communication through language, but also illustrates how ideas and values can be inspired, changed, and exchanged, how a hybrid identity can come into being through transcultural interaction. However, as pointed out above, transcultural communication is never a process free of power relations or struggles. It not only exchanges messages, but also a clash of ideas, values, and cultures — a process in which a strong culture may get the upper hand or an alternative gets into the center of focus. In this sense, naming and being named operate by analogy to the "open and indefinite power of giving significance — that is, both of apprehending and conveying a meaning" (ibid., 226). The interpellation of a subject, one might say, is a process in which power constitutes and effects itself, in which the body constitutes and is constituted by the dominant discourse.

When Samad protests against his English friend Archie's constant eyeballing, a fellow soldier sneeringly calls him "Sultan" (Smith 85). This naming brings Samad's body into a form of symbolic order, a category prescribed by the dominantly *white* discourse, and pins it to a site where it has norms and rules to obey. In Butler's term, naming "is at once the setting of a boundary, and the repeated inculcation of a norm" (Butler xvii). The designation is an "economy of stereotype" at play, as the name itself is a word dragged out of its original historical context, which is why Samad tries to refute the practice by relating the word's history and connotation. In this way he excludes himself from the category, without objecting to or protesting against their naming act; he even says that he would not mind if it were accurate (Smith 85): it is about as accurate as if he were to call his offender "Jerry-Hun fat bastard." In this equation, and when the narrator describes the offender as "adjusting his beer gut," the naming practice becomes a quality of the body. His act of correcting the usage reveals Samad's eagerness to show a superiority in historical knowledge and to expose his fellow soldiers' ignorance, an attempt from which he might gain confidence and mitigate his sense of maimed lack, to claim and affirm himself. This attempt repeatedly appears in his recourse to a historicizing narrative, telling of his family background, his heroic deeds in the army, and his university education; only when he relates and reaffirms the history could he regain his confidence, hoping to have his physical presence properly recognized and addressed. History is the root from whence his abjection of self derives, just as it is the root of colonial discourse, one in which power relations effect and naturalize the *white* body, as the ideal and intelligible body. What he does in his irritatingly "luxurious" and "too soft" manner of articulation (ibid.) is to retell the history of the hegemonial *white* body as "fat bastard," to reveal an alternative enunciation.

In Irie's case, naming as correlation between language and body is more about the word's usage and connotation, which reflect different perceptions of reading history and the world. When her class discusses Shakespeare's sonnets about the unnamed Dark Lady, which acknowledge that black "bore not beauty's name" (Sonnet 127), Irie asks the teacher whether the Lady is *black*. This is a crucial question for Irie, because Sonnet 132 in which the speaker swears that "beauty herself is black" suggests that Irie for her part, who has an Afro-Caribbean complexion, might be recognized as a beauty even in the land which favors England's Rose. However, her *white* teacher (Mrs. Roody) firmly and with a brief reflection answers, "no, [...] she's dark," based on the reasoning that in the 1600s there were probably no Afro-Caribbean people in Britain and Shakespeare was "unlikely to have written a series of sonnets to a lord and then a slave" (Smith 272). By transfer, Irie is almost identified as a slave girl. The teacher is unaware, of course, that further research has indicated that the Dark Lady might possibly be of "exotic origin and black skin" and have existed in real life with an authentic individual name (Habib and Salkeld 148). The answer given by Irie's teacher shows disregard, perhaps inadvertently, for the position and contribution of people of color in British history. It inscribes history on the skin, intersecting with social class and gender, showing how a specific concept of whiteness can be constructed by excluding records of people of color from the central institutions of power, erasing their presence from view, from the act of "looking" as reading. The teacher enhances the body's boundaries and exacerbates Irie's self-abjection. As a consequence, Irie is left with her feeling of being invisible in the mirror of England, where blacks' figures and names are purged into transparence.

Body Rewriting

According to Crossley, Merleau-Ponty holds that "embodied action [...] is based in 'habit' (i. e. acquired skills, schemas and techniques) and these habits are drawn, in part at least, from a social stock or habitus" (Crossley, "Body-Subject" 101). On the one hand, this concept recognizes embodied action as our being-in-the-world and its active participation in the world, "social, embodied action with the production of meaning" (ibid.). On the other hand, it indicates the influence of social and discursive context on habits, and thus of cultural differences on embodied actions, as a basis for embodied differences in transcultural communication. Rooted in historical discourse, such differences are embedded in the body. Meanwhile, as both Foucault and Merleau-Ponty talk about the body's visibility and the effects of history, even though the body's unintelligibility is amply discussed in their works, the implication is that some bodies may be excluded from visibility or intelligibility under a power system's discursive regime and execution. In the process of transculturation, the bodies of people of color may thus be neglected and overlooked in the process of transcultural communication, raising the question how to make them visible in the dominantly *white* discourse.

Samad remains invisible, unintelligible in the post-World-War-II era in his new land. Though he is a university graduate, he cannot find an adequate job in London because of his crippled hand. He can only work as a waiter in a restaurant run by his cousin. In most nights, he faces verbal abuse from another waiter and must endure condescension from his boss; he adheres to the irregular time schedule, which almost turns him into a nocturnal animal away from the sun and from his wife (see Smith 54 – 58). He is excluded, isolated, and alienated. This drives him to have "the urge, the need, to speak to every man, and [...] explain constantly, constantly wanting to reassert something, anything" that he is not actually a waiter but a university student, also a soldier, a married man, and a Muslim (ibid., 58). He even wants to have "a large white placard" hanging in front of him to assert his other identities, his merits, and his pride, because all these except the identity of being a waiter are not important in others' eyes, all being erased by his social identity as a waiter. He has the strong urge to define, voice, and constitute himself outside the boundary of waiting on customers, outside the identity that society confers on him. We also hear of disbelief that, as a Bangladeshi, he has served in the army during the world war (ibid., 172).

This depressing awareness of being invisible in the new land comes to its climax when his crippled hand is cut and drips blood without a stop. If the accident that crippled his hand symbolizes Samad's bodily seizure and psychological trauma caused by history and colonial discourse, the hand's bleeding at this time signifies his discomfort, his depression, his self-abjection, and his feeling of alienation in the new land. The bleeding is a wound ripped open, on the vestiges of colonial discourse, a new wound representing new hurt, new trauma. If the crippled and senseless hand represents Samad's being accustomed to colonial discourse, the bleeding wound represents his regaining of the sense and awareness of the painful suppression characteristic of postcolonial discourse, an awakening of agency. Moreover, the different wounds show how, in the post-war era, relations between the colonizer and the colonized dissolve and transfer into relations of class. Differences in social status and class in the postcolonial age replace or conceal difference and prejudice of 'race' to become a representation and result of one's hard work, one's ambition, one's intelligence, and also one's own luck. It is not a social problem — it is more of a personal issue, written on the hand.

In the face of the new wound, of alienation, depression, and of hegemonic discourse, Samad's first reaction is to write his name on the world, more precisely to write it with blood on a chair and to strengthen it with a knife (Smith 505). This is owing to Samad's strong desire to assert his presence in the new land and owing to his urge to challenge, resist, and release his anger against the hegemonic discourse, the symbolic order which deliberately overlooks his presence, his contribution, and his voice. Writing with blood is his declaration of his presence in the world, his resistance to injustice, and his airing and ventilation of anger, depression, and self-abjection. It is his way of communicating with the world through the body in a manner of "social inscription" (as quoted above), and his attempt at transculturation.

However, Samad later regrets his acts, because he realizes that by bloodwriting his name on the chair he is "becoming like them," that is, "like the Englishmen who named streets in Kerala after their wives, like the Americans who shoved their flag in the moon" (ibid., 505–506). It suddenly dawns upon him that writing his name on the chair is similar to Britain's or America's actions of invading lands, claiming territories, and demonstrating dominance, similarly to what Britain has done in the colonial era. His writing could be a similar act of naming, which imposes power without respecting the alternatives. Samad's relations with the chair can be seen as intercorporeal interaction: the act of writing is a sign of claiming space, of taking and invading. "The body manifests the stigmata of past experience"; desires, failings, and errors may "join" in a body for sudden expression, but may just as often "efface each other" (Foucault, "Nietzsche" 148).

Division and Descent

This moment of regret marks Samad's realization of a failure of transculturation and his wish to end the circle of hurting. His abandonment of writing his name symbolizes an attempt to stop hurting and revenging, to find compromise instead of an "eye for an eye, a tooth for a tooth" circle, to try to escape a binary separation and antagonism. Yet this sudden "enlightenment" is also a sudden realization of the prescribed failure of ascending on the social ladder by following a similar path, and the beginning of an effort to find his own way of living. If it is impossible for Samad during the war to ascend toward becoming one of the British by following their ways to assert his presence and gain intelligibility of his body, in the new land he is reluctant and unwilling to do so. He takes to religion, "kneeling and praying" (Smith 505), experienced and performed through the body's posture. To some extent, religion here serves as a way of redemption, a way of overcoming weakness, a way of healing and saving oneself after psychological trauma and physical laceration in the strange land. It is at this moment that Samad realizes the limits of himself, defined through secular society.

His religious belief plays a crucial role in his mid-life crisis, in his affair with Poppy Burt-Jones. If his bodily desire symbolizes an uncontrolled, unconscious yearning for being *white* British, the religion which symbolizes his past and his children who symbolize the future protect or prevent him from the desire. His extramarital affair with Poppy motivates him to send one of his sons back to Bangladesh, to keep the heritage of his "good blood" alive, though this turns out to be only temporary. And it enables him to be a more pious believer. Through his intersubjective or intercorporeal communication with Poppy, Samad painfully comes to realize that his identification with the British has already taken place. He is "a mixed-up thing [...] Brown and old on the outside, white and fresh on the inside" (ibid., 166). The time he spends with Poppy is a time of transition and vacillation in his identification, a time when he feels "divided" and "split" (ibid., 179), when he realizes his multiple identifications, and experiences both fulfillment of desire and torture from the desire. This period seems to be a liminal space in which he dwells, a feeling of being in-between, a sense of belonging nowhere — a vivid illustration of gaps and differences beneath hybridity's surface.

Samad's hybrid identity is embodied in his physical desire and psychological dilemma, but this clearly does not work: the body is "the locus of a disassociated Self," a "volume in perpetual disintegration" (Foucault, "Nietzsche" 148). He turns and adheres to one side in the end, the one in which he has his own language, in which he feels most comfortable and true to himself, through which he can distinguish and assert his presence in the new land. His return to religion and his adherence to the binary separation of body and soul, Britain and Bangladesh, born healthy but crippled during the war, are to some extent a way of resisting cooperation with the given power structures, a way of proclaiming his uniqueness, of exposing the fissures in normativity. The bigger the gap between the identity elements, the more powerful his resistance might be, which in a way foreshadows his son's turning to fundamentalism. For Samad, then, religion is a way to make his voice heard, his body visible, his presence acknowledged.

What is also available for Samad is his past, not only as an individual but in terms of his descent. Transcending his individuality, for him this becomes a "means to translate and name the world" as spoken of above. It offers him a means to constitute, to sustain and maintain himself, to find the pillar and meaning of his life, to overcome self-abjection and out-of-placeness in his process of transcultural communication *with* or his transculturation *in* the land. The past serves as ventilation, a reminder, possibly a placebo in alleviating his dissatisfaction, disappointment, and despair regarding his currently depressing and suffocating life in the new land. Samad accordingly uses history as his way of bodily rewriting, resisting the dominant discourse — which is that of "blank pancake English faces." The mutual look as these faces and Samad's eye each other empowers his Foucaultian discovery of a subjectivity that would otherwise be denied him: "[D]escent attaches itself to the body" (ibid., 147). The attachment takes shape in Samad's insistence on telling the story of his great-grandfather Mangal Pande, who, as he relates it, shot the first bullet against the British army. If mainstream representations depict him as a mutineer, traitor, and drunkard, in Samad's terms he is a hero (Smith 251–252). By narrating his great-grandfather, in a semi-humorous way as "the tickle in the sneeze," with a narration that doesn't leave out the ancestor's "large unsightly ears," also by persuading the boss of a bar to hang up his picture, Samad reinvents the body in reconstituting history, and thus his own identity. The story of Mangal Pande with its "tickle" serves as a new language, one that belongs to Samad and enables him to reveal to the reader how the marginalized is excluded from the only domain that is intelligible to "pancake faces." It is a language that, as Merleau-Ponty has described it, does not determine thought "from without" the body.

Hybrid Re-education

The question was raised above whether differences or conflicts are observable beneath the surface of hybridity. I discussed hybridity as an unavoidable result of transcultural communication, since it represents a conflicted and ever-changing identification. While Samad in the novel experiences and performs hybridity through his body, he eventually chooses his previous cultural background, his religion as a final spiritual home. A hybrid identity, it appears, is not the solution. Yet Irie, who negotiates her identities by leaving family history behind, reconstructing history and home for herself (see O'Leary 50), is evaluated as positive example in a multicultural era (see, for instance, Childs 12). But is a hybrid identity possible, and achievable for people of color in transcultural communication?

As a teenage girl whose presence, attractiveness, and even value is denied in this land, Iris tries to become visible, to empower and entitle herself, by repudiating the Afro element in her. She thinks that only when she limits herself entirely to a place within the body's *white* boundaries, conforms to the majority's cultural norms and rules and meets these aesthetic standards, can she attract attention, become popular, and gain a measure of influence. Irie comes to think she can only look attractive by looking *white*, by killing her Afro elements and having straight and red hair — hoping for "new cultural phenomena" as described by Ortiz. Thus, Irie decides to go to a hairdresser, demanding to get rid of the hair she hates (see Smith 277). This act is not only a result of accumulated self-abjection, but also a decision made in the hope of being acknowledged and accepted in the transculturation process. However, when she strives to conform to an English Rose ideal, she meets another critique. She is criticized for not being true to herself. When Irie meets Neena and her lesbian girlfriend Maxine after her hairdressing, what Irie encounters is not the praise she expects, but the ridicule that she looks "like a freak" and appears like "The Negro Meryl Streep" (Smith 283). A gap opens between what she thinks she is and what others see her as being. This corresponds to Crenshaw's claim that "the social power in delineating difference need not be the power of domination; it can instead be the source of social empowerment and reconstruction" (Crenshaw 1242). Neena's and Maxine's comments function as an act of delineating her difference and an attempt to impose boundaries on her body in relation to cultural background, yet they show another possibility for Irie: "The Afro was cool, man. It was wicked. It was *yours*" (Smith 285). This is not only telling Irie to acknowledge and accept herself as she is, but also shows her another world and belief system, one she can possess. The pain she encounters during the hairdressing symbolizes her realization of her own body, her awareness of her being. Who will she want to be after her transculturation effort? The hairdressing is a turning point in her understanding and recognition of a self lost in transculturation.

An important reason why Irie has her hair re-done is her wish to be noticed by Millat, Samad's younger son, to attract his attention and achieve his admiration, while Millat is always hanging around with *white* girls. Millat attracts her not only because of their shared history, but also because of his rebellious acts, his "dangerous" demeanor, with a courage that she lacks to voice herself. This corresponds to the double mechanism and power system that Irie integrates into herself: the *white* post-colonial discourse and the patriarchal system. These two make her neglect her inner self and replace it with seemingly "right" and adequately "British" norms to obey. In the big mirror of British society, the realization of her body regulates her transculturation process, her desire, her body's materialization, in a self-estrangement and self-division process. That is why Neena says to Irie, "You've got to re-educate yourself. Realize your value, stop the slavish devotion, and get a life [...]" (ibid., 285). Unconsciously integrating the discourse of transculturation, Irie lives a life programmed as the Other, without trying to find herself.

This is the case, too, in Irie's interaction with the Chalfens. If Irie's attempt to conform to the norms and standards of attractiveness is a reflection of oppressive body discourses, her involvement with the Chalfens make her think of living in another's skin. They seem to be a typical middle-class, British-Jewish family, "who dealt in the present, who didn't drag ancient history around like a chain and ball, [...] who were not neck-high and sinking in the quagmire of the past" (ibid., 326), even though they are also immigrants. Her wish to "merge with them" (ibid., 328), to have "their Englishness. Their Chalfenishness" (ibid.), reflects her ultimate and hidden wish to be purely British — "to the pure all things are pure." Her wish to be a Chalfen, who for her are "more English than the English" (ibid.), reflects her transculturating desire: she feels like "sneaking into England [...] wearing somebody else's uniform or somebody else's skin" (ibid.), even though she was born and grows up in England. Obviously, the body (as quoted above) is the site of "social inscription" as Irie's alienated effort to be British is established by the body; she thinks she can become visible through the other's skin. Yet there is a sense in which her contact with the Chalfens is also a desire for protection from her idea of the past, contrasting with Samad. She wants to escape the past's heaviness, which is everywhere but also nowhere, for it seems to her that there are so many secret histories that no one talks about but that are present all the time. She envies this family, because they only have "neutral spaces. And not this endless maze of present rooms and past rooms and the things said in them years ago and everybody's old historical shit all over the place" (ibid., 514). Her wish to escape the heavy chains of history emerges in her fantasy of a bodily exchange, to "merge with the Chalfens, to be of one flesh; separated from the chaotic, random flesh of her own family and transgenically fused with another" (ibid., 342): a different concept of the intercorporeal in its relation to space. It fictionalizes not only Merleau-Ponty's characterization of the body as both sentient and sensible, but even more Foucault's description of the body as "totally imprinted by history" — together with a sobering reminder of "history's destruction of the body" ("Nietzsche" 148).

Foucault's reminder of history's imprint explains why Irie's involvement with the Chalfens and her attempted focus on the present can be little more than temporary, a self-medication, self-anesthesia, and ultimately self-deception. In being with the Chalfens, she does become part of them, but at the same time loses her own self as her voice is once again drowned, ignored, and rendered impotent. She gradually realizes that Chalfenishness will not empower her to leave her history behind, because it remains a part of her, of her own flesh, her own blood. Her effort to merge with their flesh ends when she finds that her mother does not have her own teeth. These symbolize a hidden history not known to Irie. Her escape into Chalfenishness resembles her mother's hiding of her false teeth: it is not real, not of herself; like a buried secret, the genuine history is not told but is always present, where it clashes with the desired "neutral spaces."

In this dilemma, Irie visits her grandmother's place. To some extent, the event marks Irie's first break from the shackles of both Englishness and Afro elements, a break from the binary separation of the two. It is a moment when she recognizes both in her, admits their existence, and tries to find a compromise or balance. From that moment, she repudiates her identification with either one of the two elements that are imposed on her; she starts to constitute herself out of her own will, no longer feeling torn apart. Her stay with her grandmother represents a new beginning. This also corresponds to

Irie's subsequent and fervent intercourse with the twin brothers Magid and Millat. The twin brothers can be seen as the soul and the body, the colonizer and the colonized, the white and the colored, which seem to be opposites but are in fact dependent on each other. She tries to use her body to readjust the symbolically hegemonic order of the twin brothers, a colonial order, to make up the blank or the gap that is left by colonial discourse, in order to redeem herself with her sense of being in a land that is both familiar and foreign — to reorder, revisit, and review a history "imprinted" on the body.

It is at her grandmother's place that Irie realizes that "[i]t just seemed tiring and unnecessary all of a sudden, that struggle to force something out of the recalcitrant English soil, [...] when there was now this other place" (Smith 402). Irie gradually becomes aware that she is transcultural, without needing to make any choice between being British or *black*; what she needs to do is only to accept herself with her desires. It is there that she finds stories about Jamaica, an entirely unknown but closely related place, not "neutral," one that can be constructed and read in a way that she likes, an imaginary site fully at her disposal: "a place where things simply were. No fictions, no myths, no lies, no tangled webs — this is how Irie imagined her homeland" (Smith 402). Irie's identification with Jamaica, a newly hybrid identity that enables her to become what has been called a "global soul" (Krause), signifies a condition that may be confined by certain geographical boundaries but that is also free from them. Her return to Jamaica and her child which is born there symbolize a conciliation of the two identity elements. If Magid by identification appears to represent the former colonizer and Millat the former colonized, the child is a daughter of both, whose father is not easy to determine. At the same time, her union with pale and "curly-haired" Joshua Chalfen symbolizes her identification with the British, while Jamaica signifies a return to her own self.

Conclusion

As the basis for human existence, the body represents discourse, culture, and history, by which it is constituted, restrained, and modified. We not only perceive the world through it, but also actively participate in the world by its intersubjective relations with the world, as it is our being-in-the-world. In transcultural communicative encounters, migrants from previously colonial countries may have "no face in this country, no voice in the country" (Smith 234), especially because of their bodies. In Merleau-Ponty's terms, "consciousness can do nothing without its body and can only act upon others by acting upon their bodies. It can only reduce them to slavery by making nature an appendix of its body, by appropriating nature to itself and establishing in nature its instruments of power" (*Humanism* 102). The body's physical nature is not a nature that is untouched by the mind's instruments of social coercion. When people of color consciously or unconsciously identify themselves with the colonial metropolis, they are reminded that they are foreigners, strangers, and outsiders. They are regulated and disciplined by discourse, excluded and pained by the power structure imprinted on the body.

Violence on the body comes not only from a discursive power structure, but also from the self which internalizes such discourse as consciousness. Transcultural communication or transculturation is more than a process of cultural adaptation or cultural integration, it is no less one of constituting the discourse of dominant cultural schemes within oneself. In the cases of Samad and Irie, the subtle violence imposed on the intersubjective body through eyeing and through naming meets with their desire to adapt to the metropolitan land, which makes them unconsciously fuse elements of the dominant discourse into their own body and its mentality. Yet the body luckily is an active agency, as Crossley pithily summarizes Merleau-Ponty's position:

> The body is dependent upon cultural repertoires and skills, in Merleau-Ponty's account, but is equally responsible for the reproduction of those repertoires and skills. Moreover, in this sense, it is the habituated or instituted actions of bodies which are responsible for the reproduction of the social formation and of historical time. ("Body-Subject" 104)

While a bodily discourse produces violence, it is not simply where the characters' self-abjection comes from, but also where their resistance and subversion take place. In terms of cultural hybridity, criticism has noted that Samad does not adapt well, whereas Irie is successful in finding a hybrid identity. It is undeniable that Samad turns to religion and adheres to a binary separation of two cultures. Yet it is only through their clear-cut distinction and separation that Samad can gain the strength to realize his own value. This is surely related to conditions in the colonial and post-World-War-II era. For him, the sharper the contrast between the cultural heritages, the more sense of being, the more voice and presence he gains in the dominantly *white* discourse.

As for Irie, her return to Jamaica delivers a message that the "neutral space" does not exist. What is possible is a liminal and fluid space, where her identification changes all the time and where she feels at ease with herself. What she finds is a comfort zone, one that serves as a compromise between herself and her cultural environment which is similar to Samad's state of mind. Since the prospect of a favorable adaptation mode does not exist in the first place, we should recognize their identification solutions as successful transculturations.

References

Bhabha, Homi K. "Remembering Fanon: Self, Psyche and the Colonial Condition." *Colonial Discourse and Postcolonial Theory*. Eds. Patrick Williams and Laura Chrisman. New York: Columbia UP, 1994. 112–123.

Butler, Judith. *Bodies that Matter: On the Discursive Limits of Sex*. New York: Routledge, 2011.

Childs, Elaine. "Insular Utopias and Religious Neuroses: Hybridity Anxiety in Zadie Smith's *White Teeth*." *Proteus* 23 (2006): 7–12.

Crenshaw, Kimberlé. "Mapping the Margins: Intersectionality, Identity Politics, and Violence against Women of Color." *Stanford Law Review* 43 (1991): 1241–1299.

Crossley, Nick. "Body-Subject/Body-Power: Agency, Inscription and Control in Foucault and Merleau-Ponty." *Body & Society* 2.2 (1996): 99–116.

—. "Merleau-Ponty, the Elusive Body and Carnal Sociology." *Body & Society* 1.1 (1995): 43–63.

—. "The Politics of the Gaze: Between Foucault and Merleau-Ponty." *Human Studies* 16.4 (1993): 399–419.

Fanon, Frantz. *Black Skin, White Masks*. Trans. Charles Lam Markmann. Frogmore: Paladin, 1970.

Foucault, Michel. "Body/Power." *Power/Knowledge: Selected Interviews and Other Writings, 1972–1977*. Ed. Colin Gordon. Brighton: Harvester, 1980. 55–63.

—. *Discipline and Punish*. Harmondsworth: Penguin, 1979.

—. "Nietzsche, Genealogy, History." *Language, Counter-Memory, Practice: Selected Essays and Interviews*. Ed. Donald F. Bouchard. Ithaca: Cornell UP, 1977. 139–164.

Habib, Imtiaz, and Duncan Salkeld. "The Resonables of Boroughside, Southwark: An Elizabethan Black Family near the Rose Theatre." *Shakespeare* 11.2 (2015): 135–156.

Hancock, Philip. *The Body, Culture and Society*. Philadelphia: Open UP, 2000.

Hepp, Andreas. *Transcultural Communication*. Chichester: John Wiley, 2015.

Jung, Hwa Yol. *Transversal Rationality & Intercultural Texts*. Athens, OH:

Ohio UP, 2011.

Kraidy, Marwan. *Hybridity, Or the Cultural Logic of Globalization*. Philadelphia: Temple UP, 2005.

Krause, Mine. "From 'In-Between-Identities' to 'Global Souls' in Zadie Smith's *White Teeth* and Elif Şafak's *The Bastard of Istanbul*." 22nd METU British Novelists Conference: Zadie Smith and Her Work. Middle East Technical U, Ankara, Turkey. 26–27 March 2015.

Loomba, Ania. *Colonialism / Postcolonialism*. 2nd ed. London: Routledge, 2005.

Merleau-Ponty, Maurice. *Humanism and Terror*. Boston: Beacon, 1969.

—. *Phenomenology of Perception*. Trans. Colin Smith. London: Routledge, 2002.

O'Leary, Joanna. "Body Larceny: Somatic Seizure and Control in *White Teeth*." *Reading Zadie Smith: The First Decade and Beyond*. Ed. Philip Tew. London: Bloomsbury Academic, 2014. 39–52.

Shakespeare, William. *The Norton Shakespeare*. Ed. Stephen Greenblatt. New York & London: Norton, 1997.

Smith, Zadie. *White Teeth*. London: Penguin, 2001.

15

Small-Town Family as a Battlefield: Reading Cultural Influences in Alice Munro's "Chaddeleys and Flemings"

Zhou Yi
Shanghai International Studies University

Summary: This chapter holds that Canada's literary tradition of "small-town fiction" reflects a national psyche of "in-betweenness," and Alice Munro's focus on small-town family can be traced to the same origin. Taking "Chaddeleys and Flemings" as a case example, the chapter examines the multiple cultural influences on Munro's archetypal small-town family. It points out that the maternal Chaddeley aunts represent a connection to "England and history," as the power they enjoy is related to an English mercantilism tradition. The paternal Flemings, on the other hand, represent a physiocracy tradition of Scotland, Ireland, and France. The mutual suspicion among Canadians of different descendants is due to long-term commercial and agricultural inequalities existing in Canadian economic and political life. The narrator, the family's daughter, is depicted as an epitome of the country's cultural compromise, sandwiched between the influences of the maternal English and the paternal Scottish family, between the urban ideal and the rural tradition of the country. The family house is located neither in the city or the country, but at the edge of a small town. Its awkward position "in-between" isolates the family, geographically and culturally, from mainstream society. The chapter considers a further important cultural factor that emerges in the narrative and affects Canada's identity and security: the rivalry between the elitist tradition of Europe and the consumer culture of the United States. It concludes that Canada enjoys an inbred, ambiguous identity of in-betweenness, which promises a power of cultural compromise and reconstruction.

I

In 1965 Northrop Frye, Canada's most famous literary and cultural critic, published the influential "Conclusion" to *Literary History of Canada*, which was the first major attempt to give "CanLit" a tangible shape. It raised the well-known question "Where is here?" (Frye 826). At the core of Frye's argument was a nation's concern with space, both geographical and psychological. Later, Linda Hutcheon took a postmodern perspective in her attempt to explore the national preoccupation with space. She noticed that "small-town fiction" flourishes in Canada. "[T]he small town in Canadian fiction," as Linda Hutcheon puts it, "came to represent a limited and limiting society from which protagonists yearned to escape." She also noticed that "the small town, dwarfed by a hostile environment, was the setting for the struggle of the often sensitive individual against a puritanical society, often symbolized or incarnated in some patriarchal figure of authority, whose weight of guilt was internalized by the would be rebel" (Hutcheon 197). From Stephen Leacock's *Sunshine Sketches of a Little Town* to Margaret Lawrence's *The Stone Angel*, the small town encapsulates a collective unconsciousness that is unique to Canadian people.

Alice Munro is one of Canada's most critically acclaimed authors and one of the world's best short story writers. Her most important contribution to Canada's literature, even to world literature, is her literary exploration of the metaphoric meaning of a Canadian small-town mindset. Munro herself was born in Wingham, a very small town of south-western Ontario, and she spent most of her life in similar small towns nearby. Her best stories, by general agreement, are mostly set in small Canadian towns. Only a few of her works are given to descriptions of urban life in Toronto and British Columbia. Munro created her own Munro Tract. As Dennis Deffy puts it, "The Munro Tract is a written-over district in Ontario bounded by lakes Huron and Erie on the west and south, the towns of Goderich on the north and London in the east. A transparent overlay of the Munro Tract would largely match the boundaries of the Huron Tract, first developed by the Canada Land Company in 1829" (Deffy 197). Munro's focus regarding the small town is usually on its intermediary position between the city and the country, between the urban and the rural, the modern and the traditional, as a symbol of cultural/ economic confrontation and compromise. She once described the awkward feeling of the small town in an interview as being "outside the whole social structure [...] in this kind of little ghetto [...] It was a community of outcasts. I had that feeling about myself" (Ross 23).

That feeling of marginality is also strongly felt by the small-town family in Munro's stories. For her half century's writing, Munro has created an archetypal Ontario family, a Protestant one with a cultural division: a Scottish father and an Irish mother. The family type is quite representative of rural Ontario in Munro's time. The couple is always emotionally alienated from each other. In a sense, that alienation between the father and mother symbolizes an internal separation within Canada's Protestant community. The family house is very often located at a very awkward position neither "in" nor "out of" the town. It will be at the outskirts of the town, at the end of a town road, very close to the country. That is another symbol of the family's in-betweenness. The couple usually has two children, a realistic boy who will successfully step into the mainstream society when he grows up, and a sensitive girl who is the artist and will forever struggle with her ambiguous identification as a small-town girl. And the grown-up sister and brother will suffer a similar alienation, which is metaphorically rooted in the country's cultural incompatibility.

It is noteworthy that, when Munro creates her small-town family, she draws heavily on her own family. The setting is always very much like the landscape of her childhood, Wingham, Huron County, Ontario, be it Tuppertown in "Walker Brothers Cowboy," or Jubilee in "The Peace of Utrecht." By happenstance, Munro herself is Presbyterian Scots on her father's side and Anglican Irish on her mother's, both sides being the descendants of the 1810–1820s immigrant exodus pouring into Canada after the Napoleonic wars. There was an obvious difference in life perspectives between Munro's father, Robert Laidlaw, and her mother, Anne Chamney. Robert was not a very ambitious man, while Anne was intelligent and held strong aspirations. The couple's difference reflects the different worldviews of the Presbyterians and Anglicans. As Robert Thacker has pointed out, "the Ontario Scots were people who lived austere and well-ordered lives, who worked hard and followed a reasonably strict way of being. The Irish, by contrast, did some of the same but were generally freer" (Zhou). But at the same time, Munro faithfully records the other cultural influences that changed the country's history and help shape today's Canada, such as the British, the French, and the American.

I intend to take one of Munro's short stories as a case example to examine the writer's artistic dealing with the small-town family and its cultural differences. I will argue that Munro's focus is not local geography in the physical sense, but a Canadian sentiment featured in the country's cultural imagination. Munro imbues the genre of small-town fiction with a unique national psyche by presenting the family as a battlefield where different cultural influences vie with each other for domination. Munro's small-town protagonists are mostly outcasts in the mainstream society, trapped by globalization and modernization, lost between the material and the spiritual, desiring wealth and recognition while fearing loss and betrayal. They suffer an ambiguous identification based on their cultural in-betweenness. After they eventually leave the small town and settle in a big city, they still pay constant visits to the old family house as spiritual pilgrimages for internal peace and comfort. The small-town family, nevertheless, is the epitome of Canadian society.

II

"Chaddeleys and Flemings" is the leading story of the collection *The Moons of Jupiter* (1982). The story consists of two parts: "Connection" and "The Stone in the Field." The first part was originally published in *Chatelaine* and the second in *Saturday Night* in 1979. In the collection, the two parts appear tight-knit and well-balanced. They are actually "mirror stories," as Coral Ann Howell puts it, with "two parts representing the double strain in Janet Fleming's inheritance" (71). Janet is the character who tells the story. Together, the parts construct a symmetrical beauty, with one telling the story of "city visiting the town — city revisited," and the other of "town visiting the country — country revisited."

In "Connection," the first part of the story, the visit of four Chaddeley cousins, who represent the English side of Janet's family, brings a hilarious carnival to the narrator's town family. The narrator describes the Chaddeley aunts thus: "Cousin Iris from Philadelphia. She was a nurse. Cousin Isabel from Des Moines. She owns a florist shop. Cousin Flora from Winnipeg, a teacher; Cousin Winifred from Edmonton, a lady account" (Munro 1). Here, city and profession across national borders are the primary identity label of the Chaddeley aunts. Philadelphia is the most international and metropolitan, followed by Des Moines, the capital of Iowa. Both are American cities. Winnipeg and Edmonton are, of course, major Canadian cities, Edmonton being the capital city of Alberta and a famous tourist destination. In comparison to these cities, the narrator's hometown, Dalgleish of Huron County in Western Ontario, only holds a population of 2,000 people, rendering it comparatively insignificant.

Aunt Iris, who comes from Philadelphia, is no doubt the leader of the sisters. She drives on her own to pick up the others: "She drove a 1939 Oldsmobile. She had driven to Winnipeg to collect Flora, and Winifred, who had come down from Edmonton by train. Then they all drove to Toronto and picked up Isabel" (ibid., 2). Iris is also the most daring (evidenced in her willingness to relieve her bladder in the open air of nature), as well as the most vigilant and experienced of the sisters (she possesses the knowledge that to leave the car at any time in the barren Northern Ontario town puts the women in danger of being raped by loggers). As a nurse, she has witnessed many celebrities, their joys and sorrows, partings and reunions. In a symbolic way she feels she has almost witnessed the ugliness of the whole of Philadelphia's high society, "the top society of Philadelphia. Not at their best" (ibid., 6). Iris almost insinuates that she possesses the God-like power to give life to and visit death upon many people. Her profession brings her a sense of superiority. She feels she can laugh at rich people and control them in the ward, when they are weak and vulnerable. Iris also shows off her professional ethics. She claims that she never keeps a dime belonging to a patient. At the same time, a dying and libertine stage actor's courtship makes her feel proud of her womanly charm. In short, Iris seems to embody the trinity of power, ethics, and charm of the big city, and that makes her feel free to criticize the small town.

The other aunts, too, have their respective advantages of life: "Winifred said that she had seen things too. The real truth, the real horrible truth about some of those big wheels and socialites came out when you got a look at their finances" (ibid., 6). Winifred's career, in a similar way, provides her with the advantage of seeing the ugliness hidden behind lives of luxury and dissipation.

It is worth noting that none of the Chaddeley aunts are married:

"Maiden ladies, they were called. Old maids was too thin a term, it would not cover them" (ibid., 1). As unwed women, the Chaddeley aunts' positions are not at home, but in the society. They possess professional lives and power typically associated with men, and the hierarchical relationships between them are determined by the magnitude of the cities that they respectively represent. The American consumer city leads (Philadelphia), followed by the Canadian consumer city (Edmonton), as a copy of the United States city. But Dalgleish, the Canadian small town, always remains in last place, silently in the shadows.

From the cultural perspective, the Chaddeley aunts bring to the narrator's mother not only a connection to the modern cities, but also a connection to their cultural inheritance, a connection "to England and history." The Chaddeleys' ancestors came from England, and they accordingly concluded that they enjoy a social superiority over Scottish or Irish descendants:

> It is a fact that Canadians of Scottish — which in Huron County we called Scotch — and Irish descents will tell you quite freely that their ancestors came out during the potato famine, with only the rags on their backs, or that they were shepherds, agricultural laborers, poor landless people. But anyone whose ancestors came from England will have some story of black sheep or younger sons, financial reverses, lost inheritances, elopements with unsuitable partners. (Ibid., 7)

Accordingly, the Chaddeleys' grandfather, an English "gentleman," is regarded by his offspring as proof of their family's noble origin. Janet's mother and the Chaddeley aunts love to talk about his mysterious past: he had been a student at Oxford, but lost all the money that his family sent him by gambling. (There is another possibility: he made a servant girl pregnant, was compelled to marry her, and then took her to Canada.)

These conjectures are fraught with cultural misunderstandings. The Chaddeleys think of distant European city life as indulgent and rife with sensual pleasures, a sharp contrast with the rigid and conservative small-town life of Canadian society. They also speculate that their family estates were close to Canterbury (in association with the famous "Canterbury pilgrims" and "Canterbury bells"), or "were in the west of England," with the name Chaddeley being related to Cholmondeley — Lord Cholmondeley. Their family might be a branch of the Cholmondeley family, or a French family: "It was originally *Champ de laiche*, which means field of sedge. In that case the family had probably come to England with William the Conqueror" (ibid., 7). The conjecture ensures a glittering family history as well as an innate tragedy: "Every one of them believed, whatever the details, that there had been a great comedown, a dim catastrophe, and that beyond them, behind them, in England, lay lands and houses and ease and honor" (ibid., 8). Put another way, the Chaddeleys believe that they lost their wealth and honor because they were the victims of an irresistible tragic force that they could do nothing to change, leaving them with a lingering sense of melancholy. As described by Margaret Atwood in her famous *Survival*, this victim mentality is a typical reflection of a collective Canadian mindset. And yet the victim mindset also provides the Chaddeleys with moral sublimity: as victims, pure and innocent lambs, they are not perpetrators. In keeping with this, their grandfather's idleness becomes an enviable approach to life in the eyes of the Chaddeley children. Their grandfather's snobbish attitude meets the family's psychological need for a superior social status: "He had the air of a gentleman, was widely read, and full of rhetoric and self-esteem" (ibid.). His children take pride in supporting their "gentleman" father, though they dare not have more than one or two children of their own because of a lack of money: "His children did not balk at supporting him; they sank into their commonplace jobs, but pushed their own children [...] out to Business School, to Normal School, to Nurses Training" (ibid.). Thus a rigid concept of social classification derived from distant Europe is falsely transplanted to Canada. Despite their ancestors perhaps having been impoverished and oppressed, and their own place turning out to be actually at a social margin, the Chaddeleys nonetheless endeavor to copy the hierarchy, classification, and discrimination of the European world into Canadian society.

At any rate, the exquisite food coming with the aunts from the big city creates a ceremonial atmosphere: "Tins of coffee, nuts and date pudding, oysters, olives, ready-made cigarettes" (ibid., 3). On top of that, "a five-pound box of chocolates." Such a feast creates so much excitement in the narrator's poverty-stricken house that, long after it is over and all the chocolates are eaten, the empty chocolate box is still carefully kept and enshrined "in the linen drawer in the dining room sideboard," as a symbol of sacredness waiting in vain for "some ceremonial use that never presented itself" (ibid.). In the cold wintertime, the narrator "[sniffs] at the cups, inhaling their smell of artifice and luxury," and imagining the list of ingredients: hazelnut, creamy nougat, Turkish delight, golden toffee, peppermint cream. Those foods bring to the narrator and her family a feeling of luxury, a solace bestowed by a higher culture.

As well as the food, the clothing that the Chaddeley aunts wear has a similar culturally symbolic effect on the family. They dress their plump bodies in tight-fitting corsets, stockings, silky jersey dress, face powder, rouge, cologne, and tortoise-shell combs. As gifts, they bring the narrator's family stockings, scarves, and blouses, as well as the latest white organdy pinafores. In the narrator's young eyes, the Chaddeley aunts who are city dwellers are embodiments of a type of lofty, other-worldly new women. They are powerful, fearless, sophisticated. They not only smoke like men, they enjoy the men's power.

III

In sharp contrast are the six Fleming aunts. These aunts live in the backcountry, completely isolated from the outside world. The Flemings represent a Scottish tradition: men are created equal. They hold a plain view of nature derived from laborers. Generations of poverty and suffering make them accustomed to mutual help and protection. In contrast to the Chaddeleys, who aggressively seek power and fortune, the Flemings are introverted and defensive. If the Chaddeleys represent a connection to outward social power, the Flemings represent a connection to inward peace. For them, the blood ties are their unbreakable bond, and the land is the object for which they would put their lives on the line. Threatened by the corrosion of external change, however, the Flemings move toward an extreme: their Scottish pioneer ethic goes dour, and they become blind, suspicious, filled with hatred, frightened of change. Any innovation would be interpreted negatively as opportunism. Their way of life, a small-scale peasant economy as against the large-scale market economy, is too fragile to maintain under the influence of globalization. As they refuse to participate in commercial activities, they accordingly lose their ability for self-expression and self-protection.

Symbolically, the fate of the Flemings embodies the sentiment on the part of Canadians who value physiocracy. In Canada, such English-speaking Scottish or Irish descendants, as well as the French-speaking French descendants, mostly came from traditional farming families. They are representative of the country's "agricultural economy." However, the wealth and power of Canadian society in history has largely been concentrated in the hands of English descendants, who value mercantilism and represent Canada's cities. To a certain extent, the long-standing mutual suspicion and "two solitudes" between French Canadian and British Canadian are due to the long-term commercial and agricultural inequalities existing in Canadian economic and political life. The confrontation and difference between the Chaddeleys and Flemings embody the scramble of cultural influences that has long existed in Canada: the descendants of England as a cultural representation of urban influence, and the descendants of Scotland, Ireland, and France as cultural representations of rural influence.

The Fleming aunts are very shy and introverted. Even when greeted by kin, they behave as nervously as if being given a royal reception, and have to rely on a great deal of self-control to avoid a hasty retreat. When the narrator visits them, she cannot not help noticing that their room is almost empty except for the clean, solid, and clumsy family furniture; no refreshment is provided for visitors. She notices that the Fleming aunts' hair is in a plain style, they wear no makeup, they are hunched in shapeless clothes and act awkwardly even with the most ordinary small talk. In the Fleming aunts' house, food and clothing are stripped of all their cultural meaning. Food is no longer an attitude toward life, and clothing is no longer a status indicator. They are what they originally were: food is sustenance, something to keep one from becoming hungry, and clothing is simply clothing, something to keep one from becoming cold. Any trends and fashions would be bleached pale at the hands of poverty, and time seems to have stopped.

Here in the story, the narrator's admiration for the Chaddeley aunts dramatically shifts into the relationship between herself and the Fleming aunts, with a totally reversed sentiment. The narrator admires her Chaddeley aunts, who maintain a high sociocultural profile, while she examines her Fleming aunts' life from a lofty cultural stance. To her, the Chaddeley aunts and Fleming aunts represent opposing cultural forces. At one pole is the city, which represents a frenzied pursuit of modernization. The city dwellers enjoy all the advantage of consumerism, but will also go astray in their pursuit of materialistic goals. At the other pole is the country, which is physically remote from urbanity and suffers from scarcity and social deprivation, but conserves traditional values. The narrator thus eventually finds herself caught, willy-nilly, between the innate contradictory cultural heritages of her father's family and her mother's family, with her own family house being the battlefield.

IV

It is typical of Munro's stories that the narrator's house is neither located in the city or the country, but in a small town, a place awkwardly "in-between." It is no exception in "Chaddeleys and Flemings." The narrator's family house is not even in the center of the small town Dalgleish, but at the edge of it, "at the end of a road" (Munro 6). Farther, there is "some scrubby land," "mall wooden houses" and "flocks of chickens and children," leading to "wide fields and pastures," and "the curve of the river" (ibid.). The family house is "an old brick house of a fair size," which looks decent from outside whereas its inside has fallen into disrepair. It can hardly provide the family with shelter from wind and rain. In fact, the narrator's family is neither rich nor poor, neither prominent nor humble. It is an archetypal family of a Canadian small town, because it highlights a marginalized position of "in-betweenness."

This awkward position causes an identity crisis for the narrator's mother. She finds great difficulty in acquiring a sense of belonging to the local community because the house is at the fringe of the town's territory. To compensate for her lack of a sense of place, she resorts to her kinship connection to construct a sense of superiority. To the mother, the Chaddeley aunts' visit is not only a maintenance of the connection by blood, but also a display of social connection. The kinship entitles her to share the power enjoyed by her other family members. The connection links the adventurous and prosperous city with the backward and stagnant small town. Its significance is symbolic. Because of the connection, the mother no longer identifies herself as an ordinary housewife but as a sister of the risk-takers. She now stands beside women who are in control of wards, classrooms, shops, and financial affairs. She stands beside those who hold power.

Dreaming of such power herself, the mother imitates her cousins' behavior. She equips herself with their second-hand clothing, and ambitiously embarks on an antique business: she finds local antiques from the rural areas and sells them to the big city

(Toronto). She thinks she can be a successful businesswoman, make a fortune, lead a good life. The good life that she yearns for, in short, is a life of materialism and consumerism of the kind that the city can offer. But as Baudrillard points out, consumption is not only the use of the sign values, but also symbolic values. The end of consumption is not for the satisfaction of real needs, but for realizing the symbolic meaning of products, for satisfying some ever-created and ever-invited desires. So the mother is foreordained to failure Desires will never be fully satisfied. In the end, the mother has to quit her business because she becomes ill and her business partner is "put in chains and thrown into prison." The failure forever traps the mother in an ambiguous middle, an awkward in-betweenness. She eventually dies miserably in Dalgleish, struggling in vain to get rid of the curse of the small town: an innate tendency toward compromise.

Trying to avoid her mother's fate, her daughter as narrator is determined to leave her hometown. She endeavors to enter the city, as her city aunts are such transforming presences. She wants to reconstruct her identity through geographical and social migration, through her occupation and consumption of a new space. Education helps her in finding a way into the city, and her marriage provides double legitimacy for her new urban identity. It is the narrator's small-town background that helps her attract her husband, who comes from a wealthy family and enjoys social privileges but possesses a "beggar maid complex." The small town and country are interpreted in modernization as a highly abstract cultural symbol, because the city needs something solid and stable to balance its rapid development, to give its ever-changing life a meaning of historical coherence, to compensate for a felt deficiency in the soul. The country might be too unruly to be tamed into a romantic and nostalgic imagination, but the small town, with its in-betweenness, its nature of compromise, easily becomes the best fantasy object against which the city determines its progress.

However, it turns out that the beauty of the small town (as well as the country) is only to be appreciated from a distance. Once the city actually confronts the town, it steadily consolidates its superiority as power center by reminding the town of its inferior position. Usually the inequality is internalized through cultural difference. Among all the cultural symbols, language appears to be the most revealing identity indicator. The urban accent that is accepted and practiced in the commercial world becomes the standard, while other dialects are held up to ridicule. In the story, whenever the narrator's husband receives a call with Dalgleish dialect, he immediately adopts an attitude of suspicion, as if he were treating a virus. The narrator and her husband eventually become estranged. Whereas she enjoys a comfortable urban upper class life, she is forever haunted by her small-town background, her accent, and her lifestyle. She always lacks the sense of belonging, just as her mother felt. She lives in a big house in an upscale neighborhood, but she has no car for herself and is bound by endless family responsibilities. She cannot build her own circle of friends, and she is void of any real connection with the outside city world. In this sense, the narrator is not fully accepted by the center. She is left along the marginal border between the center and the margin. She, too, suffers a complex of in-betweenness and placelessness.

The narrator finally reaches her epiphany through two visits: city revisited and country revisited. Aunt Iris, retired and alone, visits the narrator and her prosperous lawyer husband in Vancouver. This time the narrator notices that "[t]here was a bit of the Ottawa Valley accent still in [Aunt Iris's] voice, something rural." Upon this visit, the narrator, now seeing through her husband's eyes, is disappointed to find that Aunt Iris is actually mediocre and vulgar. Aunt Iris's accidentally dialectal expressions, such as "all out of puff" or "carrying the lard," exposes her inferior background. The important "connection," which the narrator has yearned for all her childhood, seems ridiculous now, and Aunt Iris, if she is not a bragger, turns out to be only a poor creature building her entire life on meaningless conjectures. The narrator also senses a disappointment with urban social relations. In the noisy, busy, and calculating city, interpersonal relationships appear shallow and transient. Blood ties, once regarded as the most important connection in the rural town, are inevitably weakened in the city by urban mobility. This visit helps the narrator to see through the city's good looks, and, as Coral Ann Howell points out, "Janet's buried family loyalties burst out in grotesque form: she throws the dish with the remains of a lemon meringue pie in it at his [i.e., her husband's] head" (73): the visit triggers the eventual breakdown of her marriage.

Years later, when she is long divorced, the narrator pays another visit to the Fleming aunts' old house. This second visit makes her reflect on the value of the country life. The old family house has long since been owned by others, and people change as time passes. Large-scale modern agricultural production has replaced the small-scale traditional family farming. Farm people are no longer traditional farmers. Instead, they are good at calculating risk and return on investments, as well as expanding production. The narrator cannot help remarking that "a farmer was just like a businessman nowadays, wasn't he?" (Munro, "The Stone in the Field" 34). But upon this return to the country, the narrator experiences a deep and seemingly indestructible spiritual connection to the land and its traditions. The self-enclosed and self-contained country makes her nostalgic because of its non-functionality, non-materiality, purity, and perpetuity. She finally understands her Fleming aunts. She understands that the Fleming aunts' taking care of a poor hermit of unknown origin did not occur out of love or out of any specific purpose; they cared for the hermit because it is their way of living: labor and mutual caring *are* their life.

At the end of the story, the narrator realizes the double cultural influences that the Chaddeleys and Flemings aunts have exerted on her. The maternal Chaddeleys represent the urban ideal, while the paternal Flemings represent the rural tradition. As personification of the two contradictory forces of urbanity and wilderness, the narrator owns an ambiguous identity of in-betweenness.

V

If we take into account the symbolic meaning of geographical space, the repellent attitude that the narrator's husband assumes toward Aunt Iris suggests a form of cultural resistance couched in nationhood. The husband originates from a wealthy upper-class Vancouver family, while Aunt Iris, as discussed earlier, represents the American city of Philadelphia. As a post-colonial country, whether in the period of "New France" or British North America, Canada has long existed as a frontier of European civilization. From the United States perspective, Canada is further north; it is more remote, desolate, and its people are more likely to feel helpless and timid before the imposing forces of nature. Andrew Malcolm observes in *The Canadians*:

> [M]any immigrants went to the United States with the specific goal to do something they could not do elsewhere — to practice a particular religion for example, like the Pilgrims [...] Many of Canada's immigrants were simply fleeting something — the Irish potato famine, the Highland clearances in Scotland, persecution

> against Indians in Kenya, or, in the case of some English nobility, a somewhat sullied reputation back home. The latter were called remittance men because they were not trying to create much of a new life in Canada; they lived, instead, off remittances from home. (Malcolm 59)

Self-referentially, Canada has been, and remains, highly dependent on the other cultural traditions. As Malcolm puts it, "being Canadians usually means also maintaining a simultaneous strong emotional tie to another country" (66). Canada needs an external cultural center, a reference, to assure itself where it is. It also tries to build its own civilization on the reproduction of the social order of the mother country.

In Canada's emotional imagination, Europe is so influential in daily life that it is by no means a faraway symbol. Instead, Europe is a real, closely-felt existence. It stands as the center of power and of culture. London, Paris, Cambridge, Waterloo, St. Petersburg — these important European city names can easily be found on the map of Canada, specifically of Ontario. Magdalene Redekop, speaking of Munro's "Scottish Nostalgic Grotesque," notices the connection:

> Look at the road map of Huron County, Ontario, and you will find that Wingham (the place where Alice Munro grew up) and Clinton (where she lives now) are in the middle of a region generously sprinkled with Scottish names: Culloden, Fingal, Kincardine, Melrose, Iona, Dungannon, Ailsa Cragg, New Dundee, and many more. Of course, Ontario also has a Dublin, a Stratford, a Paris, and even a Sparta (not to mention Brantford, named after the Mohawk chief Joseph Brant), but there is no question that the area is especially resonant with displaced Scottish history. (21)

Redekop points out the explicitly Scottish references in Munro's stories, emphasizing that the Scottish connection needs to be seen as more than a blurry background for interpretations of Munro's fiction. In fact, not only Scotland, other European regions, too, also help construct the Canadian cultural imagination. Europe, in short, is the most important identity reference for Canadians. Today, well-off Canadian families like sending their children to Europe for higher education.

Yet at the same time, the United States has replaced Europe as the world's power center. In a sense, the powerful cultural development of the United States makes "modernization" a synonym of "Americanization." American values which are based on mass consumption attack the European tradition of elitism in an unprecedented way. In Andrew Malcolm's words, Canadians are "forced to develop in the towering shadow of a superpower. They are bombarded daily by the overpowering cultural, economic, political, and even athletic influence of a dynamic and sometimes boorish United States [...]" (60). As a close neighbor, Canada shares in American economic prosperity. In fact, Canada not only shares continental space, but also the language and even its history with the United States. The two countries are inextricably linked, as it is the American Revolution that gave birth to both the United States and Canada. United States prosperity is a cultural temptation that is difficult for Canada to resist or avoid. American television, films, radio, advertisements, newspapers, novels, and music pour freely into Canada. The close proximity is an advantage and a threat. The biggest difference between a distant center and a close center lies in that the latter might swallow the individual at any time, whereas the former will not. The war of 1812 made Canadians forever cautious of the United States. They maintain a degree of guardedness against the cultural invasion and assimilation from the United States. Hugh Innis points out: "So conscious are we of the presence and power of our big neighbor, that the nationalism of Canadian people often seems anti-American rather than pro-Canadian" (1). In this perspective, the confrontation in Munro's story between the cautious husband and the outspoken Aunt Iris from Philadelphia is emphatically symbolic of the conflict between the European elite's culture of hierarchy and the American mass culture of carnival.

In this situation, what will the narrator, the epitome of the country's "in-betweenness," choose for her future? She witnesses the shallowness of Aunt Iris's pretension, while she cannot tolerate her husband's patronizing complacency. Unable to find sympathy with either, the narrator feels herself neither "in" nor "out of" any intimate relationship. She cannot rely on a solid emotional connection to solve her identity crisis. Eventually she assumes a rebellious disposition to reject her old self. She gets divorced, returns to Toronto, and starts a career as a documentary scriptwriter. The salary is not very good, but she finds inner peace by collecting, reexamining, and retelling local stories. Here the narrator is not only able to register the changing interpretation of her own family history, but also the shifting significance of local history. In so doing, she creates her own space of signifying power by recognizing a meaningful gap in the Grand Narrative. The few scraps of words appearing in old local newspapers, fragmentary and heterogeneous facts buried in the gaps of histories, gradually unfold before her eyes. The narrator eventually experiences an epiphany: she reconciles herself to her small-town background, and establishes a truce between the two halves of her split self.

The focus on the center, from a philosophical reflection, is without exception based on ignorance of the margin. Once the margin is in the limelight, it enjoys its own stage. It is no longer satisfied with existing as the center's insignificant attachment. It de-centers the center. Compared to the United States, which is highly urbanized, commercialized, and modernized, and based on clearly-defined core values of assimilation, Canada is to some extent more loosely united by separate regions, towns, and communities. Each region features its own narrative myths and ethical standards, a situation that is reflected in Canadian literature, which has long been argued by critics as not consisting of any unified literary tradition. As William John Keith maintains, "[t]he Maritimes, Newfoundland, Quebec, Ontario, the Prairies, British Columbia, the Northern Territories: all these distinctive areas can boast their own literary tradition" (26). The core spirit embodied in the dispersed pattern of Canadian regional literary traditions is a post-colonial attitude that transcends the limitation of the binary opposition of center and margin. Positioned in a non-central "in-betweenness," Canada resists the possibility of cultural assimilation by fostering its distinctive regional literatures. In Munro's story, the narrator's choice suggests the philosophical imagination of the power of places on the cultural margin, the places "in-between."

This chapter was completed by the author with funding from and as part of meeting the requirements of a Chinese National Ministry of Education research project. 本文为 2015 年教育部青年项目"加拿大文化视阈下的艾丽丝·门罗研究"阶段性成果, for MOE Project Number 项目批准号 15YJC752051.

References

Atwood, Margaret. *Survival: A Thematic Guide to Canadian Literature*. Toronto: House of Anansi, 1972.

Baudrillard, Jean. *For a Critique of the Political Economy of the Sign*. Trans. Charles Levin. Candor, NY: Telos P, 1981. (Originally published 1972.)

Deffy, Dennis. "Too Little Geography; Too Much History: Writing the

Balance in ' Meneseteung '." *National Plots: Historical Fiction and Changing Ideas of Canada*. Eds. Andrea Cabajsky and Brett Josef Grubisic. Waterloo, ON: Wilfrid Laurier UP, 1987. 197–213.

Frye, Northrop. "The Conclusion." *Literary History of Canada: Canadian Literature in English*. Vol. 3. 2nd ed. Ed. Carl F. Klinck. Toronto & Buffalo: U of Toronto P, 1976. 821–849.

Howells, Coral Ann. *Alice Munro*. Contemporary World Writers. Manchester: Manchester UP, 1998.

Hutcheon, Linda. *The Canadian Postmodern: A Study of Contemporary English-Canadian Fiction*. Toronto: Oxford UP, 1988.

Innis, Hugh, ed. *Issues for the Seventies: Americanization*. Toronto: McGraw-Hill Ryerson, 1972.

Keith, William John. *Canadian Literature in English*. London & New York: Longman, 1985.

Kröller, Eva-Marie, ed. *The Cambridge Companion to Canadian Literature*. Cambridge: Cambridge UP, 2004.

Malcolm, Andrew H. *The Canadians*. New York: Times Books, 1985.

Redekop, Magdalene. "Alice Munro and the Scottish Nostalgic Grotesque." *Essays on Canadian Writing* 66 (1998): 21–43.

Relph, Edward. *Place and Placelessness*. London: Routledge, 1976.

Ross, Catherine Sheldrick. *Alice Munro: A Double Life*. Toronto: ECW Press, 1992.

Shields, Rob. *Places on the Margin: Alternative Geographies of Modernity*. London: Routledge, 1991.

Toye, William, ed. *The Oxford Companion to Canadian Literature*. Toronto: Oxford UP, 1983.

Zhou, Yi. " Alice Munro and Canadian Literature: An Interview with Professor Robert Thacker." 26 Oct. 2014. Web. 15 June 2016.

丁林棚：《加拿大地域主义文学研究》，北京：北京大学出版社，2008。

黄仲文、张锡林：《加拿大英语文学简史》，南京：南京大学出版社，1991。

王晓德：《美国现代大众消费社会的形成及其全球影响》，载《美国研究》2007 年第 2 期，第 48–67 页。

Section Four

Variations of Cross-Cultural Transfer

16

"All the races": Reassessing the American Community Masque

Michael STEPPAT
University of Bayreuth

Summary: A fresh assessment of a striking event in American drama appears possible, based on research in several U.S. archives: the non-commercial civic masque *Caliban By the Yellow Sands*. Employing well over a thousand players, it was produced in New York in May 1916, while world war was threatening to engulf the U.S., and later in Boston. It was chiefly devised by New York dramatist Percy MacKaye, who spoke of the project as extending the scope of art by "the inexhaustible material awaiting the dramatist's muse in the folklore poured from overseas into America through our immigrant population." With an open-ended stimulus, the masque was expected to empower cultural communities to operate through "constructive imagination" for the purpose of "creating the international mind" — and for "the horizon of cosmopolitan promise." By integrating people from a wide range of communities as active cast members, MacKaye claimed such a production would "help unite all classes and all beliefs in a great cooperative movement for civic expression through dramatic art." While influential modern critics have given the performance rather unfavorable assessments, others have not considered the work as a whole. The masque's design provokes challenging questions: doesn't it subject immigrants to neo-colonial obligations of an Anglo-Saxon culture in America? What position is actually assigned to the ethnically varied immigrant groups? Finding an answer requires careful attention to the resources of intercultural research.

1. "Twenty Nationalities"

New York dramatist and poet Percy MacKaye declared in 1912 that he wished to widen his art " by the inexhaustible store of material awaiting the dramatist's muse in the folk-lore which is poured from overseas into America through our immigrant population, now ignored or stamped out by ignorant derision" (*Civic* 75). The tercentenary of William Shakespeare's death a few years later, in spring 1916, gave him an opportunity for such widening. Yet it turned out to raise some conceptual problems — not only at the time but also for modern scholarship. It is important to recall that, although Shakespeare was hardly an American dramatist, his work was understood in the nineteenth and at times in the twentieth century to be a significant part of American culture owing to a shared linguistic and cultural heritage with England.① In Michael Bristol's analysis, Shakespeare is or at least has long been " an American institution"; interpreting Shakespeare and interpreting American political culture are "mutually determining practices" (1, 3). We can understand the tercentenary, at a time when world war was raging in Europe, as an instance enabling mutual interpretation. The Drama League of America took it as a marvelous occasion to celebrate the English bard with events across America, with plays, masques, festivals, pageants, music, dancing, and many other forms (see Roberts, "Shakespeare" 354). There was a curious sense of cultural, even national appropriation: "[T]here is a quality attaching to American recognition of the Shakespearean tercentenary that even British celebrants can not possess"; Anglo-Saxons and Celts apart, "mankind of every race and blood emerge from America's melting pot joint heirs of this matchless

---

① For the way works of Shakespeare were required reading during the 19th century "[f]rom the frontier homesteads in the West to city schools in the East," to teach children from different national backgrounds "to read and speak the unifying American English," see Sturgess (146). "As America moved inexorably toward the Pacific Ocean, Shakespeare was seldom far behind" (Vaughan and Vaughan, *Shakespeare* 72); in major cities Shakespeare clubs "kept a broad cross-section of middle class Americans reading the plays" (ibid., 90).

treasure" (Periwinkle).② Prominently among the events, the Drama League envisioned a large-scale production in New York, and invited MacKaye to devise it.

Diversity and Paradox

The reason for approaching MacKaye was that he had become well known for creating a vast, pageant-like masque for the city of St. Louis in 1914 which had attracted an audience of approximately 400,000 people. Thus MacKaye seemed to have proven his capacity for large-scale spectacle with a peculiar mixture of highbrow as well as popular appeal. Clearly the Drama League was hoping for something on a similar scale. But New York with its large immigrant population from a growing range of origins was different — as was the occasion. In the non-commercial event that MacKaye began preparing to honor the English bard, accordingly, about a dozen ethnic groups were to take part (see MacKaye, *Caliban* 152). He had proclaimed that the dramatic art of American diversity "shall be the richer and mightier for every positive contribution of distinctive experience and tradition which each member shall conserve from his own inheritance and bring to it — the Asiatic, the European, the American, each contributive of his peculiar zone and meridian of wisdom [...]" (MacKaye, *Playhouse* 93).③ An art form thus enriched can be discovered "in America, if we shall look around us with fresh eyes, and if, with fresh vision, we peer into that Yankee past which produced us, and beyond to the horizon of cosmopolitan promise which is our destiny to come" (ibid., 94). Cosmopolitanism, for that matter, has in our time become a prominent topic for the

---

② William Chauncy Langdon's Dramatic Tribute of 1916 puts the following words in the mouth of American writer and politician Meredith Nicholson, imagined as speaking to Shakespeare: "In this Republic, that was undreamed of in your day, and in this commonwealth that arose from the ashes of the hunters' campfires, your name is loved even as in your own England. No day passes in which words of yours are not spoken on this young soil" (20). George Santayana wrote a witty, tongue-in-cheek essay "Shakespeare: Made in America" in *The New Republic* (27 Feb. 1915: 96–98).

③ This declaration actually echoes one by African-American poet and social reformer Frances E. W. Harper in 1892: "There are scattered among us materials for mournful tragedies and mirth-provoking comedies, which some hand may yet bring into the literature of the country, glowing with the fervor of the tropics and enriched by the luxuriance of the Orient, and thus add to the solution of our unsolved American problem" (282). Thus MacKaye's impulse has an earlier, perhaps not even White American origin.

International Association for Intercultural Communication Studies (IAICS). The challenge for MacKaye was to integrate people from a wide range of immigrant communities, whose native language was not necessarily English,④ as active cast members, "to help unite all classes and all beliefs in a great cooperative movement for civic expression through dramatic art" (MacKaye, *Caliban* xx). More characteristically available for immigrant entertainment in New York were dance halls, movies, and saloons (see Erenberg). MacKaye asserted that participating in drama productions would awaken a people instead to "self-government in the activities of its leisure," which is identical with "democratic life" (*Civic* 15, 17). The Shakespeare masque, when completed, would indeed rely on co-operation with ethnic communities. One of the actors described how "the representatives of all the races, classes, conditions in the great city" formed a range of community groups for the event (qtd. in MacKaye, *Epoch* 2: 482). The *Boston Evening Transcript* explained that, besides autochthonous Americans and peoples from the British Isles, the principal peoples represented were "Greek, Italian, Armenian, German, Hebrew, Polish, Irish, [...] Lithuanian, Russian, French and Spanish"; in fact for many weeks "citizens of twenty nationalities and as many religions" had been rehearsing (Baynes).⑤ The same critic went so far as to declare that the masque was not offered "by the black men or the white men," it was offered "by all of them." Horace Kallen, who would later become one of the founders of the Intercultural Communication concept, at this time (1915) highlighted the autonomous and dissimilative character of America's immigration groups.

The inclusion of many ethnic groups then exposes a fundamental paradox, a semiotic gap: how and for what purpose could anyone expect these diverse metropolitan communities to join forces at all in the celebration of an old-worldly artist? Would the expectation not amount to imposing on the immigrant communities a progressivist,

---

④   For the immigration situation in New York around this time, see Rosenwaike (especially 90–97, 109–119), Kessner (esp. 32–43, 84–99), and Foner (esp. 79–89, 142–149). In the 1910s, commercialization of everyday life was more pronounced than in previous decades; the growth of urban, commercial, also multiethnic popular culture generated anxieties and tensions for many citizens, challenging America's traditional sense of itself (see for instance Blanke 3).

⑤   Moderwell confirms the cooperation of "twenty nationalities" for the masque's New York presentation.

culturally hegemonic claim with an ideologized Anglo-Saxon bias?[6] I will address this question by taking a closer look at the actual performative event, in the context of MacKaye's own theoretical manifestos and contemporary reception. We can activate a chronotopal perspective when we reflect that "[e]very engagement with a Shakespearean text is necessarily intercultural. The past really is another culture [...]" (Tatlow 5). What's more, cultural transfer processes form a central component of Intercultural Communication, as "productive reception" of artifacts in a different cultural domain (see for instance Lüsebrink Chapter 5). In the following analysis, a few impulses from cross-cultural psychology in conjunction with a branch of interaction studies will become especially useful.

2. A Community Masque

What MacKaye offered was an adaptation of the American pageant tradition.[7] His concept led to the creation of an allegorizing community masque which carried the title *Caliban by the Yellow Sands*. The masque quarried Shakespeare's *The Tempest*, while radically changing its genre, structure, and characters. It was certainly a spectacular event, which received extensive press tracking during its preparation and then its production. The sheer scale had no precedent in New York: at least 1,500 individual performers were active; one could add to this figure the necessary supportive

Figure 1

The program cover of the 1916 production of *Caliban*

---

6   For the context of Progressivist attitudes toward immigration, see Higham (for instance 116ff., 186ff.). Coppélia Kahn (263) describes the hardly realistic Progressivist "conception of immigrants as passive and malleable under the uplifting influence of an anglicized American culture."

7   For the context of the American pageant movement, see especially Glassberg and Prevots.

staffs.[8] The premiere was witnessed by an audience of probably well over 10,000. The performances were repeated every evening for two weeks until about 200,000 audience members had actually seen and heard *Caliban*. Subsequently the production moved on to Boston. In the masque's dominant layer of plot development, the mage Prospero lands on an island named Yellow Sands (reconfigured from *The Tempest*) and soon begins a perplexing and erratic effort to educate youthful Caliban, a semi-human native, to civilized conduct.[9] A closer look shows that the main accent is not so much on Prospero's teaching but rather, with a subtle yet significant shift of agency, on "Caliban seeking to learn the art of Prospero" (*Caliban* xvii). The following is a brief overview of the work's structure. On the yellow sands the action unfolds in three layers, corresponding to acting levels:

(1) The first is the so-called Masque Proper, comprising a Prologue and three Acts. It takes place on a Middle Stage, where the selected group of characters who are re-imagined from *The Tempest* perform. Over this looms the image of the idol Setebos, Caliban's bestial sire; beneath is the opening of Caliban's cave. We see the spirit Ariel, a native of the island who has become Prospero's servant, about to be devoured by Setebos, when Prospero's daughter Miranda arrives and announces her father's approach. Fascinated with Miranda, Caliban soon lusts for a chance to breed offspring, until her father's spectacular entrance saves her from his clutches. He crushes Setebos, whereupon his educative program begins. The method is highly unusual: it's performative art.

(2) Caliban (and actually Miranda too) is offered a string of disjointed scenes mostly but not only from Shakespeare's plays of various genres, excerpts that are spawned by Prospero's imagination. These scenes are presented on a second acting level, an Inner Stage or separate recess, which features so-called "Cloudy Curtains" representing Prospero's mind. It is

---

[8] Franck (161 – 163, 165) gives a valuable account of the economic and organizational context of the masque's production. She also lists the main sponsors, a number of whom have no Anglo-Saxon descent. In the 1917 Boston production of the masque, "[m]ore than 5000 persons participated in the cast [...]" ("Storm"). The figure is confirmed by Baynes.

[9] Lorini (*Rituals* 238) describes this educative program as being in "curious" agreement with G. Stanley Hall's recapitulation theory, which is also outlined in Cavallo (55 – 60) and Lorini ("Progressives"). The assumption treats Caliban as a human individual, not as an allegorical character in a dramatic work. Not being a literary scholar, Lorini ignores the genre of allegory.

Figure 2
The masque's stage depiction of Setebos

raised above the Middle Stage. These Prosperonian scenes are keyed more or less closely to the plot of the Masque Proper — actually the connection is sometimes rather loose.

(3) Compounding the scenes, Prospero shows Caliban three partly non-speaking Interludes, aligned in at least some cases with the action, that exemplify the history of theater — but only as far as "a jocund festival" of England's Elizabethan period. (This development of Prospero's art does indeed speak to an Anglo-Saxon cultural bias.) These Interludes take place on the third and by far the largest level: the stadium's Ground Circle, which is equated with the Yellow Sands. These are "mottled with shadowy contours of the continents of the world" (xxx), from whence the national and civic groups converge. Whereas professionals are given the roles of the characters adapted from Shakespeare, many hundred amateurs, coached and guided by volunteer community leaders (see Prevots 80), enact the Interludes in chorus, pantomime, music, and dance, and partly the inset scenes too. This is where the ethnic communities become active, a decisive extension of the cast.

Figure 3

The setting of the inner stage with cloudy curtains

"More Visions"

For a number of these inset performances and Interludes, Caliban appears to be an attentive though somewhat naive learner. Yet a peripety shatters that educative program when certain inset scenes spark a rebellious, even warlike impulse in Caliban, empowering him to take Prospero and Miranda (the old world, as it were) captive — ending the third and final Act. Yet that does not end the masque. At this crisis, the allegorical Spirit of Time takes over. Time is Caliban's home — since the shifting Yellow Sands are clearly identified as "a great hour-glass, flowing with luminous sands" (xxx). Prospero's Interludes were crowned by evoking an idyllic English Mayday; with his defeat, such Anglo-Saxon centrism flops. Hence, Time now launches a huge parade, as Epilogue, enacted by the massive amateur cast in national/ethnic groups, who this time unfold the history of theater and acting all the way down to Henrik Ibsen, thus to the present. We learn that MacKaye's plan for the masque originally extended to representing the theater of "Persia, India, China" (Roberts, "Shakespeare" 360). The whole masque becomes remarkably autoreferential, theater quoting and staging itself, to prepare for a final self-celebration of the participating communities. Out of the English group Time foregrounds a modest Shakespeare, a mere simulacrum, one whom Prospero drapes in his own cloak. He can hardly mean the gesture to be empowering for the

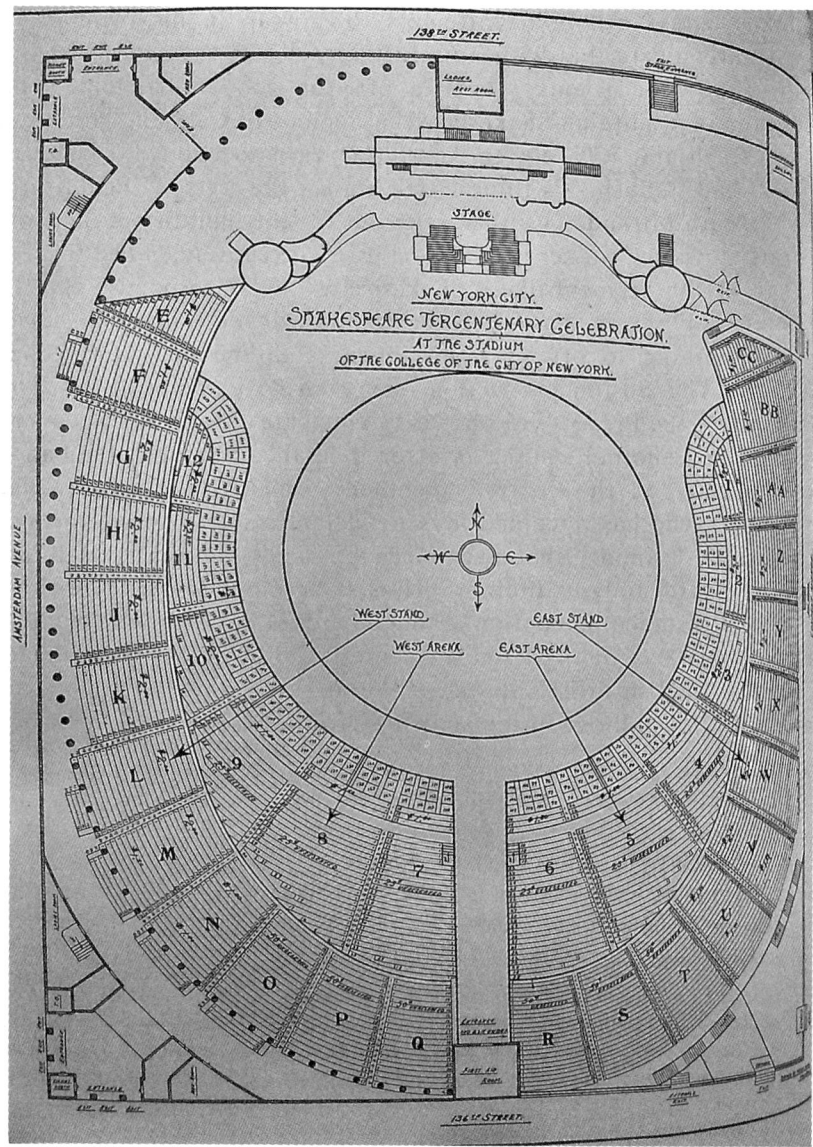

Figure 4
The stage position and seating plan of the New
York production at Lewisohn Stadium

bard. Since Miranda has explained earlier that Prospero's enfolding persons in his cloak means that he "holds us now/In his great art" (*Caliban* 16–17), the mage is now claiming the like hold on

"Shakespeare," whom he attempts to enwrap in his own arts.⑩
Apparently aware that he has no further place in the action, at this
point the mage silently shuffles off for good, abandoning his
daughter in a quite un-Shakespearean manner to Caliban. The latter
comes forth and calls out to Time: "I yearn to build, to be thine
Artist/And stablish this thine Earth among the stars —/Beautiful!"
(145). With Miranda, Caliban cries out for the plurality of "[m]ore
visions — visions" rather than for the bard's deceptively unified figure.

It is the figment-like "Shakespeare" who responds. But he
presents only the famous speech beginning *Our revels now are ended*:
he has nothing to offer — this amounts to the masque's second
ending. (The Boston production may even have scrapped the bard
altogether; see Prevots (213 n. 12)). Yet again, that is not all. As an
alternative, another ending is offered in the Program: Caliban is
now placed "at the centre" together with Ariel, Miranda, and
Prospero (who has remained present), significantly coming forth to
a position "[amid] the assembled thousands." Edward Hall has
recommended studying literary scripts as "a source of data" for shifts
in spatial distance perception, though he does not expressly mention
allegory (100). Coming from the center, Caliban picks up an image
from the English artist's speech ("We are such stuff/As dreams are
made on") to call out to the audience crowd:

> You, you, my fellow dreamers in the dark,
> We which are one, you millions that are me,
> Like as our dreams shall we ourselves become! [...]
> Together let us dream another world
> Beyond the tempest's pall — a strong, new world
> Builded with brothers' hands.

---

⑩　In the Preface, MacKaye explains that he is converting the "art of Prospero"
in *The Tempest* into the "art of Shakespeare in its universal scope," which he
defines as "that many-visioned art of the theatre" (*Caliban* xv). This is not
quite an equation of Prospero with Shakespeare. Later, in 1927 after having
moved on to other projects, MacKaye curiously misquotes a concluding
passage from his own masque, as if his recollection of its particulars is dim.
Among the misquotes is "*the only light remains on the figure of Prospero*"
(instead of Shakespeare) — as Caliban's "only immortal hope" (2: 483). But
this merely serves the general declaration that, when "all human aspiration"
asks for vision, "it must ask it of Genius" such as Prospero or Shakespeare,
an asking that is answered by the "Great Discovery" of the potential in
aspiration's own being.

　　The Shakespeare figure introduced in Conant's masque (1916), who also
becomes associated with Prospero (40), has a far more substantially centered
voice in much of *Will O the World*.

He calls on the thousand and more performers to kneel with him in tribute to the Shakespearean spirit of "dreams."⑪ And the masque's choirs sing

> Kindle where the dreams of Man
> Lift their master's lyre.
> Dreams of the world! — behold
> How they glister the night with their cloth of gold
> Where the spirits dance on the yellow sands
> And the children of earth clasp hands!

3. Research Situation

When modern scholarship has not just offered a general introduction to the plot and the historical situation of the *Caliban* masque, it has focused on certain critical aspects. Vilma Potter in 1996 discussed the work in the context of MacKaye's drama concepts, especially concerning notions of democracy, and suggested that it functions as "an affirmation of the superiority of English tradition" (76). In an influential study, Thomas Cartelli in 1999 offered an assessment of the American renegotiation of Shakespeare at this time, in which MacKaye's concern was "how best to 'Americanize' the newly arrived masses of immigrants and introduce them to the standards and obligations of Anglo-Saxon culture"; the masque then appears as "an internal or domestic colonizing venture" with a "largely anti-democratic bias" (63, 74, 75). With a similar approach, Coppélia Kahn in 2000 focused on "the longstanding question of what transformed an immigrant into an American" (258) and the contemporary Nativist-Progressivist debate as context for the masque. She found not only that the masque "expressly denies Caliban his aspiration to artistic visions of his own," but also that it "coheres all too well with the Anglo-Saxon vision of America into which many reformers expected immigrants to blend" (269, 270).

Rather differently, Diana Henderson in 2003 in a short discussion spoke of "the explicit allegory of this celebration of art" and MacKaye's "'faith' in the communal powers of art" (224, 226). Then, Monika Smialkowska commented on the masque's "representations

---

⑪ Long before this, in Act 1 already Caliban was described as having "dreams within" (48), as being "full of dreams" (63), which are thus not generated in the first place by "Shakespeare"'s speech.

of history and its uses of Shakespeare and the Shakespeare canon," concluding that it "transforms history from a set of particular events into a grand moral narrative" ("Shakespeare" 18, 22). In a further important essay, Smialkowska discussed the masque's world war context for the work's "optimistic, pacifist message": "With Caliban's submission to Prospero and Shakespeare at the end of the show, Art conquers War," while the Boston production after America's entrance into the war was more strongly involved in "rallying support for the U.S. war effort" ("Conscripting" 196, 197). While this body of research has greatly helped our understanding of the masque with its sociocultural situation, in the following it will form a recurring focus because in some respects it falls short of being satisfactory. Inevitably, a number of quotations from the critical discussion will be required to clarify the analytical needs.

The Caliban "Type"

The first such respect is the basic question, who (or what) is Caliban? MacKaye himself identifies him with "that passionate child-curious part of us all [whether as individuals or as races], grovelling close to aboriginal origins, yet groping up and staggering [...] toward that serener plane of pity and love, reason and disciplined will" (*Caliban* xv). He is nothing less than "the protagonist of aspiring humanity" (xvi). The concept appears designed to appeal to virtually the entire audience and the readers. If this embraces the critic as well, it can be said to speak to Patrice Pavis's appraisal of the interculturalism of the theater's hourglass, which "forces the analyst to reconsider his own cultural parameters and his viewing habits, to accept elements he does not fully understand [...]" (*Theatre* 5). However, Potter narrows MacKaye's concept somewhat, equating Caliban with "the masses, the immigrants whose lives in America were generally contaminated by vulgar commercial entertainments" (71). And Cartelli (80) goes further in this direction when he supposes that MacKaye's Caliban represents the mass of immigrants and hence (193, n. 11) considers the masque consistent with the blatant racism of sociologists such as Edward A. Ross in 1913, for whom "the Caliban type" designated immigrants of "obviously low mentality," ones "out of place," "oxlike men" who are "thick in the sluiceways of immigration" (Ross 285, 286).[12] Not

---

[12]   See Higham (109 – 110) for a historical assessment of Ross's attitudes. Coppélia Kahn (268) speaks of Caliban as "the cultural — and racial — Other" of Anglo-American culture.

unlike this, Madison Grant in 1916 contended that "the altruistic ideals [...] and the maudlin sentimentalism that has made America 'an asylum for the oppressed,' are sweeping the nation toward a racial abyss" (228). Without closer analysis of the depiction, what justification is there for taking MacKaye's dramatic character to be "the Caliban type," as if the masque were the work of Edward Ross? In *The Tempest*, one can read Caliban as a second-generation immigrant, but in the American masque his native cave opens directly onto the sands, rendering him autochthonous — there is nothing to suggest clearly that his ancestry is not native, unlike Prospero who has had to make "many a starry journey" to find this land (*Caliban* 16).

If Caliban cannot be simply identified with immigrants, should we by contrast assume a colonial enterprise in which a MacKayan Caliban "symbolized colonized nations before they received the blessings of western culture and civilization" (Vaughan and Vaughan, *Shakespeare's* 114)? Prospero would then be a colonist who forces advanced civilization's light upon the benighted native. That, however, wouldn't square with the masque either. The hundreds from among the ethnic communities who form the Interludes and the concluding theatrical parade, and who are thus decisive for Caliban's education, can by no stretch of the imagination be read as a colonizing army. Efforts to redefine the masque's Caliban have on the whole not been convincing.

4. Neo-colonial Obligations?

If this Caliban is hardly an immigrant, can we really assume that the masque serves to introduce immigrants to neo-colonial "obligations of Anglo-Saxon culture"?[13] What are the alleged obligations that

---

[13] Carlyle had much earlier been able to muse about future "Nations of Englishmen," being "of one blood and kind" with Shakespeare, "[f]rom Paramatta, from New York, wheresoever" (110 - 111). As against MacKaye's, other Tercentenary productions are more straightforwardly Anglocentric, such as those by Carroll, Langdon, and Conant. There is no space here for further comparison. Im (237-238) is among critics who stress that the mystification of Shakespeare productions in terms of a "universal performative force" may actually be a mode of "cultural imperialism." The criticism is picked up by Pavis in 2010 ("Intercultural"). The universalizing topos tends to deny what intercultural transversalism calls a "journey of difference without arrival" (Jung 32).

Prospero embodies? With radical binarism, MacKaye's Prospero, to counter the oxlike Caliban type, has been regarded as echoing Moses and Christ, hence as "the unquestioned source and force of goodness" with consistently "wise governance," so that Caliban must forever "exist in a dependency relationship" with him (Cartelli 68, 72, 75). The allegory would then suggest that the new immigrants must remain under the thumb of a haughtily "wise" Anglo-Saxonism; there would be no room for any ambivalence in MacKaye's starry, old-worldly journeyer Prospero. Is the assessment justified?

One could argue that Prospero turns out to be a poor educator. This is one chief respect in which the present analysis differs from previous ones. As explained above, his endeavor is to educate Caliban to become a civilized individual, by means of a range of scenes taken mostly from Shakespeare's plays of various genres. In a climax which Smialkowska describes as being meant to "criticise and exorcise" a propensity for violence on Caliban's part ("Shakespeare" 24),[14] Prospero's teaching rises to a scenic lesson "how noblest natures/Are moved to tiger passions" (Caliban 136). This occurs when he offers Caliban nothing less than "the blast of war" from Shakespeare's historical play Henry V, which might indeed be cathartic but for a blatant call to "imitate the action of the tiger" (138). That beast has been introduced as none other than Caliban's sire, who is "half tiger" and has "tiger-jaws," while "War" is Setebos's priest.[15] Prospero's imperative to do as Caliban's father does makes him, not the son, difficult to distinguish from the "colossal and primitive" idol, so that the mage himself sparks the violent rebellion which undoes him: "Now Setebos returns" (139).[16] We need to remember the world war situation. MacKaye observes,

---

[14] Cartelli (69) justly observes that "the scenes themselves generally fail to deliver the lessons in civility Caliban is presumably meant to master," yet without letting that affect his appraisal of Prospero. Instead, the failure is due to "oxlike" Caliban's backsliding and inability to grasp such lessons.

[15] Not noticing the tiger, Shattuck (307) inaccurately describes MacKaye's Setebos as "bull-like, dragon-like," thus missing the image connections and consequently failing to find much coherence in the masque. A "bull" image does occur once (Caliban 19), but in its context it is as metaphorical as Caliban's being "dog-like" (ibid.); there is no dragon in the masque.

[16] Potter (76) offers a perceptive side-glance: "not only barbed wire and machine guns, but poison gas and aerial bombardment are features of Prospero's 'western' world." Engler (103) documents ways in which Henry V was actually being used by both Britain and Germany to support their official war causes.

"Over seas [...] War, Lust, and Death are risen in power to restore the primeval reign of Setebos" (ibid., xiii). Caliban's final speech in the Program, accordingly, defines an American sense of diminishing space that calls for urgent action: "night rolleth towards us, Yet we will drive the night back with our dreams." As already mentioned, Edward Hall recommends studying literary scripts for such historical shifts in spatial distance perception, without considering allegory (100). Diana Henderson, at any rate, well observes that the masque "is not written from the superior position of either Prospero or Shakespeare," since it shows awareness of " the seeming 'backsliding' of all civilization" (225). A parallel with his own reign, in fact, is drawn by Prospero himself: "The will of Setebos is matched with mine/To rule our world" (26).

Matched Values

Here, as in related contexts, we might bear in mind that "observations do not refer to objects of an independent reality" (Barad 170), that objects of observation hardly exist outside the agency and specific vantage point of investigation and inquiry. In seeking a fresh observation form linked with the masque's semantic import, and to do justice to the depicted plot climax, we can draw transversally on an adapted concept of Basic Individual Values in the context of cross-cultural psychology. It then turns out that both Prospero and Setebos assert a value of power dominance (authority and control over others), as analyzed by Shalom H. Schwartz ("Refining" 200), a *matched* value. The power value has a subtype that appears adaptable to the masque: controlling events through one's assets, which can be economic or, not wholly separable, " intellectual resources" (Schwartz, "Refining" 200, 248; "A Theory" 162). The resources in our case are especially the masque's inset drama scenes, a currency which becomes contested as rival forces aim to impose their "readings" on the characters — as the exclusively desirable way toward a rewarding life in Yellow Sands with its people from "the continents of the world."

We need to keep in mind, all the while, that we are dealing with literary allegory, which intensifies sociocultural realism to negotiate between what cross-cultural research distinguishes as individual-level values and nation-level values (see Knafo et al.; also Schwartz, "Studying" 314). We can then agree that "using such social science frameworks for values or identity mapping may provide helpful tools for analyzing literature [...]" (Kulich 135).

The concept of Cultural Value Orientations understands the power value as "mastery," with a purpose to change the social environment and attain group or personal goals (Schwartz, "A Theory" 141). In all situations, the rival cultures embodied by Setebos and Prospero seek to subject the *personae* to their own ideological goals. The masque reveals the fallacy of a seemingly linear power value. Both antagonists induce the likes of their dominance motive in Caliban when he is enjoined to imitate the tiger, exposing how such a conjunction can only fail owing to its inner antinomy.

"Wise" Prospero

Nonetheless, critics have been notably reluctant to associate Prospero, the "source of goodness," with any disaster. Cartelli (70) subtly dislocates the agency when he speaks of "MacKaye's decision," hence apparently not Prospero's, to place the militant *Henry V* scene where it appears. Within the masque's dialogue, it is Prospero who "sends" the scene at this point (136). The minor dislocation is more significant than it appears in serving to preserve an idealization of Prospero, whereas the masque has begun the opposite process of debunking his status.[17] The question of debunking is crucial for any understanding of the masque's development toward its final interpellation of the ethnically mixed participant and audience crowd. When Ariel, speaking for Prospero, announces the warlike scene, no critic has seen any internal confusion in his verses: "Image of Strife, may never more/Your like draw near! /Pageant of long-forgotten War,/Appear!" (137). For Smialkowska ("Shakespeare" 24), this expresses the show's "pacifistic intention," yet when one listens closely the verses confound logic in equating a wish that strife should never more approach with a command for war's entrance. For the perception and meaning of spatial distance, Hall (we might remember) has urged looking carefully at textual microstructure (94ff.). Doing so will reveal the ambivalence that, at this crucial moment, engulfs Prospero as the show's sender, whose "wise governance" is arguably crumbling. Perhaps the Cloudy Curtains that represent his mind in the masque are to be understood as *cloudy* indeed, opaque, muddy. Unlike Shakespeare, MacKaye

---

[17]   Smialkowska ("Conscripting" 196) maintains that "*Caliban* condemns warlike sentiments as capable of corrupting" noble natures, and stresses ("Shakespeare" 24) the "pacifistic intention of the show." She is silent about Prospero's role in this context.

does not give any precise origin for Prospero, freeing him to associate the character in general terms with the loftiest cultural and moral claim intertwined with a deadly call to arms. He introduces him from the start as composed of ambivalent "masks/Of joy and sorrow" (9).

Self-Verification Clash

But is the staging of the tiger-passions scene right here without any allegorical motivation? We need to look at a plot detail. Just before this, Caliban has drawn mostly on his own energies to turn against the lures of War (126), an incident critics have ignored. He is puzzled by War's bait "Miranda shall be thine," since Miranda has just taught him, remarkably enough, not only that she loves him but that their love "knows not *mine* and *thine*, But only *ours*" (124). At this highly sensitive juncture, Prospero can think of nothing better than to offer him a scene that harbors a thinly veiled mockery and thus steers the masque directly toward the tiger-passions climax. The key scene is taken from the comedy *Merry Wives of Windsor*, featuring a supposedly lascivious Falstaff wearing great horns. Watching closely, Caliban soon senses whom Falstaff stands for, that his earlier and even his present self is being made fun of, since the pinching of Falstaff now revives the earlier plaguing of Caliban. When Ariel "silverly" commends this "fairy sport for laughter," Caliban hears his past being employed to engulf his present. His responses grow bitter: "Mocketh me, mocketh me, ah! — A man with horns And heart of monster!" (133). Before long he is choking with resentment. One might gather that the masque demonstrates how "silverly" comedic laughter and sport can thinly veil some underlying psychic and physical violence. While Coppélia Kahn (268) offers no account why Caliban is moved to passion, Potter (76) inexplicably asserts that Caliban is "sexually aroused" by the comedy scene.

We should look for a different explanation. A grasp of the plot situation here, after all, has bearing on the attitude toward what has been called America's "great unwashed" (see below). We are unlikely to go far wrong if we assume that, following Prospero, Caliban becomes locked with him in a contest for perception confirmation: each wants perceivers to see him as he would see himself, and accordingly rejects whatever does not confirm his self-conception (see Swann). Across cultures, each *persona*'s self-view enables him to "maintain a sense of continuity, place, and coherence" (Seih et al. 169). The mage throughout has a highly positive self-view, Caliban largely so despite moments of self-criticism ("now — am mud": 74).[18] Experimental psychology shows that persons "impute more accuracy to positive than negative evaluations" by others, a tendency that may be self-enhancing but may also reflect "honest assessments of the extent to which the evaluations matched their self-views" (Seih et al. 172). Craving for coherence and place, like those around him, Caliban sees himself deprived through mockery of any positive evaluation. At this stage in the plot, the deprival would amount to an inaccurate assessment. Yet the lordly mage will allow no doubt as to his sound judgment. The masque is rapidly building up to a disruption of any continuity.

The mutual self-verification engagement reveals a perceptual split. In a cognitive performance charged with emotive energy, it forms a highly effective run-up to the explosive plot peripety in which Caliban attacks and conquers Prospero and his servants. His rage, which has been presented as being the condition of the "huddled masses" and of "New York's great unwashed" (Cartelli 75), is not simply inborn, it is readable as a state that the haughty mage has thrust upon him. Here again, the object of observation depends on the agency or vantage point of inquiry. When a point is chosen, the object will show a corresponding face. Some of its features act in a particular way under observation — coming under erasure, for instance, as being paltry or negligible. Whereas criticism has described Caliban as being "ape-like" and childishly "destructive" throughout (as in Coppélia Kahn 275), is the capacity that he shows for poetic energy really erasable as in his responses to Miranda, whom he tropes "Spring-i'-the-air" (17) and reflects or possibly sings, "The moon hath a face/And smileth on the lily pools, but hath/No lily body withal [...]" (18)? It is at least as likely that his response to the alleged "obligations" is a process rather than a condition, one that needs analysis.

5. Moment of Change

When "fairy laughter" triggers "tiger passions," the masque spirals

---

[18]   At this juncture, remarkably enough Miranda refuses to accept Caliban's self-doubt and seeks to bolster his self-confidence by calling him "star-dust." This enables him to counter put-downs thereafter with "'Tis lies!" (*Caliban* 78).

downward back in time to Setebos's tiger rule. And that means back to the opening. Fittingly enough, that is when the allegorical Spirit of Time takes over from Prospero, whose endeavors have gone awry. Staged as "a great hour-glass," Yellow Sands turns out to be a terrain on which both temporal and value orientations can flip.⑲ That is because the setting's "continents of time" become a Bakhtinian chronotope of island as

Figure 5
The Yellow Sands as "Altar of the Time" in the New York production

---

⑲ Patrice Pavis in the 1990s famously offered a concept of the hourglass of theater, to which he devoted a whole work, as defining "intercultural transfer between source and target culture" (*Theatre* 5) — his immediate focus being mostly on recent European adaptations. The concept is somewhat binary and linear, not designed to cover some theater forms that only emerged toward the end of the 20th century. Sequential as it appears, the hourglass is continuously inverted so as to "flow indefinitely from one culture to another," questioning "every sedimentation" (ibid.). It has further implications. The sands of the transferable "layers of culture" are made of a "hybridization of races and traditions" (5, 6); how they become rearranged is not prefigured, being regulated by "their passage through some dozen filters put in place by the target culture and the observer" (4). The perceived rearrangement, that is, depends on the observer's procedure. By the same token, as Pavis maintains, "intercultural communication needs *reception-adapters*, 'conducting elements' that facilitate passage from one world to the other" — especially theater directors who "make one aware of differences" (16). The hourglass model thus has some analytical value for MacKaye's masque. As Finelli among others confirms, the model "works for productions that transfer materials" by adaptation (65).

threshold, "a transitional space between two worlds. Temporally, it presents a suspended moment of change or crisis," to "destabilize and distort" any source material "in order to undermine the specific ideological perspective of its source" (Collington 189, 192). That moment happens when a beaten Prospero slinks away, giving way to a "Shakespeare" figure who appears only to intone the end of his revels. Smialkowska ("Shakespeare" 25) acutely observes that, since the figure is "transferred to the same plane of existence" as the dramatic characters, the masque "empties him of inherent meaning." The emptying is chronotopal, the masque's engagement with Shakespeare reminding us that the past "really is another culture" (Tatlow 5) — as L. P. Hartley would famously suggest in 1953. Yet critics have not devoted attention in their analyses to the masque's other ending, as printed in the Program and quoted above,[20] and this is a further respect in which the present analysis differs from previous ones. We should at least briefly come back to that alternative, which shows the destabilizing of source material together with MacKaye's escaping what Adichie would perhaps call the danger of a single story.

The Embedded Individual

We can draw again on the adapted concept of Basic Individual Values to explain how, coloring the masque's preceding structure, Caliban here opens the finale to overcome the earlier power/dominance motivation in favor of new key values which are very close to universalism-as-societal-concern (equal opportunity and "believing that immigrants deserve the same rights as citizens") with benevolence-as-dependability (trustworthy membership of an ingroup, voluntary bonding) (see Schwartz, "Refining" 203–204, 211, 234, 251). These translate into allegory, and thus beyond individual relevance, when Caliban identifies himself with the players as well as with the huge

---

[20]   Thomas Cartelli (193 n. 10) and Coppélia Kahn (281 n. 25) mention the alternative ending only in their notes, quoting very short excerpts from Green's incomplete rendering, without connection to their interpretations of the masque. Smialkowska ("Shakespeare" 24 – 25) contends that the inset scenes' "potentially multiple meanings," which are liable to differing interpretations by Caliban and by Prospero, may not support Shakespeare's cultural authority, which is transferred "to those who interpret him." Yet regrettably she does not discuss the alternative ending, which can be read as opening the finale beyond the characters' differing interpretations of Shakespeare's own work.

   In the alternative, for that matter, Prospero remains on stage to announce and give way to the appearance of Shakespeare's "spirit."

and ethnically mixed audience, and indeed the common "millions" coming together to form America. The verse in the masque's program as quoted above strengthens a culturally relevant value orientation toward "embeddedness," in which individuals are regarded as "entities embedded in the collectivity [...] restraining actions that might disrupt in-group solidarity," on the "assumption that a person's roles in and obligations to collectivities are more important than her unique ideas and aspirations" (Schwartz, "A Theory" 140–141; for partial replication, see Vauclair et al. 193). The Caliban *persona* stands for what Schwartz with a suggestive theater analogy calls "role players embedded in groups" ("Mapping" 344).

As in the cultural value concept, this blends well in the masque's design with hierarchy. That is understood as a reliance on "ascribed roles to insure responsible, productive behavior" and an acceptance of "unequal distribution of power, roles, and resources as legitimate" (Schwartz, "A Theory" 141). We can find the reliance expressed by MacKaye's belief not so much in Prospero's lordship, but in a non-commercial "consecrated leadership of Genius," artistic guides and sources of inspiration for the common people, not for all time but until the people discover "the Aristocrat potential" in their own being (*Epoch* 2: 483–484). Not too differently, Schwartz suggests that "democratic institutions may foster cultural mastery, because they demand more active participation by individuals and groups and make it worthwhile" ("Mapping" 368). The masque's other ending thus offers a glimpse of an elaborated value orientation for America's culturally varied communities. To sustain it, Caliban calls on the people to use their dreams to fashion another world beyond Shakespeare's work (transparently invoked as "the tempest's pall"). There will be no continuing hierarchical claim or aid from the Anglo-Saxon bard — or Anglo obligations.㉑ As Patrice Pavis declares, as if responding to the masque: "After the sand has filtered from one bowl of the hourglass to the other, the spectators are the

㉑ Coppélia Kahn (269–270) asserts that the masque "expressly denies Caliban his aspiration to artistic visions of his own"; only "watching Shakespeare's visions" can possibly free him from brutality. This reading is founded on a claim that the *Our revels now are ended* lines are "echoed by the large choir and orchestra," so that the whole masque bars Caliban from creative desire. Yet that is not exactly what happens in the masque when Ariel's choirs pick up only two later lines beginning *We are such stuff* (146). The Shakespeare figure apart, no cast members expressly announce an ending of revels. Such minutiae are not merely hairsplitting when they support a general interpretation.

final and only guarantors of the culture which reaches them, whether it be foreign or familiar" (*Theatre* 18). And American poetess Florence Ripley Mastin writes, "The audience itself is Caliban."

English Hegemony

Yet isn't there still a subtle ideological dominance? Assuming there is not much aid from the Anglo-Saxon bard, and if the text and plot do indeed show a failure of attempted "Anglo" centrism, don't the masque's speeches and dialogues make use of hegemonic English? Seeing that MacKaye spoke of having initially "devised a structure in which the English language, spoken by actors, is an essential dramatic value" (*Caliban* xxv), Coppélia Kahn (271) highlights an "Anglo-Saxon America" that requires immigrants to "adopt English tradition as the foundation of American culture".[22] Yet she does not note that, in order to carry the masque's "community meaning" beyond English to what he expressly characterizes as New York's polyglot population, MacKaye in a quite up-to-date move (as characterized by Henderson 226) loses no time in commissioning the masque's immediate translation into Italian, Yiddish, and German (see *Caliban* 152), though we have no clear record whether and how any of these versions were subsequently performed.[23]

In the Preface to a civic ritual that he devised for new citizens, MacKaye does suggest a linguistic centrism: "[A]t the altar of our English-speaking tradition of liberty gather the manifold cultures,

---

[22] On Americanization in the later 19th century through "the English language and the influential cultural text supplied by the American publishers of Shakespeare," see Sturgess (116). In the masque's performance, the Anglo-Saxon civility materializing in the speaking roles was, ironically enough, the element least effectively received. As Coppélia Kahn (272) notes, some reviewers complained that, despite the installation of sounding boards and actors' vocal exertions, the huge stadium made it difficult for those seated further from the playing area to hear, let alone understand much of the dramatic dialogue. We do hear in *The New York Times* that "the voices of the players come faint but clear if the wind is right [...]" ("MacKaye's Masque"). *The New York Dramatic Mirror* is lenient on the indistinctly heard dramatic poetry's effect: "[...] perhaps it gained beauty and mystery in the lurking shadows and under the starlit sky" ("The First"). As against such difficulties, at any rate the music composed by Arthur Farwell for the masque was highly praised, and could be heard even at the times when it was played very quietly, up to almost 400 feet away (see Graziano 305).

[23] Potter (76) and Cartelli (73) acknowledge the translations, though the latter objects that the initiative would "little profit" those community members who lacked the skill or money to buy and read the versions.

languages, arts and crafts of all peoples" (*New* 14). Nonetheless, an express subjugation to English is not easy to find within the ritual itself, so that the initiative of offering the masque in various languages in the following year becomes noteworthy. It may be fair to say that MacKaye was ambivalent about a linguistic hegemony whose stability he did not consistently support. There is an ethnic aspect to consider. Whereas it has been maintained that the masque was designed to reassert "America's status as a bastion of Anglo-Saxon culture" when that status was being "threatened" by what Henry James called "the Hebrew conquest" (Cartelli 77), it may be worth recalling that the production's actual venue, the City College of New York and its stadium, provided for the educational needs largely of Russian Jews and of German Jews (see Jackson 228). What is more, as Smialkowska ("A democratic" 8) well observes, "Anglo-American exceptionality was being sponsored by Americans who were naturalised," and who were of largely Jewish-German origin.

Community Input

But is there no Bakhtinian "transitional space" between the artist's dominance and the community's part? Within the masque's structure, Prospero's Interludes rarely grant the community actors dramatic speech in presenting the history of theater, unlike the professionalized Masque Proper and the inset scenes. It has hence been declared that the Interludes are delegated to "mute figurants" who represent "still unintegrated latecomers to the feast of Anglo-American civility" (Cartelli 66). And it has been claimed that, because MacKaye's own central role as writer and organizer "belies" any community, there is in the whole masque "no community input into either script or production" (Coppélia Kahn 275). These assessments are somewhat overstated. The Interludes feature Choruses, which are clearly described as performed "by community participants," numbering about sixty amateurs (*Caliban* xxx, 168) who are not exactly mute but are granted several stanzas of lofty Sophoclean dramatic poetry to chant (for instance 170−171). In terms of community input, Smialkowska ("A democratic" 5) points to the Jewish names of participants recorded in the Program; for that matter, the latter also records a number of Italian and German names. Even so, John Collier at the time of the masque was surely right in critiquing that "the shortness of time made it impossible to reassemble into the definite and ambitious structure of this pageant-drama such elements of local and racial group-life as do exist in richness unparalleled in Greater New York"; the event, accordingly, "was not a folk-product or a communal product" (344–345).

And yet we learn from a press report that MacKaye left smaller, probably non-speaking parts of the masque to be composed by community groups, coming close to an autopoietic feedback loop: "In some cases, the local group will take a certain section of the masque, lasting five minutes or so, and work it out as its contribution to the local celebrations" ("New York Gets").[24] This has a further dimension: a Don Giovanni scene-plot within the second Interlude "is being enlarged, under Mr. [Ernest] Peixotto's direction, into the spring festival of the MacDowell Club, performed locally at its clubhouse, lasting an hour and a half [...]" (*Caliban* 153). Evidently community spin-offs from the masque's own structure were being actively encouraged, as a part of the community drama idea. We could acknowledge that these are as yet not more than inchoate moments of change to move both performance and composition slightly closer to what MacKaye called *democratic life*.

6. Demos and Drama

Community input is central in MacKaye's own concept of the art form that he was propagating. His key term is Demos, which stands for democracy's people. In the somewhat turgid manner of the day, he commended the Demos for having faith "in the Aristocrat potential in his own passional being — the austere *Artist* of Democracy" (*Epoch* 2: 483). Such faith is a trust in "the consecrated leadership of Genius, whose touchstone is creative art" (ibid., 2: 484). Its home is "the democracy of excellence, not the democracy of mediocrity" (qtd. in Kilmer SM13). We have this categorization likewise in MacKaye's civic ritual, in which he speaks of "those enlightened ideals of *the new citizenship* which stand not for the

---

[24]   As *The New York Times* described it, when MacKaye proposed a representation of Renaissance Italian theater, for instance, the MacDowell Club picked up the idea and fashioned such a production for its spring performance: "when the time for the masque comes, the MacDowell Club will fit neatly into the whole scheme" ("New York Gets").

Recommendations for the casting of pageants tended to "reinforce the distinctions" between local and ethnic groups, for the purpose of facilitating their working together (Glassberg 113), which was the case also with *Caliban*. Even so, outside formal rehearsal situations there turned out to be much "fraternizing" ("Behind") and "mingling" (Baynes) between the various groups.

levelling away of all world-cultures to leave bare an American mediocrity, but for the welcoming of all world-cultures to create an American excellence" (*New* 14). In 1916 Otto H. Kahn, who was a banker and chairman of the Mayor's Honorary Committee for New York's Shakespeare Celebration, in similar terms (6) rejected a "false democracy" which "seeks or tends to establish a common level of [7] mediocrity," preferring a democracy which "strives to lead us all onward and upward to an ever higher plane."

Figure 6

Percy MacKaye.
Courtesy of Dartmouth
College Library.

In MacKaye's artistic version of this idea, when the people with their varied cultural backgrounds look up to artistic Genius, the latter stirs a similar potential in Demos's mind. A discourse of art based on "elimination of private profit by endowment and public support" transversally intersects the democratic and the migrant arguments (MacKaye, *Civic* 15). While the trope of aristocratic leadership hardly sounds democratic, it leads back to a democratic population's inner constitution:㉕ the populace cannot but aspire to rise "to lordly reason" (*Caliban* 26), enabling art's inspiration to awaken a people to the achievement of "lordlier self-government" (MacKaye, *Civic* 83). In the masque, once again, Caliban can accordingly be identified with the "millions" of the commoners who are ready to awaken to art — and in the same process to self-government. No longer radically strange, Caliban is placed inside an order that is well within the democratic people's boundary (see Waldenfels). We should see this against a backdrop of Progressive

㉕ Cartelli (81) asserts that MacKaye is arguing for "aristocratic entitlement" which marks a "clear-cut separation" from "the immigrant hordes." MacKaye's own feudalizing tropes, however, carry no demarcation against Demos's "groping Aspiration." The discussion is prefigured, at some distance, in the philosophical fragments of Novalis, who in 1798 fused his fanciful idea that "[e]very person should become an artist" with playful aristocratic troping (*Faith and Love* No. 39, 95 – 96): "A true prince is the artist of artists"; the "regent" becomes "a diverse spectacle, where stage and parterre, actor and spectator are one, and he himself is poet, director, and hero of the play." Prince, artist, and commoner slide into each other. More relevant perhaps is Willa Cather's pronouncement in 1894, likewise playing with a monarchic/aristocratic trope, that "a poet's consummation and crown is that the ideal shall be real to him" (1: 42).

belief in democratic arts culture, what Van Wyck Brooks in 1915 called "the current of Transcendentalism," a world of ideals which was running side by side with the prevailing "current of catchpenny opportunism" (9; see also Bradley 10).

The International Mind

What means, then, is best suited for bridging the chasm between Genius and democracy? For MacKaye it was the dramatic masque, which as he came to think differs from the pageant by including poetry and a plot (as in *Caliban* xvii-xviii or the later *Wakefield* 105–106). Staging some allegorical subject, it involves large numbers of participants, a majority of them amateurs. It has "a structure of potential interrelated pantomime, music, dance, lighting, acting, song [choral and lyric], scene values, stage management and spoken words" (*Caliban* xxiii). Innovative theater reformers like Gordon Craig, MacKaye acknowledged, advocated dropping speech from theatrical works (ibid., xxiv). Doing so would have made his own task easier given the age's technical limitations in amplifying sound — and would have perhaps enabled him to escape the later charge of Anglo-Saxon presumption.

   Yet he insisted, for better or worse, on aiming to reach "the soul of the audience," which could only happen through the spoken word. Ironically enough, as it turned out, the masque achieved acclaim mainly on the strength of the Interludes and the music, at the expense of speeches and dialogues which were difficult to hear and may not have conveyed all that much meaning to the huge audience.[26] At any

---

[26]   The visual effects turned out to be the masque's highlight, created in a state-of-the-art manner by stage artist Joseph Urban from Vienna. Reviewing the premiere, *The New York Times* explains: "The lights [...] worked half the beauty of the evening. Now the yellow sands were fairly bathed in hot sunlight as the Egyptians trod their ritual measures; now you saw only the cool, white temple of Miranda singled out of the darkness. Now the entire floor was marked with a straight path of light with Isadora Duncan dancing along it; now contrasting lights of amber, of silver, and of blue played on Brutus in his tent. [...] The musical aspects of the masque were especially satisfactory. [...] The interludes, with their hundreds of participants in bright costumes, were particularly well liked" ("MacKaye Masque"). *The Literary Digest* quotes *The Evening Sun*: "[...] it was the pageants of the interludes that made the mask a success" ("The Shakespeare" 1701). Of the costumes in the Interludes, Roberts ("Rehearsing" 484) says: "[...] the movement and the drapery of the people passing up and down the pathway from each side of the stage and also on the stage itself was full of a poignant beauty beyond the power of any producer to arrange without motion." (485) Each Interlude was "planned in a typical, striking color scheme."

rate, MacKaye was confident that adapting the masque form would enable "poetry for the masses" (*Playhouse* 113) to satisfy an "elemental instinct for art" among all women and men in the street (*Civic* 174). The concept is influenced to some extent by Richard Wagner (for whom drama is the "expression of a joint artistic longing" which "can only parley with a common receptivity").⑦

MacKaye was convinced that the multiple ethnic groups that were expanding America's social composition had communal aspirations which needed strengthening by drama " *of* and *by* the people" (*Caliban* xviii).⑧ This is the way to form not only a nation, as contemporary press reviews commended, but more importantly what Columbia University president Nicholas Murray Butler called an "international mind" (MacKaye, *Community* 6). MacKaye is honest enough not to claim he has actually achieved art production "by the people," which remains a "desired potential" rather than a proven fact; his utopian concept remains somewhat oblique to the *Caliban* masque.⑨

The concept's original form did not long survive America's involvement in the world war. The cultural climate thereafter shifted in new directions. Later generically related works were different in kind, as in Robert Frost's somewhat ironic *Masque of Reason* and *Masque of Mercy* in the 1940s. One reason may possibly be aesthetic quality — MacKaye's allegorical style at times sounds ponderous and labored, at least some decades later. At the time critics were divided: Peyser offered a scathing comment on the

---

⑦ See Wagner's short chapter *"Communion of players and audience"* (especially 78). The context is the comprehensive work of art.

⑧ Matthew Arnold almost anticipates MacKaye's concept (78–79): Culture "is not satisfied till we *all* come to a perfect man; it knows that the sweetness and light of the few must be imperfect until the raw and unkindled masses of humanity are touched with sweetness and light." Arnold continues, "those are the flowering times for literature and art [...] when the whole of society is in the fullest measure permeated by thought, sensible to beauty, intelligent and alive." Arnold does not go so far as to speak of art "of and by the people"; moreover, MacKaye gives the stronger form of the idea an interethnic turn. Dickinson, however, soberly records the skepticism of those who hold that "[t]o assume for the people en masse the possession of creative powers would be to falsify all that we know of the creative process," and tends to believe one cannot "create beauty in a caucus" (45, 46).

⑨ According to *The New York Times*, when Lear de Bessonet staged a production of *The Tempest* at New York's Delacorte Theater in September 1913, she did so in order to pay tribute to MacKaye's "utopian vision" (Leland).

script's literary quality (3), whereas Clayton Hamilton in *Vogue* found the script "more than adequately written" (1 July 1916, qtd. in Green 69), and *The New York Times* called it "graceful, eloquent, and worthy" ("MacKaye Masque"). Potter (78) is lenient: "MacKaye did not write down to his audience." The masque's success, at any rate, did convince the city authorities to enable Lewisohn Stadium to become an "outdoor performance space": "for over forty years this functioned as an endowed civic theatre where tickets were inexpensive and great art was available for the masses" (Prevots 70).

Conclusion

Some years ago, the Slovak comparative literary scholar Dionyz Durisin highlighted what he called genetic (contactual) relationships between literatures. In this view, it is "essential to start from the determining role of the recipient literature" (121–122), since "[t]he properties of a work of art become concrete only in relationship to the recipient" (316). Studying such concretion is of central value, for Durisin, to literary comparatistics. Contactual relationships, to use this terminology, are of similar value for Intercultural Communication, where they are embraced in approaches to embodied culture and the transfer of signifying objects. Few areas of study enjoy the same strong position in both — and for that matter in Patrice Pavis's hourglass model. Despite some flaws, *Caliban* can be said to exemplify the recipient's determining role, the stadium audience rather than Shakespeare's *Tempest*. It is also a case of director's theater, more trans- than acculturated Shakespeare (see Im 242). Caliban needs to start weaving his own dream from the "stuff" of which he has caught glimpses, but not only he, as the community's ethnically varied millions will need to weave theirs. From another angle, we might recall that "interculturality reduces the tension between cultural identity and diversity, and enhances human creativity" (Xiaodong Dai 110).

As Caliban's own voice differs from Prospero's and Shakespeare's, one might ask whether he is not fumbling toward what Deleuze and Guattari have called "the language of sensations, or the foreign language within language that summons forth a people to come" (176). As a form of what transversal thought would call incursive disclosure, the open-ended stimulus serves not only what press reviews heralded as "the solidity of the nation" (Baynes). More precisely, it empowers cultural communities to operate through "constructive imagination" (MacKaye, *Community* 5). For MacKaye, that is identical with a synergy of "communities with communities," for "creating the international mind" (ibid., 6) — the term *intercultural* was not yet born. For Diana Henderson, the masque "prefigures a quite active strain" in 20th-century theater, claiming Shakespeare "as a force for artistic internationalism" (226). The synergy moves along a path which invites comparison with that of Eugene Jolas, for those "always amerigrating on a long journey": "Ero americáno and all my friends were the aliens." It is the immigrant groups that play a decisive role in the artistic aspiration together with the civic education of the American Demos. In this lost art form, they receive an occasion to celebrate the process. And to celebrate themselves.

References

Arnold, Matthew. *Culture and Anarchy and Other Writings*. [1867–1868.] Ed. Stefan Collini. Cambridge: Cambridge UP, 1993.

Bakhtin, M. M. "Forms of Time and of the Chronotope in the Novel: Notes toward a Historical Poetics." *The Dialogic Imagination: Four Essays*. Ed. Michael Holquist. Trans. Caryl Emerson and Michael Holquist. Austin: U of Texas P, 1981. 84–258.

Barad, Karen. "Meeting the Universe Halfway: Realism and Social Constructivism Without Contradiction." *Feminism, Science, and the Philosophy of Science*. Eds. Lynn Hankinson Nelson and Jack Nelson. Dordrecht: Kluwer, 1996. 161–194.

Baynes, Ernest Harold. "'All the World's a Stage,' From Poetry to Fact." *Boston Evening Transcript* 18 July (1917): Pt. 2, p. 5.

"Behind the Scenes at Caliban." *The Boston Daily Globe* 15 July 1917: 51.

Blanke, David. *The 1910s*. American Popular Culture Through History. Westport, Conn., & London: Greenwood, 2002.

Bradley, Patricia. *Making American Culture: A Social History, 1900–1920*. New York: Palgrave Macmillan, 2009.

Bristol, Michael D. *Shakespeare's America, America's Shakespeare*. London & New York: Routledge, 1990.

Brooks, Van Wyck. *America's Coming-of-Age*. New York: Huebsch, 1915.

Carlyle, Thomas. "The Hero As Poet." 12 May 1840. *On Heroes, Hero-Worship, and The Heroic in History*. Ed. Henry David Gray. New York & London: Longmans, Green, 1906.

Carroll, Armond. *A Pageant and Masque for the Shakespeare Tercentenary*. Atlanta: Atlanta Center, Drama League of America, 1916.

Cartelli, Thomas. *Repositioning Shakespeare: National Formations, Postcolonial Appropriations*. London: Routledge, 1999.

Cather, Willa. *The World and the Parish*. Willa Cather's Articles and Reviews, 1893 – 1902. Ed. William M. Curtin. Vol. 1. Lincoln: U of Nebraska P, 1970.

Cavallo, Dominick. *Muscles and Morals: Organized Playgrounds and Urban Reform*, *1880–1920*. Philadelphia: U of Pennsylvania P, 1981.

Collier, John. "Caliban of the Yellow Sands: The Shakespeare Pageant and Masque Reviewed Against a Background of American Pageantry." *The Survey* 1 July (1916): 343–350.

Collington, Tara. "The Chronotope and the Study of Literary Adaptation." *Bakhtin's Theory of the Literary Chronotope: Reflections*, *Applications*, *Perspectives*. Eds. Nele Bemong, Pieter Borghart et al. Ghent: Academia, 2010. 179–193.

Conant, Isabella Fiske. *Will O The World: A Shakespearean Tercentenary Masque*. [Wellesley, Mass.] 1916.

Dai, Xiaodong. "Out of a Dialogical Dilemma: The Construction of Interculturality." *Intercultural Adaptation（I）: Theoretical Explorations and Empirical Studies*. Intercultural Research Vol. 6. Eds. Xiaodong Dai and Steve J. Kulich. Shanghai: Shanghai Foreign Language Education Press, 2012. 97–114.

Deleuze, Gilles, and Félix Guattari. *What is Philosophy?* Trans. Hugh Tomlinson and Graham Burchell. New York: Columbia UP, 1994.

Dickinson, Thomas H. *Playwrights of the New American Theater*. New York: Macmillan, 1925.

Durisin, Dionyz. *Theory of Literary Comparatistics*. Bratislava: Veda Slovak Academy of Sciences, 1984.

Engler, Balz. "Shakespeare in the trenches." 1992. *Shakespeare and Race*. Eds. Catherine M. S. Alexander and Stanley Wells. Cambridge: Cambridge UP, 2000. 101–111.

Erenberg, Lewis A. *Steppin' Out: New York Nightlife and the Transformation of American Culture*, *1890–1930*. Chicago: U of Chicago P, 1981.

Finelli, Patrick Michael. "Paralinguistic and Kinesic Codes of Performance: An Intercultural *Gilgamesh*." *Journal of Literature and Art Studies* 1.1 (2011): 65–78.

"The First Nighter." *The New York Dramatic Mirror* 3 June 1916: 8.

Foner, Nancy. *From Ellis Island to JFK: New York's Two Great Waves of Immigration*. New Haven: Yale UP, 2000.

Franck, Jane. "*Caliban* at Lewisohn Stadium, 1916." *Shakespeare Encomium*. Ed. Anne Paolucci. New York: City College, 1964. 154–168.

Glassberg, David. *American Historical Pageantry: The Uses of Tradition in the Early Twentieth Century*. Chapel Hill: U of North Carolina P, 1990.

Grant, Madison. *The Passing of the Great Race or The Racial Basis of European History*. New York: Charles Scribner's Sons, 1916.

Graziano, John. "Community Theater, *Caliban by the Yellow Sands*, and Arthur Farwell." *Vistas of American Music*. Eds. Susan L. Porter and John Graziano. Detroit Monographs in Musicology/Studies in Music, No. 25. Warren, MI: Harmonie Park Press, 1999. 293–308.

Green, William. "*Caliban by the Yellow Sands*: Percy MacKaye's Adaptation of *The Tempest*." *Maske und Kothurn* 35 (1989): 59–69.

Hall, Edward T. *The Hidden Dimension*. 1966; New York: Anchor Books, 1982.

Harper, Frances E. W. *Iola Leroy, or Shadows Uplifted*. 1892. Introd. Hazel Carby. Boston: Beacon P, 1999.

Henderson, Diana E. *"The Tempest* in Performance." *A Companion to Shakespeare's Works*. Vol. 4. Eds. Richard Dutton and Jean E. Howard. Malden, MA: Blackwell, 2003. 216–239.

Higham, John. *Strangers in the Land: Patterns of American Nativism, 1860–1925*. 2nd ed. New Brunswick: Rutgers UP, 2002.

Im, Yeeyon. "The Lure of Intercultural Shakespeare." *Medieval and Early Modern English Studies* 15.1 (2007): 233–253.

Jackson, Kenneth T., ed. *The Encyclopedia of New York City*. New Haven & London: Yale UP, 1995.

Jolas, Eugene. *Words from the Deluge*. New York: Gotham Book Mart, 1941.

Jung, Hwa Yol. *Transversal Rationality & Intercultural Texts*. Athens: Ohio UP, 2011.

Kahn, Coppélia. "Caliban at the Stadium: Shakespeare and the Making of Americans." *Massachusetts Review* 41.2 (2000): 256–284.

Kahn, Otto H. *Art and the People: Remarks by Otto H. Kahn at the Shakespeare Tercentenary Celebration Dinner in New York City, May 4, 1916*. New York: Shakespeare Tercentenary Celebration Committee, [1916].

Kallen, Horace. "Democracy versus the Melting-Pot: A Study of American Nationality. Part 1." *The Nation* 18 Feb. (1915): 190–194.

Kessner, Thomas. *The Golden Door: Italian and Jewish Immigrant Mobility in New York City, 1880–1915*. New York: Oxford UP, 1977.

Kilmer, Joyce. "Percy MacKaye Predicts Communal Theatre: That Is What the Shakespeare Masque Means, Says Its Author — Poetry and Drama Becoming Democratic, He Declares." *New York Times Magazine* 14 May (1916): SM: 13–14.

Knafo, Ariel, Sonia Roccas and Lilach Sagiv. "The Value of Values in Cross-Cultural Research: A Special Issue in Honor of Shalom Schwartz." *Journal of Cross-Cultural Psychology* 42.2 (2011): 178–185.

Kulich, Steve J. "Constructing Dynamic Theoretical Frames for Contextual Intercultural Identity Analysis." *Identity and Intercultural Communication (II): Conceptual and Contextual Applications*. Intercultural Research Vol. 3. Eds. Steve J. Kulich and Xiaodong Dai. Shanghai: Shanghai Foreign Language Education Press, 2012. 105–154.

Langdon, William Chauncy. *In Honor of Shakespeare: A Dramatic Tribute for the Shakespeare Tercentenary Celebration of Indiana University, at Bloomington Indiana, April Twenty Sixth Nineteen Sixteen*. Bloomington: Indiana U, 1916.

Leland, John. "Turning Chaos Into Theater, With a Cast of 200." *New York Times* 30 Aug. 2013. Web. 17 July 2016.

Lorini, Alessandra. "The Progressives' Rhetoric on National Recreation: The Play Movement in New York City (1880–1917)." *Storia nordamericana* 1 (1984): 34–71.

—. *Rituals of Race: American Public Culture and the Search For Racial Democracy*. Charlottesville: UP of Virginia, 1999.

Lüsebrink, Hans-Jürgen. *Interkulturelle Kommunikation: Interaktion, Fremdwahrnehmung, Kulturtransfer*. 4te Auflage. Stuttgart: Metzler, 2016.

MacKaye, Percy. *Caliban by the Yellow Sands*. New York: Doubleday, 1916.
—. *The Civic Theatre in Relation to the Redemption of Leisure: A Book of Suggestions*. New York: Mitchell Kennerley, 1912.
—. *Community Drama, Its Motive and Method of Neighborliness: An Interpretation*. Cambridge, MA: The Riverside P, 1917.
—. *Epoch: The Life of Steele MacKaye*. 2 vols. New York: Boni & Liveright, 1927.
—. *The New Citizenship: A Civic Ritual*. New York: Macmillan, 1915.
—. *The Playhouse and the Play*. New York: Macmillan, 1909.
—. *Saint Louis: A Civic Masque*. Garden City, New York: Doubleday, Page, 1914.
—. *Wakefield: A Folk-Masque of America*. Washington DC: United States George Washington Bicentennial Commission, 1932.
"MacKaye Masque a Rare Spectacle." *The New York Times* 25 May 1916: 11.
"MacKaye's Masque Seen From Above." *The New York Times* 29 May 1916: 9.
Mastin, Florence Ripley. *Green Leaves*. New York: James T. White, 1918.
Moderwell, Hiram Kelly. "The Playwright Who Has the Largest Audiences." *New York Times* 19 Dec. 1915: X9.
"New York Gets Ready to Honor Shakespeare." *The New York Times* 19 Mar. 1916: SM12.
Novalis. *Philosophical Writings*. Trans. and ed. Margaret Mahony Stoljar. Albany: State U of New York P, 1997.
Pavis, Patrice. "Intercultural Theatre today (2010)." *Forum Modernes Theater* 25.1 (2010): 5–15.
—. *Theatre at the Crossroads of Culture*. Trans. Loren Kruger. London & New York: Routledge, 1992.
Periwinkle, Pauline. "Tercentenary of Death of Shakespeare in April." *Dallas Morning News* 3 Apr. 1916: 13.
Peyser, Herbert F. "New York's First Community Masque Notable Spectacle." *Musical America* 24.5, 3 June 1916: 1, 3–4.
Prevots, Naima. *American Pageantry: A Movement For Art and Democracy*. Ann Arbor, Mich.: UMI Research P, 1990.
Program of the Community Masque Caliban by the Yellow Sands, by Percy MacKaye. New York: The New York City Shakespeare Tercentenary Celebration Committee, 1916.
Roberts, Mary Fanton. "Rehearsing a Community Masque, What Artists Did For It, and What It Did For the Public." *The Craftsman* 30.5 (Aug. 1916): 483–488.
—. "Shakespeare — The Man of Wisdom: Our National Celebration in His Honor." *The Craftsman* 29.4, Jan. 1916: 347–363.
Rosenwaike, Ira. *Population History of New York City*. Syracuse: Syracuse UP, 1972.
Ross, Edward Alsworth. *The Old World in the New: The Significance of Past and Present Immigration to the American People*. New York: Century, 1914.
Schwartz, Shalom H. "Mapping and Interpreting Cultural Differences around the World." 2004. *Value Frameworks at the Theoretical Crossroads of Culture*. Intercultural Research Vol. 4. Eds. Steve J. Kulich, Michael H. Prosser and Weng Liping. Shanghai: Shanghai Foreign Language Education

Press, 2012. 339–379.

—. "Studying Values: Personal Adventure, Future Directions." *Journal of Cross-Cultural Psychology* 42.2 (2011): 307–319.

—. "A Theory of Cultural Value Orientations: Explication and Applications." *Comparative Sociology* 5.2–3 (2006): 137–182.

Schwartz, Shalom H. et al. "Refining the Theory of Basic Individual Values." 2012. *Value Dimensions and Their Contextual Dynamics Across Cultures.* Intercultural Research Vol. 5. Eds. Steve J. Kulich, Weng Liping and Michael H. Prosser. Shanghai: Shanghai Foreign Language Education Press, 2014. 191–262.

Seih, Yi-Tai, Michael D. Buhrmester, Yi-Cheng Lin, Chin-Lan Huang and William B. Swann, Jr. "Do people want to be flattered or understood? The cross-cultural universality of self-verification." *Journal of Experimental Social Psychology* 49 (2013): 169–172.

"The Shakespeare Community-Mask." *The Literary Digest* 10 June 1916: 1700–1701.

Shattuck, Charles H. *Shakespeare on the American Stage.* Vol. 2: *From Booth and Barrett to Sothern and Marlowe.* Washington, D.C.: Folger Books, 1987.

Smialkowska, Monika. "Conscripting Caliban: Shakespeare, America, and the First World War." *Shakespeare* 7.2 (2011): 192–207.

—. "'A democratic art at a democratic price': The American Celebrations of the Shakespeare Tercentenary, 1916." *Transatlantica* 1 (2010): 2–11.

—. "Shakespeare in History, History through Shakespeare: *Caliban by the Yellow Sands.*" *Multicultural Shakespeare: Translation, Appropriation and Performance* 4.19 (2007): 17–27.

"Storm Breaks Over Caliban." *The Boston Daily Globe* 3 July 1917: 1, 5.

Sturgess, Kim C. *Shakespeare and the American Nation.* Cambridge: Cambridge UP, 2004.

Swann, William B., Jr. "The self and identity negotiation." *Interaction Studies* 6.1 (2005): 69–83.

Tatlow, Antony. *Shakespeare, Brecht, and the Intercultural Sign.* Durham, NC: Duke UP, 2001.

Vauclair, Christin-Melanie, Katja Hanke, Ronald Fischer and Johnny Fontaine. "The Structure of Human Values at the Culture Level: A Meta-Analytical Replication of Schwartz's Value Orientations Using the Rokeach Value Survey." *Journal of Cross-Cultural Psychology* 42.2 (2011): 186–205.

Vaughan, Alden T., and Virginia Mason Vaughan. *Shakespeare in America.* Oxford: Oxford UP, 2012.

—. *Shakespeare's Caliban: A Cultural History.* Cambridge: Cambridge UP, 1991.

Wagner, Richard. *Wagner on Music and Drama.* Eds. Albert Goldman and Evert Sprinchorn. Trans. H. Ashton Ellis. New York: Dutton, 1964.

Waldenfels, Bernhard. "The Boundaries of Orders." *Philosophica* 73 (2004): 71–86.

—. *The Question of the Other.* Hong Kong: Chinese UP, 2007.

17

From Social Norms to Law: Translational Dysfunction and Palimpsest in *The Contract* and *The Merchant of Venice*

SUN Yan

Shanghai International Studies University

Summary: The anonymous Chinese Yuan-based drama *He Tong Wen Zi* or *The Contract* and William Shakespeare's comedy *The Merchant of Venice* (ca. 1598) both develop their plot and thematic significance around a "contract," and resolve the major dramatic conflict in a courtroom. An examination of the two plays in relation to one another allows us to discern convergences in legal histories when law supersedes social norms as a new social order organizer, while revealing how the two legal cultures diverge in relating law to mercy: in *The Contract*, as a coordination; in *The Merchant of Venice*, as a dichotomy. Cultural similarity and difference here become complexly interrelated. The difference of legal philosophies represented in the two dramas is further illuminated by the way in which a leading modern Chinese translator renders the court scene in *The Merchant of Venice*, which in this cultural transfer becomes reconstructed so as to resemble the rather different situation depicted in the court scene in *The Contract*. In negotiating between languages of remote cultural and philosophical heritages, the widely accepted and influential translation "chooses" to palimpsest the source culture with the target culture.

Transition: Expansionism and Mercantilism in Yuan China and Elizabethan England

Both the Yuan dynasty (1271–1368) in China and later the Elizabethan era in England (1558–1603) witnessed an increased popularity and production of dramatic art. The Yuan dynasty witnessed a considerable development of drama because of support from the Mongol nobles, commercial prosperity, involvements of literati, and audiences' fondness (see Wang Yunxi and Gu Yisheng 866). The drama form popular in this dynasty used lyrics set to northern tunes, and was called Yuan drama or Zaju （杂 剧）(see Feng 83).[1] Yuan-era playwrights, such as Guan Hanqing and Wang Shifu, were renowned in Yuan China no less than William Shakespeare and Ben Jonson came to be in Elizabethan England. Yuan playwrights created works that have been repeatedly adapted and performed from the time they were released until the present day in China. Both Yuan China and Elizabethan England underwent transitions toward more mercantile economies while their territories were significantly expanding.

The Yuan dynasty was the ruler of a Mongolian state, the first minority dynasty to rule China in its entirety. Kublai Khan, founder of the Yuan dynasty, was an expansionist, during whose reign the nation covered an extremely vast territory, partly drawing the basic outline of China's present territory. Due to their nomadic lifestyle, which was very different from that of the Chinese people they ruled, the Mongolian leaders abandoned their long-held physiocracy for mercantilism.[2] Commercial activities within and outside the territory were encouraged and protected (see *Inner Mongolia* 88). With a unified national market established, commerce-related sections in

---

[1]   Properly, in Yuan drama, only one character has a singing role, a mark of the evolution of the form from the Sung period "recitation" of songs interspersed with prose narrative sections. Each act of a Yuan drama consists of a sequence of song patterns set to a given key. Dialogues carry the action of the play and coordinate with the poetic song patterns. A coordination of song, dialogue (monologue) and actions defines the mood, paints word pictures, and conveys inner emotions of the central figure (see Birch 391). In order to appeal to audiences, Yuan dramas based their plots on stories familiar to the audience.

[2]   See Wu Lan and Liu Zhenjiang. Although beyond the scope of this chapter, it can be argued that mercantilism, because of its creation of commercial relations with strangers rather than neighbors, is one condition that instigates the transformation from pre-modern to modern social formations.

the national economy such as handicrafts, trade, transportation and related activities gained new momentum for development (see Xiao 17). Paper currency was issued and circulated within the entire nation.③ Commercial prosperity served as a means to strengthen the ties among the five sub-empires of the great Mongol Empire; ④ it also created the logistics for the Mongol armies that were continuously trying to push the empire's borders farther and farther outward.

The Yuan dynasty's mercantilist and expansionist inclinations in China were shared by Elizabethan England. As Peter Ackroyd notes in his history of sixteenth-century England,

> In the reign of Elizabeth, the commerce of England was greatly increased with spices and perfumes from India, ermine and steel from Russia. [...] As a result of all these activities London was fast overtaking Antwerp as the European capital of trade and finance. [...] [T]he mariners of England sailed down the western coast of Africa and the eastern coastline of the New World. In the 1560s Sir John Hawkins made three successful voyages to the African continent, where he opened the unhappy trade in slaves, and crossed the Atlantic to Hispaniola and the Spanish colonies in America. At the beginning of the next decade Sir Francis Drake made three journeys to the West Indies. On his last expedition, from a summit of a mountain on the Isthmus of Darien, he caught sight of the great Pacific. So the map of the world was slowly being unrolled. (2: 867, 875–876)

Domestically, loans with interest began to be legalized in 1545 and became common in the 1580s; after the enclosures of common lands, villagers and debtors became masterless vagabonds who were then shipped overseas as indentured laborers or conquistadors (so to speak) in the colonial armies or navies (see Graeber, Chapter 11). In England, as in China, the mobility accompanying an emerging

---

③ The Mongols, who ruled China from AD 1271 to 1368, maintained a paper currency system, which was only abandoned in the seventeenth century. Money is another institution, like explicitly articulated legal precepts, that assumes commerce and intercourse between strangers. For the relation of money to strangers, see Graeber 270.

④ The Mongol Empire was the largest contiguous land empire in human history. Beginning in the Central Asian steppes, it eventually stretched from Central Europe to the Sea of Japan, covering Siberia in the north and extending southward into Indochina, the Indian subcontinent, the Iranian plateau, and the Middle East (see Weatherford 6). Historians disagree on the size of the Mongol Empire, as the Empire was never free of inside conflicts, esp. among tribes led by Genghis Khan's sons (see Chen Dezhi).

commercial economy weakened social connectedness and hence the community observance that curbed violations of social norms, which in turn made the emergence of law necessary and unavoidable. Elizabethan England, like Yuan China, thus represents a transition from the pre-modern Middle Ages to modernity, featuring an abstraction and mechanical operation of social institutions (see Toulmin, Chapter 1).

From Social Norms to Law: The Rise of Law as Dispute Resolution

A social norm is defined as a rule that is not enforced by an official system or courts but one that is complied with as the way things are done within a community (Posner 1997). Behaviors that are not in accordance with social norms are punished by sanctions such as ridicule, gossip, ostracism and related forms; social norms are enforced by non-official agency, being internalized and simply "lived": community members observe/supervise each other's behaviors and hence deter any breaking of social norms with the threat of being identified as deviant and punished; alternatively, a community member recognizes the "self-evident" moral inappropriateness of violating social norms, and refrains from breaking them. When outer observance and inner moral self-restraint fail to stop violations, however, the community will issue social sanctions to censor violators; when social sanctions fail to deter the breaking of social norms, another form of regulation in the shape of law becomes necessary.

This social transformation has been described in some detail by legal scholar Yoshinobu Zasu. "The ability of the members of a community to observe each other," he observes, "can be interpreted as a measure of the community's social connectedness" (382). In other words, the ability to easily observe another person's actions implies that either the connectedness among community members is strong or the relationship between them is close-knit. If social connectedness is high (low), the society is deemed pre-modern (modern). Social connectedness in pre-modern society is strong, and the expected level of punishment imposed by social norms is high. As a result, undesirable acts are deterred. In this environment, law, which is costly, is not required. There is only a slim possibility that law can improve such a society's adherence to norms. In other words, social norms and law are substitutable, and there is no reason for the existence of costly formal regulations. In contrast, social connectedness in modern society is weak, and the expected level of punishment by social norms is low. In such a society, the effect of social norms monitoring undesirable acts declines. As a result, such acts are insufficiently deterred. In this environment, law is required even if it is costly — hence the emergence of law. Law complements social norms in such a society, enabling the society to arrive at a more desirable outcome owing to the existence of law. This idea is consistent with a historical assertion that there has been a gradual displacement of informal regulation by formal regulation (see Yoshinobu Zasu).

In Yuan China as in Elizabethan England, fast territorial expansion and prospering commerce and trade resulted in mobilities of labor and commodities which accelerated the rise of law as dispute resolution together with the gradual withdrawal of social norms. The courtroom resolutions in the anonymous Yuan drama *The Contract* (uncertain date) and William Shakespeare's comedy *The Merchant of Venice* (ca. 1598) capture the inclination for legal sanctions to rise over social sanctions during geographic, economic, and social transitions.[5] In *Contract* Yangshi, who has a despised identity, trusts in the law's rigidity. Throughout Chinese dynastic feudal history (1100 BC-AD 1911), a woman's faithfulness to her husband had been promoted, as indicated by the famous saying "A wife should remain faithful to the husband till her death" — for instance in Liu Xiang's *Biographies of Exemplary Women* (列女传) (quoted in Liu Yuqing). A woman who gets married more than once (even after her legitimate husband dies), as Yangshi chooses to do, could hardly avoid being the focus of contempt. After her husband dies, Yangshi marries Liu Tianxiang, whose younger brother Liu Tianrui, to earn a living, leaves with his wife Zhangshi and three-year old son Liu Anzhu (henceforth shortened as Anzhu) in a poor harvest year. Upon their departure, with village Head Li as witness, Liu Tianxiang and Liu Tianrui sign a contract claiming that the Liu clan's properties and real estates are jointly owned, so that Liu Tianrui can later claim his share upon his return. Liu Tianrui and his family go to Xiama Village (下马村) where Zhang Bingyi, a local esquire

---

[5] *The Contract* is of uncertain date and is based on a *Huaben* novel in the Sung Dynasty (960-1279), portraying an upright judge named Judge Bao (see Li Jianming 60). *The Contract* was transformed into a vernacular novel and compiled in *Slapping the Table in Amazement* (拍案惊奇) by Ling Mengchu (1580-1644) in the Ming Dynasty (1368-1644) (see Hanan 138).

without offspring, kindly allows the family to stay in his hotel.
Zhangshi and Liu Tianrui become terribly sick, however, and die
one after another, leaving three-year old Anzhu an orphan. As he
faces death, Liu Tianrui entrusts Zhang Bingyi with Anzhu and the
contract. Keeping his promise, fifteen years later Zhang Bingyi tells
Anzhu about his family and about his deceased parents' wishes to be
buried in the Liu clan's graveyard. Anzhu carries his parents' coffins
back to the Liu clan, whose wealth has increased largely due to their
new pawn store business, which is run by Yangshi. He is then
confronted with Yangshi, who has a plan involving the clan's wealth
for her daughter Chouge (from the previous marriage). The
paternal-line male-heir family property inheritance norm, however,
denies Yangshi and her daughter Chouge any inheritance rights to
Liu clan properties. Chouge is legally barred from inheriting any
properties from the Liu clan unless several circumstances arise to
render altering the inheritance sequence possible and meaningful:

(a) Liu Anzhu's departure from the town in a poor harvest year (as
the only male successor in the clan, this son of Yangshi's
husband's brother is the only legitimate heir to the family
fortune);

(b) matrilocality between Chouge and a young man (the offspring in
matrilocal marriage carry the maternal family name, the Liu
clan's family name, unlike other situations);

(c) the financial success of the Liu clan's pawnshop.⑥

The absence of Liu Anzhu may thus cancel the inheritance priority
he enjoys and grant Chouge the rights to inherit the Liu clan's
properties under the condition (b). A contract previously signed
between Liu Anzhu's father and Yangshi's husband in this situation is
the only proof of Anzhu's identity, and hence of his inheritance
priority. For this reason, when Anzhu returns, Yangshi decides to
challenge the social norms that jeopardize Chouge's inheritance
rights by deceiving Anzhu about the contract. After securing the
contract, to drive Anzhu away, Yangshi attacks him with a stick and
injures him in the head. In the court, Judge Bao leads Yangshi to

---

⑥ Originating in the fifth century and driven by mortgages, *dangpu* (当铺)
were set up by politicians, aristocrats, wealthy businessmen, and even temple
monks who hoped to profit from interest rates and make money. *Dangpu*,
both private and governmental, thrived for nearly all of China's long history.
However, they mostly targeted poor lower-class people, providing small loans
and some money in exchange for gold, silver, and copper. See Yong.

believe that Anzhu has died from the injury she inflicted, and rules that she shall suffer a death penalty for murder unless she provides evidence to prove her family ties to Anzhu. Yangshi presents the contract in the court as a proof of the relationship, only to find that Anzhu is alive. Judge Bao then rules that Anzhu is the legal heir to the Liu clan. Yangshi is fined one thousand pounds of copper. Chouge and her husband are ordered to move out of the Liu clan's houses, and have no entitlement to any of the clan's properties.

In *Merchant*, the Jewish money-lender Shylock arranges with the Venetian Antonio, who declares himself bound for a large sum that his intimate friend Bassanio owes, having needed it to woo the wealthy heiress Portia, to nominate a forfeit "for an equal pound/Of your fair flesh to be cut off and taken/In what part of your body pleaseth me" instead of the usual interest — a "merry bond" (I. iii. 145–147, 169). It subsequently turns out that the forfeit cannot be avoided. In sixteenth-century Europe, where Jews were relatively few and considered evil and vampiric, a Jew's cutting a pound of bloody flesh from a Christian could not avoid giving rise to both focused attention and panicking. Such attention presses the Duke to handle the situation with caution. In other words, the Duke cannot afford to unmark Shylock's identity of being a Jew as irrelevant; he cannot pursue "blind" justice. The Hebrew "identity problem" has been discussed in this series previously (see Tian Zhang, Yali Zhou). When Shylock refuses to take the money compensation and drop the case, the Duke adjourns the court by declaring,

> Upon my power I may dismiss this court
> Unless Bellario, a learnèd doctor
> Whom I have sent for to determine this,
> Come here today. (IV.i.103–106)

While Shylock recognizes that the Duke takes sides with the majority in his community even before the court is open (IV.i.2–5), he believes that that he can rely on the law's strictness and impersonality. Shylock perceives that he needs rigidity in legal institutions in the way that unsupported and essentially powerless persons need it. He wishes to obtain total vindication and invincible power through the inflexible machinery of a public tribunal.

Resembling Shylock for his trust in the law's impersonal strictness, Yangshi treasures a firm belief in the law's strict power: the inheritance contract, as vital evidence, determines the outcome of the dispute resolution. Therefore, after she procures the contract, she fears no challenges over her fraudulent behavior. To drive Liu Anzhu away, she beats him with a heavy stick; she dismisses Community Head Li as an interferer in her family's trifles when he questions her behavior; she openly lies to the Court Judge, emphasizing her assertion with a curse against herself: "I never saw this deed. If I did, I'll suffer sore eyes" (Zhang Guangqian 293). In this, Shylock's utterance in the court echoes hers: "Till thou canst rail the seal from off my bond/Thou but offend'st thy lungs to speak so loud" (IV.i.138−139). The confidence and security that Yangshi and Shylock share are based on the belief that they own the vital legal document — the contract — and thus the law would work, mechanically, in their favor (see also Harmon 81 − 114 on the significance of contracts and bonds in *Merchant*). Perhaps Shylock's bond in *Merchant* "cannot be a legal contract" in a strict sense (Haque and Das 77), but it is entertained as one that appears to be covered by the law until IV.1.300 when, as described below, it becomes impossible to maintain.

Besides trust in the law's strictness and impersonality as working in their favor, Yangshi the defendant and Shylock the plaintiff share more similarities:

a. Language Craft or Glib Tongue

When she is asked whether she took the contract from Liu Anzhu, Yangshi answers, "What use could I have for that piece of paper? To paste it over the window?" (Zhang Guangqian 287). Yangshi did indeed take the inheritance contract. But she covers her fraudulence by sidetracking the issue, adroitly shifting the focus of debate from whether she took the contract to the function of a piece of paper.

When he is asked why he specified one pound of flesh to be the forfeiture, Shylock answers,

> Pray you tell me this:
> If he should break his day, what should I gain
> By the exaction of the forfeiture?
> A pound of man's flesh taken from a man
> Is not so estimable, profitable neither,
> As flesh of muttons, beeves, or goats. I say,
> To buy his favour I extend this friendship.
> If he will take it, so. If not, adieu. [...] (II.i.158−165)

Whether Shylock is sincerely sending a signal of friendship or whether he is actually coaxing Antonio into an evil trap is not clearly known here, yet he is proven to possess a powerful language craft, which is cunning and dishonest.

In both cases, the characters' language willfully confuses the contract's denotation and connotation: Yangshi employs a strategy of casting out the contract's legal connotation, by substituting its physical existence as a piece of paper for its legal function. By equating a pound of human flesh with a pound of animal meat, Shylock tries to cover the barbarianism embodied in the connotation of the forfeiture. He then argues that the violent forfeiture he requires is something that, in the face of friendship, cannot be done with any gain.

b. Profession

Yangshi is a pawnshop (*dangpu*) owner, Shylock a usurer. Both are doing a legalized but not, in the historical context, fully moral business (see Bell, Wiesner-Hanks, especially 220ff., and Woodbridge). A pawnshop was a form of usury in ancient China. With official or indirect official connections, a pawnshop would derive high profit by taking advantage of the customer's urgent need (see Yong 42). The work of money as a medium of exchange between people — based upon social norms of relationships — and the work of money as an impersonal commodity to be "rented" for interest are confused in these dramatic characters' livelihood as well as language. In both jobs — taking material pledges in the place of communal caretaking — neighbors come to be treated as strangers, as is the case in strict and impersonal law.⑦

c. Double Identities

Yangshi has a double identity as community member and twice-married woman, while Shylock has a double identity as Venetian citizen and Jew. Yangshi's and Shylock's first identities are based upon impersonal law rather than community values. However, their other identity as twice-married woman and Jew mark them as outsiders to be despised. As a citizen/community member, Yangshi is permitted to enter wedlock and assist in running the pawn store and

---

⑦　Graeber describes the origin of "impersonal markets, born of war, in which it was possible to treat even neighbors as if they were strangers" (288). This is both the cause and result of making the medium of exchange into a commodity that itself can be traded; but it is also closely related to *impersonal* justice, whether it be "blind" or superhumanly "penetrating."

also manage the store. But as a twice-married woman, Yangshi is detested: "Her mouth was sweeter than a honey pot," but she is actually a "foxy shrew" (Zhang Guangqian 286). The social norms of Confucian Chinese society required a woman to remain faithful to her husband during the husband's life and after his death. Remarriage, when it occurred, needed to go through strict procedures under the supervision of related clans rather than an impersonal legal system. Widowed women, if they maintained their widowhood to death, had the chance of being officially awarded with honorable titles and even honorific arches. Remarried widows were detested, and were frequently depicted as lustful, cold-hearted, and dishonest, as indicated by the above images. An "unfaithful" woman in a Confucian society was as much an outsider as a Jew was in the nominally Christian world of the sixteenth and early seventeenth century. As a citizen, Shylock is allowed to run his usury business and, seemingly impersonally, enter into contracts and litigation. But because of his second identity, Shylock is spat upon, spurned, and cursed as an essential outsider, a cut-throat dog.

The identity of being outsiders is negative social mark imposed by the community in which the characters live, which they cannot choose freely. In their societies, Yangshi and Shylock are trapped by their identities, which are by their nature social and cultural rather than individual. As in their language and the social work, in their very persons Yangshi and Shylock embody the confusion of social norms on the one hand and strict and impersonal law on the other. In *Contract* and *Merchant*, Yangshi and Shylock are identified as social parasites (one as pawnshop owner and the other as usurer) and outsiders (one as a twice-married wife and the other as a Jew), who meet with negative judgments and negative social responses from the community. Under these circumstances, fear of being punished by social sanctions should perhaps be able to deter Yangshi and Shylock from outwardly challenging or breaking the implicit norms that govern interpersonal behavior. In the two dramas' unfolding plots, however, the degree of Yangshi's and Shylock's internalization of social norms declines. In each drama, their "undesirable" acts are insufficiently deterred by social norms. Hence they challenge social norms and resort to the law. The emergence of law and the gradual replacement of informal institutions by formal legal structures are thus clearly represented.

Despite the different understandings of how law and morality are related to each other, the two court judges employ tricks, which reveal the uneasy combination of social norms and statutory law. Judge Bao designs a trick when he makes Yangshi believe in Liu Anzhu's death, so that Yangshi no longer worries about Anzhu's possibility of inheriting family wealth. But then she feels the immediate threat to her life from Anzhu's death. With quotes from the criminal code, Judge Bao asserts to her

> If you were related, you'd be his elder generation and he'd be your younger generation, and then you wouldn't have to pay with your life even if you had killed ten of them. It could only be judged as an accident. And the punishment would be no more than a fine. But if you were not related, you certainly know that "Those who owe debts must pay back money; those who kill must pay with own lives." (Zhang Guangqian 295–296)

Yangshi has to weigh gains and losses. She surrenders the key evidence, the contract, and admits to having struck him. In this way, Judge Bao applies the law to facts that the court has just witnessed, and at this moment Yangshi realizes she has fallen into the judge's entrapment. Judge Bao's assertions are thus based on Confucian *Li*, to be explained below, and mercy is embedded within the applied law. The judge's trick aims at revealing family and interpersonal relationships rather than personal character. As for Portia, who enters disguised as a legal expert named Balthazar, she firmly refutes the possibility of bending the law, and assures Shylock of his right to claim the pound of flesh from Antonio's body. It is only upon the confirmation of his right by the judge that Shylock starts to sharpen the knife and prepare for the cutting. Possibly, Shylock may have intended to perform a show of cutting flesh but to refrain, mercifully and theatrically, at the last moment, but that is purely a matter of the role's interpretation. This process of preparation is later used as evidence in court against him. Portia designs a trap when she first relaxes Shylock's alertness, whereupon Shylock confirms the legitimacy of his right to the flesh. Thus, Shylock presents in the court, in front of the public eye, both his intention and his preparatory action for killing via the fatal cutting; then Portia applies the law to the "facts" the court has just witnessed and doesn't need to further verify Shylock's identity, which, in the impersonality of statutory law, is superseded by impersonal acts. Yet Shylock's own intention may possibly have been to commit a circumcision rather than a physically fatal cut (see for instance Reik 358–359). At any rate, at the moment Shylock realizes his own

words and actions betray him in court, he falls into the trap. Portia
makes Shylock's loss possible through technically rigid interpretation
of Venetian law provisions in IV.i.300–307 and then the following
passage which may be Shakespeare's addition to his major source
material:

> The law hath yet another hold on you.
> It is enacted in the laws of Venice,
> If it be proved against an alien
> That by direct or indirect attempts
> He seek the life of any citizen,
> The party 'gainst the which he doth contrive
> Shall seize one half his goods; the other half
> Comes to the privy coffer of the state,
> And the offender's life lies in the mercy
> Of the Duke only, 'gainst all other voice. [...] (IV.i.342–351)

The applied law here refers to statutory law. Haque and Das
maintain that the play reveals how "law itself can be modified by the
authority" (86), but the emphasis is actually on displaying a legal
literalism. The characters in the earlier play appear to be more fully
embedded within social norms than those in *Merchant*, even while
both plays display the combination of social norms and statutory law.

After the court traps unfold fully and verdicts are declared, a
stunning similarity emerges between Yangshi and Shylock: extreme
verbal frugality in contrast with their previous verbal craftsmanship.
In *Contract*, after the court verdict is declared, not a word is
allocated to Yangshi; in *Merchant*, a very few lines in Act IV and
no line at all in Act V are assigned to Shylock. Several explanations
can be provided to explain Yangshi's and Shylock's abrupt shift from
eloquence to silence: firstly, they are too shocked and overwhelmed
by unexpected changes in court to say anything; secondly, they
realize they are trapped and defeated and it's of no use to utter
more; thirdly, they immediately protest and argue against the
verdicts' rationality, but their legal existence is denied and their
voices are accordingly lost, to the judge and also to the audience;
fourthly, the playwrights consider justice to be properly restored so
that the parties who have lost can't or shouldn't issue any complaint.
None of the above speculations may be fully adequate. However, the
metamorphosis from eloquent speaker to wordless listener reveals a
transformation in both Yangshi and Shylock: their legal identity can
be denied, so that they are easily subjugated to legal invisibility. In
this way, the power of social norms and statutory law seem to

converge, at the expense of character continuity.

The legal language's linguistic fixity and certainties necessarily conceal the fluidities of experience and the prejudices of the community where the law is created, interpreted, and enforced. By resting their cases heavily on legal technicality, Yangshi and Shylock bestow trust in an unworthy place. Yangshi's trust in the law's power is betrayed by Judge Bao's application of the law's spirit. The law's letter is mechanically interpreted to refute Shylock's petition. In these plays, different interpretation methods of law are appropriated to realize the aim of the group, which in turn is able to control the judicial system's operation. Thus the statutory law, as it is practiced in these dramas written at moments of cultural transition, is not a correction of the unfairness of social norms, but is the reinforcement of social norms.

Law and Mercy: Coordination or Dichotomy?

The interpretation of the law in *Contract* and *Merchant* sheds light on how Chinese and English legal traditions were similar during a transitional period. Inter-textualizing the two dramas may reveal where the two legal traditions diverged. Liu Anzhu in *Contract* exclaims after Judge Bao announces the verdict:

> His Majesty is, to the weak and poor,
> The life sustaining drizzle[8] from on high.
> To him we owe our life and loyalty. (Zhang Guangqian 300)

He draws a parallel between the court verdict and the rain and dews falling from heaven, so that he deems mercy to be the Emperor's endowment. In *Merchant*, both plaintiff and judge deem the law inflexible and unbendable. Shylock insists on the enforcement of the bond and offers no compromises, uttering "[...] And by our holy Sabbath have I sworn/To have the due and forfeit of my bond./If you deny it, let the danger light/Upon your charter and your city's freedom" (IV.i.35–38). He has as strong a belief as Antonio has in the Duke's inability to deny the law (III.iii.26–31). The legal doctor and semi-official judge (Portia, whom Bassanio has just married) counters Bassanio's beseeching the Duke to "wrest once the law to your authority" with the argument:

---

[8] "为甚么皇恩不弃孤寒辈,似高天雨露垂,生和死共戴荣辉"(Zang 435). Zhang Guangqian's translation here simplifies "雨(rain)" and "露(dew)" as drizzle.

> There is no power in Venice
> Can alter a decree establishèd.
> 'Twill be recorded for a precedent,
> And many an error by the same example
> Will rush into the state. (IV.i.213–217)

These lines highlight the law's technicality and inflexibility. In the court, however, Portia leads up to this by resorting to mercy to ease the law's harshness in some of the play's most famous lines:

> The quality of mercy is not strained.
> It droppeth as the gentle rain from heaven
> Upon the place beneath. It is twice blest:
> It blesseth him that gives, and him that takes.
> 'Tis mightiest in the mightiest. It becomes
> The thronèd monarch better than his crown.
> [...] It is an attribute to God himself,
> And earthly power doth then show likest God's
> When mercy seasons justice. (IV.i.179–184, 190–192)

Her statements present the law and mercy in terms of a dichotomy: the law doesn't inherently include ethical ingredients; no Venetian power can bend or alter Venetian law; mercy is God's attribute, while the earthly monarch is denied the right to use mercy to destroy the law.[9] Therefore, following the Old Testament, Portia analogizes mercy as gentle rain falling from heaven, divine and not secular. In *Merchant*, the law stipulates who can grant mercy, but mercy is not an inherent part of the law. Mercy appears as the foremost of all God's attributes, and for that very reason it cannot but be an attribute of humanity, in God's image. The book of Psalms is full of praise for divinity in the form of God's mercy. Since mercy's source is God, humans, whether Duke or Jew, would show the imprint of God within themselves (as in Seneca, *De Clementia* 1.19 or in a petition of the Convocation to Queen Elizabeth I in 1580).

Previously, then, Portia implicitly appealed to Shylock's desire to be like God, authorized to grant or deny forgiveness and to distribute vengeance and recompence (see Leimberg 178); now she emphasizes that granting mercy is a reflection of God's image inside the human soul, specifically as dispensed by the Duke (actually a

---

9 "Mercy" as used here actually has an etymological connection with mercantile objects which are given or lent out, a "paradoxical identity" which is basic to the play's structure (Leimberg 178). The giving and taking suggest the idea of a contract.

stronger privilege in this English play than the historical ruler of Venice enjoyed), while refusal to grant mercy is to discard God's imprint in humanity. Portia also implies, in this way, that the laws of Venice are in alignment with God's rules, owing to the specific place of mercy, and accordingly have a rational foundation. Her invocation of mercy may be opportunistic and "self-interested" (Miller 83, similarly for instance Moody 82−83), and indeed her whole approach to the legal situation speaks as much of her complex characterization as of the actual legal culture constructed in the play, be it Venetian or English (see also Posner 152). The trial in any case starts with her claims about the nature and source of the virtue of mercy, which become the essence of Portia's pleading (see also Leimberg 161).

Liu Anzhu and Portia thus converge in the function of mercy while diverging in the source of mercy, even as they strikingly use the same imagery.[10] The differentiation is, in a sense, a representation of the legal and philosophical divergence between Chinese and European jurisprudences. In conventional Chinese legal philosophy, Heaven (*Tian*) was believed to be the Almighty ruler of the natural, the human, and the spiritual world. The emperor in each dynasty, who was deemed to be a son of Heaven (*Tian-zi*) and the agent of Heaven, was granted exclusive earthly power. The emperor appointed officials to administer particular areas within the nation's territory. Officials were granted executive, legal, and judicial power, and traced their authority and legitimacy back to the emperor and from thence to Heaven.[11] As local chief justices, the officials were required to hear and judge all cases under their jurisdictions, whether the case was of civil or criminal nature. In

---

[10] Zhang Longxi speaks illuminatingly of the complex relationship between cultural difference and similarity, especially when individual differences are seen in relation to collective ones. See also his chapter in this volume.

[11] *Keju* or Imperial Examination System was an examination system in ancient China, through which officials were examined and selected. It was first adopted in the Sui dynasty (581−618) and lasted through the Qing dynasty (1644−1911). Intellectuals who wanted to be an official were required to take multi-tier examinations. The final imperial examination was under direct supervision of the emperor of the dynasty. Only *Gongshi* were qualified to take the exam. The matriculation had three levels of excellence. The first level, granted to three candidates, conferred *Jinshi*. The second level conferred *Jinshi status*. The third level conferred *Jinshi status as well*. The benefits of reaching these levels were both sentimentally and materially shared by relatives, one's clan, and even one's town members of the immediate family. See Liu Haifeng.

The Contract (and in most of his judicial opinions in other works),
Judge Bao starts with the emperor's ruling principle(s) and then
applies the principle(s) to the case under trial:

> All on your knees! Listen to my judgment!
> His Majesty espouses a harmonious world,
> And approves particularly filial sons.
> I appoint Zhang Bingyi this country's Magistrate,
> And confer the title of "Virtue" on his wife.
> A hundred silver pieces is for Elder Li
> To bring about his daughter's wedding with Anzhu.
> As Liu Anzhu has proved himself a filial son,
> He's entitled to wear a jinshi's gown and hat.
> His parents shall be buried in the family graves
> With an inscribed stele erected by their tomb.
> Liu Tianxiang is found guilty of disowning kins,
> But he is granted a pardon because of age.
> His wife deserves the sentence of a long jail term,
> But she may atone for her misdeed with a fine.
> Her live-in son-in-law belongs not to the Lius,
> And must be expelled immediately from the house.
> Posters are to be put up in and out of town
> To manifest the fairness of imperial laws. (Zhang Guangqian 299-
> 300)

The court bestows on the plaintiff Liu Anzhu the contract rights —
the rights related to his identity. Beyond the contract rights, he is
rewarded with official candidate status and an honorary monument
in memory of his deceased parents. For Judge Bao, collaboration
thus characterizes the relationship between the law and mercy, while
for "Judge" Portia, following a European tradition as in *Processus
Belial* (ca. 1473), antagonism characterizes the situation between
them. Willson has maintained that Portia represents "the reconciliation of
Justice and Mercy," even that "'Mercy' is Justice" (711) in the
play, yet a comparative reading with *Contract* shows that such an
equation would be misleading.

From Law to Social Norms: Re-Confucianization of Chinese Law

On the one hand, territorial expansion and commercial prosperity in
Yuan China as in Elizabethan England weakened the social
connectedness that helped social norms to organize social order,

paving the way for the law to rise as a new social order organizer. On the other, in defining how the law is related to mercy, Chinese legal philosophy diverges from its western counterpart. Based on the presumption that the law and mercy are co-ordinates, with mercy subjugated to the Emperor's power, Chinese legal philosophers, especially with a Confucian orientation, transformed mercy into an ideal state-ruling craft, termed *Li*, thus activating the Confucianizing process of law (see Xu 38). ⑫ The minority-ruled Yuan dynasty interrupted the process by separating the law from *Li* and elevating it as a major society organizer. However, with the Yuan dynasty replaced not long afterwards by the Ming dynasty, a mercy-based, or *Li*-based, state-ruling pattern was resumed with the Confucian Renaissance. The law's Confucianization has been shaping Chinese jurisprudence thenceforth. The manner of defining how the law is related to mercy thus helps to understand how two legal cultures view the law's function and what, besides the geographic gap, caused these legal cultures to take the routes they took.

In China, from as early as the Zhou dynasty (c.1046−256 BC), Chinese philosophers began to realize the necessity of coordination between social norms and law, with priority placed on the former (see Yu et al. 46). ⑬ Confucianized social norms (*Li*) were taken as an irreplaceable supplement to law (*Fa*) and incrementally assimilated into law. At the urging of imperial scholar Dong Zhongshu (179−104 BC), Emperor Wu (156 − 187 BC) adopted Confucianism as the imperial state ideology and established the Han Imperial Academy to train government official candidates who would be tested on Confucian classics. Confucian classical texts enjoyed imperial sponsorship, while other schools of thought lost ground (see Ho 76). Han dynasty governments sponsored the assimilation of *Li* into *Fa* (law). This process came to its height during the Tang dynasty (618−907) through codifying *Li* into statutes (see Yu et al. 56). As *Tang Lu*

---

⑫   *Li* （礼）consists of the norms of proper social behavior as taught by fathers, village elders, and government officials. The teachings promoted ideals such as filial submission, brotherliness, righteousness, good faith and loyalty. *Li* practices have been revised and evaluated over time to reflect the emerging views and beliefs found in society. Although these practices may change, which happens very slowly, fundamental ideals remain at the core of *Li*, which largely relate to social order. Within Confucian texts, three works comprise the primary teachings of rites. These works include *Yi Li*, *Li Ji*, and *Zhou Li*. The large textual coverage of *Li* reportedly includes 300 major and 3000 minor rules of ritual (see Fan Ruiping 143−144; Wang Wenjin 321).

⑬   This principle was called *Ming De Shen Xing* （明德慎刑）.

Shu Yi states, virtue and morality have become the foundation of government and education, while laws and punishments are the operative agencies of government and education. Both the former and the latter are necessary complements to each other, just as it takes morning and evenings to form a whole day, and spring and autumn to form the whole year.[14]

Thus law and *Li* were complements, with law being lowered below *Li*. This pattern was sustained till the end of the Song dynasty (920–1279). Yuan China (1271–1368), the first wholly-minority-rule dynasty, altered deep-rooted traditions. Yuan leaders implemented ethnically based hierarchies, with Mongolian ethnicity on the top and Han at the bottom (see Xiao 17–18). Han Chinese Confucian classics lost favor from the Mongolian regime, hence also the Confucianized *Li*-and-law-coordinated legal philosophy. Yuan China's extremely fast territorial expansion demanded stronger logistic support. The continuously held policy in previous dynasties of "Supporting agriculture, suppressing commerce" was an obstacle to achieve the purpose. Henceforth, policies were issued to stimulate business and trade, and laws and regulations were enacted to run the society. Yuan China thus saw the rise of law itself as a new society organizer, and the separation of law from Confucianized social norms. This is the context in which Yangshi in *Contract* recognizes the rise of law, and seizes it as a chance to alter life for herself and her daughter, which was formated by Confucian social norms.

However, Yuan China was a short-lived dynasty. The subsequent Ming dynasty (1368–1644) quickly achieved a Confucian renaissance, named Neo-Confucianism. Neo-Confucianism traced its origin back to the Song dynasty, and was, therefore, also called "Song (dynasty) and Ming (dynasty) philosophy." The short interruption caused by the Yuan dynasty in the dominance of Confucian thought was not deep and durable enough to cleanse the Confucian influences that permeated the society's every fiber. In *Contract*, as against Yangshi, who challenges the Confucian social norms, Liu Anzhu chooses Confucian social norms over the law as direction for his behavior.

Liu Anzhu advocates *Li*. As explained above, Yangshi cheats him out of the contract, beats him, drives him out, and his Uncle

---

⑭   "德礼为政教之本，刑罚为政教之用，犹昏晓阳秋相须而成者也。" The reference is to Chapter *Ming Li* in *Tang Lü Shu Yi* (唐律疏议). This translation is by Chen En-Cheng. (See also Yu et al. 56).

Liu Tianxiang declines to recognize him. When in the court Judge Bao orders Liu Anzhu to beat his uncle, Anzhu refuses, excusing his refusal as follows:

> [The Jade Hooks]
> He and my father are brothers by blood.
> How can I take the stick to punish him?
> One can't go against his conscience or heaven's way
> — he is the uncle, I nephew.
> I didn't come to seize or share his wealth,
> But to fulfill the calling of a son.
> How can I act in an unfilial way? (Zhang Guangqian 294)

The Confucian classic by Zeng Zi commends "self-cultivation, regulating the clan, governing the country, and establishing peace throughout the world,"⑮ arguing that the world's peace and the country's stability are based on harmoniously self-regulating clans. To achieve harmony, clan members need to cultivate Confucian virtue — *Li*, which, as explained above, enjoins individuals to proper behavior based on their roles and place in feudalistic society. Confucian scholars advocate a strict hierarchy of superiors and inferiors within a clan: the elders and the male members are superiors, while the young and the female members are inferiors. An inferior's injuring his/her superior is a severe crime.

The cherishment of clan ties is shared by another character in *Contract*, Li Ding Nu, daughter of the community head Li.⑯ She is betrothed to Liu Anzhu already in the womb by their respective

---

⑮ "古之欲明明德于天下者,先治其国;欲治其国者,先齐其家;欲齐其家者,先修其身;欲修其身者,先正其心。"From *Da Xue* by Zeng Zi, as in < http://ctext.org/liji/da-xue>. The original assessment of the ancients is as follows (2): "Wishing to cultivate their persons, they first rectified their hearts. Wishing to rectify their hearts, they first sought to be sincere in their thoughts. Wishing to be sincere in their thoughts, they first extended to the utmost their knowledge. Such extension of knowledge lay in the investigation of things. Things being investigated, knowledge became complete. Their knowledge being complete, their thoughts were sincere. Their thoughts being sincere, their hearts were then rectified. Their hearts being rectified, their persons were cultivated. Their persons being cultivated, their families were regulated. Their families being regulated, their states were rightly governed. Their states being rightly governed, the whole kingdom was made tranquil and happy." Confucius's student Zeng Zi (or Zeng Can) recorded and edited Confucius's words to compose the *Da Xue*. (See Zeng Zi 3-4).

⑯ Here Li (李) is the surname for the community head. It is one of the most popular surnames in China. This is different from *Li*, the systematic social and cultural institutions governing behaviors as explained in Note 12.

parents. She agrees to marry Liu Anzhu, without any resistance, despite their having never met each other. Marriage arranged by parents was a tradition in China until as late as the 1920s. *Li* forbids inferiors to defy superiors. To warn off potential transgressors, *Li* bars an eloping woman from legally becoming the wife of the man with whom she elopes (*Qi*), and it permits her only to become the man's concubine (*Qie*).[17] A young woman who elopes with a man is debased by both the man's clan and her own. The most influential statute in Chinese history as well as in Asian history, *Tang Lü Shu Yi*,[18] specifies: "*Qie* is a humble woman, and the law allows her to be bought and sold. If a man insists on marrying a *Qie* as *Qi*, he and the *Qie* are to be condemned to one and a half year's imprisonment" (Zhangsun 256).

　　Yuan China and Elizabethan England thus saw the rise of law as a new social order organizer. As they held contrasting views about how law is related to mercy, the two societies developed divergent legal philosophies and judicial frameworks. The Confucianization of law before the Yuan dynasty and Re-Confucianization of law after that dynasty systematically embedded Confucian social norms in law. Law was transformed as an instrument to achieve Confucian morals and values. Western and specifically English jurisprudence, deeming the relationship between law and mercy in terms of a dichotomy, incrementally separated law from social norms and enabled it to gain greater independence.

Palimpsest: Translational Cultural Overwriting

The divergence in the relationship between law and mercy can be seen even more clearly in the Chinese translation of *Merchant*. Zhu

---

[17] In ancient China it was common for economically successful men to have several concubines, women who cohabit with men without being married. The concubine's position was inferior to the wife's. The concubine was heavily dependent on the wife's disposition and the favor of her "husband." A concubine could improve her position by producing an heir, although her son would be inferior to legitimate children by the legal wife. "不待父母之命，媒妁之言，钻穴隙相窥，逾墙相从，则父母国人皆贱之。"(See Fu 92–93).

[18] The statute was in force during the period 618–907. This statute was drafted and passed in the Tang dynasty, and was believed to be the hallmark of legislation history in ancient China. Its impact was sustained till the end of China's ancient period, with governments in successive dynasties generally choosing to regard the statute as the fundamental document so that only some modifications were necessary. (See Zheng et al. 189–190).

Shenghao's translations of Shakespeare's works have been the most widely circulated and accepted among all Chinese translations. In 1978, *The Complete Works of Shakespeare* were published, as the first foreign writer's complete works ever in China (see Zhu Hongda and Wu Jiemin 17). Scholarly and amateur readers alike tend to acknowledge that the top choice of Chinese translations of Shakespeare's works is that of Zhu Shenghao (see Chen Caiyu 1). All the dramas offered in this collection give evidence of Zhu Shenghao's (1912–1944) specific interpretations, his manner of "free translation" (Sun 140).

Just one instance will have to serve in the present context to show the extent of Zhu Shenghao's interpretation in cultural transfer. In the Venetian court, Shylock declares "If you deny it, let the danger light/Upon your charter and your city's freedom" (IV.i. 37–38). Zhu Shenghao translates this as

> If Your Highness (*Dian Xia*) won't allow me the forfeiture, you are showing contempt to the charter. I will go to the capital Dadu[19] to sue you, requesting cancellation of your city's privileges (*te quan*).[20]

The translator changes Shylock's way of addressing the Duke into *Dian Xia* (Your Highness), revealing the ancient Chinese respect for and even fear of a court judge. When conducting a trial, the judge would sit behind a large table, with the prosecution and defense made to kneel in front of the table and to address the judge as *Qing Tian* (Clear Sky), *Da Ren* (Big Man), *Dian Xia* (Your Highness), or *Bi Xia* (Your Majesty). In feudal China, "all the land under the heaven belongs to the emperor and all the people to the boundary of the earth are the emperor's subjects."[21] Therefore, there is no possible place that is beyond the emperor's control in which to enjoy "freedom." All that one can enjoy is an endowment, that is, special favors from the Emperor. In Zhu Shenghao's version, the very word "freedom" is translated as "*te quan*" (特权, meaning

---

[19] Dadu was the capital city where the Emperor resided in the Yuan dynasty. Each dynasty in ancient China established special institutions such as *Yi Que* (诣阙) in the Han dynasty and then *Deng Wen Gu* (登闻鼓) and *Yao Che Jia* (邀车驾) in the Yuan and Tang dynasties. The Yuan dynasty government allowed people to appeal to higher courts or even to the emperor if they were denied justice in local courts.

[20] Zhu Shenghao's rendering is "要是殿下不准许我的请求,我就到京城上告去,要求撤销贵邦的特权."

[21] The Chinese poetic lines are as follows, "溥天之下,莫非王土;率土之滨,莫非王臣." (See Kong Zi 614).

privileges), the connotation of which is actually closer to the opposite. The adding of "I will go to the capital Dadu to sue you" transforms Shylock from a firm law-believer to a disobedient appellant, thus subjugating the law under the emperor's authority while believing the law is bendable to realize virtue. This instance illustrates how Confucianized Chinese legal philosophy deems law and mercy as a supplementary whole, both being subjected to the emperor's power, whereas the English legal philosophy recognizes law and mercy as divided, with mercy beyond the monarch's power. Zhu Shenghao's translation thus overwrites this latter philosophy with Chinese legal philosophy; similar further instances could be found. The method is similar to what has been called "domesticating" rather than "foreignizing" (Venuti 188). Is the translator attempting to resist what may have been thought of as a dominance of English-speaking culture? Very likely, according to Emily Apter, the reader "assumes the good faith effort" of the translator "to deliver an authentic copy of the original" (Apter 167). Yet while such faith may be disappointed, law's questionable translatability may then suggest for the reader that "one redefines oneself in the course of renegotiating one's relation with the other and, ultimately, with oneself — always bearing in mind, of course, that the other cannot be preconstituted in its otherness prior to the encounter" (Legrand 43).

Zhu Shenghao had widely recognized literary talents in both the English and the Chinese language, so that his rendering is by no means a product of willful ignorance. He translated Shakespeare's works with a war hero's devotion, with the determination to refute the Japanese invaders' teasing of China as such a cultureless country as not to have quality translations of Shakespeare's works (see Zhu Hongda and Wu Jiemin 21). Zhu Shenghao declares his principle as follows: "I will try to retain the spirit of the original as far as I possibly can; if this cannot be achieved, I will at least try to convey the intentions of the original, using fluent, plain Chinese; as to word-for-word 'hard' translations, I dare not venture to go along with" (Preface to *Complete Works of Shakespeare*, trans. Sun 139). Bermann speaks of translations as "linguistic negotiations occurring over time, each a poiesis, each establishing a new inscription and, with it, the possibility of new interpretation" (Bermann 6). Going further, Emily Apter asserts that "all translations are in some sense 'forgeries,' since they pretend to a contract of fidelity they never keep" (Bermann and Wood 91). With his knowledge of both the source culture and the target culture, with his extreme devotion, with his apparent clear-mindedness in seeking to retain the "spirit" and the "intentions" of a source text, Zhu Shenghao was nonetheless hardly able to surmount overarching cultural differences. That would be even less possible for his readers to achieve. After many years in which market forces were able to select and eliminate different translated versions of Shakespeare's works, versions preceding Zhu Shenghao's were attracting only a very limited readership, except for research purposes; even some versions later than Zhu Shenghao's are fading out of readers' sights (Li Weimin, "Permanent Shakespeare" 14). The higher rate of reception of Zhu Shenghao's translation among Chinese readers, as against other more "accurate" or "faithful" versions, indicates the slim possibility for cultural translation that does adequate justice to Otherness, especially between languages of remote cultural heritages. When it comes to the fundamental legal principle of how law is related to mercy, a highly sensitive translation may easily dysfunction.

In a more general sense, Pierre Legrand invites us to consider that "justice itself can be redeemed if we respect the gaps between laws, just as literary translation respects the gaps between languages" (Bermann and Wood 11–12). Does it? Jacques Derrida has suggested ways in which *Merchant* shows that translation "is the law; it even speaks the language of the law beyond the law, of the impossible law, represented by a woman who is disguised, transfigured, converted, travestied, read *translated*, into a man of the law"; thus all translation implies "an insolvent indebtedness," with all the paradoxes of "a *bond* and a contract" (183). In our case, that contract is indeed, as Derrida declares, "impossible and asymmetrical." Yet the seeming insolvency disguises the translator's subtle empowerment in the shape of overwriting. Instead of achieving a universalist poetics, a widely influential and accepted translation palimpsests the source text culture, as it were, with the target text culture.

The bulk of the chapter was finished during a research period at John Jay College of Criminal Justice, CUNY, as a visiting scholar. This chapter was supported by Shanghai International Studies University Research Funds (KX181103/QJTD14WX001).

References

Ackroyd, Peter. *Tudors: The History of England from Henry VIII to Elizabeth.*

New York: Thomas Dunne, 2013.

Apter, Emily. "Translation with No Original: Scandals of Textual Reproduction." *Nation, Language, and the Ethics of Translation*. Eds. Sandra Bermann and Michael Wood. Princeton: Princeton UP, 2005. 159–174.

Bell, Dean Phillip. *Jews in the Early Modern World*. Lanham, Md.: Rowman & Littlefield, 2008.

Bermann, Sandra. Introduction. *Nation, Language, and the Ethics of Translation*. Eds. Sandra Bermann and Michael Wood. Princeton: Princeton UP, 2005. 1–10.

Birch, Cyril, ed. *Anthology of Chinese Literature*. New York: Grove, 1965.

Chen Caiyu. "Editor's Remarks." *Thirty-one Dramas of Shakespeare Translated by Zhu*. Hangzhou: Hangzhou Industry and Trade UP, 2011.

Chen Dezhi. "On the Title, Year and Domain of the Yuan Dynasty." *Journal of Beifang Ethnic University* 87.3 (2009): 5–14.

Chen En-Cheng. "Han Fei's Principle of Government by Law." *Chinese Culture* 1.4 (1958): 91–103.

Derrida, Jacques. "What Is a 'Relevant' Translation?" Trans. Lawrence Venuti. *Critical Inquiry* 27 (2001): 174–200.

Fan Jiachen. *The Contract* (《包龙图智赚合同文字》). *Notes to Bao Gong Yuan Drama*. Jinan: Qi Lu P, 2006. 271–293.

Fan, Ruiping. "Confucian Ritualization: How and Why?" *Ritual and the Moral Life: Reclaiming the Tradition*. Eds. David Salomon, Ruiping Fan and Ping-cheung Lo. Heidelberg: Springer Dordrecht, 2012. 143–158.

Fang Yong. *Meng Zi*. Beijing: Zhonghua, 2015.

Feng Yuan-chun. *A Short History of Classical Chinese Literature*. Beijing: Foreign Language P, 2009.

Fu Perong. *Notes to Meng Zi*. Beijing: The East Publishing House, 2012.

Graeber, David. *Debt: The First 5000 Years*. New York: Melville House, 2011.

Hanan, Patrick. *The Chinese Short Story: Studies in Dating, Authorship, and Composition*. Cambridge, Mass.: Harvard UP, 1973.

Haque, Ziaul, and Snigdha Das. "The Evil Bond in William Shakespeare's *The Merchant of Venice*: The Source of Irrationality." *International Journal on Studies in English Language and Literature* 2.9 (2014): 73–91.

Harmon, A. G. *Eternal Bonds, True Contracts: Law and Nature in Shakespeare's Problem Plays*. Albany: State U of New York P, 2004.

Ho, Norman P. "Confucian Jurisprudence in Practice: Pre-Tang Dynasty Panwen (Written Legal Judgments)." 22 *Pacific Rim Law and Policy Journal* 49 (2013): 49–111.

Hou Xinyi. *History of Chinese Legal Thought*. Beijing: China U of Political Science and Law P, 2012.

Inner Mongolia Classical Statutes and Sociology Institute. *Genghis Khan's Code and Research*. Beijing: Commercial P, 2007.

Kong Zi (Confucius). *Book of Poetry*. Trans. Xu Yuanchong. Beijing: China Intercontinental P, 2012.

Legrand, Pierre. "Issues in the Translatability of Law." *Nation, Language, and the Ethics of Translation*. Eds. Sandra Bermann and Michael Wood. Princeton: Princeton UP, 2005. 30–50.

Leimberg, Inge. "*What May Words Say ...?*" *A Reading of* The Merchant of Venice. Madison, NJ: Fairleigh Dickinson UP, 2011.

Li Jianming. "The Story of a Bond: From the Story-telling Scripts in Song Dynasty to the Dramas in the Yuan Dynasty." *Journal of Yangzhou University (Humanities & Social Sciences)* 13.2 (2009): 60–65.

Li Weimin. *The History of Shakespeare Criticism in China.* Beijing: China Drama P, 2006.

—. "Permanent Shakespeare, Permanent Zhu Shenghao: The Specific Value of Zhu Shenghao's Translation of Shakespeare's Plays." *Shandong Foreign Language Teaching Journal* 4 (2013): 13–18.

Liu Haifeng. "On the Meaning of Imperial Examination and Its Time of Origination." *Journal of Xiamen University (Arts & Social Sciences)* 5 (2008): 70–91.

Liu Yuqing. "The Implied Meaning of Jujiu (osprey) in Guanju of The Book of Songs." *Journal of Peking University (Humanities and Social Sciences)* 2 (2004): 71–80.

Miller, William Ian. *Eye For an Eye.* Cambridge UP, 2006.

Moody, A. D. "The Letter of the Law (III.iii–v; IV.i)." *The Merchant of Venice: Critical Essays.* Ed. Thomas Wheeler. London: Routledge, 1991. 79–102.

Posner, Richard A. "Law and Commerce in *The Merchant of Venice.*" *Shakespeare and the Law: A Conversation Among Disciplines and Professions.* Eds. Bradin Cormack, Martha C. Nussbaum and Richard Strier. Chicago: U of Chicago P, 2013. 147–155.

Reik, Theodor. *The Search Within: The Inner Experiences of a Psychoanalyst.* New York: Farrar Straus and Cuhady, 1956.

Seneca, Lucius Annaeus. *De Clementia.* Bohn's Classical Library Edition. London: George Bell, 1900.

Shakespeare, William. *The Norton Shakespeare.* Ed. Stephen Greenblatt. New York & London: Norton, 1997.

Sun, Yanna. "Translating Methods of Shakespeare in China." *English Language Teaching* 2.2 (2009): 138–140.

Tian Zhang. "Bewilderment and Rebirth in Jewish Identity: Cultural Identity Construction in *The Assistant* by American Jewish Writer Bernard Malamud." *Identity and Intercultural Communication (II): Conceptual and Contextual Applications.* Intercultural Research Vol. 3. Shanghai: Shanghai Foreign Language Education P, 2012. 353–362.

Toulmin, Stephen. *Cosmopolis: The Hidden Agenda of Modernity.* Chicago: U of Chicago P, 1992.

Venuti, Lawrence. "Local Contingencies: Translation and National Identities." *Nation, Language, and the Ethics of Translation.* Eds. Sandra Bermann and Michael Wood. Princeton: Princeton UP, 2005. 177–202.

Wang Wenjin. *Notes to Li Ji.* Beijing: Zhonghua Book Company, 2001.

Wang Yunxi and Gu Yisheng, eds. *A New History of Chinese Literary Criticism.* Trans. Zhang Siqi. Beijing: Foreign Language P, 2013.

Weatherford, Jack. *Genghis Khan and the Making of the Modern World.* Trans. Wen Haiqing and Yao Jiangen. Chongqing: Chongqing Publishing House, 2009.

Wiesner-Hanks, Merry E. *Early Modern Europe, 1450 – 1789.* 2nd ed. Cambridge UP, 2013.

Willson, Michael Jay. "View of Justice in Shakespeare's The Merchant of Venice and Measure for Measure." *Notre Dame Law Review* 70.3 (1993):

695–726.

Woodbridge, Linda. *Money and the Age of Shakespeare: Essays in New Economic Criticism*. New York: Palgrave Macmillan, 2003.

Wu Lan and Liu Zhenjiang. "The Mercantilism of Genghis Khan and Kublai Khan." *Forward Position* 111 (2012): 111–113.

Wu Shuchen. *The Origin and Evolution of Chinese Law*. Beijing: People's P, 2013.

Xiao Qiqing. *Ethnicities, Culture and Keju in Yuan China*. Taipei: Linking, 2008.

Xu Yanbin. *Rationality Construction of Li and King's Power — Based on Pre-Tang Historical Documents*. Beijing: China Social Science P, 2011.

Yali Zhou. "Moses and the Israeli National Identity." *Identity and Intercultural Communication (II): Conceptual and Contextual Applications*. Intercultural Research Vol. 3. Shanghai: Shanghai Foreign Language Education P, 2012. 329–352.

Yong Fang. "Dangpu: A Commercial Usury in Ancient Society." *Commercial Research* 3 (1991): 42–44.

Yoshinobu Zasu. "Sanctions by Social Norms and the Law: Substitutes or Complements?" 36 *Journal of Legal Studies* 36.2 (2007): 379–396.

Yu Ronggen, Long Daxuan and Lu Zhixing. *A Research on Traditional Chinese Jurisprudence: A Perspective of National Heritage*. Beijing: Beijing UP, 2004.

Zang Jinshu. *Collections of Yuan Drama*. Vol. 2. Beijing: Zhonghua Book Company, 1958.

Zeng Zi. *The Great Learning (Da Xue)*. Beijing: Foreign Language and Education P, 2011.

Zhang Guangqian, trans. *Selected Plays from the Yuan Dynasty*. Beijing: Foreign Language P, 2010.

Zhang, Longxi. "The Complexity of Difference: Individual, Cultural, and Cross-Cultural." *Interdisciplinary Science Reviews* 35.3–4 (2010): 341–352.

Zhangsun Wuji. *Tang Lu Shu Yi*. Beijing: Zhonghua Book Company, 1983.

Zheng Jixu, Ji Yong and Qu Guangkang. *King of Codes: Tang Lu Shu Yi and Chinese Culture*. Kaifeng: Henan UP, 2005.

Zhu Hongda and Wu Jiemin. "Zhu Shenghao's Translating Principles and Accomplishments in the Translations of Shakespeare's Works." *Jiaxing College Journal* 17 (2005): 17–22.

Zhu Shenghao (朱生豪). *Shashibiya quan ji* (The Complete Works of Shakespeare). 11 vols. Beijing: renmin wenxue chubanshe, 1978. Nanjing: Yilin, 2001.

18

Dialogical Hermeneutics as an Alternative Model for Literary Imagination: A Critique of Ethical Criticism

Inge VAN DE VEN
Tilburg University
Tom VAN NUENEN
King's College London

Summary: A combination of cosmopolitanism and empathy can be problematic. In an essay about the attacks of 9/11/2001, British author Ian McEwan makes an appeal to our human capacity for love and imagination: only thinking oneself into the minds of others, the strangers who are remote from us in space and situation, makes morality possible. Literary critics such as Martha Nussbaum and Wayne Booth argue that literary narratives can make us more empathic, by offering the experience of living vicariously through the textualized other. This is all the more relevant for intercultural contact zones. Yet when we transfer feelings of empathy from fiction to life, can we avoid projecting onto the other our own thoughts and feelings, thus reducing the other to the self? The authors argue that Hans-Georg Gadamer's ontological hermeneutics, which explains that the cultural or historical strangeness of artworks can never be suspended, avoids this trap. To rethink the notion of intercultural and interpersonal empathy with the textualized character, as the other, the authors offer a new reading of McEwan's award-winning novel *Saturday* (2005).

1. Empathy Through Literature

Cosmopolitanism and empathy make for a problematic combination. The recognition of a radical humanistic plurality or "inclusive differentiation" (Beck, *Cosmopolitan* 5), and the mutual global interdependence and responsibility that follow from it (see Fine 2), acquire a new urgency in the face of globalization. The constant awareness of innumerable faceless strangers and their fates that it produces sometimes seems a regrettable attainment: moral ambivalence has taken over comfortable ignorance. The ethical challenge of our age is characterized by the abundance and intrusive impact of mediated encounters with the lives of strangers, remote from us in space and situation. Simon Cooke assesses this challenge in the following way:

> If we can characterize modernization and globalization as creating an increasing network of connections, as expanding the surface area of our interpersonal and intercultural contact zones, then the ethical imperative today is one in which we are required, not only to respond to a given situation as it occurs — to respond to an encounter in our immediate environment (with sympathy) — but to incorporate in our ethic a sense of what is happening elsewhere. (Cooke 166)

Narrative fiction, it has often been argued, has an important role to play here. In an essay published in *The Guardian* as a response to the attacks of 9/11/2001, titled "Only love and then oblivion," British author Ian McEwan makes an appeal to our human capacity for love and imagination. McEwan charges the terrorists with a "failure of the imagination" and a lack of the natural capacity for empathy that makes us human: "If the hijackers had been able to imagine themselves into the thoughts and feelings of the passengers, they would have been unable to proceed. [...] Imagining what it is like to be someone other than yourself is at the core of our humanity." Empathy, projecting the self into another's situation in order to come to a deeper understanding of that other person, is what ethical behavior is founded on, so the argument goes. Accessing such a terrible event through the news does not allow for such comprehension. We can only begin to understand the meaning of it as we "fantasize ourselves into the events" and pose the question "What if it was me?" "[T]o think oneself into the minds of others," McEwan continues, is what makes morality possible. It is the "essence of compassion." Engaging with ethical events in which we are not directly implicated incites us to fashion imaginative reconstructions. This imaginative exercise, then, can be fostered by reading literary prose. McEwan insists elsewhere that the novel is "empathy in its purest form," for it allows us to inhabit the mind of the other and experience what it feels like to be this other (qtd. Vervaet).

McEwan is not alone in underscoring the relation between literary narrative or narrative fiction and empathy. Literary critics like Martha Nussbaum and Wayne Booth argue that literary narratives can make us more empathic, by offering the experience of living vicariously through the (textual) other while also retaining a distance, enabling the reader to reflect on complex situations. This is thought to expand our capacities of ethical judgment in real life. But the conditions for this expansion may be more complex than that, especially in light of the lure of self-imposition, or substituting one's own mental attitude for the unknown attitude of others (Freud 130–131). In this process of trying to place the self in the others' position, how do we make sure that we do not inadvertently project our own thoughts and feelings onto this other, and thus reduce the other to the self? When it comes to understanding across cultures or ideological boundaries, questions like these receive a special weight.

In this chapter we expand upon a number of theories on empathy and literature (Todorov, Nussbaum, and Carroll) which we critically assess. These critics, associated with the school of "ethical criticism," argue for the use of literary narrative as a field of demonstration and testing ground for responsible and rewarding human conduct. We aim to demonstrate the shortcomings of this model for the relation between literature and empathy through a reading of McEwan's novel *Saturday* (2005). Then we will present an alternative model for this relation on the basis of Hans-Georg Gadamer's dialogic hermeneutics.

2. Dialogical Hermeneutics and the Literary Imagination

A dominant way of thinking about the relation between literature and empathy is that reading literature can incite us to sympathize with humans in general, as literary reading contributes to a more full-fledged, balanced and complex definition of what it is to be human. In "What is literature for?" Tzvetan Todorov elaborates on the work of philosopher Richard Rorty, who sees the redemptive value of literature in the way it diminishes our egotism or self-satisfaction, the illusion of self-sufficiency. Reading literary works, according to Rorty, is like meeting new people, "with the important difference that we can discover right away what they are like inside" (Todorov 27). Through these encounters, Todorov has it, literature "lets each of us fulfill our human potential" (ibid., 17). He locates literature's power to attain this understanding in the way we attempt to become familiar with the ideas, feelings, and viewpoints of characters, and as such this can train the reader's humanity, make her an "expert in being human" (ibid., 31).

In a well-known work on the relation between literature and ethics, *Poetic Justice* (1995), philosopher Martha Nussbaum states that a good judge should be able to take an empathic stance in complex ethical situations, and that reading literary texts provides an excellent training to this end. The way she sees it, "[l]iterary works that promote identification and emotional reaction cut through those self-protecting stratagems, requiring us to see and to respond to many things that may be difficult to confront — and they make this process palatable by giving us pleasure in the very act of confrontation" (*Poetic* 6). The ethical benefit of literature, for her, is the experience of living vicariously through the (textual) other while retaining a distance, enabling the reader to reflect on complex situations. This is thought to expand our capacities of ethical judgment in real life, because we obtain an understanding of the uniqueness of every situation. In training our judgments, empathy, the "imaginative exercise of putting oneself in [another] person's place" (Nussbaum, *Upheavals* 342), supports an extension of our ethical concerns. Ethical considerations should be founded on as comprehensive and full-fledged a notion as possible of the people involved, their stories and motivations. This, as Nussbaum is convinced, ultimately leads to a better treatment of the other:

> if you really vividly experience a concrete human life, imagine what it's like to live that life, and at the same time permit yourself the full range of emotional responses to that concrete life, you will (if you have at all a good moral start) be unable to do certain things to that person. Vividness leads to tenderness, imagination to compassion. (Nussbaum, *Love's* 209)

Noël Carroll considers narrative fiction to be the "ethical" medium par excellence, by virtue of the numerous gaps enclosed in it, waiting to be filled in by the reader ("Moderate" 419–420). Among the feelings and thoughts employed to make the story intelligible are ethical ones, *antecedent* ethical concepts to be precise: "moral emotions and judgements that narratives typically call upon audiences to fill in are generally already in place. Most narrative artworks do not teach audiences new moral emotions or new moral tenets. They activate pre-existing ones" (Carroll, *Beyond* 299). In "enlarg[ing] our powers of recognition with respect to abstract virtues and vices" (ibid., 286), works of literature function as a kind of laboratory, an ethical playground in which we can experiment to our hearts' content. The focal point of these experiences is the literary character, with whom we empathize or identify (Nussbaum, Todorov), whose lives we "try out" (Booth 485) or whose experiences we simulate or "empathically reenact" (Currie).

We argue that this metaphor of the laboratory, in which normative sentiments are always defined *a priori*, and in which empathy is considered the chemical mixture of an "activation strategy," leads to a reductionist attitude toward humanistic morality. It posits imagination as a categorical variable. A more fruitful approach, to our minds, can be found in the ontological hermeneutics of Hans-Georg Gadamer. The importance of interculturality in a hermeneutic perspective has been theorized before. In this respect we point the reader to Vince Marotta's work on cross-cultural understanding and subjectivity in intercultural hermeneutics. He uses Gadamerian hermeneutics to formulate an alternative conception of the in-between subject and cross-cultural interpretation. He shows that the cross-cultural subject is situated within the intercultural encounter rather than dwelling above it.

Carroll's notion of the "gaps" of ethical meaning leads naturally to Gadamer's theory on the interpretation of art, which is based on the insight that there is an "insuperable difference between the interpreter and the author" (Gadamer 296). Gadamer's distinctive approach to interpretation revolves around the notion of *dialogue*: the process of entering into a productive "conversation" with the work of art. Following Martin Heidegger in his decommissioning of the subject-object paradigm, Gadamer notes that the engagement with artistic representations needs to be a fundamentally reflexive exercise. By interpreting a text, we lay bare and question our own prejudices. In contrast to the positivist Enlightenment tradition in which subjectivity has to be left 'at the door' when commencing the analysis, Gadamer urges us to understand the existentialist tenet that our prejudices are a function of our deep involvement and convergence with the world — and that they are necessary for any productive interpretative act. The only way to draw our prejudices into view, he suggests, is by their *provocation* when a text addresses us in its strangeness or unintelligibility (ibid., 198).

By extension, a proper hermeneutic attempt amounts to, in Gadamer's parlance, a *fusion of horizons*: a convergence of vantage points of both reader and text. This constitutes a rejection of both subjectivism and relativism; the locus of hermeneutics is a space of vacillation, an *in-between* (ibid., 295). We are familiar with the artwork because it stands in a tradition, and yet its cultural or historical strangeness can never be suspended. In fact, "the circle of whole and part is not dissolved in perfect understanding but, on the contrary, is most fully realized" (ibid., 293). What at first appears alien in the text can, upon close inspection, come to present a richer context of meaning. We gain a better and more profound understanding not only of the text but also of ourselves; what art ultimately offers is Aristotelian *phronesis*, practical wisdom, concerning our own existential condition. However, and importantly, Gadamer does not suggest that we simply transpose ourselves into the horizon of the text. He compares this to a conversation in which one has only to get to know the other, in which no agreement is sought and horizons cannot coalesce. Empathy, understood as such, is not enough. Instead, we are effectuating and producing a tradition in which both artwork and hermeneutical consciousness are implicated. It is this search for commonality, understood as a recognition in the face of strangeness, on which Gadamer notes:

> Hermeneutics must start from the position that a person seeking to understand something has a bond to the subject matter that comes into language through the traditionary text and has, *or acquires*, a connection with the tradition from which the text speaks. (Ibid., 295, emphasis ours)

That is, understanding the tradition from which an artwork speaks is no precondition to its total understanding. The further the distance between interpreter and artwork, the more space for tradition to unfurl. Temporal distance thus becomes a productive condition for understanding. "It is not a yawning abyss but is filled with the continuity of custom and tradition, in the light of which everything handed down presents itself to us" (ibid., 297). At this junction, we should add that this not only goes for history, with which Gadamer concerns himself: the deeply *unfamiliar* phenomena we face — be they historical, cultural, or personal — are always coming at us through a sprawling of centrifugal connections of meaning. Gadamer's insistence on "understanding the tradition from which we come" (ibid., 305) may lead one to criticize him for his Western-centric approach, but we are at once reminded that he does speak about the formation of *one* horizon, but rather the meeting of several:

> The hermeneutic task consists in not covering up this tension by attempting a naive assimilation of the two but in consciously bringing it out [...] Historical consciousness is aware of its own otherness and hence foregrounds the horizon of the past from its own. (Ibid.)

Thus, when further on he notes the importance of "applying the text to be understood to the interpreter's present situation" (ibid., 307), this does not mean that we are to take over the textual horizon. Instead, "the interpretive activity considers itself wholly bound by the meaning of the text [...] it objectifies tradition and methodically eliminates the influence of the interpreter and his time on understanding" (ibid., 328–329). *Phronesis*, here, means that we apply the textual meaning insofar as we can recover it primarily to ourselves.

There is no need for epistemological pessimism in the face of Gadamer's concerns. After all, he takes care to emphasize the "fore-conception of complete-ness" (ibid., 294), the human presupposition that the artwork we are facing is, essentially, understandable. It exemplifies *Dasein's* involvement with and tacit understanding of the world. Yet, this also means that in our hermeneutic attempts we are drawn into the play of something much larger than what is immediately evident to our subjective consciousness. And the way in which we should familiarize ourselves with the "other" should, then, not be to transplant her into an instantly recognizable horizon but to recognize her distance and immerse ourselves in her strangeness, in the hope that we may "understand in a different way, if we understand at all" (ibid., 296). This position of epistemic modesty, to reiterate, does not preclude meaning-making across the borders of space, time, and thought, but it does force us to rethink the notion of intercultural and interpersonal empathy with the text — or, for that matter, the literary character. This opens the possibility of a literary critique informed by what Xie Ming in 2014 has termed an "intercultural hermeneutics": the theory and practice of interpretation between cultures. With this in mind, we now turn to a close reading of Ian McEwan's *Saturday*: a novel which, to our mind, exemplifies the problems of an approach to (intercultural) empathy as transposing oneself into the mind of the other.

3. *Saturday* and the Problem of Intersubjectivity

Saturday is inspired by the notion of ethics as placing oneself in the other's shoes, which is present at two levels. As a novel it grants us the experience of vicariously living a day in the mind of the middle-aged neurosurgeon Henry Perowne. On a diegetic level, Perowne in turn struggles to obtain an empathic attitude to the other. In an ongoing stream-of-consciousness narrative entirely in the present tense we are witness to this character's every thought presented in free indirect discourse. Perowne is a privileged man who leads a happy life with his wife and two children. Yet he is aware of the fact that modern luxuries and comforts are precarious goods, and that harmonious communities such as his are fragile. *Saturday* explores to what point we can buttress ourselves against disharmony creeping in from the world outside — outside our minds, our houses, our families.

Although his daughter Daisy keeps striving to educate his sensibility, Perowne seems to grant literature only a referential function. The novel is "too humanly flawed, too sprawling and hit-and-miss to inspire uncomplicated wonder at the magnificence of human ingenuity, of the impossible dazzlingly achieved" (*Saturday* 68). It lacks the "purity" of science and music. After all, who needs stories to defamiliarize the world when "[t]he times are strange enough. Why make things up?" The world that Perowne tries to grasp is too complex, too strange as it is: "it interests him less to have the world reinvented; he wants it explained" (ibid., 66).

To come to such an explanation, Perowne approaches the world with rationalism and pragmatism as his armor. As "professional reductionist" he is positive that the "invisible folds and kinks of character" have been "written in code, at the level of molecules" that "resist any humane attempts to change individuals' fates" (ibid., 272). The mechanics of the brain are clear to him, whereas the complexities of the individual consciousness remain a mystery. While he debunks religious faith as simply "a problem, or an idea, of reference. An excess of the subjective, the ordering of the world in line with your needs, an inability to contemplate your own unimportance" (ibid., 272), his own devotion to science does not give him the solution to this "problem." The brain does not teach him about ethics, and his anxious feelings about justifying his prosperity, a debt to faceless others still to be paid, his desire for an impossible measure of control over his life and mind, all point to similar "reference" problems: Perowne himself is stuck for an answer vis-à-vis the friction between his personal life and the world around him. There are no pre-made guidelines for what it means to be "human" now; even science falls short.

Therefore it is unsurprising that Perowne's pragmatic ideal of simplicity bestows on him a relentless sense of ambivalence concerning global politics and ethics. He "can't feel, as the members [of the anti-war march in Hyde Park] themselves probably can, that they have an exclusive hold on moral discernment" (ibid., 73). Ethical responsibility, even more muddled, messy, imperfect, and tainted by "the human" than literature, makes him uneasy, enforces his inclination to *turn away*. Still, as Emmanuel Levinas has reminded us, "the other haunts our ontological existence and keeps the psyche awake, in a case of vigilant insomnia. Even though we are ontologically free to refuse the other, we remain forever accused, with a bad conscience" (Kearney 64). This is an apt description of Perowne's state of anxiety. He refuses to engage with it, opts for consolation, for a refuge in a withdrawn liberalism. The biography of Darwin that his daughter made him read "[a]t times [...] made him comfortably nostalgic for a verdant, horse-drawn, affectionate England" (*Saturday* 6). At these moments of reflection on his life and the responsibilities of his position in society, he often flees into a longing for simpler times, when one could permit oneself an attitude of careless naiveté:

> How restful it must once have been, in another age, to be prosperous and believe that an all-knowing super-natural force had allotted people to their stations in life and not to see how the belief served your prosperity — a form of anosognosia — a useful psychiatric term for lack of awareness of one's own condition. Now we think we do see, how do things stand? After the ruinous experiments of the lately deceased century, after so much vile behavior, so many deaths, a queasy agnosticism has settled around these matters of justice and redistributed wealth. No more big ideas. (Ibid., 74)

And this is one rule he seems to embrace: Perowne indulges in the small pleasures of life. In fact, he may be a materialist when it comes to brain and character, and he may miss the point of literature, but he is very receptive to aesthetic pleasure. Upon Bach and Coltrane he bestows "a ruthless, nearly inhuman element of self-enclosed perfection" (ibid., 68), and he admires the work of Rothko, Parker, and Hodgkin, revealing a preference for the abstract, non-representational in art, a Kantian "free" or pure beauty. What he stands truly in awe of is *perfection*, devoid of the uncertainties that belong to the domain of the human. He finds it in the brain, in the beauty of the tentorium, the arachnoid, the globus palladus (ibid., 11, 57, 227); while performing the "art of neurosurgery" (ibid., 255) in the operating theatre, he inhabits the "pure present ... that dissolves all sense of time" (ibid., 266), with "the pleasure of knowing precisely what he is doing" (ibid., 250). He finds it in the "biological hyperspace" of sexual intercourse with his wife (ibid., 51), in a game of squash, and even in his everyday surroundings. In art as well as in life, Perowne admires harmony, orderliness, flawless mechanisms, configurations where every element has its *own place*. What Perowne admires can be described as a Kantian purposive purposelessness; the five hundred pages of *The Origin of Species* amount to the most beautiful story imaginable, because it all "fits"; Science and abstract art — free and pure — are juxtaposed to literature and the complex moral world, muddled and flawed. Located in art, nature, and the human brain, this harmony is least likely to be found where *subjectivities* come into play. He connects the transcendence, the perfect clarity and harmony in his son's music, to a balance and harmony absent from life. And since this larger cohesion will always remain a utopia, he withdraws and sticks to his private joys, subscribing to the philosophy of his eighteen-year-old son:

> When we go on about the big things, the political situation, global warming, world poverty, it all looks really terrible, with nothing getting better, nothing to look forward to. But when I think small, closer in — you know, a girl I've just met, or this song we're doing with Chas, or snowboarding next month, then it looks great. So this is going to be my motto — think small. (Ibid., 34–35)

This strategic "small thinking" is connected to Perowne's nostalgia for more naïve times, and his tendency to close off his consciousness from otherness. Pondering the alleged feelings of the fish he will prepare for dinner, he contemplates these issues: "[t]his is the growing complication of the modern condition, the expanding circle of moral sympathy. Not only distant peoples are our brothers and sisters, but foxes too, and laboratory mice, and now the fish" (ibid., 127). Perowne will not comply and opts for ignorance: "If they're alive and in pain, he isn't to know" (ibid., 177). His empathy is selective and does not travel: "[f]or all the discerning talk, it's the close at hand, the visible that exerts the overpowering force. And what you don't see ... That's why in gentle Marylebone the world seems so entirely at peace" (ibid., 127). There are no guidelines, no terms of selection, determining to whom we extend our humane feelings: Animals? Murderers? The mentally deranged? Terrorists? But once we allow empathy to trickle down in our consciousness, its appeals are bound to increase: mercy and responsibility are inherently non-selective. And as Jacques Derrida reminds us in *The Gift of Death*, this boundlessness of responsibility is essential: there are infinite responsibilities, and they are all absolute and immediate in their demands (Derrida 72). In the real world there are consequences to actions, even the ones we do not take — ethical responsibility makes demands on us before we choose to withhold it, to *not* relate, as Perowne finds out a little later.

4. Closing the Circle: Hidden Cultural Anxieties in *Saturday*

The threat looming over him during this day presents itself in the form of the outsider Baxter, representing the inability to guard ourselves from intrusions and the irrationality of chance. After a minor car accident, where his diagnosis of Baxter's Huntington's disease — "biological determinism in its purest form" (*Saturday* 93) — saves Perowne from a beating, Baxter is humiliated and bent on revenge. He follows Perowne home, holds his family hostage with a knife, and threatens to rape his daughter Daisy, whom he commands to read a poem from the proof copy of her own collection. Unable to undergo this ultimate humiliation, on a hint from her grandfather she instead recites Matthew Arnold's "Dover Beach" (see Appendix), which she knows by heart. On hearing this mid-Victorian poem, Baxter goes through a dramatic mood swing. Ecstatic and genuinely moved, he demands a second reading, whereupon he undergoes an instant transformation — despite the poem's gloomy message, he is spellbound by its beauty, which occasions in him a metamorphosis "from lord of terror to amazed admirer" (ibid., 223). The aesthetic experience fills him with a new zest for life: he now wants to participate in the made-up program that will cure his disease, giving the Perownes the chance to overpower him. Afterwards, Henry regrets having treated the intruder as a neurological diagnose instead of a human, to have imagined the story of Baxter's disease but not his life. Although Baxter has broken the nose of his father-in-law, put a knife to his wife's throat, and almost raped his daughter, the surgeon fixes his injury and chooses not to press charges. Baxter's genetic condition is sentence enough, he decides.

"On closer examination of the crucial scene in which Baxter's consciousness is transformed through Daisy's recitation Dover Beach," it is noteworthy that what happens to him in this experience remains a mystery to the reader. This moment, like the rest of the day, we experience from Perowne's viewpoint. Triggered by his recognition of Baxter's emotive reaction to art, Perowne comes to see him as a human being despite of his "simian" appearance (ibid., 88) — as Kathleen Wall has pointed out: "Baxter is human, not animal!" (Wall 785). For the first time, he comes to imagine Baxter's story, tries to attain an understanding of the man behind the genetic affliction. He asks himself what it would be like to stand in his shoes. The act of imagining the story behind his intruder points him to the similarities between Baxter and himself — both can be touched by aesthetics; for both, the world is a dark and scary place; and Baxter lives Perowne's ultimate fear, the unraveling of consciousness.

This recognition of Baxter's humanity, however, does not really amount to a discovery of "what the man is like inside": it is an attempt at understanding by *incorporating the other into the same*, by fashioning a narrative construction of his consciousness. Of course, Perowne could never succeed in seeing the world through Baxter's eyes, understanding his experience of life: probably, Baxter is not even capable of such a lucid understanding of *himself*. And due to the exclusive focalization of events through Perowne, his opponent remains a one-sided figure, a flat character, for the reader as well. We cannot *but* see him as a medical "case," because that is all we know of him. As Edouard Glissant has declared in *Poetics of Relation*,

> the self's opacity for the other is insurmountable, and, consequently, no matter how opaque the other is for oneself (no myth ever provides for the legitimacy of the other), it will always be a question of reducing this other to the transparency experienced by oneself. Either the other is assimilated, or else it is annihilated. (49)

Imposing one's perspective on the other is an act of assimilation and appropriation.

Instead of an openness to Baxter's unique being, it is a recognition of *sameness* that awakens Perowne's compassion and inspires him to a deed of balancing the wrongs done to his attacker, to recreate a symmetry which will finally redeem Perowne and rid him of his guilt. With his operation on Baxter, described in great aesthetic detail, symmetry is arrived at on multiple levels in the novel, resolving the narrative tension as well as the different forms of guilt plaguing the protagonist: guilt for misleading Baxter with his professional power, for his high social standing, for winning the genetic lottery. This "balancing act," while giving the novel thematic and structural closure, allows Perowne to reinstate an ethical balance — in an exceptional achievement of harmony between form and content. This well-rounded aesthetic harmonization represents a subjective narratorial consciousness which would be easy to submit to a deconstructive reading.

Perowne himself cannot relate to Baxter or come to a true understanding. It is the *poem* that intervenes, and to which Baxter relates. Although Baxter is more capable of reacting to this poem than Perowne is, it becomes painfully clear that it symbolizes a community that for him will remain forever out of reach. Despite his momentary exaltation, the aesthetic experience only inscribes his alienation from the Perownes' universe. This starts with the experience being based on deception, on making him believe the poem to be Daisy's. Falling into this trap, his illiteracy becomes his downfall. His enchantment has the meaning of a distraction, facilitating his expulsion. Even if he does have an imagination, the uncouth man does not *belong*. As Elaine Hadley reminds us, "[t]his is decidedly not Baxter's novel — Baxters rarely, even now, have novels about them, and his confirmed case of Huntington's disease, although in its early stages, only renders him more definitively beyond the investments of the ideal of withdrawal and self-fulfillment the poem epitomizes" (Hadley 93).

The choice of "Dover Beach" by Matthew Arnold is telling in this respect. In this poem, as in *Saturday*, the literary imagination plays an important thematic role. Contrasting the fleeting moment of the present with the past, "Dover Beach" clothes the past in images that prepare us for a gloomy fate, posing an immersion in the tenderness of the present moment as our only escape. With past time as our burden, the fragility of the joy of life is revealed. Between past and present, the poem installs literary imagination as a gateway. It suggests that the imagination is our only way to achieve true happiness in an ignorant world. It is a sharing of this experience with our loved ones, who are similarly capable of imaginative understanding: "knowledge, shaped by the well-educated imagination, leads to understanding, understanding to empathy, and empathy to true love" in the face of the imminent threat to intricate happiness from outside (Lancashire 4).

Arnold's "ignorant armies clash[ing] by night" (the poem is printed in full as an appendix to the novel) are omnipresent as peripheral omens in *Saturday*: the anti-war marchers, the armies preparing an invasion, the ominous presence of al Qaeda, the mentally deranged and drug addicts populating the streets of London. In the face of all this chaos, what is left to rely on is secluded happiness. This should justify Perowne's resolve to refrain from opening his consciousness to the other outside his immediate circle. Such an awareness comes without guarantees, amounts to an even greater risk in already threatening times. Therefore, instead of extending one's own consciousness, an inward move is opted for. And this retreat is what literature promises here: it offers consolation and redemption.

This, finally, leads us back to McEwan's views of the novel: the "love" that the world lacks in Arnold's poem is associated with the empathic imagination that was juxtaposed to the terrorists' "fanatical certainty, misplaced religious faith, and dehumanising hatred" (McEwan, "Only"). The emphasis on love at a personal level in the absence of divine intervention is *Saturday*'s ethical answer: it is a simple, "pure" ethics answering to a complex, messy, impure status quo. Arnold's poem stages a persistent liberal humanist fantasy that has not lost its power: the fantasy of withdrawal. This celebration of the present is invoked in Perowne's operation on Baxter, when he finds himself in a state of serenity, "delivered into a pure present, free of the weight of the past or any anxieties about the future" (*Saturday* 258).

If this is the world view that triumphs in *Saturday*, it does so through an evasion of the original threat posed — the spectacle of the planes Perowne sees through his bedroom window at the outset — and the subsequent installment of a substitute threat that is finally overcome. As most critics have noted, *Saturday* is far more about 9/11 than we are led to believe: Baxter, "a man who believes he has no future and is therefore free of consequences" (ibid., 210), allegorically evokes the hijackers (Sharp 39), as "a kind of echo of the hatred and anger of the disenfranchised, militant, impoverished Third World" (Siegel 34). Baxter's vengefulness for Perowne's prosperity and health, culminating in an attack on his family, is the equivalent of anti-Western sentiment culminating in "an attack on our whole way of living" (*Saturday* 32). He is a relatively manageable opponent by comparison (driven by defect genes instead of beliefs). If Baxter is indeed a stand-in for a bigger threat, this only reinforces the fantasy-character of bestowing on him imaginative faculties and aesthetic sense. In that case, the novel seems to carry out a strategic, but grave, evasion. The concretization and personalization of a greater cultural climate of anxiety provides an opportunity for sidestepping the original ethical issues at stake. As Susan Sontag claims,

> [a]ll modern wars [...] are cast as clashes of civilizations — culture wars — with each side claiming the high ground and characterizing the other as barbaric. The enemy is invariably a threat to "our way of living," an infidel, a desecrator, a polluter, a defiler of higher or better values. The current war against the very real threat posed by militant Islamic fundamentalism is a particularly clear example. Terrorism is now conflated with barbarism. (Sontag 196–197)

This is precisely what *Saturday* effectuates by redeeming Baxter with poetry. The real, eluded other haunting this novel remains barbaric, inhuman, deprived of imagination, and incapable of love. Therefore, there is no need to attempt to *respond* to this other, to enter into a dialogue with him. The curiosity we may feel toward him, with Perowne, is one of theoretical apprehension. There is no *phronesis* because there is no attempt at fusing our horizon with his. Instead, the author, by way of his protagonist, has effectively transposed his own horizon, involving the universalizing demand of "imagination," into the abnormal other. McEwan has set up a *deus ex machina* of the redemptive power of poetry to bring across the point that Baxter, unlike the 9/11 hijackers, does not lack imagination: "He isn't an Arab after all" (Sharp 15). But when evil is a lack of imagination, giving the source of evil the capability to imaginatively respond to art makes for a consolation that, in the context of 9/11, is phantasmatic.

In this decision to conclude a novel that stages the ethical complexities of our contemporary world with a contrived enactment of consolation and redemption, McEwan inadvertently draws attention to the fallibility of his conception of ethics. "Stylistically," Dominic Head argues, "the novel makes a bold attempt to engage with the immediacy of human consciousness, and it is in this way that *Saturday* finally stakes a claim to a share of the ethical high ground on behalf of the literary intervention" (Head 98). But since it offers the reader a "slice of mind" of a normative, empowered character, the limits of this project become apparent. Such a novel could hardly have been written from the perspective of a Baxter or an Arab extremist. If what separates us from zealous barbarians is our ability to imagine ourselves in the position of others, it would be far more vital to explore the minds of such characters.

Where Perowne has trouble dealing with the complexity, the lack of purity and harmony of the world as compared to abstract art or science, McEwan ultimately falls into the same trap in creating a self-enclosed, perfectly balanced story out of its heterogeneous material. In his linkage of aesthetics to neurosurgery, and in his attempt to make one mind transparent, to make us live vicariously through the imagination, he finds a way of not having to deal with the essential opacity of otherness. His desire for symmetry goes against singularity. Parallel to Perowne's recognition of *the same* in Baxter, of a generic humanity, we are given a character to whom we can relate for reasons of recognition: to guilt and anxiety, for instance. *Saturday* gives us what we want, as John Banville has noted: it was well-received by Western readers who are reassured at a time when they are "shaken in [their] sense of themselves and their culture" (Banville 27). Ironically, a novel about the imagination's triumph over ethical complexities loses itself in fantasy.

Conclusion

Our reading of *Saturday* ends on a critical note. Still, because this fantasy is incapable of answering to the "real" anxieties informing it, something valuable is revealed about the shortcomings of McEwan's faith in love and the imagination as the consoling power of literature. These redemptive values seem an oversimplified answer to the ethical complexities of the post-9/11 world he has so subtly and intricately captured in his book. We are reminded of Ulrich Beck's analysis of the destruction of the World Trade Center, in which he notes that the West lacks the language to accurately describe it. Yet the event, a sure sign of globalization, also signifies a "global community of fate" to which humanity is now bound (Beck, "Terrorist" 42). Elsewhere, Beck talks about the fundamental term he wants to attach to the cosmopolitan perspective, with which he leads us back to Gadamer: that of the *dialogic imagination*. "By this," Beck notes, "I mean the clash of cultures and rationalities within one's own life, the 'internalized other'. The dialogic imagination corresponds to the coexistence of rival ways of life in the individual experience" (Beck, "Cosmopolitan" 18).

By contrast, dissecting the brain as a metaphor for mapping psychological motivations, both linked to a pure, abstract aesthetics, does not entail a transformation of the self. Nothing of the self is gambled by the neurosurgeon, nor by the moral agent imagining what it would be like to be another. More than ever, the contemporary world demands an acknowledgement of the *opacity* of the other, the *impossibility* of fully penetrating the other's consciousness.① This is precisely the point that Gadamer makes: recognition in the face of strangeness demands that we do not dissolve the hermeneutic circle but "fully realize" it (Gadamer 293). It is no coincidence that Perowne fails in this mission when McEwan, having chosen the easiest "other" at hand, a "barely-other," as his focal point, needs a structural manipulation to complete his mission.

As we have seen, McEwan's novel offers a poignant reflection on the current state of ethical anxiety, and on a thoroughly ambivalent, complex global situation in which politics and ethics are concerned. It also offers an insightful illustration of the fact that the extension of empathy is not as easy as it might sound. Perowne's attempt to come to a true understanding of his opponent in the novel is described as an effort towards empathy. He almost literally asks McEwan's question in *The Guardian*, "What if it was me?" He construes a narrative of Baxter's life and fills in the gaps with his own memories and fears, only to accomplish a recognition of a general humanity. He does not "discover" what this man "is like inside," as Todorov's account of empathy went. We have argued that such a discovery is impossible to begin with, due to the opacity of otherness. The ethical effect to which this attempt at empathy finally

---

① Making an analogous point in the field of translation studies, Emily Apter in *The Translation Zone* (2006) precisely critiques such optimistic humanist notions that one can translate a "source text" in a transparent and straightforward fashion, arguing, by contrast, that translation is non-transparent, opaque.

amounts is a balancing deed, a restoration of symmetry.

On a second level, the reader has been invited to inhabit a "slice" of the mind of Perowne, a rich, educated Western-European plagued by global guilt and ethical confusion — a mind probably not utterly alien to the average reader of McEwan. Due to the exclusive focalization of events through Perowne, his opponent remains a one-sided figure, a flat character. Baxter lives a sentence, he is to be pitied, he is unpredictable and dangerous, but can be easily overcome due to his lack of cultural education. What is more grave, the real, eluded other haunting this novel is inscribed as *beyond* empathy, as not deserving of an empathic response, as inhuman.

What does all this tell us about the ethical project of empathically inhabiting the mind of another, of projecting the self in her situation in order to come to as comprehensive and full-fledged an understanding as possible of this person, her stories and motivations? Empathic identification is filling in the gaps in your understanding of the other by projecting your*self*, your *own* memories and feelings into them. This ultimately entails an attempt at understanding based on a recognition of sameness, incorporating the other into the same, reducing the other to the self. In *Civilization and its Discontents*, Freud has phrased it in the following way: "We shall always tend to view misery objectively, that is to project ourselves, with all our demands and susceptibilities, into their conditions, and then try to determine what occasions for happiness or unhappiness we should find in them" (Freud 130). This mode of perception is blind to variation in subjective sensitivity, and "substitutes our own mental state for all others, of which we know nothing" (ibid., 131). Similarly, when we transfer feelings of empathy from an aesthetic object to an actual human and ask "what if it was me?", the self remains firmly placed in the center of its consciousness. We cannot "map" the psyche of the other.

In this chapter we have therefore offered an alternative perspective by operationalizing Gadamer's dialogical hermeneutics to rethink the notion of intercultural and interpersonal empathy with the literary text or the character — and, by extension, the other. Ethical critics like Nussbaum, Carroll, and Todorov argue for the ethical benefits of imaginatively placing the self in the position of the other. We have critiqued such views for performing a *reduction*: of otherness and difference to sameness and symmetry, and of singularity to generality. Often, this act of imagining the story of the other by finding similarities, points of convergence, amounts to a recognition of universal humanity in an attempt at understanding by incorporating the other into the same. With reference to the Appendix on "Intercultural Concepts of Identity" in this volume, an analogy suggests itself with the concept of universalization for participants in the context of an intercultural exchange, as developed in the theory of intercultural personhood. But as we have stressed throughout our critical close reading of McEwan's novel, symmetrical harmonies are unlikely to be found where subjectivities are concerned.

Gadamer, by contrast, began by pointing out the limits of such an enterprise. He precisely foregrounds the difference, the gap between interpreter and other. He does not suggest that we simply transpose ourselves into the horizon of the text. He compares this to a particular kind of conversation: one has only to get to know the other, no agreement is sought, and horizons cannot coalesce. When confronted with unfamiliar phenomena (and we have suggested throughout that this applies to cultural artefacts, literary characters, and human beings), understanding can only be attained in a dialogue, a productive conversation in which the other is able to talk back. This entails making the self, the familiar, strange, as much as familiarizing oneself with the other's viewpoint. By interpreting a text, we get the chance to question our own prejudices, which are requisite for any productive interpretative act. These can only come into view when they are provoked by a text or an "other" that addresses us in its strangeness or unintelligibility. The dialogical fusion of horizons renders the familiar (our own horizon, codes, traditions) strange.

We have argued that encountering the (historical or cultural) "other," rather than transplanting her into an instantly recognizable horizon, entails a recognition of *distance* and an immersion into this other's strangeness, in the hope that we may understand differently. In this manner, intercultural hermeneutics can become a space of vacillation, an *in-between*, through which we ideally gain a better and more profound understanding: not only of the text but also of ourselves and our own cultural contexts.

References

Apter, Emily. *The Translation Zone: A New Comparative Literature*. Princeton & Oxford: Princeton UP, 2006.
Banville, John. "A Day in the Life." [Review of *Saturday*.] *New York Review of Books* 26 May 2005. Web. 15 Apr. 2010.

Beck, Ulrich. "The Cosmopolitan Society and Its Enemies." *Theory, Culture & Society* 19.1–2 (2002): 17–44. Web. 25 Mar. 2017.

—. *The Cosmopolitan Vision*. Cambridge: Polity P, 2006.

—. "The Terrorist Threat." *Theory, Culture & Society* 19.4 (2002): 39–55. Web. 25 Mar. 2017.

Booth, Wayne. *The Company We Keep: An Ethics of Fiction*. Berkeley: U of California P, 1988.

Carroll, Noël. *Beyond Aesthetics: Philosophical Essays*. Cambridge: Cambridge UP, 2001.

—. "Moderate Moralism versus Moderate Autonomism." *The British Journal of Aesthetics* 38 (1998): 419–424.

Cooke, Simon. "'Unprofitable Excursions': On the Ethics of Empathy in Modernist Discourses on Art and Literature." *Ethics in Culture*. Eds. Astrid Erll, Herbert Grabes and Ansgar Nünning. Berlin: Walter de Gruyter, 2008. 153–170.

Currie, Gregory. "Realism of character and the value of fiction." *Aesthetics and Ethics: Essays at the Intersection*. Ed. Jerrold Levinson. Cambridge: Cambridge UP, 1998. 161–181.

Derrida, Jacques. "The Gift of Death." *The Gift of Death & Literature in Secret*. Trans. David Willis. Chicago: U of Chicago P, 2008 [1999].

Fine, Robert. *Cosmopolitanism*. New York: Routledge, 2007.

Freud, Sigmund. *Civilization and its Discontents*. Trans. David McLintock. London: Penguin Classics, 2001.

Gadamer, Hans-Georg. *Truth and Method*. 2nd ed., trans. Joel Weinsheimer and Donald G. Marshall. London & New York: Continuum, 2004 [orig. 1960].

Glissant, Edouard. *Poetics of Relation*. Trans. Betsy Wing. Ann Arbor: U of Michigan P, 1997.

Hadley, Elaine. "On a Darkling Plain: Victorian Liberalism and the Fantasy of Agency." *Victorian Studies* 48.1 (2006): 92–102.

Head, Dominic. *Ian McEwan*. Manchester: Manchester UP, 2007.

Kearney, Richard. "Ethics of the Infinite." Interview with Emmanuel Levinas. *States of Mind: Dialogues with Contemporary Thinkers*. New York: New York UP, 1995. 47–70.

Lancashire, Ian. "Commentary to Matthew Arnold's 'Dover Beach.'" 2009. Web. 1 Apr. 2010.http://rpo.library.utoronto.ca/poem/89.html.

McEwan, Ian. "Only love and then oblivion: Love was all they had to set against their murderers." *The Guardian* 15 Sept. 2001. Web. 15 Apr. 2010.

—. *Saturday*. London: Vintage, 2006 [2005].

Marotta, Vince. "Intercultural Hermeneutics and the Cross-Cultural Subject." *Journal of Intercultural Studies* 30.3 (2009): 267–284.

Nussbaum, Martha C. *Love's Knowledge: Essays on Philosophy and Literature*. New York: Oxford UP, 1990.

—. *Poetic Justice: The Literary Imagination and Public Life*. Boston: Beacon P, 1995.

—. *Upheavals of Thought: the Intelligence of the Emotions*. Cambridge: Cambridge UP, 2001.

Sharp, Ellis. "Barbaric Document: The Politics of Ian McEwan's Saturday." May 2006. Web. 15 Apr. 2010. http://barbaricblogspot.com/2005/02/politics-of-mcewans-saturday_04.html.

Siegel, Lee. "The Imagination of Disaster." [Review of *Saturday*.] *The Nation* 280.14 (24 Mar. 2005). Web. 5 Apr. 2010.

Sontag, Susan. "Literature Is Freedom" (The Friedenspreis Acceptance Speech 2004). *At the Same Time: Essays and Speeches*. Eds. Paolo Dilonardo and Anne Jump. London: Hamish Hamilton, 2007. 192–209.

Todorov, Tzvetan. "What is literature for?" *New Literary History* 38 (2007): 13–32.

Vervaet, Steven. Interview with McEwan. *Humo*. Web. http://www.rpe.ugent.be/Vervaet.html.

Wall, Kathleen. "Ethics, Knowledge, and the Need for Beauty: Zadie Smith's *On Beauty* and Ian McEwan's *Saturday*." *University of Toronto Quarterly* 77.2 (2008): 757–788.

Xie, Ming, ed. *The Agon of Interpretations: Towards a Critical Intercultural Hermeneutics*. U of Toronto P, 2014.

Appendix

Matthew Arnold, "Dover Beach" < https://rpo.library.utoronto.ca/poems/dover-beach#22>

1 The sea is calm to-night.
2 The tide is full, the moon lies fair
3 Upon the straits; — on the French coast the light
4 Gleams and is gone; the cliffs of England stand,
5 Glimmering and vast, out in the tranquil bay.
6 Come to the window, sweet is the night-air!
7 Only, from the long line of spray
8 Where the sea meets the moon-blanch'd land,
9 Listen! you hear the grating roar
10 Of pebbles which the waves draw back, and fling,
11 At their return, up the high strand,
12 Begin, and cease, and then again begin,
13 With tremulous cadence slow, and bring
14 The eternal note of sadness in.

15 Sophocles long ago
16 Heard it on the Ægean, and it brought
17 Into his mind the turbid ebb and flow
18 Of human misery; we
19 Find also in the sound a thought,
20 Hearing it by this distant northern sea.

21 The Sea of Faith
22 Was once, too, at the full, and round earth's shore
23 Lay like the folds of a bright girdle furl'd.
24 But now I only hear
25 Its melancholy, long, withdrawing roar,
26 Retreating, to the breath

27 Of the night-wind, down the vast edges drear
28 And naked shingles of the world.

29 Ah, love, let us be true
30 To one another! for the world, which seems
31 To lie before us like a land of dreams,
32 So various, so beautiful, so new,
33 Hath really neither joy, nor love, nor light,
34 Nor certitude, nor peace, nor help for pain;
35 And we are here as on a darkling plain
36 Swept with confused alarms of struggle and flight,
37 Where ignorant armies clash by night.

Appendix

Appendix

Introductory Explanation

Michael STEPPAT and Steve J. KULICH

Some if not most of this volume's readers are likely to be more familiar with literary studies than with intercultural research. Accordingly, they may hardly be acquainted with recent developments in the fields of intercultural study, which have been explored and presented in many influential publication outlets across the globe and also in previous volumes in this series. It may therefore be helpful to provide a brief and introductory overview of a few such developments, ones which we believe have a considerable potential for a better understanding of literary works that depict encounters across cultures.

Working together across two continents, Mine Krause and Shen Weiwei, who are at home in both disciplinary fields, have chosen to highlight especially identity theories for this purpose, as a starting point, not only because theories with this focus have played a prominent role in previous volumes but also because they are currently turning out, as some chapters in this volume show, to be suitable for casting new light on problems of literary analysis. On the wide terrain of intercultural communication, there are nonetheless still further identity concepts, beyond which one can easily find numerous other theories and topics that may well prove to have methodological value for the study of literary works in various genres. No single essay could attempt to do justice to all such possible avenues of inquiry.

While this volume's readers may be well acquainted with many branches of the world's literary canon, and very likely with the problematic nature of any canon formation, the development in recent decades not only of what can be called intercultural literature but especially of a dynamic and rapidly maturing body of theory as framework for the analysis of such literature may not be so familiar. For this reason, a short overview of the development aims to give an introductory insight. Like the identity concepts, this is an ongoing process, which we can expect to reveal new facets and grow further branches in the years ahead.

The two Appendix sections have points of correspondence with the volume's individual chapters, but they are also designed to suggest further perspectives. Because of their introductory quality, they may be taken on their own, offering some elementary insights into important developments as well as the common ground between intercultural and literary study.

Intercultural Concepts of Identity

Mine KRAUSE
(Paris)

SHEN Weiwei Vivian
(Hangzhou Medical College and Shanghai
International Studies University)

Some Themes of "Culture"

This brief appendix attempts to suggest the potential usefulness of selected identity theories in Intercultural Communication for the purposes of literary study. Intercultural Communication can be defined as a symbolic exchange process whereby individuals from two or more different cultural communities negotiate shared meanings in an interactive situation (see Ting-Toomey, 2007 ed., 16–17). Over the past three decades, the field of Intercultural Communication in the U.S. and Europe has seen a proliferation of theories, research methods, and concomitant paradigms. In China, this field has developed even faster in recent years, and scholars have found that the study of Intercultural Communication has witnessed a history of booming growth (see, for instance, Peng and Sun).

Before we introduce some selected identity theories in the context of Intercultural Communication, it is important to clarify what "culture" is — not only because culture is often considered the core of Intercultural Communication, but because it is the context where identity is formed and constructed, immersed and situated. The important connection between culture and identity studies becomes especially salient in the age of globalization. Renowned anthropologist Bronislaw Malinowski has considered culture as "the most central problem of all social science" (588); indeed, as Raymond Williams finds, "[i]t played a crucial role in definitions of 'the arts' and 'the humanities'" (17). According to Kroeber and Kluckhohn's classic and comprehensive study of definitions of culture in 1952, which collected and analyzed most of the existing definitions, at the time we already had 164 representative definitions of culture, and more than 300 identified definitions that carry similar meanings (149). It is clear, then, that "culture is flexible in its usage and defined in a number of different ways" (Rosaldo x). Culture is an elusive and dynamic concept that takes on different shades of meanings and a variety of components. Consequently, a singular definition of culture is not advisable because any one definition turns out to be too restrictive (see Baldwin and Lindsley).

Martin and Nakayama summarize three different approaches to definitions of culture, as illustrated in the chart below. Among the three approaches, the social science/functional approach is of major significance in this field: "Positivist views and treatment of intercultural communication continue to dominate our field's academic journals while critical scholars have been forced to seek alternative outlets [...]" (Moon 44–45). Therefore, most intercultural studies need support from empirical and positivist research for solid evidence, and unlike the literary discipline, purely critical thinking and observation will not, in many cases, be readily accepted in this context.

Three Perspectives on Defining Culture

Social Science/functional	Interpretive/anthropological	Critical
Culture is: Learned and shared Patterns of Perception	Learned and shared Contextual symbolic meanings	Heterogeneous, Dynamic Site of Contested meanings
Source: Adapted from Martin and Nakayama (86)		

Martin and Nakayama (86–90) describe social science scholars (mostly psychologists and sociologists) as identifying cultural variations and recognizing cultural differences in many aspects of communication, but not often considering conceptualizations of culture. Interpretive researchers (such as anthropologists and sociolinguists) emphasize that communication should be examined for the influence of cultural context. Critical scholars recognize the power to communicate as a significant factor in shaping culture, as well as the contested nature of cultural boundaries. However, Dreama G. Moon describes what used to be a "general devaluation" of critical paradigms from the perspective of "traditional" scholarship (Moon 44–45). At any rate, the three perspectives are equally important for us to see the landscape of Intercultural Communication more clearly, since they can help us analyze and interpret literary works by borrowing fruitful developments therefrom.

Building on Kroeber and Kluckhohn's classic volume in 1952, Faulkner, Baldwin, et al. (30) identify seven main themes of different definitions of "culture" as:

A. a structure or patterns, in terms of a system or framework of elements (e.g., ideas, values, behavior, symbol systems, or organizational forms or any combination of these).

B. a "function" theme that sees culture as a tool for achieving some end such as adapting or surviving or controlling a different group.

C. a process, with definitions that focus on the ongoing social construction of culture and the practice of sense-making or of relating to Others.

D. a product of meaningful activity, such as art or architecture. This embraces products of representation/signification, like artifacts and cultural "texts" that are mediated or otherwise.

E. refinement/"cultivation": Forms of moral progress, with stages of development that divide the civilized from the savage; or the study of perfection through civilization. This includes instruction, the care that is given to development of the mind, and refinement (e.g., of a person).

F. group membership such as country, or social variations among components of pluralistic societies of our time.

G. power/ideology, with political and ideological dominance. This definition is commonly used for purposes of critical Intercultural Communication studies. It may also include awareness of a fragmentation of elements, a theme often found in postmodernist scholars' research.

Many themes of culture have been widely acknowledged, though not all have been studied in equal depth. A brief overview of reconceptualizations of culture is offered by Kulich and Weng (16–17). Cultural identity formation under conditions of the capitalist era and of a consumer society has been less often the concern of Intercultural Communication. A rewarding field of inquiry is the relationship between cultural identity and performativity (see Fine and Speer, Njogu, Wyer et al.).

Identity theories and their conclusions that are drawn from functional/social science as well as from interpretive and critical approaches tend to be somewhat different from received literary identity concepts. Many intercultural theories are multi-/inter-disciplinary empirical studies from disciplines like intercultural psychology, sociology, communication, and sometimes gender studies. Since literary theories have absorbed concepts not only from social sciences, such as psychoanalysis, sociology, and psychology, but also from fields such as anthropology, cultural studies, gender studies, and a range of others, it might be meaningful to relate the different but connected disciplines to each other, perhaps even hybridize them, by exploring their commonalities.

In the following, we will briefly summarize some influential identity theories developed in the context of Intercultural Communication that may prove useful for the analysis of identity problems in intercultural literary texts.

I. Identity Management Theory

Identity Management Theory (IMT) was first developed by William Cupach and Tadasu Imahori in 1993. Focusing on face and face-work, Cupach and Imahori argue that the way individuals present "face" (signifying a socially situated identity) reveals aspects of their identity, while identity is relational (with relational partners) as well as cultural. Maintaining face appears as a natural and inevitable condition of human interaction, and intercultural communication competence should include an individual's ability to negotiate mutually acceptable identities in interaction successfully (116). IMT suggests that people manage their identities in various ways at different junctures of relationships. The theory proposes that there are three highly interdependent and cyclical phases of intercultural relationships which are based on unique features of identity management in each phase: trial, enmeshment, and re-negotiation. Cupach and Imahori assume that intercultural competence goes and develops through these phases. The first phase consists of "trial-and-error" processes of finding identities, in which communicators share some similarities. The second phase involves enmeshment of individuals' identities into "a mutually acceptable and convergent relational identity, in spite of the fact that their cultural identities are still divergent" (ibid., 125). The third phase involves the increased ability of intercultural communicators to work out face problematics and dialectics based on a salient relational identity, accompanied by increased symbolic and rule convergence (see Imahori and Cupach 205). Cupach and Imahori state that the three phases are "cyclical." This reminds us of Young Yun Kim's "stress, adaptation, and growth dynamics" which communicators go through to become "intercultural," which we will introduce further below.

Such dynamic/cyclical phases can be observed in mother-daughter relations as presented in several Asian American novels. Since several Asian American novels vividly describe family conflicts between a Chinese-born mother and an American-born daughter, we can speak of value discrepancy and cultural conflict.

> For example, Maxine Hong Kingston's *The Woman Warrior* has spawned a new sub-genre of Asian American fiction: matrilineage (see Grice). The novel is a collection of memoirs by the "I" narrator in five chapters, each of which features a story by her mother. At the beginning, the narrator recounts the first of the stories her mother once told her, and at this time both communicators are trying to find their commonalities and differences. This is a "trial-and-error" process. Then, a cultural conflict arises when the narrator cries out to her parents that she is not going to be the girl they would arrange her to be, as she would not care about her mother's opinion because she is adopting American values. Eventually the narrator comes to terms with her mother after hearing more about her background, trying to understand the culture of her time. In this segment, a "re-negotiation" of the cultural identity can be observed. Since the publication of *The Woman Warrior*, more fiction about maternity has appeared, most of which includes a focus on mother-daughter relationships. Amy Tan's *The Joy Luck Club* (1989), Canadian Chinese writer Sky Lee's *Disappearing Moon Café* (1990), and Gish Jen's *Mona in the Promised Land* (1996) all belong to this kind.

II. Critical and Interpretive Cultural Identity Negotiation Theory

Mary Collier's Cultural Identity Negotiation Theory (CINT) aims to build knowledge about the communicative processes that individuals use to construct and negotiate their cultural group identities and relationships in particular contexts. Early versions of the theory, when it was named "Cultural Identity Theory," emphasized an interpretive theoretical perspective, social construction, and individuals' discursive accounts of experiences. Collier's aim is to learn how to increase the number and quality of relationships that can promote inclusion and social justice. Focusing mainly on marginalized and underprivileged groups, namely South African groups and gender issues in the U.S., the major methodology Collier adopts is critical discourse analysis as well as a postcolonial approach. She endeavors to fuse the interpretive and critical approaches in her work. Thus, after 2000 CINT became broadened to incorporate a critical perspective and to draw attention to contextual structures, ideologies, and status hierarchies (see Collier's articles, but also Myers and Collier, Thompson and Collier). This is why "negotiation" has become a key term included in the concept. The critical approach as employed here uncovers structures of domination and the ways hierarchy is maintained and how it is resisted, in order to indicate means to emancipate those who are unjustly subjugated. Scholars with a critical perspective often investigate discursive means enabling ideologies of oppression: "This is partly a matter of how power relations are exercised and negotiated in discourse" (Fairclough and Wodak 272).

Collier defines culture as dynamic, communal, and contested group identifications that emerge as shared locations of speaking, acting, and producing. She believes that cultural identifications are co-created with others through interaction. Individuals have a range of cultural identities that may perform in the interaction, including national, racial, ethnic, class-related, sex- and gender-based, political, religious, and others. The cultural identities are contingent, contextualized, and they are temporary. They are also sculpted through institutional policies and practices, disciplined by social norms; they implicate and are implicated by issues of power and ideology since all discourses are enacted within relations of power (see West). In social interaction, individuals come to be culturally identified through social conduct, in relationship to and with others who have similar but also different locations. This identification occurs within complex contexts in which histories, institutions, ideologies, laws, economic circumstances, political policies, and organizational practices are influential.

Stressing the role of contextual negotiation of multiple identities and relationships, Collier's more recent theory development highlights the material and social consequences of cultural identity negotiation, and increasingly turns attention to concerns with social equality and justice. Collier proposes that cultural identities are negotiated within a social context, and are affected not only by historical events and political conditions but also by such considerations as who is present and the situation or site of interaction or public discourse. CINT thus wants to show how political histories and governmental or institutional actions are described by representatives of marginalized and privileged groups. The concept aims to uncover systems of oppression as well as to transform oppressive structures, institutions, and relationships (Collier, "Cultural" 262).

> Bharati Mukherjee's *Jasmine* tells the story of an Indian girl Jasmine who has come to America with a beautiful American dream. However, suffering from her illegal existence, she is forced to flee from East Florida to Iowa, and finally toward the Western coast, where she eventually finds her home. In the narrative, issues such as gender, identities, and power relations create cultural conflicts, acculturative stress, stereotypes, sexual and racial discrimination imposed in the course of Jasmine's seeking a new home, as she fights for equal rights and seeks to negotiate a new citizenship. She suffers from mistreatments and inequality, but never stops fighting for her new life. She negotiates with her social environment, with world views and values, and eventually succeeds in hybridizing cultures and fusing Self with Other. Meanwhile, in the process of her identity negotiation, her intercultural communication competence improves and her capacity for adaptation grows.

III. Identity Negotiation Theory

Identity negotiation was first proposed by psychologist William B. Swann. While the negotiation of identity is a general concept that has been in existence for as long as there have been intergroup and interpersonal differences, Identity Negotiation Theory (INT) was proposed by Stella Ting-Toomey. INT proposes that identity is viewed as an explanatory mechanism for the intercultural communication process, as reflective self-images that are constructed, experienced, and communicated by individuals within a culture and in a particular interaction situation. The concept of negotiation is defined as a transactional interaction process whereby individuals in an intercultural situation attempt to assert, define, modify, challenge, and/or support their own and others' desired self-images (see Ting-Toomey, 1999 ed., 40). A communicator attempts to evoke her/his own desired identity in the interaction; s/he also attempts to challenge or support the other's desired identity. Ting-Toomey also adapts the concept of "mindful" (as against "mindless") stereotyping for her purpose, understood as a learned process of "cognitive focusing" which leaves room for a person's willingness to change loosely held images. Ting-Toomey makes several assumptions in constructing INT: cultural variability influences the sense of self; self-identification involves security as well as vulnerability; identity boundary regulation, which motivates behavior, involves a tension between inclusion and differentiation. Additionally, managing the dialectic of inclusion and differentiation influences the coherent sense of self, which in turn has an impact on individuals' resourcefulness in communicating — i. e., "the knowledge and ability to apply cognitive, affective, and behavior resources appropriately, effectively, and creatively in diverse interaction situations" (Ting-Toomey, "Communicative" 74).

Inspired by INT, Ronald Jackson developed his "Cultural Contracts Theory" and defines the negotiation of cultural identity as

> a bargaining process in which two or more individuals consider the exchange of ideas, values, and beliefs. [...] *Negotiation of cultural identity* is a process in which one considers the gain, loss, or exchange of their ability to interpret their own reality or worldview. (*Negotiation* 10)

Intercultural relationships may or (alternatively) may not be coordinated, depending on the dynamics involved such as power relations, boundaries, cultural loyalty, group identification, maturity, and related factors. The cultural contracts paradigm that Jackson proposes seeks to make sense of identity effects or outcomes as necessary end products of identity negotiation. He distinguishes three contract typologies: ready-to-sign contract (assimilation), quasi-completed contract (adaptation), or co-created contract (mutual valuation). Generally, identity negotiation involves a conscious and mindful process of shifting one's worldview and/or cultural behaviors. Gish Jen's *Mona in the Promised Land*, her second novel, relates a range of intra-family identity negotiation processes, as discussed in Shen's chapter in this volume.

IV. Intercultural Personhood

Living between cultures sooner or later naturally leads to various kinds of identity crisis. Especially in the last decades, this topic has also become of particular interest in the field of literature. In certain cases, the attachment to and identification with one's own cultural roots gradually loses importance during the integration process. However, there are also cases in which the exact opposite is true: a clinging to one's customs and traditions can sometimes be observed when one fears a confrontation with a different culture.

There are several theories explaining the reactions that are triggered by the sensation of cultural in-betweenness. One of them is the concept of "intercultural personhood" (also called "intercultural identity") which was introduced by Young Yun Kim. She describes the state of intercultural personhood as "[...] a way of relating to others that conjoins and integrates, rather than separates and divides" (Kim, "Intercultural Personhood" 405). For Kim, the phenomenon of intercultural identity explains that "as individuals advance in the cross-cultural adaptation process, their identity orientations undergo a gradual and largely unconscious transformation toward less categorical and more complex ones. That is, individuals become better able to see the common humanity among different cultures and ethnicities and locate the points of consent and complementarity beyond obvious difference and contention" (Kim, "Cross-Cultural" 2009). "Intercultural personhood" is based on the "General System Theory" (1968) of Ludwig von Bertalanffy, who argues that all human beings are "open systems" which are flexible and therefore likely to change under certain circumstances: "Every living organism is essentially an open system" (Bertalanffy 39). As such, these systems are able to interact freely with their environment and to evolve, resulting in a non-static and fluid identity. Taking Berry, Kim and Boski's "Theory of intercultural adaptation and adjustment" into account, it seems that reaching the state of intercultural personhood is easiest for integrators who reconstruct their identity in another country while combining traditional as well as new cultural elements.

The ability to engage in intercultural dialogue, i.e., communicating across cultural identity boundaries and eventually transcending them, increases the probability of achieving intercultural personhood. However, in the course of a direct confrontation with other cultures, moments of psychological stress can occur that might favor a regression toward separation or even marginalization. After all, questioning one's own traditions naturally causes a sensation of insecurity. Not without reason, Kim ("Globalization") emphasizes that a development toward intercultural personhood is not linear and smooth but rather characterized by a " stress-adaptation-growth dynamic," alternating phases of acculturation (learning) and deculturation (unlearning), integration and disintegration, as well as progression and regression. Every confrontation with a stressful situation in a foreign culture causes a step back ("draw back").

> Such a "draw back" can be observed for example in Jhumpa Lahiri's novel *The Namesake*. Ashima Ganguli, who once used to tutor schoolchildren in Calcutta and taught them "to pronounce words like *sign* and *cough*" (Lahiri 7), makes a grammar mistake in front of a native speaker, which causes a moment of embarrassment: "Patty smiles, a little too widely, and suddenly Ashima realizes her error, knows she should have said 'fingers' and 'toes'. This error pains her almost as much as her last contraction. [...] in Bengali, a finger can also mean fingers, a toe toes" (Lahiri 7). Nurse Patty's smile obviously makes Ashima feel like a stranger whose linguistic competence (compared to a native speaker's) is not sufficient. Drawbacks like the one described here later on often generate adaptive energy which then results in a "leap forward." Old and new cultural patterns blend and thus lead to a continuous reinventing process of one's own identity.

The term "culture shock," which Kim uses in the context of her "stress-adaptation-growth dynamic," should in our opinion be replaced with John W. Berry's more positive term "acculturative stress." Berry ("Acculturation") explains that the notion of "shock" has rather negative connotations, while the term "culture" suggests that this shock is a reaction to one culture only (cf. Berry 708). However, the expression "acculturation" implies the interaction of at least two cultures. It also includes both positive and negative aspects, thus matching Kim's "stress-adaptation-growth dynamic" with its alternating draw-backs and leap-forwards. In contrast to Berry, Kim describes acculturation as "a process over which each individual has a degree of freedom or control, based on his or her predispositions, pre-existing needs and interests" (Kim, "Globalization" 87). Whether in situations of acculturative stress individuals confronted with another culture are really able to control their identity development is nevertheless rather questionable.

According to Kim's theory, gaining intercultural personhood means being more open-minded, self-aware, and eager for cultural learning while the self-other orientation becomes open-ended, adaptive, and transformative. In other theories (acting on the assumption that human beings are open systems), attributes like "bicultural," "multicultural," "multiethnic," or "hybrid" serve to describe similar identity tendencies. The main difference between these and the concept of intercultural personhood is that the latter focuses on individuation: participants of an intercultural exchange regard themselves and the members of other cultures involved in the interaction as individuals first, and not primarily as members of a group with specific cultural traits. As Kim puts it, they see "[themselves] and others on the basis of unique individual qualities rather than categorical stereotypes" (Kim, "Globalization" 89). This individuation goes hand in hand with the notion of universalization, which highlights common aspects of humanity shared by all human beings in spite of existing cultural differences. This universal element can also be found in other concepts including "multicultural personhood" (Peter Adler) or "hybrid identity" (Homi Bhabha).

Intercultural Communicative Competence

In this context, it seems worth pointing out that intercultural personhood should always be seen in connection with intercultural communicative competence (ICC). ICC is the "ability to communicate and interact across cultural boundaries" (Byram, *Teaching* 7), even though it should be stressed that these boundaries cannot be clearly defined. Michael Byram's Intercultural Competence Model turns out to be useful for the analysis of intercultural interaction. According to Byram and Fleming, language and culture are inseparable notions. "Language learning is culture learning" (Byram and Fleming 42), so that both need to be taught together. In Khaled Hosseini's novel *And the Mountains Echoed*, we find the following observation about the relation between language and culture: "[Abdullah] said that if culture was a house, then language was the key to the front door, to all the rooms inside. Without it, he said, you ended up wayward, without a proper home or a legitimate identity" (Hosseini 417). By explaining the meaning of words, proverbs, idiomatic expressions, dialects, language registers, and the like, one needs to provide cultural knowledge as well: "The language holds the culture through the denotations and connotations of its semantics" (Byram and Fleming 94).

In Byram's model (see *Teaching* 34), the following elements are taken into consideration: skills (interpreting and relating, discovering and interacting), knowledge (of self and other, interaction, individual and societal), education (political and cultural), attitudes (the ability to relativize the self and to value the Other). According to this approach, certain attitudes, including openness and curiosity, are necessary to successfully engage in intercultural interaction. At the same time, some kind of self-distance is required in order to see one's own culture from an outsider's point of view. Kohlberg et al.

call this skill "decentering," a stage that facilitates understanding other cultures. Byram also stresses that the ability to "decenter," i.e., to perceive one's own and other cultures from an insider's and outsider's point of view and question the values and beliefs that come with them, is an important step in the process of intercultural learning and communication. His notion of "tertiary socialisation" that helps "learners to understand new concepts (beliefs, values and behaviors) through the acquisition of a new language" should also be considered in this context. The new insights provided here "challenge the taken-for-granted nature of their existing concepts" (Byram, *From Foreign* 113 f.), and make foreigners acquire intercultural competence while interacting with native interlocutors.

By learning more about other cultures, the distance between "us" and "them" — despite possible temporal regressions in the identity development — is gradually reduced, and "the Other" after a while appears less frightening. Ideally, during this development cultural habits are re-examined on both sides. As a result of intercultural exchange, diversity is experienced as enriching. The notion of a "pure" culture is gradually replaced by a blend of religious, ethnic, cultural, and linguistic traditions. Consequently, the cultural boundaries of which Byram speaks (*Teaching*) become so blurred that they could almost be called non-existent. Nevertheless, Kim correctly claims that in spite of this continuous transformation process, the "cultural base of an individual identity is not going to disappear until the end of one's life, even if one wanted to remove it" (Kim, "From Culture" 434).

> Taking this statement into account, certain aspects of the concept of "assimilation" (including losing one's accent, for instance) might need to be revisited. The character development of Mustafa in Elif Shafak's *The Bastard of Istanbul*, for instance, would prove that despite the wish of complete assimilation, certain linguistic reflexes seem to remain that are related to one's original roots (see also Krause's chapters in this volume). Having refused to speak Turkish in America for 20 years, Mustafa is overwhelmed when suddenly confronted with his mother tongue. The language he wanted to "remove" from his life will always be a part of him, despite all his efforts to assimilate. In the case of Magid in Zadie Smith's *White Teeth* (see also Yuan's chapter in this volume), a complete assimilation is also prevented, here by family members. By changing his name from Magid Iqbal to Mark Smith, Magid tries to be "more English than the English" (Smith 406), but his father

Samad always manages to bring him back to reality: "I GIVE YOU A GLORIOUS NAME LIKE MAGID MAHFOOZ MURSHED MUBTASIM IQBAL! ... AND YOU WANT TO BE CALLED MARK SMITH!" (Ibid., 151). Similarly, Gogol in Jhumpa Lahiri's *The Namesake* tries to change his name to Nikhil in order to be called Nick as if he were an ordinary American without an "exotic" background. His attempts to wipe out a part of his identity are only partly successful, since his family keeps reminding him of his origins.

A slightly different case of assimilation can be found in Khaled Hosseini's novel *And the Mountains Echoed*. Timur came from Afghanistan to the United States with his family when he was still a little boy. Like Magid in *White Teeth*, he decides to change his name after a while: "In the States, Timur goes by 'Tim.'" He changes his name after 9/11 and claims that he has nearly doubled his business since" (Hosseini 153f.). When he visits Afghanistan to take care of his family's house, however, he easily turns into "Timur" again and acts as if he had been living in this country all his life. The reasons for his cultural adaptability seem to be rooted in a kind of opportunism. Where the concrete lines of assimilation really lie is questionable here. Taken as a whole, all these instances show that there are various types of assimilation and that complete assimilation is nearly impossible.

Finding a Scale

As pointed out before, Kim's concept of intercultural personhood is of interest because it not only highlights universal, but also individual elements of intercultural identity. According to the author herself, terms like "meta-identity," "cosmopolitan," and "transcultural" identity (Kim, "Globalization" 89) are similar to her idea of intercultural personhood. Xiao-Dong Dai claims that "[a]s soon as people are exposed to other cultures, intercultural personhood begins to germinate." Considering this statement, one of the weak points of Kim's theory (also mentioned by Margaret Jane Pitts) is that she does not make clear how to measure intercultural personhood. In this context, it might be helpful to find out to which degree a person who is regarded as "multicultural" or "hybrid," for example, acquires "intercultural personhood." It should also be clarified whether integrators (as described by Berry, Kim and Boski) do not *per se* already possess a certain degree of "intercultural personhood."

For an adequate measuring, we suggest creating a scale which explains the gradual development toward intercultural personhood stage by stage. This scale should also include the general attributes that are gained and lost at each step, for instance in the language learning process or in the learning and unlearning of certain rituals.

> Gish Jen's Mona in *Mona in the Promised Land*, for example, can be described as a character on the way toward intercultural personhood, since she succeeds in combining different (sometimes even contradictory) cultural elements like Catholic, Jewish, Chinese, and American while reconstructing her identity. The same is true for the character development of the Armenian-American Armanoush in Elif Shafak's *The Bastard of Istanbul* and also of Turkish student Ömer in Elif Shafak's *The Saint of Incipient Insanities*. A similar cultural blend can partly be observed in the character Ashima from Jhumpa Lahiri's *The Namesake*, who wishes "there were mustard oil to pour into the mix." Here, an Indian ingredient like mustard oil is mentioned together with American ingredients like "Rice Krispies and Planters peanuts" (Lahiri 1), all serving as a metaphor for an intercultural mix. With regard to eating culture, the integration process is more or less successful, but drawbacks can still be observed now and then, even during the development toward intercultural personhood. It goes without saying that each character evolution is different, but it might be helpful in certain cases to name the stages toward intercultural personhood by using an adequate scale.

With regard to Kim's concept, Pitts also criticizes that achieving intercultural personhood is presented as something "good and possible for most people" (Pitts 400), but there is no indication of an alternative approach in case the state of intercultural personhood is not reached. As a last problem, Pitts states that Kim's theory does not include enough empirical data. Even though Kim ("Globalization") refers to some empirical studies she carried out in 2001 and adds a few more recent case illustrations (among them intercultural writers and musicians), the examples she gives are not sufficient. Thus it is true that Kim's theory is lacking in certain respects, but it still provides us with insightful information on the dynamic, evolutionary, and transcending nature of identity. Without doubt, her concept is also useful for the analysis of literature, as it can be applied to novels dealing with intercultural conflict situations and the development of a "well-balanced" identity.

> Among the partly aforementioned examples that come to mind in contemporary literature are Zadie Smith's *White Teeth*, Elif Shafak's *The Bastard of Istanbul*, *The Saint of Incipient Insanities*,

and *Honour*, Gish Jen's *Typical American* and *Mona in the Promised Land*, as well as Jhumpa Lahiri's *The Namesake*. Some of the characters in these novels who are characterized by an in-between identity undergo the "stress-adaptation-growth dynamic," with positive or negative outcomes, depending on the case. Now and then, the state of intercultural personhood is reached, generally after a direct confrontation with family roots and the past. How important it is to deal with one's cultural origins is illustrated in Khaled Hosseini's novel *And the Mountains Echoed*: "But it is important to know this, to know your roots. To know where you started as a person. If not, your own life seems unreal to you. Like a puzzle. [...] Like you have missed the beginning of a story and now you are in the middle of it, trying to understand" (Hosseini 410).

Like the concept of Peter Adler, Kim's is based on a constructivist view of cultural communication. In her theory, there seems to be nothing between the individual and the universal perspectives. It is especially the focus on the individual rather than on cultural patterning and historical consciousness that makes Kim's approach interesting, but at the same time maybe also sometimes problematic for the literary analysis of fictional characters who are coping with intercultural identity conflicts. There is a risk of oversimplification, since applying Kim's theory might reduce characters to individual persons, neglecting the fact that "persona" has always been a mask through which another voice speaks. After all, individual consciousness and cultural patterning factors cannot be strictly separated.

Kim's idealistic idea of a self that becomes "stretchable" in an intercultural environment, thus enabling individual internal growth and continuous self-renewal, is at any rate accompanied by more permeable cultural boundaries, which means that with regard to this aspect it goes a step further than Byram's theory. In the age of globalization, new ways must be found to welcome cultural diversity, show empathy in cross-cultural conflict situations, and adapt to different cultural contexts without entirely losing oneself. Kim's concept can be regarded as one of the recent approaches that make it possible to incorporate difference into one's own unique worldview without risking alienation.

Excursus: A Conceptual Dilemma? (SHEN Weiwei Vivian)

Between Intercultural Communication and the study of literature there seems to be a considerable gap, which there has hardly ever been any effort to bridge. But does the gap really exist? There are many intercultural theories that study interactions between people from different cultures or co-cultures. Such interactions happen in our daily life, but also in many literary works that we value. Such literature makes a reader think and feel. It opens a reader's eyes, brings vivid images of another time and place to her or his mind. Though personal and particular, literature of high quality touches something universal, moral, and inspiring that resonates within the minds of readers in many different cultural contexts, like an epiphany. We may understand what Frank R. Leavis called "the Great Tradition" as offering "a reminder of time, and therefore of the possibility of change in a society whose consumerist ethos denies both" (Day 63); Leavis's own critical readings have been said to "refuse the reductions and conformities of mass culture, promoting instead the virtues of multiplicity, complexity and difference" (ibid., 2). At another level, an elementary academic textbook claims that "literature is a way to experience a way of life, a time period, a culture, an emotion, a deed, an event that you are not able, willing [...], or capable of encountering in any other manner" (McGee 2). Are there, embedded in such perceptions, no commonalities with at least some of the concerns of Intercultural Communication? Increasingly, researchers are ignoring traditional disciplinary demarcations. Kettemann and Marko (2003) highlight the transcending of boundaries between literary studies and "media and communication studies, musical studies, sociology, psychology, political science, etc." (13).

But it is not that simple. In the case of Intercultural Communication studies, it is important to be aware that they are supported by empirical studies, making use of such tools as surveys, interviews and questionnaires, and related methods. Scientists in this field need to demonstrate their evidence, especially statistical data; otherwise, they will not be able to prove any hypotheses, theorems, or assumptions. Are not literary analyses, by contrast, based on a reader's perception, and are hence chiefly phenomenological and subjective? Would not such a perception be spurned by any Intercultural Communication expert with social science experience? Such an expert will ask (and has already asked) legitimate questions concerning how one can possibly ensure the validity of any literary analyses, how one can prove any interpretive argument, especially considering that literary works are fictional. This can easily push a reader seeking to gain insights from both fields into a dilemma.

In this situation, the critical approach of Halualani and Nakayama is encouraging. It points incisively to the problems that traditional approaches of Intercultural Communication encounter, and introduce a concept of interculturality that combines all three major intercultural perspectives, the functional, interpretive, and critical (for these, see Martin and Nakayama 51). Halualani and Nakayama call for more studies through a critical lens on topics such as race, language inequalities, local-to-global articulations, diasporas, and much more:

> How do we take the larger collection of critical intercultural communication research, informed by multiple theoretical and perspectival traditions and spread across various fields of communication scholarship and outside disciplines, and engage these works in meaningful and productive dialogue around insights, conclusions, and question-probing and provide these with a deeper, integrated focus to have important metacritical conversations that characterize the continual development of perspectives and forms of scholarship (as even in the case of critical theory, cultural studies work, postcolonial perspectives, feminist studies, among others)? (10)

Perhaps a way can be found, after all, to take a postcolonial perspective together with critical studies of power and hegemony, to enable integrative textual/literary analysis with an intercultural approach to contribute to the scope of critically oriented Intercultural Communication studies. Cannot intercultural issues in literature be clearly and solidly investigated without a necessity for empirical quantification?

Of course, literary study has a long disciplinary history, with its own rich development of analytical methods. Yet it is not so clear whether these address all problems of critical understanding. One might ask, for instance, whether there is anything that current literary identity theories/approaches lack? Are there questions that intercultural identity theories can help answer? Could intercultural theories with a social science orientation contribute at all to a clearer understanding of literary works and their fictional world? Literary study and social science theories do come together at times for a multidisciplinary methodology. For example, as a concept of relevance to Intercultural Communication, "cultural shock" was introduced by U.S. anthropologist Kalervo Oberg to refer to the experience of adjusting to a foreign environment (see also the discussion of this concept above). Since then, social psychologists among others have attempted to identify the basic pattern of cultural shock by means of empirical studies. A W-curve has been devised in that "the sojourner tends to undergo a decline in adjustment shortly after entering a foreign culture, which is followed by a recovery stage with a resultant increase in adjustment; then, on returning home, the sojourner undergoes another decrease in adjustment followed by a second stage of recovery" (Brein and David 216; see also Berry). The experience had been explored at length and with great insight in literary works by authors of international fame. In the English language, Henry James's *The American* (1877), E. M. Forster's *A Passage to India* (1924), and going back in history Shakespeare's *Othello* (1603/1604) are just a few examples of corresponding experiences. Lewis and Jungman have anthologized a collection of short fiction as case studies of culture shock. In another connection, when Sigmund Freud embarked on his research concerning the neuro-system, he did not expect that his theories would be widely accepted in the literary field and even adapted for literary theory. Yet many of his conclusions that were drawn from clinical cases were employed for the understanding of literary works of all genres.

Literary representations of intercultural experience obviously do not meet the predictive methodological requirements of social science. Yet a pattern of mutual correspondence is observable also in the educational field. In many countries high schools, universities, even elementary schools often use selected literary works or popular movies as teaching materials for the purpose of inter-/cross-cultural communication teaching and training, to improve students' intercultural competence and awareness in the era of globalization and to meet requirements of multicultural diversity (see Cai, Fox, Mohammadzadeh, Mekheimer and Aldosari, Pandey; also a number of academic theses). Many scholars have realized the important connection between multicultural literature and Intercultural Communication needs. The purpose of using literature to teach both language and culture is to develop students' intercultural competence (see Savignon, Göbel and Helmke). Mohammadzadeh explains the reason for introducing literature in advanced language teaching as follows:

> Students who use postcolonial reading strategies achieve higher levels of multicultural literacy. [...] When we expose students to multicultural literary texts, we will encourage them to gain a literacy to compare and analyze the cultural viewpoints and values of East and West. [...] When students examine the themes of a multicultural novel or short story, they can connect the various conflicts and

cultural issues which took place between the discourses within a text to the similar conflicts in other pertinent fiction, newspapers, historical texts, and other non-fictional literary texts. Therefore, the texts used in these courses are no longer seen as a work of literary text to be valued only in aesthetic terms, but as a compilation of opposing discourses which are related to conflicts that expand well outside the boundaries of a normal text. (24)

"Students" function as a subgroup of "readers," so that the explanation easily extends beyond the educational domain. In terms of a "knowledge acquisition pathway," Bruno Latour contends that observable reality is closely connected to the form and agency of representation or observation, so that there is never a "gap between representations and reality" (Latour 94). It is very likely that the legitimacy of connecting literature and the analysis of non-fictional experience can be seen in this light.

Theories such as Shalom Schwartz's Cultural Value Orientations or Mark Orbe's and Regina Spellers's Co-cultural Theory, to name just a few, have a suggestive potential for literary interpretation. There is no space here to explore these connections in more detail. If we consider such instances as Stella Ting-Toomey's Identity Negotiation Theory (INT) and Ronald Jackson's Cultural Contract Theory, it is clear that these are intended for intercultural training and intercultural competence improvement, rather than for any literary analysis. They are interpersonal, functional, and also interpretive, and are accordingly supported by empirical research. Literary study has not so far made use of them or any of their branches. But, while remaining fully aware of their non-literary methodology and purpose, one could ask whether they have any adaptable elements and findings as one turns to interculturally oriented literature. In literary representations of cultural interaction, differential power relations are usually diagnosed carefully — while such relations are also an intrinsic part of the intercultural negotiation process. Since Jackson's concepts, standing in for numerous other interculturally communicative approaches, are specially designed for race and ethnic studies, building on Ting-Toomey's INT, it is difficult to see why an innovative doorway should not open toward the needs of fictional analysis.

References

Baldwin, John R., and Sheryl L. Lindsley. *Definitions of Culture: Conceptualizations*

From Five Disciplines. Urban Studies Center, Arizona State U, Tempe, AZ, 1994.

Berry, John W. "Acculturation: Living successfully in two cultures." *International Journal of Intercultural Relations* 29 (2005): 697–712.

Berry, John W., Uichol Kim and Pawel Boski. "Psychological Acculturation of Immigrants." *Cross-cultural Adaptation: Current Approaches*. (International and Intercultural Communication Annual 11.) Eds. Young Yun Kim and William B. Gudykunst. Newbury Park: Sage, 1987. 62–89.

Bertalanffy, Ludwig von. *General System Theory: Foundations, Development, Applications*. New York: George Braziller, 1968. Revised ed. 1973.

Brein, Michael, and Kenneth H. David. "Intercultural Communication and the Adjustment of the Sojourner." *Psychological Bulletin* 76.3 (1971): 215–230.

Byram, Michael. *From Foreign Language Education to Education for Intercultural Citizenship: Essays and Reflections*. Clevedon, Buffalo, Toronto: Multilingual Matters, 2008.

—. *Teaching and Assessing Intercultural Communicative Competence*. Clevedon: Multilingual Matters, 1997.

Byram, Michael, and Michael Fleming, eds. *Language Learning in Intercultural Perspective: Approaches Through Drama and Ethnography*. Cambridge: Cambridge UP, 1998.

Cai, Mingshue. *Multicultural Literature for Children and Young Adults: Reflection on Critical Issues*. Westport, Conn.: Greenwood P, 2002.

Collier, Mary J. "Cultural Identity Theory." *Encyclopedia of Communication Theory*. Eds. Stephen W. Littlejohn and Karen A. Foss. Vol. 1. Thousand Oaks, CA: Sage, 2009. 260–262.

—. "Enacting and Contesting Privilege: Cultural Identifications in South African Focus Group Discourses." *Western Journal of Communication* 69 (2005): 295–318.

—. "Research on Cultural Identity: Reconciling Post-Colonial and Interpretive Approaches." *Cultural Identity and Intercultural Communication*. *International and Intercultural Communication Annual*. Ed. Dolores Tanno. Thousand Oaks, CA: Sage, 1998. 122–147.

—. "Theorizing Cultural Identifications: Critical Updates and Continuing Evolution." *Theorizing about Intercultural Communication*. Ed. William B. Gudykunst. Thousand Oaks, CA: Sage, 2005. 235–256.

—. *Transforming Communication About Culture: Critical New Directions*. Thousand Oaks, CA: Sage, 2002.

Cupach, William R., and Tadasu T. Imahori. "Identity Management Theory: Communication Competence in Intercultural Episodes and Relationships." *Intercultural Communication Competence*. Eds. Richard L. Wiseman and Jolene Koester. Newbury Park, CA: Sage, 1993. 112–131.

Dai, Xiao-Dong. "Intercultural personhood and identity negotiation." *China Media Research* 5.2 (2009). Web. 15 July 2016. http://www.thefreelibrary.com/Intercultural + personhood + and + identity + negotiation.-a0215410902.

Day, Gary. *Re-Reading Leavis: Culture and Literary Criticism*. Houndmills, Basingstoke: Macmillan, 1996.

Fairclough, Norman L., and Ruth Wodak. "Critical Discourse Analysis." *Discourse Studies: A Multidisciplinary Introduction*. Ed. Teun A. van Dijk. Vol. 2. London: Sage, 1997. 258–284.

Faulkner, Sandra L., John R. Baldwin et al. "Layers of Meaning: An Analysis of Definitions of Culture." *Redefining Culture: Perspectives Across the Disciplines*. Eds. John R. Baldwin et al. Mahwah, N.J.: Lawrence Erlbaum, 2006. 27–52.

Fine, Elizabeth C., and Jean H. Speer, eds. *Performance, Culture, and Identity*. Westport, CT: Praeger, 1992.

Fox, Frampton F. "Reducing Intercultural Friction through Fiction: Virtual Cultural Learning." *Intercultural Journal of Intercultural Relations* 27 (2003): 99–123.

Göbel, Kerstin, and Andreas Helmke. "Intercultural Learning in English as Foreign Language Instruction: The Importance of Teachers' Intercultural Experience and the Usefulness of Precise Instructional Directives." *Teaching and Teacher Education: An International Journal of Research and Studies* 26 (2010): 1571–1582.

Grice, Helena. *Negotiating Identities: An Introduction to Asian American Women's Writing*. Manchester: Manchester UP, 2002.

Halualani, Rona Tamiko, and Thomas K. Nakayama. "Critical Intercultural Communication Studies: At a Crossroads." *The Handbook of Critical Intercultural Communication*. Eds. Thomas K. Nakayama and Rona Tamiko Halualani. Malden, Mass. & Chichester: Wiley-Blackwell, 2010. 1–16.

Hosseini, Khaled. *And the Mountains Echoed*. London: Bloomsbury, 2014.

Imahori, Tadasu T., and William R. Cupach. "Identity Management Theory: Facework in Intercultural Relationships." *Theorizing about Intercultural Communication*. Ed. William B. Gudykunst. Thousand Oaks, CA: Sage, 2005. 195–210.

Jackson, Ronald L. II. "Cultural Contracts Theory: Toward an Understanding of Identity Negotiation." *Communication Quarterly* 50.3–4 (2002): 359–367.

—. *The Negotiation of Cultural Identity: Perceptions of European Americans and African Americans*. Westport, CT: Praeger, 1999.

Jen, Gish. *Mona in the Promised Land*. New York: Alfred A. Knopf, 1996.

—. *Typical American*. London: Plume, 1992.

Kettemann, Bernhard, and Georg Marko. "Filling the Reflecting Pool: The Self-analysis of English and American Studies." *Expanding Circles, Transcending Disciplines, and Multimodal Texts: Reflections on Teaching, Learning and Researching in English and American Studies*. Eds. Bernhard Kettemann and Georg Marko. Tübingen: Gunter Narr, 2003. 13–18.

Kim, Young Yun. "Beyond Cultural Identity." *Intercultural Communication Studies* 4.1 (1994): 1–23.

—. "Cross-Cultural Adaptation Theory." *Encyclopedia of Communication Theory*. Eds. Stephen W. Littlejohn and Karen A. Foss. Thousand Oaks, CA: Sage, 2009. 244–248.

—. "From Culture to Interculture: Communication, Adaptation, and Identity Transformation in the Globalizing World." *Intercultural Communication: A Reader*. 14th ed. Eds. Larry A. Samovar, Richard E. Porter, Edwin R. McDaniel and Carolyn Sexton Roy. Boston: Cengage Learning, 2015. 430–437.

—. "Globalization and Intercultural Personhood." *Intercultural Communication: A Reader*. 13th ed. Eds. Larry A. Samovar, Richard E. Porter and Edwin R. McDaniel. Boston: Cengage Learning, 2012. 83–94.

—. "Ideology, Identity, and Intercultural Communication: An Analysis of

Differing Academic Conceptions of Cultural Identity." *Journal of Intercultural Commmunication Research* 36.3 (2007): 237–253.

—. "Intercultural Personhood: An Integration of Eastern and Western Perspectives." *Intercultural Communication: A Reader*. 14th ed. Eds. Larry A. Samovar, Richard E. Porter, Edwin R. McDaniel and Carolyn Sexton Roy. Boston: Cengage Learning, 2015. 405–417.

Kingston, Maxine Hong. *The Woman Warrior: Memoirs of a Girlhood Among Ghosts*. New York: Alfred A. Knopf, 1976. Vintage International, 1989.

Kohlberg, Lawrence, Charles Levine and Alexandra Hewer. *Moral Stages: A Current Formulation and a Response to Critics*. Contributions to Human Development 10. Basel: S. Karger, 1983.

Kroeber, A[lfred] L., and Clyde Kluckhohn. *Culture: A Critical Review of Concepts and Definitions*. Cambridge, Mass.: Peabody Museum, 1952.

Kulich, Steve J., and Weng Liping. "Introduction: Value Dimensions, Dynamic Contexts, and Beyond." *Value Dimensions and Their Contextual Dynamics Across Cultures*. Intercultural Research Vol. 5. Eds. Steve J. Kulich, Weng Liping and Michael H. Prosser. Shanghai: Shanghai Foreign Language Education Press, 2014. 1–24.

Lahiri, Jhumpa. *The Namesake*. New York: Mariner Books, 2003.

Latour, Bruno. "A Textbook Case Revisited — Knowledge as a Mode of Existence." *The Handbook of Science and Technology Studies*. Eds. Edward J. Hackett, Olga Amsterdamska et al. 3rd ed. Cambridge, Mass.: MIT Press, 2008. 83–112.

Leavis, Frank R. *The Great Tradition: George Eliot, Henry James, Joseph Conrad*. London: Chatto & Windus, 1948.

Lee, Sky. *Disappearing Moon Cafe: A Novel*. Vancouver: Douglas & McIntyre, 1990.

Lewis, Tom J., and Robert E. Jungman, eds. (1986). *On Being Foreign: Culture Shock in Short Fiction. An International Anthology*. Yarmouth, Maine: Intercultural Press, 1986.

Malinowski, Bronislaw. "Review of Six Essays on Culture by Albert Blumenthal." *American Sociological Review* 4 (1939): 588–592.

Martin, Judith N., and Thomas K. Nakayama. *Intercultural Communication in Contexts*. 5th ed. New York: McGraw-Hill, 2010.

McGee, Sharon James. *Analyzing Literature: A Guide for Students*. Longman. Web. 16 July 2016. http://wps.ablongman.com/wps/media/objects/327/335558/AnalyzingLit.pdf.

Mekheimer, Mohamed Amin A., and Hamad S. Aldosari. "Impediments to Cultural Teaching in EFL Programmes at a Saudi University." *Journal of Intercultural Communication* 26 (2011). Web. 17 July 2016. http://www.immi.se/intercultural/nr26/mekheimer.htm.

Mohammadzadeh, Behbood. "Incorporating Multicultural Literature in English Language Teaching Curriculum." *Procedia Social and Behavioral Sciences* 1.1 (2009): 23–27.

Moon, Dreama G. "Critical Reflections on Culture and Critical Intercultural Communication." *The Handbook of Critical Intercultural Communication*. Eds. Thomas K. Nakayama and Rona Tamiko Halualani. Malden, Mass. & Chichester: Wiley-Blackwell, 2010. 34–52.

Mukherjee, Bharati. *Jasmine*. New York: Grove P, 1989.

Myers, M., and Collier, Mary J. (2006). "Toward Contingent Understandings of

Intersecting Identifications Among Selected U. S. Interracial Couples:
Integrating Interpretive and Critical Views." *Communication Quarterly* 54
(2006): 487–506.

Njogu, Kimani, ed. *Culture, Performance, and Identity: Paths of Communication in Kenya*. Nairobi: Twaweza Communications, 2008.

Oberg, Kalervo. "Cultural Shock: Adjustment to New Cultural Environments."
Practical Anthropology 7 (1960): 177–182.

Pandey, Satish. "Using Popular Movies in Teaching Cross-Cultural
Management." *Special Issue of European Journal of Training and
Development* 36.2 (2012): 329–350.

Peng, Shi-yong. "Intercultural Communication Research in China: Status
Quo, Problems, and Suggestions." *Journal of Hunan Univ.* (Social
Sciences) 19.4 (2005): 86–91. In Chinese.

Pitts, Margaret Jane. "Intercultural Personhood." *Encyclopedia of Identity*.
Eds. Ronald L. Jackson II and Michael A. Hogg. 2 vols. Thousand Oaks,
CA: Sage, 2010. 398–402.

Rosaldo, Renato I. "Foreword: Defining Culture." *Redefining Culture:
Perspectives Across the Disciplines*. Eds. John R. Baldwin, Sandra L.
Faulkner et al. Mahwah, N.J.: Lawrence Erlbaum, 2006. ix–xiii.

Savignon, Sandra J. "Beyond Communicative Language Teaching: What's
Ahead?" *Journal of Pragmatics* 39 (2007): 207–220.

Shafak, Elif. *The Bastard of Istanbul*. London: Penguin, 2007.

—. *Honour*. London: Penguin, 2012.

—. *The Saint of Incipient Insanities*. New York: Farrar, Straus and Giroux,
2004.

Smith, Zadie. *White Teeth*. London: Penguin, 2000.

Sun, Youzhong. "Intercultural Mass Communication: A New Frontier for
Intercultural Communication Research." *Intercultural Communication
Theory Exploration and Practice* [跨文化交际理论探索与实践]. Shanghai:
Shanghai Foreign Language Education P, 2012.

Swann, William B. "Identity Negotiation: Where Two Roads Meet." *Journal
of Personality and Social Psychology* 53.6 (1987): 1038–1051.

Tan, Amy. *The Joy Luck Club*. New York & Toronto: Penguin, 1989.

Thompson, J., and Mary J. Collier. "Toward Contingent Understandings of
Intersecting Identifications Among Selected U. S. Interracial Couples:
Integrating Interpretive and Critical Views." *Communication Quarterly*
54.4 (2006): 487–506.

Ting-Toomey, Stella. *Communicating Across Cultures*. New York & London:
Guilford P, 1999. Shanghai: Shanghai Foreign Language Education P,
2007. 2nd ed. 2019.

—. "Communicative Resourcefulness: An Identity Negotiation Theory."
Intercultural Communication Competence. Eds. Richard L. Wiseman and
Jolene Koester. Newbury Park, CA: Sage, 1993. 72–111.

West, Cornel. "The New Cultural Politics of Difference." *The Cultural
Studies Reader*. Ed. Simon During. 2nd ed. London: Routledge, 1999.
256–270.

Williams, Raymond. *Marxism and Literature*. Oxford: Oxford UP, 1977.

Wyer, Robert S. et al., eds. *Understanding Culture: Theory, Research, and
Application*. New York & London: Taylor & Francis, 2009.

The Challenge of an Intercultural Literature

Michael STEPPAT
University of Bayreuth

Steve J. KULICH
Shanghai International Studies University

Mapping a Research Field

Collaborating across academic cultures (German, U.S., and Chinese), we seek to explore a mutual cross-fertilization between literary studies with a comparative orientation and recent research on Intercultural Communication. These perspectives, as we find, have considerable potential for integration into a distinctive research field of "intercultural literature." The Introduction to this volume has offered a hypothesis, referring to the work of pioneering scholars in the field of intercultural literary studies, that is designed to explain the fruitfulness of an intercultural approach for comparative literary studies and for analyses of inter- or cross-cultural encounters, as depicted in literary works, that might draw on Intercultural Communication research.

   We would like to suggest that the role of intercultural literature as it has developed strongly in Germany is perhaps paradigmatic, and at least noteworthy. An adapted concept of hybridity, originating in English and American studies, has become central for the intercultural focus of German literary studies. Germany gradually moved toward becoming a multicultural society since the 1950s. From this experience, a distinct cultural position of literature has emerged, which could be of interest and possibly instructive for other countries that are likewise not burdened with an imperial past and/or that may be facing new ethnic and cross-cultural openings as a potential factor in their social development. To bridge these possibilities, there may be possible points of comparison and contrast with Chinese migrant writing.

As Germany faced the challenge of absorbing a growing variety of immigrant population groups, the political and cultural status of such groups has not automatically been categorized as inferior or as subject to a need for development. This does not mean that their status is free from any hegemonic discourses or social differences — far from it. But the immigrant groups were not mute, nor were they silent; a significant number of immigrants have shown literary interests. This is precisely how and why a new body of literature came into being, sometimes treated as a new literary genre. Its implications reach further than any historical particulars of immigration history in one country as might be true in other colonial instances.

From Guest Workers' Literature to Migrants' Literature

About 1980, a generic title was proposed for such literature: "writings of the affected/impacted" (Literatur der Betroffenheit). The term became influential; it expresses the situation of several population groups affected by harsh and oppressive conditions, and the term has been paraphrased as "literature of dismay." Those affected by such conditions include not only laborers but foreigners, women, homosexuals, and the disabled. The label calls attention to economic exploitation and social discrimination affecting a range of social groups whose members were not always aware of what they had in common, among them workers of all ethnic backgrounds, including native or autochthonous workers. The purpose was therapeutic and cathartic, also aiming for insight and self-criticism on the part of readers who were not members of the groups affected. Biography and autobiography were suitable genres for this purpose, co-constructed (as it were) by the reading public. But the label was superseded a few years later by an extensively argued concept of "foreigners' literature": it designates literature written by foreigners and created in or in relation to the host country. Foreigners could be labor migrants, third-world refugees, or system migrants from political régimes that were geographically close and were felt to be oppressive. Though the term extends to migrants who have the host country's passport and who speak the country's language as their second language, it also includes migrants who have settled in the country, so that the term may be misleading. There is an alternative concept, "immigrant literature," which highlights integration into the host society's literary culture, but also implies a form of appropriation by that society. For this reason, some scholars prefer the neutral-sounding term "migrants' literature" — which calls attention to authors' biography rather than their works, enabling influences from the writers' native culture to become an object of study. This is almost synonymous with "migration literature," a form of writing that concerns itself with the subject of migration, which is treated and aesthetically shaped from a committed viewpoint, the perspective of oppressed minorities. While migration can be considered as a form of escape from harsh conditions, however, not all migration patterns are covered by such motives. What is more, migrants' literary works in their native language and in the host country's language, or even including both, are worthy of attention, since these enable fruitful comparisons. Also, literature created by second-generation immigrant authors, who are not immigrants themselves — this has been thought of as *littérature décentrée* in relation to a country's mainstream culture. Any single generic label can thus easily fall short of the range and richness of literature produced in such contexts. It has come to be considered as the potential germ of a new world literature, with variable contact and interaction points between natives and foreigners. This understanding might offer the latter a natural place in the context of a language that is still new to them and that they can perhaps help to shape. In this context one might, with Jing Tsu, critique the unquestioning assumption of linguistic nativity, which is not simply a given or received privilege, and think of language as a medium of access rather than a right to identity.

Intercultural Narrative Forms

In terms of literary genres, the materials that are and can be analyzed by intercultural literature studies, in principle, belong to all conceivable genres and subgenres. In forming a disciplinary canon, genres and works tend to be analytically embraced when they represent and reflect on culture and cultural meeting grounds. Prominent are narrative works representing travel, exile, migration, or colonial experience; the genres include utopias, adventure fiction, robinsonades, or postcolonial literature. Poetry of various subgenres and also dramas are no less suitable forms. The boundary between generic devices is a permeable one. A range of forms such as variation, alienation, parody, pastiche, collage, polyphony, carnivalization, rereading, rewriting classical texts, and writing back are represented among intercultural literary works. As a consequence, comparisons between national literatures, external comparisons, are being superseded by a study of hybrid mixtures in literary culture. The original meaning of comparative literary studies as such has shifted accordingly.

Multilingualism and Dialogicity

Beyond the focus on one country as topographical and linguistic space, a particular case of intercultural writing can be singled out as paradigmatic: it arises from the pluricultural and multilingual character of a region on the very fringe of any dominant language influence, or between such influences, one which functions as contact and conflict area of cultures with different languages. On the surface, literature with such origins may seem to resemble that of bilingual authors who write works in one language at a time (such as Samuel Beckett, Vladimir Nabokov, Rainer Maria Rilke, or Stefan George), or works in which classic authors use quotations from different languages (such as T. S. Eliot or Ezra Pound, and in certain genres Qian Zhongshu). But the literature in question makes use of the sociolinguistic situation of regional everyday life, which can be called diglossia with di-ethnicity, with bilingual code-switching; the rich-text "language in everyday use" approaches of Dell Hymes or Gerry Philipsen offer research applications. It is a strategically significant procedure for "minor literature," the literature of national minorities. Nationally related ascriptions for such literature ienvitably fail, since the works do not belong to any single literature with such boundaries. The participating languages form an intercultural dialogue, which calls into question problematic traditions and value systems. Mikhail Bakhtin's concept of dialogicity, the co-presence of different languages or voices within a polyphonic novel, is relevant in that the voices express different ideological standpoints, opposing value positions and cultural concepts — such as hegemonic and minority culture, official and popular culture. A de-hierarchizing of official culture is embedded in such dialogicity. The growing field of critical intercultural studies (as in Nakayama and Halualani, 2010) focuses on analyzing such phenomena. Leading on from this focus, in fact, is a call for a renewed form of comparative literary study to adopt such a dialogic concept of literature, studying the crossing of borders in dialogic multilingualism and the interplay within individual literary works. Dialogicity may be understood as forming a particular stage in a larger process. An initial stage would then be an experience of aliennness as such, before any textual communication can be set in motion. On this experience, a second stage can build and become effective, a stage formed of a communicative situation in which each partner needs the stranger's or Other's dissent in order to shape her/his own discourse.

At this point, intercultural literature's significance finds its systematic place: in accordance with the semiotics of Mikhail Bakhtin and also of Yuri Lotman, we might assume that multilingualism is a material condition of literary bilinguality, which means that it is capable of becoming — if it has not already become — a constitutive factor of culture as such in a world of mobile migration. In this sense, multilingual literature is not a special (or peripheral) case but more generally a vital condition for literary culture that is not limited by regional boundaries.

Culture and Communicative Interaction

An understanding of the quality of literature as just described depends on the concept of "culture" that one adopts. There is more involved than the collective and relative stability of group cultures or a distinction between high and low culture, as often studied in social science discourses. For many in our hybridized and cross-border world, the concept of "home culture" is in itself problematic. A more fruitful concept would be open to a focus on persons: cultures as ensembles of societal experiences, thought patterns, and practices impacting on people; it may extend to a "site of struggle" for the recognition and legitimation of meaning, or "a mental toolkit of subjective metaphors" that is liable to mass media manipulation. It is essential, we may gather, to be non-essentialist, looking beyond homogeneous cultures toward the way cultural patterns are connected to persons with their ambivalent and even reversible cultural orientations. Being perceived as an identifiable person has become a central problem in a world in which fears of exclusion are dominant. By means of the enactment of symbolic structures, cultural practice serves to make the specifics of individuals visible, which can extend to recognizing an individual's right to be different. A result of the cultural practice is imaginary representation of the transitory nature of human existence, in the modern experience of mobility and acceleration. Here is a conceptual site for literature in culture's social communication process. That is because cultural identities, like ethnic identities, are largely constituted and manifest themselves in the sign structure of texts, enabling these to become culture's exhibition and representation. In thinking beyond cultural boundaries, and in reflecting on the relevant literature's rapid development, intercultural literary study has a cognitive and critical interest that might enable it to offer a modest scholarly contribution to the overarching challenge of culture per se, which has been called the overcoming or at least diminishing of barbarism.

Aesthetic of Rhizomatic Circulation

To set off intercultural literary production from other types of minority literature, the consideration of what has been called foreign authors' literature — a key segment of intercultural writing — has moved beyond the usual schema of marginal or subaltern cultures, which tends to assume members' single identity and also tends to focus on their subaltern character. By contrast, this kind of literature is characterized by heterogeneity and openness toward external influences, since it forms a network or rather a mobile and intermediate space in relation to autochthonous writers' literary forms. Accordingly, there are cultural overlaps in terms of an author's definition of her/his own position: the borders toward the mainstream majority are blurred and in motion. It is a deterritorialized literature, in the sense of Deleuze and Guattari, in a foreign environment. The literary works sometimes have an aesthetic quality that differs from that of autochtonous writers, though not always; hence they sometimes function as carriers of innovation. Comparative literature scholars have argued that the rhizome model developed by Deleuze and Guattari is especially apt: the rhizome is non-hierarchical, without an organizing memory, and is defined by a circulation of conditions. These features correspond to the literature's aesthetic configuration.

The configuration comes about owing to cultural contacts and intersections of cultural traditions, enabling an intercultural aesthetic in which no clear distinction between individual cultural layers is possible. A rhizomatic jumbling of the familiar and the foreign applies not only to the literary form, but also to subject matter: both the familiarity of home and the experience of foreignness are represented — not as a binary opposition (this is decisive) but rather as an in-between state, as both one and the other. We can thus observe a deconstructive circulation between spaces rather than a decision between them, so that migration presents an opportunity to meet the Other and to experience oneself as the Other for someone.

The aesthetic of intercultural literature that has emerged is inseparable from the larger development of cultural studies. That raises the question: how capable are each of us to cope with different symbolic forms of any culture that is increasingly on the move? Intercultural literature as a field and function of academic inquiry may conceivably gain an important place for exposing and cultivating intercultural awareness in the literatures written by "the Other" in non-colonizing societies. It may even serve as a stimulus for rethinking some types of comparative literature studies in China.

Differences and Analogies: Chinese Diasporic Literature

If we ask about points of comparison and contrast with Chinese literary culture, the closest comparison that is possible thus far is with the literature created by emigrants. When these write in the host culture's language, they tend to be treated as belonging to (for instance) American or Canadian rather than Chinese literature proper. Yet, as Aijun Zhu shows, for Sino-American writers of both sexes Chineseness has multiple meanings: as against discourses of authenticity, it is a "political and cultural negotiation between essentialized interpellations" from the western culture and from China too (40). Since most emigrants have migrated from China as their cultural center, and spread around the world, their periphery, they are often thought of as diasporic. Research shows that, for transmigrants to Southeast Asia, diasporic spaces tend to be place-centered as well as network-based with porous boundaries, allowing individual activity spaces, inviting comparison with the spatial understanding of migrant authors in the German context. A disarticulation of identity from natal and national resources is a condition common to these literatures. In the research context, the concept of diaspora has consequently been thought inadequate, an alternative approach being the "heteroglossia" of Sinophone culture. Discussion of the cultural position of Chineseness as against diaspora is becoming as lively as the debate about migrant literature in the German context. The relationship between the transnational category which is meaningful here and the transcultural paradigm which is relevant in the German as well as the postcolonial context would need further study for a comparative analysis of migrant literary production (see also Arndt's chapter in this volume). The dominant themes and motifs of fictional writing that exemplifies a duality of selfhood include several that, cultural specifics apart, form mirror images to German migrant literature: a struggle to enter the larger society, the quest for a place in the host culture's life, the migrant's positive or negative impact on the host culture, exploration of cultural identity, conflicts between culturally bound values, views on interracial marriage, the pursuit of a dream of mobility, and the generational relationship. We might ask whether and how these fictional treatments could be open to a rhizomatic analysis in comparison with migrant writing in German literary culture.

References

Amodeo, Immacolata. " *Die Heimat heißt Babylon* ": *Zur Literatur ausländischer Autoren in der Bundesrepublik Deutschland*. Opladen: Westdeutscher Verlag, 1996.

Bakhtin, M. M. "Forms of Time and of the Chronotope in the Novel: Notes toward a Historical Poetics." *The Dialogic Imagination: Four Essays*. Ed. Michael Holquist. Trans. Caryl Emerson and Michael Holquist. Austin: U of Texas P, 1981. 84–258.

Deleuze, Gilles, and Félix Guattari. *A Thousand Plateaus: Capitalism and Schizophrenia*. Trans. Brian Massumi. London & New York: Continuum, 2004.

Jing Tsu. *Sound and Script in Chinese Diaspora*. Cambridge, Mass.: Harvard UP, 2010.

Lim, Shirley Geok-Lin. "Immigration and Diaspora." *An Interethnic Companion to Asian American Literature*. Ed. King-Kok Cheung. Cambridge: Cambridge UP, 289–311.

Ma, Laurence J. C., and Cartier Carolyn, eds. *The Chinese Diaspora: Space, Place, Mobility, and Identity*. Lanham, Md.: Rowman & Littlefield, 2003.

Nakayama, Thomas K., and Rona Tamiko Halualani, eds. *The Handbook of Critical Intercultural Communication*. Malden, Mass., & Chichester: Wiley-Blackwell, 2010.

Steppat, Michael, and Steve J. Kulich. "Considering Intercultural Literature:

A Mature Field of Study." *Intercultural Communication: German and Chinese Perspectives*. Perspectives of the Other: Studies on Intercultural Communication. Eds. Jürgen Henze, Steve J. Kulich, and Z. Q. Wang. Wiesbaden: VS Research/Springer Fachmedien (forthcoming).

Zhu, Aijun. *Feminism and Global Chineseness: The Cultural Production of Controversial Women Authors*. Youngstown, N.Y.: Cambria P, 2007.

About the Authors

Shola Adenekan is currently a researcher and tutor in African literature and films at the Faculty of Linguistics and Literature, University of Bremen, Germany. Prior to that, he was a postdoctoral researcher in African literature at the University of Bayreuth, Germany. Before moving to Germany in 2013, he was a Vice-Chancellor postdoctoral fellow at the University of Leeds, England. He completed his Ph.D. at the University of Birmingham, England (Class of 2012), where he also taught classes in African literature and arts. Dr. Adenekan moved to England from Nigeria in the mid-1990s, and had his university education there. His current research focuses on the intersectional links between class, gender, sexuality, and politics as well as the representation of these discourses in a variety of literary and performing arts genres. Dr. Adenekan has also been working as a journalist since 2002, and used to work as a freelance for BBC News Online, *The Guardian*, *The Times Higher*, *Times Educational Supplement*, Jobs.ac.uk and the *Christian Science Monitor*. He is the publisher of an online magazine Thenewblackmagazine.com.

Susan Arndt is Professor of Anglophone Literatures at the University of Bayreuth. Previously, she was a Research Fellow at St. Antony's College (Oxford), and held scholarly positions at Humboldt University Berlin, the Center for Literary and Cultural Studies in Berlin, and the University of Frankfurt/Main. She has acted as Speaker of the Academy of Advanced African Studies at Bayreuth. The book publications that she has authored or edited include *Die 101 wichtigsten Fragen: Rassismus* (2014), *Afro-Fictional In(ter)ventions* (2014), *Theatre, Performance and New Media in Africa* (2007), *Worlds and Words: African Writers on Literature*, *Theatre und Society* (2007), *Africa, Europe and (Post)Colonialism* (2006), *The Dynamics of African Feminism* (2002), *and African Women's Literature, Orature and Intertextuality* (1998). Her research interests include transcultural literary studies, critical whiteness and critical race research, postcolonialism and intersectionality, and African women's writing.

Shirin Assa has been engaged with cultural identity and the literary poetics thereof. Holding a Bachelor of Arts degree in Spanish Language and Literature from Allameh Tabataba'i University (Tehran/Iran), she completed her Master of Arts in Intercultural Anglophone Studies at the University of Bayreuth (Germany), where she received the 2016 national DAAD (German Academic Exchange Service) Award as best foreign student. She has pursued doctoral studies at Georgetown University, Washington, and is a member of the Bayreuth International Graduate School of African Studies. She is intrigued by alternative models of collective consciousness nationally, culturally, and gender-wise. With a special interest in postcolonial and diaspora studies, Assa reflects upon world literature and in particular female writings. Assa has contributed to the 41st Annual Conference of the African Literature Association and to the Bayreuth Academy of Advanced African Studies.

Sandra L. Bermann is Cotsen Professor of the Humanities and Professor of Comparative Literature at Princeton University, and serves as Master of Whitman College. In addition to articles and reviews in scholarly journals, she is author of *The Sonnet Over Time: Studies in the Sonnets of Petrarch, Shakespeare, and Baudelaire*; translator of Manzoni's *On the Historical Novel*; editor with Michael Wood of *Nation, Language, and the Ethics of Translation*; and editor with Catherine Porter of *A Companion to Translation Studies*. Her current projects focus on lyric poetry, translation, the intersections between twentieth-century historiography and literary theory, and new directions in the field of comparative literature. A recipient of Whiting and Fulbright Fellowships, Prof. Bermann has been a visiting scholar at the Institute for Advanced Study in Princeton and the Columbia University Institute for Scholars at Reid Hall in Paris. At Princeton, she chaired the Department of Comparative Literature for many years, served as Master of Stevenson Hall, co-founded the Program in Translation and Intercultural Communication, and led the President's Working Group on the Bridge Year Program. She completed a term as President of the American Comparative Literature Association in 2009.

Fu Lin received her Bachelor of Arts degree in English Language and

Literature from Heilongjiang University (China) and a Master of Arts degree in Intercultural Anglophone Studies from the University of Bayreuth (Germany). In October 2010, she joined the International Ph.D. program "Cultural Encounters" at the University of Bayreuth and successfully defended her doctoral dissertation on "Trauma in Chinese North American Fiction" with Magna Cum Laude honors in 2015. She was awarded the DAAD (German Academic Exchange Service) research grant for her doctoral studies and BayCHINA (Bavarian Academic Center for China) Visiting Scholar grant for her research visit at Shanghai International Studies University. Her research interests include transnational migration and diaspora, memory and trauma studies, Anglophone Chinese literature in North America and the UK, and Victorian literature. Since 2012, she has been a member of the cooperative research project between the University of Bayreuth and Shanghai International Studies University on "Identity and Intercultural Communication: Perspectives on America."

Mine Krause graduated with a double Ph. D. in Comparative Literature from the Universities of Bayreuth (Germany) and Pau (France) in 2009. During her studies, she worked as an assistant in the Literature and Linguistics departments of Bayreuth, Ankara, and Granada. Her doctoral thesis on scandal and *angst* in the works of Albee, Pinter, Ionesco, and Genet was published in a scholarly book series by Peter Lang in 2010. In the same year, an article on Pinter's *Ashes to Ashes* followed in Merle Tönnies's *Das englische Drama der Gegenwart*. Her analysis of Elif Shafak's culinary language appeared in the *Journal of Turkish Literature*. She participated in the 22nd METU British Novelists Conference on Zadie Smith's work in Turkey, where she compared identity concepts in Zadie Smith's *White Teeth* and Elif Shafak's *The Bastard of Istanbul*. Since 2013, Mine Krause has been a member of an international research cluster at the University of Bayreuth together with Shanghai International Studies University, where she currently focuses on the different forms of intercultural identity. For "The International Symposium On Literature, Comparative Studies, Interculturality: America and Beyond" in Shanghai she delivered a keynote speech in 2015. Her research interests include intercultural communication, immigrant literature, and culinary culture.

Steve J. Kulich is Distinguished Professor at Shanghai International

Studies University, Director of the SISU Intercultural Institute, Editor of *Intercultural Research*, and Academic Coordinator for the SISU MBA program. He received his M.A. from the University of Kansas and his Ph. D. from Humboldt University of Berlin, Germany. In his 40 years in Asia and 26 years in Shanghai, he has pioneered intercultural training courses, M.A. and Ph.D. programs at SISU, and has helped organize ten international Intercultural Communication conferences. With Michael Prosser, he has edited the *International Journal of Intercultural Relations* 2012 (4) " Special Issue: Early American Pioneers of Intercultural Communication." He is on the Editorial Board of the *Intercultural Communication Series*, *Intercultural Communication Research*, and the *Journal of Middle East and Islamic Studies* (*in Asia*). Prof. Kulich's work has been published in *Intercultural Communication Studies*, *China Media Research*, *International Management Review*, *China Media Reports Overseas*, *Cross-cultural Psychology Bulletin*, *The International Scope Review*, and by Edgar Elgar Press (in Xu and Bond's *Handbook of Chinese Organizational Behavior*, 2012), Oxford University Press (in Bond's *Handbook of Chinese Psychology*, 2nd ed., 2010), Sage (in Littlejohn's and Foss's *Encyclopedia of Communication Theory*, 2009), Hong Kong University Press, Higher Education Press, FLTRP, SFLEP, and Yunnan People's Press, as well as his 2002 columns in *English Salon* and *Shanghai Scene*. He has been honored with a "Special Contribution Award" (CAFIC, 2011) and twice with the Magnolia Award (Silver 2007, Gold 2011) from the Shanghai government, as well as a national "Favorite Foreign Teacher" Award (2014). With his team, he has been chiefly responsible for developing and running China's first international partnership Massive Online Open Course with FutureLearn. He is President-Elect of the International Academy for Intercultural Research (IAIR). (2019–2021).

Mao Sihui received his B.A. in English Language and Literature and M.A. in British and American Literary Studies from Guangzhou Institute of Foreign Languages, now called Guangdong University of Foreign Studies (GDUFS), his second M. A. in Contemporary Literary and Cultural Studies from the University of Lancaster, UK, and his Ph.D. in Comparative Literature — Film Culture from the University of Hong Kong, China. He taught various English subjects at GDUFS from 1982 to 2000 (as Dean of the Faculty of English Language and Culture from 1998 – 2001), translation and culture courses at the Department of Translation, Hong Kong Lingnan University, from 2001 to 2003 and then directed the MPI-Bell Centre of English, Macao Polytechnic Institute from 2003–2015. In March 2015, he started his new job as Director of the English Language Centre and Professor of English and Comparative Cultural Studies, Shantou University.

Prof. Mao has been Vice President of the Sino-American Comparative Culture Association of China since 2000, President of the Federation of Translators and Interpreters of Macao since 2007, Executive Director of the International Association for Intercultural Communication Studies (IAICS) since August 2014, and was a Council Member of International Translators Federation (2011–2014). He taught B.A., M.A., and Ph.D. courses at GDUFS and HK Lingnan University, such as "Modern British and American Drama," "Contemporary Critical Theory," "Comparative Cultural Studies," "Film Culture," "Translation for the Media," "Translation of Texts in Popular Culture," "Culture and Translation." He has supervised many M.A. and six Ph.D. theses to completion.

His major publications include *Technologising the Male Body: British Cinema 1957–1987* (1999), *New Perspectives: Contemporary Literary and Cultural Studies* (2000), *Decoding Contemporary Britain* (2003), *Literature, Culture and Postmodern Transformations: 8 Case Studies from William Shakespeare to James Bond* (2009). He was General Editor of the *New Topics in Contemporary Cultural Studies Series* (6 vols., Sun Yat-sen University Press, 2007–2009), co-edited with Doreen Wu a special issue for the journal of *Critical Arts, Media Discourses and Cultural Globalisation: A Chinese Perspective* (Routledge & UNISA, 2011), and co-authored three books on *English for International Communication Series: International Conference Communication* (2013); *Paper Writing and International Publication* (2014); *Literature Reading and Translation* (forthcoming), all published by the Foreign Language Teaching and Research Press, Beijing. Prof. Mao has also published dozens of academic journal papers and book chapters in literary, cultural, and translation studies. He has recently finished a research project on *Representations of Macao in Contemporary Cinema* and is now working on *Transcultural Competence in ELT and Intercultural Communication*.

Patrick Oloko is a Senior Lecturer in the Department of English, University of Lagos, Nigeria, where he started his teaching career in 1999 as an Assistant Lecturer. His specialization is African postcolonial literature, gender and cultural studies. He obtained his Bachelor's Degree in English and Literary Studies from the University of Calabar, Nigeria, in 1991 and his M.A. and Ph.D. degrees in English, majoring in African women's writing, from the University of Lagos in 1995 and 2003 respectively. Dr. Oloko is the editor of two collections of essays on two prolific but understudied Nigerian writers: *In Theory and In Practice: Engaging the Writings of Hope Eghagha* (2015) and *The Fiction of Akachi Adimora-Ezeigbo: Issues and Perspectives* (2008). He has co-edited a special issue of the *Journal of African Media Studies* (Vol.7 No.1, 2015) titled "Across Media: Mobility and transformation of cultural materials in the digital age." Dr. Oloko has been the recipient of fellowships, research and travel grants such as the Cadbury Visiting Fellowship of the University of Birmingham, UK (2010); the German Research Council grant for his study of publishing in early postcolonial Nigeria (2010/2011) at the Goethe Universität, Frankfurt/Main, and the Point Sud travel grant to conduct a workshop on Popular Culture, funded by the Deutsche Forschungsgemeinschaft and held in Ougadougou, Burkina Faso (2013). He was the Regional Coordinator (Lagos) of the European Research Council FP7 Research Grant on the project *The Cultural Politics of Dirt in Africa: 1880-Present*, working with Professor Stephanie Newell (formerly of Sussex, now at Yale) as Principal Investigator.

Shen Weiwei Vivian (沈维维) is Associate Professor in the Foreign Language Department of Hangzhou Medical College and Ph.D. in a joint program of the School of English Studies at Shanghai International Studies University and the University of Bayreuth. Her academic research focuses mainly on Intercultural studies and Asian American literature. In cooperation with Prof. Steve J. Kulich and Prof. Michael Steppat, she is on her way to exploring and contributing an innovative perspective to the combination of Intercultural Communication and Literary Studies. Her recent publications include "The Third Space in Nie Huangling's *Mulberry and Peach* and Bharati Muhkerjee's *Jasmine*" (2015), "'I am Heathcliff!': Identity in *Wuthering Heights* from a Psychoanalytical Perspective" (2013), and "Differences and Analogies: Chinese Diasporic Literature" (forthcoming). Her paper "Hybridity and Third Space in Bharati Mukherjee's *Jasmine*" was presented in the Panel on "Gender Study and Communication" at the 21st International Conference of the International Association for International

Communication Studies (IAICS) at Hong Kong Polytechnic University in 2015.

Michael Steppat served as Chair of Literature in English at the University of Bayreuth, Germany, until he achieved Emeritus status in 2015. He also holds a Professorial position of honor in Moscow from the Russian Federation's Ministry of Higher Education and Science. He has been appointed regular visiting professor at Shanghai International Studies University, extending to advisor functions, as well as visiting professor at other Chinese universities and at Fu Jen Catholic University, Taipei (China). After receiving his Ph.D. from the University of Münster (Germany) and later his "Habilitation" both from Münster and from Free University of Berlin, he was a Fulbright scholar at the University of Texas at Austin, then research professor at Arizona State University. He has repeatedly been awarded the Myra and Charlton Hinman Fellowship of Amherst College and Folger Shakespeare Library, Washington DC; he has also been granted the position of a Scholar-in-Residence at the John W. Kluge Center of the Library of Congress. He has served in a number of administrative functions, including the Academic Dean's position in his Faculty for many years. To move in a new direction, he developed an internationally cooperative graduate program of Intercultural Anglophone Studies. His book publications include *Americanisms: Discourses of Exception, Exclusion, Exchange*; *Chances of Mischief: Variations of Fortune in Spenser*; *The Critical Reception of Shakespeare's Antony and Cleopatra*; editions of several Renaissance Latin dramas; co-editorship of the New Variorum edition of Shakespeare's *Antony and Cleopatra*; and a monograph on the early work of St. Augustine of Hippo. A collaborative volume on *Writing Identity: The Construction of National Identity in American Literature* (Moscow City University) extends this range. As appointed member of the MLA's editorial team for the New Variorum Shakespeare, he has the honor of continuing to edit assigned plays. Spurred by an invitation from the London School of Economics and Political Science in 2011 to organize a workshop, which turned out to be a first-rate learning experience, Prof. Steppat has increasingly devoted attention to intercultural studies in connection with literature. In 2012, he became Primary Investigator in a Bavarian government-sponsored Sino-German cooperative program on "Identity and Intercultural Communication: Perspectives on America." He has recently co-authored an article on "Considering

Intercultural Literature: A Mature Field of Study" (*German and Chinese Perspectives on Intercultural Communication and Competence*, ed. Jürgen Henze), and has given papers and conducted workshops on intercultural literary study at various international institutions and conferences in recent years.

Sun Yan gained her Ph. D. in English Literature at Shanghai International Studies University. She is also Judicial Master at the Law School of Fudan University. In 2007–2008 she was a Fulbright visiting scholar at Mississippi Valley State University, and in 2014–2015 visiting scholar at John Jay College of Criminal Justice, City University of New York. Her publications include *EU and Africa from Historical and Cultural Perspectives: Britain and Western Africa* (Shanghai Foreign Language Education Press, 2015) as well as an article on "Judicial Realism and William Brown's *Clotel.*" She has authored the Afanti and Little Donkey Series (Fudan University Press) and translated the Afanti and His Family Series as well as the Little Cricket Gery Series.

Inge van de Ven is Assistant Professor of Online Culture in the Department of Culture Studies at Tilburg School of Humanities (Netherlands). She previously completed research at the Education for Learning Societies Center and taught in the Comparative Literature department at Utrecht University. She has been a member of the Innovational Research Incentives project Back to the Book. Her dissertation is titled *Monumental Novels in a Global and Digital Age* (2015). Major areas of interest are literary theory, literature and film, literature and new media, digital culture, and narratology.

Tom van Nuenen is a Teaching Fellow of Digital Media and Culture in the Department of Digital Humanities, and Research Asso ciate in the Department of Informatics, at King's College London. He teaches popular culture and digital methods, and performs research into forms of reading and writing travel in online ecologies. He has held a Visiting Fellowship at the University of Western Sydney (2016) and Shanghai International Studies University (2017) and elsewhere. His articles have appeared in *Tourist Studies*, *Games and Culture* and *The Journal of Popular Culture*, and he is currently co-writing a chapter in the *Cambridge History of Travel Writing*.

Yuan Mingqing has obtained a Master of Arts degree from Shanghai

International Studies University with a focus on Intercultural Communication, and a Master degree in Intercultural Anglophone Studies from the University of Bayreuth (Germany), in a cooperative international program. She is currently a member of the Bayreuth International Graduate School of African Studies. Her research interests are in the areas of African and diasporic African literatures, postcolonial studies, as well as transcultural and postcolonial readings of Shakespeare.

Zha Mingjian is Professor of Comparative Literature and Translation Studies at Shanghai International Studies University (SISU). He is Dean of the School of English Studies, and Director of the Center for Comparative Literature at the Institute of Literary Studies. His pen name is Shi Yi or Wei Hang. After studying at East China Normal University, Fudan University, and SISU, Zha received his Ph.D. in Translation Studies at Lingnan University in Hong Kong. He was a Fulbright Visiting Scholar at Harvard University. His major research interests are the history of translated literature, theories of comparative literature, and comparative cultural studies. His publications include *A History of Translated Literature in Modern China* (1898 – 1949) and *A History of 20th-century Foreign Literary Translation in China*.

Zhang Longxi holds an M.A. in English from Peking University and a Ph.D. in Comparative Literature from Harvard University. He had taught at Peking, Harvard, and the University of California, Riverside, and is currently Chair Professor of Chinese and Comparative Literature at the City University of Hong Kong. Professor Zhang was elected a foreign member of the Royal Swedish Academy of Letters, History and Antiquities in 2009 and a foreign member of Academia Europaea in 2013. He serves as an Advisory Editor of *New Literary History*, and an Editor-in-Chief of the *Journal of World Literature*. He has published more than 20 books and numerous articles in both English and Chinese in East-West comparative studies. His major English book publications include *From Comparison to World Literature* (SUNY, 2015), *Unexpected Affinities: Reading across Cultures* (Toronto, 2007), *Allegoresis: Reading Canonical Literature East and West* (Cornell, 2005), *Mighty Opposites: From Dichotomies to Differences in the Comparative Study of China* (Stanford, 1998), and *The Tao and the Logos: Literary Hermeneutics, East and West* (Duke, 1992).

Zhou Yi is Associate Professor at the Intercultural Institute and Center for Canadian Studies, Shanghai International Studies University. She specializes in contemporary British and American Literature and Culture studies. Her publications include *Understanding Alice Munro* (2014), China's first monograph on Alice Munro, "Canadian Cultural Psychology in Alice Munro's Short Stories" (2014), and "On Annie Proulx's Western Writing" (2009). She is the recipient of the 2012 Special Award of Canadian Studies by Canada's Department of Foreign Affairs and International Trade. In 2014, Guy Saint-Jacques, Canadian Ambassador to the People's Republic of China, hosted a book talk at his official residence to present Dr. Zhou's research on Alice Munro. Her other honors include a China Scholarship Council scholarship to McMaster University (Canada, 2014−2015), the Shanghai Excellent Doctorate Dissertation Award, and The Association for Canadian Studies in China Excellent Doctorate Dissertation Award. Dr. Zhou currently leads a project of the Chinese Ministry of Education, and a university-level team project. She is the peer-reviewer for the CSSCI journal *Foreign Literature*.

About the Series

The *Intercultural Research* book series of the SISU Intercultural Institute (SII) of Shanghai International Studies University (SISU) aims to be a publication in the tradition of an "annual" with each volume (or pair of volumes) focusing on one important topic or theme central to the historical or ongoing development of intercultural communication. With this goal mind, *Intercultural Research* has and continues to seek to publish seminal, cutting edge chapters on the state of the intercultural field in a specific area.

In seeking to cover and help map out the "state of the art" on the designated domain, each volume (or pair of volumes) aims to include diverse theoretical or applied research from indigenous or comparative cultural, intercultural, or cross-cultural approaches, highlight varied paradigms or investigative methodologies on that subject, and provide pertinent "history and status" overviews that track developments, note or critique trends, and suggest important directions for further research developments. The series thus aims to provide a benchmark reference for assessing the current state of the field and an impetus for stimulating future research development on each specified topic.

While seeking to broadly encompass diverse international approaches to any given topic, because of being published in China, the series seeks to especially consider non-Western perspectives. Each volume aims to incorporate contributions that may have greater relevance to studies in other Asian or Chinese societies. For those domains deemed to merit two volumes, the second companion volume generally includes a focus related to Chinese theories and applications (and some chapters or volumes may on occasion be published in Chinese).

In line with international publishing standards for social science and communication studies, *Intercultural Research* has adopted the editorial policies of the *APA Publication Manual* (6th ed.) or *MLA Handbook* (8th ed.) (these volumes on literature) along with specific guidelines developed for the integration of Chinese names and Chinese language publications. These "SII APA Integrated Chinese Editing" standards (two documents) can be found on the web site of the Institute (**http://en.sii.shisu.edu.cn**) along with model citation, reference, and layout examples. Information on intended future volumes may also be found on the web page. Further inquiries or comments may be addressed to the editors or to the Institute staff at:

icinstitute@shisu.edu.cn

Intercultural Research 跨文化研究

A thematic academic monograph series
produced by the SISU Intercultural Institute（SII） 上外跨文化研究中心

Series Editors：*Steve J. Kulich*，*Michael H. Prosser*

Volumes in the Series